AGREEMENTS

Combining rigorous philosophical analysis with a deep knowledge of law, this study of agreements illuminates legal doctrine by philosophical theory and vice versa. Against the prevailing philosophical view of agreements, the book argues that they are to be understood in terms not of promises but of offer and acceptance. Topics covered include the obligations associated with agreements; the practical reasoning that leads parties to make and perform agreements; the relation between agreement and intention; and the reasons the state has to intervene in agreements. There are also separate chapters devoted to doctrines of agreement in the law of contract, competition and conspiracy.

OLIVER BLACK is Visiting Professor of Philosophy and Law at King's College London. He is also a practising solicitor, working as Counsel at Linklaters LLP, where he is head of the UK procurement law practice. He has taught at Cambridge and been a fellow at the University of California, Berkeley. He is the author of *Conceptual Foundations of Antitrust* (Cambridge University Press, 2005) and has published articles on a variety of topics in philosophy and law.

AGREEMENTS

A Philosophical and Legal Study

OLIVER BLACK

CAMBRIDGE
UNIVERSITY PRESS

CAMBRIDGE UNIVERSITY PRESS
Cambridge, New York, Melbourne, Madrid, Cape Town,
Singapore, São Paulo, Delhi, Mexico City

Cambridge University Press
The Edinburgh Building, Cambridge CB2 8RU, UK

Published in the United States of America by Cambridge University Press, New York

www.cambridge.org
Information on this title: www.cambridge.org/9780521885607

First published 2012

Printed in the United Kingdom at the University Press, Cambridge

A catalogue record for this publication is available from the British Library

Library of Congress Cataloguing in Publication data
Black, Oliver, 1957–
Agreements : a philosophical and legal study / Oliver Black.
p. cm.
Includes bibliographical references and index.
ISBN 978-0-521-88560-7 (hardback)
1. Contracts – England. 2. Contracts – Philosophy. I. Title.
KD1554.B53 2012
346.4202′2 – dc23 2012002689

ISBN 978-0-521-88560-7 Hardback

CONTENTS

ACKNOWLEDGEMENTS

I am grateful to the friends and colleagues who have helped with this book, and in particular to Bill Allan, David Bailey, Annette and Jerry Barnes, Jon Barton, Sophie Botros, Jessica Boyd, Kenneth Campbell, Simon Evnine, Edmund Fawcett, Donald Franklin, Alex Gregory, Michael Grenfell, Chris Hughes, Richard Linenthal, Oke Odudu, David Ormerod, David Owens, Alex Paseau, John Phillips, Tom Pink, Olga Ramírez Calle, Joseph Raz, Mark Textor, Carole Thomas, Richard Whish and Helena Wright. Special thanks go to my wife Jenny, for cheerfully enduring neglect.

Introduction

So far as I know, this is the first book devoted to agreements as such. The sparsity of the literature is suprising, given the number and importance of agreements: they form one of the main types of social bond, they are central to the law, and they are prominent in various theoretical domains such as the theory of co-operative games and social contract theories of political obligation.[1] I shall consider agreements from both a philosophical and a legal perspective, the aim being to illuminate legal doctrine by philosophical theory and vice versa.

Philosophers have written more about promises than about agreements:[2] one explanation may be the prevalence of an assumption that the latter can be easily understood in terms of the former. The main thesis of this book is that agreement is best understood in terms not of promises but of offer and acceptance. Contract lawyers will not be surprised by the positive half of the thesis but may baulk at the negative half, for in the law of contractual agreement the ideas of offer, acceptance and promise are often and unhappily combined. Chapter 1 attacks promise-based accounts and Chapter 2 defends an offer–acceptance account. The remaining chapters of the book's philosophical part discuss, among other topics, the obligations associated with agreements, the practical reasoning that leads parties to make and then to perform agreements, and the reasons the state has to enforce, prohibit or promote certain types of

1 In these domains the concept of an agreement or of a contract is more often presupposed than examined. Game-theoretic accounts of bargaining throw some light on the nature of an agreement, but co-operative solutions such as Nash's assume an enforceable agreement between the parties: Nash (1950); Dixit and Skeath (1999), chap. 16. As to the social contract, Hobbes gives a brief account of a contract as 'the mutual transferring of right': Hobbes (1968), 192. Hume distinguishes a strong and a weak sense of 'contract': Hume (1963), 454 f. Rawls makes some remarks on the appropriateness of the term to describe his own theory: Rawls (1972), 16.

2 A recent book of philosophical essays on promises and agreements (Sheinman (2011c)) is typical: only one of the sixteen contributions is primarily about agreements.

agreement. The legal part explores doctrines of agreement in the law of contract, competition and conspiracy. At the end of this Introduction there is a fuller survey of the chapters.

I hope that, as befits a cross-disciplinary study, each chapter will be interesting to specialists and comprehensible by beginners, but the latter should note that the discussion, although introductory, is not always elementary (the denser passages can be skimmed or skipped without losing the thread of the argument) and that this is not a textbook; in particular, the chapters in Part II are not digests of their respective legal areas or even of the doctrines of agreement within those areas. I have included only those topics that have stimulated me. The book also has little to say about the history and anthropology of agreements and of understandings of agreement: it is about agreements as *we* understand them – 'we' being the author and likely readers.[3] In partial compensation for those omissions, the footnotes are liberal in their suggestions for further reading.

Analysis and conditions

In the last century philosophers often saw their task as one of analysis: a question of the form 'What is it for . . . to . . . ?' about some philosophically interesting topic – 'What is it for someone to know something?', 'What is it for one thing to cause another?' – was understood as a request for an analysis of what it is for . . . to . . . , an analysis often being understood in turn as a non-trivial but analytically true statement that certain conditions are necessary and sufficient for . . . to . . . . If, for example, the statement 'Knowledge is justified true belief' is analytically true, it is an analysis of knowledge; more explicitly, if '<X knows that P> if and only if <X has a justified true belief that P>' is analytically true, it is an analysis of what it is for X to know that P.[4] The statement that <X knows that P> if and

3 On the philosophical use of 'we', see Foster (1957).

4 It perhaps goes without saying that <one thing is necessary for another if and only if the second is sufficient for the first> and that <if and only if it is the case that if P then Q – equivalently, that P only if Q – then (roughly speaking, at least) the actual or merely possible fact that P is sufficient for the actual or merely possible fact that Q>. A fact can be represented by a nominalisation of a declarative sentence. Such a sentence – 'Fluffy is sleeping' – can be nominalised in various ways: 'the fact that Fluffy is sleeping', 'for Fluffy to be sleeping', 'Fluffy's sleeping', and so on (see O. Black (2004b), 273; O. Black (2005b), 172 f.). Whether conditions, necessary or sufficient, are best conceived as facts is debatable (see J. Kim (1971), 71), but there is no need to resolve the issue here; on the nature of facts, see further section 3.2 below. For convenience, I shall sometimes refer to conditions with

only if <X knows that P>, although analytically true, is not an analysis, as it is trivial.

Analytic truth is built into this definition of analysis,[5] so that a statement of conditions that is not analytically true – and a fortiori a statement that is false – is not an analysis but at best a purported analysis. On a broader definition, such a statement could be an analysis but would not be a correct one. A corresponding point applies to the requirement of non-triviality. 'Analytically true' has been used to mean various things. On a Kantian account, analytic truth is truth by virtue of conceptual containment:[6] if the biconditional about knowledge is analytically true, the concept of knowledge contains, in some sense, the concepts of justification, truth and belief. That goes easily with the view that analysanda are concepts,[7] but other views assign them to different ontological categories: the analysandum in the example might be held to be the meaning of 'knows', or the property of knowing, or facts or states of affairs involving knowledge, or something else.

The search for analyses, thus defined, is no longer a popular philosophical project. Grounds for the decline in popularity include the paradox of analysis, scientific essentialism, scepticism about analytic truth, and the simple failure to find agreed sets of necessary and sufficient conditions for philosophically interesting analysanda.[8] As regards the example, Gettier argued persuasively that justified true belief is not enough for knowledge.[9] With those grounds in mind, I propose only a sufficient condition for agreement and do not assert that the statement of sufficiency is analytically true.[10]

phrases that do not readily apply to facts; e.g., I shall talk of something's being sufficient for agreement, or for a contract, or for a concerted practice, rather than for the fact that X and Y agree / contract / engage in a concerted practice. The analysis of conditionality is pursued in section 1.22 below.

5 For the view that analyses are not analytically true, see M. Zimmerman (1996), 77.

6 Kant (1929), 48 ff. For a survey of other meanings, see Bealer (1998).

7 For a recent defence of conceptual analysis, see Jackson (1998a), esp. chap. 2.

8 The paradox of analysis: Langford (1952). Scientific essentialism: Putnam (1975). Scepticism about analytic truth: Quine (1961); M. White (1950); for a defence, see Grice and Strawson (1991). For an example of disagreement over necessary and sufficient conditions, see n. 9 below. On philosophical analysis generally and its shortcomings, see Hanna (1998); Papineau (2009); H. Lewis (1963), esp. chap. 1; Searle (1969), 55; Williamson (2007), chaps. 1 ff.

9 Gettier (1967). Contrast Ayer (1956), 34; Chisholm (1957), 16.

10 For the view that philosophical theses are not analytic, see Papineau (2009), 2 ff.; Williamson (2007), chaps. 3 f. Papineau (20 ff.) differs from Williamson (chaps. 5 ff.)

Roughly put, the thesis is this: X and Y agree with each other if X makes to Y an offer which Y accepts. (The 'with each other', in this and similar phrases, will usually be omitted from now on; in Chapter 8, for example, it should be read into 'act jointly', 'have a concurrence of wills' and 'engage in a concerted practice'.) Since the condition is only sufficient, not necessary, for agreement, it allows the existence of agreements the parties to which do not meet it; but, for most or at least many agreements, and for all or at least most paradigmatic agreements, the parties do meet the condition. For at least some agreements for which the condition does not hold, either the parties meet it if minor adjustments to it are made or the parties stand in a certain relation to a set of 'normal agreements', i.e., agreements the parties to which do meet it. In the first case their meeting the revised condition, and in the second their so standing in that relation, is sufficient for them to agree.

These claims will be refined, amplified and explained below and in the following chapters. I call the full account 'the offer–acceptance model'. 'The promise model' signifies its foil, the view that promises are necessary and/or sufficient for agreement. A more precise statement of the promise model is that there are kinds of promise, Kpx and Kpy, such that X's giving to Y a promise of kind Kpx and Y's giving to X a promise of kind Kpy are severally necessary and/or jointly sufficient for X and Y to agree.

Whether the offer–acceptance model is taken to be an analysis of what it is for parties to agree depends on the definition given of analysis. On the narrow definition above, the model is not an analysis, but a definition broad enough to classify it as one would not be strained. It might be objected that a true, but possibly not analytically true, statement of a sufficient condition does not, without more, amount to an analysis: 'If a thing is a robin, it is a bird' is not an analysis of what it is for something to be a bird. Even if that is conceded, the objection misses its mark, for the model provides more: in particular, I shall maintain that its central thesis, duly expanded, follows from constitutive rules of agreement, and I entertain the suggestion that these rules, and hence the thesis, are analytic truths. In the following chapters I label as analyses various propositions – including certain propositions, true or false, that give conditions for agreement – but the term is one of convenience only and does not import a developed definition or theory of analysis. (Chapter 2 contains further discussion of possible requirements for an analysis.) Similarly, if questions

in holding also that philosophical knowledge is a posteriori, i.e., based on the same kind of empirical evidence as are theories in the natural sciences.

of the form 'What is it for . . . to . . . ?' are understood as requests for analyses on the narrow definition, the model is not a correct answer to the question 'What is it for parties to agree?' But a broader understanding of such questions – either as requests for analyses more broadly defined or as not being requests for analyses at all – admits the model as a correct answer to the particular question, even if, because the model gives only a sufficient condition, the answer is not a complete one.

The statement that a certain condition is sufficient for parties to agree is not an answer to such epistemic questions as whether anyone knows, or what evidence there is, that they do; a theme of the book, prominent in the second part, is the importance of distinguishing between evidence, and conditions for the existence, of an agreement. The model nevertheless provides material to answer such questions, for often a way of telling whether two people agree is to see whether one of them makes to the other an offer which the other accepts. This epistemic claim does not exclude other ways of telling – for example, by asking one of the parties or some other knowledgeable person (but his knowledge may in turn be based on his witnessing an acceptance of an offer) – or entail the false contention that it is always easy to ascertain whether one party accepts another's offer: there might be perceptual obstacles, or it might be debatable, as a matter of interpretation, whether the parties' actions amount to offer and acceptance. The interpretive issue is especially likely to arise in relation to implied or tacit agreements; such agreements, and certain aspects of interpretation, are discussed in Chapter 8.

Preliminary clarifications

Some distinctions, assumptions and conventions will apply throughout the book. The topic is agreements to do things ('active' agreements), not agreements as to fact ('factual' agreements): if X and Y agree that Everest is the highest mountain, their agreement cannot – unless the circumstances are strange – readily be understood as one to do anything. The content of a factual agreement may be false, so factual agreements are not 'factive' in the sense philosophers often give to that word.[11] Questions left open are whether one kind of agreement is in some sense reducible to the other,

11 See Adler (2002), 39; Alvarez (2010), 41 n. 9; Dancy (2000), 131 ff.; Williamson (2000), 21. By contrast, Thomas Pink, in a talk on 'Promises, Agreements and Obligations', given at a conference of the Institute of Philosophy (London, 2009), used 'factive promise' to signify a promise as to fact, but allowed that the content of such a promise may be false.

whether both are reducible to something else, whether there are here not only two kinds but also two concepts of agreement and/or two meanings of 'agree', and whether the distinction is exhaustive of agreements.

A negative answer to the last question might invoke an agreement between X and Y that their secretaries will arrange a meeting: it is not an agreement as to fact, but nor are the parties agreeing to do anything: it is their secretaries who will make the arrangement. A plausible response is that the description of the agreement is elliptic: it is more accurate, but perhaps not wholly so, to say that they agree to *cause* their secretaries to arrange a meeting – an ordinary active agreement. Cases such as this normally arise only where the parties believe that they have relevant power over the other agents mentioned in the elliptic description. Whether or not the distinction is exhaustive, active and factual agreements are in the following respect not mutually exclusive: parties may both agree to do something and agree that as a matter of fact they will do it.

An argument that the distinction is superficial or illusive might invoke statements that appear to mention both an active agreement and a factual one. It might be said, for example, that in the statement 'X and Y agree both to meet at noon and that Everest is the highest mountain' the phrase 'X and Y agree' is not a syllepsis but has a unitary meaning. Against that, it is plausible to hold that the making of an active agreement and the making of a factual agreement are different speech acts (as to which, see Chapter 1): in particular, active agreements, but not factual agreements, are typically made by acts of offering and accepting.

The distinction is fairly clear at an intuitive level, but not easy to capture in theoretical terms other than those of the offer–acceptance model itself. Two bases for it might be proposed: one concerns the parties' mental states,[12] the other the agreement's content. As to the former, a suggestion is that the parties to an active agreement intend its content – or that each intends a possible action of his that is specified in the content – whereas the content of a factual agreement is believed by the parties. The suggestion fails. As regards its first half, another theme of the book is that intention and active agreement are only loosely connected and that bad law results from the belief that the connection is tighter; examples of such bad law are given in the last two chapters. Clearly X's and Y's intending to meet at noon is not sufficient, but nor – as will be made clear in Chapter 5 – is it necessary, for them to agree to meet then.

12 For the claim that mental states, specifically intentions, may determine the illocutionary force of speech acts, see Strawson (1971a), discussed in section 5.15 below.

As regards the suggestion's second half, the intuitive notion of factual agreement is not precise enough to answer the question whether their believing that Everest is the highest mountain is necessary and/or sufficient for them factually to agree that it is; different answers flow from different proposals to refine intuition. It is trivially both necessary and sufficient on the simple proposal that ≪X and Y factually agree that P> if and only if <X and Y both believe that P≫, but stronger proposals remove the sufficiency and weaker ones the necessity. For example, a stronger proposal may require in addition that each party communicate his belief to the other, or know the other to share the belief, or that it be common knowledge (explained in Chapter 1) between them that they share it. On one weaker proposal, <X and Y factually agree that P> if they do not believe that P, but merely assume that P for the sake of argument – possibly even an argument by reductio ad absurdum to the negation of P – or conjecture or hypothesise or speculate that P.[13] If they agree to make the assumption, they also have an active agreement.

As to the other basis for the distinction, it might be suggested that active agreements do, and factual agreements do not, concern possible future actions of the parties. That suggestion also fails. It is true that normally, if X agrees to φ, φing is a possible action of his which he would perform after making the agreement; but, as noted above, X may agree that as a matter of fact he will φ. Thus φing's being a possible future action of X is at most necessary, not sufficient, for it to be the case that an agreement by X that X will φ is active. Arguably it is necessary only that X *think* that φing is such an action: varying the example at the end of the previous paragraph, it might be said that, if X and Y agree to believe, rather than to assume, that P, they may have an active agreement even though belief is not an action.[14] In that case it might also be argued, from the premiss that an obligation concerns a possible action of the obligor, that their agreement imposes no obligations on them (see Chapter 3).

Another suggestion is that whereas the content of a factual agreement is a proposition, represented by a 'that'-clause, the content of an active agreement is non-propositional and – as I assumed when introducing the distinction – is represented by a 'to'-clause. The suggestion is consistent with the fact that an active agreement may have a logically complex, and in particular a conditional, content (X and Y might agree this: to meet at

13 For a broad use of 'believe' that covers all such states, see Alvarez (2010), 126.

14 The literature on deciding to believe is relevant here. See Adler (2002), chap. 2; Noordhof (2001); Raz (1999); B. Williams (1973), 147 ff.

noon if it is sunny) but as it stands it too is inadequate, for the content of an active agreement may be represented by a 'that'-clause: as explained below, I shall assume that active agreement is a propositional attitude. The content of a factual agreement is not, however, represented by a 'to'-clause; so, if the active/factual distinction is exhaustive, the fact that the content of an agreement is represented by such a clause is sufficient for the agreement to be active. Questions remain as to when clauses of different forms represent the same content[15] – it seems that, at least on certain conditions, the same content is represented by 'to meet at noon' and 'that they will meet at noon' – and whether the linguistic feature just identified is intrinsic to, or merely an indicator of, the active/factual distinction. The distinction is reflected also in other idioms: generally, for example, 'have an agreement' and 'in agreement' respectively signify active and factual agreement.[16]

The word 'agreement', applied to active agreements (from now, save where indicated, the only kind at issue) may signify the making of an agreement – i.e., the acts by which the agreement is made – or the resultant state of agreement, or the content of the making or of the state;[17] more rarely, it may signify the fact that the acts are performed, or the fact that the state exists,[18] or a document which records the acts, the state, the content, and/or the facts. Similarly, 'X and Y agree that P' may mean that X and Y make an agreement, or that they are in a state of agreement, that P. I shall draw these distinctions only where necessary. For convenience I shall talk about the content of an agreement, rather than about the

15 A sample of the literature on problems in the notion of content, in particular those concerning indexical terms such as 'I' (as to which, see the main text below): Bach (1987), chaps. 1 f.; Burge (1977); J. Campbell (1994), chaps. 3 f.; Cassam (1994); Castañeda (1999), esp. chap. 2; Evans (1982), chaps. 5 f.; Forbes (1989); King (2008); Peacocke (1986); Perry (1993); Recanati (1993), chaps. 5 f.; Shoemaker (1984); Shoemaker (1996), pts. 1 and 4.

16 On being in agreement, see S. Smith (2004), 188 f., quoted in Chap. 7 n. 59 below; see also n. 20 to that chapter. Smith appears to identify being in agreement with 'agreement in judgment': ibid., 181 n. 22. See also S. Smith (2005), 56 f. For a use of 'in agreement' to signify active agreement, see the passage from Peel (2007), para. 20–058, on *Byrne* v. *van Tienhoven*, quoted in section 7.31 below.

17 Compare Alvarez (2010), 3 f., 87 f., 125 on the importance of the act/object distinction as regards belief and desire.

18 Alvarez (2010), 47 f., 99, 126 observes that gerundial phrases, such as 'my believing that', can obscure the distinction between a mental state and the fact that a person is in that state. A similar point applies to 'our agreeing that', but the state of agreement is mental in only a loose sense: see Chap. 9 n. 23 below.

content of the making or of the state of agreement. Corresponding points apply to offers, acceptances and promises.

The statement that a party performs an agreement, contract, promise or obligation, or just that he performs, means that he does the thing he agrees, contracts, promises or is obligated to do. A distinction can be drawn: if X agrees to rob the bank, 'X does the thing he agrees to do' is true if and only if 'X robs the bank' is, but the two do not mean the same. Since, however, the distinction is for the most part not needed (it arises in Chapter 3), I shall usually ignore it. Talk of performance extends to certain agreements, contracts, promises and obligations with logically complex content, and in particular to conditional ones: if X agrees <to rob the bank if the police are not there>, he performs if and only if he robs the bank. As explained in Chapter 1, there are kinds of compliance such that he may comply with the conditional agreement even if he does not rob the bank; compliance, of those kinds, is therefore not the same as performance.[19] 'Performs' and 'complies with' could be defined to mean the same in such contexts, but to do so would obscure useful distinctions. In English criminal law, statutory conspiracy is defined in terms of an agreement's being 'carried out': Chapter 9 identifies carrying out with performance.

I shall assume, again for convenience, that agreeing, offering, accepting and promising, and also certain states such as intending, believing and desiring, are propositional attitudes, i.e., that their contents are propositions;[20] 'attitude' here has a wide meaning which covers acts as well as states. As already noted, 'agree that' can signify an active agreement; similarly, 'X promises to' can be rewritten as 'X promises that he will', 'X intends to' as 'X intends that he will', and so on. 'Offer that' and, in the context of active agreements, 'accept that' are clumsy, but the clumsiness is bearable because, first, the assumption as to propositional content can be eliminated and, second, as explained in Chapter 2, 'offer' and 'accept' are to be understood broadly. I shall similarly assume that the content of an obligation is a proposition, so that an obligation can be represented in

19 Compare M. Zimmerman (1996), 105, which distinguishes 'satisfaction', 'fulfilment' and 'maintenance' of obligations.

20 This is a common view in philosophy: see, e.g., Cappelen and Hawthorne (2009); Salmon and Soames (1988), 1. Merricks (2009a), which gives other references, argues that belief is a propositional attitude, but follows Brewer (2006) and Montague (2007) in arguing – but on different grounds – that neither fear nor desire is; see also Alvarez (2010), 67, and Ben-Yami (1997). For difficulties with the theory of Cappelen and Hawthorne, see Brogaard (2009).

the form 'X is obligated that P':[21] the points about convenience, clumsiness and eliminability apply here too.[22] I shall slide between 'to' and 'that' as style dictates.

Chapter 2 also maintains that, where an agreement is made by one party's making to the other an offer which the other accepts, the content of the offer, the acceptance and the agreement typically has the form 'X does Ax and Y does Ay'. As in this case, I often – and in particular when specifying contents – use the timeless present and pretend that co-referring expressions, and schemata for them, are intersubstitutable: in logical jargon, the pretence is that contexts such as 'agrees that . . . ' are referentially transparent. For present purposes those simplifications are convenient and harmless, but at least in some cases they are unidiomatic or inaccurate. (On certain accounts of the nature of propositions, it might be argued that the falsity of the pretence of transparency follows from the assumption that agreeing etc. are propositional attitudes.) Suppose that you agree to take the plane that leaves at 9.30. Suppose also that – although you do not know this – the plane will explode when it takes off. Then, roughly, 'the plane that leaves at 9.30' and 'the plane that will explode when it takes off' refer to the same thing. But, in normal circumstances, we are inclined to deny that you agree to take the plane that will explode when it takes off. Perhaps there is a weak sense of 'agree' in which you do, and a stronger and more usual one in which you do not. Another example, which reverts to schemata: instead of saying that the content of X's offer, Y's acceptance and their agreement is that <X does Ax and Y does Ay>, it is often more accurate to say that (i) the content of X's offer is that <he will do Ax and Y will do Ay> and (ii) the content of Y's acceptance that <X will do Ax and he (Y) will do Ay>. Here, on a narrow concept of content, the contents of the offer and the acceptance are distinct and the agreement arguably has two contents.[23] One basis for adopting such a narrow concept is the thought that X might believe that he is not X, in which case he would likely deny his offer to be that X will do Ax etc. On the simplifying assumptions, offer, acceptance and agreement all have the same content.

21 Compare Broome (2000), 79, on *ought*. For criticism of this approach, see M. Zimmerman (1996), 63 f., invoking a distinction between binding and non-binding senses of 'ought'. For that distinction, see ibid., 2 ff., 91, and works cited there. Harman's 'evaluative' sense (Chap. 6 n. 55 below) is non-binding.

22 M. Zimmerman (1996), 63 ff. rewrites certain principles of deontic logic in terms that do not make the assumption. On deontic logic, see Chap. 3 n. 25 below.

23 See n. 15 above.

As already indicated, I rank ease above precision where it is safe to do so. I switch casually between the material mode (talk about things) and the formal mode (talk about language), without always marking the distinction, and I am mainly careless about such differences as those between a kind, a concept, a conception, an idea, a notion and a meaning, and between an analysis, a definition, an account, an understanding and a theory: narrowly speaking, for example, two kinds of agreement might be covered by the same concept of agreement or meaning of 'agreement', and the same definition of agreement might be used in two theories or accounts of agreement. I am similarly nonchalant in the use of symbols, some of which have already been introduced. The letters X and Y are schemata for names of people and of other potential agents; further letters are used in multipartite cases. The symbols Ax, Ay, etc. are schemata for names of the agents' respective actions. Greek letters – φ, χ, . . . – are schemata for verbs of action. 'Action' has a broad meaning, which includes omissions, and I use 'action' and 'act' interchangeably. The same applies to talk of action and talk of conduct or behaviour. 'Action', 'conduct' and 'behaviour' are not always interchangeable: in particular, 'action' often is a count-noun, but 'conduct' (in the relevant sense) never is, and 'a behaviour' is mainly restricted to scientific and quasi-scientific contexts. 'Conduct' and 'behaviour' also are normally used in respect of longer stretches of time than 'action' is. Those differences are not material for my purposes.

The letters P, Q, . . . are schemata for sentences and for names of propositions expressed by the sentences. Distinctions can be drawn between a sentence, a statement and a proposition,[24] but I use these words loosely – for example, in talking of a schema as a proposition. Bracketed numbers – (1), (2), . . . – are used both to name and to abbreviate the sentences, and schemata for sentences, that they introduce; in the case of the schemata for sentences, the bracketed numbers are also used as schemata for names of propositions expressed by the sentences. A single numerical sequence runs throughout the book; as I often use numbers only, a list of the numbered propositions (strictly, sentences and schemata) is given at the end, for ease of reference. (The table of contents, which includes all headings of sections, should also aid navigation. Section numbers – 1, 1.1, . . . – are given without brackets, the number before the point indicating the chapter. Given this convention, there should be no confusion between

24 See Haack (1978), chap. 6; Lemmon 1966b. King (2008) is a study of the nature of propositions.

sections of the book and sections of statutes, to which I sometimes refer.) In complex constructions I sometimes use angle-brackets < > to clarify the scope of propositional attitudes and of logical constants ('and', 'or' etc.). Italics are used to denote concepts – for example, the concept *ought*. Other symbols and conventions will be explained as they are introduced, or their meaning will be clear from the context.

Schemata are placeholders: 'X does Ax' does duty for sentences such as 'George pays £5', 'The content of Y's belief is that P' for sentences such as 'The content of Ann's belief is that George pays £5', and 'the fact that P' for referring expressions such as 'the fact that George pays £5'. Much of the discussion will be in schematic terms, because schemata import generality: the statement that if X makes to Y an offer which Y accepts then X and Y agree implies that if any two parties meet that condition then they agree. Some philosophers reject generalism in ethics and certain branches of the theory of action,[25] but I have not encountered a particularist theory of agreement. In any event, I assume the possibility of stating correctly a condition for agreements in general. If the offer–acceptance model is correct, it realises that possibility.

Overview of the chapters

Part I of the book deals with philosophical issues. Chapter 1 attacks the promise model by arguing against analyses according to which promises are sufficient for agreement. The first section applies speech act theory to give a brief account of the nature of promises: I locate them in a broader class of undertakings, distinguish active promises – the kind at issue – from factual ones (the distinction corresponds to that between active and factual agreements), discuss the relations of promises to intentions and to obligations, and use the connection with obligation to explain why promises cannot be withdrawn or accepted.

The following section, which opens with the thesis – defended in Chapter 2 – that agreements typically have conjunctive content, examines analyses proposing that unconditional promises are sufficient for agreement. The analyses fail because they breach criteria of adequacy discussed later. The failure prompts the thought that conditional promises are sufficient for agreement. A proposal in this vein is that <X and Y agree that <X does Ax and Y does Ay≫ if, first, X promises to Y that if Y does Ay then

25 See Dancy (1993), esp. chap. 4; B. Hooker and Little (2000). McKeever and Ridge (2006) is a generalist response.

X does Ax and, second, Y promises to X that if X does Ax then Y does Ay. One problem for such analyses is that they create a mismatch of content: the promises' content is conditional, the agreement's is conjunctive. The particular analysis just stated faces three further objections: it breaches criteria of adequacy, it represents at best a peripheral kind of agreement, and it creates a divergence of compliance conditions. The last objection is that, whereas the parties comply with their respective promises if neither does anything, only if both parties perform do they comply with the agreement. The discussion of the objection distinguishes weak from strong compliance.

If neither unconditional promises alone nor conditional promises alone are sufficient for agreement, it might be suggested that mixed promises are sufficient: one party gives a conditional promise and the other responds with an unconditional one. I consider two analyses of this kind, each of which again creates a mismatch of content. Further problems arise from four criteria for the adequacy of an analysis of agreement: Symmetry, Obligation, Simultaneity and Interdependence. One analysis breaches all of them, the other breaches at least two. The most serious problem is posed by Interdependence – breached by both – which, in Gilbert's formulation, provides that if one party defaults on his performance obligation then the other ceases to have his original performance obligation.

Options are to live with the breach, to revise the mixed-promise account, to produce a quite different promise-based analysis, or to analyse agreement otherwise than in terms of promises. Option one is unpalatable. Option two covers two possibilities: revision of the analyses, or of normative principles used in the argument that Interdependence is breached. I review proposals of these kinds and show that they fail. Under option three I consider, and reject, further analyses in terms solely of conditional promises. The conclusion is that analyses which purport to give a sufficient condition in terms of promises fail to capture the paradigm cases of agreement.

Chapter 2 pursues option four, by developing the offer–acceptance model. A more accurate statement of its central thesis is that, given certain conditions, X and Y agree if X makes to Y an offer which Y accepts. Since it is not the case that an offer and an acceptance in those conditions are sufficient for a promise, the offer–acceptance model implies that promises are not necessary for agreement and thus completes the case against the promise model.

The chapter starts by stating the analysis more precisely, noting that 'offer' and 'accept' have broad meanings similar to the meanings of, respectively, 'propose' and 'assent' and distinguishing sufficient conditions for the making and for the state of agreement. I then amplify the claim that the statements of those conditions follow from constitutive rules of agreement. The next section outlines the account, pursued in Chapter 3, of the obligations arising from agreement: roughly, if X and Y agree that <X does Ax and Y does Ay>, then X's obligation is to do Ax and it ceases if Y releases X from it or if Y does not do, or it is clear that Y is not going to do, Ay.

There follows a discussion, applied later, of the functions of agreement. An agreement is a device the main function of which is to enable, and agreements do enable, rational self-interested parties to benefit from each other's actions; a secondary function is to ground obligations on the parties to perform. Offer and acceptance likewise have functions, the main one of an offer being to put it in the power of the offeree, by accepting, to make an agreement with the offeror; the main function of an act of acceptance, to make such an agreement. Offer and acceptance also have functions corresponding to those of agreement; for example, they have the indirect function of enabling offeror and offeree, if rational and self-interested, to benefit from each other's actions.

The offer–acceptance model meets the four criteria of adequacy, but faces various objections: that it does not fit agreements of certain kinds; that offer, acceptance and agreement are themselves promises; that the model fails to capture the conditionality of agreements; that its account of the parties' obligations is defective; that it imports the presupposition of a rule-defined practice; and that it is circular. I answer all these.

Chapter 3 examines in more detail the obligations of agreement. If X and Y agree that <X does Ax and Y does Ay>, then, subject to certain provisos, X has a performance obligation, i.e., an obligation to do Ax. The main question is what the ground of that obligation is. I explain the notion of a ground, distinguishing complete grounds, which are minimal sufficient conditions, from partial grounds, which are proper parts of complete grounds, and direct from indirect grounds. I also consider the relations between grounding and supervenience and between grounds and reasons.

The next section, as well as clarifying and defending the thesis that X has the obligation, surveys various theories of the obligation's ground. The section after that addresses a problem raised by the claim that the obligation is a moral one: since the claim is general, it implies that in every case of agreement there exists a ground of a moral performance obligation on X, but in some cases there appears to be no such ground. I review a number of possible responses. The best is to maintain that in every case the fact of agreement, FA, is itself a ground of a performance obligation on X, and that in some but not all cases some other fact, FM, grounds a moral performance obligation on X. If the obligation grounded in FA is moral, X has a moral performance obligation in every case; if not, he has a performance obligation in every case but a moral one in only some.

As regards FM, a pluralist view is plausible: the grounds of X's moral performance obligation vary from case to case. A candidate for FM is a fact to do with Y's reliance on X. Two objections to reliance-based theories are that they get things the wrong way round – Y relies on X because X in agreeing obligates himself to do Ax – and that they misidentify the time at which X's obligation arises, which is when the agreement is made, not when Y acts in reliance. I answer both of these before discussing a harder objection, that the fact that Y in doing Ay relies on X to do Ax is neither a complete ground nor even a partial ground of X's obligation. It is not a complete ground, as it is not a sufficient condition. Where it is a part of a sufficient condition, the remaining parts are sufficient; so the original condition is not minimally sufficient and hence not a complete ground; and so the fact of reliance is not a partial ground. I consider responses which purport to specify a minimal sufficient condition of which the fact of reliance is a proper part. Although these specifications have intuitive appeal, the conclusion is left open, for intuitions as to the grounds of obligations are uncertain. In principle at least, a more powerful approach would be to derive a specification from a general theory of moral obligation, but such a theory is beyond the scope of the book.

After considering some other candidates for FM – to do with harm, benefit, fairness and assurance – I return to the thesis that FA, the mere fact of agreement, grounds a performance obligation, even if not a moral one, on X. The explanation why it does so is that a constitutive rule of agreement is that the parties are obligated to perform. Two objections to this explanation are that it trivialises the obligation and that it is shallow. I answer both, the answer to the first giving some reason to hold that a performance obligation grounded only in FA is moral. I also answer two objections to the thesis itself – the first, that X is obligated only if he recognises the device of agreement; the second, that the thesis misses the obligation to 'play the game' of agreement.

Chapter 4 analyses reasoning that would lead rational X and Y to make and then to perform an agreement that <X does Ax and Y does Ay>. The main types of reasoning discussed are instrumental and deontological. If X and Y are narrowly and exclusively self-interested, they will not be moved by deontological considerations as such, but their instrumental reasoning may still refer to their obligations.

As regards the making of an agreement, whether each party wants the other to perform or – as in an agreement for solving a co-ordination problem – each wants both to perform, they may reason in accordance with the schema: (i) I want that P; (ii) the best means to its being the case that P is for me to φ; (iii) other things are equal; so (iv) I will φ. If the reasoner believes that (i)–(iii) and intends that (iv), his reasoning is correct in the sense that the set of his mental states that have the premisses as contents normatively requires his mental state with the conclusion as content. X, for example, may correctly reason: I want that Y does Ay; the best means to Y's doing Ay is for me to offer to Y that <I do Ax and he does Ay>; and so on.

To establish the second premiss, he may in turn reason in three steps: if I offer, then Y does Ay; my offering is a means to Y's doing Ay; my offering is the best means to Y's doing Ay. I set out the premisses for the first step, which itself covers three moves – from offer to acceptance, from acceptance to agreement and from agreement to Y's doing Ay. As to the second and third steps, I discuss the relation between conditionality and instrumentality and identify an assumption of commensurability in the transition from 'means' to 'best means'.

Once the agreement is made, X's reasoning to performance may instantiate the schema: (i) I am obligated to φ; (ii) other things are equal; so (iii) I will φ. Preliminary reasoning to the relevant instance of (i) may use the premiss 'If I and Y agree that <I do Ax and he does Ay>, then I am obligated to do Ax'; this is an indexical variant of the principle discussed in Chapter 3 and, like that principle, is subject to provisos. Given that, as explained in Chapter 3, X's obligation to do Ax is grounded in a reason for him to do Ax, X may alternatively reason in accordance with a variant of the schema, which replaces (i) with: there is a reason for me to φ.

X may otherwise reason instrumentally to performance, his reasoning relating either to the agreement at hand or to other agreements. In either case it may again follow the first schema. Reasoning of the former type may be based, as with X's reasoning to the offer, on the desire that Y perform, or that both parties perform, or it may be based on the desire to avoid certain consequences, such as legal sanctions or a rebuke, that would occur if X did not perform. In the latter case, the reasoning may be based on this thought: X makes future agreements if he maintains a reputation for trustworthiness, and he maintains that reputation if he performs the present agreement.

Other kinds of reasoning to the making and the performance of agreements include reasoning from expressive considerations and from conditional intentions. The appendix to the chapter discusses the question how agreements are possible and rebuts an argument which purports to show that the making of an agreement involves a vicious circle or a vicious infinite regress.

Chapter 5 deals with various topics that have legal implications. The first is the relation between, on the one hand, a person's offering, accepting or agreeing and, on the other, his intentions. I argue that various conditionals purporting to connect them are, with a couple of possible exceptions, false. Subjects raised in the discussion include the conditions for sincere agreement, and the distinction – pursued in the chapter's appendix – between internally and externally conditional intentions. The general distinction between internal and external conditionality, which arises at various points in the book, is explained in Chapter 1.

The second topic is the identity of agreements: the basic idea, which needs elaboration to cover complex cases, is that agreements are identical if and only if they are made by the same parties at the same time and have the same content. Then I consider logical properties of agreement, specifically properties concerning conjunction and closure. As to the former, I argue that there is no conditionality in either direction between the propositions '<X and Y agree that P> and <X and Y agree that Q>' and 'X and Y agree that <P and Q>'. As to closure (defined in the chapter), I maintain that agreement by X is not closed under simple conditionality, that for sufficiently strong forms of necessity it is closed under necessary simple conditionality known by X, and that a comparison between agreement and intention throws light on intermediate cases.

Agreements to agree are the next topic. I show that the account of the obligations arising from agreements implies a clear distinction between agreement to agree to φ and agreement to φ; in particular, it is not the case that the former is merely a special case of the latter in which the details of the agreement have not been specified, or that if X agrees to agree to φ then X agrees to φ. The final section discusses agreements with oneself: after rejecting various specious examples, I maintain that certain cases can plausibly be described as such an agreement – in particular, an agreement in which a person acts in two capacities or is subject to certain epistemic limitations.

Chapter 6 discusses reasons for the state to enforce, prohibit or promote certain types of agreement. The first section, after arguing that reasons can correctly be imputed to the state, distinguishes the activities that the state has reason to perform from those that are proper for it to perform; the distinction is pursued in the appendix to the chapter. By 'enforcement' I generally understand the state's provision of an apparatus – the courts and other institutions – which the parties to a contract can use to enforce it; 'contract' is short for 'contractual agreement', and the discussion of enforcement is limited to these because the main agreements enforced by the state are contractual. The chapter is thus a bridge to the discussion, in the first chapter of Part II, of agreements in contract law.

Reasons for enforcement may be consequential or deontological. Consequential ones relate to the achievement of goods or to the avoidance of bads. The goods may result from the performing or the making of contracts, or from neither. They may consist of benefits enjoyed, expressive acts, or the performing of obligations. Benefits – which may be enjoyed by the parties to the contract or by others, and may or may not be intended by the parties when the contract is made or performed – may be caused by, or in some other way result causally from, the performing or the making of contracts, whereas expressive acts and the performing of obligations are likely to be results of some other kind, perhaps involving a relation of constitution.

For each category of good, the argument is the same: (i) the state's enforcing contracts is a means to G; (ii) G is good; (iii) if (i) and (ii), then the state has a reason to enforce contracts; so (iv) the state has a reason to enforce contracts. As to the mechanism underlying (i): roughly, in the case of goods that result from the performing of contracts, enforcement reduces the likelihood that there exists an outweighing consideration that would stop a contractual party from performing. For example, his desire not to perform may be stronger than his desire that the other party perform; but, given that contracts are enforced, the former desire needs to be weighed against not only the latter but also the desire to avoid the possible consequences of enforcement.

The benefits resulting from contractual performance are varied, but I cast doubt on the claim that welfare, in either an economic or a philosophical sense, is one of them. As to goods, resulting from such performance, that consist of expressive acts or the performing of obligations, examples are the expression of mutual commitment by the parties to a marriage contract and the performing of obligations to do the things specified in the contract. Goods that result just from the making of contracts are miscellaneous, fact-specific, relatively rare and generally minor. Other arguable goods, which do not result from the performing or the making of a contract but may provide a reason for enforcement, include the contractual parties' exercise of autonomy, the state's expressing a positive valuation of contracts, and a reliable framework for exchange.

Deontological reasons concern the things the state has an obligation or duty to do, that it would be right for it to do, that it ought to do, and so on. Such reasons for enforcement depend on the normative foundations of the state: if, for example, you take the state to be a product or expression of the divine will, you may find such a reason in the ground of a duty derived from the duty to obey God. 'Ideal utilitarianism' assimilates deontological reasons to consequential ones.

Reasons for the state to prohibit or promote certain types of agreement are of the same kinds as those for enforcement. For example, the state has reason to prohibit conspiracies, which are discussed in Chapter 9, in that its doing so prevents or reduces the bad results of performing or just making them; prohibition also arguably has the good result of expressing disapproval; and it may be held that the state has a duty to prohibit them. Similar reasons may be argued to apply to the cartels prohibited by competition law: see Chapter 8. Marriage contracts are a type of agreement which some would argue the state has reasons to promote; consequential reasons alleged might, for example, relate to emotional and economic goods.

The three chapters of Part II concern doctrines of agreement in the law of contract, competition and conspiracy. Save where indicated otherwise, the topic is English law (in the case of competition, the provision in question is an import from the Treaty on the Functioning of the European Union (TFEU)); but I refer to other jurisdictions in order to illuminate certain points.

The offer–acceptance model takes its concepts of offer and acceptance from the law of contract, and so it may seem that agreements, modelled thus, and contracts are sure to coincide. But an agreement is neither sufficient nor necessary for a contract; even where an agreement is a contract, it can be hard to identify the offer and the acceptance; and offer and acceptance seem to be missing from some contractual agreements. Chapter 7 explores and explains these divergences. Another problem is that the cases and commentaries often describe contracts in terms of promises: if contracts are agreements, that approach revives the objections to the promise model. I propose responses consistent with the offer–acceptance model.

A special case is the doctrine that in certain circumstances a contract is constituted by independent promises. The rule is that neither party to such a contract can rescind for failure by the other to perform. I examine various versions of the independent/dependent distinction. On one analysis, it concerns the reason why someone gives a promise; on others, it concerns the conditionality of a promise. The analysis in terms of reasons conflicts with contract law's doctrines of offer and acceptance and of consideration. All the conditional analyses provide a justification for the rule, but certain of them – in terms of external conditionality – unduly limit the availability of rescission. An analysis in terms of internal conditionality is therefore proposed. Contracts constituted by independent promises form the basis of two arguments that an agreement is unnecessary for a contract. I also show it to be false that, if one party's promise *depends* on the other's, then the parties agree.

Article 101 TFEU prohibits certain anticompetitive agreements and concerted practices. Chapter 8 examines the nature of agreements within the meaning of Article 101, having regard also to the corresponding provision in US law – section 1 of the Sherman Act. A phrase that has become canonic in EU jurisprudence is 'concurrence of wills', the Court of First Instance (CFI) finding in *Bayer* that 'the concept of an agreement within the meaning of Article [101] . . . centres around the existence of a concurrence of wills'. I review various readings of that claim and object that, on all the readings, it is either false or uninteresting; the objection is argued for readings on which there is a simple relation of conditionality between agreement and concurrence of wills, the latter being understood in terms of intention. I then reject an account of agreement in terms of 'common intention'. These results support the thesis that bad law results from the drawing of too tight a connection between agreement and intention. The conclusion is that the competition authorities would do better to talk in terms of offer and acceptance.

The rest of the chapter deals with issues on the boundaries of agreement. One is the relation between agreements and concerted practices. I propose a 'joint action model' according to which most or at least many concerted practices involve communication; the model is developed by means of a Gricean analysis of degrees of communication. I argue that this account is better than a thinner one which maintains that the reason for engaging in a concerted practice is to reduce uncertainty. The next section shows how the authorities use the concept of a 'single overall agreement' to deal with complex cartels, and how that approach is accommodated by the offer–acceptance model of agreement.

Agreements and concerted practices are forms of collusion, which contrasts with unilateral action. In a series of decisions, the European Commission argued with increasing audacity that certain seemingly unilateral actions constituted vertical agreements, i.e., agreements between entities at different levels of the supply chain; this approach was endorsed by the courts until, in *Bayer*, the CFI found that the Commission had pushed the boundaries of agreement too far. I review the jurisprudence and consider how it might be cast in terms of offer and acceptance rather than concurrence of wills.

Oligopolies – markets in which there are few sellers – raise another question as to the distinction between collusion and unilateral action. According to the theory of interdependence, sellers in such a market may engage in anticompetitive conduct that is parallel but unilateral: the 'oligopoly problem' is how, if at all, competition law should deal with such conduct. In particular it risks falling into a gap between Articles 101 and 102 TFEU: the former normally does not apply if the conduct is unilateral, the latter does not apply if the firms are not dominant. It might be argued that, since the category of collusion includes tacit as well as explicit agreements, the problematic cases are less common than at first appears; but this argument fails on various accounts of tacit agreement. A more fruitful approach is to reduce the problem by expanding the category of agreement and/or that of a concerted practice. I pursue that approach, applying (to both categories) the Gricean analysis of degrees of communication and (to the category of concerted practices) an analysis of degrees of correlation.

Chapter 9 deals with agreements covered by the criminal law of conspiracy, and in particular those falling within section 1(1) of the Criminal Law Act 1977 – a provision open to various readings, depending on the scope given to certain phrases. The criminal law draws a serviceable but problematic distinction between a crime's actus reus and its mens rea, the actus reus of conspiracy being the agreement itself. Various doctrines about conspiratorial agreement are mutually consistent – that the actus reus is complete once the agreement has been made, that the agreement need not be made before actions are taken to carry it out, that the accused must perform overt acts which manifest his intention, that no overt act need be done in pursuance of the agreement, that communication is necessary, that the only evidence of a conspiracy may comprise actions constituting the relevant substantive crime, and that the relevant concept of agreement is subjective. On the last point, the criminal law of conspiracy differs from contract law, which uses an objective concept of agreement, but I reject an argument from the difference between conspiracies and contracts to the conclusion that the offer–acceptance model does not fit conspiratorial agreements. I also show how the model accommodates complex conspiracies, just as it accommodates complex cartels, and I consider the ways in which the cases and commentaries distinguish a single complex conspiracy from a plurality of simpler ones.

The chapter discusses difficulties that relate to the duration of a conspiracy, to the 'course of conduct' which section 1(1) states that the parties agree shall be pursued, and to the theses that a conspiratorial agreement must have a 'material object' and that the parties must collaborate on a project. Conditional agreements cause particular problems, which are clarified, but not eliminated, by distinguishing between internal and external conditionality of the agreement and between conditionality of the agreement and conditionality of performance.

Conspiracy's mens rea – which according to one view comprises an intention to agree, an intention to carry out the agreement, and intention or knowledge as to any circumstances forming part of the substantive offence – is also problematic, the literature being marred by failures to distinguish clearly between agreement and intention. The same fault – in particular, a failure to recognise that a person who agrees to do something may not intend to do it – appears to underlie the doctrine of 'unilateral' conspiracy, which is recognised in the USA. A rough definition of such a conspiracy is: X does something with the intention of, and believing that he is, making an agreement with Y to commit a crime, but in fact there is no agreement. Unilateral conspiracy is either self-contradictory (if it is a conspiracy without an agreement) or a commonplace (if it is an agreement which one of the parties does not intend to carry out).

PART I

Philosophy

1

Promises

Various expressions have been used, in and outside legal contexts, to try to illuminate the nature of agreement – examples are 'meeting of minds',[1] 'common intention',[2] 'mutual assent',[3] 'mutual consent,'[4] 'consensus'[5] and 'understanding'[6] – but most are unhelpful, as their meaning is unclear. Against the promise model[7] this objection is fairly weak, for we have a reasonable grasp of the meaning of 'promise'. The model fails for other reasons. This chapter argues against that version of the model which maintains that promises are sufficient for agreement. The next chapter presents the offer–acceptance model, the main thesis of which is that in certain conditions offer and acceptance are sufficient for agreement. Since offer and acceptance in those conditions are not necessary for promises,

1 Gordley (1991), 136; Kahn (1955); Nussbaum (1936), 920 ff.; Plowden (1792), i, 1 ff.; von Mehren (1992), paras. 153, 187; Chap. 8 n. 10 and Chap. 9 nn. 2 and 26 below.

2 Beatson (2002), 27; Orchard (1974), 343 (also, at 339, 'common purpose' and 'common object'); Chap. 8 n. 10 and Chap. 9 nn. 34 and 126 below. 'Joint' or 'shared' is sometimes used instead of 'common', and 'intent' instead of 'intention'. On the difference between 'joint' and 'common', see section 8.2 below.

3 Gordley (1991), 135. See further Chap. 2 n. 3, Chap. 7 n. 12, Chap. 8 n. 53 and Chap. 9 n. 36 below.

4 Domat (1713), bk. 1, Introduction; Gordley (1991), 109; Orchard (1974), 340. See further Chap. 7 n. 14, Chap. 8 n. 53 and Chap. 9 n. 37 below.

5 Allen (2009), 225; Beatson (1986), 21; Peel (2007), para. 8–078; Simester et al. (2010), 290; Chap. 3 n. 73, Chap. 8 n. 10 and Chap. 9 nn. 2 and 23 below.

6 Ashworth (2009), 453; Fitzpatrick (1993), 1180; Macdonald and Thompson (2003), 99; Marcus (1977), 950 n. 89, 956; Orchard (1974), 299, 301 f., 340; Chap. 8 n. 10 and Chap. 9 n. 35 below.

7 In the philosophical literature on agreement, the orthodox view, so far as one exists, is that agreements can be understood in terms of promises: see Atiyah (1981), 204 f.; Bach (1995); Baier (1985), 199; Binmore (1994), 60; D. Lewis (1969), 34, 35, 84; Prichard (2002c); Radford (1984), 582; Raz (1984), 203; Robins (1984), 105; Sheinman (2011a); S. Smith (2005), 35 f.; Velleman (2000a), appendix; Velleman (2000b). For a dissenting view, see Gilbert (1996a) and Gilbert (1996d). Gilbert (2000a), 59 ff. brings promises and agreements together under the heading of joint commitment. For promise-based accounts of the nature of contracts, see section 7.5 below and the references there.

Chapter 2 dispatches the promise model, by establishing that promises are neither necessary nor sufficient for agreement.

1.1 The nature of promises

I shall not attempt a full theory of promises,[8] but some general remarks will be useful. Promises are one kind of undertaking;[9] other kinds include oaths and vows.[10] Distinctions, drawn in the Introduction, concerning agreements apply also to promises: in particular, 'promise' may signify the act of making a promise, the resultant state of promising, or the content of the act or the state, and there is a distinction between active and factual promises. In the normal case, if X says to doubting Y 'I promise that Everest is the highest mountain', he is not promising to do anything – certainly not to make true a proposition of geography; rather, he is assuring Y as to a matter of fact. For the most part I am concerned only with active promises, although factual promises will arise again in the discussion.

The making of a promise is a speech act – 'speech' here including writing and certain non-verbal forms of communication such as gestures.[11] It might be suggested that, as regards communication, promises differ from certain other undertakings such as vows: a promise must, but a vow need not, be communicated – or at least the promisor must intend to communicate. But if you make a private vow there is a sense in which you are talking to yourself, even if silently, and so this may be considered a limiting case of communication. To make a vow is thus different from, say, forming an intention.[12] On one definition, a vow is a promise to God:

8 Sheinman (2011c) is a collection of essays on the topic. On changes in the concept of a promise, see J. Cartwright (1984), 247.

9 S. Smith (2005), 1 talks of 'an agreement, promise, or other undertaking', which implies that promises are a subclass of undertakings; see further Chap. 2 n. 51 below. Prichard (2002f), 259 says that 'undertake', 'promise' and 'agree' are all 'equivalent'. Compare Trollope (2004), 168: 'That is all very well; but is she to give any undertaking? Do you intend to exact any promise from her?'

10 On oaths, see Aquinas (1894), II f, q 89; S. Smith (2004), 186. On vows, see Aquinas, ibid., q 88; de Moor (1987), 109; Fried (1981), 40 ff. Smith suggests that 'offers to the world', e.g., an offer of a reward, are like oaths, and (in S. Smith (2005), 60 f.) that they are like vows. Offers of that kind are discussed in section 7.36 below.

11 For the same approach in the rhetorical tradition, see Skinner (1996), 108 f.

12 Some philosophers hold that all thinking consists of computations on sentences in the 'language of thought'. Whether or not that is true, it does not erase the distinction between talking to oneself and other forms of thought. Fodor (1975) proposes the language-of-thought hypothesis; see also Fodor (2008). For criticism, see Searle (1984).

a vow in that sense is more obviously communicative. The questions can be left open (but see further the next paragraph) whether every giving of an undertaking is a speech act, whether every giving of an undertaking is communicative and whether every speech act is communicative (see further sections 8.2, 8.5 and 9.21, which maintain that speech acts are typically forms of communication): the answers depend on the breadth of the definitions given to the terms.[13]

The theory of speech acts is a well-developed branch of the philosophy of language.[14] The central idea is that a speaker need not, or not primarily, be stating that something is the case, but may be performing any of a number of types of act.[15] One classification,[16] in terms of the attitude expressed by an utterance – 'utterance' has a broad sense corresponding to that of 'speech' – distinguishes 'constatives' (stating, answering, conjecturing etc.), 'directives' (advising, asking, permitting . . .), 'acknowledgements' (apologising, greeting, thanking . . .) and 'commissives' (agreeing, guaranteeing, inviting . . .). Promising is a commissive. It is plausible to hold that every giving of an undertaking is a commissive, in which case, if every commissive is a speech act, every giving of an undertaking is a speech act. A single utterance may constitute speech acts of more than one type: 'It's hot in here' may be both a statement about the temperature and a request to change it. I shall write indifferently of an utterance's constituting or being a speech act: that is shorthand for statements of the form 'In/by uttering U, X performs speech act A'. (On the 'in'/'by' distinction, see section 2.1, which entertains a narrower definition of constitution, in terms of 'by' rather than 'in'.) For each type the theory distinguishes propositional content, illocutionary force[17] and perlocutionary effect: if X says to Y 'I will feed your cat', the content of his

13 On the various senses of 'communication', see O. Black (1992); O. Black (2005a); O. Black (2005b), chap. 5; Gilbert (1989), 214 ff.; Habermas (1981), vol. 1; Habermas (1998); section 8.32 below. Bach (1998), 81 f. says that some speech acts are not primarily acts of communication: rather their function is to affect institutional states of affairs, an example being a judge's ruling or act of sentencing. These are acts that Austin called performatives: Austin (1970a).

14 The classics are Austin (1962) and Searle (1969). See also Bach and Harnish (1979); Cole and Morgan (1975), vol. 3; Gazdar (1979); G. Green (1989); B. Harrison (1979), chap. 10; Holdcroft (1978); Levinson (1983); Lycan (2000), chap. 12; Searle (1965); Searle (1979); Travis (1975); Tsohatzidis (1994).

15 See Wittgenstein (1958), para. 546: 'Words are also deeds'. For an application of that insight, see Skinner (1996), 8.

16 In Bach and Harnish (1979).

17 Searle (1969), 70 proposes various 'continua' of illocutionary force.

speech act is (roughly) that he will feed Y's cat; the act's illocutionary force is, in appropriate circumstances,[18] that of promising to feed Y's cat; and its perlocutionary effect may, depending on the context, be to reassure Y.[19]

Various questions remain controversial – for example, how to interpret sentences with explicit prefaces that specify the type of speech act performed, such as 'I promise that . . . '[20] (it is of course possible, as the example shows, to promise without saying 'I promise' or words with the same meaning, just as it is possible to agree without saying 'I agree'[21]), and to what extent illocutionary force is determined, on the one hand, by convention or constitutive rules and, on the other, by intention (see further section 5.15 and, on constitutive rules, section 2.2). The latter question forms part of a more general one about the place of intentions in speech acts. Clearly, in the standard case, the agent intends to produce the utterance – the sound, mark or movement that is the act's physical realisation – but normally he has at least one intention of a more complex nature. On one view, he has a Gricean intention, i.e., an intention to produce an effect in another person by means of that person's recognition of the intention.[22] Searle, for example, maintained that X's utterance of a sentence in the presence of Y constitutes <a promise by X to Y that X will φ> only if X intends, first, that his utterance of the sentence will produce in Y a belief that X intends to φ and, second, that the production of the belief will be by means of Y's recognition of X's intention to produce the belief.[23]

Gricean intentions will be discussed at various points in this book. The content of the one just mentioned relates to another intention of X's,

18 Searle (1965), 231 ff. and Searle (1969), 57 ff. propose conditions that an utterance must meet in order to be a promise.

19 Searle (1969), 71 maintains that some illocutionary verbs (such as 'request') are, and others (such as 'promise') are not, definable in terms of the perlocutionary effect intended by the speaker.

20 See L. Cohen (1964). On one account, the speaker both performs a speech act and describes himself as doing so: see Bach and Harnish (1979); Cresswell (1973). For other responses, see Ginet (1979); Lycan (1984), chap. 6; Lycan (2000), 181 ff.

21 Searle (1969), 68 hypothesises that, wherever the illocutionary force of an utterance is not explicit, it can be made explicit. On agreeing without saying so, see Hay (2006), 880.

22 Grice analysed meaning in those terms: see Grice (1989d); Grice (1989e); section 8.32 below. For overviews of Grice's programme, see B. Harrison (1979), chap. 11; Lycan (2000), chap. 7; A. Miller (1998), chap. 7.

23 Searle (1965), 236. The formulation is modified in Searle (1969), 60.

to φ, which Searle regards as distinguishing a sincere from an insincere promise;[24] but, as Searle notes, an insincere promise is a promise none the less.[25] A sincere promisor may be in a mental state stronger than mere intention – perhaps resolve. The title 'commissive' may suggest that the relevant mental state is commitment, but at least in one sense of the word a commitment is itself a speech act the sincerity of which requires a mental state.[26] Section 5.11 will argue that the sincerity conditions for an agreement are more intricate than the one that Searle proposes for a promise.

Roughly, if X promises to φ, X is obligated to φ: in that sense his undertaking is an undertaking of an obligation.[27] The obligations associated with promises will be discussed in more detail in section 1.2312. A formulation more accurate than the one just given is: the fact that X promises to φ grounds the fact that X is obligated to φ. The terminology of grounding is explained in section 3.2. If 'grounds' signifies a complete ground, which is a kind of sufficient condition, the principle in its revised form may still have exceptions, and so a better version is: the fact that X promises to φ and that condition C obtains grounds the fact that X is obligated to φ – where C excludes the exceptions. Possible exceptions – this does not purport to be a complete list – are cases where X is unable

24 Searle (1965), 235 describes this as 'the most important distinction'; Searle (1969), 60, as 'the distinction'.

25 Searle (1965), 237; Searle (1969), 62. In the terminology of Austin (1962), 14, it is 'infelicitous'; in that of Searle (1969), 54, 'defective'. Searle says (ibid.) that an insincere promisor intends that his utterance will 'make him responsible for intending' to do the thing promised. It is unclear what that means.

26 Searle (1969), 58 describes 'I promise' as a device for commitment. Compare Bach (1995), 606 f. The US Restatement (Second) of Contracts (1981), para. 2 defines a promise in terms of a commitment; the opposite approach is taken in Binmore (1994), 161 and Binmore (1998), 47. On commitment, see Chap. 3 n. 149 below.

27 Searle (1969), 60 says that the 'essential feature' of a promise is that it is the undertaking of an obligation to perform a certain act: 'I think that this condition distinguishes promises (and other members of the same family such as vows) from other kinds of illocutionary act'. Mintoff (2004), 49 takes it as uncontroversial that 'every promise generates an obligation'. M. Zimmerman (1996), 146 talks of an obligation of fidelity, describing it as prima facie and conditional: '*if* one makes a promise (or some other sort of commitment) to φ, then one has a *prima facie* (and *not* necessarily overall) obligation to φ'. (Emphasis in original, schematic letters changed. Scanlon's 'principle of fidelity' (Chap. 3 n. 128 below) concerns different, but related, obligations.) On conditional obligations, see n. 33 below; on prima facie obligations, Chap. 3 n. 89 below.

to φ,[28] or his φing would be immoral,[29] or the promisee does not want X to φ,[30] or X is coerced into giving the promise,[31] or it is based on an innocent but fundamental mistake, perhaps resulting from deception.[32] If

28 See Atiyah (1981), 155 ff; Brandt (1964), 377, noting that the phrase 'duty by', as opposed to 'duty to', is used in cases of impossibility; DeMarco and Fox (1992), 49 f.; Driver (1983); Driver (2011) (promises to do the impossible commit the agent); Martinich (1987); D. Ross (1939), 109; Searle (1965), 235 and Searle (1969), 60, which state that a sincere promisor believes it is possible for him to do the act promised; Sinnott-Armstrong (1987), arguing that one can be obligated to do the impossible; Sinnott-Armstrong (1988b); Woozley (1981), 290, arguing that one can promise to do something one knows to be impossible but that such a promise creates no obligation to perform. On agreements to do the impossible, see section 2.3, Chap. 3 n. 83 and Chap. 9 n. 10 below.

There is a large literature on the broader and related question whether 'ought' implies 'can'. See, for example, Frankena (1950); McConnell (1989); Montefiore (1958); Shaw (1965); Widerker (1991); M. Zimmerman (1996), 40 ff., 79 ff. On the special case of self-imposed impossibility, see Henderson (1966), 106; Richman (1983), 85; Robinson (1971), 252; Sinnott-Armstrong (1988a), 116 f.; Stocker (1971), 314; A. White (1975), 149; M. Zimmerman (1996), 95 ff.

For the application of the doctrine of mistake, in English contract law, to contracts that are impossible to perform, see Peel (2007), paras. 8–003 ff.; on impossibility as a ground of frustration of contract, ibid., paras. 19–008 ff.; on the distinction in this context between impossibility and impracticability, ibid., paras. 19–032 ff.; also S. Smith (2005), 171 ff. On the prominent place of impossibility in the German law on breach of contract, see Zweigert and Kötz (1998), 488 ff. On the treatment of impossibility in French contract law, see Nicholas (1992), 116, 205 ff. On the Pandect School's view of impossibility in contract, see von Mehren (1992), para. 24.

29 See Altham (1985), which argues that wicked promises do not obligate; Chisholm (1964), 152, which states that someone who promises the forbidden is required to, but should not, keep the promise; Christiano and Sciaraffa (2003), 489, referring to known impermissibility (see also 497); DeMarco and Fox (1992), 50 f.; Gilbert (2006), 229 ff., which argues that immoral promises obligate but may not morally bind or require the promisor to perform (on bindingness, see section 3.6 below); Hart (1958), 102 ('[m]orals like law may have principles of "public policy" and render "void" a promise that from the start involved doing something patently immoral'); Hart (1982), 255; Stocker (1970), 618.

30 See McMahon (1989), 241, which discusses promises that would thwart the promisee's purposes; D. Ross (1939), 110; Searle (1965), 233 f.; Searle (1969), 58 f.

31 Christiano and Sciaraffa (2003), 489 states that a promise made and accepted under 'deeply unfair conditions' does not generate obligations. See also Chwang (2011); Fried (1981), 97 ff.; Gilbert (1996a) (coerced agreements are possible); Gilbert (2006), 228; McMahon (1989), 241; Simmons (1984), esp. 809 ff. (coerced agreements are impossible). On duress and undue influence in contract law, see section 7.12 below.

32 On deception, see A. Barnes (1990); A. Barnes (1992); A. Barnes (2007); Harrington (2009); MacCormick (1983); McMahon (1989), 241; Martin (2009); Shute and Horder (1993). See also Chap. 3 n. 69 and section 9.4 below, on the ethics of veracity. On mistake and misrepresentation in contract law, see sections 7.12 and 7.21 below and n. 28 above. DeMarco and Fox (1992), 51 ff. discusses other situations in which a promise is 'degenerate', e.g., promising the unlikely, the ridiculous, the distasteful or the superfluous; compare Chap. 9 n. 95 below, on conspiracies subject to fanciful conditions.

Y is rich but deceives X into believing that Y is a beggar, and on that basis X promises to pay Y five pounds, it appears that X has no obligation to pay the money. It might be suggested that, whatever X may say or do, he does not in fact make a promise in this last situation, or that if he does make one it is implicitly conditional – that he will pay five pounds to Y if Y is very poor – and grounds a correspondingly conditional obligation.[33] Both suggestions are mistaken. As to the latter, X's promise is not internally conditional: its content is not a conditional proposition. All promises are externally conditional, in the sense that there are certain conditions on which a promise, whatever its content, exists: for example, a trivial necessary condition is the existence of the promisor. (For corresponding points about agreements and intentions, see sections 2.63, 5.11 and 9.26.)

The distinction between internal and external conditionality will recur in the book. In the case of promises, it can be represented as one between the respective scopes of 'X promises that' and 'if'. Roughly, where the former includes the latter, there is an internally conditional promise; where the converse is true, the promise is externally conditional. In the simplest case 'X promises that if P then Q' represents an internally conditional promise, 'If P then X promises that Q' an externally conditional one. The same distinction applies to other types of speech act, to propositional attitudes and to obligations.[34] (Internally conditional obligations associated with promises and agreements are considered in sections 1.2312, 1.5 and 3.3.) Unless the distinction needs to be drawn, I shall in this context use 'conditional' to signify internal conditionality.

The fact that a promise obligates the promisor (this is shorthand for the fuller formulation) explains why a promise normally cannot be withdrawn. On a natural understanding of 'withdraw', if X withdraws his promise he releases himself from any obligation arising from the promise. (Talk of an obligation's 'arising from' or 'deriving from', or being 'created by' or 'imposed by' or 'generated by', or being 'under', a promise or agreement can be explicated in terms of grounding.) But it is of the nature of an obligation that the obligor cannot release himself from it; that is a conceptual truth, but the 'cannot' signifies not a conceptual impossibility

33 On the varieties of conditional obligation, see Feldman (1986), chap. 4; Jackson and Pargetter (1987); M. Zimmerman (1996), chap. 4.

34 On the distinction in respect of promises, see Gilbert (1996d), 632 f. It is applied to questions, commands and bets in Dummett (1973), 338 ff. and to intentions in Tuomela (1995), 122 f. The question whether an obligation is unconditional – internally or externally – is distinct from the question whether the obligation motivates; the distinction is blurred in Gilbert (1996d), 319, 328 f.

but what may be called a normative disability.[35] Where a contingency excluded by C obtains, this obstacle to withdrawal does not apply, for, other things equal, X has no obligation; thus it seems that in the example, absent other obstacles, X can withdraw his promise if he learns that Y is rich.

It is more debatable whether the promisee can release the promisor from the promise and hence from the obligation that it creates:[36] the answer may turn on the circumstances, but it appears that in the normal case a release is possible. From now on I assume normality in that respect. It might be suggested that the promisee's releasing the promisor is one of the contingencies excluded by C, but it might be argued, as follows, that the suggestion obscures a distinction. Grant it to be false that, say, if X promises to do something he is unable to do, he is obligated to do it. If he so promises, then, other things equal, he is in a state of promising but without an obligation. If, however, he promises to do something and the promisee releases him from the promise, then, other things equal, he is no longer in a state of promising. Whether that is right depends on the conditions, which I shall not try to specify, determining the duration of states of promising. (Section 2.3 considers the duration of obligations arising from agreements.)

The promisee cannot *accept* the promise in the sense in which an offer may be accepted,[37] although he may do so in the sense, for example, of becoming aware of it or of being content to receive it. A sense might also be proposed in which acceptance is the default situation where he does not release the promisor. (In the case of the five pounds, Y can accept the money, but that is not an acceptance of the promise.) This aspect of promises too is connected to their relation to obligations. An offer to do something does not by itself ground an obligation on the offeror

35 I do not assume any sharp boundary between conceptual and other truths; see the Introduction above on analyticity as conceptual containment and on scepticism about analytic truth. If the categories in Hohfeld (1985) are extended from the legal to the normative, a normative disability is the opposite of a power and is correlative to an immunity. (For a different concept of normative power, see Raz (1972).) On the objection that such an extension presupposes an obsolete conception of the normative in terms of divine law, see Chap. 3 nn. 20 f. below.

36 Raz (1977), 211 appears to assume that the promisee can release the promisor.

37 'The typical and appropriate response to a promise is not "I accept" or "I agree", but "thank you"': S. Smith (2005), 57. On the question whether a promise is binding only if accepted, see Gordley (1991), 80 ff.; McMahon (1989), 243 ff. In Roman law, Justinian's Digest distinguished 'pollicitations' from 'promises', the former being promises made and not accepted: see A. Simpson (2007), 15.

to do it: a function of acceptance, when an offer has been made, is to impose such an obligation (see section 2.4). There is no room for such a function when a promise has been given, for without an acceptance the promise obligates the promisor. Thus the 'cannot', in the statement that the promisee cannot accept the promise, differs from the 'cannot' in the statement that the promisor cannot withdraw it: the latter signifies a normative disability, the former a functional redundancy.

1.2 Promise-based analyses

1.21 Unconditional promises

An agreement between X and Y typically has, explicitly or implicitly, a conjunctive content:[38] 'X will make the beds and Y will wash the dishes', 'X will pay £10 to Y and Y will transfer ownership of his book to X', 'X and Y will meet on the steps of St Paul's at noon' – which implies that both X will be there at noon and Y will be there at noon. In the timeless idiom explained in the Introduction, the content is represented schematically by:

(1) X does Ax and Y does Ay.

Consider:

(2) X and Y agree that (1).

On a very simple analysis:

(3) (2) if:
 (a) X promises to Y that X does Ax; and
 (b) Y promises to X that Y does Ay.

(On independent promises in contract law, see sections 7.6–7.64.) This analysis and the ones that follow are intended only to display the structure of the interaction between X and Y: it is not suggested that X and Y need use the words 'I promise [etc.]'. The exchange is likely to be more informal – for example: X: 'Why don't you wash the dishes and I'll make the beds'. Y: 'Fine'. Indeed, as indicated in section 1.1, X and Y may use no words, their promises being constituted by other actions. Nevertheless it is a point against the promise model, and in favour of the offer–acceptance model,

38 On this point I agree with Sheinman (2011a), 366.

that an exchange of the kind just mentioned appears on its face to amount to an offer and an acceptance rather than to a pair of promises.

In any event, the pair of promises in (3) is insufficient for agreement. This objection, obvious on its face, follows from the fact that the analysis breaches criteria for the adequacy of an analysis of agreement. For example, Gilbert's criterion of Interdependence provides that 'if one party defaults on his performance obligation, the other ceases to have his original performance obligation';[39] by the principle stated in section 1.1, if X gives his promise (and C obtains), then, whether or not Y does Ay, X is obligated to do Ax; so the analysis breaches Interdependence.[40] A parallel objection applies to a variant of (3) in which (1) is the content of each party's promise. The criteria and the relevant principles of obligation are discussed more fully in sections 1.231–1.2314 and 1.5.

1.22 Conditional promises

Since it appears that no other unconditional promises are sufficient for X and Y to agree, it might be proposed that conditional ones are sufficient. But it is obscure how promises with conditional content can yield an agreement with unconditional content of the form (1). The objection might be avoided by maintaining that the content of typical agreements is conditional: in the earlier example, 'X will pay £10 to Y and Y will transfer ownership of his book to X' is a loose rendering of 'X will pay £10 to Y if and only if Y will transfer ownership of his book to X'. (Compare section 5.5.) But that misrepresents the typical case; section 2.63 shows that the conditional aspects of agreement do not normally relate to the content.

There are various ways of analysing agreement in terms of conditional promises; for example, the conditionality may be external or internal, and one party's promise may be conditional on the other's giving a promise or on his performing it. A simple thought is:

(4) (2) if:
 (a) X promises to Y that if Y does Ay then X does Ax; and
 (b) Y promises to X that if X does Ax then Y does Ay.

39 Gilbert (1996d), 317; see also Gilbert (1996a), 291 and compare Fried (1981), 117. Gilbert (1996a), 291 and Gilbert (1996d), 316 propose a stronger version of Interdependence: if either party defaults, he nullifies the obligations of *both* parties. In French law a distinction is sometimes drawn between interdependent and reciprocal obligations: see Nicholas (1992), 43.

40 This objection applies to Sheinman's more elaborate account in terms of unconditional promises. His response is to dilute Interdependence: Sheinman (2011a), 389 ff.

Assume for simplicity a 'material implication' analysis of the conditional: <if P then Q> if and only if either not P or Q, and hence if and only if not both P and not Q. The nature of conditionals is a debated issue in the philosophy of logic; this book uses whichever analysis is easiest in the context, with the proviso that it should be a reasonable approximation and not distort the discussion. Later chapters will use the arguably more realistic 'strict implication' analysis: <if P then Q> if and only if <necessarily, either not P or Q>, and hence if and only if it is not possible that both P and not Q. On the assumptions, which hold in classical logic and are made here, that <P if and only if it is true that P> and that ≪not P> if and only if it is false that P>,[41] the two analyses can be reformulated in terms of truth values or in mixed terms; for example, as regards material implication, '"If P then Q" is true if and only if either it is false that P or it is true that Q' – the conditional is thus said to be a truth function of its antecedent (the 'if'-clause) and its consequent (the 'then'-clause) – or '"If P then Q" is true if and only if either not P or Q'. Both the material-implication analysis and the strict-implication analysis face difficulties – notably the so-called paradoxes and, as regards the versions in terms of truth and falsity, the more radical objection that conditionals do not have truth values – but for present purposes those can mainly be ignored.[42] One of the paradoxes will arise in section 8.121.

An objection to (4) is that it likewise breaches criteria of adequacy; another is that in any event it represents at best a peripheral kind of agreement. If X and Y give their promises, one or other is likely to press to make the position clear: X might say 'So, do we have an agreement that I do Ax and you do Ay?' If Y replies 'Yes', they have an agreement of a kind different from that represented by (4). The different kind is captured by the offer–acceptance model, presented in the next chapter.

41 For logics in which those assumptions do not hold, see Haack (1974), chap. 3.

42 Jackson (1991) is an introduction to the philosophy of conditionals; see also E. Adams (1975). For the paradoxes of material implication, see Grice (1989a); Grice (1989b); Grice (1989c); Jackson (1998b). For those of strict implication, see J. Bennett (1954); J. Bennett (1965); Duncan-Jones (1935); Geach (1958); Hughes and Cresswell (1968), 39 f., 335 ff.; C. Lewis and Langford (1959), 174 f., 248 f., 503 ff.; Lewy (1950), 195; Lewy (1958); Nelson (1930); J. Pollock (1966); Smiley (1959); Strawson (1948); von Wright (1957). Edgington (1991) denies that indicative conditionals have truth values. On the question whether counterfactual conditionals have determinate truth values, see D. Lewis (1973), 66 f., 91 ff.; Mendola (1987), 127 ff.; M. Zimmerman (1996), 60 (which considers the implications for attributions of obligation). On conditional obligations, see n. 33 above; on paradoxes of conditional obligation, see M. Zimmerman (1996), 122 ff. and works cited there.

A third objection adverts to the distinction, drawn in the Introduction, between performance and compliance. That X does Ax and Y does Ay is necessary and sufficient for them to perform the agreement, for them to comply with it, and for them to perform their promises; but, although it is sufficient for them to comply with the promises, it is not necessary, for they may comply if neither does anything.[43] It is hard to see how the promises can be sufficient for the agreement if their conditions for compliance diverge in this way.

As regards X's promise, the objection can be formalised as an argument to the negation of (4) from the premisses:

(5) X complies with the agreement only if he does Ax.
(6) X complies with his promise if Y does not do Ay.
(7) It is not the case that if Y does not do Ay then X does Ax.
(8) If (4) then, if X complies with his promise, X complies with the agreement.

The most contentious premiss is (6), which follows from the proposition that, if someone promises that if P then he φs, then he complies with the promise if either not P or he φs.[44] One response to (6) is to point out that, if X fails to do Ax, he runs the risk of failing to comply with the promise: that happens if Y does Ay. So, if X wants to comply and is not certain that Y does not do Ay, he does Ax.[45] (Compare section 5.11 on cases where one party to an agreement is uncertain as to the other's performance.) The response fails for two reasons: the conditional just stated both has a false antecedent in some instances and is consistent with (6).

A better response distinguishes kinds of compliance. Here compliance with promises is at issue, but the same distinction applies to compliance with agreements, obligations and so on; given the importance of compliance in an account of agreement and of its relations to other phenomena, the response has an interest beyond that of the present objection. If a simple kind is in question then, if X promises that P, <he complies with the promise if and only if he acts in such a way that P is true>. (Section 8.122 considers a kind of compliance that involves the parties' acting

43 S. Smith (2004), 181 raises the related but different objection that, if X and Y make promises that are conditional on each other, neither party is obligated to do anything. Compare the objection, concerning breach of obligations, to the offer–acceptance model: section 2.64 below.

44 Compare Broome (2001b), 180 on conforming to normative requirements. See further Chap. 4 nn. 5 and 27 below.

45 Compare Sheinman (2011a), 394 n. 43.

with certain intentions.) There are a weak sense and a strong sense of this biconditional's right-hand side. In the weak sense, <X acts in such a way that P is true> if and only if <X performs some action and P is true>; the strong sense adds the condition that X's performing the action makes P true. We may thus talk of weak and strong compliance. 'Action', as noted in the Introduction, includes omissions. 'Makes P true' can be left unanalysed.[46]

X either does or does not do Ax, and so X performs some action in the relevant broad sense. (I draw no distinction between not doing and omitting to do.) Suppose that Y does not do Ay. Then, by the material-implication analysis, the content of X's promise is true. So X performs some action and the content of the promise is true. So X weakly complies with the promise. But he does not strongly comply, for his performance of the action does not make the content true: the content is true by virtue of the falsity of its antecedent, and the antecedent is falsified by Y's not doing Ay. (The assumption is that whatever falsifies the antecedent of a material conditional makes the conditional true.) So (6) is true for weak but false for strong compliance. Provided that the other premisses are true, the objection succeeds for weak but fails for strong compliance.

In further defence of (4) it might now be argued that the objection's success as regards weak compliance is Pyrrhic, as the concepts of weak and strong compliance are artifices that fail to reflect the intuitive notion of compliance.[47] X strongly complies with the content P of his promise if and only if X performs an action that makes P true. But, the argument goes, the truth of the right-hand side of this biconditional is not sufficient for compliance according to the intuitive notion; a fortiori the truth of the right-hand side of the biconditional characterising weak compliance is not sufficient. To see the insufficiency in the case of strong compliance, suppose that X promises to Y that if X hears a noise then X will shout. X does not comply with his promise if he plugs his ears, even if by so doing he makes false the antecedent of the promise's content and thus makes the content true. The reason is that by plugging his ears X undermines the promise's point.

46 On truth-making, see Armstrong (2004); J. Fox (1987); Mellor (2000), 771; Mulligan et al. (1984); Restall (1996); B. Smith (1999). For scepticism about the concept, see Merricks (2007); Merricks (2009b).

47 On the place of intuitive judgments in philosophy, see Earlenbaugh and Molyneux (2009); A. Goldman (2007); Knobe and Nichols (2008) (from the approach of 'experimental philosophy'); Papineau (2009), 12 ff.; Williamson (2007), chap. 7.

Four objections to this argument are that it confuses compliance with performance; that the intuition it invokes is frail; that at least on certain understandings of a promise's point, and of undermining the point, a promisor may comply with his promise even if he undermines its point;[48] and that the argument confuses the words X utters with the promise he gives. As to the last objection, the example is thinly described, but it might be imagined that X and Y are hiding in the jungle and surrounded by enemies. If X says 'If I hear a noise, I'll shout', he expects Y to take him to intend (perhaps via a Gricean mechanism) to make Y believe that he will warn Y of danger. It is plausible to say that making Y believe this is the, or a, point of X's utterance and of the promise he gives in uttering those words. The point will be achieved only if Y takes X to mean more than he says, i.e., to be giving the conjunctive promise (Px1) that X will listen out for a noise and if he hears one he will shout. If X plugs his ears, the first conjunct, and hence the whole content, of Px1 is false. In that case X neither strongly nor weakly complies. Nor does X comply according to the intuitive notion. So the example, expanded thus, does not show that the concepts of strong and weak compliance conflict with the intuitive notion.

If, however, X merely promises (Px2) that if he hears a noise he will shout, he strongly and weakly complies by plugging his ears; but, although intuition is less confident here, it is plausible to say that he also complies according to the intuitive notion. So again there is no conflict. Of course the circumstances in which both parties take X to be giving Px2 would be odd: we might imagine that Y is a doctor giving a motor co-ordination test to X. A scene more readily suggested by the argument is one in which X and Y are back in the jungle but X is one of the enemy and makes his utterance in order to mislead Y: not wanting to utter a falsehood, he plugs his ears and jesuitically maintains that he intended his words literally. It might be suggested that X here breaches an implied promise not to mislead Y; if that promise is mixed up with Px2, the mistaken result emerges that by plugging his ears X breaches Px2. But again the result rests on a confusion, as well as on the debatable claim that there is any such implied promise.

This objection depends on the material-implication reading of 'if' in X's utterance and in Px1 and Px2. The defender of (4) might now say

48 Bacchus's gift to Midas, if it involved a promise, is arguably an example. The witches' prophesies to Macbeth are arguable examples concerning factual rather than active promises. Alex Gregory drew my attention to cases of this kind.

that the reading is another artifice: 'if' normally signifies not merely that the antecedent is false or the consequent true, but that there is good reason to infer the consequent from the antecedent.[49] If the two promises are understood thus, the result for Px1 stays the same: regardless of the conditional second conjunct of Px1's content, X's plugging his ears makes false the first conjunct and X thereby fails to comply strongly, weakly or according to the intuitive notion. But, the defence runs, the result for Px2 changes. Assume that X's making his utterance provides a good reason to infer that X will shout from the proposition that he hears a noise. If X plugs his ears, our intuition is that he does not comply with Px2. Nor does he strongly comply, for his plugging his ears does not make it true that there is good reason to make that inference. But he weakly complies, for he performs some action and the content of Px2 is true. Weak compliance thus diverges from intuitive compliance.

There are two flaws in this defence. First, if Px2's 'if' is given the proposed strong reading, it is not intuitively clear that X fails to comply with Px2; my intuition, at least, is uncertain. Second, it may be retorted that it is the strong, not the material-implication, reading of 'if' that is an artifice. That raises the old debate over the relation between conditionality and material implication, which I shall not pursue. The standard argument for their equivalence appeals to rules of implicature.[50] (Such rules might be invoked to justify Y in taking X to be giving Px1 in making his utterance.) If that or some other argument works, no persuasive reason has yet been given for rejecting the concept of weak – or strong – compliance. In that case the earlier conclusion stands: the objection from (5)–(8) succeeds for weak but fails for strong compliance.

Given the other objections, (4) should in any event be rejected. On the material-implication analysis, it is no use complicating the clauses of (4) so that (i) X promises that <if, if X does Ax then Y does Ay, then X does Ax> and (ii) Y promises the converse.[51] Since on that analysis ≪if, if P then Q, then P> if and only if P>, the content of X's promise is equivalent to 'X does Ax' and that of Y's to 'Y does Ay', and hence the content of each party's promise is equivalent to that of his promise in (3). Objections to (3) extend to the revision of (4); there is no need to develop the point, but it is worth noting that it does not depend on the implausible claim that promising is closed under biconditionality. (On

49 See Strawson (1963), 35 ff., 82 ff. 50 See the essays by Grice in n. 42 above.
51 Compare Radford (1984), 580 f. A more elaborate complication of the conditionals is proposed by Prichard (2002c) in an account of exchange.

closure, see section 5.32, which argues that agreement is not closed under conditionality.)

1.23 *Mixed promises*

It appears, then, that neither unconditional promises nor conditional promises are sufficient for agreement. In earlier work[52] I tried to avoid the dilemma by developing the thought that, if X gives to Y a conditional promise and Y responds with an unconditional one, then X and Y agree.[53] An analysis along those lines is:

(9) (2) if:
- (a) X promises to Y that, if Y promises to X that Y does Ay, then X does Ax (call this promise Px);
- (b) Y promises to X that Y does Ay (call this promise Py);[54]
- (c) Y's reason for giving Py is that X gives Px; and
- (d) X has the justified belief that (b),

(2) being the proposition that X and Y agree that (1) <X does Ax and Y does Ay>. In a simpler variant, Ax is conditional not on Py but on Ay:

(10) (2) if:
- (a) X promises to Y that if Y does Ay then X does Ax;
- . . . ,

the other clauses remaining the same, with the references adjusted accordingly.[55] Clause (c) of each analysis is intended to capture the idea

52 O. Black (2004a); O. Black (2005b), chap. 4.

53 Mintoff (2004), 56 ff. offers a similar analysis in terms of intentions rather than promises.

54 Raz (1984), 203 seems to hold that (a) and (b) are sufficient for an agreement. Raz appears to take the same view of (a) and (b) in (10) below. He explicitly disregards the distinction between the internally and the externally conditional (which, in the case of duties, he conflates with a distinction between present and future duties): ibid., 196 n 1. Bach (1995), 606 f. likewise seems to say that an agreement may involve promises of the forms in (a) and (b) in (9). In Gilbert (1996d), 327, case 8, read as involving an internally conditional promise, instantiates (9)(a) and (b). Surprisingly, Gilbert does not examine a case instantiating the corresponding clauses of (10).

55 A fictional agreement which arguably instantiates (10) is described in *The Way We Live Now*: 'a treaty had been made between Mr Longestaffe, the father, and Georgiana, the strong-minded daughter. The daughter on her side undertook that the guests should be treated with feminine courtesy. . . . In return for this the Longestaffe family were to be allowed to return to town.' When Mr Longestaffe later breaches the agreement, Georgiana remonstrates: 'Did you not promise that we should go back if we would come down and entertain these people?' Trollope (1982), 160, 197. On another reading, the words 'In

that, for the parties' promises to amount to an agreement, Y must give his in response to X's.[56] 'Y's reason' includes the case where Y has more than one reason[57] and the case where X's giving Px is only part of Y's reason. There are various kinds of reason and various theories of reasons.[58] The kind in question comprises motivating practical reasons.[59] On one theory, such reasons are facts[60] and so the phrase 'that X gives Px' in (c) signifies the fact that X gives Px. Another theory has it that such reasons are mental states of the agent: on that account, the phrase might be taken to signify, more elliptically, Y's belief that X gives Px, or a compound of that belief and some desire.[61]

Clause (c) is plausibly read as entailing that Y's giving Py is based on the reason. I favour an account of basing in terms of causal explanation:

return for this the Longestaffe family were to be allowed to return to town' represent part of the content of Georgiana's undertaking, in which case the agreement instantiates (4).

56 Compare Mintoff (2004), 56, 62, which says that one party makes an unconditional decision 'because' of a belief as to the other party's intended action.

57 Alvarez (2010), 127 f. discusses such cases.

58 On some theories, distinct kinds of reason are marked by distinct idioms: see O. Black (1987), 93 ff. It might be said, for example, that 'a reason for X to φ' signifies a normative reason, 'a reason for which X φs' a motivating reason, and 'a reason why X φs' an explanatory reason. A debated question is whether the distinction between these kinds of reason is an ontological one or a distinction between roles played by the members of a single ontological category; for example, it might be said that, whereas normative reasons are facts, motivating reasons are mental states, or that facts may play the role either of normative or of motivating reasons. On that question, see Alvarez (2010), chap. 2, which distinguishes the normative, the motivating and the explanatory, and argues that the distinction is one of roles. Dancy (2000), 2 makes the similar point that 'the single notion of a reason' can be used to answer normative questions and questions of motivation. See further nn. 60 f. below and Chap. 3 n. 48 below.

59 On the concept of motivation, see Alvarez (2010), 53 ff.; Mele (2003); Peters (1958).

60 See Alvarez (2010), 3, 40 ff.; contrast Bittner (2001), 69. Alvarez takes facts to be the same as true propositions: Alvarez (2010), 151 ff. On the metaphysics of facts, see Chap. 3 n. 37 below.

61 The distinction is similar to that in Dancy (2000), 14 f. between 'psychologistic' and 'anti-psychologistic' theories of reasons for action. Dancy is an anti-psychologist, but holds (ibid., 131 ff.) that explanation by motivating reasons is not factive; he would therefore deny that such reasons need be facts, unless there can be non-existent facts. On the meaning of 'factive', see n. 11 to the Introduction above. For the more general view that an explanans need not be true, see van Fraassen (1993), 278. For other anti-psychologistic accounts of reasons, see Alvarez (2010); Bittner (2001); McDowell (1982); Stout (1996); Stout (2005); Stoutland (1998). For the 'Hume-Davidson' theory that a motivating reason is a compound of belief and desire, see Davidson (1980a); see also R. Audi (2001), 66 on 'conative groundedness'. For an overview of the debate, see Chang (2004). For the theory that belief can generate desire, see O. Black (1994), 78 f.; T. Nagel (1970), chap. 5. Dancy (1993), chaps. 1 ff. argues that belief by itself can motivate action; compare Alvarez (2010), 258 ff.

roughly, Y's giving Py is explained by the fact that there is an appropriate causal chain from the reason to the giving of Py.[62] To say that there is a causal chain from A to B is to say that A stands to B in the proper ancestral of the relation . . . causes . . . , or of some other causal relation; on an informal definition,[63] this means that A bears the relation to B, or bears the relation to C, which bears the relation to B, and so on. The requirement that the chain be appropriate is intended to exclude cases in which the chain involves grossly irrational mental processes, or even no mental processes at all, on Y's part. An account of appropriateness need not be attempted here,[64] but an arguably necessary condition in this case is that Y believe that X gives Px,[65] in which case a mental state enters into the basing relation even if it is not itself a reason.[66] In normal cases of agreement, not only does Y have the belief, but his belief is justified or amounts to knowledge.

It might be objected that (9) should mention not only Y's reason but also X's – not for giving Px but for doing Ax. Suppose that, first, <X knows that <if Y gives Py, Z forces X to do Ax≫, where Ax is something that X hopes not to do and believes it would be bad for him to do; second, X, in order to alert Y, tells Y that if Y gives Py then X does Ax; and third, for the reason that X tells this to Y, Y maliciously takes advantage of X's predicament by giving Py. Then it seems that the condition in (9) is met, but X and Y do not agree that they respectively do Ax and Ay. One proposal is to exclude this case by rewriting the consequent of (a) to say that X, for the reason that Y gives Py, does Ax. But the proposal is unnecessary because the case is not a counterexample to (9). X's utterance is not an

62 In O. Black (1987), 108 ff. and O. Black (1988), 429 the account is used to explicate the notion of one belief's being based on another. It accommodates the theory (as to which see Davidson (1980c) and Evnine (1991), chap. 2) that only events, not facts or states, are causes. Causal theories of basing are common; see, e.g., Armstrong (1974), chap. 6, esp. 79 ff.; Pappas (1979); B. Williams (1973). For other theories of basing, see O. Black (1987), 104 ff., which gives references.

63 Quine (1979), 215 ff. gives a formal definition of the proper ancestral.

64 Peacocke (1979), chap. 2 proposes one. Stout (2005), chap. 6 impugns explanations of action that invoke causal chains.

65 Here is a point – additional to the distinction between promises and offer/acceptance – at which contract law may diverge from these analyses of agreement, for there is doubtful authority in English law for the rule that a contract may be created by a party's accepting an offer of which he is ignorant: *Gibbons* v. *Proctor* (1891) 64 LT 594, 55 JP 616 (compare *Neville* v. *Kelly* (1862) 12 CB (NS) 740); sections 7.13 and 7.36 and Chap. 7 n. 119 below. The rule can be squared with the analyses if ignorance is taken to be the absence of knowledge rather than of belief.

66 Dancy (2000), 126 ff. appears to accept this. See n. 61 above.

active promise that if Y gives Py then X does Ax: rather, it is a conditional prediction – perhaps also a warning and/or a factual promise. A similar reply can be made to the corresponding objection to (10).

As already noted, (c) arguably implies that Y believes that X gives Px. It might be proposed that a similar condition be imposed on X – that X believe that Y gives Py – for otherwise, the reasoning goes, the analyses fail to capture the fact that agreement involves a meeting of minds. This step can generate a regress: if X must believe that Y gives Py, perhaps Y must believe that X believes this, and perhaps X must believe that Y believes that X gives Px, and so on. Such thinking motivates the addition of a clause attributing to X and Y the common belief that they respectively give Px and Py and perhaps also that Y's reason for giving Py is that X gives Px. Roughly, to say that <X and Y have the common belief that P> is to say that <X believes that P>, <Y believes that P>, <Y believes that X believes that P>, <X believes that Y believes that P>, and so on. Corresponding definitions apply to other propositional attitudes.[67]

How far one should go along that path depends first on how strong a sense 'meeting of minds' has and second on whether agreement involves a meeting of minds[68] in that sense. The answer to the first question is partly a matter of stipulation, for the phrase is more venerable than clear (see above) and it can be given a meaning thin enough to apply to the conditions in (9) and (10). A clause attributing common belief to X and Y is needlessly strong, save perhaps for an artificially narrow concept of agreement: if the condition in (9) or (10), with the addition of the clause,

67 The one most often discussed is common knowledge. Gilbert's account of an agreement attributes common knowledge to the parties: Gilbert (1996a), 285; see also Gilbert (1996h), 109. On common knowledge generally, see Aumann (1976); Binmore and Brandenburger (1990); Geanakoplos (1992); Heal (1978); D. Lewis (1969), 52 ff.; Milgrom (1981); Nielsen (1984); Parikh and Krasucki (1990); Schiffer (1972), chaps. 2 f.; Schiffer (1987), 245 f.; N. Smith (1982).

68 The view that a meeting of minds is not needed for a contract to exist is supported by the doubtful rule in n. 65 above that a contract may be created by a party's accepting an offer of which he is ignorant, and also by the better entrenched converse rule that a contract may arise if the offeror is ignorant of the acceptance: see sections 7.13 and 7.31 and Chap. 7 n. 119 below; also Beale (2008), para. 1–004, which cites *Byrne* v. *Van Tienhoven* (1880) 5 CPD 344 in support of the principle that a contract can arise where the parties are not 'ad idem'. It appears to be a principle of English contract law that where the offeree believes the offeror to have the relevant intention – that the offer is to become binding on acceptance (see Peel (2007), para. 2–003, discussed in section 7.11 below) – it is not necessary, for a contract to exist, that the offeror be aware of the offeree's belief (*The Hannah Blumenthal* [1983] 1 AC 854, 924; Beale (2008), para. 2–004). That pulls against a requirement of common belief.

is sufficient for X and Y to agree, it is also partly redundant. To add such a clause would also raise the general difficulties with common propositional attitudes, notably that it seems psychologically unrealistic to suppose that people ever have them.[69] A more attractive proposal is to include just a clause to capture the idea that not only Y but both parties are aware of what is going on.[70] That is the purpose of (d), which says that X has the justified belief that Y gives Py.

1.231 Criteria of adequacy

There is a good argument, as follows, that (9) and (10) are better than (4) (the analysis in terms of conditional promises) in the respect that neither (9) nor (10) creates a divergence of compliance conditions. The parties comply with the agreement if and only if both X does Ax and Y does Ay. Assume (9) and that X and Y respectively give Px and Py. If (9) then if and only if X complies with Px and Y with Py do they comply with the agreement. So if and only if X complies with Px and Y with Py do they comply with the agreement. X complies with Px if and only if either Y does not give Py or X does Ax. (From now on, unless stated otherwise, weak compliance is at issue and the material-implication analysis assumed.) So X complies with Px if and only if X does Ax. Y complies with Py if and only if Y does Ay. So <X complies with Px and Y with Py> if and only if both X does Ax and Y does Ay. The compliance conditions for the agreement and the promises in (9) are thus the same. A similar argument applies to (10).

(9) and (10) nevertheless raise the problem mentioned in section 1.22, of a mismatch between the content of the agreement and the contents of the promises. Further problems arise from four criteria that may be proposed for the adequacy of an analysis of agreement: Symmetry, Obligation, Simultaneity and (one already stated) Interdependence.[71] (10) breaches all of them, and (9) breaches at least two, in this sense: it is

69 See Schiffer (1987), 246. Proposals for psychologically realistic forms of common knowledge or belief are found in J. Bennett (1976), 127; Kemmerling (1986); Loar (1981), 250; Tuomela (1995), 41 ff. On the broader issue of a person's having an infinity of beliefs, see O. Black (1987), chap. 8; O. Black (2003b).

70 A strong version of this idea is embodied in Gilbert's '"knowledge of agreements" assumption' that, if a person enters into an agreement, he knows that he does: Gilbert (1996a), 284. On the possibility of entering an agreement unintentionally, see sections 5.1, 5.12, 8.12 and 9.3 below.

71 The last three, and a 'rescission' criterion, are discussed in Mintoff (2004), 45 ff. Mintoff recasts the criteria in terms of reasons rather than obligations. On rescission, see further n. 89 below.

not the case that, if the parties meet the condition stated by the analysis to be sufficient for agreement, they meet the condition specified by the criterion. Hence either the analyses are inadequate or the criteria are. I shall argue for the first alternative. The thesis is that, although questions can be raised about the criteria, the fact that the analyses breach Interdependence is strong reason to hold that at best they cover peripheral cases of agreement.[72] Such cases aside, the form of the argument is this: each analysis says that, if the parties meet its condition, they agree; if they agree, their obligations are interdependent; it is false that, if they meet the condition, their obligations are interdependent; so both analyses are false. I start with (9).

1.2311 Symmetry The idea of Symmetry is that both parties do the same thing.[73] It is hard to make this precise, but there is no need to, as it is clear that the criterion is breached by (9). The content of Px is conditional and that of Py is not; whereas Y gives Py for the reason that X gives Px, the converse need not be true; and, although X has the justified belief that Y gives Py, Y may not have the justified belief that X gives Px. So much the worse, it might be replied, for Symmetry: (9) does, and the criterion does not, reflect the fact that normally, in the making of an agreement, one party – X in the analysis – 'goes first'[74] (see further section 1.2313).

1.2312 Obligation The remaining three criteria have been proposed by Gilbert, as part of an argument against the view that an agreement is an exchange of promises.[75] These criteria are intuitively more persuasive, although it is a weakness of Gilbert's discussion that Gilbert says little

72 Mintoff (2004), 50 maintains that Interdependence poses 'the central problem' for the view that an agreement is an exchange of promises.

73 Radford (1984), 581 talks of the 'parallel nature' of the things said by the parties, but in effect Radford rejects Symmetry.

74 Compare Bach (1995), 606 f.

75 Gilbert describes these as criteria for the adequacy of a 'model' of agreement: Gilbert (1996d), 315 ff. For present purposes there is no need to decide whether a model in Gilbert's sense, which she does not define, is the same as an analysis. As noted in the Introduction above, I use 'analysis' as a term of convenience only; the Introduction also explains my use of 'model'. Gilbert's sense of 'model' may be the same as or similar to the one I used in O. Black (2003c), 65; O. Black (2004a), 78 f.; O. Black (2005b), 4 f.

For a legal example of the 'exchange of promises' view, see *Mulcahy* v. *The Queen* (1868) LR 3 HL 306, 317, a case on conspiracy: 'When two parties agree to carry [a design] into effect, the very plot is an act in itself, and the act of each of the parties, promise against promise, actus contra actum, capable of being enforced, if lawful, punishable if for a criminal object or for the use of criminal means'.

about their sources. She might, for example, have argued that the criteria somehow flow from the purposes served by the concept of agreement[76] or by agreements themselves.

She expresses Obligation by saying that 'the agreement directly generates the relevant performance obligation for each of the parties' – a performance obligation, which she appears to view as unconditional, being 'an obligation to perform the specified act'.[77] The specified acts in (9) are Ax and Ay. (It might be argued that, even though Ax is the act specified for X, a distinction exists between X's obligation to perform the specified act and his obligation to do Ax; but that issue can be ignored. A parallel issue is discussed in section 3.3.) To decide whether (9) meets Obligation, principles of obligation are needed. The following is rough (see section 1.1) but serviceable:

(11) If someone promises that P, then he is obligated that P.

(11) follows, given certain supplementary premisses, from the proposition that the fact that someone promises that P grounds (to be more accurate, the fact is a complete ground of) the fact that he is obligated that P: on grounding, see the brief discussion in section 1.1 and the longer one in section 3.2. The question can be left open whether the obligation here is moral; section 3.4 discusses the corresponding question about the obligations associated with agreements. Assume that it is of the type to which Gilbert's criterion refers.[78] Substitution instances of (11) are:

(12) If someone promises that he φs, then he is obligated that he φs;[79]
(13) If someone promises that if P then he φs, then he is obligated that if P then he φs.[80]

76 Compare the approach taken to knowledge in E. Craig (1990), chap. 1, and to truth in B. Williams (2002), and see further section 4.4 below.

77 Gilbert (1996d), 315.

78 Gilbert (1996a), 299 f. allows that the obligations of agreement are pro tanto, i.e., can be outweighed (see further Chap. 3 n. 89 below, and compare Zimmerman on the prima facie nature of the obligation of fidelity (n. 27 above)) and doubts that they are moral. See also Gilbert (1996d), 336; Gilbert (1996f), 79; Gilbert (1996h), 108 f.; Gilbert (1996i), 181; Gilbert (2000a), 61; Gilbert (2006), 224; Mintoff (2004), 49. Gilbert (2004), 108 suggests that promissory obligations may be neither moral nor legal. On the moral nature of the obligation to keep a promise, see Robins (1984), 108 f. Raz (1977), 225 denies that promissory obligations as such are moral. See also Atiyah (1981), 110, 138 ff.; Finnis (1980), 308; Narveson (1967), 193; Searle (1969), 188 (quoted in Chap. 3 n. 141 below).

79 Raz (1984), 202 states a similar principle.

80 An obligation of this form is similar to a 'normative requirement' in Broome's sense, but the applicable normative concept in the latter case is *ought* rather than *obligation*: see

It might be objected that (11) confuses a purely externally conditional obligation with one that is internally conditional:

(14) Whether or not someone promises that P, he is obligated that if he promises that P then P.

A corresponding issue as to the external/internal distinction arises in respect of the obligations associated with agreements: that issue is discussed in section 3.3. Here it is enough to note first that, whether or not (14) is true, (11) is plausible and second that, if (14) is the only relevant principle, (9) and (10) breach Obligation; in particular, whereas Y's performance obligation is unconditional, (14) and clause (b) of each of the two analyses together imply only that Y has the conditional obligation, to do Ay if Y promises to do Ay. (Here and elsewhere I slide, for convenience, between 'obligation that' and 'obligation to'; see the Introduction on the propositional content of obligations.)

Gilbert does not explain what she means by 'directly generates', but it appears that (9) meets Obligation so far as Y is concerned: by (9)(b), Y promises that he does Ay; so, by (12), Y is obligated to do Ay. X, however, gives the conditional promise in (9)(a); hence by (13) he has the conditional obligation, to do Ax if Y promises to him that Y does Ay. But that is not X's performance obligation, which is simply to do Ax: compare the point about (14). Absent any other relevant principle, (9) breaches Obligation.[81]

One response is to elaborate (13) into a more controversial principle which is not a substitution instance of (11):

(15) If someone promises that if P then he φs, then:
 (a) he is obligated that if P then he φs; and
 (b) if P then he is obligated that he φs.

((12) and (15) are elaborated respectively in sections 7.632 and 7.633.) The obligation in (15)(a) is, and that in (15)(b) is not, internally conditional; both are externally conditional – the former on the promise, the latter on both the promise and P. If P, (b) allows the detachment of the proposition

Chap. 4 n. 5 below. On the relation between *ought* and *obligation*, see Chap. 3 n. 87 and Chap. 6 n. 54 below. For reservations about internally conditional obligations, see Gilbert (1996d), 319.

81 A particularist as to obligation might hold that, even if no principle applies, X may have an obligation. On particularism, see n. 25 to the Introduction above.

that the promisor has an internally unconditional obligation.[82] Given (15) and a suitably generous reading of the criterion, (9) meets Obligation so far as X is concerned; for, by (9)(a), (9)(b) and (15)(b), X is obligated to do Ax. In that case (9) meets Obligation, for it does so as regards both X and Y.

1.2313 Simultaneity The next criterion is Simultaneity: the parties to an agreement acquire simultaneously their obligations that derive from it.[83] (12), (13) and (15) say nothing about the times at which the obligations they mention arise, but temporal references can plausibly be introduced,[84] thus:

(16) If at T1 someone promises that he φs, then at T1 he gets an obligation that he φs;
(17) If at T2 someone promises that if at T3 event E occurs then he φs, then at T2 he gets an obligation that if at T3 E occurs then he φs.
(18) If at T2 someone promises that if at T3 E occurs then he φs, then:
  (a) at T2 he gets an obligation that if at T3 E occurs then he φs; and
  (b) if at T3 E occurs, then at T3 he gets an obligation that he φs.

Temporal references can likewise be introduced into (9) (see further section 2.64). Using names for times that match those in the principles (so that T1 = T3):

(19) <At T1 X and Y agree that (1)> if:
  (a) at T2 X promises to Y that, if at T1 Y promises to X that Y does Ay, then X does Ax;

82 On the detachability of normative conclusions, see Broome (2000), 79 ff.; Broome (2001a); Broome (2001b); Broome (2002), 94; Broome (2004); Chap. 4 n. 3 below. On the varieties of such detachment, see Feldman (1986), 90 f.; Greenspan (1975), section 2; A. Price (2008), 164; Vorobej (1986), 20; M. Zimmerman (1996), chap. 4 (esp. 128 ff.), 146, 160 ff., 200 ff. See also the example of the driver, in section 1.5 below.

83 Gilbert (1996a), 290 and Gilbert (1996d), 315 f. Gilbert may – her wording is not clear – have in mind a stronger criterion, that the parties both acquire and lose their obligations at the same time. If so, the following discussion is unaffected. The distinction between lasting for the same period and lasting for adjoining or overlapping periods seems to resolve the conflicts between requirements of simultaneity and succession that Benson (2001c) finds in contract law. It thus avoids the need for the baffling solution Benson proposes, that '"[s]imultaneity" must . . . mean something other than "at the same time"' (148) and that '[v]alue is the unity of temporal succession and simultaneity' (195). On concurrent obligations in contract law, see also Nicholas (1992), 42.

84 On the time of an obligation, see Castañeda (1977); Chellas (1980), 195 ff.; Feldman (1986); H. Goldman (1976); Prichard (2002g); Prior (1957); Sinnott-Armstrong, (1985); Thomason (1981); van Eck (1982); M. Zimmerman (1996), 82 ff.

(b) at T1 Y promises to X that Y does Ay;
(c) and (d) as before.

X's promise normally precedes Y's, and so T2 precedes T1. By (19)(b) and (16), Y gets a performance obligation at T1; by (19)(a) and (17), X gets a conditional obligation at T2; so, if (16) and (17) are the only relevant principles, (19) breaches Simultaneity. By (19)(a) and (18)(a), X gets the same obligation at T2; by (19)(a), (19)(b) and (18)(b), X gets a performance obligation at T1; and so X gets the conditional obligation before, but his performance obligation at the same time as, Y gets Y's performance obligation. Hence, if (18) applies, (19) meets Simultaneity provided that the criterion is understood, as Gilbert appears to intend it, to concern only the performance obligations of the parties.

Her statement in support of Simultaneity, that '[i]n many cases, a given party will have no desire to take on some particular obligation before the other party has taken on a corresponding obligation',[85] can be reconciled with the fact that, by (18), X gets a conditional obligation before Y gets Y's performance obligation, for the obligations may be said not to 'correspond'. In any event, if X wants to make an agreement with Y, X must be willing to take the steps needed to achieve that – specifically, the defender of (19) may say, to give his promise and thereby to get a conditional obligation. (Compare the point in section 1.2311, that one party goes first.) Since the obligation is only conditional, it is not burdensome unless and until at T1 Y promises. It might be argued that the conditional obligation implies certain unconditional obligations on X – in particular the obligation not to put himself in such a position that, if at T1 Y promises, X is unable to do Ax – and that in some circumstances such obligations are a burden on X. Whether or not that is true, it is consistent with Simultaneity if the criterion is understood as above.

1.2314 Interdependence Gilbert's third criterion is Interdependence. To repeat: 'if one party defaults on his performance obligation, the other ceases to have his original performance obligation'.[86] It might be argued that (9) meets the criterion in respect of a default by Y: as explained in section 1.2312, if the only principle bearing on X's obligations is (13), X does not get a performance obligation; and there is no difference between his not getting one and his ceasing to have one. The reply is that there is a difference: if he does not get one, then either it is false that he ceases

85 Gilbert (1996d), 315 f. 86 See n. 39 above.

to have one or the question of cessation does not arise. On either view, (9) breaches Interdependence. In any case, as already noted, if (13) is the only relevant principle then (9) breaches Obligation.

If instead (15) applies, it appears that (9) breaches Interdependence so far as a default by Y is concerned. By (9)(a), (9)(b) and (15)(b), X has a performance obligation: nothing in the analysis or in the normative principles so far proposed implies that this obligation falls away if Y fails to do Ay. A possible reply is that, if Y fails to do Ay, Y thereby ceases to promise to do Ay, in which case (15)(b) ceases to generate the performance obligation on X. (Compare the discussion, in section 7.633, of the caducity of promises.) There is no need to consider whether the reply can be sustained – specifically, by reintroducing temporal references and/or by distinguishing the act from the state of promising – for it is clear that the analysis breaches Interdependence as regards default by X: by (12), whether or not X does Ax, if Y gives Py then he has a performance obligation. It makes no difference that, as (9)(c) provides, Y's reason for giving Py is that X gives Px. Hence (9) breaches Interdependence.

Gilbert's case for Interdependence is based on our 'common understanding'[87] of agreement, but it may be questioned whether we do commonly understand that agreements meet the criterion. At least in some cases it seems that, if one party defaults on his performance obligation, the performance obligation of the other party persists; for example, the agreement might so provide. Cases that support Interdependence include agreements of co-ordination – as where the parties agree to meet at a certain place and time (see sections 1.21 and 4.1) – for in those instances a breach by one party makes the other's performance pointless;[88] but such cases do not sustain Interdependence as a general criterion for the adequacy of an analysis of agreement. The performance obligations of the parties in (9) still meet a looser criterion: Y's performance obligation arises from a promise which he gives for the reason that X gives a promise which, together with Y's promise, creates X's performance obligation.

The following points may be made against Interdependence. English contract law provides that a breach justifying rescission[89] does not

87 Gilbert (1996d), 316. 88 Compare Gilbert (1996d), 335 f.

89 The use of 'rescind' and its cognates in this context has been criticised (see Furmston (2007), 691; Peel (2007), para 18–001; Treitel (2003), 759 f.) but is a common and convenient shorthand for those remedies that, broadly, absolve the injured party from compliance with obligations under the contract that have not accrued. See the cases cited in Chap. 7 n. 123 below. Sections 7.6–7.633 discuss rescission of contracts that are constituted by independent promises.

automatically determine a contract and that, where a contract is rescinded, the injured party remains liable to perform obligations that accrued before rescission. Moreover, a distinction should be drawn between those obligations that Y has and those that it is fair for him to have: it can be granted that, if X defaults, it is unfair for Y to be obligated to do Ay, but it does not follow that Y is not thus obligated. Obligations are often unfair. Examples can be found among cases (unlike the present one) in which an obligation arises otherwise than from a promise of the obligor, such as certain obligations to look after one's parents; but it seems that an obligation created by a promise may also be unfair, for example where someone who, through no fault of his own, is poor and ill promises to pay a rich doctor for treatment. Duress (as to which, see section 7.12) may exclude an obligation,[90] but there need be no duress in cases of this kind. The unfairness to Y is mitigated by the fact that X's default does not free X from all obligations relating to the agreement: in most cases he is obligated to compensate Y – in a broad sense of 'compensate' which includes apology, for example. (See further sections 2.3 and 2.64.)

Interdependence may need refinement, but in essence it is highly plausible and not dislodged by the points just made. Taking them in reverse order: Where X is obligated to compensate Y, X may breach this obligation in turn, but by (12) Y remains obligated to do Ay, and that is just as hard to accept. The distinction between being obligated and being fairly obligated can be admitted, but Interdependence does not presuppose a confusion of the two. The summary of English contract law's rules of rescission is too crude; when elaborated[91] they seem as close to Interdependence as to its negation. Here is a fuller, but still compressed, statement. If X and Y have a contract and X fails to perform a condition precedent or a concurrent condition, such failure justifies Y's refusal to perform for so long as the failure continues, but it does not in itself justify an outright refusal by Y to perform or to accept further performance from X; such justification exists only if X's failure either is serious enough to justify rescission or falls within an exception to the requirement of serious failure. In the special case of independent promises – discussed in sections 7.6–7.64 – a breach does not justify rescission by the other party. Where rescission is justified, Y has an option to rescind; the contract terminates only if Y exercises the option. If he does so, he is released from the contractual obligations which he was to perform in the future, but remains bound by those that accrued before rescission.

90 See n. 31 above.

91 The rules are set out in Peel (2007), chap. 18.

1.232 Analysis (10)

(10), which differs from (9) in that Ax is conditional not on Py but on Ay, fares worse than (9) against the four criteria. In every case where (9) fails, so does (10); but whereas it can be argued that if (15) applies then (9) meets Obligation, and that if (18) applies then (9) meets Simultaneity, (10) fails – absent any other relevant principle – in those circumstances. As to Obligation, (10) and (15) together imply that if Y does Ay then X is obligated to do Ax: on no plausible reading does it follow that the agreement 'directly generates' X's performance obligation. As to Simultaneity, in the case of (10) T1 is normally not the same as T3: (10) (elaborated temporally, in the same way as (19)), (16) and (18) together imply that, whereas Y gets his performance obligation when he promises, X gets his at the time – usually later – when Y does Ay.

1.3 A trilemma

The claim that promises are sufficient for agreement faces objections, whether the promises are taken to be unconditional, conditional, or – as maintained by the most promising analyses – a mixture of both. Options are to live with the breach of the criteria, to revise the mixed-promise account, to produce a quite different promise-based analysis, or to analyse agreement otherwise than in terms of promises. Option one is unpalatable. The rest of this chapter considers options two and three. The next chapter will pursue option four.

1.4 Revision of the mixed-promise analyses

Option two itself covers two possibilities: revision of the analyses or of the principles of obligation. The former divides in turn: one proposal is to change (9) and (10) so that each states not a sufficient condition, but a condition of some other kind, for agreement; an alternative is to revise the clauses on the analyses' right-hand side. As to the first proposal, an obvious thought is that the first 'if' in each of (9) and (10) should be replaced by 'only if'. But none of the promises in the analyses is necessary for X and Y to agree that (1) <X does Ax and Y does Ay>. Section 2.1 explains that, given certain conditions, they thus agree if X makes to Y, and Y accepts, an offer that (1); the promises are unnecessary for the offer, the acceptance, or the obtaining of the relevant conditions, and hence unnecessary for the agreement. (Section 2.62 deals with the objection that offer, acceptance and agreement are themselves promises.) Other versions of the first proposal which invoke conditions of greater complexity do no better.

As to the second proposal, one idea is to combine the approaches of the two analyses, so that one party's promise is conditional on the other's promise whereas the other's is conditional on the first party's action:

(20) (2) if:
- (a) X promises to Y that, if Y gives to X the promise in (b), then X does Ax; and
- (b) Y promises to X that if X does Ax then Y does Ay,

where (2) is the proposition that X and Y agree that (1). As in the case of (9) and (10), there is a good argument that (20) does not create a divergence of compliance conditions; but (20) creates a mismatch of content and it breaches criteria of adequacy. For example, if (13) is the only relevant principle, Obligation is breached: neither party has a performance obligation. If (15) applies, Interdependence is breached: X has a performance obligation whether or not Y does Ay.

Another idea is to keep (9) and (10) separate from each other but in each case to expand clauses (a) and (b), the thought being that, if each party's promise provides in addition that only if the other party performs does the promisor perform, there is no breach of Interdependence.

(21) (2) if:
- (a) X promises to Y that:
  - (i) subject to (ii), if Y gives to X the promise in (b) then X does Ax;
  - (ii) if Y does not do Ay, then X does not do Ax;
- (b) Y promises to X that:
  - (i) subject to (ii), Y does Ay;
  - (ii) if X does not do Ax, then Y does not do Ay;

  . . .

(22) (2) if:
- (a) X promises to Y that:
  - (i) subject to (ii), if Y does Ay then X does Ax;
  - (ii) if Y does not do Ay, then X does not do Ax;

  . . .

The analyses might be further expanded to cover the situation in which it is clear that the other party is not going to perform, but the present version – in which the content of Y's promise, and of X's promise in (22), is equivalent to the proposition that <Y does Ay if and only if X does Ax> – is accurate enough. (21) and (22) are like (20) in creating a mismatch of content and breaching criteria of adequacy; for example, as to Obligation, no plausible principles of obligation imply that, if the parties give their respective promises, they have performance obligations that are, in any plausible sense, directly generated by the agreement. In addition, there is a divergence of compliance conditions, as can be shown by an argument parallel to the one used in section 1.22 to make the same point against (4), the simple analysis in terms of conditional promises.

The proposed revisions of the analyses' clauses are thus no improvement. So far as I can see, any other such revision leads to an outcome at least as bad.

1.5 Revision of the principles of obligation

The other approach within option two is to revise the principles of obligation.[92] Those in question are:

(12) If someone promises that he φs, then he is obligated that he φs.
(13) If someone promises that if P then he φs, then he is obligated that if P then he φs.
(15) If someone promises that if P then he φs, then:
  (a) he is obligated that if P then he φs; and
  (b) if P then he is obligated that he φs.

It might be objected that (13) is too weak: if someone promises that if P then he φs, then he is obligated not merely that if P then he φs, but that if P then, for the reason that P, he φs.

One reply is that his having the stronger obligation does not preclude his having the weaker one – on the contrary, if obligation is closed under the conditional (as to which, see section 3.3), his having the weaker follows from his having the stronger – and so the amplified principle does not impugn (13). An alternative and plausible view is that the weaker obligation is the only one created by the promise: if he φs only for some different reason, he thereby both complies with and performs both the promise and the obligation. It can be conceded that, if he fails to pay adequate attention to that obligation, he is at fault; the fault might perhaps

92 One possibility, which I do not pursue, under this head is to develop a subjective theory of obligation: see Chap. 2 n. 20 and Chap. 3 n. 57 below.

be described in terms of a meta-obligation (which might, in order to avoid a potential regress, be taken to apply to itself) to pay attention to his obligations.

A similar objection, and similar responses, apply to (15); but (15)(b), which distinguishes (15) from (13), exposes (15) to a further objection. Suppose that X, who is driving a car, promises to Y, his passenger, that if Y asks X to stop then X does so. Y asks X to stop. By (15)(b), X has an unconditional obligation to stop. But, if it is unconditional, the following is false:

(23) If Y does not ask X to stop and X does not stop, then X complies with his obligation.

But (23) is true and hence (15) is false.

The objection combines two confusions, between internally and externally conditional obligations and between an obligation's being unconditional and its having a condition that is met. X's obligation is not internally conditional; in particular, there is no proposition Q such that, by (15)(b), X is obligated that if Q then he stops. But, as (15)(b) makes clear, the obligation is externally conditional: if Y asks X to stop, X is obligated to stop. Of course it has been assumed that the condition is met, but that does not make the obligation unconditional. Given that it is thus externally conditional, and given an additional assumption, it follows – contrary to the objection – that (23) is not true. The assumption is that Y's asking or not asking X to stop is the sole factor determining whether X has an obligation to stop. In that case Y's asking X to stop is a necessary as well as a sufficient external condition of X's having such an obligation. Hence, if Y does not ask X to stop, X does not have an obligation to do so. Similarly, if Y does not ask X to stop and X does not stop, X does not have an obligation to stop. If he does not have such an obligation, he does not comply with one (just as, if a person does not get an obligation, he does not cease to have one: see section 1.2314). So, if the antecedent of (23) is true, the consequent is not. So (23) is not true. A related basis for this conclusion is that 'his obligation' in (23) is naturally read as having existential import, i.e., as implying that X has an obligation to stop. Given the above assumption, the implied proposition is false where the antecedent of (23) is true. On this reading it might be said that (23) is not false but lacks a truth value;[93] hence my cautious claim that (23) is not true.

93 See Strawson (1963), 184 ff.; Strawson (1971b), 11 ff.

The main argument that (9) and (10) breach Interdependence was that, by (12), if Y gives Py then, whether or not X does Ax, Y has a performance obligation. (12) might be denied on the basis of this thesis: the fact that someone promises to φ is only a partial ground of the fact that he is obligated to φ, the complete ground being the conjunctive fact that he so promises and the promisee acts in reliance on him to φ. The relevant instance of (12) now expands to:

(24) If:
(a) Y gives Py; and
(b) X relies on Y to do Ay,
then Y is obligated to do Ay.

'Relies', in (b) and elsewhere, is short for 'acts in reliance on'; (b) might be amplified to specify that the reliance is to X's detriment,[94] but the present version is good enough. Suppose that, in a situation to which (9) or (10) applies, Ax is the only candidate for a possible action in reliance by X. Then, if X does not do Ax, (24)(b) is false and hence (24) does not imply that Y has a performance obligation. Assume that no other sufficient condition for Y to have one is met. Then Y does not have such an obligation. Contrary to the argument from (12), therefore, it is not the case that if Y gives Py then, whether or not X does Ax, Y has a performance obligation.

This response faces difficulties. First, the fact of reliance is arguably not even a partial ground of obligation: see section 3.51. Second, Interdependence provides that 'if one party defaults on his performance obligation, the other ceases to have his original performance obligation'. Nothing in the description of the contemplated situation implies that Y gets a performance obligation. If he does not get one, he does not cease to have one: see above. So the response does not establish, even in that situation, that (9) and (10) meet Interdependence. Third, neither (9) nor (10) mentions action in reliance; that is as it should be, for, whether the making or the performance of the agreement is in question, it is at best doubtful that in every case the parties rely on each other.[95] Assume this analysis of reliance:

(25) <X, in doing Ax, relies on Y to do Ay> if:
(a) X does Ax;
(b) X has the goal Gx;
(c) If X does Ax, then Gx is achieved if and only if Y does Ay;

94 See Chap. 3 nn. 64 and 112 below.

95 O. Black (2005b), 164 f. argues that performance need not involve reliance.

(d) X believes (c);
(e) X believes that Y does Ay; and
(f) (a) because <(b), (d) and (e)>.[96]

The discussion can be restricted to reliance in performance, as only that is at issue in the response based on (24). Imagine that X and Y, who share a house, agree that <X will make the beds and Y will wash the dishes>. It may be argued as follows that X, in making the beds, does not rely on Y to wash the dishes. Suppose that X's goal is (and that he knows that it is) merely that the beds get made and the dishes washed: it does not matter to him who does the chores. Suppose also that, if Y fails to wash the dishes, the cleaner will wash them. Then it is not the case that <if X makes the beds, his goal is achieved if and only if Y washes the dishes>. Hence the relevant instance of (25)(c) is false. Likewise X may believe that, if Y fails to wash the dishes, the cleaner will wash them. If so, and if X is rational, X does not believe the relevant instance of (c), in which case the relevant instance of (d) is false. X may also not believe that Y will wash the dishes: he knows Y to be lazy and unreliable. In that case the relevant instance of (e) is false. X may have been going to make the beds anyway, in which case, if 'because' in (f) means 'only because', the relevant instance of (f) is false. If 'because' means 'at least partly because', the relevant instance of (f) is still false if that of (d) or (e) is false.

Since (25) gives only a sufficient condition for reliance, X's not meeting the relevant instances of all of (c)–(f) does not entail that he does not rely on Y to wash the dishes; the objection needs to show that X meets no other sufficient condition. Moreover, the examples are controversial. As to (c) and (d), it might be replied that, even if X's main goal is just that the beds get made and the dishes washed, X must also have the more specific goal that he make the beds and Y wash the dishes; otherwise he would have no reason to make the agreement with Y. But, if this goal is taken to be Gx, the relevant instance of (c) is a tautology and hence true. Given that it is a fairly simple one, X is likely to believe it, at least in the dispositional sense of 'believe' (roughly, he would assent to it if he were thinking about it), in which case the relevant instance of (d) is

96 This analysis is used in O. Black (2005b), chap. 5. As explained there, an analysis of 'strong' reliance is produced by adding: (g) X can do Ax*; (h) if X does Ax*, Gx is achieved even if Y does not do Ay; (i) if X does Ax, X does not do Ax*; (j) X believes (g), (h) and (i). O. Black (2004b) uses the analysis of strong reliance. On the nature of reliance, see also Hertzberg (1988); Holton (1994); Lagenspetz (1992); MacCormick (1982), 195 ff.; McMahon (1989), 239; Regan (1985); Rotenstreich (1972); Stoljar (1988); Strasser (1985). On the problems of defining reliance, see Atiyah (1986c), 31.

also true. It might be objected that the nature of belief is such that a belief cannot have a tautology as content; but, even if that is true, (d) may plausibly be amplified to accommodate the exceptional case where (c) is tautologous. As to (e), if X does not believe that Y will wash the dishes, why did he enter into the agreement? Perhaps he believed it then but has since ceased to do so, or perhaps he merely hopes that Y will wash them – but in that case X meets a weaker but still plausible version of (e) which includes mental states falling short of belief. A more persuasive example is one in which the agreement is legally enforceable (unlikely in this domestic situation – see section 7.21), X does not even hope that Y will perform, but X entered into the agreement in reliance on the law to provide a remedy for Y's breach. Here there is reliance by X, but not on Y to perform.

There is no need to pursue the dialectic further. If it is true that in some cases the parties to an agreement do not rely on each other, (24) is irrelevant to their performance obligations in those cases. The response based on (24) therefore fails to exclude the possibility of the relevant principle's implying that in those cases (9) and (10) breach Interdependence. If they breach it there, they breach it tout court, for the criteria of adequacy are general.[97] The advocate of (24) might reply that, if neither party relies on the other, neither gets a performance obligation.[98] The reply is implausible and in any event fails to square the cases of non-reliance with Interdependence: as already noted, a party who does not get a performance obligation does not cease to have one.

A different proposal is to build exceptions into the principles of obligation, to cover situations where the promise in question is given as part of an agreement. As regards (9), the relevant instances of (12) and (15) expand to:

(26) (a) Subject to (b), if Y gives Py then Y is obligated that he does Ay.
(b) If clauses (a), (c) and (d) of (9) are met, then Y's obligation ceases if X does not do Ax.

(27) (a) Subject to (b), if X gives Px then:
(i) X is obligated that if Y gives Py then X does Ax; and
(ii) if Y gives Py then X is obligated that X does Ax.

97 A particularist might deny this. Compare n. 81 above.

98 Atiyah might accept this consequence where neither party has paid a price to the other: Atiyah (1979b), chap. 1.

(b) If (b)–(d) of (9) are met, then X's obligation ceases if Y does not do Ay.

These revisions clash with the intuitive judgment that, unless a promise is conditional on the promisee's doing a certain thing, it is normally not the case that if he does not do that thing then the obligation ceases. (It is frivolous to reply that the obligation ceases if the promisee releases the promisor and that releasing is the same as not not releasing.) Absent any separate reason to reject the judgment, the revisions are ad hoc devices to avoid the problem of Interdependence. It might be suggested that a separate reason for (26) is the fact that, as (9)(c) provides, Y's reason for giving Py is that X gives Px: from this, it may be said, it follows that if X does not do Ax then Y's obligation ceases. But it does not follow; and in any case the defence cannot be extended to (27), for (9) does not provide that X's reason for giving Px is that Y gives Py.

Revision of the principles of obligation has been no more successful than revision of the analyses as a means of repairing the mixed-promise account.

1.6 Conditional promises again

Option three is to produce a quite different promise-based analysis of agreement. It might be suggested that analyses in terms only of conditional promises have been dismissed too quickly. This part of the chapter briefly reviews some further variants of (4), sampling the objections they face. A reminder:

(4) (2) if:
  (a) X promises to Y that if Y does Ay then X does Ax; and
  (b) Y promises to X that if X does Ax then Y does Ay.

(2) is the proposition that X and Y agree that (1) <X does Ax and Y does Ay>. One proposal is to reverse the direction of conditionality in (4)(a) and (b):

(28) (2) if:
  (a) X promises to Y that, only if Y does Ay, X does Ax; and
  (b) Y promises to X that, only if X does Ax, Y does Ay.

One objection to this analysis is similar to the third objection to (4). Unlike that objection, however, the present one applies to both weak and strong compliance: X weakly and strongly complies with the promise if he does not do Ax, for in that case he makes true the promise's content – equivalent to 'If X does Ax, Y does Ay' – by making false its antecedent. This objection, and the others below that concern a divergence of compliance conditions, can be formalised as in section 1.22, using premisses that correspond to (5)–(8).

The next proposal is to amend (4) so that each party's promise is internally conditional on the other's promising rather than performing:

(29) (2) if:
- (a) X promises to Y that, if Y promises to X that Y does Ay, then X does Ax; and
- (b) Y promises to X that, if X promises to Y that X does Ax, then Y does Ay.

(29) is in the same case as (4) as regards a divergence of compliance conditions. Suppose, as is compatible with (a) and (b), that Y does not promise to do Ay. Then the content of X's promise is true, as it is a conditional the antecedent of which is false. X therefore weakly complies with the promise, for he performs some action; in particular, he gives the promise. He does not strongly comply, for the antecedent is made false, and hence the content made true, by an action – here an omission – of Y, not of X. In any event, (29) represents at best a peripheral kind of agreement. X's promise to do Ax is conditional on Y's promising to do Ay. As already noted, (a) and (b) do not imply that Y gives that promise. A corresponding point applies to Y. Given this, even a supporter of the promise model is unlikely to accept that the promises which, by (a) and (b), the parties do give are sufficient for an ordinary agreement.

Standing to (28) as (29) stands to (4) is:

(30) (2) if:
- (a) X promises to Y that, only if Y promises to X that Y does Ay, X does Ax; and
- (b) Y promises to X that, only if X promises to Y that X does Ax, Y does Ay.

This analysis fails because each party weakly and strongly complies with his promise if neither performs.

Corresponding to the foregoing conditional analyses are ones in terms of purely externally conditional promises. The counterpart of (4) is:

(31) (2) if:

(a) if Y does Ay, then X promises to Y that X does Ax; and

(b) if X does Ax, then Y promises to X that Y does Ay.

(32), the counterpart of (28), reverses the direction of conditionality in (31)(a) and (b). These analyses fail because they propose absurdly weak sufficient conditions for agreement. If Y does not do Ay, (31)(a) is true; if X does not do Ax, (31)(b) is true; so, according to (31), it is sufficient that X and Y respectively do not do Ax and Ay. According to (32), by parallel reasoning, it is sufficient that neither party gives the specified promise.

The counterpart of (29) is:

(33) (2) if:

(a) if Y promises to X that Y does Ay, then X promises to Y that X does Ax; and

(b) if X promises to Y that X does Ax, then Y promises to X that Y does Ay.

(34), the counterpart of (30), is the same as (33) but with (a) and (b) reversed. As well as facing the objection just raised to the previous two analyses, (33) and (34) breach Interdependence in the case where either party gives his promise. Suppose that X promises to Y that X does Ax. By (33)(b), Y promises to X that Y does Ay. By (12), whether or not X does Ax or Y does Ay, X is obligated to do Ax and Y to do Ay.

Another possibility is to revert to internally conditional promises, but to formulate the conditions in terms of the parties' epistemic states. For example:

(35) (2) if:

(a) X promises to Y that, if X does not have good reason to believe that Y does not do Ay, then X does Ax; and

(b) Y promises to X that, if Y does not have good reason to believe that X does not do Ax, then Y does Ay.

(Compare the suggestion, set aside in section 1.4, that (21) and (22) be revised to cover the situation where it is clear that the relevant party is not going to perform.) Since 'P if not Q' is equivalent to 'P unless Q', the content of X's promise is equivalent to 'X does Ax unless X has good reason to believe that Y does not do Ay', and similarly for Y's promise. Variants might be proposed – for example, to make 'good' stronger or more precise; or to expand the antecedent of the conditional in (a) either to provide that, or that X believes that, Y does Ay, or to provide that X believes that he does not have good reason to believe that Y does not do Ay (and correspondingly for the conditional in (b)); or to replace the mention of reasons with one of evidence, justification or knowledge; or to introduce temporal references, perhaps so that the promises' contents are equivalent to propositions of the form 'P unless and until Q'.

Whatever the precise formulation, the proposal fails. In the first place, (35), like all analyses in terms of internally conditional promises, raises the earlier problem of a mismatch between the content of the agreement and the contents of the promises (see sections 1.22, 1.231 and 1.4); but in this case the problem is especially stark, as the content of an agreement does not normally concern the parties' reasons for belief. In the second place, (35) creates a divergence of compliance conditions. Suppose that X has good reason to believe that Y does not do Ay. Then the content of his promise is true because its antecedent is false. Since X performs some action, which need not be Ax, he weakly complies with the promise. If he omits to do Ax, the omission may give him good reason to believe that Y does not do Ay. In that case the omission falsifies the antecedent; so it makes the content true; so X strongly complies with the promise.

There is no persuasive basis for a reply that, if X has good reason – at least at the time when the agreement is supposedly made – to believe that Y will not perform, X does not truly agree. Such appeal as that reply has derives from a confusion with one or other of two propositions. The first is that X's obligation to do Ax ceases if it is clear that Y is not going to do Ay: see section 2.3 and compare Interdependence. The second – elaborated in Chapter 5 – is that, in certain circumstances, part of a sufficient condition for the sincerity of X's agreeing is that, at the time the agreement is made, X intend this: to do Ax unless he has good reason to believe that Y will not do Ay. As with promises, an insincere agreement is an agreement none the less.

1.7 Conclusion

It would be tedious and fruitless to examine further conditional analyses. None of (28)–(35) is an improvement on (4), and (4) is unsatisfactory. I can think of no other promise-based analysis that would avoid the objections. The result is that, although such analyses may represent certain outlying sorts of agreement, a different approach is needed to capture the paradigm cases.

2

Offer and acceptance

2.1 Elements of the offer–acceptance model

Of the four options listed in section 1.3, the last is to analyse agreement otherwise than in terms of promises. The analysis I propose uses concepts from the law of contract.[1] A rough statement is: X and Y agree if X makes to Y an offer which Y accepts. As mentioned in the Introduction, 'agreement' may signify, among other things, the making of an agreement, the resultant state of agreement, or the content of the making or state. 'Offer' and 'acceptance' can each be given corresponding senses: thus 'offer' can mean the speech act of offering, the resultant state of offering – as in 'my offer still stands' – or the content of the act or state. As also mentioned in the Introduction, I shall for convenience talk about the content of an agreement, offer or acceptance, rather than about the content of a making, act, or state. The parties make the agreement by offering and accepting, i.e., by their speech acts of offering and accepting; those acts normally result in a state of agreement (for an arguable exception, see below); and the content of the offer, of the acceptance and – as noted in section 1.21 – of the agreement is typically a conjunctive proposition[2] of the form:

(1) X does Ax and Y does Ay.

To accommodate contents of form (1), 'offer' and 'accept' must be understood broadly: perhaps 'propose' and 'assent' would be happier terms.[3]

1 For the view that the concept of agreement is infused with contract law, see Atiyah (1986l), 2; de Moor (1987), 115. See further Chap. 7 n. 111 below.

2 Contrast S. Smith (2005), 36, 50, which represents an offer as conditional. Smith notes (50) that in contract law a conditional acceptance fails to count as an acceptance; he distinguishes (n. 37) a conditional acceptance from a conditional contract.

3 F. Pollock (1885), 9 describes a contractual offer as a proposal, as do S. Smith (2004), 180 and S. Smith (2005), 36. A standard definition of an acceptance in English contract law is that it is a final and unqualified expression of assent to the terms of an offer: Peel (2007), para. 2–015. Markesinis et al. (1997), 47 describes a contractual agreement in German law

The relevant concepts of offer and acceptance are tolerably clear at an intuitive level,[4] and in developing the analysis we can help ourselves to, without accepting all, the detailed rules of offer and acceptance provided by contract law (and described in section 7.13); hence my preference for this terminology.

Instead of saying that the parties make the agreement *by*, we might more awkwardly say that they do so *in*, offering and accepting. A nice question is when 'by' or 'in' is the appropriate word in contexts such as this, for they are not always intersubstitutable: compare 'he woke the children by [not in] slamming the door' and 'he used a lot of force in [not by] slamming the door'. A possible answer[5] is that 'by' signifies that one action is in some sense constituted by another, whereas 'in' signifies that a single action is being described in two ways. (Contrast the use of 'constitute' in section 1.1 to cover cases both of 'in' and of 'by'.) Pursuit of the 'in'/'by' distinction would lead further than necessary into the philosophy of action, and so I simply use, mainly without comment, whichever word is the more natural in the context.

Both the making and the state of agreement are subject to conditions beyond the offer and the acceptance, and hence a more accurate analysis is:

in terms of proposal and assent. On assent as an element of agreement in various areas of law, see sections 7.11, 7.13, 7.37, 8.13, 9.2 and 9.22 below.

4 Compare *Prior* [2004] EWCA Crim. 1147, paras. 15, 36. The judge at first instance, in his directions to the jury, said '[T]here is nothing technical or legalistic about the word "offer", it is a normal English word in common usage and you treat it as such'. The Court of Appeal talked of 'this simple English word'. The case concerned an 'offer to supply' a controlled drug; it can be assumed that, given certain conditions (see the main text below), if such an offer is accepted then there is an agreement to supply. Even if an offer to supply in this context is different from an offer that, if accepted, results in an agreement, they are clearly similar.

Sheinman (2011a), 393 f. n. 41 objects to an earlier version of my account (O. Black (2007)), which he summarises as the view that agreements are 'accepted offers'. That is inaccurate, for an offer – accepted or not – is not itself an agreement. The objection is that 'the notion of such a conjunctive offer is no simpler than the notion of the agreement it seeks to explain'. As set out in the Introduction above and in section 2.2 below, I 'seek to explain the notion of agreement' only in the sense of specifying a sufficient condition, and constitutive rules, of agreement. The project does not require that the concepts used in the specification be simpler than that of agreement. See further section 2.66 below for a reply to the objection, which Sheinman may have in mind, that the concepts of offer and acceptance cannot be grasped by someone who does not grasp the concept of agreement.

5 Proposed by Simon Evnine in correspondence. The door-slamming examples are Jessica Boyd's. Austin (1962), chap. 9 discusses the relation between this distinction and that between illocutionary force and perlocutionary effect, as to which see section 1.1 above.

(36) <X and Y make an agreement that (1)> if:
(a) X makes to Y an offer that (1);
(b) Y accepts X's offer; and
(c) condition CM obtains.

(37) <X and Y have an agreement that (1)> if:
[(a) and (b) as in (36)]; and
(c) condition CS obtains,

'have an agreement' in (37) signifying the state of agreement. CM and CS are placeholders for conditions that include ones specified by informal counterparts of certain rules of contract law; for example, CM excludes the possibility that X withdraws the offer before Y accepts it. On a narrow view of acceptance, this possibility is excluded by (b): the argument is that an offer can be accepted only if it exists at the time of the purported acceptance and that if an offer is withdrawn it ceases to exist at the time of withdrawal. On a narrow view of *agreement*, motivated perhaps by the thought that agreement involves a meeting of minds (see section 1.23), CM provides that X is aware of Y's acceptance. Another possible condition is that Y communicates his acceptance to X: this condition is not implied by the propositions that acts of acceptance are speech acts and that every speech act is communicative, for the latter proposition (left undecided in section 1.1) leaves open the identity of the person, if any, to whom the communication is made. On the treatment in English contract law of offeree's communication and offeror's awareness, see sections 7.13 and 7.31.[6]

CS includes CM and is a placeholder for further conditions: for example, it both excludes the possibility that the agreement itself has terminated – perhaps by a further agreement between the parties – and covers the provision, which could be made explicit by the introduction of tenses into (37), that the state of agreement is no earlier than, and usually starts from, the time at which Y's act of acceptance is completed. Normally there is a making of an agreement if and only if there is a state of agreement; 'there is' here is again a timeless present and the 'normally' acknowledges arguable but peripheral counterexamples such as the case, which CS is naturally taken to exclude, where (i) X's offer provides that the agreement would lapse at a given time and (ii) Y completes his act of acceptance at that time. Even here it might be said that there is a state of

6 See also Chap. 1 n. 68 above.

agreement, albeit an instantaneous one; but a generous reading of 'state' is needed if 'instantaneous state' is to avoid self-contradiction.[7]

(36) and (37) give only sufficient, not necessary, conditions for agreement, as the parties to some agreements do not meet them; but, in the case of most or at least many agreements, the parties do meet the conditions. For *paradigmatic* agreements, 'most or at least many' can be strengthened to 'all or at least most'. The class of paradigmatic agreements coincides roughly with that of things that ordinary people would unhesitatingly judge to be an agreement; this is vague (what makes a person ordinary, what are the circumstances in which the judgment is made, how quickly must it be made in order to be unhesitating?[8]), but the vagueness does not empty of content the thesis in the preceding sentence.

As I shall argue, for at least some agreements – paradigmatic or not – for which the conditions do not hold, either the parties meet the conditions if minor adjustments to the conditions are made or the parties stand in a certain relation to a set of 'normal agreements', i.e., agreements the parties to which do meet the conditions (again, possibly subject to minor adjustment of the conditions). Certain agreements with more than two parties fall into the first category; 'wheel' agreements, discussed in section 2.612, fall into the second. In the first case the parties' meeting the revised conditions, and in the second their so standing in that relation, is sufficient for the parties to make and to have an agreement.

Ignore, for the moment, the first category and the possible minor adjustments, and suppose both that all non-normal agreements fall into the second category and that there is just one relevant relation, R1 – which might be a disjunction of other relations. Define a relation R2 thus: parties stand in R2 to a set of normal agreements if and only if either they stand

7 Joshua and Jordan (2004), 653 seems to assume that agreements and contracts are acts rather than states: 'a conspiracy is constituted by an agreement ... but it is the result of the agreement, rather than the agreement itself, just as a partnership, although constituted by a contract, is not the contract, but the result of it. The contract is instantaneous; the partnership may endure as one and the same partnership for years. A conspiracy is a partnership in criminal purposes'. Read narrowly, the passage is compatible with the view of an agreement or contract as a state, for one state can result from another; but that view sits uneasily with the claim that a contract is instantaneous. See further Chap. 8 n. 5 and Chap. 9 nn. 22 and 29 below.

8 On the philosophical use of paradigm cases, see Donnellan (1967), 39 ff.; Martinich (1998), 145. On the 'central case method' in the analysis of agreements and promises, see Sheinman (2011b), 9 ff. On paradigm-related reasons for interpretations, see section 8.51 below. The statement that, if A is a paradigmatic F, ordinary people would unhesitatingly judge A to be an F needs qualification, as Fs may form a recondite class about which ordinary people know nothing. The converse conditional is also false: a three-legged pig is not a paradigmatic pig, but ordinary people may unhesitatingly judge it to be a pig.

in R1 to that set or they are parties to a normal agreement. In the latter case they may be said to stand in R2 to the unit set of that agreement. We now have a condition both sufficient and necessary for agreement: parties agree if and only if they stand in R2 to a set of normal agreements. If the biconditional is read in terms of material implication, it concerns only actual agreements; if in terms of strict implication, it also concerns merely possible agreements; and the assumptions from which it is inferred need to be read accordingly. (On material and strict implication, see section 1.22.) Absent an illuminating specification of R1, of course, the result is purely formal. A partial specification is given in section 2.612, and a fuller one in section 9.27.

Cases of offer and acceptance with the meeting of CM and CS but without agreement would be counterexamples to (36) and (37). I can think of no such case, but, if one were alleged, (36) and (37) could be defended by qualifying them to exclude cases of the relevant kind or by arguing, as regards the case at issue, that CM or CS was not met, or that there was no offer or no acceptance, or that there was an agreement. Such a defence would be supported by the fact that application of the words 'offer', 'accept' and 'agree' is an interpretive exercise that involves judgment;[9] but the defence would need to avoid the further objection that it trivialised (36) and (37) by giving an ad hoc definition to one or more of those words. The strength of the defence would depend in part on the example proposed, but also on the extent to which (36) and (37) fit other situations: given that in general people agree if they meet the specified conditions, there would be reason – not necessarily an overriding reason – to doubt that the case at issue was a counterexample. A high general level of fit thus gives normative force to the offer–acceptance model in hard cases.[10]

2.2 Constitutive rules

(36) and (37) are intended as straightforward statements of sufficient conditions – their surface meaning – but can also be read as constitutive

9 On interpretation of an utterance as an offer or an acceptance, see Tiersma (1994); on legal interpretation, Chap. 8 nn. 158 ff. below.

10 In Rawlsian terms, the offer–acceptance model marks a reflective equilibrium between theory and pre-theoretic judgments: Rawls (1972), 20 f., 48 ff., 120, 432; discussed in Daniels (1979). Compare O. Black (2003c), 65; O. Black (2004a), 78 f.; O. Black (2005b), 4 f. (on models); Goodman (1973), 66 f.; Hyman (2006), 81; Korsgaard (1996a), chap. 2 (on 'reflective endorsement'); Papineau (2009), 23; Searle (1969), 55 (on idealisation in analysis); Wittgenstein (1974), 76; Chap. 3 n. 118 below.

rules of agreement, with the purport, roughly, that the holding of the relevant sufficient condition counts as the parties' making/having the agreement.[11] It makes for clarity to give a separate and explicit formulation of the rules. The one corresponding to (36) is:

(38) X's making to Y an offer that (1), Y's accepting X's offer and CM's obtaining together count as X's and Y's making an agreement that (1).

The following points may need qualification, but I pass over the details. Assume that a constitutive rule can be the antecedent of a conditional. Then if (38) then (36). (37) is connected in the same way to its corresponding constitutive rule. For simplicity, ignore CM and CS. If X's φing counts as X's χing, then, by φing, X χs. If this principle is expanded to cover bipartite cases, then, as noted in section 2.1, by X's making to Y an offer that (1) and Y's accepting X's offer, X and Y make an agreement that (1). Developing a suggestion from that section: if, by φing, X χs, then X's φing constitutes his χing. If this principle is likewise expanded to cover bipartite cases, X's making to Y an offer that (1) and Y's accepting X's offer together constitute X's and Y's making an agreement that (1). It is plausible to hold that the same sense of 'constitute' is in play in this statement and in the statement that (38) is a constitutive rule of agreement.

Other constitutive rules of agreement are the rules specifying conditions under which one party makes an offer and the other accepts it; various other informal counterparts of rules of contract law, such as rules on frustration and mistake and rules specifying conditions for which CM and CS are placeholders; and the rule – roughly stated here and amplified in the next section – that the parties to an agreement are obligated to perform it. The rule of obligation, unlike (38) and at least some of the others, is a mandatory rule.[12]

11 Searle (1965), 224 and Searle (1969), 34 f. note that constitutive rules sometimes have the form 'A counts as B'. Searle attributes the 'counts as' formulation to Max Black.

12 Searle (1965), 224 says that constitutive rules sometimes, and regulative rules generally, have the form 'Do so-and-so' or 'If P, do so-and-so'; compare Searle (1969), 34, which says that regulative rules 'characteristically' have, or can be 'comfortably paraphrased' in, those forms. On regulative rules, see the main text below. A mandatory rule need not be expressed by an imperative, or by 'must' or a similar verb: the mandatory rule in Snakes and Ladders, discussed in the next paragraph of the main text, could be written 'A player whose counter lands on the head of a snake moves it to the end of the snake's tail'. The question can be left open whether mandatory rules are ever appropriately expressed in terms of counting-as. The mandatory/counting-as distinction is different from the

I shall not provide a full account of constitutive rules, but a sketch will be helpful. To use a well-worn analogy, the constitutive rules of agreement are like those of a game:[13] the rule of obligation can be compared to the rule of Snakes and Ladders that, if a player puts his counter on the head of a snake, he must move it to the end of the snake's tail; (38) is similar to the rule that the first player to put his counter on square 100 is the winner – or, to be more explicit, that his being the first player to put his counter on square 100 counts as his being the winner. On a narrow view of rules, statements such as this and (38) are not rules, but there is no persuasive reason to adopt the narrow view.[14] Just as the rules of Snakes and Ladders may be said to define the game, so (38) and others may be said to define agreement.

Searle distinguishes constitutive from regulative rules by saying that whereas regulative rules regulate a pre-existing activity – one of his examples is 'When cutting food, hold the knife in the right hand' – constitutive rules constitute, and also regulate, an activity the existence of which is logically dependent on the rules.[15] His formulation needs refinement; in particular, it is unclear what 'logically dependent' means. One suggestion

prescriptive/descriptive distinction in C. Wright (1992), 15, and both are different from the constitutive/regulative distinction.

13 See Williamson (1996), 489 ff.; Williamson (2000), 238 ff. Rawls (1967), Searle (1965), 238 and Searle (1969), 63 draw the analogy for promises. Searle decribes it as 'tiresome' but as 'holding up remarkably well'. Contrary to the suggestion in Cavell (1979), 296 there is no confusion here between a game and a move in a game; compare C. Wright (1992), 15 on the distinction between a practice and a move within it. (A related confusion, arguably perpetrated by Strawson (1971a), 36, is between a game and the practice of playing a game. On practices, see section 2.65 below.) Acts of offer, acceptance and performance might be said to be moves in the game of agreement. On constitutive rules generally, see further Textor (2010b); Williamson (1996) (on the normativity of such rules – see further Chap. 3 n. 140 below – and on their relation to conventions and necessary conditions); C. Wright (1992), 15 f. On the implicit rules of board games, see Bergström (2010). Games have not only constitutive rules but also a point, e.g., fun; analogously, agreements also have functions, discussed in section 2.4 below.

14 On the philosophy of rules, see O. Black (1996c), 341 ff.; Hart and his commentators (n. 64 below); Pettit (2002); Rawls (1967); Raz (1990), 58 ff.; Sartor (2000), 589 n. 1; Schauer (1991); Twining and Miers (1991), esp. chap. 3. There is a large literature stemming from Wittgenstein's remarks on rule-following: notable texts are G. Baker and Hacker (1984); Hindricks (2004); Holtzman and Leich (1981); Kripke (1982); McDowell (1979); McGinn (1984); Waismann (1965), chap. 7; Wittgenstein (1958), paras. 143 ff. On the application of those remarks to legal theory, see Bix (1993), chap. 2.

15 Searle (1965), 224; Searle (1967), 112; Searle (1969), 33 ff., 185 f. Searle draws on Kant's distinction between regulative and constitutive principles (Kant (1929), 210 f., 450 ff., 515 ff., 546 ff.) and on the distinction in Rawls (1967) between the 'summary' and the 'practice' conceptions of rules. See also C. Johnson (1975), 315 f.

is that such rules are analytic truths,[16] in which case it is a short step to the thesis that (36) and (37) are also analytic. But it may be objected that rules, or at least mandatory rules, are not happily classified as truths, analytic or not: this claim, combined with certain accounts of conditionality, such as the truth-functional one in section 1.22, could be used to argue against the assumption above that a constitutive rule can be the antecedent of a conditional. The discussion need not be pursued, for, although the concept of a constitutive rule and the distinction between a constitutive and a regulative rule are rough,[17] they are serviceable for present purposes.

2.3 Obligation

Neither X's offer nor Y's acceptance by itself grounds an obligation on either party to perform[18] – although in certain circumstances an offer may, in the absence of an acceptance, create some other obligation on the offeror, for example to keep the offer open for a certain period,[19] or to remain able to perform if the offer is accepted (compare the similar point in section 1.2313) – but in the normal case (a qualification assumed henceforth) each has a cancellable obligation: roughly, X's is to do Ax[20] and it ceases in various circumstances – in particular, if Y releases X from it or if Y does not do, or it is clear that Y is not going to do, Ay – and conversely for Y. I draw no distinction between an obligation's being cancelled and its ceasing.[21] 'It is clear that' can be amplified in various

16 Compare Martinich (1985), 117, which asserts it to be analytically true that a person who promises to φ thereby puts himself under an obligation to φ. See also Searle (1965), 224 on the 'quasi-tautological' character of constitutive rules and on their relation to analytic truths: Searle (1969), 191. For criticism, see McNeilly (1971); also Raz (1977), 212, which queries the analyticity of the statement that one ought to keep one's promises. On analytic truth, see the Introduction above.

17 For criticism of the distinction, see Atiyah (1981), 118 ff.; Cavell (1979), chap. 11; Raz (1990), 108 ff.; Stocker (1970), 605 n. 4. Rawls accepts that there are borderline cases in which it is difficult or impossible to decide which of his two conceptions of a rule applies (see n. 15 above).

18 Hohfeld (1985), 545 f. holds that a contractual offer creates a liability against, but not an obligation on, the offeror and that it creates a correlative power in favour of the offeree.

19 For the rules on withdrawal and revocation of contractual offers in various jurisdictions, see Chap. 7 nn. 30 f. below.

20 Prichard (2002b), 97 maintains that an obligation is not to perform an action but to set oneself to perform it. See further Chap. 1 n. 92 above and Chap. 3 n. 57 below.

21 For distinctions that have been drawn in this area, see Chap. 3 n. 88 below. In the context of a discussion of the difference between immediate and remote obligation, M. Zimmerman (1996), 107 ff. denies that obligations can be cancelled. See further nn. 26 f. below.

ways, for instance in terms of X's beliefs and his reasons for them. (Compare the discussion of analyses (21), (22) and (35) in sections 1.4 and 1.6.) Other circumstances in which the parties' obligations cease include frustration through supervening impossibility,[22] and termination of the agreement in accordance with its terms. In certain situations, covered by a suitably broad definition of an abnormal case, it appears that one party's obligation may persist even if the other party fails to perform; for example, as noted in section 1.2314, the agreement might so provide. As before, these claims can be read either as ordinary statements of conditions or as constitutive rules. They are intended in both senses.

The obligations can be specified more accurately if times are assigned to the offer, the acceptance and the actions that X and Y agree to perform.[23] (Compare the discussion of Simultaneity in section 1.2313.) Suppose that at To X makes an offer which at Ta Y accepts: more precisely, To and Ta are respectively the times at which the act of offering and the act of accepting are completed. The agreement thus comes into being at Ta. The content of the agreement is that <at Tx X does Ax and at Ty Y does Ay>. (In some instances the time for Ax and/or Ay is unspecified.) Normally it is the case both that To precedes Ta and that Ta precedes Tx and Ty. Tx may be earlier or later than or simultaneous with Ty.[24] At Ta X gets an obligation to do Ax at Tx. Unless one of the cancelling conditions obtains, it continues up to Tx.[25] If at Tx X does Ax, at Tx the obligation ceases if it has not already done so. If at Tx X does not do Ax, at Tx it likewise ceases[26] but is replaced by an obligation – also cancellable – on X to compensate Y for the failure,[27] in the broad sense of 'compensate' noted in section 1.2314.

22 Compare Chap. 1 n. 28 above, on promising the impossible.

23 On the time of an obligation, see Chap. 1 n. 84 above.

24 On the order of contractual performance, see S. Smith (2005), 192.

25 Compare M. Zimmerman (1996), 111 ff. on the 'supersession' of an obligation. See further Chap. 3 n. 88 below.

26 In Zimmerman's terminology, 'the fulfilment or nonfulfilment of an immediate obligation trivially counts as its extinction': M. Zimmerman (1996), 113. See n. 21 above.

27 Compare M. Zimmerman (1996), 174 ff. on residual obligations. In the law on rescission of contract (as to which, see Chap. 1 n. 89 above), the new obligation is to pay damages: see the cases cited in Chap. 7 n. 123 below. Compare S. Smith (2005), 169, which discusses the view that an ordinary contractual undertaking 'is in effect' two undertakings: to use one's best efforts to bring about the promised result (compare Prichard's view in n. 20 above) and to make good whatever losses might be suffered if, despite those efforts, the result is not achieved. The differences are that the offer–acceptance model concerns agreements, not contracts (on the relation between the two, see Chap. 7 below); the model does not connect agreements to undertakings; the present analysis concerns obligations, not undertakings; and the primary obligation is strict, not an obligation to use best efforts.

At any time from Ta to Tx, the obligation, if it has not ceased already, ceases if (i) Y releases X from it, (ii) Ty occurs and Y does not do Ay then, or (iii) it is clear before Ty that (ii) is the case. Y's obligation is symmetric with X's. Just as the law of contract amplifies the concepts of offer and acceptance, so its rules of performance and breach[28] – such as the rules of rescission described in section 1.2314 – can be used to refine further this account of the parties' obligations. The account will be developed in Chapter 3.

2.4 Functions

(36) and (37) give conditions for there to be an agreement, but do not say what an agreement is *for*. In outline, it is a device the main function[29] of which is to enable rational self-interested parties to benefit from each other's actions.[30] 'Benefit' here has a thin sense: a drug addict may benefit from a supply of heroin in that it satisfies his craving, even if on balance he

28 For the rules in English law, see Beale (2008), pts. 7 f.; Peel (2007), chaps. 17 f. For other jurisdictions, see Zweigert and Kötz (1998), chaps. 35 f. For theories of the times at which offer and acceptance take effect, see von Mehren (1992), paras. 182 ff. See further section 7.6 below.

29 On the concept of a function, see Bigelow and Pargetter (1987); Cummins (1975); Godfrey-Smith (1993); Godfrey-Smith (1994); Griffiths (1993); Hempel (1965); Kitcher (1988); Millikan (1984); Millikan (1993), esp. chap. 1; E. Nagel (1961), chap. 12; Parsons and Carlson (2008), 72, 75; Preston (1998); Sober (1993), chap. 3; Woodfield (1975); L. Wright (1973); L. Wright (1976).

30 Compare the 'economic'/'utilitarian' justification for the enforcement of contracts, discussed in S. Smith (2005) (and in section 6.2111 below): 'Thus interpreted, contract law's essential purpose is to secure cooperation in human behaviour, and particularly in exchange' (4; see also 22). 'Essential purpose' seems much the same as 'function', and for present purposes the distinction between agreement and contract can be ignored, as can the fact that Smith is directly concerned with contract law rather than with contracts themselves. His account is nevertheless more restricted than mine in one respect, as it seems that the benefits ensuing from agreement need not involve co-operation or exchange, at least in any narrow sense of those words. (On the relation between exchange and contract, see section 7.1 below.) In another respect his account is less restricted, as it does not explicitly refer to parties who are self-interested; but such a reference seems to be implied.

As discussed in Chap. 6 n. 39 below, Smith also considers a 'moral'/'individualist' justification for enforcement. 'The concept of a promissory obligation,' he writes, 'is one of humanity's greatest moral inventions. The idea that merely by uttering some words – "I promise" – individuals can put themselves under obligations to do things for other individuals represents the triumph of trust and cooperation over greed and self-interest' (22; see also 29). That is an overstatement, for a virtue of promises and agreements is that they reduce the need for trust in dealings with self-interested parties. If self-interested X agrees to φ, Y may need to trust him to keep to the agreement; but that may be easier

would do better not to take it[31] (see further sections 4.11 and 6.2111, the latter of which contemplates a fuller sense of 'benefit'). In many cases an agreement is not necessary in order for people to benefit from each other's actions: if X is willing to pay £10 to Y for Y's book, Y is willing to transfer ownership of his book to X for £10, X and Y are facing each other and respectively holding a £10 note and the book, and they are able-bodied and of equal strength, then they can simultaneously hand each other the note and the book and thereby benefit.[32] The example concerns objects that are, in Hume's phrase, 'present and individual', but in other cases the procedure does not work. One relates to objects that Hume calls 'absent or general',[33] another to the exchange of services:

> Your corn is ripe today; mine will be so tomorrow. 'Tis profitable for us both, that I should labour with you today, and that you should aid me tomorrow. I have no kindness for you, and know you have as little for me. I will not, therefore, take any pains upon your account; and should I labour with you upon my own account, in expectation of a return, I know I should be disappointed, and that I should in vain depend upon your gratitude. Here then I leave you to labour alone: You treat me in the same manner. The seasons change; and both of us lose our harvests for want of mutual confidence and security.[34]

Hume gives his example in a discussion of promises, but it is equally relevant to agreements: if the parties agree that each will help with the other's harvest, each will perform and both will benefit. The main mechanism for this is the parties' reasoning (examined in Chapter 4) to the making and the performance of an agreement and their acting on the conclusions of that reasoning.

Corresponding to the thesis about function is one about effect: not only is it the main function of agreements to enable rational self-interested

than trusting him to φ in the absence of an agreement. Compare the example, in section 7.38 below, of the promise by deed.

31 Compare O. Black (2005b), 43; Dagger (1982); Scanlon (1993a), 38; Scoccia (1987), 588. See also Chap. 3 n. 112 below.

32 S. Smith (2005), 108 maintains that all exchanges are simultaneous. That is false or presupposes an unusually restricted concept of exchange. Atiyah (1986g), 75 says more cautiously that exchange 'can be a purely present transaction'. On 'conditional transfers', see S. Smith (2005), 75 and see further section 7.33 below.

33 Compare Stoljar (1988), 205 f.

34 Hume (1978), 520 f. See also Atiyah (1981), 31, 135; Hart (1961), 192 f.; Kimel (2003), chaps. 1, 3; Kötz (1997), 5 ff. (which maintains that division of labour is a source of contract law, via a Mainean route from status to contract); McMahon (1989); Robins (1984), 105; S. Smith (2004), 112; S. Smith (2005), 3 f.; Zweigert and Kötz (1998), 327.

parties to benefit from each other's actions, agreements also do so enable them. Both theses need to be modified to provide for exceptions. As to effect, the carrying out of a particular agreement may fail to benefit one or both parties; or it may enable them to benefit in only a thin sense of 'enable', as they would have performed the actions in question even if they had not agreed to do so (compare the example of the housemates, in section 1.5). Some agreements do not, at least primarily, have the function described: arguably the main function of a marriage agreement, for example, is to enable the parties to express their commitment to each other (see further sections 4.3, 6.2112 and 6.3). Even in a standard case, the parties' desires may diverge from the function of the agreement: the desire that leads X to enter into the agreement may be that Y do Ay, not that X and Y benefit from each other's actions. If X is purely self-interested, he may not care whether Y benefits.

I maintain in sections 3.4 and 3.6 that the fact that parties agree is a ground of obligations on them to perform. The grounding of such obligations can be viewed as a secondary function of agreements, in the sense that its fulfilment is a means to the fulfilment of the primary function. The fact that the means-end relation (discussed in sections 4.11, 6.21 and 6.211) obtains here is itself grounded in the parties' possible reasoning to performance. In outline the connection is this: if X and Y agree respectively to do Ax and Ay, the fact of their agreement grounds obligations on them to perform; so they can reason, in ways described in section 4.21, from those obligations to intentions to perform; if they have those intentions, they perform; if they perform, they benefit from each other's performance. If X and Y are narrowly and exclusively self-interested, they will not be moved by deontological considerations as such, but their reasoning to performance may still refer to their obligations.

Offer and acceptance likewise have functions. The main one of an offer is to put it in the power of the offeree, by accepting, to agree with the offeror; the main function of an act of acceptance is to make such an agreement. Offer and acceptance also have functions corresponding to those of an agreement: an offer has the function of putting it in the power of the offeree, by accepting, to impose obligations on the parties; an acceptance, of imposing such obligations; and both have the indirect function of enabling offeror and offeree, if rational and self-interested, to benefit from each other's actions. Variants of the functions corresponding to those of an agreement can be specified by restricting them to one party; for example, it can be said that functions of an acceptance are to impose an obligation on the offeror and to enable the offeree to benefit from the offeror's actions.

2.5 Criteria of adequacy

Subject to minor qualifications, the offer–acceptance model meets the four criteria of adequacy discussed in sections 1.231–1.2314: Symmetry, Obligation, Simultaneity and Interdependence. Symmetry, which provides that both parties do the same thing, is indeterminate, for sameness is relative to description: X and Y do the same thing in making the agreement that (1), but different things in that X offers and Y accepts. If that difference is a violation of Symmetry, the criterion is too stringent. Once the agreement is made, there is symmetry between the parties, albeit not in respect of their doing anything: they both have an agreement with the same content (subject to the complexities noted in the Introduction) and each is obligated to perform his part.

The model meets the other criteria by virtue of the constitutive rule of obligation. The Obligation criterion provides, in Gilbert's words, that the agreement 'directly generates' the parties' performance obligations.[35] Although the words are unclear, it seems that the model meets the criterion: section 3.6 maintains that the mere fact of agreement grounds the obligations, the explanation being that the rule of obligation is constitutive of agreement. From the moment the agreement is made, each party has a performance obligation (see section 2.3), and so the model meets Simultaneity, which provides that the parties get their obligations at the same time. Interdependence provides that, if one party defaults on his performance obligation, the other ceases to have his original performance obligation. The model meets this criterion by virtue of the cancellability of the parties' obligations (section 2.3 again). The obligations' temporal features, including their cancellability, are specified by the constitutive rule. These criteria, or the claim that the model meets them, need qualification to exclude performance obligations grounded in certain facts other than the mere fact of agreement: this point is developed, as regards reliance-based obligations, in section 3.51.

2.6 Objections and replies

Objections may nevertheless be raised: that the model does not fit agreements effected by a third party, multipartite agreements or agreements formed by a fluid process or by voting; that offer, acceptance and agreement are promises, and hence not only is the model consistent with the promise model but problems canvassed in Chapter 1 recur; that the

35 Gilbert (1996d), 315.

offer–acceptance model fails to capture the conditionality of agreements; that the account of the parties' obligations shares a fault with analyses in terms only of conditional promises; that the model wrongly implies that the existence of an agreement presupposes a rule-defined practice; and that it is circular.

2.61 *Varieties of agreement*

The first objection is that the offer–acceptance model does not fit agreements of certain kinds. If the objection means that the parties to such agreements do not meet the conditions in (36) and (37), the objection is misconceived, for those conditions are proposed only as sufficient, not as necessary, for an agreement. Moreover, the model accommodates agreements for which the conditions do not hold: I shall argue, as announced, that, for at least some such agreements, either the parties meet the conditions if minor adjustments to the conditions are made or the parties stand in a certain relation to a set of normal agreements – the parties to which do meet the conditions (with or without minor adjustments to the conditions) – and that in the first case their meeting the adjusted conditions, and in the second their so standing in that relation, is sufficient for them to agree. I also argue that, as regards certain forms of conduct for which the conditions in (36) and (37) appear not to hold, either the conduct does not amount to an agreement or the conditions hold after all. (This approach is used also in sections 7.4, 8.4 and 9.27.) For convenience, the discussion will be in terms of (37) and the state of agreement, but the same points apply to (36) and the making of an agreement.

2.611 Intervention by a third party

Suppose that X and Y cannot agree what to do. In order to settle things, Z proposes to both of them that X do Ax and Y do Ay. X and Y say OK. It seems that there is an agreement between X and Y but that neither makes an offer that the other accepts.[36] In a variant of the example, Z presents X and Y with a document which, when they sign it, records an agreement between them; as noted in the Introduction, the document itself may at that point be called an agreement.

One response is to say that Z makes an offer which X and Y accept, and so the agreement has three parties: only a minor change to the condition in (37) is needed for it to fit such a case. The interpretation strains the

36 See S. Smith (2005), 36.

normal meaning of 'offer', but it was acknowledged in section 2.1 that 'offer' in this context has a broad sense similar to the sense of 'propose'. Z's intervention, described above as a proposal, is an offer in that broad sense. The example still diverges from (37) in that the content of the offer, the acceptances and the agreement does not specify an action by the offeror; but again it has been allowed that such an action is typically, not always, specified by the content.

Alternatively it may be argued that the condition fits the situation without amendment, for X and Y agree with each other to abide by Z's proposal. It might be, for example, that X and Y are representatives of, respectively, a company and a trade union in dispute, that X proposes to Y that they settle the issue by referring it to an arbitrator, Z, and that Y accepts the proposal. Of course the situation need not be like that; Z might simply come along and make his proposal. But even here there is likely to be an offer by X that is accepted by Y. X may say to Y 'What do you think of Z's idea: shall we go along with it?' and Y may say 'Yes', or they may achieve the same result less articulately, say by eye contact. Offer and acceptance are speech acts but, as noted in section 1.1, 'speech' in this context can be non-verbal. In the odd situation where X and Y merely respond to Z and do not interact at all with each other, there may be no agreement between them (but see the discussion of 'wheels' in the next section).

2.612 Multipartite agreements

The condition as it stands does not fit agreements with more than two parties. Some agreements that may appear to be multipartite are in fact bipartite and hence raise no issue: if a corporation with more than one member is party to an agreement, the agreement may still have only two parties, for the corporation is a single party. There are various kinds of genuinely multipartite agreement, and the condition fits some of them with only minor revision; for example, as just indicated, three people have an agreement if – subject to conditions covered by CS – one makes an offer to the other two which they accept.

More recalcitrant is the 'wheel', where X and Y have an agreement with each other by virtue of the fact that each has an agreement with Z. Such cases arise in all the areas of law covered in Part II of this book. An arguable example from contract law is *The Satanita*,[37] a case about a

37 [1895], 248 (Court of Appeal), affirmed sub nom *Clarke* v. *Dunraven* [1897] AC 59 (House of Lords). The passages quoted in nn. 38 and 44 below are from the Court

regatta. The defendant and the claimant entered their yachts for a race, each having signed a letter, to the secretary of the club that organised the regatta, undertaking to obey certain rules. There was held to be a contract between defendant and claimant,[38] but it is not clear from the judgment whether an agreement was also found[39] and, if so, whether there was found to be an offer and an acceptance. (The gaps between contract, agreement and offer and acceptance are explored in Chapter 7.) It is doubtful that the competitors had agreements even with the club, for it seems that the only reason to think that they did was that their letters contained undertakings.[40] Promises are a species of undertaking, as noted in section 1.1, and the objections in Chapter 1 to promise-based analyses of agreement extend to analyses in terms of undertakings generally.[41]

In the case of at least some wheel agreements, each of the 'spokes' X and Y has an agreement with the 'hub' Z for which the condition in (37) holds, but it is artificial to say that the agreement between the spokes comprises even a deemed offer and acceptance. In particular, X and Y need not know of each other's existence,[42] and in many situations one could equally well say that X offers and Y accepts, or the opposite, or that

of Appeal's judgment. For wheel agreements in competition law, see *Argos/JJB* [2006] EWCA Civ 1318, para. 31, discussed in section 8.32 below; Hay (2006), 882. The British Institute for International and Comparative Law has run a project on the treatment of such agreements in competition law. On their treatment in the criminal law of conspiracy, see section 9.27 below.

38 Some of the statements by the judges are unclear. Lord Esher said 'The first question raised is whether, supposing [the yacht] to have broken a rule, she can be sued for that breach of the rules by the owner of the competing yacht which has been damaged; in other words, Was there any contract between the owners of those two yachts? Or it may be put thus: Did the owner of the yacht which is sued enter into any obligation to the owner of the other yacht, that, if his yacht broke the rules, and thereby injured the other yacht, he would pay damages? It seems to me clear that he did . . . ' (255). The trouble is that the phrases 'in other words' and 'or it may be put thus' connect questions that can have different answers.

Contrast this case with *Ellesmere* v. *Wallace* [1929] 2 Ch 1, where it was held that persons who entered horses for races organised by the Jockey Club had contracted with the club but not with each other. On multilateral contracts arising from membership of a club or other unincorporated association, see Peel (2007), paras. 2–077, 14–010 f. See further n. 44 below.

39 Phillips (1976), 500 appears to say that an agreement was found.

40 Each wrote 'I undertake that, while sailing under this entry, I will obey and be bound by the sailing rules of the Yacht Racing Association and the by-laws of the club'.

41 The discussion in O. Black (2003d); O. Black (2004a); O. Black (2005b), chap. 4 and O. Black (2007) is in terms of undertakings.

42 In *Argos/JJB* (n. 37 above), the Court of Appeal seemed to say (at para. 31) that, in order for X and Y to have an agreement with each other, they must be aware of each other's agreements with Z.

each both offers and accepts, or that they make cross-offers.[43] Also, where there are more than two spokes, it is unclear whether their respective agreements with the hub give rise to a single multipartite agreement or to another set of bilateral agreements.[44] Nevertheless, although the fact that each of X and Y has an agreement with Z which the condition fits is not enough for X and Y to have an agreement with each other, they stand in a certain relation to the set of those agreements, and their doing so is enough. To characterise that relation the courts invoke a cluster of conditions[45] – arguably none of them necessary, although in conspiracy law the requirement of a 'scheme' or 'common purpose'[46] is often prominent. The issue is discussed further in section 9.27, which applies a similar approach to other complex agreements such as 'chains' and 'forks'; see also section 5.2 on the identity of agreements, and section 8.4 on complex cartels.

2.613 Fluidity and voting

An agreement may arise through a fluid process that does not clearly involve offer and acceptance. Imagine that X, Y and Z are the members of an office management committee. At a meeting of the committee X says 'We need a new printer on the first floor. The one we have keeps jamming'. Y: 'It's not so bad – I don't think we need a new one'. Z: 'If we are to get a new one, we'll need to find out about prices, servicing and so on'. X: 'I'll make some inquiries'. At the next meeting, X reports: 'The Lexmark is the best value'. Z says 'OK, why don't I order it'. X and Y say nothing in reply and the meeting moves to the next point on the agenda.

43 Peel (2007), para. 2–077 reviews and rejects various attempts to represent the facts of *The Satanita* (n. 37 above) in terms of offer and acceptance. Phillips (1976), 502 quotes F. Pollock (1950), 5 in this context: 'the exclusive pursuit of the analytical method in dealing with legal conceptions always leads into some strait of this kind, and if the pursuit be obstinate, lands us in sheer fiction'.

44 In *The Satanita* (n. 37 above), 260 f. Lopes LJ seemed to contemplate a multipartite contract, for he said that there was 'a contract between the owners of the competing yachts amongst themselves, and that contract was an undertaking that the owner of one competing yacht would pay the owner of any other competing yacht injured by his yacht all the damages arising . . .'. 'Between' in its narrow sense signifies a relation with two terms, whereas 'amongst' implies more than two, and so 'a contract between the owners of the competing yachts amongst themselves' is unclear: it could mean a contract just between the claimant and the defendant or a contract to which all participants (presumably there were more than two) in the race were parties. 'Any other competing yacht' suggests, however, that the judge had the latter in mind, for it would be odd for a contract just between claimant and defendant to include a provision to pay damages to other participants. On the difficulty of proving the existence of numerous agreements, see the quotation from Whish in section 8.4 below.

45 On clusters, see section 9.27 below. 46 See section 9.27 below.

Cases similar to this are familiar in contract law, which discusses them in terms of a distinction between precontractual negotiations and the formation of a contract, or more specifically between an invitation to treat and an offer: see section 7.13. On one view of the example, there is no agreement: Z makes a unilateral decision to place the order. How plausible that view is will depend on facts about Z's seniority, the committee's procedures and so on. On another view, his utterance of the words 'OK, why don't I order it' constitutes an offer, and the silence of the other parties an acceptance. (Sections 7.13 and 7.4 deal with silence as a form of acceptance and, more generally, as a means of forming a contract.) As noted in section 2.1, the determination whether an utterance is an offer involves interpretation, but that does not trivialise the second view, for interpretation is subject to constraints.[47] If, as is plausible to hold, the second view is correct, the case is one of an offer to more than one person. As explained in section 2.612, only a minor change to the condition in (37) is needed for it to fit such cases.

Fluidity in complex cartels and complex conspiracies is discussed in sections 8.4 and 9.27. Here I consider another issue which arises from a variant of the example. Suppose that the committee makes decisions by majority vote. Z says: 'I propose that I order the printer. Let's vote on it'. Z and X vote in favour, Y against. It might be said that here is an agreement without an offer or that, even if there is an offer, Y agrees without accepting. One response is to deny that decisions by majority vote are, without more, agreements; for example, *pace* social contract theorists, it seems artificial to say that the members of the British electorate agree with each other to put a certain political party into power. If it is allowed that there is an agreement in the present example, the first half of the contemplated gloss is answered as in the discussion, in section 2.611, of interventions by a third party: 'offer' has a broad sense which covers Z's utterance. As to the second half, Y may be said to accept the proposal by not resigning from the committee. His being on the committee may of course itself be the result of an agreement to which the condition in (37) applies as it stands.

2.62 *Offer, acceptance and promise*

The second objection starts from the premiss that offers and acceptances are kinds of promise.[48] This implies that, if the offer–acceptance model

47 On reasons for interpretations, see section 8.51 below.

48 Sheinman (2011a), 381 maintains that an offer, once accepted, transforms into two promises, respectively by the offeror and the offeree, and that it causes the first of these;

is true, there are – contrary to the conclusion of Chapter 1 – kinds of promise, Kpx and Kpy, such that X's giving to Y a promise of kind Kpx and Y's giving to X a promise of kind Kpy are sufficient for X and Y to agree. (In the present discussion, CM and CS can be ignored.) Therefore, given the premiss, the offer–acceptance model implies the promise model; so, contrary to the Introduction's description of the latter as the foil of the former, it is wrong to represent the models as opposed to each other. Moreover, <an offer by X to Y that (1)> is a promise by X to Y that <if Y does Ay, X does Ax>; and an acceptance by Y of that offer is a promise by Y to X that Y does Ay. We have therefore returned to analysis (10) of section 1.23 and to its problems.

The premiss of the objection is undermined by important differences between promises on the one hand and offers and acceptances on the other. Roughly, a promise differs from an offer in that a promise does, but an offer does not, ground an obligation and an offer can, but a promise cannot, be accepted or, before acceptance, withdrawn (see section 1.1). If the fact that an offer does not ground an obligation is not obvious, it may help to revert to the terminology of proposal and assent. If X says to Y 'I propose this: I make the beds and you wash the dishes', he does not thereby obligate himself to make the beds. He might do in odd circumstances, for example where he has previously told Y that if he says those words he is to be understood as promising to make the beds; but in that case X's 'proposal' is a promise. Acceptances are like promises as regards acceptance and withdrawal, but like offers as regards obligation: normally acceptance of an offer is sufficient for an agreement and thus for an obligation, but the ground of the obligation is the fact of agreement, not the fact of acceptance.

As explained below, the nature of these distinctions is the same as that, described in section 1.1, of the relevant theses about promises: the one about obligation is based on the account of obligation to be given in Chapter 3, the one about withdrawal relates to normative powers and disabilities, and the distinction as to the possibility of being accepted is based on function. They need qualification, but the caveats do not undermine the proposition that neither an offer nor an acceptance is a promise. For example, as noted in section 2.3, an offer to φ may, in conjunction with other factors, obligate the offeror to keep it open for a certain period, but it does not obligate him to φ. Also it was noted in

Sheinman may also think, but does not say, that it causes the second. He says that the acceptance, when complete, likewise transforms into those two promises; it is unclear whether he thinks that it causes either of them.

section 1.1 that, where a person promises to φ, an obligation on him to φ may be lacking if he is unable to φ, or it would be immoral for him to φ, and so on: in such cases it seems that the promise may be withdrawn. The position appears similar for acceptances.[49]

As with promises, the features of offer and acceptance that concern the possibility of being withdrawn or accepted are connected to the relations borne by offer and acceptance to obligation. The arguments that follow may need qualification of the kinds just mentioned, but I shall state them baldly. Consider the proposition that an acceptance cannot be withdrawn. Y's acceptance of X's offer is sufficient for an agreement, which grounds obligations on X and Y. If Y withdrew his acceptance, the agreement and the obligations would cease, and so Y would release himself from his obligation. But an obligor is normatively disabled from releasing himself. So an acceptance cannot be withdrawn. This argument – which is similar to the one for promises in section 1.1 – does not apply to the withdrawal of an offer before acceptance, because an unaccepted offer is not sufficient for an agreement. Absent any other argument, there is no reason to deny that an offer can be withdrawn before acceptance.

As to the possibility of being accepted, the connection is mediated by the functions of offer and acceptance. One function of an offer is, as noted in section 2.4, to put it in the power of the offeree, by accepting, to impose obligations on the parties; so, if the offer fulfils its function, the offeree can accept it. The conclusion that offers can be accepted follows on the assumption that they fulfil the function. Although an acceptance presupposes an offer, there is no parallel argument from acceptance's function of imposing obligations on the parties to the proposition that an acceptance can be accepted, and there seems no other reason to believe that proposition; indeed, it threatens an infinite regress, albeit a benign one as the infinity is merely potential. (The stronger claim, that for an agreement to exist an acceptance by one party must be accepted by the other, entails, when joined to the premiss that an agreement exists, an actual infinity of acceptances and a seemingly vicious regress.[50]) The

49 On the scope for revoking an acceptance in various systems of contract law, see von Mehren (1992), paras. 190 ff. On the distinction between revocation and withdrawal, see ibid., para. 134; n. 54 below; Chap. 7 n. 30 below.

50 The distinction between the potential and the actual infinite is due to Aristotle: Aristotle (1983), bks. 3 f.; A. Moore (1990), 39 ff. On a plausible view, a regress involving an actual infinity need not be vicious: for an example, see section 3.2 below. On infinite regresses, see O. Black (1987), chap. 2 and O. Black (1996b), which build viciousness into the definition of an infinite regress (and contain further references). Other authors use

same result can be reached from the primary functions of an offer and an act of acceptance. That of an offer is to put it in the power of the offeree, by accepting, to agree with the offeror; so, if the offer fulfils this function, the offeree can accept it; but again there is no parallel argument from the primary function of an act of acceptance – to make such an agreement – to the conclusion that an acceptance can be accepted.

Since two of the distinctions align acceptances with promises, and only one with offers, it might be suggested that an acceptance is more like a promise than like an offer and therefore can reasonably be classified as a promise. That requires a stretch of the meaning of 'promise', but even if it is stretched to cover both offers and acceptances[51] the objection does not work. A version of the problem – identified in sections 1.22, 1.231, 1.4 and 1.6 – of a mismatch of content recurs: if offer and acceptance have the content (1), they do not respectively have the contents 'if Y does Ay, X does Ax' and 'Y does Ay'; so there is no return to analysis (10) of section 1.23. In any case, if offers and acceptances are promises, they are special in the respects just identified; but the promise model is naturally understood to concern ordinary promises; so the objection fails because it confuses different sorts of promise.

If the objector maintains that the promise model covers both ordinary and special promises, the reply is that, since the meaning of 'promise' has to be stretched to cover offer and acceptance, the defence reduces the model's interest. That is not to say that the extension of meaning is groundless, as if one were to stretch the meaning of 'cat' to cover the number 2; acceptances, at any rate, are similar to promises in the respects identified. But, if the meaning of 'cat' were stretched to cover all domestic animals, it would be uninteresting to be told that Fido is a cat, even though there are significant respects in which cats (in the usual sense) and dogs

definitions that admit benign infinite regresses: see, e.g., Russell (1979), 348 f.; Yalden-Thomson (1964), 505. See further Chap. 4 n. 35 below. Compare the distinction between vicious and benign circles: n. 69 below.

51 For the view that offer and acceptance are undertakings, see Benson (2001c), 139, 149; de Moor (1987), 116 ff.; Stoljar (1988), 206. Section 1.1 above maintains that promises are a kind of undertaking. S. Smith (2005), 36 seems to say that an offer may have an undertaking as its object: 'the offer is a proposal by the offeror to undertake to do or abstain from doing something'. (See also 37. See further n. 52 below and compare the implication in Ormerod (2008), 413 that an agreement is the object of an offer and an acceptance. Mintoff, like Ormerod, writes of an offer or acceptance of an agreement: Mintoff (2004), 58. For similar locutions in competition law, see Chap. 8 nn. 44 f. below.) S. Smith (2004), 172 says 'the language of offer and acceptance is the language of promising, broadly understood'.

are alike. It is no more interesting to be told that promises, in a similarly stretched sense of 'promise', are sufficient for agreement. This response is consistent with the statement in section 2.1 that the offer–acceptance model uses broad senses of 'offer' and 'accept': in the first place, even if a broad sense is a stretched sense, the senses of these terms are not stretched so far; in the second, as explained in that section, these senses are rooted in the doctrines of contract law.

The meaning of 'promise' is more plausibly stretched to cover agreements than to cover offers or acceptances,[52] for it can be argued that agreements share all three specified features with promises: they ground obligations and cannot in the relevant senses be withdrawn or accepted. An agreement is made in part by, but is not the object of, an acceptance.[53] The point about withdrawal is debatable: a party can withdraw *from* an agreement, but that can be distinguished from withdrawal of the agreement itself; nevertheless, the former is one way of terminating an agreement and there seems little difference, beyond one of idiom, between termination and withdrawal of an agreement.[54] If an agreement is a promise, it is sufficient for a promise; so, it may be objected, the promise model is true whether or not the offer–acceptance model is true. Again the conclusion is that it is wrong to represent the models as opposed to each other.

The Introduction formulated the promise model thus: there are kinds of promise, Kpx and Kpy, such that X's giving to Y a promise of kind Kpx and Y's giving to X a promise of kind Kpy are necessary and/or sufficient for X and Y to agree. Even if an agreement between X and Y is a promise, it is debatable whether either party gives a promise to the other: an alternative view is that they form a 'plural subject' which gives a promise to itself (see further section 8.121). If that view – however it is

52 S. Smith (2005), 1 talks of 'an agreement, promise, or other undertaking' (see Chap. 1 n. 9 above). This indicates that Smith regards an agreement as itself an undertaking but not as a promise; compare ibid., 3, where he describes contracts as 'voluntary undertakings', and 56, where he describes agreements as 'mutual undertakings'. At 36 he writes that the parties 'agree to mutual undertakings', which seems to say that an agreement – rather than, or as well as, being an undertaking – has undertakings as its object. As mentioned in n. 51 above, he uses a similar locution in relation to an offer. S. Smith (2004), 56 deliberately assimilates agreements to promises, save when dealing with the bilaterality of contracts (180 ff.). See further Chap. 7 nn. 87 and 110 below.

53 Contrast the view of Mintoff and Ormerod: n. 51 above.

54 As regards offers, von Mehren (1992), para. 134 distinguishes withdrawal from revocation, the former occurring before, the latter after, the offer has legal effects. Granted that both are kinds of termination, withdrawal and termination of an offer are different, even if an offeror may terminate an offer in or by withdrawing it. On the revocation of acceptances, see n. 49 above. On the 'in'/'by' distinction, see section 2.1 above.

to be understood[55] – is right, the promise model needs to be expanded in order for the objection to work. Even if it is thus expanded, the objection shares faults of the previous one: if an agreement is a promise, it is a special one[56] – in particular, either there is more than one promisor or the promisor is a plural subject or some other special thing – whereas the model is naturally understood to concern ordinary promises; and, if the model covers special promises, its interest is reduced. In the present case the second fault is glaring: an agreement is sufficient for a promise, the promise is from a special class, the class is the class of agreements, and so an agreement is sufficient for an agreement.

The objector might now maintain that the promise model amounts merely to the thesis that agreements and promises are alike in the three specified respects. As already explained, the thesis is debatable as to the possibility of withdrawal; but, even if it is true, the objection fails. The manoeuvre merely redefines the model and in a way that again reduces its interest.

2.63 *Conditionality*

According to the offer–acceptance model, the content of the offer, the acceptance and the agreement is a conjunctive proposition of the form (1) (X does Ax and Y does Ay). The next objection is that a mere conjunction fails to capture the conditionality of agreements.[57] A bad argument for conditionality is that it is imported by the doctrine of consideration in contract law; the doctrine is briefly described in section 7.1, which notes that it has been invoked to support the view that a contract is an exchange or bargain. The thesis that consideration is conditional implies at most that contracts, not contractual agreements, let alone all agreements, are also conditional. (See section 9.22 for two meanings of 'contractual agreement'.) Moreover, as explained in sections 7.2–7.38, neither an agreement nor consideration is either necessary or sufficient for a contract.

55 Gilbert (1989), 382; Gilbert (1996a), 292 claim that the parties constitute a plural subject, but in conversation Gilbert has said that 'plural subject' is itself a mere label. See further Gilbert (1989), 17, chap. 4. See also List and Pettit (2011) on corporate agents.

56 It might be called a joint promise, but that should not be understood to mean that the parties, in performing the promise, meet the condition in (199) (section 8.31 below) for joint action. That condition includes mutual reliance, and it was argued in section 1.5 above that the parties in performing the agreement need not be relying on each other to perform. See further section 8.5222 below.

57 For one expression of the conditionality, see S. Smith (2004), 168 f., quoted in section 7.11 below.

Every agreement is externally conditional, in the sense that there are certain conditions on which an agreement exists; for example, it would not exist if its parties did not exist, and it ceases to exist when the conditions for its termination are met. (Section 1.1, which explains the distinction between external and internal conditionality, makes a corresponding point about promises, and section 5.11 about intentions.) Furthermore, the model accommodates various conditional relations connecting offer, acceptance, the parties' obligations, their actions in performance of the agreement and their beliefs and intentions as to those actions. In some cases the conditionality is external, in others internal.

As to offer and acceptance, Y accepts X's offer only if X makes an offer. On a narrow view of acceptance, Y accepts the offer, rather than merely purporting to do so, only if the offer is not withdrawn before the relevant time: see section 2.1. Normally, Y accepts X's offer only if Y believes that X makes the offer. His having the belief arguably follows from the fact, which normally obtains, that Y's reason (understood widely, as in section 1.23) for accepting the offer is that X makes the offer: the connection is the same as the one traced, in the discussion of clause (c) in analyses (9) and (10) of section 1.23, between Y's reason for giving the promise Py and his belief that X gives Px. It was suggested that Y's giving Py is based on the reason; the corresponding suggestion is that Y's acceptance is based on the reason that X makes the offer. If basing is a matter of causal explanation, as stated there, and the relevant causal relation is one of conditionality,[58] there is another respect in which the acceptance is conditional. Even if some other account of basing is correct, it is plausible to hold that the relation is conditional, in which case the conclusion still follows.

Conversely, in the normal case, although the acceptance itself is not a necessary condition of the offer, X makes the offer only if he believes it sufficiently likely that Y accepts it – the threshold of sufficiency depending on the cost to X of making the offer and the benefit he gains from Y's acceptance. To be more precise, the content of X's belief is that the probability of Y's acceptance if X makes the offer is high enough; so the belief, on which the offer is conditional, is itself internally conditional. Again, X's reason for making the offer is normally that Y's acceptance, given the offer, is sufficiently likely; as with the acceptance, on the assumptions that the offer is based on the reason and that basing is conditional there is another respect in which the offer is conditional.

58 D. Lewis (1986) gives a theory of causation in terms of counterfactual conditionals. See further Chap. 4 n. 16 below.

Each party's obligation is externally conditional on the other's performance, by virtue of the obligations' cancellability: X's obligation is to do Ax and it ceases if Y does not do, or it is clear that Y is not going to do, Ay – and conversely for Y. If, as suggested in section 2.3, 'it is clear that' is amplified in terms of the relevant party's beliefs and his reasons for them, X's obligation is conditional on his beliefs, and his reasons for those beliefs, as to Y's performance, and vice versa.

Ax and Ay may also be conditional on each other. A form of reasoning, described in section 4.22, that may lead X to do Ax includes the premiss 'The best means to Y's doing Ay is for me to do Ax'. If the premiss is true, and if the means-end relation is conditional, there is a conditional relation between the two actions. As noted in section 4.11, no entailment obtains in either direction between 'A means to its being the case that P is for me to φ' and the simple conditional 'If I φ then P'; but it is suggested there that the means-end relation can be analysed in terms of causation or constitution, in which case it is conditional if they are. Normally, if reasoning from the premiss leads X to do Ax, Ax is based on X's belief in the premiss; so, if basing is understood as above and the relevant causal relation is conditional, Ax is further conditional on X's belief in a conditional relation between Ax and Ay. 'Belief in' here has a de re sense:[59] X may believe of the conditional relation that it obtains, without believing that it is conditional; but, if he believes that there is a conditional relation between Ax and Ay, his belief is internally conditional. All the points about X, in this paragraph and the next, have counterparts applying to Y.

Section 4.3 shows how X may reason to performance from an intention, concerning a conditional relation between Ax and X's epistemic state in respect of Ay, which he may have at the time the agreement is made and which, as explained in section 5.11, is in certain circumstances sufficient for X to agree sincerely. He may intend, for example, <to do Ax at Tx if and only if at Tx he knows that at Ty Y does Ay> or <to do Ax at Tx unless at Tx he has good reason to believe that at Ty Y does not do Ay>, where (as in section 2.3) Tx and Ty are the times that the agreement specifies for X and Y respectively to perform. The conditionality of the content of these intentions is compatible with the thesis that the agreement's content is unconditional: some who think that an agreement has a conditional content may do so because they confuse the contents of the agreement and of the parties' intentions. As noted in the Introduction, the connection

59 Gallois (1998) is an introduction to the various distinctions that go under the title de re / de dicto. See further Chap. 9 n. 82 below.

between intention and agreement is a loose one. (See further sections 5.1, 8.1–8.2 and 9.4.)

2.64 Breach of obligation

These conditional aspects do not expose the offer–acceptance model to the objection to analyses using only conditional promises, that the parties comply if neither does anything; but it may be argued that the model falls to an analogue of that objection, which applies to the obligations arising from the agreement. The new objection is that, if both parties fail to perform, they do not breach any such obligation.[60] X's obligation to do Ax ceases, it has been said, if Y does not do Ay. That entails, as has been noted, that X's obligation is externally conditional: if Y does not do Ay, X does not have the obligation and a fortiori does not breach it. Suppose that Y does not do Ay. Then, absent any other ground for an obligation on X to do Ax, X has no such obligation. Suppose that X does not do Ax. Then he does not breach such an obligation. By parity of reasoning, Y does not breach an obligation to do Ay. Absent any other obligation arising from the agreement, X and Y breach no such obligation in failing to perform.

The objection ignores the temporality of the obligations and thus fails to distinguish between a party's never having an obligation and his ceasing to have one. Assume, as before, that Ta is the time at which Y accepts and hence the agreement is made and that Tx and Ty are the times for X and Y respectively to do Ax and Ay. Assume also that Tx precedes Ty. It was granted in section 2.3 that X ceases to have his obligation – unless it has ceased already – at Tx and, at any time from Ta to Tx, if either Y releases X from it or it is clear that at Ty Y does not do Ay; but, from Ta to the earliest time at which any of those cancelling conditions obtains, X is obligated to do Ax. Suppose that the earliest is Tx, at which time X does not do Ax. He thereby breaches his obligation and cancels Y's. Y on that basis decides not to do Ay. In that case neither party performs, but one of them is in breach of an obligation arising from the agreement.

The abnormal case might arise in which neither party gets an obligation, or at most each gets one that exists for a bare instant. That happens if at Ta a cancelling condition obtains in respect of both parties; for example, it is clear that both X and Y are not going to perform. If neither performs, it can here be said that the parties breach the agreement without breaching any

60 Compare Smith on interconditional promises: Chap. 1 n. 43 above.

obligation associated with it. The same can be said in the more common case where the parties do not perform and, at some time later than Ta but before Tx and Ty, their obligations cease. If the objector resists the idea that the parties can breach an agreement without breaching obligations, the situation can be redescribed in either of two ways. First, it might rather artificially be said that in both these cases there are obligations that are breached – evanescent obligations in the former case – but that at the time of breach the obligations have ceased. Second, a distinction might be drawn between breaching an agreement and not performing it:[61] a party breaches an agreement if and only if he both does not perform it and breaches an obligation arising from it. Compliance might then be defined in opposition either to non-performance or to breach. (On the varieties of compliance, see sections 1.22 and 8.122.) There seems, however, no good reason to deny that an agreement can be breached without a breach of obligation.

It is worth noting that the specification of times does not save analyses (9) and (10) in section 1.23 from the objection that they breach Interdependence. Consider Y's promise to X (in clause (b) of those analyses) that Y does Ay. If times are introduced, (b) becomes: at Tp Y promises to X that at Ty Y does Ay. This also elaborates clause (b) of analysis (19) (section 1.2313), which specifies only the time of the promise. Most of the things true in the case of offer and acceptance are true of Y's promise: normally, at Tp Y gets an obligation to do Ay at Ty; unless a cancelling condition obtains, it continues up to Ty; if at Ty Y does Ay, the obligation ceases if it has not already done so; if at Ty Y does not do Ay, it also ceases, but is replaced by an obligation to compensate; and, at any time from Tp to Ty, the obligation, if it has not ceased already, ceases if X releases Y from it. In contrast to the previous case, however, it is false that, if in that period either Tx occurs and X does not do Ax at Tx or it is clear before Tx that this is the case, then Y's obligation ceases. So there is still a breach of Interdependence.

2.65 *A practice of agreement*

Another objection is that the talk of constitutive rules (section 2.2) implies that the existence of an agreement presupposes a practice defined by

61 Compare Zweigert and Kötz (1998), 488 on a distinction, made for a different purpose, between breach and non-performance of a contract.

rules.[62] That cannot be right, the objection runs, for when the first agreement was made there was no such practice.[63] (Section 4.4 considers the converse objection, that the practice presupposes an agreement.) The answer is that the discussion of constitutive rules did not mention practices: the thesis was simply that agreement is defined by rules. Rules can exist without a practice of obeying them;[64] to continue the analogy used in section 2.2, if you invent a game, setting out the rules, the rules exist whether or not the game is ever played.

Suppose, however, that the objector could establish that the thesis entails that the existence of an agreement presupposes a practice of agreement. The point about the first agreement would still be fallacious: it might as well be argued that not every human being has human parents, as the first human did not. Just as humans evolved from other species, the practice of agreement may have evolved from simpler arrangements.[65] The objector might concede this but maintain that nevertheless there must at some past time have been an agreement – between two cavemen, say – without a practice of agreement. The reply is that a practice can be more or less extensive, complex, articulated or entrenched:[66] we have a

62 Compare the view of promising as a rule-governed practice: Husi (2011); Melden (1956); Rawls (1967); Searle (1965); Searle (1967); Searle (1969), chap. 8. That should be distinguished from the theory, associated with Hart, that some rules are themselves practices (see n. 64 below) and from the theory that the obligations concerned depend on practices (see Altham (1985), 15; compare Atiyah (1981), 129). The latter distinction is blurred, as regards promissory obligation, in MacCormick (1982).

63 For objections to the corresponding view of promises (n. 62 above), see Altham (1985), 13 (concerning the claim that this is a matter of the meaning of 'promise'); Atiyah (1979b), 654; Atiyah (1981), 106 ff. (but with an exception for wholly executory promises, 121 f.); Cavell (1979), chap. 11; DeMarco and Fox (1992); de Moor (1987), 105 ff.; Downie (1985), 259 ff.; Gilbert (1996a), 296; MacCormick (1982); Raz (1972), 100; Raz (1977), 214 f.; Robins (1984), 110 ff.; Scanlon (1990); Scanlon (1998), chap. 7; Scanlon (2001), 86 f. (the law of contract is, but promising is not, a social institution – a view similar to that in de Moor (1987); on institutions, see n. 66 below).

64 This is an objection to some versions of the 'practice theory' of rules. Compare the claim in Stocker (1970), 622 that the rules of promising differ from those of law in that the former do not cease to be rules through disuse. See also Rawls (1967), 164 n. 1 on blueprints for practices. On the practice theory, see Hart (1958), 88; Hart (1961), 54 ff., 86 ff., 96 ff., 244. For criticism, see Bayles (1992); R. Dworkin (1978), chaps. 2 f.; Gilbert (2000c); Gilbert (2006), 185 ff.; MacCormick (1978), 275 ff.; MacCormick (1981), chap. 3; Raz (1990), 49 ff.; Sartorius (1987).

65 One thought is that agreements to do evolved from agreements in doing: see Atiyah (1981), 116, which draws on Hume (1978), 490. See also Hume (1963), 455 on the evolution of the social contract.

66 On the meaning of 'practice', see McNeilly (1971), 75; Rawls (1967), 144 n. 2. On practices generally and their normative characteristics, see C. Wright (1992), 15 ff. On a practice's

developed practice of agreement, cavemen may have had a cruder one. If it were conceded that an agreement presupposes a practice of agreement, it could be said that whether the two cavemen agreed depends on how crude the practice was at the time: if it was similar enough to ours, they had an agreement or a proto-agreement; if it fell too far short, they had no agreement but only an ancestor of one.

The objector might abandon the argument about practices and claim – recycling the example of the cavemen in support – that an agreement can exist without rules. The reply is similar to the one just given: even if the two cavemen did not have the constitutive rules described in section 2.2, they could have had cruder ones, possibly just for the nonce.[67] In that case, likewise, whether they agreed depends on how nearly their rules approached ours.

2.66 Circularity

The final objection is that the promise model is better than the offer–acceptance model in that the relevant concepts of offer and acceptance are in the following sense dependent, but that of a promise is not, on the concept of agreement: the concept of a promise can be grasped, but the concepts of offer and acceptance cannot, by someone who does not grasp the concept of agreement.[68] Substitution of 'agree' for 'contract' in a standard definition of a contractual offer yields: an offer is an expression of willingness to agree on specified terms, made with the intention that it is to become binding as soon as it is accepted by the person to whom it is addressed (see section 7.11). Agreement is supposed to be analysed in terms of offer and acceptance, the concepts of which depend on that of agreement – a vicious circle.[69] (A fierce form of the objection is that the

sphere of validity, see Altham (1985), 7. The statement about practices is true also of institutions, the concept of which is sometimes used in this context. See Altham (1985), 15 f.; Cavell (1979), 292 ff.; Hanfling (1975); Hare (1967), 122; MacCormick (1982), 191 ff.; Scanlon (2001), 86 f.; Searle (1967), 111 ff.; Searle (1969), 50 ff. (on institutions as systems of constitutive rules). Mackie (1977), 80 ff. distinguishes abstract descriptions of an institution from its 'concrete reality'; compare Rawls on blueprints for practices (n. 64 above).

67 This possibility may conflict with the claim in Raz (1990), 49 that a rule is necessarily general; whether there is a conflict will depend on the standard of generality. See further Chap. 3 n. 55 below. On the philosophy of rules, see n. 14 above.

68 See n. 4 above.

69 For the distinction between vicious and benign circularity, see Keefe (2002). Compare the distinction between vicious and benign infinite regresses: n. 50 above.

concept of acceptance is identical to that of agreement. Answers are, first, that the offeror may agree but does not accept and, second, that (as noted in section 2.62) the fact of agreement, not the fact of acceptance, grounds performance obligations on the parties. These points are consistent with the fact that, on the conditions in (36), Y agrees by accepting.)

One response, which might be based on the thought that a promise, if it is to obligate the promisor, must be accepted by the promisee, would be to maintain that the concept of a promise can likewise be grasped only by someone who grasps the concept of agreement. The underlying thought was dismissed in section 1.1 (see also section 2.62), and in any event the response would worsen the case for the promise model without improving that for the offer–acceptance model. A better approach is to reject the claim that the concepts of offer and acceptance depend on that of agreement.

The objection rests on a definition of dependence according to which this is true: one concept depends on another if the first cannot be grasped by someone who does not grasp the second. Given the strict-implication analysis of conditionality, the proposition may be rewritten as:

(39) Concept C1 depends on concept C2 if <if X grasps C1, then X grasps C2>.

The definition fails to recognise that grasp of a concept is a matter of degree.[70] To accommodate that fact, dependence could be defined either as binary, in terms of threshold degrees of grasp, or as itself a matter of degree. An example of a definition of the former kind is one according to which the following is true for specified values of N1 and N2:

(40) C1 depends on C2 if <if X grasps C1 to degree N1, then X grasps C2 to degree N2>.

A plausible thesis is that, although the concepts of offer and acceptance cannot be fully grasped, they can be grasped to a fair degree, by someone who has no grasp of the concept of agreement. If the thesis is taken together with the offer–acceptance model, it is also plausible to hold that the concepts of offer and acceptance and the concept of agreement provide mutual illumination in the sense that a person's grasp of the first two concepts may support or improve his grasp of the third, and vice versa. The thesis is supported by the proposition that connections can be

70 Gateways to the literature on concepts are Carey (2009); Fodor (1998); Peacocke (1992), chap. 1; G. Rey (1998).

traced between, on the one hand, the concepts of offer and acceptance and, on the other, further concepts which themselves can be grasped to a fair degree by someone who has no grasp of the concept of agreement.[71] That proposition too is plausible. In the first place, contract law's highly developed rules of offer and acceptance connect the concepts of offer and acceptance with numerous other concepts – such as those of undertaking, guarantee, conduct, advertisement, display, silence and ignorance – which can be fairly grasped without a grasp of the concept of agreement. In the second, it is arguable that the concepts of offer and acceptance used in the offer–acceptance model evolved from other, simpler, concepts of offer and acceptance which themselves can be fairly grasped without a grasp of the concept of agreement: compare the point, in section 2.65, about the evolution of the practice of agreement. If one caveman holds an arrowhead out to another and the other one takes it, there may be said to be an offer and an acceptance, but it might also be said that there is no agreement between them, not even a proto-agreement, to the effect that, say, the offeror allows the offeree to keep the object. The claim is debatable – if there are primitive offer and acceptance, might there not also be primitive agreement? – but, given the point about the contractual rules of offer and acceptance, need not be settled.

The thesis can likewise be expressed in conditional terms:

(41) If X fully grasps the concepts of offer and acceptance, then X has some grasp of the concept of agreement.
(42) It is not the case that, if X has a fair grasp of the concepts of offer and acceptance, then X has some grasp of the concept of agreement.

Given (40), whether (41) and (42) imply the claim that the concepts of offer and acceptance depend on that of agreement turns on the values given to N1 and N2. If a grasp to degree N1 is a full grasp and a grasp to N2 is one to a degree above zero, then, on the assumption that 'some grasp' in (41) and (42) likewise signifies a grasp to a degree above zero, the claim follows from (41). If a grasp to N1 is a fair grasp and a grasp to N2 is the same as before, the claim does not follow from (41) and (42). It is reasonable to give the latter values to N1 and N2, in which case, absent some other argument for the claim, the claim may be rejected.

Other responses turn on the nature of analysis and on the relation between analysis and dependence. The core of the objection may be

71 Compare Textor (2010a).

represented as an argument, to the claim that the offer–acceptance model is not an analysis, from the premisses:

(43) In an analysis, the concepts in the analysans do not depend on those in the analysandum.

(44) In the offer–acceptance model, the concepts in the supposed analysans depend on those in the analysandum.

Variants would talk of a correct or an adequate analysis; the present version might be read as building correctness or adequacy into the concept of analysis. (Compare the comments in the Introduction on the relations between analytic truth, analysis and correct analysis.)

In the Introduction I made only some brief remarks about analysis; one of them was that, although I would label as analyses certain propositions that gave conditions for agreement, the term was one of convenience only. Pursuant to that approach, it may be denied that the model purports to be an analysis in whatever sense is at issue in the objection: if it does not, the objection is irrelevant. It does not follow that the model is uninteresting, for a statement of sufficient conditions and of constitutive rules can be interesting whether or not it is an analysis.

Given (40), (41) and the assumption that the offer–acceptance model is supposed to be an analysis, the first pair of values given to N1 and N2 make (44) true. Grant those values to the objector. They import a broad definition of dependence: it is plausible to think that, according to such a definition, more concepts depend on other concepts than would be the case according to a definition imported by the second pair of values. For the objection to avoid failure for equivocation, the same broad definition must be read into (43), in which case (43) is true only if a correspondingly narrow definition is given of analysis. There seems no good reason for such a narrow definition: its adoption would be merely a device to make trouble for the offer–acceptance model. To secure the truth of (43) given a broader definition of analysis, dependence could be given a narrower definition – for example, one imported by the second pair of values. Again, the same definition of dependence must be read into (44). Given that definition, (44) has not been established. The challenge to the objector, then, is to supply plausible definitions of dependence and of analysis that establish both his premisses. Unless that challenge is met, and absent some other argument for his claim that the offer–acceptance model is not an analysis, the claim may be rejected.

3

Obligation

3.1 Questions about obligation

There are many questions about obligation.[1] What is it for someone to have an obligation?[2] (As noted in the Introduction, questions of this form can be understood in various ways.) What does the word 'obligation' mean? In what kinds of situation do obligations arise? What is the relation between moral and other types of obligation? How does moral obligation relate to law, including divine law? What are the relations of obligation to agency, to coercion, to responsibility and to blame and other forms of criticism? Is obligation a reason-giving feature of an action or is it the force of the justification generated by such a feature?[3] What are the logical properties of statements of obligation? How can we know that someone has an obligation?

There is also a wide range of views. Various writers note that the etymology of 'obligation' (*ob-ligare*) includes the idea of a bond,[4] and some have drawn attention to the distinction between being bound (a normative matter) and feeling bound (a matter of psychology).[5] Hart suggests

1 For a taxonomy of such questions in the context of contract, see S. Smith (2004), 43 ff. Smith distinguishes an 'analytic' question about the nature of contractual obligation from a 'normative' question 'about the justification, if any, for contractual obligations' (43). The normative question appears either to correspond to my question of grounds (section 3.2 below) or to be a request for the justification of the fact or proposition or belief that a certain fact is the ground of a contractual obligation.

2 A variant, addressed in M. Zimmerman (1996), x, is: What is it for an act to be obligatory?

3 For promises, Woozley (1981), 289 f. distinguishes the force of obligation from the force of guarantee.

4 Gilbert (1996a), 295; Hart (1961), 85; Mackie (1977), 74; Nicholas (1962), 158; Warnock (1971), 94. '[T]he precise figure is not that of two persons bound by a chain, but of *one* person bound, the other end of the chain lying in the hands of another to use if he chooses': Hart (1967), 58 (Hart's emphasis). See also A. Campbell (1954), 31; Skinner (1996), 389 f., on Hobbes's use of such metaphors.

5 Gilbert (2000c), 71, 81; Gilbert (2006), 189; Warnock (1971), 95 f. On the feeling of obligation, see Prichard (2002a), 10 ff.

that the psychological/normative distinction is marked by a difference in meaning between 'is obliged' and 'has an obligation':[6] if X threatens to shoot Y unless Y gives his money to X, Y is obliged, but under no obligation, to hand it over. With this distinction in mind, I use 'is obligated', but not 'is obliged', as a synonym for 'has an obligation'.[7] (I also continue to shift, as convenience dictates, between 'obligation to' and 'obligation that': on the propositional content of obligations, see the Introduction.) Brandt, who distinguishes obligation from duty,[8] maintains that the paradigmatic use of the word 'obligation' is in talk about promises, agreements or the acceptance of benefactions.[9] According to him, three features of such contexts are that a roughly specifiable service is 'required'[10] of one person; two

6 Hart (1958), 89, 95 f., which distinguishes both from 'is physically compelled to'; Hart (1961), 80 f. Hart writes that the meaning of the statement that a person has an obligation (moral or legal) is connected in two ways to social rules: the existence of the rules is the normal background for the statement, and the function of the statement is to apply a rule to a person by calling attention to the fact that his case falls under it. (Hart connects the second point, however, with the coercion characteristic of moral rather than legal obligation: see n. 18 below.) The rules in question, according to Hart, have three distinctive features: the pressure to conform is high, the rules are thought important because they are believed to be necessary to the maintenance of social life or some highly prized feature of it, and it is generally recognised that the conduct they require may conflict with the desires of the person to whom they apply: Hart (1961), 83 ff. As to the last feature, compare Gilbert (2006), 30 ff.; see further n. 12 below. For other elements of Hart's account, see nn. 18 f. below.

7 Compare McNeilly (1971), 64 on the phrase 'obligate myself'.

8 As do O. Black (2004b), 280 f.; O. Black (2005b), 180 ff.; Hart (1958), 103; Hart (1967), 56 n. 1; Searle (1978), 87; B. Williams (1993), 7. It is common to ignore, wittingly or unwittingly, the distinctions between obligation and duty. Examples of conscious fusion are Gilbert (2004), 87 f.; L. Green (2002), 514 n. 1; Pothier (1802), 2; Raz (1977), 210; D. Ross (1939), 43; Wellman (2004), 97 n. 1; Whiteley (1952), 96.

9 Brandt (1964), 377 f., 386 ff. Brandt also makes a number of points which he describes as 'grammatical' (376 ff.). Compare the suggestion in Gilbert (2006), 37 that the original meaning of 'obligation' tied it to transactions such as promises and agreements. On the broadening use of 'obligation' over time, see Brandt (1964), 375 ff.; Gilbert (2006), 26; Gilbert (2000a), 65. On the genealogy of obligation, see n. 21 below.

10 Brandt (1964), 387; inverted commas in original. In one sense of 'requirement', every obligation is a requirement but not vice versa: see Gilbert (2004), 88; n. 138 below. Chisholm (1964) takes the concept of requirement as an 'ethical primitive' which is used to illuminate various other concepts, including obligation. On Broome's concept of a normative requirement, see Chap. 4 n. 5 below; on requirements of rationality, see A. Price (2008). An obligation is not simply a moral requirement, for there are non-moral obligations: see nn. 18 f. below. Contrast Robins (1984), 109, which restricts the concept of obligation to moral cases. Gilbert (2006), 161 uses 'moral requirement' to indicate a moral obligation that is context-sensitive: see n. 99 below. Gilbert writes (ibid., 29) that a reference to what one ought to do, or should do, rather than what one is obligated to do, is equivalent to a reference to what is rationally required. On the relation between *ought* and *obligation*, see n. 87 below.

parties are involved, the one who is required to perform the service and the one for whom, or at whose bidding, the service is to be performed;[11] and a prior transaction – for example, the making of an agreement – is the source of the relationship.[12]

As regards moral obligation,[13] Prichard holds, and Ross appears to hold, that it is irreducible.[14] Brandt proposes five characteristics of a moral obligation:[15] it is a matter of conscience; it commands community-wide support; failure to perform, without excuse, reflects on character; it is a matter of principle; and it has high stringency. Hart proposes three: dependence on the actual practice of a social group,[16] possible independence of content,[17] and a connection with

11 On the 'directed' or 'relational' character of obligations, see Brecher (2002), 111; Gilbert (1996a), 295; Gilbert (2004), 87; Gilbert (2006), 35 ff., 161 ff.; Nicholas (1962), 99 ff., 158; Hart (1967), 56 n. 1; Robins (1984), 108; D. Ross (1930), 22; D. Ross (1939), 76; Warnock (1971), 111 f.; M. Zimmerman (1996), 6 ff., 178 ff., distinguishing mere obligation and obligation-to, and suggesting that self-regarding obligations may fall between the two. (Compare de Moor (1987), 119 ff. on the 'special bond' created by a contract.) Darwall (2010) distinguishes this character from the 'second-personal' nature of obligations, as to which see Darwall (2006), 26 ff., chap. 5; Darwall (2011). On the distinction between perfect and imperfect obligations, the latter not being directed/relational, see Gilbert (2006), 36, 162; Grotius (1925), bk. 1, section 4; Korsgaard (unpub.), 5 f.; Mill (1910b), 46; Pothier (1802), 2; M. Zimmerman (1996), 38 ff., 233 f. As to the distinction between 'for' and 'at the bidding of', see the discussion, in section 3.52, of parties to and beneficiaries of agreements.

12 Compare Hart (1967), 58, which talks of 'the transaction or antecedent situation or relations of the parties'. For another general account, see Gilbert (2006), which proposes three features of obligation: to have an obligation is to have sufficient reason to act (27 ff.; on the relation between obligations and reasons, see section 3.2 below); obligations are independent of personal inclinations and self-interest (30 ff.; see further n. 147 below); and they are recalcitrant to the obligor's will (34).

13 M. Zimmerman (1996), 2 suggests that moral and non-moral obligation may be analysed in similar terms. Compare Feldman (1986), chaps. 5, 7.

14 Prichard (2002d), 169. Ross is committed to this view by his theses that the concept of the right is irreducible and that 'right' means the same (subject to a minor qualification) as 'morally obligatory': D. Ross (1930), 3 f.; see further n. 87 below. D. Ross (1939), 43, omits 'morally'. On the irreducibility of *right* and *ought*, see also Sidgwick (1907), 31 ff. On the irreducibility of moral concepts generally, see Hutcheson (1969), 305; R. Price (1948); Korsgaard (1996b), 66.

15 Brandt (1964), 381 f.

16 On the social character of obligation, see R. Adams (1999), 233. For Hart's account of the social rules to which obligations, moral and legal, have a special connection, see n. 6 above. Note 19 below cites the list in Hart (1961) of the features that distinguish moral rules.

17 See also Coleman (2001), 121 ff.; Gilbert (1996a), 296; L. Green (2002), 516; Hart (1967), 56 n. 1; Hart (1982), 254 f., 255 ff.; Raz (1972); Raz (1977), 223 ff.; Raz (1990), 70.

coercion.[18] Legal obligations, according to Hart, are normally human artefacts that are created, varied and extinguished by means of rules of particular kinds.[19] A long tradition ties the concept of moral obligation

18 Hart (1958), 100 ff. By contrast with legal obligation, 'the coercion characteristic of moral obligation takes the form not of the infliction of harm or the use of force but primarily of the exposure of the individual to reminders that he has failed to comply with rules regarded by the social group as a matter of serious importance and to demand [*sic*] that he should comply' (102 f.). On the connection between coercion and the concept of wrong, see Mill (1910b), 45. Hart (1967), 56 n. 1 gives a different list of the main characteristics of moral obligations: they may be voluntarily incurred or created, are owed to special persons, and arise not from the character of the actions that are obligatory but from the relationship between the parties.

A list of 'what must be true, on broadly semantical grounds, of anything that is to count as . . . moral obligation' is given in R. Adams (1999), 235 f.: we should care about complying with it; it should be something we can be motivated to comply with; it should ground reasons for compliance (see further n. 56 below); breach justifies blame; and compliance and opposition to breach should be publicly inculcated. At 244 f. Adams maintains that a conception of moral obligation imposes a certain kind of critique of reasons for complying with a demand: whether such an obligation exists depends on the value of (a) the social bond from which the reasons arise, (b) the characteristics of the person making the demand and (c) the demand itself. An assessment of (c) must consider the value of the action demanded, the appropriateness of the sanctions implied and the value of the demand's relational history and wider social significance. Condition (c) is at best in tension with Hart's thesis of content-independence.

Darwall (2006), 26 f. states that moral obligations are categorical and overriding and involve a distinct kind of accountability; see also Darwall (2010) and n. 50 below. The thesis that they are categorical has been prominent since Kant: see Kant (1969). For the opposing view, see Foot (1978).

19 On Hart's view of the relation between moral and legal obligation, see Hart (1961), chaps. 8 f., esp. 163 ff. Hart identifies four features that distinguish moral rules from legal and other social rules: importance (169 ff.), immunity from deliberate change (171 ff.), the voluntary character of moral offences (173 ff.) and the form of moral pressure (175 f.). For discussion of his distinction, see MacCormick (1981), chap. 5; Simmonds (1986), chap. 5. The most prominent challenge to Hart's theory has been from Dworkin: see R. Dworkin (1978), chaps. 2 f.; for discussion, see M. Cohen (1984), esp. pt. 1; Guest (1992), esp. chap. 5. On the relation between moral and legal obligation generally, see Coleman (2001), esp. pts. 2 f., discussed in Christiano and Sciaraffa (2003); C. Johnson (1975); Woozley (1981), 289. On the idea that moral obligation should be conceived in terms of law, so that legal obligation is conceptually prior, see Hart (1958), 83 f.; Mill (1910b), 45; Prichard (2002d), 169; D. Ross (1930), 12; D. Ross (1939), 3; Zagzebski (2002), 455. On the connection between moral obligation and divine law, see nn. 20 f. below.

As to other types of obligation, R. Adams (1999), 234 f. maintains that there are non-moral obligations other than legal obligations, e.g., financial obligations. At 243 Adams identifies a 'premoral conception' of obligations as constituted by certain social facts. Brandt (1964), 381 holds that all types of obligation have a common core; see also Raz (1977), 225 on the desirability of a unified account of moral and non-moral obligation. Korsgaard (1996a), 255 ff., chap. 3 distinguishes non-moral obligations, based on our contingent identities, from moral ones based on our identity as human beings;

to that of a divine command or law,[20] Anscombe maintaining the tie to be so close that, given the decline of belief in God the lawgiver, the concept of moral obligation has become unintelligible.[21] Pink,[22] who follows the natural-law theorists in arguing that obligation is a force – of 'demand' – rather than a reason-giving feature, nevertheless holds that moral obligation 'involves' a reason[23] that is both demanding and 'agency-specific', i.e., is a reason only for acting or refraining from acting; he links these two features to the point that moral obligation is associated with blame, which he connects in turn to responsibility.[24]

for criticism, see O. Black (2006), 284 n. 16. See also Horton (1992), chap. 6 on the role of identity in constituting political obligation. Searle (1978), 87 says that obligations can be divided into legal, financial, social, moral, parental etc., and that the classes are not in general exclusive. McPherson (1967), 26 f., 77 f. distinguishes moral, political and legal obligation. Gilbert (2006), 27 notes the variety of types of obligation and queries whether a useful account can be given of them all. Gilbert (2000a), 65 suggests that obligation may be a family-resemblance concept. On such concepts generally, see Bambrough (1968); Wittgenstein (1958), para. 66; Wittgenstein (1972), 17 f. On the notion of family resemblance in a legal context, see Bix (1993), 143, 146 f., 170 f.

20 A recent champion of this tradition is Adams: R. Adams (1987); R. Adams (1999), pt. 3. Quinn (2002) criticises Adams's theory. A sample of earlier writings: J. Locke (1965), bk. 1, chap. 3; bk. 2, chap. 28; Pufendorf (1934), 91; Suárez (1944), 54 ff. For Hobbes's place in this tradition, see LeBuffe (2003); Warrender (1957).

21 Anscombe (1997), esp. 31; see also Alvarez (2010), 11. It is unclear why Anscombe holds that, for a non-believer, statements of moral obligation are unintelligible rather than false. Brandt (1964), 381, alluding to her view, uses the word 'meaningless'. On obligation as a 'fiction', see Zagzebski (2002), 455. Pink (2004), 167 ff. maintains that Anscombe's objection wrongly presupposes the 'feature' rather than the 'force' model of obligation (see the main text below). Anscombe might reply that the idea of a force of demand only makes sense on the assumption that someone – God – makes the demand. On the scope for dialogue between believers and non-believers as to which actions are wrong, see R. Adams (1987), 117 ff.

Another moral genealogist who, for different reasons, holds that our moral concepts have become detached from the framework that made sense of them is MacIntyre: see MacIntyre (1985). The framework identified by MacIntyre is Aristotelian, whereas Anscombe contrasts Aristotelian virtue-oriented ethics, which she favours, with the approach based on divine law. On genealogy as a philosophical method, see Nietzsche (1966); B. Williams (2002), chap. 2. B. Williams (1993), chap. 10 contends that ethical theory overemphasises and distorts the concept of obligation, but Williams concedes that there is a useful 'everyday' notion of obligation (174), which he connects to reliance (185). See further n. 71 below. On reliance as a ground of obligation, see section 3.51 below.

22 Pink (2004); Pink (2007).

23 Gilbert (1996a), 288 makes a similarly weak claim, that if X has an obligation then X has a reason.

24 On the connection between obligation and blame, see also R. Adams (1999), 235 (at 238 ff. Adams discusses the connection between obligation and guilt); Brandt (1958). On the connections between obligation, blame and responsibility, see also Darwall (2006),

Differing views as to the logic of obligation are embodied in the systems of deontic logic, which formalise reasoning involving normative concepts.[25] Various answers have likewise been given to the epistemic question; for example, certain intuitionists, such as Prichard, hold that we somehow just see that someone has an obligation,[26] whereas some non-cognitivists would deny that we can know that someone has an obligation, on the basis that there is nothing to know. According to these philosophers, judgments of obligation, and other normative and evaluative judgments, do not express beliefs and are neither true nor false; rather, to say that X is obligated to φ is to express an emotion or attitude towards X's φing.[27]

3.2 The ground of an obligation

Another question concerns grounds.[28] If X has an obligation to φ, the fact that he has it is grounded in some other fact about him[29] – for example,

28, chap. 5; Darwall (2010). B. Williams (1993), 177 f., 192 ff. maintains that morality overemphasises blame and the voluntary. On Hart's view of the voluntary character of moral offences, see n. 19 above.

25 See Chellas (1980), chap. 6; Chisholm (1974); Goble (1993); Hilpinen (1970); Hilpinen (1981); Horty (2001); Jackson (1985); Lemmon (1965); Powers (1967); von Wright (1963), esp. chaps. 8 ff.; von Wright (1968). For criticism of deontic logic generally, see Sayre-McCord (1986); M. Zimmerman (1996), 63. Deontic logic is standardly treated as a branch of modal logic, which concerns necessity (analogue of the obligatory) and possibility (analogue of the permissible). For modal logic, see Chellas (1980); Hughes and Cresswell (1968), (1984); Kuhn (1998); Lemmon (1966a); Mints (1992).

26 'The sense of obligation to do . . . an action of a particular kind is absolutely underivative or immediate': Prichard (2002a), 12. On the varieties of ethical intuitionism, see R. Audi (1996); Frazier (1998).

27 A crude version of non-cognitivism is the emotivist theory in Ayer (1947), chap. 6. Emotivism is refined in Stevenson (1944); see also Stevenson (1959). Another prominent form of non-cognitivism is Hare's prescriptivism: see Hare (1952); Hare (1963); Hare (1981). More recent non-cognitivist theories are Blackburn's quasi-realist projectivism and Gibbard's norm-expressivism: Blackburn (1984), chap. 6; Blackburn (1993a), pt. 2; Blackburn (1998a); Gibbard (1990). An ancestor of such theories is found in Hobbes (1983), 119, 150; see Skinner (1996) 279 f. For an overview of non-cognitivism and its place in meta-ethics, see A. Miller (2003), chaps. 1, 3 ff.

28 On grounding, see P. Cameron (2008); Hofweber (2009); Oliver (1996); Paseau (2010). On the relation between definition and ground, see D. Ross (1939), 27 f., 57 f. Compare the distinction in Prichard (2002d), 164 between the criterion and the nature of obligation.

29 Sophie Botros pointed out, in conversation, that a deontologist might deny this in the case of general obligations. He might hold for example that, even if the fact that X is obligated to φ is grounded in the fact that he promised to φ, X's general obligation to perform his promises is not grounded in any other fact about X. For present purposes the thesis of

the fact, or some elaboration of it, that he promised to φ (see section 1.1), or that φing is part of his job or station (here we might talk of duty as well as, or instead of, obligation[30]), or that his father told him to. So, if X has an obligation, the question is: what grounds the fact that he has it?

As just indicated, grounding is most easily conceived as a relation between facts,[31] and so the canonical form is 'the fact that P grounds the fact that Q'; but, for brevity's sake, I shall sometimes say that obligations, rather than facts about them, have grounds. By 'ground' I shall usually mean a complete ground. This, roughly, is a minimal sufficient condition[32] – i.e., just enough, but no more – for the grounded fact, but not every minimal sufficient condition is a complete ground: merely causal or truth-functional conditions, for instance, do not qualify. The relevant kind of condition is not readily characterised in other terms; in particular, it is like other philosophically interesting subjects in resisting analysis of the narrow sort described in the Introduction.[33] It might be thought that since a complete ground is sufficient for an obligation, and an obligation is sufficient for a complete ground, each is necessary and

grounding – expressed in proposition (51) below – can be left unqualified. The ground of an obligation is different from a broader obligation of which the first obligation is an instance; that distinction is blurred in LeBuffe (2003), 16. On obligations with different degrees of generality, see Scanlon (1998), 295. See further n. 134 below.

30 On 'my station and its duties', see Bradley (1927), chap. 5. See also O. Black (2004b), 280; O. Black (2005b), 180 ff.; Brandt (1964), 387 ff. L. Green (2002), 533 suggests that there may be no general obligation to perform the duties of one's station: rather they may be 'justified' piecemeal by different considerations in different cases. 'The apparent general duty may simply be an intermediate conclusion summarising a range of unrelated reasons, including the dependence of others on one's performance.' Dependence in this sense is close to reliance, as to which see section 3.51 below; for a different sense, see nn. 33 and 46 f. below.

31 P. Audi (unpub.), 2 treats grounding a relation between facts, in turn conceived as 'obtaining states of affairs'. On conditions as facts, see n. 4 to the Introduction above.

32 See Marc-Wogau (1962), 213 ff. The concept is elaborated in Mackie (1974), 62; Mackie (1993), 34 ff.; O. Black (2004b), 275; O. Black (2005b), 175 f.

33 In particular, analyses in terms of causation or modality (i.e., necessity and possibility) are not promising. On the causal approach, see Blackburn (1998b), 315; Broome (2000); Cavell (1979), 250; Mackie (1977), 41. A modal analysis is likely to face an analogue of the paradoxes of strict implication: see Chap. 1 n. 42 above. My pessimism is shared by Stocker (see Stocker (1970), 610 n. 10) and apparently by Dancy, who writes of 'resultance' that '[a]ll we can do is to gesture towards it' (Dancy (1993), 73). Resultance appears to be the inverse of grounding, i.e., one thing results from another if and only if the second grounds the first: see n. 42 below. J. Kim (1993a), 53 talks of 'dependence', a notion which Kim suggests is central to our conception of the world as a system or structure; see further nn. 46 f. below. (Contrast Green's sense of 'dependence': n. 30 above.) 'Determination', in Broome (2000), 80, seems to be the same as or similar to grounding.

sufficient for the other. That is inaccurate. Suppose that the fact F is a complete ground of the fact that X is obligated to φ. Then F is sufficient for the fact that X is obligated to φ, and the latter fact is necessary for the former. The fact that X is obligated to φ is sufficient for there to be some fact or other that is its ground; but it may not be sufficient for F, and so F may not be necessary for the fact that X is obligated to φ.

A partial ground is a fact that is a proper part of a complete ground. Since a complete ground is minimally sufficient, no partial ground is sufficient. Another distinction is between direct and indirect grounds: fact 1 may be directly grounded in fact 2, which is directly grounded in fact 3, which thus indirectly grounds fact 1.[34] Provided that such a chain does not lead in a circle or extend to infinity,[35] it ends in an ultimate ground of fact 1. Thus a distinction between ultimate and intermediate grounds can be defined in terms of that between direct and indirect grounds.

These statements, and others that will be inferred from them, can be made more precise,[36] but an informal account is good enough. The statements have implications for the metaphysics of facts, for example that facts have parts. I shall go no further into a theory of facts[37] – which would deal with such questions as how facts relate to propositions[38] and states of affairs[39] and whether there are (in some sense of 'are') non-existent facts[40] – than to assume, for simplicity, that only an existent fact can be a ground; that <the fact that P exists if and only if P>; that <P

34 Compare Dancy (1993), 74 on 'resultance trees'; Chap. 6 n. 40 below. The claim in P. Audi (unpub.), 2 that grounding is transitive, can be refined: transitivity holds for indirect but not for direct grounding. To say that a relation *R* is transitive is to say that, if A bears *R* to B, and B to C, then A bears *R* to C.

35 J. Kim (1993b) rejects the idea of 'an endless descending series of valuations'. On infinite regresses generally, see Chap. 2 n. 50 above and Chap. 4 n. 35 below; on infinite regresses of explanation, n. 148 to this chapter.

36 To avoid trivial counterexamples, the concept of a partial ground needs to include or to be supplemented by a condition of independence: see O. Black (2004b), 274 ff.; O. Black (2005b), 175 f.

37 For an introduction to the metaphysics of facts, see Loux (2002), 164 ff. The nature of facts bears on the time at which an obligation or its ground exists – an issue at the heart of an objection to reliance-based theories of the obligation to perform an agreement: see section 3.51 below.

38 According to Alvarez, facts are true propositions: see Chap. 1 n. 60 above.

39 P. Audi takes facts to be obtaining states of affairs: see n. 31 above.

40 On things that are but do not exist, see Meinong (1915); Meinong (1972). Meinong's theory was famously criticised in Russell (1956), 45. Note 4 to the Introduction above contemplates merely possible facts.

if and only if it is true that P>; and that, where P and Q are distinct, the fact that P is a proper part of the fact that <P and Q>. (The second assumption and the third, which was made in section 1.22, each generate a seemingly benign infinite regress,[41] as 'the fact that P exists' and 'it is true that P' can each be substituted for 'P'.) Since a ground is sufficient for the fact it grounds, it follows that, if the fact that P grounds the fact that Q, then: the fact that P exists; if P then Q; P; Q; and the fact that Q exists.

In one terminology, grounding is the inverse of supervenience,[42] but 'supervenience' has been used to mean many things.[43] Often it signifies a relation of covariance, the idea being that, if two things have the same properties in one class, they have the same properties in another;[44] for example, it is often said that if two actions have the same non-normative or non-evaluative properties then they have the same normative or evaluative ones,[45] so that they could not differ merely in the respect that one was obligatory and the other not. A number of covariance relations have been distinguished, and it may be that some are and others are not connected to the relation of grounding;[46] but all of them, and their inverses, are distinct from that relation.[47]

41 See Chap. 2 n. 50 above and Chap. 4 n. 35 below.

42 That seems to be the assumption in M. Zimmerman (1996), 216. A bears the inverse of the relation *R* to B if and only if B bears *R* to A.

43 Dreier (1992), 13 deplores the 'confusing menagerie'. J. Kim (1993a), 77 distinguishes supervenience from definition, reduction and explanation. Klagge (1988) distinguishes 'ontological' from 'ascriptive' supervenience.

44 See J. Kim (1993a); J. Kim (1993b); J. Kim (1993c); J. Kim (1993e). Covariance may be synchronic – a relation between properties of different things at the same time – or diachronic, a relation between properties of the same thing at different times. I know of no one who believes that synchronic and diachronic covariance of the relevant kinds may come apart. Blackburn says that he can think of no argument that they do: Blackburn (1993b), 115.

45 Blackburn (1993b); Blackburn (1993c). Wiggins (1998), 197 is sceptical as to any 'general and illuminating' principle of the supervenience of values. For a rejection of supervenience in the aesthetic domain, see Scruton (1974), 36 and the discussion in MacKinnon (2000) and MacKinnon (2001).

46 J. Kim (1993a) and J. Kim (1993e) argue that a certain form of covariance is necessary but not sufficient for dependence; DePaul (1987) argues that it is not sufficient; see also J. Kim (1993c). On dependence in this sense, see also n. 33 above and n. 47 below. Some philosophers appear to think that dependence and both synchronic and diachronic covariance go together: see Blackburn (1998b), 236; Davidson (1980e), 214; Hellman and Thompson (1975), 558; MacKinnon (2001), 60 f. Klagge (1984), 371 shows how, on Blackburn's view, it is natural to move from dependence to covariance.

47 A point stressed by Dancy (1993), 77 ff. J. Kim (1993e), 148 maintains that covariance is a mere 'surface' relation indicating the presence of a dependence relation the explanation

What is the connection between the ground of an obligation to do something and a reason to do it? There are various kinds of reason – as noted in section 1.23, which discussed motivating practical reasons. Here the relevant reasons are practical, but normative rather than motivating.[48] An attractive theory is that such a reason is a triple of <fact, agent, action-type>,[49] but I shall for convenience talk of facts as reasons. (Section 1.23 also entertained the theory that motivating reasons are mental states rather than facts; that theory, whatever its merits as an account of motivating reasons, is arguably less plausible in the case of normative ones.) Consider the situation where the fact that P grounds an obligation on X to φ. Here the fact that P is a reason for X to φ, but also a reason for X not to act for certain conflicting reasons.[50] If, for example, the fact that X promised to φ grounds his obligation, that fact is both a reason for him to φ and a reason for him not, merely because he would enjoy doing something else instead, to break his promise.[51] That does not imply that a promise trumps every conflicting reason: if the promise is trivial, X would be justified in breaking it in order, say, to save a life.

of which may differ from case to case. J. Kim (1993b), 166 f. makes the stronger claim that the dependence relation itself differs between cases; Kim also there claims that the explanation of covariance differs between cases, but it is not clear whether he thinks that the difference in explanations of covariance is itself explained by the difference in dependence relations. See further nn. 33 and 46 above.

48 See Chap. 1 n. 58 above, which raised the question whether the distinction between kinds of reason concerns ontology or roles. If it concerns roles, the point can be rephrased in terms of reasons qua motivating or qua normative.

49 Raz (1977), 219 n. 11 says that only facts are reasons. Raz (1990), 19 says that a reason is a relation between a fact and a person. At Raz (1990), 51, in a discussion of rules, Raz writes that, strictly speaking, not a rule but the fact that there is a rule is a reason. The combination of the latter two claims yields the baffling result that the fact that there is a rule is a relation between a fact and a person. Raz may mean either that the fact that there is a rule stands in the relation to the person, or that the fact is that the rule stands in the relation to the person. On the person-relative character of reasons for action, see Alvarez (2010), 19 ff., which also argues that reasons are facts: Chap. 1 n. 60 above. On the question whether obligatoriness should be predicated of action-types or action-tokens, see M. Zimmerman (1996), 53 ff. On the distinction between types and tokens, see Chap. 5 n. 18 below.

50 Although Darwall (2010) maintains that this condition is not sufficient for obligation, Darwall holds that obligations have an overriding character: see n. 18 above.

51 Compare Gilbert on obligations' independence of personal inclinations and self-interest: n. 12 above. As mentioned there, Gilbert holds that to have an obligation is to have sufficient reason to act.

This structure was identified by Raz,[52] who distinguishes a first-order reason, to act, from a second-order reason – to act, or to refrain from acting, for a reason. Raz calls an 'exclusionary' reason a second-order reason to refrain from acting for some reason.[53] Whether an exclusionary reason excludes a certain reason depends on reasons that affect the scope of the former, a scope-affecting reason being a kind of auxiliary reason.[54] At least in certain cases where something is both a first-order reason to act and an exclusionary reason to refrain from acting for some reason, Raz calls it a 'protected' reason.[55] In the example, the fact that X promised to φ is a first-order reason for him to φ, an exclusionary reason for him not to break the promise for certain reasons, and a protected reason for him to φ. The conflicting reasons excluded by the fact of the promise depend on the associated scope-affecting reasons.[56]

3.3 Grounds of performance obligations

Consider again the schema from previous chapters:

(1) X does Ax and Y does Ay.

52 Raz (1990), chap. 1, postscript.

53 Raz (1990), 37 ff. gives examples of exclusionary reasons; see also Raz (1977), 221 ff. Compare the concept of 'peremptory' commands in Hart (1982), 253 ff. Hart derives it from Hobbes. For criticism of Raz's concept of exclusionary reasons, see Schauer (1991), 88 ff.

54 In Raz's classification, an auxiliary reason is one that is not operative, and a reason is operative if and only if its existence entails a practical critical attitude: Raz (1990), 33 ff.

55 Raz (1990), 191; see also J. Gardner and Macklem (2002), 465. Raz says that a protected reason is a 'systematic combination' of such reasons. His 'mandatory norms' are normally protected reasons: Raz (1990), 58 ff. In Raz's usage a norm, unlike a rule or principle, need not be general (49); see Chap. 2 n. 67 above.

56 This analysis is consistent with Pink's view, cited in section 3.1 above, that obligation is not a reason-giving feature, for the analysis concerns the ground of an obligation whereas Pink has in mind the obligation itself. Both Pink's view and mine seem to conflict with the thesis in R. Adams (1999), 235 that 'the nature of obligation should be such as to ground *reasons* for compliance' (Adams's emphasis). My claim is that the ground of the obligation is a reason; but Adams may be using 'ground', or 'reason', in a different sense. See also 241 where Adams writes that obligations 'constitute', and then that they 'ground', reasons for action. Searle (1978), 87 and Horton (1992), 14 say that obligations 'provide' reasons for acting. L. Green (2002), 516 says that to have an obligation is to have a reason to act or to refrain from acting. See also Gilbert (1996a), 288, 295; Gilbert (2006), 28; M. Zimmerman (1996), 150 positing a biconditional connection between prima facie obligations and 'deontic reasons'. On prima facie obligations, see n. 89 below.

Grant that:

(2) X and Y agree that (1).
(45) If (2) then X is obligated that X does Ax.[57]

The question for the rest of the chapter is what the ground of that obligation is.

There is a large literature on the grounds of obligations associated with promises and contracts, and much of it can be extended to agreements.[58] Here is a brief survey of theories, some of which will be discussed below, as to the ground of X's obligation: it is the fact that Y, in doing Ay, relies, or reasonably or detrimentally relies, on X to do Ax (see section 1.5);[59] or that X intends or believes, or it would be reasonable for him to believe,

57 Gilbert (2000a), 50 presents this as a 'datum for ethics'; see also Gilbert (1989), 380 and the works cited in n. 137 below. On the 'subjective' theory of obligation proposed in Prichard (2002b) (see Chap. 2 n. 20 above) and D. Ross (1939), chap. 7, X's obligation is conditional not on X's agreeing but on X's belief that he agrees. There is no need to pursue this, for it is at most rare for someone to make an agreement without believing that he is doing so; compare the discussion of 'sub-agreement' in section 3.6 below (concerning intention rather than belief). As mentioned in Chap. 2 n. 20 above, Prichard holds that an obligation is not to φ, but to set oneself to φ; compare the distinction in the French law of contract between an *obligation de moyens* – to take the measures that a *bon père de famille* would take to achieve the contract's purpose – and an *obligation de résultat*, to achieve that purpose (Nicholas (1992), 50 ff., 116). Prichard's view might be expressed by saying that there are no moral *obligations de résultat*. (Compare also the distinction in law between fault-based and strict liability: P. Cooke and Oughton (1993), 191 ff.; n. 137 below.) For distinctions between subjective and objective obligation, see Broad (1946), 557; Broad (1985), 125 ff., 131 f., 144, 172; Broome (unpub.); Feldman (1986), 46; Lemos (1980), 301; McCloskey (1973), 62; Russell (1970), 12 ff.; Thomson (1986), 179; M. Zimmerman (1996), 10 ff., 49 f., 110.

58 On the greater prominence of promises than of agreements in the literature, and on the lack of philosophical consensus over promissory obligation, see the Introduction above and Gilbert (2006), 223 ff.

59 Here and below I use disjunctive shorthand to talk about separate theories and facts: one theory is that the ground is the fact that Y relies; another, that it is the fact that he reasonably relies; and so on. Forms of reliance theory are found in Atiyah (1979b), 1 ff.; Atiyah (1981), chap. 7; Atiyah (1986c); Atiyah (1986e), 150; Atiyah (1986f), 111 f.; Atiyah (1986g); Atiyah (1986j), 127, 143 f., 148; Atiyah (1986l), 2 ff.; Fuller (1941), 10 ff.; Fuller and Perdue (1936); Katkov (1937), 136 ff.; Pufendorf (1934), bk. 3, chap. 5, para. 11; Scanlon (1990); Scanlon (2001), 92 f.; Stocker (1970), 617 ff. For objections, see Ardal (1976); Benson (2001c), 174 ff.; O. Black (1998); O. Black (2004b); O. Black (2005b), 169 ff.; J. Cartwright (1984), esp. 241 ff.; Downie (1985), 263 ff.; Fried (1981), chaps. 1 f., 4; Gilbert (1996a), 296; Gilbert (2004), 92; MacCormick (1982), 198; Morris (1991); Patterson (1992), esp. 399; Raz (1972), 100; Raz (1977), esp. 216; Robins (1984), 7 ff.; D. Ross (1939), 105 f.; S. Smith (2004), 78 ff.; Woozley (1981), 291. For further discussion, see Benson (2001a); P. Cooke and Oughton (1993), chaps. 2 ff., 6 ff.; Gilmore (1995), chap. 1; Kimel (2003), 27 ff.

that Y thus relies on him;[60] or that Y expects[61] or trusts[62] X to do Ax (here and for some of the following theories there are similar variations, in terms of reasonableness, detriment and X's intention or belief); or that X authorises or induces Y thus to rely, expect or trust;[63] or that Y suffers harm if X does not do Ax;[64] or that X benefits if Y does Ay;[65] or that X assures Y that X does Ax;[66] or that X voluntarily assumes his obligation in an exercise of autonomy;[67] or that X exercises a normative

60 See Knapp (1984), 940; MacCormick (1982); McMahon (1989); R. Price (1948), discussed in Fogelin (1983). For objections, see Atiyah (1981), 36 ff.; Fried (1981).

61 See Fuller and Perdue (1936), 54; D. Ross (1930), 27; Scanlon (1990); Scanlon (1998), chap. 7; Scanlon (2001); A. Smith (1978), 472. For objections, see Ardal (1976); Atiyah (1979b), 3 ff.; Atiyah (1981), 42 ff.; Atiyah (1986c), 33 ff.; Atiyah (1986e); Downie (1985), 263 ff.; Gilbert (1996a); Patterson (1992); Robins (1976), 323 ff.; Robins (1984), 7 ff., 140 ff. There is discussion in P. Cooke and Oughton (1993), chaps. 2 ff., 16, 22; Fried (1981), 16 ff.; Fuller and Perdue (1936). On the distinction between expectation and reliance, see Atiyah (1981), 32, 43; Fuller and Perdue (1936), 73 ff.; MacCormick (1982), 195; Sidgwick (1907), 443. Gilbert (1996f), 75 distinguishes a normative from a 'plain' sense of 'expect'.

62 See Atiyah (1979b), 81 ff.; Fried (1981), chap. 2; Friedrich and Southwood (2011); Hobbes (1968), chap. 14; Kimel (2003), chaps. 1 ff.; MacCormick (1982), 205 f.; Pink (2009); n. 115 below. On the relation between trust and reliance, see Atiyah (1986j), 148 n. 1; Holton (1994). On trust generally, see Baier (1986); Baier (1997), 31 ff., 77 ff.; M. Kohn (2008); Misztal (1996); Seabright (2010), 74 ff.

63 On authorised reliance, see Woozley (1981), 291; on inducement, section 3.51 below.

64 See Fuller and Perdue (1936), 54; Knapp (1984), 938 ff.; MacCormick (1982), 205; Scanlon (1998), chap. 7. On reliance that is detrimental, see Atiyah (1979b), 184 ff.; Atiyah (1981), 184 ff.; Atiyah (1986c), 20; Atiyah (1986f), 111; Scanlon (2001). On the relation between reliance and harm, see n. 112 below. For objections, see J. Cartwright (1984), 241 ff.; Fried (1981), chap. 2. For discussion, see P. Cooke and Oughton (1993), chaps. 1, 3, 6, 8 f. On the connection between obligation and harm, via guilt and alienation, see R. Adams (1999), 241.

65 See Atiyah (1979b), 1, 652 ff.; Atiyah (1981), 143, chap. 7; Atiyah (1986c); Atiyah (1986e), 150; Atiyah (1986f), 111; Fuller (1941), 812 f. For objections, see J. Cartwright (1984), 236 ff.; Fried (1981), chap. 1, esp. 3, chap. 2. On the flexibility of the concept of benefit, and the consequent blurring of the boundary between the reliance and restitution interests in contract, see Fuller and Perdue (1936), 72. For the law on unjust enrichment, see P. Cooke and Oughton (1993), chaps. 1 ff., 11. See further n. 125 below.

66 See R. Fox and DeMarco (1993), 82; Scanlon (1998), 304; Scanlon (2001), 93 ff. (the 'principle of fidelity' discussed in section 3.52 below); Warnock (1971), 98 f. For objections, see Patterson (1992).

67 See J. Cartwright (1984), 247; Fried (1981), chaps. 1 f.; Fuller (1941), 806 ff.; Korsgaard (1996b), 66; Raz (1977); Robins (1976), esp. 322; Robins (1984), 15, chap. 6; S. Smith (2004), chap. 2, 180 ff.; Trebilcock (1993). For objections, see Atiyah (1986c); Atiyah (1986g); Atiyah (1986j); Eisenberg (2001), 229 ff.; Gilbert (1996a), 286 ff. (distinguishing senses of 'voluntary'); B. Williams (1993), 7 f. For further discussion, see Benson (2001a), 5 ff. For a definition of the voluntary, see Feinberg (1973), 48. For a historical view of ethical voluntarism, see Irwin (2007–9), esp. vols. 2 f.; Korsgaard (1996a),

power;[68] or that X intends to convey a truth about his behaviour, so that his obligation is one of veracity;[69] or that if X fails to do Ax he is unjust[70] or lacks honour, integrity, fidelity or some other such virtue or desirable property.[71]

Then there are theories that purport to identify, as the ground of X's obligation, an aspect of the whole agreement, for example the fact that it represents the will of the parties,[72] or a consensus between them,[73] or a meeting of their minds;[74] or that it constitutes an exchange[75] or

1 ff. (which distinguishes voluntarism from autonomy-based theories of the source of normativity); Olafson (1967), pt. 1, esp. chaps. 1 ff.; Schneewind (1998). On autonomy, see Benn (1971); Christman (1989); Colburn (2010); Downie and Telfer (1971); G. Dworkin (1988); Frankfurt (1999); Hill (1991); Korsgaard (1996a), chaps. 1, 3; Reath (1998); Schneewind (1986); Young (1980). On voluntariness as distinguishing obligation in contract from obligation in tort, see Beale (2008), para. 1–119, which grounds the distinction in the 'will theory' of contract; see further n. 72 and sections 6.213 and 7.12 below. On voluntarism as a theory of political obligation, see Horton (1992), chap. 2.

68 See MacCormick (1982); Raz (1972); Raz (1990), 98 ff.

69 See the discussion in Gordley (1991), 73 of Aquinas and Cajetan; R. Price (1948), discussed in Clarke (1972) and Fogelin (1983); Warnock (1971), chap. 7, criticised in D. Locke (1972). For objections, see Atiyah (1981), 104 ff.; Scanlon (1998), 317 ff.; Sidgwick (1907), 303 f. D. Ross (1939), 112 f. appears to argue that the obligation of veracity depends on the obligation to keep a promise. Fried (1981), 9, 16, 78 f. compares breach of a promise with lying. On the ethics of veracity, see Bok (1989); de Chiara-Quenzer (1994); Isenberg (1964); Kupfer (1982); Mannison (1969), 143 f.; Page (1991); D. Simpson (1992); section 9.4 below. See also Chap. 1 n. 32 above, on deception.

70 This view is found in Aquinas and later scholastics; see Gordley (1991), 73 ff.

71 See Downie (1985), 269 on the 'moral obligation of honour or self-fidelity'; Warnock (1971), 113. For objections, see DeMarco and Fox (1992), 57 f.; R. Fox and DeMarco (1993), 83. One objection to theories of this kind is that they combine incommensurate concepts from different ethical traditions, the Hebraic and the Greek: see Anscombe (1997); Prichard (2002a), 17; D. Ross (1939), 3. B. Williams (1993), 178 ff. chides Ross for over-extending the concept of obligation; see also n. 21 above. A theme of Williams's book is that in certain basic respects ancient, and specifically Greek, ethical theory is superior to modern. On concern for a reputation for trustworthiness, as an element in the practical reasoning leading to performance of agreements, see section 4.22 below.

72 See Beale (2008), para. 1–119; Flume (1975), 7; Fried (1981), chap. 1. For the 'will theory' of contract, see sections 6.213 and 7.12 below. On agreement as concurrence of wills, see sections 8.1 ff below.

73 See Atiyah (1979b), 455 ff.; de Moor (1987), 115. On agreement as consensus, see Chap. 1 n. 5 above, and Chap. 8 n. 10 and Chap. 9 nn. 2 and 23 below.

74 On meeting of minds, see Chap. 1 n. 1 above, and Chap. 8 n. 10 and Chap. 9 nn. 2 and 26 below.

75 See Atiyah (1979b), 716; P. Cooke and Oughton (1993), 83 ff., 111 ff. (on fairness of exchange); Gordley (1991), 137. On exchanging, see Prichard (2002c); section 2.4 above. On agreement as an exchange of promises, see Chap. 1 n. 75 above. On exchange in contract, see section 2.63 above and sections 6.2111, 6.213, 7.1 and 7.33 below.

bargain;[76] or that it permits co-operation between the parties;[77] or that it allocates risk between them in a way that reflects their abilities to bear it;[78] or that it is economically efficient;[79] or that it transfers rights between the parties;[80] or that there is a 'categorical' rule of compliance with agreements;[81] or – a theory that approximates to part of the account offered in section 3.6 – that the agreement is an instance of an institution or practice that has constitutive obligation-generating rules.[82]

(45) follows from the premisses that if (2) then there exists a ground of the fact that X is obligated to do Ax, and that if there exists such a ground then X is so obligated. The first premiss is developed below; the second follows from assumptions made in section 3.2. (45) follows from the first premiss without the second, on the assumptions that 'the fact that X is obligated to do Ax' is used with existential import, i.e., with the implication that the fact exists, and – a consequence of an assumption made in that section – that if the fact that P exists then P. Both (45) and the first premiss are shorthand for propositions containing the provisos that the obligation has not ceased, in particular for one of the reasons described in section 2.3, and that the case is normal. The discussion is limited to cases in which the provisos are true. The latter one would trivialise (45), and the other propositions to which it applies, if no informative account

76 See Atiyah (1979b), 404; P. Cooke and Oughton (1993), 17, 35, 38; Gilmore (1995), chap. 1, 41, 44, 62 f.; Fuller and Perdue (1936), 2; Kötz (1997), 8 f. The common-law doctrine of consideration is sometimes said to express the notion that a contract is an exchange or bargain: see sections 2.63 above and 7.1 below.

77 See Atiyah (1981), 30 ff. (on a utilitarian account of promising), 135; Atiyah (1986l), 5; Kimel (2003), 28; S. Smith (2005), 3 f. This approach is rejected in Raz (1977), 215 f. On the role of agreements in securing cooperation, see section 3.6 below.

78 See P. Cooke and Oughton (1993), chap. 22; Holmes (2005), 324 ff. For objections, see Atiyah (1979b), 5; Atiyah (1986c), 36 ff.; Atiyah (1986i).

79 See Benson (2001a), 4; Buckley (1999); Craswell and Schwartz (1994); Eisenberg (2001), 235 ff.; Kötz (1997), 6, 13; Kronman and Posner (1979); S. Smith (2004), 108 ff.; S. Smith (2005), 3 f., quoted in section 6.2111 below; Zweigert and Kötz (1998), 326. For objections, see Atiyah (1986e); R. Dworkin (1986c), pt. 4. On the 'law and economics' project generally, see Posner (1986).

80 See Barnett (1986); Benson (2001c); Hobbes (1968), 192; n. 1 to the Introduction above. For objections, see S. Smith (2004), 6 ff., 97 ff. For a similar view of promises, see Gordley (1991), 73 ff.; Grotius (1925), II, xi, 1, 3 f.; Pufendorf (1934), III, v, 5 ff.

81 See Raz (1977), which gives two slightly different descriptions of a categorical rule: as 'a rule not dependent for its validity on the goals and desires of the agent' (219) and as 'a mandatory rule which applies to its subjects not merely because adherence to it facilitates achievement of their goals' (223).

82 See Fried (1981), 14 ff.; Hume (1978), bk. 3, pt. 2, section 5; Rawls (1967), 162 ff.; section 2.2 above. An objection is discussed in section 2.65 above.

of normality could be given – whether in the form of a criterion or of a list – but I shall assume an account to be available. Abnormal cases might include ones corresponding to those mentioned in sections 1.1 and 2.62 as possible exceptions to promissory obligation: other things equal, X perhaps has no obligation if he is unable to do Ax, or Ax would be immoral, or Y does not want him to do Ax, or X is coerced into agreeing, or his agreement is based on an innocent but fundamental mistake.[83]

It might be objected that (45) is inaccurate in two further respects. If (2) then X is obligated to perform the agreement; he performs if and only if he does Ax; but, the objection goes, it does not follow that he is obligated to do Ax, for it is false that obligation is closed under the biconditional; i.e., it is false that, if X is obligated to φ and X φs if and only if X χs, then X is obligated to χ. (A similar point arose in section 1.2312; on closure properties of agreement, see section 5.32.) It is no good replying that the loose use of 'perform' explained in the Introduction prevents the distinction from being drawn, for the objector will say that this merely obscures one inaccuracy by another. A somewhat better reply is that in standard deontic logic obligation is closed under the biconditional,[84] and

83 The thesis that these conditions exclude an obligation should be distinguished from the thesis that they exclude the existence of an agreement. Clearly it is possible to agree to do something immoral, but it might be argued that an alleged agreement that was coerced, or is to do the impossible, is not a true agreement. As to the former, it might be said that offer and acceptance are actions and that a person under coercion does not truly act; as to the latter, that the actions of offer and acceptance are intentional and that one cannot intend to do something one believes to be impossible. (See Davidson (1980d) for the thesis that an action is an event that is intentional under some description; Stout (2005), 3 for the thesis that 'full-blown' action is intentional; section 5.32 below for the thesis that actions are intended; section 6.1 below for the thesis that if a thing is capable of action then it is capable of intention; and section 9.2 below for the thesis that paradigmatic actions are intentional. Those are bad arguments. Coercion covers a spectrum of cases: at one end, X threatens to hurt Y's family if Y declines to agree; at the other, X presses a pen into Y's hand and forces it across the page to spell Y's name. It can be allowed that in the second case Y does not act – he could be dead – but he does act in the first; compare Nicholas (1992), 106 on violence as determining consent. Whether or not one can intend to do something one believes impossible (as to which, see Searle (1965), 235; Searle (1969), 60), one can intend to do something that is impossible in fact. See further Chap. 1 n. 28 above and Chap. 9 n. 10 below. The argument also confuses the making with the performing of an agreement.

84 The system can be axiomatised with the rule $P \rightarrow Q \vdash OP \rightarrow OQ$. For paradoxes generated by the rule, see Åqvist (1967); Føllesdal and Hilpinen (1970), 21 ff.; A. Ross (1941); M. Zimmerman (1996), 72 ff. The principle of closure is in tension with, but does not contradict, Green's claim that 'obligation imposing reasons are not transitive across ideal, or even necessary, means to their fulfilment': L. Green (2002), 537. On deontic logic, see n. 25 above.

so, if standard deontic logic accurately reflects the concept of obligation, X's being obligated to do Ax follows from his obligation to perform. Whether or not it follows, and even if the obligations are distinct, they go together in normal cases where (2) is true. For present purposes there is no need to distinguish them in such cases, and so I shall use the phrase 'performance obligation' to cover both.[85]

The other alleged inaccuracy is a confusion between a conditional and an unconditional obligation. (To be more explicit, the distinction is between an obligation that is purely externally conditional and one that is internally conditional: see section 1.2312, which raised a parallel issue in relation to principles (11)–(14).) (45) is conditional, but its consequent attributes an unconditional obligation to X. On the contrary, the objection runs, X has only a conditional obligation:

(46) X is obligated that if (2) then X does Ax.

The objection might be supported by denying that, if X is obligated that if P then Q, then if P then X is obligated that Q.[86]

One explanation for the objector's rejection of (45) might be that he identifies the proposition that X is obligated to do Ax with the proposition that X ought to do Ax[87] (see further section 6.22). At least in one sense of 'ought', whether X ought to do Ax depends on whether the reasons for him to do Ax outweigh those for him not to (section 5.1 states a parallel thesis about reasonable belief), whereas an obligation on him to do Ax

85 The distinction is similarly elided in Gilbert's definition of a performance obligation as 'an obligation to perform the specified act': Chap. 1 n. 77 above.

86 Compare Broome on normative requirements and detachability: Chap. 1 n. 82 above; Chap. 4 n. 3 below.

87 On the relation between the two, see R. Adams (1999), 234; Brandt (1964), 376 ff.; Cavell (1979), 308 f.; Chisholm (1964), 150; Flathman (1972), 34 ff.; Gilbert (2006), 29; Hart (1958), 83; Hart (1961), 83 f.; Hart (1967), 55, 62; Mackie (1977), 74; Prichard (2002d), 163; Raz (1977), 210; Simmons (1979), 7 ff.; Tunick (2002), 467; Warnock (1971), 94. Examples of their identification are found in Driver (2011), 191, in M. Zimmerman (1996), 1, where 'ought' is defined to express moral obligation, and in D. Ross (1930), 3 f.: 'if we turn to the sort of moral judgment in which we do use the word "right", such as "this is the right act", it is clear that by this we mean "this act is the act *that ought to be done*", "this act is *morally obligatory*"' (Ross's emphasis). Ross distinguishes this sense of 'obligatory' from one in which it means 'compulsory'. In the legal context, see *Lake Shore & MSR Co.* v. *Kurtz* (1894) 10 Ind App 60: 'A duty or a legal obligation is that which one ought or ought not to do'. Informal commentaries on deontic logic often identify 'it ought to be the case that' with 'it is obligatory that': Chellas (1980) does, at 190.

is grounded in a reason for him to do Ax which may be outweighed;[88] the latter point – sometimes misleadingly expressed by talk of 'prima facie' obligations[89] – is compatible with the possibility that the reason is 'protected' in Raz's sense. Given that distinction, it is not true that if X is obligated to do Ax then X ought to do Ax, nor that if (2) then X ought to do Ax. But it is a confusion to deny, on that basis, that if (2) then X is obligated to do Ax (let alone to conclude that if (2) then X is not thus obligated or, still worse, that if (2) then X is obligated not to do Ax).

An argument that (45) is false and (46) true might use the premiss that there is a symmetry between the obligations of active agreements and those of factual ones. An example, given in the Introduction, of a factual agreement was:

(47) X and Y agree that Everest is the highest mountain.

The counterpart of (45) is not true, and indeed has no clear sense:

(48) If (47) then X is obligated that Everest is the highest mountain.

But the counterpart of (46) is true:

(49) X is obligated that if (47) then Everest is the highest mountain.

88 In that case the obligation itself may be said to be outweighed. On the circumstances in which the obligation to keep a promise is outweighed or 'abolished', see D. Ross (1939), 109 ff. For distinctions between outweighing, abolishing, overriding, excluding, defeating, undercutting, superseding, extinguishing and cancelling, see Belzer (1998), 889; Chisholm (1964); Chisholm (1974); Raz (1990), chap. 1, esp. 40; M. Zimmerman (1996), 107 ff., 135 f., 162 f., 169. Outweighing is discussed further in sections 4.11 and 6.211 below.

89 This use is favoured in Brandt (1964), 377; Belzer (1998), 889; Pietroski (1993); Snare (1974); Tunick (2002), 467; Wellman (2004), 97 n. 1; M. Zimmerman (1995); M. Zimmerman (1996), 5 ff., chap. 5. The locus classicus is D. Ross (1930), 18 ff., 61ff.; see also D. Ross (1939), 84 f. Ross's use of the phrase is hedged; in particular, Ross notes that a prima facie duty is not a duty proper. For criticism, see Atwell (1978); Chisholm (1964), 150; Donagan (1977), 93; Feldman (1986), 144; Hart (1967), 62 f.; Loewer and Belzer (1991); McCloskey (1963); Searle (1978). See also Hintikka (1970), 91 ff. Partly because of the problems with the notion of prima facie obligation, some philosophers prefer 'pro tanto' to 'prima facie': see, e.g., Alvarez (2010), 12; O. Black (2004b), 280 f.; O. Black (2005b), 180 ff.; Broome (2004); Kagan (1989), 17. (Hurley (1989), 130 gives a special sense to 'pro tanto reason', in order to deal with weakness of will. On prima facie reasons, see Raz (1990), 27 f.) Broad (1985), 190 distinguishes 'component' obligations from a 'resultant' obligation. On degrees of obligation, see Prichard (2002a), 14 n. 7. On bindingness as a matter of degree, see Atiyah (1986i), 61; D. Ross (1939), 100; see further n. 147 below. On degrees of legal liability, see Atiyah (1986k), 287.

These claims are supported by the thought that, even in the case of a factual agreement or promise, an obligation concerns a possible action of the obligor. (Compare Pink's point about agency-specificity.) The alleged obligation in (48) does not, but the obligation in (49) does, concern an action of X – his agreeing. Hence, given the premiss, (46) is true and (45) is not. The argument fails for some accounts of factual agreement; for example, if the fact that X and Y believe that P is sufficient for them to agree factually that P, then, granted that belief is not an action, X's factually agreeing need not be an action (see the Introduction).

A contrary argument – I give only a sketch – uses the premiss that the obligations of active agreements are voluntary.[90] X's obligation in (45) is voluntary, for it is up to X whether or not he agrees with Y that (1) and thus assumes the obligation; but his obligation in (46) is not, for he has it whatever he does. Given the premiss, (45) is true and (46) is not. It is sometimes claimed that there is a mystery in the idea of a voluntary obligation.[91] One bad source of the claim may be a failure to distinguish (i) 'If X φs then X is obligated that X χs' from (ii) 'X is obligated that if X φs then X χs'. Another may be a failure to distinguish X's making true the antecedent of (i) – and hence, if (i) is true, his also making true the consequent – from his making true (i) itself.[92] He does the former by φing and, if (i) is a material implication, the latter by not φing. Again it may be assumed that whether or not X φs is up to him, and so thus far there is no distinction in point of the voluntary; but if (i) is read modally – say, as a strict implication – then it is unclear how X can affect its truth value. (On material and strict implication, see section 1.22.) It is likewise unclear how, on this reading, X can affect the truth value of (iii) 'If X φs then the fact that X φs grounds the fact that X is obligated to χ'.

90 See n. 67 above.

91 See Fogelin (1983), 289 f.; Horton (1992), 42 f.; Hume (1978), 516 ff. Contrast de Moor (1990), 645; Hart (1967), 56 n. 1; Hobbes (1968), 268 ('there being no Obligation on any man, which ariseth not from some Act of his own'); Pateman (1985); Prichard (2002f), 257; Robins (1984), chap. 1; D. Ross (1930), 27 ('obligations arising from acts the very intention of which, when they were done, was to put us under such an obligation'); D. Ross (1939), 76; Searle (1965), 235 f. (on the 'essential condition' for a promise); S. Smith (2004), 182; S. Smith (2005), 22, 28 f., 57; Stocker (1970), 620; Walzer (1970), x. Inconsistency of terminology is a problem in this area. For example, Hart (1958), 103 f. distinguishes 'assumed' from 'created' duties, whereas R. Dworkin (1986a), 197, distinguishing 'assumed' from 'attracted' obligations, uses 'assumed' to mean the same as, or something similar to, Hart's 'created'. On Dworkin's notion of an 'associative' obligation, see ibid. 195 ff.; L. Green (1989); L. Green (2002), 532 ff.; Utz (2004). See also B. Williams (1993), 7 f.

92 See O. Black (2006), 282. On truth-making, see Chap. 1 n. 46 above.

3.4 Generality versus morality

Whatever the truth value of (46), (45) is plausible, as is:

(50) X's obligation in (45) is a moral performance obligation.[93]

The point that it is a performance obligation was covered in section 3.3. Certain suggested features of moral obligation were mentioned in section 3.1, but there is no need here to try to draw the boundaries, no doubt vague and contestable, of morality.[94] Although (45) and (50) are both plausible, it can be argued as follows that together they imply a false proposition and hence are not both true. As stated in section 3.2:

(51) Every obligation has a ground.

So:

(52) If (2) then there exists a ground of a moral performance obligation on X.

(52), being schematic and hence general (see the Introduction), applies to every case where two parties agree that one of them does one action and the other another. Call such a case a 'relevant case'. (52) thus entails:

(53) In every relevant case, there exists a ground of a moral performance obligation on a party.

Talk of cases, and of grounds, and thus of facts, existing in them, could be made more precise – perhaps as part of a theory of facts (see section 3.2) – but is clear enough. A corollary of (53) is that in a relevant case a ground exists irrespective of the nature of the actions agreed (compare Hart on content-independence) and of the circumstances in which the agreement is made or performed. But:

93 See Chap. 1 n. 78 above.

94 See Whiteley (1960). On the relation between morality – the 'peculiar institution' – and ethics, see B. Williams (1993), chaps. 1, 10. Hart (1961), 164 maintains that the words 'morality' and 'ethics' have open texture. On open texture, see Bix (1993), chap. 1; Hart (1961), 124 f.; Margalit (1981), 141 ff.; Schauer (1991), 34 ff.; Waismann (1968), 119 ff.; Whittaker (2008), paras. 1–063 f.; Williamson (1994), 90 ff. On contested concepts, see Chap. 6 n. 10 below. On moral obligation in the law of contract, see Whittaker (2008), para. 1–001, and, in the contractual doctrine of consideration, Peel (2007), para. 3–021; on the relation between moral obligation and competition law's concepts of arrangement and concerted practice, see O. Black (1992), 204; O. Black (2005b), 168 f.; Whish (1993), 129.

(54) In some relevant cases, there exists no ground of a moral performance obligation on a party.

For example, it might be maintained, in accordance with the first of the theories listed in section 3.3, that in some relevant cases a party has a moral performance obligation grounded in the fact that the other party relies on him to perform. But in other such cases there is no fact of reliance – see the example of the household chores, in section 1.5 – and no other fact that would ground such an obligation. (Further objections to reliance-based theories are examined in section 3.51.) (53) therefore is false. Since – given (51) – (45) and (50) imply (53), one of (45) and (50) is also false.

One response distinguishes two meanings of 'ground of a moral performance obligation on a party': where a party has a moral performance obligation, the phrase could mean either a ground of the fact that he has the obligation or a ground of the fact that the obligation is moral. The thought is that on the former reading (53) follows from (45), (50) and (51), but (54) is false, whereas on the latter reading (54) is true but (53) does not follow, and so the argument fails for equivocation. It might be objected that the distinction between the two meanings quantifies illegitimately into the context 'the fact that . . .';[95] but that move is not available to the proponent of the argument against (45) and (50), for there is an implicit quantification into the same context in (53). That issue can be left for a theory of facts.

There is a more straightforward objection to each half of the claim of equivocation. As to the first reading, the objector to (45) and (50) may claim that in some relevant cases there exists no ground of any performance obligation, moral or not. (Section 3.6 gives reason to reject that claim.) If he concedes that on the second reading (53) does not follow, he may revise the argument in such a way that the counterpart of (53) (so interpreted) does follow from the preceding steps. The revised argument uses the plausible thought that, whether or not the fact that, in a given case (relevant or not), a performance obligation is moral has a ground, it depends – in a sense that need not be pursued here – on some other fact of the case. The argument runs: (45); (50); so in every relevant case there exists a moral performance obligation; in every case where there exists

95 Such quantification is problematic if the context is not referentially transparent. On transparency, see the Introduction above. On quantification into such contexts, see Linsky (1971).

such an obligation, there exists a fact (a 'moral fact') on which depends the fact that the obligation is moral; so – the counterpart of (53) – in every relevant case there exists a moral fact; but in some relevant cases there exists no moral fact; and so on.

Another response is to support (53) by looking for some fact – perhaps involving more than the relation between the parties – that both exists in every relevant case and is a 'suitable fact' in the sense that it grounds a moral performance obligation on a party, or for some fact-type that is instantiated in every relevant case by a suitable fact. The following discussion blurs the type/instance distinction by reverting, for convenience, to schemata. It might be held that one such fact is that X's failure to do Ax would damage society by weakening the general confidence in the keeping of agreements. But that fact does not exist in every relevant case, if in any; an individual breach may do little or nothing to weaken the general confidence, and in some cases may reinforce it.[96]

A different way to support (53) is, in logical jargon, to replace the EA with an AE proposition (see further section 9.27) – to say not that there is a suitable fact that exists in every relevant case, but that in every relevant case a suitable fact exists. The former proposition does, and the latter does not, imply that the fact is the same in all the cases; but the latter, like the former, implies that (53) is true. By itself, however, the AE proposition is a weak support for (53) because, absent some explanation why some suitable fact is always forthcoming, the proposition implies the existence of an odd coincidence. The coincidence is odder if not only actual but merely possible relevant cases are in question.

The next response reverts to the distinction between conditional and unconditional obligations. X, it may be said, has the conditional obligation in (46) (X is obligated that if (2) then X does Ax). That obligation is moral, and it exists whether or not X and Y agree that (1). Hence it exists in every relevant case. By (51), it has a ground. If the obligation exists in every relevant case, so does the ground. Hence the ground exists in every relevant case. But that argument fails to support (53): since the obligation is not a performance obligation, no reason has been given to think that the ground is a suitable fact. A different argument starts in the same way as the previous one, but continues as follows: if the conditional obligation exists in every relevant case, so does the fact that X has it; that

96 For the parallel thesis and objection relating to promises, see Pickard-Cambridge (1932), 154 f. and D. Ross (1939), 91 ff. D. Ross (1930), 39 uses a 'death bed' counterexample. On the dangers of reasoning from deathbed cases, see Ardal (1976), 60 f.

fact grounds a moral performance obligation on X; so (53) is true. There are two objections to this. It is at best doubtful that the fact grounds a performance obligation on X: a more detailed theory of grounding would be needed to settle the issue. Even if it does ground such an obligation, no reason has been given to think that the obligation is moral. Indeed, it is plausible to hold that, if the fact grounds a moral performance obligation on X, then:

(55) X's obligation in (46) is a moral obligation.

But an analogue of the argument against (45) and (50) can be raised against (46) and (55). To adapt the previous example: a reliance theorist might say that the obligation's ground is the fact that if (2) then Y relies on X to do Ax; but that fact does not exist in every relevant case.

Here is a better but more concessive response, which will be refined in section 3.6. In every relevant case, the fact (FA) exists that (2). In some but not all relevant cases, at least one other fact (FM) exists which grounds a moral obligation on X to do Ax and is thus a suitable fact. In section 3.6 I defend:

(56) If (2) then FA grounds an obligation on X to do Ax.

Given (56), (45) is true: see sections 3.2 and 3.3. I also consider an argument that the obligation grounded in FA is moral. If it is moral, (53) is true. If it is not moral, X has a performance obligation in every relevant case, but a moral performance obligation in only some.[97] If that is so, (53) needs to be qualified to exclude the other relevant cases. Since the unqualified (53) follows from (45), (50) and (51), and (45) and (51) have been granted, (50) must be similarly qualified.

In the relevant cases where FM exists, we might say either that X has two performance obligations – a substantive one grounded in FM, a formal one in FA[98] – or that he has a single performance obligation with two grounds. I shall use whichever locution – the first of which presupposes a narrow principle, the second a broad one, for individuating obligations – is more convenient. If the narrow principle is adopted, the phrase 'X's

97 For a similar view of promissory obligation, see Ardal (1976), 61; Raz (1977), 225; Stocker (1970), 614. Compare Gilbert (2004), 105, which distinguishes a 'primary' obligation that is 'part and parcel' of promising from 'secondary' obligations. As mentioned in Chap. 1 n. 78 above, Gilbert suggests that promissory obligations – she seems to mean the primary obligations – may not be moral or legal. See also McMahon (1989); McNeilly (1971); Searle (1969), 188.

98 See n. 136 below.

performance obligation' can still be used to refer in short form to the set of X's performance obligations. The broad principle threatens a contradiction: if FM grounds an obligation that is moral, and FA an obligation that is not, and both facts ground the same obligation, then a single obligation is both moral and not moral. Solutions are to reject the broad principle; to hold that FA grounds a moral obligation, at least in relevant cases where FM exists; or to qualify, maintaining that the obligation, as grounded in FM, is pro tanto moral and, as grounded in FA, pro tanto not moral.

3.5 Grounds of moral performance obligations

3.51 Reliance

If FA and the question whether it grounds a moral performance obligation on X are set aside, it is plausible to hold, as regards the relevant cases where X has such an obligation, that its grounds vary from case to case; that in some of those cases there is more than one ground (and hence, on the narrow principle of individuation, more than one such obligation); and that there may be no ground that is present in all those cases.[99] If this pluralist view is correct, a modest reliance-based theory of the ground of X's moral performance obligation – modest in that it purports to apply only to some relevant cases in which X has such an obligation – may also be correct.

Although a theory of that sort avoids the objection that in some relevant cases Y does not rely on X to perform, reliance-based theories, modest or not, face further problems. One complaint is that they get things the wrong way round: Y relies on X to do Ax, because X in agreeing obligates himself to do Ax.[100] An answer can be developed from the thesis that FA grounds a performance obligation, even if not a moral one, on X. In outline: Y, recognising that X is obligated on that ground, believes that X likewise recognises himself to be thus obligated; on the basis of that belief, Y believes that X reasons to an intention to do Ax (the reasoning is

99 For scepticism about theories that purport to identify a single ground, see Atiyah (1986j), 149; Kötz (1997), 8; Weir (1992), 1647. On the 'context-sensitivity' of certain moral obligations, see Gilbert (1996a), 299; Gilbert (2006), 159 ff. Compare Raz (1972), 98; Stocker (1970), 614. See also n. 25 to the Introduction above, on moral particularism.

100 This objection is raised, to reliance-based theories of promissory obligation, by Downie (1985), 266; Fried (1981), 19; see also Atiyah (1981), 37 ff. The same objection is made to expectation-based theories in Robins (1976), 323 f.; Robins (1984), 7; Warnock (1971), 99 f. See also Anscombe (1981).

described in section 4.21); on the basis of that belief, Y believes that X has the intention; on the basis of that belief, Y believes that X does Ax; given this further belief and certain other facts about Y (see the condition for reliance given by (57) and (64)–(68) below), Y relies on X to do Ax; and the fact that Y so relies grounds a moral obligation on X.[101]

Another objection is that reliance-based theories misidentify the time at which X's performance obligation arises:[102] that is the moment the agreement is made, but the theories imply that the obligation does not arise until the time when Y acts in reliance.[103] If the action in reliance is Ay, that time is normally later. Various responses are possible. One is to argue that the ground of the obligation is not the fact that Y in doing Ay relies on X to do Ax, but the fact that the making of the agreement causes Y so to rely, and that this fact starts to exist when the agreement is made. A second response is to hold that the ground is the fact, which likewise starts to exist then, that it would be reasonable for X to believe that Y so relies.[104] A third is to argue that the time when Y so relies need not be the same as the time when the fact that Y so relies starts to exist. A fourth is to drive the wedge not between the time of reliance and the time of that fact, but between the latter and the time the obligation arises – the idea, a brave one, being that an obligation may arise earlier than its ground.

The best response may be to appeal again to the thesis that FA grounds a performance obligation on X. FA and the obligation it grounds start to exist at the time the agreement is made. The fact that Y in doing Ay relies on X to do Ax, and the moral performance obligation on X that it grounds, start to exist at the later time when Y starts so to rely. This response requires a qualification to the criterion of Simultaneity (section 1.2313) or to the claim that the offer–acceptance model meets it (section 2.5); for by similar reasoning, if X in doing Ax relies on Y to do Ay, Y has a moral performance obligation that starts to exist at the time when X starts so to rely, and that time may be different from the time when Y starts to rely on X to do Ax, just as each of those times may be

101 Compare McMahon (1989). See also Scanlon's defence of his theory against the charge of circularity: Scanlon (1990), 212 f.

102 On the time of an obligation, see Chap. 1 n. 84 above.

103 See Atiyah (1981), 38 ff., criticising the proposal in MacCormick (1972) to solve the problem by reference to the probability, rather than the fact, of reliance; Patterson (1992), 399. Parallel objections and replies apply to certain other theories such as the harm- and benefit-based theories discussed in section 3.52 below. For the objection in terms of benefits, see J. Cartwright (1984), 238.

104 See Atiyah and MacCormick: n. 103 above.

different from the time when FA and the obligation it grounds starts to exist. The qualification limits the criterion, or the claim, to performance obligations grounded only in FA.

The next objection is that reliance-based theories fail to explain the cancellability of X's performance obligation, in particular where Y fails to do Ay. One thought is that, if Ay would be Y's action in reliance, X's obligation ceases because it lacks a ground. But, if the only ground of the obligation would be the fact that Y in doing Ay relies on X to do Ax, the obligation does not cease: it never arises.[105] (A similar point was made in section 1.2314.) Suppose, on the other hand, that the ground is the fact that Y performs some action, other than Ay, in reliance on X to do Ax. Then it is unclear how Y's failure to do Ay would cancel the obligation. The best response may be to concede the objection and to qualify the thesis of cancellability: Y's failure to do Ay cancels a performance obligation of X that is grounded only in FA, and the explanation is that a constitutive rule of agreement so provides. (This develops the account in sections 2.2 and 2.3.) A corresponding qualification applies to the criterion of Interdependence (section 1.2314) or to the claim that the offer–acceptance model meets it (section 2.5): compare the qualification, in the previous paragraph, relating to Simultaneity. It is plausible to hold that reliance-based theories also require a qualification to be made in relation to the criterion of Obligation; for, although that criterion is unclear (see section 1.2312), it seems that, if X's performance obligation is grounded in the fact of Y's reliance, it is not 'directly generated' by their agreement.

A more difficult objection runs as follows. The fact that Y in doing Ay relies on X to do Ax is not a complete ground, because it is not a sufficient condition, of an obligation on X to do Ax. The standard example is the story that Kant used to take his constitutional so regularly that the people of Königsberg used to set their watches by him.[106] Assume that, in order to set their watches, they relied on Kant to take his constitutional at the same time every day. It is highly implausible to claim that the fact of their reliance was sufficient for Kant to be obligated to do so. The example does not involve an agreement, but the principle transfers; for, if the fact of reliance were sufficient, any further fact, such as the presence of an

105 M. Zimmerman (1996), 107 rhetorically asks how an obligation could be cancelled unless it were already in existence.

106 See Baier (1986), 231; J. Miller (2011), 267; Simmons (1981), where the example is used to refute the 'principle of reasonable expectation' in Postow (1980). Other examples are given in MacCormick (1982), 198 and Atiyah (1981), 36.

agreement, would be immaterial. If it is suggested that the further fact could defeat the sufficiency of reliance,[107] the replies are first that, on the most straightforward understanding of sufficiency, defeasible sufficiency is a self-contradiction and second that, even if that concept is admitted, there is no reason to think that the presence of an agreement would be a defeater in this case.

The next step of the objection is to deny that the fact of Y's reliance is a partial ground of an obligation on X to do Ax. The concern, roughly stated, is that, where that fact is part of a sufficient condition of such an obligation, the remaining parts are sufficient; so the original condition is not minimally sufficient and hence not a complete ground of the obligation; and so the fact of Y's reliance is not a partial ground of it.[108] Suppose that the following are all true:

(57) Y does Ay.
(58) Y, in doing Ay, relies on X to do Ax.
(59) A failure by X to do Ax would cause significant harm to Y.
(60) X induces Y to do Ay.
(61) It would be reasonable for X to believe (57)–(60).
(62) If (57) and (58) and (59) and (60) and (61), then X is obligated to do Ax.[109]

X therefore has an obligation to do Ax. By assumptions in section 3.2, there exist 'conjunct facts' – the fact that (57), the fact that (58), . . . , the fact that (61) – and 'the first conjunctive fact' that <(57) and (58) and (59) and (60) and (61)>, each conjunct fact being a proper part of the first conjunctive fact. Assume this: the first conjunctive fact is a complete ground of X's obligation if and only if (62) meets two conditions: first, (62) is true; but, second, if any conjunct in the antecedent of (62) is deleted, the resultant conditional is false.[110] That assumption is accurate enough but could be refined – for example, to acknowledge that, as noted in section 3.2, not every minimal sufficient condition is a ground.

Applied to (57)–(62), the objection is that, although by hypothesis (62) is true, it does not meet the second of the two conditions, as the conditional resulting from the deletion of (58) from the antecedent of

107 Compare P. Audi (unpub.), 3 on the non-monotonicity of grounding.
108 See O. Black (1998); O. Black (2004b); O. Black (2005b), 169 ff.
109 For variant sets of conditions, see Benson (2001c), 174; O. Black (1998); O. Black (2004b); O. Black (2005b), 169 ff.; Scanlon (1990); Scanlon (1998), chap. 7; Stocker (1970), 617 ff.
110 On the question whether conditionals have truth values, see Chap. 1 n. 42 above.

(62) is also true. In that case the first conjunctive fact is not a complete ground – and hence (unless, as the next paragraph proposes in relation to some of the conjunct facts, those facts are parts of other complete grounds[111]) the conjunct facts are not partial grounds – of X's obligation. In particular, the fact that (58) is not a partial ground of the obligation.

A possible reply is that 'the second conjunctive fact', resulting from the removal of the fact that (59) from the first conjunctive fact (together perhaps with the substitution, for the fact that (61), of the fact that it would be reasonable for X to believe (57), (58) and (60) – an elaboration that can be ignored) exists and is a complete ground of X's obligation. Applying the same approach as before: it is true that:

(63) if (57) and (58) and (60) and (61), then X is obligated to do Ax;

but, if any conjunct in the antecedent of (63) is deleted, the resultant conditional is false. Since the fact that (58) exists and is a proper part of the second conjunctive fact, the fact that (58) is a partial ground of the obligation. (That is consistent with the claim that (58) implies (59), and in any event the implication holds only on further assumptions.[112]) Hence this modest reliance-based theory is true: if both (2) and the antecedent of (63) are true, the second conjunctive fact is a complete ground, and so the fact that (58) is a partial ground, of X's performance obligation. Further reasoning might show the obligation to be a moral one.

It might now be objected either that the antecedent of (63) is too meagre or that it is too ample. As to the first objection, the thought might be that another conjunct – that it is reasonable for Y in doing Ay to rely on X to do Ax – must be added to the antecedent in order to yield a truth. Consider

111 Compare the 'debatable assumption' in O. Black (2004b), 277 ff.; O. Black (2005b), 178 ff.

112 If the condition for reliance, given in (25) (section 1.5 above) and repeated (with trivial changes) in (57) and (64)–(68) below, is met where Y relies on X to do Ax, then if X fails to do Ax a goal of Y is not achieved. It does not follow that X's failure would cause the non-achievement of Y's goal: compare the distinction, drawn in section 4.11 below, between conditionality and instrumentality. Moreover, it is in only a thin sense of 'harm' (compare the thin sense given to 'benefit' in section 2.4 above) that a person suffers harm, let alone significant harm, if one of his goals, no matter what, is not achieved: if he wants to drink from a glass but is prevented from doing so, he normally is not harmed in any fuller sense if, unbeknown to him, the glass contains poison. The law recognises this in distinguishing between bare and detrimental/injurious reliance: see, e.g., *The Hannah Blumenthal* [1993] 1 AC 834, 916. On the forms of harm that can arise from reliance, see P. Cooke and Oughton (1993), 76 f.; on the meanings of 'harm', Feinberg (1984), 31 ff. In any event, the condition is sufficient, not necessary, for reliance, and so a person may rely without its being met.

the condition proposed in section 1.5 as sufficient for such reliance (the positions of X and Y being reversed to fit the present discussion):

(57) Y does Ay;
(64) Y has the goal Gy;
(65) If Y does Ay, then Gy is achieved if and only if X does Ax;
(66) Y believes (65);
(67) Y believes that X does Ax; and
(68) (57) because <(64), (66) and (67)>.

If this condition is met, Y might be reasonable in respect of having Gy, of believing (65), of believing that X does Ax, and/or of the connection signified by 'because' in (68). As to this last, it might be said that 'because' here signifies an appropriate causal chain and that the concept of reasonableness is included in the relevant concept of appropriateness. (On appropriate causal chains, see section 1.23.)

As to the second objection, the thought is that a conjunct may be deleted from the antecedent of (63) without falsifying the resultant conditional. In particular, it might be held that the conditional resulting from the deletion of either (60) or (61) is true; for example, if the antecedent provides that X induces Y to do Ay, the clause that it would be reasonable for X to believe (57)–(60) can be deleted salva veritate. That raises the question how 'induces' should be understood.[113] In a weak sense, if X merely causes Y to do Ay, X induces Y to do Ay; but stronger senses import an intention on X's part. A plausible thought is that X has the Gricean intention <to cause Y to do Ay, the causation working through Y's recognition of X's intention>, perhaps with certain further intentions that exclude Strawsonian situations of the kind discussed in section 8.32. If the claim that (60) makes (61) superfluous, in the respect identified, is somehow reached from the premiss that X, by virtue of inducing Y to do Ay, has the relevant intention,[114] the objection is not deflected by substitution of the arguably weaker word 'invites' for 'induces' in (60),[115]

113 The definition of 'inducing reliance' in MacCormick (1982), 195 is circular as regards inducement: '"Inducing reliance" means intentionally or knowingly inducing a person to base his conduct on expectations about one's own'.

114 The principle of loss prevention in Scanlon (1998), 300 f. and Scanlon (2001), 91, which concerns expectation rather than reliance, includes both intention and what 'one has reason to believe'. MacCormick (1982), 197 ff. takes a disjunctive approach. See also Atiyah (1981), 38 ff.

115 Downie (1985), 266 says that a promise invites but does not induce reliance, but does not explain the distinction. Atiyah (1981), 36 likewise says that promises invite reliance;

for it is just as plausible to hold that only if a person has that intention, or a similar one, does he invite. In any event, the concept of invitation does not fit the present context. If X offers to Y that (1), he perhaps invites Y to accept; but if Y does accept, thereby agreeing, and if Y then does Ay, it is more natural to say that X induces than that he invites Y to do Ay. The same applies where X accepts an offer by Y and Y performs.

Even if the objections concerning (63) are sound, they suggest that the specification of the complete ground only needs adjustment. The first objection is consistent with the thesis that, on the assumption that it is reasonable for Y in doing Ay to rely on X to do Ax, the fact that <(57) and (58) and (60) and (61) and it is reasonable for Y so to rely> is a complete ground, and hence the fact that (58) is a partial ground, of X's obligation. The second objection is consistent with the thesis that one or both of these facts is a complete ground of the obligation: the fact that <(57) and (58) and (60)>, the fact that <(57) and (58) and (61)>. Again, if either is a complete ground, the fact that (58) is a partial ground, of X's obligation.

Intuitions as to grounds of moral obligations tend to be weak and conflicting, and so it is an arid exercise to try to specify such a ground on the basis of intuition alone. In principle a more powerful approach is to derive a specification from a general theory of moral obligation,[116] but in practice the process by which consequences are inferred from moral theories is often obscure. Scanlon, for example, maintains that his contractualist theory implies various principles about those obligations that concern the expectations that we lead others to form about the things we intend to do[117] (see section 3.52), but it is unclear how his contractualist premisses imply precisely the principles he identifies: implicitly the principles seem to be based to some extent on intuition. There is in any event

Atiyah (1986k), 287 says that they 'virtually' do so; see also Atiyah (1986j), 143. S. Smith (2005), 2 talks of induced reliance. Benson (2001c), 174 appears to use 'invite' and 'induce' interchangeably in this context. Fried (1981), 11 rejects theories of promissory obligation that invoke reliance that is both invited and foreseen; Fried also connects invitation and intention. D. Ross (1939), 77 says that a promise is an 'intimation' to another person that he can rely on one. Pink (2009) says that certain promises are 'invitations to trust'; Friedrich and Southwood (2011) proposes a similar view. See further n. 62 above.

116 There are discussions of philosophical justifications for contractual obligation in Atiyah (1979b), chap. 1; Atiyah (1986d); Gordley (1991); S. Smith (2004), 46 ff. See also McMahon (1989), 239 f. on the utilitarian and deontological justifications for a principle connecting obligation and reliance.

117 Scanlon (1990), 220; Scanlon (1998), 315; Scanlon (2001), 89.

an interplay between intuition and moral theory.[118] As it is beyond the scope of this book to provide a general theory of moral obligation,[119] I shall not pursue further the questions whether, given the truth of the relevant propositions, the fact that (58) is a partial ground of an obligation on X to do Ax; if so, whether the reason is that one of the conjunctive facts discussed, or some different fact of which the fact that (58) is a part, is a complete ground of the obligation; whether some fact other than the fact that (58), but to do with Y's reliance, is a partial ground of it; and whether an obligation grounded in the relevant fact of reliance is moral.

3.52 *Other grounds*

As noted in section 3.3, there are many other accounts of the grounds of performance obligations. A simple theory of a moral performance obligation invokes (59): if a failure by X to do Ax would cause significant harm to Y, the fact that it would is a complete ground of a moral obligation on X to do Ax.[120] The harm might be due to uncompensated costs, including opportunity costs, incurred by Y in performing his part of the agreement, or to the contempt that X would show for Y in failing to do Ax.[121] The fact that in some cases X's failure to perform would not harm Y is no objection, provided that the theory is modest in the sense explained, but it might be objected that the theory confuses moral concepts: although it is normally bad and/or wrong to harm someone, we are under no obligation not to do so.[122] In any event, the theory needs

118 See Chap. 2 n. 10 above. For the view that ethical theory needs to be grounded in intuition, see D. Ross (1939), 1 ff., 82; Ross distinguishes ethics from the physical sciences in that respect. Contrast Hobbes (1983), 178, discussed in Skinner (1996), 265. For an objection to the concept of intuition in ethics, see B. Williams (1993), 93 ff. On the place of intuition in philosophy generally, see Chap. 1 n. 47 above; see also Chap. 2 n. 8 above.

119 On one view, a full theory would have a normative part, specifying obligations, or principles or categories of obligation, and a meta-ethical part dealing, e.g., with the nature of judgments of obligation. If the questions raised in sections 3.1 and 3.2 above are limited to moral obligation, those of meaning and knowledge, for instance, are meta-ethical, whereas the question of grounds is normative. For the distinction between normative ethics and meta-ethics, see Kagan (1998), chap. 1; A. Miller (2003), 1 ff. For doubts about the distinction, see Grice (1991), 29; B. Williams (1993), 72 ff. For a sceptical view of the aspirations of ethical theory, see Williams (1993), chap. 6, 148 ff.; for a similar view of theories of political obligation, Horton (1992), 14 f., chap. 7.

120 See the works in n. 64 above.

121 Compare MacCormick (1982), 205.

122 Compare Hart (1967), 56 n. 1: '"duty", "obligation", "right", and "good" come from different segments of morality, concern different types of conduct, and make different

to specify the kinds of harm in question, for it seems that it is not even wrong to inflict certain kinds of harm on others: plausible examples are just punishment,[123] some forms of interrogation to detect or avert crime, and the harm caused by fair competition.[124] Further clauses may also be needed in order to specify a complete ground – for example, the clause, corresponding to (61), that it would be reasonable for X to believe that his failure to do Ax would cause significant harm to Y.

Another approach builds on the idea, proposed in section 2.4, that each party to an agreement benefits from the other's performance: if Y does Ay, thereby benefiting X, it would be unfair for X not to do Ax, for in doing Ax he would benefit Y.[125] Again this perhaps does better as an account of the ground of the wrongness of non-performance than of that of a moral obligation to perform; but an argument that it identifies the ground of such an obligation might appeal to Brandt's observation, noted in section 3.1, that 'obligation' is paradigmatically used in relation to benefactions. A second objection is that an asymmetry of benefactions as such is not unfair, and so further explanation of the alleged unfairness is needed. A third is that the theory does not explain why, if X by doing something else could benefit Y as much as he would by doing Ax, he is nevertheless normally obligated to do Ax. A fourth – which also applies to certain reliance- and harm-based theories[126] – is that the theory confuses a party with a beneficiary: if Y's side of the agreement is to look after X's mother,

types of moral criticism or evaluation'. See also Hart (1958), 82 f. Hart's claim would be rejected by those who both identify 'right to' with 'wrong not to' and identify the latter with 'obligatory to': see R. Adams (1999), 232 and compare Mackie (1977), 76 on 'must'. Brandt (1964), 390 rejects the equation of 'obligatory' with 'wrong not to' on the basis that an obligation concerns a positive goal and is thus distinct from a prohibition. On negative obligation, see O. Black (1993). Brandt's thesis of positivity also sits uneasily with harm-based theories of the ground of X's obligation, but Brandt suggests a reconciliation (ibid., 391) by his statement that, although it is wrong to injure someone, it can be a demand on one's behaviour that one take care to avoid injuring others. Harm-based theories are, however, hard to square with Brandt's description of the paradigmatic use of 'obligation': section 3.1 above.

123 It might be denied that just punishment harms the person punished. Hegel (1952), 68 ff. is debatable authority for that denial.

124 See O. Black (2005b), chap. 2; Wolff (2002); Wolff (2006). On the arguments for and against economic competition, see Chap. 6 n. 58 below.

125 See the works cited in n. 65 above. On the related principle of fair play, sometimes invoked as a ground of political obligation, see R. Dworkin (1986a), 193 ff.; Hart (1967), 61 f.; Horton (1992), 69, 89 ff.; Nozick (1974), 90 ff. (on the problem of imposed benefits); Rawls (1964), 9 f.; Robins (1984), 10 ff.; Simmons (1979), 116 f.

126 Compare Raz (1977), 217 and Warnock (1971), 111 ff. on third parties' reliance on promises.

the mother is the potential beneficiary, but X is Y's counterparty.[127] To this it can be replied that the theory is modest in that it purports to apply only where X benefits – as he may do from Y's care for his mother.

Other candidates for grounds of a moral obligation on X to do Ax are specified by Scanlon's principles concerning expectations. An example is the 'principle of fidelity':

> If (a) X voluntarily and intentionally leads Y to expect that X will do Ax (unless Y consents to X's not doing so); (b) X knows that Y wants to be assured of this; (c) X acts with the aim of providing this assurance, and has good reason to believe that he has done so; (d) Y knows that X has the beliefs and intentions just described; (e) X intends Y to know this, and knows that Y does know it; and (f) Y knows that X has this knowledge and intention; then, in the absence of special justification, X must do Ax unless Y consents to Ax's not being done.[128]

Some of these theories identify, as grounds of X's obligation, facts that include evaluative or normative properties such as harm, benefit and unfairness. It is plausible to hold that such facts, by virtue of including such properties, in turn have grounds. The distinction between intermediate and ultimate grounds can be invoked: the theories identify intermediate grounds, but need supplementation in order to identify the ultimate ground or grounds of the obligation.[129]

A full account would specify the various grounds that might exist for a moral performance obligation on X and would place them in a general theory of moral obligation: see section 3.51. As noted there, Scanlon argues for his principles of expectation on the basis of a contractualist theory; but we could reject contractualism and keep the principles, for

127 The distinction is acknowledged in Brandt's phrase 'for or at the bidding of' (see section 3.1 above): Brandt (1964), 387. Compare Hart (1967), 57 f.; Hart however is concerned with X's right against, rather than his obligation to, Y. On the rights of third parties in contract and tort, see Kötz (1997), chap. 13; Zweigert and Kötz (1998), chap. 34. On promissory obligations to third parties, see Raz and Warnock (n. 126 above); Atiyah (1979a); Woozley (1981), 289.

128 Scanlon (1998), 304. Substantially the same principle is stated in Scanlon (1990), 208 and Scanlon (2001), 95. For uniformity I have made minor changes to the wording. For other such principles, see MacCormick (1982), 199; McMahon (1989), 239.

129 Atiyah (1979b), in distinguishing benefit-based, reliance-based and promise-based contractual liability, says that the three types 'rest on different values' (6); for example, the first arises 'from broad notions of unjust enrichment' (1). This may mean that the benefit is a direct ground and unjust enrichment an indirect ground of liability, but the wording is unclear.

example as elements of a rule-utilitarian[130] theory or a pluralist intuitionist deontology.[131] A theory of this last kind admits various grounds for X's obligation[132] and is thus consistent with the pluralist approach mentioned in section 3.51, but other theories leave room for only one. A contractualist, for example, may hold that, where X has a moral performance obligation, its ground is never, say, the fact (FF) that X's doing Ax is prescribed by the principle of fidelity, but is always the fact (FC) that X's doing Ax is prescribed by some principle, whatever it may be, that contractors meeting certain conditions could not reject.[133] Similarly, a rule-utilitarian may say that the ground is never the fact that X's doing Ax is prescribed by a specified rule obedience to which would maximise utility, but is always the fact that X's doing Ax is prescribed by some rule or other with that property. It might be suggested that FF is an intermediate ground and FC the ultimate ground; but that suggestion is confused, or uses a different intermediate/ultimate distinction. If it were correct, FF would be grounded directly or indirectly in FC. That consequent is false and the contractualist need not assert it; Scanlon's thesis is simply that the principle of fidelity is a principle of the kind mentioned in the description of FC.[134]

3.6 The fact of agreement as ground of a performance obligation

Recall:

(45) If (2) then X is obligated that X does Ax.
(50) X's obligation in (45) is a moral performance obligation,

(2) being the proposition that X and Y agree that (1) X does Ax and Y does Ay. In response to the argument that (45) and (50) together imply a falsehood, I proposed that (50) be qualified. An alternative would be to reject (45). There is, it may be said, no obligation, let alone a moral obligation, to perform an agreement as such:[135] the contrary view is at

130 On rule-utilitarianism, see B. Hooker (1990); B. Hooker (2011); Lyons (1965), chap. 4; Norcross (2011), 221 ff.; J. Sobel (1968).

131 See R. Audi (1996).

132 See D. Ross (1930), chap. 2; D. Ross (1939), 82 f.

133 See Scanlon (1982); Scanlon (1998), esp. chap. 5. Scanlon (2001), 91 talks of the validity of principles as having grounds. On contractualism generally, and the distinction between it and contractarianism, see Darwall (2003).

134 The confusion here is similar to, but not the same as, the one identified in n. 29 above.

135 Compare Atiyah (1986c), 38 ff.; Atiyah (1986e), 150. For the parallel view of promises, see Atiyah (1986l), 2 ff., and, in relation to legal obligation, Atiyah (1981), chaps. 1 f.

worst a form of fetishism and at best a useful fiction – its utility being that, if people believe it, they take seriously those cases where there is a performance obligation, whether or not they rightly identify its ground.[136] I have suggested, however, that:

(56) If (2) then FA grounds an obligation on X to do Ax,[137]

FA being the fact that (2). If (56) is true then, as noted in section 3.4, so is (45). The explanation why FA grounds X's obligation is that the rule of obligation – that the parties to an agreement are obligated to perform it – is constitutive of agreement: see sections 2.2 and 2.5. To pursue the analogy in section 2.2, the explanation is analogous to the explanation why, in the game of Snakes and Ladders, the fact that a player puts his counter on the head of a snake grounds a requirement on him to move it to the end of the snake's tail:[138] there the explanans is that the rule imposing the requirement is constitutive of the game. (56) and the rule are like (45) in being subject to the provisos granted in section 3.3, that the obligation has not ceased and that the case is normal; likewise FA, more fully specified, is the fact that <(2) and no sufficient condition for

For the thesis that there is no moral obligation to comply with a contract, see Holmes (2005), 235, 324 ff., discussed in Atiyah (1986i).

136 Atiyah (1986f), 108 ff. proposes a somewhat similar view of contractual obligation: what Atiyah calls the 'substantive reason' to perform is a benefit or induced reliance, but the existence of the contract is a 'formal reason' to hold that the benefit is worth the performance or that the reliance is reasonable. The formal reason operates as a presumption which may be irrebuttable or rebuttable. See also Atiyah (1981), chap. 7.

137 Compare Prichard (2002f), 257 on promises: 'Once call some act a promise and all question of whether there is an obligation to do it seems to have vanished'. See also Gilbert (2004), 84; McMahon (1989), 239 on the view, which McMahon attributes to Raz, that the connection between promising and obligation is immediate; Tuomela (1995), 241, maintaining that it is constitutive of the notion of agreement that an agreement creates an obligation for the parties. S. Smith (2005), 93, says that '[i]n ordinary morality, a promise or agreement is usually considered binding simply by virtue of being a promise or agreement'; the mention of ordinary morality suggests that the obligation is itself moral. See further ibid., 167 ff. on strict liability in the English law of contract (and contrast the position in French law: Nicholas (1992), 31). Gordley (1991) attributes a similar view of promises to Wolff (75 f.), and of contracts to Hobbes, Locke and various nineteenth-century jurists (116 f., 163). Some writers have held that a contract does not ground an obligation but merely provides a remedy; for objections to that view, see Whittaker (2008), paras. 1–019 f.; para. 1–021 surveys the limits of the 'binding force' of contracts. See further nn. 146 f. below.

138 Talk of obligations, rather than requirements, is usually out of place for games; Brandt would explain this by saying that games do not have the features that ground the paradigmatic use of 'obligation' (see section 3.1 above). On the relation between obligation and requirement, see n. 10 above.

the cessation of a performance obligation on X obtains and the case is normal>.

There are two objections to (56) and two to the explanation why FA grounds X's obligation.[139] I start with the latter. One of them is that, as the analogy with games indicates, the explanation trivialises X's obligation if the obligation is grounded only in FA.[140] A reply is that, if it is trivial, the triviality does not matter,[141] as in many cases X has a moral performance obligation grounded in some other fact: see section 3.4. There are, however, reasons to deny the charge of triviality. The analogy with games is no more than that: Snakes and Ladders is a childish pastime, but agreements, as noted at the start of this book, form one of the main types of social bond. Without the co-operation that performed agreements instantiate, we would be much closer to a state of nature.[142] That is not to say that every agreement benefits society; cartels and conspiracies, discussed respectively in Chapters 8 and 9, are counterexamples. (It might be claimed that in any event these agreements fall among the abnormal cases to which (56) does not apply; but cartels and conspiracies are abnormal only by a standard of normality so strict that it trivialises the claim.) The objector might grant the importance of agreements to society but maintain that it is compatible with the triviality of a performance obligation on X that is grounded only in FA: important things have trivial aspects. The reply, in outline, is that such obligations are important because they explain the social importance of agreements. The explanation, which I shall not develop, refers to deontological reasoning, mentioned in

139 Compare the literature on Searle's derivation of 'ought' from 'is': Hudson (1969); Mackie (1977), 66 ff.; Searle (1967); Searle (1969), chap. 8.

140 A frequent objection has been that Searle failed to derive a moral obligation (see previous n.): Robins (1976), 329. On the non-moral character of institutional or 'positional' obligations, see J. Cameron (1972), 318; Cavell (1979), 307 ff.; Christiano and Sciaraffa (2003), 500; Downie (1985), 259 ff. (citing A. Smith (1976), 332 f. on the distinction between the ethical and the jurisprudential points of view); L. Green (1988), 211; Horton (1992) 155 ff.; Simmons (1979), 21; Stocker (1970); Tunick (2002), 468. Compare Williamson (2000), 240 f. on the non-moral nature of the normativity of constitutive rules.

141 Searle himself writes that 'the obligation to keep a promise probably has no necessary connection with morality': Searle (1969), 188. Robins (1984), 107 ff. argues that promissory obligation is moral even if the promise is trivial; B. Williams (1993), 187 appears to take the same view. See further Chap. 1 n. 78 above.

142 On the role of promises in sustaining society, see Hume (1963), 467; Knapp (1984), 951. On co-operation, see Axelrod (1984); Axelrod (1997); Bratman (1999d); Luce and Raiffa (1989), 89; Owens (2011); Skyrms (1996), 59 ff.; M. Taylor (1987); M. Zimmerman (1992); M. Zimmerman (1996), chap. 9.

section 3.51 and developed in section 4.21, that would lead X, if he were rational, to perform.

It might be argued, perhaps in rule-utilitarian terms, that a performance obligation on X grounded only in FA is not only important but moral.[143] The version of rule-utilitarianism would need to allow – unlike the one mentioned in section 3.52 – that X's performance obligation may have a ground other than the fact that X's doing Ax is required by some rule obedience to which would maximise utility, for that fact is distinct from FA. More generally, the version would need to be weak, for it is implausible to think that agreements non-trivially maximise anything, let alone happiness.[144] (Section 6.3 discusses consequential but non-maximising reasons for the state to enforce or promote certain agreements.) It is debatable whether a performance obligation on X, grounded only in FA, has the five characteristics that Brandt proposes as features of moral obligation: matter of conscience, community-wide support, reflection on character, matter of principle, and high stringency (see section 3.1). As to the last, for example, it might be held that, even if the obligation is important in the respect stated above, it is not stringent. The question is hard to settle, for, as Brandt admits,[145] his description of the characteristics is vague.

The second objection runs as follows. The explanandum is that FA grounds X's performance obligation. Its puzzling feature is that X is bound: FA binds him to do Ax. This is the normative feature of being bound, not the psychological one of feeling bound: see section 3.1. The explanans, that the rule of obligation is constitutive of agreement, works only if it implicitly includes the proposition that X is bound in another respect – by the rule. Therefore the explanation is shallow because the puzzling feature of the explanandum recurs in the explanans.[146]

Various replies are available. One is that the explanans is adequate as stated: there is no need to add that X is bound by the rule. The objector

143 Compare the two-level theory in Raz (1977), 219 and the 'practice' conception of rules in Rawls (1967), 162 ff. At 144 n. 3, Rawls gives citations for the distinction between justifying a practice and justifying an action falling under it. See also MacCormick (1982), 206 f. for a rule-utilitarian account of obligations arising from purely executory promises (criticised in Atiyah (1981), 30 ff.); McMahon (1989), 239.

144 How implausible it is to claim that agreements maximise happiness depends on the parameters of maximisation and the breadth of the definition of happiness. See O. Black (2005b), chap. 2; Sumner (1996).

145 Brandt (1964), 382.

146 There are objections of this nature in Cavell (1979), 307; Robins (1984), 9 f., 125 ff. See also Gordley (1991), chaps. 7, 9.

might retort that, if that is true, it is so only because the explanans already entails that the rule binds X: if the rule is constitutive of agreement, anyone who agrees is bound by the rule. A second reply is that the explanandum as stated does not mention X's being bound; but the objector might say that X's having a performance obligation entails that X is bound to perform. A third is that different senses of 'bind' are at issue in explanandum and explanans:[147] since the rule binds X merely in the weak sense that it applies to him, it is in that respect no different from the non-mandatory constitutive rules of agreement that were described in section 2.2. The objector might now say that in that case the explanans is inadequate.

The objection assumes that an explanation is shallow if the puzzling feature of the explanandum recurs in the explanans. If 'shallow' is so defined that a shallow explanation is inadequate, the assumption is false; if not, the objection is harmless. Suppose that you want to know why domino 1 fell over. An adequate explanation, at least in some contexts, is that domino 2 fell over and in so doing knocked domino 1. You may go on to seek an explanation why domino 2 fell over, but this possibility does not undermine the first explanation.[148] As to the explanation of FA's grounding X's performance obligation, it is plausible to think that bindingness cannot be explained in other terms,[149] in which case the recurrence is

147 It is used in various senses and sometimes with no clear sense. Atiyah has a strong one in mind when he claims that promises are binding only in so far as the practice of promising is a fair one and operates in a fair society: Atiyah (1981), 112. Compare Rawls (1972), 343 on bindingness as presupposing the principle of fairness. L. Green (2002), 518 f. says that obligations are binding by virtue of being categorical and exclusionary. See section 3.2 above for discussion of exclusionary reasons. By 'categorical' Green means that an obligation applies to X independently of X's interests or goals; this is close to the second of the three features of obligation identified in Gilbert (2006): n. 12 above. See further Gilbert (2000c), 71; Gilbert (2006), 189, 196 f.; Raz (1977), 223. On the binding force of contracts, see Kötz (1997), 4, which blurs the distinction between the bindingness of contracts and that of agreements; Whittaker (2008), paras. 10–19 ff. On bindingness as a matter of degree, see n. 89 above.

148 On infinite regresses of explanation, see O. Black (1987), 187 ff.; P. Brown (1966), 522; Post (1980), 40 ff.

149 A different but related point is that it is no condition, on the adequacy of an explanation of something normative, that the explanans be in purely non-normative terms. One project is to try to explain bindingness in terms of commitment: see Cavell (1979), 307; Robins (1984), chap. 1; Winch (1972), 70 f. J. Cameron (1972), 318 talks in terms of the will. Fried (1981), 13 claims that the 'convention' of promising enables a person to commit himself by a promise. On commitment generally, see O. Black (2002); Blustein (1991); Liebermann (1998), 5; Peter and Schmid (2007). On commitments as protected reasons, see Raz (1990), 190 ff.; on protected reasons generally, section 3.2 above. On commitments within systems of constitutive rules, see Searle (1967), 113.

unavoidable. Nevertheless, the explanation is illuminating, as it articulates the connection – via a constitutive rule – between agreement and obligation.[150]

Of the two objections to (56), the first is this. FA is not a complete ground, as it is not a sufficient condition, of an obligation on X to do Ax: the further fact (FR) is needed that X recognises what was called, in section 2.4, the device of agreement.[151] If FA and FR both exist, there exists the conjunctive fact that <(2) and X recognises the device of agreement>;[152] this fact is a complete ground, and FA and FR, being parts of it, are partial grounds, of such an obligation. But, in some cases where (2) is true, X does not recognise the device. In such cases FR and hence the conjunctive fact do not exist. In some of those cases there exists no other complete ground, and hence FA is not a partial ground, of such an obligation. Therefore (56) is false, whether it concerns a complete ground or only a partial one.

To say that X recognises the device of agreement may be to say that X genuinely agrees. For example, if he recognises the device and says 'I offer . . . ', then, first, he is not merely pretending to offer and, second, if he offers only if he intends to do so (a thesis entertained in section 5.15), he has that intention. On this reading, the objection fails because one of its premisses is self-contradictory: there can be no case in which, although (2) is true, X does not accept the device, for in such a case X would both agree and not agree. On another reading, the statement that X recognises the device of agreement means that he holds a favourable attitude towards agreements.[153] His holding or not holding that attitude is irrelevant to his having an obligation to do Ax; in particular, there is no reason to think

On the obligations arising from joint commitments, see Gilbert (2000a), which argues that agreements are joint commitments. On commitment as an inadequate source of contractual obligation, see Gordley (1991), 244. On promise as commitment, see Chap. 1 n. 26 above; on acceptance as commitment, Chap. 8 n. 68 below.

150 To apply the pleasing analogy in L. Green (2002), 527: the fact that two rooms rest on the foundations of one house does not show that one can enter the second without passing through the first.

151 See Christiano and Sciaraffa (2003), 500, 507; Gilbert (2006), 41 f. (on 'imputed' obligations); Mackie (1977), 67 ff.; Robins (1976), 329 ff.; Searle (1969), 190 f. R. Adams (1999), 243 notes that qualifiers such as 'institutional' and 'official' are sometimes used to indicate that one does not morally endorse the obligation in question.

152 If FA is more fully specified, as above, to include the provisos, the conjunctive fact is that <(2) and no sufficient condition for the cessation of a performance obligation on X obtains and the case is normal and X recognises . . . >.

153 Compare Searle (1969), 194 ff.

that, if he holds it, the fact that he does so is a partial ground of such an obligation. Again, therefore, the objection fails.

Suppose that X offers to Y that (1), Y accepts, the other conditions for agreement (CM and CS in propositions (36) and (37) (section 2.1)) are met, X fails to perform, Y complains, and X replies that he rejects the rule of obligation and hence Y's complaint. It might be said that here X does not recognise the device of agreement. But X has a performance obligation, from which his reply does not release him, and so the example fails to show that FA is not a ground of that obligation. Suppose now that Y reminds X of his obligation and that X replies 'I reject your concept of agreement. On my concept, there is no constitutive rule of obligation'. He is thus like someone who proposes a feeble form of Snakes and Ladders, in which the players move their counters along the squares according to the number on the die but ignore the ladders and snakes. Here too it might be said that X does not recognise the device of agreement; but his reply misses its mark. It can be granted that a device of 'sub-agreement' may be specified by dropping the rule of obligation, and that if X sub-agrees to do Ax he is not ipso facto obligated to do Ax; but whether or not X sub-agrees, or takes himself or intends to be merely sub-agreeing, he also agrees to do Ax; so the rule of obligation applies and he thus has the obligation. If he intends only to sub-agree, he does not intend to agree; but it will be shown in section 5.12 that a person can agree without intending to. Again, therefore, the example fails to establish that FA is not a ground of the obligation.

The other objection to (56) is that it misses the fundamental obligation to 'play the game' of agreement.[154] Here, the objection goes, the analogy with ordinary games breaks down – there being no obligation, say, to play Snakes and Ladders.[155] If the alleged obligation is to perform agreements,

154 Compare Vitek (1986) on Hume's theory of promising. On the distinction between obligations imposed by rules and the obligation to play by the rules, see Robins (1976), 331; Christiano and Sciaraffa (2003), 506 ff., where it is used to impugn the theory in Coleman (2001), esp. chaps. 7 and 11, that legal obligation is explained by law's being a 'shared cooperative activity' in the sense proposed in Bratman (1999a), pt. 2.

155 Whether there is a requirement to continue playing an unfinished game may depend on the game's rules. If, for example, they include a constitutive rule requiring play to continue till one player wins, the structure is the same as that identified for the performance obligation grounded in FA: a requirement is grounded in the fact that the player is playing the game; the grounding is explained by the rule's being constitutive of the game; and there may also be a moral obligation, grounded in some other fact (perhaps to do with the other player's reliance), to continue playing. In the case of a game, the moral obligation is likely to be weak – i.e., in Raz's terminology explained in

it is not missed by (56), which concerns the ground of X's performance obligation. If it is to make agreements, without more, the analogy holds, as no such obligation exists.[156] In certain circumstances – for example, where a negotiator is instructed to reach a deal – a person is obligated to make an agreement: (56) misses such obligations, and any other obligation alleged to be at issue, in the sense that it says nothing about them. That is no objection, for (56) concerns a different obligation.

section 3.2 above, to exclude few conflicting reasons. The game's rules might however include, in place of that rule, the non-mandatory one that whichever player meets a certain condition is the winner. The version of Snakes and Ladders on the website of the Museum of Childhood is of that kind: 'the game ends when a throw lands a player exactly on 100'. Absent any other ground in such a case, there is no requirement to continue playing.

156 Compare M. Zimmerman (1996), 146 on the absence of an unconditional requirement to make a commitment.

4

Practical reason

Section 2.4 stated that an agreement is a device for enabling rational self-interested parties to benefit from each other's actions, and that the main mechanism for achieving the relevant benefits is the parties' reasoning to the making and the performance of the agreement and their acting on the conclusions of that reasoning. The present chapter analyses reasoning that would lead rational X and Y to make an agreement with each other that:

(1) X does Ax and Y does Ay,

and the reasoning that, once they have made the agreement, would lead them to perform it.[1] Such reasoning may be instrumental or deontological or fall within some other category, and each party may reason in more than one way. Instrumental reasoning is available to parties who are self-interested, but, as noted in section 2.4, a person who is narrowly and exclusively self-interested will not be moved by deontological considerations as such. He may however be concerned, say, to perform an obligation if to do so is a means of promoting his interests, in which case his instrumental reasoning may refer to the obligation.

4.1 Making the agreement

The benefits to X may flow either simply from Y's doing Ay or from the combination of Y's doing Ay and X's doing Ax. An example of the first case is an agreement of sale: if X and Y agree that Y sells his car to X for £500, it is no benefit to X to part with the money, but he benefits from Y's transferring the ownership of the car. An example of the second is an

1 O. Black (2004a), 89 ff. and O. Black (2005b), 111 ff. give accounts of such reasoning in the context of the promise model of agreement.

agreement for solving a co-ordination problem:[2] if they agree to meet on the steps of St Paul's at noon, X benefits from their both being there at that time, but he would not benefit from Y's turning up alone.

4.11 *Desired performance by the other party*

In the first case, each party may reason according to the schema of instrumental reasoning:

(69) (a) I want that P.
(b) The best means to its being the case that P is for me to φ.
(c) Other things are equal.
So:
(d) I will φ.[3]

Normally, someone who reasons according to (69) has a desire that P, beliefs that (a), that (b) and that (c), and an intention that (d); more strictly, he has mental states the contents of which respectively have those forms.[4] It can be assumed that those states are propositional attitudes; as

2 On co-ordination problems, see Gilbert (2006), 33, 205 f.; D. Lewis (1969), chap. 1; McMahon (1989), 244; Schelling (1980), 89 ff.; S. Smith (2004), 188, 192; Ullmann-Margalit (1977), 77 ff.

3 (69) modifies the schema (PR) in O. Black (2004a), 90 and O. Black (2005b), 113. It is similar to the schema of best-means reasoning in Broome (2002), 107: the main differences are that Broome takes the reasoner to intend one of the premisses and that (69) contains the premiss that other things are equal. (Reasoning from intention is considered in section 4.3 below.) At 108 Broome notes the need to explicate the notion of the best means. (69) is similar in other respects to the schema for practical reasoning in R. Audi (1989), 99, the main difference being that the conclusion in Audi's schema is normative: 'I should φ'. For strictures on the detachment of normative conclusions in means-end reasoning, see the works by Broome cited in Chap. 1 n. 82 above.

4 On some accounts of practical reasoning, it does not conclude in an intention; Audi's is a case in point. Bratman (1987), 152 ff. maintains that it concludes in a choice, but Bratman also says 'One's choice in favour of an overall scenario will involve one's coming to have some intentions or others' (155) and 'one's choosing an overall scenario will itself involve one's coming to have dispositions characteristic of certain intentions' (160). It is unclear what Bratman takes the relation between these two formulations to be. See also Bratman (1990), 29. Raz (1990), 28 holds that a practical inference concludes with a 'there is a reason to' statement or an 'ought' statement. On the relation between intentions and ought-judgments, see McPherson (2009), 64 ff.; Wedgwood (2007), 25 ff. Anscombe (1974), 19 says that 'the conclusion of a practical syllogism is an action or decision'. Aristotle, according to certain commentators, holds that the practical syllogism issues in action: see Broome (2001b), 175 and contrast R. Audi (1989), 17 ff.; the evidence is reviewed in Charles (1984), 90 ff. Central passages in the controversy are Aristotle (1912), 701a; Aristotle (1962), 1147a25 ff. For surveys of the philosophy of practical reasoning, see Millgram (2001); Raz (1978).

noted in the Introduction, the assumption is convenient but eliminable. 'I want that P' in (a) makes it explicit in the case of desire; the formulation is unidiomatic, but 'I desire that P' is good English and no distinction is drawn here between wanting and desiring (but see below).

Adopting concepts from Broome, I say that reasoning from beliefs that (a)–(c) to an intention that (d) is correct in the sense that the set of mental states of the reasoner that have the premisses as contents 'normatively requires' his mental state with the conclusion as content, this in turn meaning that the reasoner ought to see to it that if he has those states then he has this one.[5] (If it is objected that a set of mere beliefs cannot normatively require an intention, the reply in essence – I shall not develop the point – is that the difficulty is removed by the nature of the beliefs' contents, and in particular by the fact that (a) concerns a desire of the reasoner.) By contrast, the following theoretical meta-reasoning, in which each step is believed by the reasoner, is incorrect: X believes that (a); X believes that (b); X believes that (c); so X intends that (d). Beliefs with those premisses as contents do not normatively require a belief that X intends that (d); for X might himself violate a normative requirement, in believing that (a)–(c) while failing to intend that (d).[6]

It is plausible also to say, using another idea of Broome's, that reasoning from beliefs that (a)–(c) to an intention that (d) is made correct by the 'formal' relations between (a)–(d); but so far that is only a label. 'Formal' covers more than logical validity, for '(a)–(c); therefore (d)' is not logically valid.[7] Validity (a matter of the relations between the contents of the reasoner's mental states) is thus not necessary for correctness (a matter of the relations between the states themselves[8]). Nor is it sufficient: for example, 'P; if P then Q; so Q' is valid, but a desire that P and a belief that if P then Q do not normatively require an intention that Q, and so it is incorrect to reason from the desire and the belief to the intention.[9]

'Means', in (b) and elsewhere, is limited to means available to the reasoner; there is no need here to develop an analysis of availability. (b) is

5 Broome (2000); Broome (2001a); Broome (2001b); Broome (2002) (which builds correctness into the definition of reasoning); Broome (2004). The 'see to' locution is used also in Feldman (1986), 37.

6 Compare Broome (2001a); Broome (2002), 87 f.; contrast von Wright (1978).

7 Compare Broome (2001b), 182.

8 On the distinction of levels, compare Broome (2002), 89. The distinction is obscured in Broome (2000), 81, which talks of normative relations between propositions and uses the form 'P requires Q'; but see ibid., 79.

9 Broome (2002), 90 ff. uses a different counterexample.

a strong premiss, as 'the best', in the intended sense, entails uniqueness: only one means can be the best, but more than one can be good or good enough.[10] It might be suggested that, if 'a good' or 'a good enough' is substituted for 'the best', the corresponding reasoning in accordance with the revised (69) is also correct. Those variants, and a weaker reading of 'the best' in which it covers ties for first place, raise the question – which I shall not pursue – how the reasoner decides to φ rather than to do one of the alternatives, where they exist.

Premiss (c), which will be important in section 6.211, is needed to exclude, inter alia, cases of outweighing – as where, in a simple case, the reasoner wants that P less than he wants not to φ. An intuitive concept of outweighing includes considerations of probability, so that a weak desire may outweigh a stronger one if the former is, or is believed by the reasoner to be, much more likely than the latter to be fulfilled. (On the relation between instrumentality – i.e., the means-end relation – and probability, see below (this section and section 4.22); the topic arises also in sections 6.211 and 6.3. If it is objected that there are various means-end relations, 'the means-end relation' can be read as signifying their disjunction.) Without an informative description of the kinds of 'thing' that need to be equal, (c) makes the schema fairly trivial, but that does not matter for the present purpose.

Suppose that X is the potential offeror. A natural way to represent his reasoning in accordance with (69) is:

(70) I want that Y does Ay.
(71) The best means to Y's doing Ay is for me to offer to Y that <I do Ax and he does Ay>.
(72) Other things are equal.
So:
(73) I will offer to Y that <I do Ax and he does Ay>.

For brevity I give a separate number to the indexical[11] variant of (1) in (71) and (73):

(74) I do Ax and he does Ay.

10 On reasoning about the good enough, see Byron (1998); Byron (2004); Simon (1957); Simon (1978); Simon (1983); Slote (1990), 471. Another suggestion is to substitute 'a necessary', but then the reasoning is correct only if the reasoner assumes the proposition – which (c) could be read as including – that whatever other conditions are necessary are also met.

11 On indexicals, see n. 15 to the Introduction above.

To take the example from section 4.1, X reasons: I want Y to transfer to me the ownership of his car; the best means to his doing so is for me to offer to Y that I pay him £500 and he transfers the ownership to me; other things are equal; so I will make the offer. The example was introduced in terms of benefits, whereas (70) concerns a desire.[12] 'Benefit' can be given a thin sense in which a person benefits if he fulfils any of his desires, either because the thing desired or because the fulfilment of the desire is a benefit in that sense: compare the example of the drug addict, in section 2.4.[13] The converse, however, is false: something may benefit someone without his desiring it in any sense. (There is arguably a loose sense in which a person 'wants' everything that benefits him; compare 'You want to turn right at the traffic lights'. If so, this is a point at which 'want' and 'desire' are not interchangeable.) For simplicity's sake, however, I shall pretend here that benefits and the objects of desire coincide. (The distinction is applied in section 6.2111.)

Once X, having reasoned from (70)–(72) to (73), has made his offer, Y may reason:

(75) I want that X does Ax.
(76) The best means to X's doing Ax is for me to accept X's offer.
(72) Other things are equal.
So:
(77) I will accept X's offer.

For either party to reason in this way, he must first establish the relevant instance of (69)(b) (the best means to its being the case that P is for me to φ). In each case the argument has three main steps. For X they are: if I offer then Y does Ay; my offering is a means to Y's doing Ay; my offering is the best means to Y's doing Ay. A weaker variant of the first step would use a relation of conditional probability rather than the simple conditional. In its present form, the step – which itself covers three moves, from offer to acceptance, from acceptance to agreement and from agreement to Y's doing Ay – is made from premisses (78)–(84):

12 The distinction is blurred in Atiyah (1981), 142 ff.

13 Compare also the point, in Chap. 3 n. 112 above, that it is in only a thin sense of 'harm' that a person suffers harm if he fails to achieve one of his goals.

(78) If:
 (a) I offer to Y that (74); and
 (b) condition C1 obtains;
 then Y accepts my offer.

C1 excludes such possibilities as that Y does not want to make an agreement, at least on the terms offered by X, that he is unaware of X's offer, that he is mentally or physically unable to accept, and so on. (78) is underpinned, in the following sense, by Y's reasoning (75)–(76)–(72)–(77): (78) follows from the assumption that, first, if (a) and (b) are true then Y carries out that reasoning and, second, the intention that (77), in which Y's reasoning concludes, is reliable in the sense that if Y forms it then he acts on it.

(79) C1 obtains.
(80) If:
 (a) I offer to Y that (74);
 (b) Y accepts my offer; and
 (c) C2 obtains;
 then I and Y agree that (74).

C2 covers the same matters as CM and CS in the offer–acceptance analysis ((36) and (37) (section 2.1)); for example, it excludes the possibility that X withdraws the offer before Y accepts it.

(81) C2 obtains.
(82) If:
 (a) I and Y agree that (74);
 (b) C3 obtains; and
 (c) Y is reliable;
 then Y does Ay.

C3 excludes various contingencies that would justify Y in omitting to do Ay; they overlap those, discussed in section 3.3, that prevent him from being obligated to do Ay. (c), which ensures that, absent such contingencies, Y performs, is underpinned in the following sense by Y's reasoning, in one of the ways described in sections 4.2–4.22, from his agreeing to do Ay to his doing Ay: (c) follows from the assumption that, first, if (a) and (b) are true then Y carries out that reasoning and, second, the intention in which the reasoning concludes is itself reliable in the sense that if Y forms it then he acts on it. Read thus, (c) is a narrow claim relating only to the present agreement; in practice X is likely to believe that Y is reliable in a wider range of situations. The same applies to the assumption above that Y's intention that (77) is reliable. Two points have now been identified at which X's reasoning is underpinned by Y's. Y's reasoning is correspondingly underpinned by X's, but there is no vicious circle:[14] the point is simply that each party may base his premisses on further assumptions about the other's reasoning and behaviour.

The final two premisses of the first step in X's reasoning are:

(83) C3 obtains.
(84) Y is reliable.

It follows that:

(85) If I offer to Y that (74), then Y does Ay.

The second step is from (85) to:

(86) A means to Y's doing Ay is for me offer to Y that (74).

Unless artificial meanings are in play, there is no entailment in either direction between (85)'s generalisation – 'If I φ then P' – and (86)'s, 'A means to its being the case that P is for me to φ'. Nevertheless it seems clear that (85) can be supplemented so as to entail (86). The additional premisses needed depend on the nature of instrumentality, an issue that will not be pursued here;[15] the obvious approach is to analyse it in terms of causation or constitution (as to which, see sections 1.1 and 2.1). Let the relevant instances of those premisses, whatever exactly they are, be granted to X.[16]

The final step of X's reasoning is from 'means' to 'best means':

(87) No other means to Y's doing Ay is at least as good as my offering to Y that (74).

(71) (the best means to Y's doing Ay is for me to offer to Y that <I do Ax and he does Ay>) follows from (86) and (87) on the assumption

14 On circularity, see Chap. 2 n. 69 above.
15 For an introductory discussion, see R. Audi (1989), 30 ff.
16 This approach will be judged cavalier by someone who takes instrumentality to be quite different from conditionality. Such a person might, for example, hold that the former is a kind of causation and that causation cannot be analysed in terms of conditionality. On the latter claim, see Menzies (2008); Sosa and Tooley (1993). As mentioned in Chap. 2 n. 58 above, D. Lewis (1986) gives a theory of causation in terms of counterfactual conditionals.

that other means are commensurable, in respect of their goodness, with X's making the offer; there is no need here to amplify the relevant concepts of commensurability and goodness.[17] In some situations there is redundancy of means, whether in the form of overdetermination or of pre-emption: roughly, there is overdetermination where two independent means are present, pre-emption where one is present but, if it were not, the other would be.[18] (Such cases could be excluded by a narrow definition of means. Overdetermination and pre-emption arise again in section 6.211.) In such a situation (87) is false if the other means is at least as good.

Y's reasoning to (76) (the best means to X's doing Ax is for me to accept X's offer) is similar. It likewise has three main steps: if I accept X's offer, then X does Ax; my accepting is a means to X's doing Ax; my accepting is the best means to X's doing Ax. The first step covers two moves: from acceptance to agreement and from agreement to X's doing Ax. The first step of each party's reasoning can be stated in abbreviated form, on the assumption (restricted as necessary) that the conditional is transitive.[19] X's reasoning is: if I offer then Y accepts; if Y accepts then we agree; if we agree then Y does Ay; so if I offer then Y does Ay. Y's reasoning is: if I accept then we agree; if we agree then X does Ax; so if I accept then X does Ax.

4.12 Desired performance by both parties

An economical proposal is to reuse, so far as possible, the account of the reasoning in the first case, where each party wants the other to perform, in order to analyse that in the second, where each wants both to perform. As regards X, a suggestion in this vein is to prefix to his reasoning an argument to (70) (I want that Y does Ay) from the premiss that he wants that <he does Ax and Y does Ay>. It might be objected that there is

17 On commensurability, see Broome (1978); Broome (1990b); Broome (1990c); Chang (1997); Seung and Bonevac (1992); Stocker (1990), chap. 7; M. Zimmerman (1996), 58.

18 On the forms of causal redundancy, see D. Lewis (1986), 199 ff.

19 On transitivity, see Chap. 3 n. 34 above. Strict implication (defined in section 1.22 above) is transitive: C. Lewis and Langford (1959), 125 (the 'Principle of the Syllogism'). Unrestricted transitivity does not hold for counterfactual conditionals: D. Lewis (1973), 32 ff.; Stalnaker (1991), 38. Consider also this counterexample, which I owe to Anthony Gottlieb, to the transitivity of indicative conditionals: if I go to the party with the Queen, I go to the party (necessarily true); if I go to the party, I go alone (contingently true); so, if I go to the party with the Queen, I go alone (necessarily false). On the philosophy of conditionals, see Chap. 1 n. 42 above.

no such thing as reasoning to a desire:[20] practical reasoning concludes in intention, theoretical reasoning in belief, tertium non datur. The objection is confused because, as noted in section 4.11, although (70) concerns a desire of X's, his reasoning in the previous section is from a belief that (70).[21] The required preliminary reasoning is thus theoretical reasoning which concludes in a belief.

In one version of the suggestion, X's preliminary reasoning runs:

(88) I want that <I do Ax and Y does Ay>.
(89) If I do Ax and Y does Ay, then Y does Ay.
So:
(70) I want that Y does Ay,

where X believes each of its steps. His reasoning then continues with (71)–(73). (88)–(89)–(70) instantiates:

(90) (a) I want that P.
(b) If P then Q.
So:
(c) I want that Q.

Reasoning from beliefs that (a) and that (b) to a belief that (c) is, normally at least, incorrect, for it may be that (a) and (b) are true but (c) false: I want to possess your watch; I shall possess it only if I steal it from you; but I do not want to steal it, as you are my friend and I know that you value it. It might be replied that I have a pro-tanto desire to steal it which is outweighed by a desire not to hurt you; but that is a contrived response, for in any normal sense of 'desire' I may well have no desire to steal the watch.[22] (90) could be saved by adding 'Other things are equal' to the premisses, but that would threaten the schema with vacuity. The objection is not to ceteris paribus clauses as such; otherwise it would apply also to (69)(c). Rather the point is that here the substantive content of the clause seems to amount to (90)(c): the things that have to be excluded are all things incompatible with the reasoner's wanting that Q.

20 Broome, in one of his Jacobsen lectures at the University of London in 2010, stated a doubt that there is any correct reasoning with desires.
21 Compare Broome (2002), 97 ff. on 'normative ascent'.
22 Alvarez may think that her thin sense of 'want' applies to such cases: Alvarez (2010), 55, 95, 119. They do not involve 'proper desires' in the sense explained in Schueler (1995), 49; Schueler (2003), chap. 2.

The qualification 'normally at least', at the start of the previous paragraph, allowed the possibility that, in special cases, reasoning from beliefs that (a) and that (b) to a belief that (c) is correct: an arguable example is 'I want that P; if P then P; so I want that P'. Against this it may be said to be in only an artificially thin sense of 'see to it' that the reasoner ought to see to it that if he believes the premisses then he believes the conclusion, for the conclusion is one of the premisses. The issue need not be pursued, for it is clear that, even if such special cases exist, they do not include X's reasoning from beliefs that (88) and that (89) to a belief that (70).

A simpler thought is that X may reason directly from a belief that (88) to a belief that (70) without using (89), according to the schema:

(91) (a) I want that <P and Q>.
So:
(b) I want that Q.

It might be objected that (91) can likewise lead from truth to falsity, for example in the case of complementary goods: I may want a pair of shoes without wanting a left shoe.[23] The objection confuses the desire for a left shoe with that for just a left shoe. On the plausible assumption that desire distributes over conjunction (see further section 5.31), it is also plausible to hold that, for any substitution instance of (91), reasoning from a belief with the premiss as content to a belief with the conclusion as content is correct. It might be suggested that the principle of distributivity is needed as a further premiss believed by the reasoner; but it makes no difference whether it is treated as a premiss or as a rule of inference.[24]

A still simpler thought is that there is no need to add preliminary steps to X's reasoning from (70), for his complete reasoning can conform to (69):

(88) I want that <I do Ax and Y does Ay>.

(92) The best means to its being the case that <I do Ax and Y does Ay> is for me to offer to Y that (74).

23 Compare the application of the 'entire contracts' rule by Sir George Jessel MR in *Re Hal & Barker* (1878) Ch D 538: 'if a shoemaker agrees to make a pair of shoes, he cannot offer you one shoe and ask you to pay half the price'.

24 On the folly of trying to represent every inference as a premiss, see Carroll (1895). Carroll's paradox is discussed in Russell (1979), 34 f.; Takahiro (1999); Winch (1958), 57.

(72) Other things are equal.
So:
(93) I will offer to Y that (74).

Y's reasoning to acceptance has the same form. As in the first case, X needs to establish the relevant instance of (69)(b), here (92). The main steps – I shall not pursue the details – correspond to those of the argument to (71): if I offer then <I do Ax and Y does Ay>; my offering is a means to this; my offering is the best means. It is no objection to (92) that, in order for it to be true that (1) X does Ax and Y does Ay, X must not only make the offer but also do Ax; for, on the relevant concept of 'best means', A's being the best means to B does not entail that A alone is enough for B. That is consistent with the assumption, in section 4.11, that 'the best' entails 'better than any other'.

4.2 Performing the agreement

Once X and Y have made an agreement, their positions are symmetrical (on the Symmetry criterion, see sections 1.2311 and 2.5), and so an analysis of the reasoning to performance need only consider one party. Suppose that:

(2) X and Y agree that (1).

X may use deontological or instrumental reasoning to reach an intention to do Ax.

4.21 Deontological reasoning

He may reason in accordance with the schema:

(94) (a) I am obligated to φ.
(b) Other things are equal.
So:
(c) I will φ,[25]

25 S. Smith (2005), 23 notes that parties often perform contracts because they believe they have a moral obligation to do so. (94) is the same as the schema (NR) in O. Black (2004a), 92 and O. Black (2005b), 114. The schema of normative practical reasoning in Broome (2001b), 181 is similar, but uses 'ought to' instead of 'am obligated to' and does not have

with preliminary reasoning to the relevant instance of (a), thus:

(95) I and Y agree that (74).
(96) If (95) then I am obligated to do Ax.
So:
(97) I am obligated to do Ax.
(72) Other things are equal.
So:
(98) I will do Ax.

X's reasoning (95)–(96)–(97)–(72)–(98) is correct if X intends that (98) and believes each of the other steps. (95) is an indexical variant of (2), and (96) of (45) (section 3.3). As with that proposition, (96) and (97) are to be read as subject to the provisos that the obligation has not ceased and that the case is normal. Those provisos could alternatively be taken to be covered by (72), which also accommodates the fact, noted in section 3.3, that an obligation can be outweighed.

He may otherwise reason in accordance with:

(99) (a) There is a reason for me to φ.
(b) Other things are equal.
So:
(c) I will φ,

with preliminary deontological reasoning to the relevant instance of (a). Section 3.2 explained that if X is obligated to do Ax then his obligation is grounded in a reason for him to do Ax; to be more accurate, the fact that he is so obligated is grounded in a fact which is an element of a triple, of <fact, agent, action-type>, which is a protected reason for him to do Ax. X may therefore reason as follows:

(95) I and Y agree that (74).
(96) If (95) then I am obligated to do Ax.
(100) If I am obligated to do Ax, then there is a ground of that obligation.
(101) If there is a ground of that obligation, then there is a reason for me to do Ax.

the provision that other things are equal; on the relation between *ought* and *obligation*, see Chap. 3 n. 87 above. Compare also principle 2 in M. Smith (1994), 12.

So:
(102) There is a reason for me to do Ax.
(72) Other things are equal.
So:
(98) I will do Ax.

As before, the reasoning is correct if X intends the final step and believes its predecessors. As to (100), it could be suggested that, although if X has an obligation to do Ax then there is a fact grounding the fact that he has it, there might not be a fact grounding the fact – if there is one – stated by X's words 'I have an obligation to do Ax'. This possibility is excluded by an assumption as to the indexical insensitivity of facts – that 'I φ', said by X, and 'X φs' state the same fact. (Compare the assumption, in the Introduction, that co-referring expressions are intersubstitutable in the specification of contents.) This assumption, which needs refinement, could be backed by a theory of facts[26] (see section 3.2).

Reasoning that leads to the application of (99) need not use the concept of obligation, but could instead directly invoke a fact that is a ground of X's obligation and hence a reason for X to do Ax. In that case the reasoning is only indirectly deontological. (It is directly so if the category of the deontological is taken to include reasons: the boundaries of the category are debatable. See further section 6.22.) Section 3.6 maintained that, subject to the provisos above, if (2) (X and Y agree that (1)) then one such fact is the fact that (2). X may therefore reason thus:

(95) I and Y agree that (74).
(103) If (95) then the fact that (95) is a reason for me to do Ax.
So:
(104) The fact that (95) is a reason for me to do Ax.
So:
(102) There is a reason for me to do Ax,

and so on as before. Again the reasoning is correct if X intends the final step and believes its predecessors. The move to (103), from the thesis that if (2) then the fact that (2) is a reason for X to do Ax, is secured by the above assumption of indexical insensitivity. If it is objected that only on

26 See Chap. 3 n. 37 above.

the assumption that 'the fact that (95)', in (103) and (104), has existential import does (102) follow, the answer is that the assumption is secured by the principle stated in section 3.2, that the fact that P exists if and only if P.

The correctness of reasoning in accordance with (99) is consistent with Broome's view that correct reasoning is a matter not of giving or discovering reasons but, as explained in section 4.11, of meeting normative requirements.[27] Beliefs that (99)(a) and that (99)(b) normatively require an intention that (99)(c); but, although (a) mentions a reason, neither the fact nor the belief that (a) need itself be a reason. (On the question whether reasons are facts or mental states, see sections 1.23 and 3.2.)

4.22 Instrumental reasoning

If X reasons instrumentally to performance, his reasoning may relate to the agreement at hand or to other agreements. In either case it may again follow (69) (I want that P; the best means to its being the case that P is for me to φ; other things are equal; so I will φ). Reasoning of the former type may be of three kinds: it may be based, as with X's reasoning to the offer, on the desire that Y perform or the desire that both parties perform; or it may be based on the desire to avoid certain consequences that would occur if X did not perform. The first kind runs:

(70) I want that Y does Ay.
(105) The best means to Y's doing Ay is for me to do Ax.
(72) Other things are equal.

27 Broome (2002), 92 f.; Broome (2004); see also Broome (2000); Broome (2001a). Broome explains the difference between a reason and a normative requirement by the ways in which they weaken an 'ought': a reason is an 'ought' weakened by being made pro-tanto; a normative requirement, an 'ought' weakened by being made relative. A reason is thus slack but absolute, whereas a normative requirement is strict but relative. X might have reasons to φ and other reasons not to φ, but whether he ought to φ is determined by the balance of considerations (see section 3.3 above). If X's φing normatively requires him to χ, he is subject to a conditional 'ought': he ought to see to it that if he φs then he χs (see section 4.11 above). Broome's thesis is most clearly supported by an example of theoretical reasoning. Suppose that X believes that P, from which Q can be validly inferred. It does not follow that he has reason to believe that Q – Q might be an absurdity – but his believing that P requires him to believe that Q, and hence he ought to see to it that if he believes that P then he believes that Q. On natural understandings of conditionality and compliance (see section 1.22 above), one way of complying with the requirement is for him to cease to believe that P. Contrast Alvarez (2010), 159, which maintains that the premisses of practical reasoning are reasons for which the agent performs the action in which the reasoning concludes.

So:
(98) I will do Ax.

Although 'the best' signifies uniqueness, (105) is compatible with premiss (71) (the best means to Y's doing Ay is for me to offer to Y that <I do Ax and he does Ay>) in X's reasoning to his offer, for the best means can change between the time before and the time after the offer.

For X to apply (69), he must first establish (105). Given that the parties' instrumental reasoning to the making of the agreement has already been set out at length (sections 4.11–4.12), X's reasoning here can be presented more briefly. The obvious course is for him to invoke Y's performance obligation:

(106) If I do Ax, then Y has an obligation to do Ay.
(107) If Y has that obligation, then Y does Ay.
So:
(108) If I do Ax, then Y does Ay.

(105) is reached by adding whatever premisses are needed to move from a proposition of the form 'If I φ then P' to one of the form 'My φing is the best means to its being the case that P': compare the step, in section 4.11, from (85) to (71).

It might be objected that, whether or not X does Ax, Y is obligated to do Ay: that is so because the fact that (2) – i.e., that X and Y agree that (1) X does Ax and Y does Ay – grounds an obligation on Y to do Ay, just as it grounds one on X to do Ax (see section 3.6). In that case, the objection runs, either (106) and (108) are false or the step from (108) to (105) is more problematic than the step from (85) to (71). A long reply would consider the concepts of conditionality and instrumentality at issue; a short one is that the objection ignores the proviso that the obligation has not ceased – which it normally does if X does not perform. (This reply could be refined by applying the discussion, in section 2.3, of the order of performance; see also the discussion of Interdependence, in section 1.2314.) As to (107), X may reach it in turn by an argument concerning deontological reasoning carried out by Y. In outline: if Y has the obligation, he recognises that he has it; if he recognises this, he carries out reasoning that relevantly instantiates (94) (I am obligated to φ; other things are equal; so I will φ) – i.e., (97)–(72)–(98) with 'Ay' substituted for 'Ax'; if he carries out that reasoning, he intends to do Ay; if he so intends, he does Ay; hence, if Y has the obligation, he does Ay.

Such reasoning does not fit all agreements. If, at the time X is considering whether to do Ax, he knows that Y has already done Ay, (105) is then true in at best only a thin sense of 'means'. Even if the agreement provides for X to do Ax before Y does Ay, Y may not be able to tell whether X has performed, in which case it may be false that if Y has an obligation to do Ay then he recognises that he has it. (Compare the discussion, in section 5.11, of the epistemic conditions for sincere agreement.) Even if he recognises that he has it, he will not carry out the deontological reasoning if he does not care about the obligation. Moreover (106)–(108) concern sufficient conditions, whereas in some cases the relations are merely probabilistic: compare the probabilistic variant, in section 4.11, of X's reasoning to the making of the agreement. If in those circumstances X carries out the reasoning described, believing the premisses and intending the conclusion, his reasoning is correct in the specified sense – the beliefs normatively require the intention – but it may be unsound in that at least some of the beliefs are false.

If X wants both himself and Y to perform, he may reason in a similar way, the first two premisses being:

(88) I want that <I do Ax and Y does Ay>.
(109) The best means to its being the case that I do Ax and Y does Ay is for me to do Ax.

The supplementary reasoning is also similar to that in the previous case, for the move from (105) to (109) is trivial.

The third kind of reasoning relating to the agreement at hand uses premisses to the effect that X wants to avoid certain consequences that would flow from his not performing and that the best means of avoiding them is for him to do Ax. If the agreement is a contract, the consequences may include legal remedies (see sections 6.211 and 7.1); in other cases, they may comprise either a rebuke from Y or other forms of social pressure. X's reasoning might begin:

(110) I want to avoid a rebuke.
(111) The best means to my avoiding a rebuke is for me to do Ax.

Supplementary reasoning to (111) may involve deontological considerations even though it is instrumental and even if X is narrowly and exclusively self-interested: if I do Ax, I perform an obligation; if I perform an obligation, I avoid a rebuke; so, if I do Ax, I avoid a rebuke; so, by the necessary additional premisses, the best means to my avoiding a rebuke is for me to do Ax. The first premiss of the supplementary reasoning can in turn be reached from propositions already mentioned: I and Y agree that (74); if we do, I have an obligation to do Ax; so I have an obligation to do Ax; if I do Ax, I perform that obligation; so, if I do Ax, I perform an obligation. Again, such reasoning does not fit certain cases, for example where no one cares whether or not X performs. (Section 3.3 entertained the possibility that, if Y does not want X to perform, X has no obligation to do so.)

The remaining case (which is also an instance of the previous kind of reasoning) relates to other agreements:

(112) I want to make agreements in future.
(113) The best means to my making future agreements is for me to do Ax.
(72) Other things are equal.
So:
(98) I will do Ax.

Supplementary reasoning, stated roughly, to (113) may run: I make future agreements if I maintain a reputation for trustworthiness in performing agreements; I maintain such a reputation if I do Ax; so I make future agreements if I do Ax; so my doing Ax is the best means to my making future agreements.[28]

As before, such reasoning does not fit all agreements. The supplementary premisses usually need to be diluted from strict conditionality into probability – in particular, normally X's doing Ax only makes it more likely, and perhaps not more likely than not, that he maintains a reputation for trustworthiness – and, even when they are reformulated in probabilistic terms, they may be false in some circumstances; for example, there may be some reason, unrelated to Ax, why X is certain to lose his reputation. As noted in section 4.11, there may be redundancy of means: for example, X is charming enough to persuade

28 Compare Morris (1991), 825 on promise-keeping as a way of preserving reputation. On concern for reputation as a motive for compliance with contracts, see Posner (2001), 52 and S. Smith (2005), 23; as obviating the need for a contract, see Kötz (1997), 7, which also considers pledges and securities as means of securing performance. At 14, Kötz argues that a concern for reputation may deter a party from negotiating a contract beyond a certain level of detail and, in the event of breach by the other party, from standing on his legal rights. See further Chap. 6 n. 13 below.

people to make agreements with him even if he has a bad reputation. If trusting to charm is at least as good a means as doing Ax, (113) is false.

4.3 Other types of reasoning

The foregoing discussion covers common types of correct reasoning to the making and the performance of agreements, but is not exhaustive: rational parties may be led by other considerations. Their reasoning to the making of an agreement need not be instrumental otherwise than in a thin sense. For example, they may make one because in doing so they perform a certain sort of expressive act:[29] in making an agreement to marry they may express their commitment to each other. It is plausible to hold that either the making of the agreement is a non-causal means to the expressive act or the making and the expression are identical, in which case the former is a means to the latter in only a limiting sense. (See section 2.1, on the 'in'/'by' distinction, and compare section 6.21 on identity as a limiting case of resultance.) Another possibility is that X reasons to the making of an agreement from a deontological premiss, perhaps to the effect that his social position or his relationship with Y obligates him to make it. If X is Y's closest friend and Y asks X to agree to look after Y's child if Y should die, X may agree to do so on the basis of an obligation of friendship, even though he does not want to.

Deontological reasoning has already been discussed in the case of performance (section 4.21), and expressive considerations may also apply there: those that lead a couple to agree to marry may likewise lead them to marry. A party may also reason to performance from a conditional intention which may be sufficient for his agreement to be sincere. For example, as explained in more detail in section 5.11, if (2) (X and Y agree that (1) X does Ax and Y does Ay) then, in certain circumstances, X's agreement is sincere if X has this intention: to do Ax if and only if he knows that Y does Ay. X may therefore reason thus:

(114) I will do Ax if and only if I know that Y does Ay.
(115) I know that Y does Ay.

29 On the mutual consistency of expressive and instrumental concerns, see Smart (1999) and works cited there.

So:

(98) I will do Ax.

The reasoning is correct if X believes that (115) and intends that (114) and that (98); and, in contrast to previous cases, (98) is entailed by (114) and (115).

Another situation is that in which X has a concern to be true to his word; this is distinct from the concern, mentioned in section 4.22, to maintain a reputation for trustworthiness. If X has a stringent conception of truth to one's word, he may perform even if he knows that Y has defaulted and even if Y's default has cancelled X's obligation to perform. X's reasoning to performance may be of a kind already considered – deontological if his thought is that it is obligatory to keep one's word, or instrumental if he wants to keep his word – or it may constitute an intermediate or compound case in which the concern is part of his self-ideal.[30]

4.4 Appendix: the possibility of agreements

A common form of philosophical question is how such-and-such is possible, where the thing at issue seems to exist but to be excluded by other things. We seem to have free will, but it seems to be excluded by the fact that our actions are causally determined; we seem to know about the external world, but knowledge seems impossible in the light of sceptical arguments; and so on.[31] A correct answer to such a question explains the possibility at issue. Here the question is how agreements are possible. It may seem that, in order for the practice of agreement to have arisen, people must first have agreed to abide by the practice, in which case there is a vicious circle or a vicious infinite regress.[32] (Section 2.65 considered the converse objection, that an agreement presupposes the practice.)

Amplified thus, the question embodies a fallacy of composition. The practice of agreement is the general making and performance of agreements. Even if, for any agreement, the question arises how it is possible,

30 On ideals and their connection with identity, see O. Black (2002), 22; Parfit (1984), 327 f.

31 Kant (1929) was concerned with the question how synthetic a priori knowledge is possible, i.e., how we can know certain non-analytic truths without appeal to experience. On analyticity, see the Introduction above. For a discussion of this form of philosophical question, see Nozick (1981), 8 ff.

32 On infinite regresses of explanation, see Chap. 3 n. 148 above; on infinite regresses generally, Chap. 2 n. 50 above and n. 35 below; on circularity, Chap. 2 n. 69 above.

there need be no further question as to the possibility of agreements generally. There is a parallel here to the cosmological argument for God's existence. In one of Aquinas's versions, the argument in essence is that, since there cannot be an infinite series or circle of causes and effects, there must have been a first cause, which was God.[33] Leibniz further maintained that there must be a sufficient reason not only for each member of the causal series, but for the series itself.[34] Whatever the merits of Leibniz's claim, the justification of its analogue here is unclear: if, for each agreement, it can be explained how that agreement is possible, there seems no room for an explanation, in addition, of the possibility of agreements in general. A variant of the response is to say that, although the question can be asked about, and an explanation given of, that possibility, their content is exhausted by that of questions and explanations concerning individual agreements.

The question can, however, be understood in terms of individual agreements. Suppose that two people recognise that they would benefit from an agreement with each other. How are they to reach a position from which the agreement can be made? An obvious thought is that one of them proposes they make the agreement and that the other says OK. But the proposal is an offer and the response an acceptance. In that case (granted the conditions in (36) and (37) (section 2.1)) there is a prior agreement about which the same question arises. These reflections point to the general proposition: parties make an agreement only if they first make an agreement to make that agreement. This proposition generates a vicious infinite regress.[35]

33 This is Aquinas's 'second way': Aquinas (1894), I, 15. Kenny (1969) surveys Aquinas's five ways. Hick (1971), chap. 3 is an introduction to versions of the cosmological argument.

34 Leibniz (1934a), 9; Leibniz (1934b), 32.

35 It bears some analogy to the claim in Prichard (2002f), 259 f. that the obligation to keep a promise derives from a prior general promise. (Prichard there says that 'promise' and 'agree' are 'equivalent': see Chap. 1 n. 9 above.) Prichard's claim, however, concerns the obligation, not the promise to which it attaches.

In the schema proposed in O. Black (1996b) for an infinite regress argument, the proposition answers to the premiss of 'generation': if a thing has the property F, it bears the relation *R* to a thing that has F. The other premisses in the schema are: 'existence', that something has F; 'linearity', that *R* has an irreflexive proper ancestral (this excludes circles of things bearing *R* to each other); and 'finitude', that there is no sequence with infinite range, each element of which has F and bears *R* to its successor. (On the distinction between an infinite sequence and a sequence with infinite range, see ibid., 100.) The argument proceeds by reductio ad absurdum to the negation of one of the premisses, by deriving a contradiction between the premiss of finitude and the other premisses. On infinite regresses, see Chap. 2 n. 50 above.

Agreements to agree are common enough and, as explained in section 5.4, are distinct from first-order agreements; but people rarely if ever agree to agree to agree, and agreements of still higher order seem a purely theoretical possibility. In any event, agreements to agree are not a universal precondition for the making of agreements. In order to reach a position from which to make an agreement, X and Y need not make a prior agreement:[36] X may simply make an offer to Y; if Y accepts the offer, then (granted condition CM in (36) (section 2.1)) they make an agreement. The same is true if it is conceded – against the argument in the last paragraph but one – that an explanation is needed for the possibility of the practice of agreement: X proposes to Y, or to a group, that they make agreements with each other; Y, or the group, accepts and they thereby make an agreement which applies to itself. This is the limiting case of a circle, but there seems nothing vicious about it. If some reason, perhaps invoking a paradox, is given to hold that an agreement cannot apply to itself, it can still be said that the agreement in question applies to every other agreement.

Of course this account is presumably mythical; a more realistic one is that the practice of agreement evolved from simpler arrangements: see section 2.65. (It was noted there that a practice can be more or less extensive, complex, articulated or entrenched. It was not denied that a practice of agreement exists; the point was that its existence does not follow from that of an agreement.) It is reasonable to think that a certain level of sociability and trust must exist among the relevant people in order for the practice to be started and sustained. That might be thought to call into question the thesis, in section 2.4, that the main function of agreements is to enable rational self-interested parties to benefit from each other's actions. But there is no conflict, for rational self-interest does not exclude sociability and trust.

Someone who finds these responses simplistic may press for an account of the processes that lead X to offer and Y to accept. But that has already been given in the description of the practical reasoning leading to the making of an agreement (sections 4.1–4.12 and 4.3). The objector may now ask how each party can be sure that, if the agreement were made, the other would perform: if a party lacks that confidence, he will not make an agreement (compare the point about trust). But that is false; people often make agreements when they are not sure of the other party's performance.

36 Nor need they negotiate: see von Mehren (1992), para. 129. On the boundary between negotiation and contract, see section 7.35 below.

(Again compare the discussion in section 5.11 of the epistemic conditions for sincere agreement.) In any case, each party may have good evidence of the other's reliability. In particular, X may have good evidence for (84); this might include evidence for the two assumptions identified, in section 4.11, in the specification of the sense in which (82)(c), which is the same as (84), is underpinned by Y's reasoning from his agreeing to do Ay to his doing Ay.

The objector may now say that, if an agreement is possible, it is possible for the parties to grasp the concept of agreement. Doubt is cast on that conditional by the argument in section 5.12 that one may agree without intending to, but even if the conditional is true it jeopardises its antecedent only if its consequent is moot. There are two questions here: the broader one – beyond the scope of this book – is how it is possible for anyone to grasp a concept;[37] the narrower, how the concept of agreement could have arisen. I shall assume that the concept is a human creation, but the response can be revised to accommodate the theory that concepts exist independently and are merely discovered. In theory someone could have dreamt up the concept of agreement, as one can invent a game: he might have said 'I define an agreement as follows', then stated the constitutive rules of agreement (see section 2.2), and then explained the purpose of the concept by identifying the advantages of making and performing agreements. The hypothesis is excluded if language itself presupposes an agreement; whether it is excluded if language presupposes a *tacit* agreement depends on whether a tacit agreement is an agreement, as to which see section 8.521.[38] In any event, this account, like that of an individual's instituting the practice of agreement, is presumably only theoretical; it is more likely that the concept developed gradually as the practice likewise developed. (Compare the discussion, in section 2.66, of the evolution of the concepts of offer and acceptance.) The processes may have been dialectically entwined, changes in the concept prompting changes in the practice and conversely.

37 See Chap. 2 n. 70 above.

38 On the difference between linguistic conventions and norms of 'quasi agreement', see Gilbert (1996h).

5

Intention and other topics

This chapter deals with various topics that have legal implications: the relations between agreement and intention; the conditions for the identity of agreements; the logical properties of agreement; agreement to agree; and agreement with oneself.

5.1 Intention

A question that will be important in the chapters on competition law and conspiracy law concerns the relation between, on the one hand, a person's offering, accepting or agreeing and, on the other, his intentions. The general question as to the place of intentions in speech acts was aired in section 1.1, and the final objection to the offer–acceptance model, in section 2.66, talked of an offeror's intention that the offer, upon acceptance, become binding. Consider again:

(1) X does Ax and Y does Ay.

The question now is which of the following conditionals are true:

(116) If X agrees with Y that (1), then X intends to do Ax.
(117) If X agrees with Y that (1), then X intends to agree with Y that (1).
(118) If X offers to Y that (1), then X intends to do Ax.
(119) If X offers to Y that (1), then X intends to offer to Y that (1).
(120) If Y accepts X's offer that (1), then Y intends to do Ay.
(121) If Y accepts X's offer that (1), then Y intends to accept X's offer that (1).

I assume for convenience a strict-implication analysis of the conditional: <if P then Q> if and only if it is not possible that both P and not Q. The type and strength of possibility can be left unspecified and the paradoxes of strict implication disregarded. (On the analysis of conditionality, see section 1.22. As noted there, this analysis can be reformulated in terms of truth values or in mixed terms, for example: 'If P then Q' is true if and only if it is not possible that both P is true and Q is false.) The conditionals will be taken to concern the acts, rather than the states, of agreement, offer and acceptance, but the discussion can be extended to the states, as normally there is an act if and only if there is a corresponding state: this point was made, as regards agreement, in section 2.1. Sections 8.12 and 8.122 will consider conditionals about compliance.

There are various kinds of intention. A common distinction, rough but serviceable, is between prior intentions (which have not, or not yet, been put into action), intentions in action (doing something intentionally) and further intentions (the ends to which the agent views the action as a means).[1] The assessment of the conditionals will distinguish the first two kinds but disregard further intentions. Intentions are sometimes confused with motives, desires and results, but examples make the differences clear: from the motive of hatred, X insults Y, but hatred is not an intention;[2] X desires to eat a cake, but as he is on a diet he does not intend to; with the intention of scoring a bull's-eye, he throws a dart, but the result is that he misses the board.[3]

Some branches of law, such as the English criminal law of conspiracy, use a subjective concept of agreement – roughly, one that has regard to the content of the parties' minds – whereas others, such as the English law of contract, use an objective concept according to which – again roughly – the existence and/or the content of an alleged agreement depends on the belief which a suitably placed reasonable man would have as to

1 Duff (1990), 38 draws the same distinction in different words. For taxonomies of intention, see Allen (2009), 74 (basic, specific and ulterior); O. Black (1995), 357 (narrow and imputed – see further n. 31 below); O. Black (2005b), 124 (formal, content-specific and ulterior); Bratman (1987), chap. 8; de Moor (1990) (substantive and formal – see further Chap. 7 n. 92 below); J. Gardner and Jung (1991); Law Commission (2007), paras. 4.34 ff.; von Mehren (1992), paras. 43 ff. (subjective and objective). Mintoff (2004), 51 distinguishes between 'accounts' of intention. On the relation between intentions and goals, see Alvarez (2010), 93 ff.

2 In *Wai Yu-tsang* v. *R* [1991] 4 All ER 664, 671 f. Lord Goff distinguished intention and motive, characterising them respectively as immediate purpose and underlying purpose. There are arguably senses of 'intention' and 'purpose' that coincide (see the discussion in Allen (2009), 297 of *Hollinshead* [1985] AC 975); but a motive need not be a purpose, although it may be related to one. On motives, see Alvarez (2010), 59 ff.; Anscombe (1963), 18 ff.; Kenny (1963), chap. 4; A. White (1968), 14.

3 On the similar distinction – important in competition law – between the object and the effect of an agreement, see O. Black (2005b), 115 ff.

whether an agreement has been made and/or what has been agreed[4] (see sections 7.37 and 9.22). Parallel subjective/objective distinctions can be drawn for offer, acceptance and intention. The characteristics of the reasonable man for present purposes are debatable, but it is plausible to say at least that (i) he believes a proposition if and only if it is reasonable for him to believe it, (ii) whether that is reasonable depends on whether the reasons for him to believe it outweigh those for him not to (compare the reading of 'ought' in section 3.3), (iii) those reasons depend on his circumstances and (iv) it may be reasonable for him to believe the proposition even though it is false. (Section 8.121 makes the stronger claim that he may believe a proposition that cannot be true.) These four theses would need to be expanded and supplemented to constitute a full account;[5] other claims about the reasonable man will be considered in section 5.13.

The subjective/objective distinction, together with the one between prior intention and intention in action, yields at least four readings of each conditional – more than four if one word is read subjectively and another objectively. It would be dreary to scrutinise each conditional on each reading, and so I shall summarise the results and choose a few cases for closer review. The summary is that, with arguable exceptions in the cases of (119) and (121), all the conditionals are false[6] and some of the readings are strained. (116), (118) and (120) are naturally read in terms of prior intention and face some similar objections; (117), (119) and (121) are naturally read in terms of intention in action, and some objections to these are likewise similar to each other. The results are not affected by the subjective/objective distinction.

The connection between agreement and intention is thus, as noted in the Introduction and in section 2.63, a loose one.[7] As sections 8.1–8.2 and 9.4 will show, bad law results from the belief that it is tighter.

5.11 First case: (116) – subjective concepts, prior intention

The first case is:

4 Whether in competition law the concept of agreement is objective, and if so in what sense, is discussed in Chap. 8 n. 33 below.

5 On reasonableness and its relation to rationality, see M. Black (1983).

6 Hence the conditionals have truth values. For the contrary view of certain kinds of conditional, see Chap. 1 n. 42 above.

7 That is a problem for the theory, proposed in Mintoff (2004), that an agreement is an exchange of intentions.

(116) If X agrees with Y that (1), then X intends to do Ax,

read subjectively and in terms of prior intention. Assume that the agreement is made by X's making to Y an offer which Y accepts; let Ta be the time of acceptance, i.e., the time at which Y completes his act of acceptance, and hence the time at which the making of the agreement is completed; and expand (1) to the proposition that <at Tx X does Ax and at Ty Y does Ay>. As noted in section 2.3, Ty may or may not be later than Tx, but normally both are later than Ta. If (116) is read in terms of prior intention, it is natural to understand its consequent as stating that X has the intention at Ta. So (116) becomes:

(122) If at Ta X agrees with Y that <at Tx X does Ax and at Ty Y does Ay>, then at Ta X intends to do Ax at Tx.

(122) is false because it is possible that at Ta X agrees with Y that <at Tx X does Ax and at Ty Y does Ay> but does not have the specified intention. He might instead intend to breach the agreement.

One response is that (122) can be repaired by amending its antecedent to state that X *sincerely* agrees. Our intuitive concept of sincerity, and of sincere agreement in particular, is unclear[8] but surely weaker than the one imported by the response, which accordingly fails for falsity or artificiality. The unconditional intention in the consequent of (122) is arguably necessary for X's agreement to be sincere in the special case where at Ta X believes that at Tx he does not have any information as to whether at Ty Y does Ay; but in other circumstances X's agreement is sincere if X has only a conditional intention as to Ax. For example, it is plausible to hold that if the following conditions all obtain then it is sincere: the antecedent of (122) is true; at Ta X believes that at Tx he knows whether at Ty Y does Ay; and at Ta X's intention is <to do Ax at Tx if and only if at Tx he knows that at Ty Y does Ay>. Equivalently, if the first two conditions obtain, then, if the third does, X's agreement is sincere. It is likewise plausible to hold that if these conditions all obtain then it is sincere: the antecedent of (122) is true; at Ta X believes that at Tx he is unable to tell for sure whether at Ty Y does Ay; and at Ta X's intention is <to do Ax at Tx unless at Tx he has good reason to believe that at Ty Y does not do Ay>. (These conditional intentions were mentioned in sections 2.63 and 4.3.) Usually but not always, X's epistemic access at Tx to Y's doing or failing to do Ay at Ty is, and is believed by X at Ta to be, better if Ty precedes Tx than if Tx precedes Ty.

8 On the concept of, and changing attitudes to, sincerity, see Trilling (1972), chap. 1.

Even if the sets of conditions in the two examples need to be supplemented in order to be sufficient for X's agreement to be sincere, it is clear that the required supplements would not imply the consequent of (122) and hence would not undermine the refutation of the response as to sincerity. Since the principle supported by the examples – that in certain circumstances X's agreement is sincere if X has a conditional intention – concerns a sufficient condition for sincere agreement, the principle gives no reason to suppose that the amended (122), which states a necessary condition, can be salvaged by modifying its consequent to include conditional intentions. Nor is that supposition supported by the claim, also plausible, that in each example X's having the conditional intention is a necessary part of a sufficient condition for his agreement to be sincere. That one thing is a necessary part of a sufficient condition for another is no reason to believe that the former is necessary for the latter.

Three scholia: First, section 1.1 stipulated that, in the relevant context, 'conditional' signifies internal conditionality. The present discussion makes clear that 'conditional intention' means 'internally conditional intention' – an intention with conditional content. All intentions are externally conditional, in the sense that there are certain conditions on which an intention, whatever its content, exists. A corresponding point is made in section 1.1 about promises, and in sections 2.63 and 9.26 about agreements; the appendix to this chapter discusses further the difference between internally and purely externally conditional intentions. Second, there is a distinction (which will be important in the discussion of 'unilateral conspiracy' in section 9.4) between agreeing insincerely and pretending to agree – for example, when joking, or acting in a play. As with promises, an insincere agreement is an agreement none the less[9] (see sections 1.1 and 1.6). That is not true of a pretend agreement: the word 'pretend' here is an alienans predicate, like 'fool's' in 'fool's gold'.[10]

9 Mintoff (2004), 48, argues that Gilbert's understanding of agreements implies the contrary.

10 On alienans predicates, see Geach (1967), 64. On joking agreements, see Mintoff (2004), 45. On joking offers, see *Kray* [1992] 2 Archbold News 3; *Prior* (Chap. 2 n. 4 above), para. 24. On joking promises, see Ardal (1976), 56; Hume (1978), 523 f.; Searle (1965), 232 f. (largely repeated in Searle (1969), 57). Ardal writes 'That one does not mean one's utterance as a promise does not entail that it may not be legitimately taken as a promise'. (Compare Strawson in n. 16 below.) That leaves the question whether an utterance legitimately taken as a promise may nevertheless not be a promise. Among the conditions Searle claims to be necessary and sufficient for an act of promising are normal 'input' and 'output' conditions – 'the large and indefinite range of conditions under which any kind of serious linguistic communication is possible. "Output" covers the conditions for

Third, the examples indicate that the conditional intention bearing on a party's sincerity depends on the circumstances. The first intention looks too strong in the circumstances specified for the second: if at Ta X believes that at Tx he is unable to tell for sure whether at Ty Y does Ay, doubt is cast on the sincerity of X's agreement if at Ta his intention is <to do Ax at Tx if and only if at Tx he knows that at Ty Y does Ay>. Given that the range of potentially relevant circumstances and intentions is wide – perhaps open-ended – there is no simple condition for the sincerity of agreement. In that regard agreements are arguably unlike promises: as noted in section 1.1, Searle maintains that sincere promises are distinguished by the fact that the promisor intends to perform the promised action.

5.12 Second case: (117) – subjective concepts, intention in action

Now consider:

(117) If X agrees with Y that (1), then X intends to agree with Y that (1),

read subjectively and in terms of intention in action. The relevant action is X's offering to Y that (1), and so (117) becomes:

(123) If X agrees with Y that (1), the agreement being made by X's making to Y an offer which Y accepts, then X in making the offer intends to agree with Y that (1).

(On the distinction between 'by φing' and 'in φing', see section 2.1.) (123) is false because it is possible that X agrees with Y that (1) but does not have the intention. In particular, the following situation – call it the Bluff – is possible: X does not want to agree with Y; he is convinced that Y would not accept an offer that (1); his only intention in making the offer is to embarrass Y; but Y accepts and thus the agreement is made. (In another example X intends only to 'sub-agree', in the sense given in section 3.6.)

This refutation has the structure: possibly P; if P then <Q and not R>; so possibly <Q and not R>; so not <if Q then R>. Both steps use the strict-implication analysis of the conditional and the first is an instance of

intelligible speaking and "input" covers the conditions for understanding'. The examples he gives include the condition that the parties are not either joking or acting: it is unclear whether he views this as an input condition, an output condition, or both. On 'infelicities' of performative utterance, see Austin (1962), chaps. 2 ff. On 'tests of earnestness' in the law of contract, see Kötz (1997), chap. 4; on the intention to create legal relations in that context, Chap. 7 n. 45 below. On 'genuine' offers in the context of conspiracy, see n. 12 below.

the more general form: possibly P; Q if P; so possibly Q. The substitution instance, informally stated, is: it is possible that X and Y instantiate the Bluff; if they do, X agrees with Y that (1) and does not intend to agree with Y that (1); so it is possible that X thus agrees and does not thus intend; so it is not the case that, if X agrees with Y that (1), X intends to agree with Y that (1). The next case elaborates this structure.

5.13 Third case: (117) – objective concepts, intention in action

Read objectively, (117) becomes:

(124) If the reasonable man (RM) believes that X agrees with Y that (1), then RM believes that X intends to agree with Y that (1),

which could in turn be expanded, as in (123), to specify that X's intention is an intention in making his offer. The objective versions of (116)–(121) all have the form 'If RM believes that Q, then RM believes that R'; this formulation is more convenient than the more precise 'If a suitably placed reasonable man believed that . . . '. A proposition of this form can be refuted from the strict-implication analysis of the conditional with premisses that are relevant substitution instances of the following:

(125) It is possible that RM believes that <P and if P then <Q and not R>>.

(126) If RM believes that <P and if P then <Q and not R>>, then RM believes that <Q and not R>.

(127) If RM believes that <Q and not R>, then <RM believes that Q> and <RM believes that not R>.

(128) If RM believes that not R, then RM does not believe that R.

The instances relevant to (124) are true either as they stand or with minor changes that do not undermine the refutation, and so (124) is false. The instance of (125) is:

(129) It is possible that RM believes that <X and Y instantiate the Bluff and if X and Y instantiate the Bluff then <<X agrees with Y that (1)> and <X does not intend to agree with Y that (1)>>>.

The possibility might be realised if, for example, RM, while in a position from which it was obvious that the Bluff was occurring, reflected on its implications for X's intentions. The truth of (129) is compatible with the fact that in other possible circumstances – say, where RM has convincing evidence that the Bluff is not occurring – it is not reasonable for him to hold the belief in question: see clause (iii) of the description of RM, in section 5.1.

(126)–(128) are plausible, and their relevant instances more so. Each of (126)–(128) might be deduced from an assumption which has some plausibility but which does or may either need qualification or import a concept of the reasonable man that is unnecessarily strong for the concept's legal purposes. For (126) the assumption is that RM believes all logical consequences of the propositions he believes; for (127), that his beliefs distribute over conjunction; for (128), that his beliefs are consistent.[11] Given that <RM believes a proposition if and only if it is reasonable for him to believe it>, the last assumption implies that, if two propositions are inconsistent, one of them is such that it is not reasonable for him to believe it. Nevertheless he may have some reason to believe it.

5.14 *Fourth case: (118) – subjective concepts, intention in action*

An example of a strained reading of a conditional is a subjective reading, in terms of intention in action, of:

(118) If X offers to Y that (1), then X intends to do Ax.

(118) is naturally understood to concern a prior intention, which X has at the time he makes the offer, to do Ax later:[12] see the first case, in section 5.11. If (118) concerns intention in action, it expands to:

11 Compare J. Barnes (1969); Evnine (2008), 80 f.; Routley and Routley (1975), 218 f.

12 Compare *Prior* (Chap. 2 n. 4 above), in which the issue was whether the appellant had 'offered to supply' a controlled drug. One question before the court was whether, to constitute the offence in question, an offer must be 'made genuinely in the sense that the offeror intends to fulfil it and expects to be able to do so' (para. 16). This suggests that there are non-genuine offers that falsify (118). It is unclear whether the definition of 'made genuinely' is meant to refer to an unconditional intention or to an intention that is conditional on the acceptance of the offer; if the former, the definition is implausible or 'genuine' has a special sense. Compare the discussion of sincerity in section 5.11 above. Someone seeking to reconcile (118) with *Prior* might reply that 'non-genuine' is alienans (n. 10 above) or point out that the precise words in para. 16 are 'whether to qualify as an offer for this purpose: 1) it must be made genuinely in the sense . . . ' and that 'it' here refers not to an offer, but to an utterance that is an offer only if the utterance is made genuinely. That reading is hard to square both with the definition that follows of 'made genuinely' and with the statement in para. 20 that 'the offence is committed whether or not the *offer* is genuine' (emphasis added). It is also unclear what the genuine/non-genuine distinction amounts to as applied to utterances. Paras. 4 and 26 f. of the judgment consider the different question whether, to commit the relevant offence, the offeror must intend the offeree to *believe* that the offer is genuine.

(130) If X offers to Y that (1), then X in making the offer intends to do Ax.

It is hard to make sense of (130)'s consequent. A plausible thought is: <X in φing intends to χ> only if X believes that in or by φing he χs. The thought is false if 'X in φing intends to χ' is interpreted to mean that X, at the time he φs, intends to χ; but that interpretation erases the distinction between intention in action and prior intention. If the thought is true, the consequent of (130) is true only if X believes that in or by making the offer he does Ax. Except in odd circumstances, he would be unlikely, and wrong, to believe that. Even if the thought is false, it would be odd for the consequent of (130) to be true. Even if the consequent is true, (130) is false, for it is possible that the antecedent is true and the consequent false.

5.15 Fifth case: (119) – subjective concepts, intention in action

Now take:

(119) If X offers to Y that (1), then X intends to offer to Y that (1),

read subjectively and in terms of intention in action, so that it expands to:

(131) If X offers to Y that (1), then X in making the offer intends to offer to Y that (1).

This conditional is credible, but there are arguable counterexamples such as the old story (the Auction) in which X, ignorant of the practice at auction houses, waves in greeting at Y, the auctioneer, and is taken thereby to make a bid.[13] Our intuitive concept of an offer is too loose to settle such cases. One option is to tighten it by distinguishing strong offers, for which (131) is true, from weak ones, for which it is false, and a concept of very strong offers could be specified on which the truth of (131) is analytic. A reading of (131) as analytically true might be argued to condemn any attempt to explicate (131) to a vicious circularity or a vicious infinite regress. In one version, the objection – which need not be pursued – is that the concept of an intention to offer includes the concept of an offer

13 Compare Stocker (1970), 619. Warnock (1971), 116 f. considers cases in which 'I have given something to be understood – for instance, that I will marry my landlord's daughter – by pure inadvertence or misapprehension – being simply unaware, for instance, that to shake a girl's right hand is the way, in this society, formally to signify betrothal'. On the treatment of auctions in English contract law, see Peel (2007), para. 2–008.

and that, if the truth of (131) is analytic, the concept of an offer includes that of an intention to offer. (Compare the objection of circularity in section 2.66. On analytic truth, see the Introduction.)

Strawson argued that, whereas the illocutionary force of some speech acts is conventional, that of others is due to the speaker's having a Gricean intention in utterance.[14] If the distinction is accepted,[15] the possible counterexamples to (131) appear to fall on the conventional side of the line.[16] Nevertheless it is possible in principle for X to make an offer with Gricean illocutionary force while not intending to make an offer. I shall not pursue the question how the illocutionary force of an offer might be explained in Gricean terms.

5.16 Sixth case: (119) – objective concepts, intention in action

The objective counterpart of (131) is:

(132) If RM believes that X offers to Y that (1), then RM believes that X in making the offer intends to offer to Y that (1).

14 Strawson (1971a). 15 Strawson allows intermediate cases: ibid., 37 f.

16 That seems true of Strawson's own example of an unintentional speech act – the case of the player of bridge who lets slip the word 'redouble' without meaning to redouble: 'if the circumstances are appropriate and the play strict, then he *has* redoubled (or he may be *held* to have redoubled)' (ibid., 36, emphasis in original; compare Ardal in n. 10 above). The words in parenthesis suggest that Strawson is not confident that this is an unintentional speech act. Strawson rejects Austin's thesis that 'the successful performance of an illocutionary act involves the securing of uptake', i.e., that it involves 'bringing about the understanding of the meaning and of the force of the locution' (Austin (1962), 115 f.; Strawson (1971a), 24). Strawson would therefore probably deny that the other players' holding the utterer to have redoubled is necessary for him to have redoubled. The words in parenthesis quoted above suggest that Strawson also doubts that it is sufficient.

His objection to Austin's thesis runs thus: 'surely a man may, for example, actually have made such and such a bequest, or gift, even if no one ever reads his will or instrument of gift. We may be tempted to say instead that at least *the aim, if not the achievement*, of securing uptake is an essential element in the performance of the illocutionary act. To this, too, there is an objection. Might not a man really have made a gift, in due form, and take some satisfaction in the thought, even if he had no expectations of the fact ever being known? But this objection at most forces on us an amendment to which we are in any case obliged, viz. that the aim, if not the achievement, of securing uptake is essentially *a standard, if not an invariable*, element in the performance of an illocutionary act' (ibid., 30; emphasis in original). The second objection misses its mark, as aims and expectations need not coincide (but see the discussion, in section 5.32 below, of the concept of intention in English criminal law). Applied to the present discussion, the passage suggests that Strawson denies the proposition 'If X offers to Y that (1), then Y understands X to offer that (1)' but accepts 'Normally, if X offers to Y that (1), then X intends Y to understand X to offer that (1)'. (Compare the second proposition with the second of the two questions in *Prior*: n. 12 above.) Both of these are distinct from (119).

This conditional can be refuted by an argument with the structure described in the discussion of (124). The relevant instance of (125) is:

(133) It is possible that RM believes that <X and Y instantiate the Auction and if X and Y instantiate the Auction then <<X offers to Y that (1)> and <X in making the offer does not intend to offer to Y that (1)>>>.

Even if that belief is false, RM's circumstances might make it reasonable for him to hold it; so (133) is true. (132) is arguably true if read as concerning very strong offers: on that reading, it might be deduced from the assumption that RM believes the analytic consequences of all the propositions he believes. But that assumption either needs qualification or uses an unnecessarily strong concept of the reasonable man (compare the discussion of (126)–(128)).

5.17 Converse conditionals

Corresponding to each of (116)–(121) is a conditional in which antecedent and consequent are reversed; for example, the converse of (116) is 'If X intends to do Ax, then X agrees with Y that (1)'. Each of the converse conditionals can be read in the various ways described in section 5.1, and each is false on each of its readings, some of which are strained. The falsity of (116)'s converse is obvious.

5.2 Identity

Another important question for the areas of law discussed in the second part of the book concerns the conditions for the identity of agreements. For example, if W, X, Y and Z are found to be parties to a single agreement, the legal consequences for them may be more serious than if the agreement between W and X is found to be distinct from that between Y and Z. The question is what the identity conditions are, not the epistemic question how we can tell whether they are met.[17] 'Agreements' here means states of agreement, and the thesis is that the identity conditions for such a state refer to the making and the content of the agreement.

17 Talk of identity 'criteria', which is common in philosophy, blurs this distinction. For example, in the later writings of Wittgenstein, and in work influenced by them, 'criterion' appears to cover both existence and evidence. See Albritton (1968); Shoemaker (1963), 3 ff.; Wittgenstein (1972), 24 f.

A first thought is that agreements are identical if and only if they have the same parties and content. But suppose that in 2010 X and Y make an agreement to visit Aleppo in 2020, in 2014 they forget their agreement and in 2018 they make an agreement with the same content. One might say that the second agreement is the same as the first, but intuition suggests that they are distinct, in which case the proposed condition of identity is insufficient. The counterexample is excluded by adding the requirement that the agreements be made at the same time. It will be shown in section 5.31 that the time at which an agreement is made may partly determine its content and hence that elements of the identity condition are interconnected.

Consider this case: X says to Y 'Let's visit Aleppo in 2020' and Y replies 'Yes, let's do that'; as soon as Y has replied, X repeats his words; and, as soon as X has done that, Y repeats his. If the parties are merely eccentric, not forgetful, it is a strain to say that they have made two agreements. A lazy response is to dismiss the case as contrived; a better one is to modify the temporal requirement to provide that the relevant token acts of offering[18] occur within a short enough time from each other, and likewise for the acts of accepting – what is short enough possibly varying according to context. The best response may, depending on further details of the case, be to deny that the second pair of utterances constitutes an offer and an acceptance and to hold instead that it constitutes a confirmation of the agreement made by the first pair.

That prompts the thought that the condition of identity, instead of referring to parties and content, might refer more economically just to token acts of offering and accepting: agreements are the same if and only if they are made by the same such acts. The economy is superficial, however, as it is plausible to hold that token speech acts have identity conditions that refer to utterers and content: such acts are the same only if they have the same content and are made by the same token utterances, and such utterances are the same only if made by the same utterer. The first of these conditionals is consistent with the statement in section 1.1 that a single utterance may constitute speech acts of more than one type. The fact that the second talks of utterers rather than parties does not affect the

18 Each party's two utterances are distinct tokens of the same type. On the type/token distinction in various contexts, see Bromberger (1992); Davies (2006), 90; Dodd (2007); Goodman and Quine (1947); Hutton (1990); Quine (1987), 216 ff.; Wetzel (1993); Wetzel (1998); Wollheim (1980), 1 ff.; Wolterstorff (1975); sections 9.1, 9.25 and Chap. 9 n. 133 below.

objection, for at least normally the parties to agreements are utterers, in the relevant broad sense (see section 1.1), and in any event a reference to utterers is no more economical than one to parties.

The suggestion that agreements are identical if and only if they are made by the same parties at the same time and have the same content is good enough for simple cases, but the law often has to deal with situations that are more complex: some were discussed in sections 2.611–2.613, and the chapters on competition law and conspiracy law will describe others. A common situation is one in which the membership of a cartel or a conspiracy changes: if, as the law sometimes finds, there is a single agreement in such circumstances, it does not meet the condition for identity. Suppose that X and Y conspire to import cocaine into the UK and that a year later Z joins the conspiracy. Initially there is an agreement between X and Y with content 'X and Y import cocaine into the UK'; later there is an agreement between X, Y and Z with content 'X, Y and Z import cocaine into the UK'. The condition needs modification if these agreements are to be found identical.

One response is to substitute 'if' for 'if and only if', but then the condition has nothing to say about such cases. Another proposal is to survey the whole period in question, to treat as a party to the agreement anyone who joins it during that period and, instead of specifying a single proposition as the agreement's content, to refer to the set of propositions that constitute its content at any time – perhaps in a way that links each one to the relevant time. That, however, presupposes further conditions of identity for agreements: what makes these people parties to, and these propositions contents of, the same agreement? The answer is that, as in the case of wheel agreements (section 2.612), the courts invoke a cluster of conditions, discussed in section 9.27; see also the discussion of complex cartels, in section 8.4.

5.3 Logical properties

5.31 Conjunction

Consider these two conditionals:

(134) If <X and Y agree that P> and <X and Y agree that Q>, then X and Y agree that <P and Q>.

(135) If X and Y agree that <P and Q>, then <X and Y agree that P> and <X and Y agree that Q>.

Both concern states of agreement and are to be understood, as before, as strict implications. The question whether they are true is legally and philosophically interesting. For example, conspiracy law has difficulty dealing with conjunctive agreements that have a conditional conjunct, such as 'We will rob a bank and if anyone tries to stop us we will shoot him'. To avoid the difficulty, some writers have proposed that such cases be broken into two agreements – one unconditional, the other conditional:[19] here, an agreement to a rob a bank and an agreement to shoot anyone who obstructs the robbery. That proposal is supported by (135).

As to the philosophical interest, the question about (134) and (135) falls within a broader question about the logical features of propositional attitudes. A plausible thesis[20] is that all such attitudes distribute over conjunction: if the thesis is correct, its instance (135) is true. (It was suggested in section 5.13 that its instance applying to the reasonable man's beliefs may be true. On the distributivity of desire over conjunction, see section 4.12; on that of intention, section 8.121.) The converse thesis, of which (134) is an instance, appears false but it, or certain of its instances applying to specific propositional attitudes, may be or approximate to something true; Evnine, for example, argues that it is rational, and characteristic of personhood, to conform to the principle 'If X believes that P and believes that Q, then X believes that <P and Q>'.[21] His thought might be adapted to make a case for the truth of (134), the idea being that it is irrational, say, to agree that P and to agree that Q but not to agree that <P and Q>. The case fails because, even if the point about irrationality is correct, (134) and (135) are merely conditional propositions, not canons of rationality. Someone might therefore falsify either proposition by failing to be rational.

Various objections might be raised to the two conditionals: some apply to both, others to just one. An objection of the first kind is based on a principle of parsimony: if they were true, there would be an unrealistic proliferation of agreements. This at best creates a rebuttable presumption against the conditionals; it does not refute them. Another objection is that they conflict with the offer–acceptance model. Suppose that X offers to Y that P, Y accepts the offer, X offers to Y that Q, and Y accepts that offer. Then – subject, here and in the examples below, to the obtaining

19 Allen (2009), 288; Simester et al. (2010), 311. See further section 9.26 below.

20 It has been rejected by some: see, for example, Priest (2005), 66.

21 Evnine (2008), chaps. 3 f. Evnine takes it as uncontroversial that belief distributes over conjunction: 74 f.

of CS (see (37)(c) (section 2.1)) – they have an agreement that P and an agreement that Q. But it does not follow that X offers to Y that <P and Q> or that Y accepts such an offer. Suppose that there is no such offer and acceptance. Then according to the model they do not have an agreement that <P and Q>. There is thus a possible situation in which X and Y agree that P and agree that Q but do not agree that <P and Q>. Hence (134) is false. A similar argument applies to (135).

There are three replies. First, it may be argued that (134) and (135) have counterparts concerning offer and acceptance, so that it does follow from the alleged counterexample both that X offers to Y that <P and Q> and that Y accepts that offer. It might, however, be objected that the counterparts are less plausible: as to (134), it seems not to follow, from the assumption that X, in order to give a choice to Y, offers that P and offers that not P, that he offers that <P and not P>. The second reply is that the model gives a condition that is sufficient, not necessary, for a state of agreement; so, even if there is no such offer or acceptance, the model does not imply that X and Y do not have an agreement that <P and Q>. The third reply has the form of the account given, in section 2.612, of wheel agreements: it is sufficient, for the parties to have an agreement that <P and Q>, that they stand in a certain relation to a set of agreements the parties to which meet the model's conditions. In the example the parties stand in such a relation to such agreements.

A third objection is based on the parties' own account of the situation. It is possible that X agrees with Y that P and agrees with Y that Q but denies that he has an agreement with Y that <P and Q>. In that case, the objection goes, there is no such agreement and it follows that (134) is false. There is a corresponding argument against (135). One way of grounding the objection is to appeal to the principle that, if a person denies that he has a certain agreement, he does not have that agreement. But the principle is false; if it were true, it would enable anyone to evade his agreements. The objector might claim to have in mind the more plausible bi- or multilateral version of the principle: if all parties to the supposed agreement deny that it exists, it does not exist. But that too is false. Suppose that X and Y make an agreement a term of which is that it cannot be terminated earlier than a year after it is made. If during that year X and Y both deny that they have such an agreement, their denial is false. The principle is not saved by the possibility that they agree an amendment which allows the original agreement to be terminated early: in the first place, such an amendment might be excluded by the terms of the original agreement; in the second, an agreement to terminate is different from a mere denial that the original agreement exists.

Another objection appeals to the identity condition proposed in section 5.2 for simple agreements: they are the same if and only if they are made by the same parties at the same time and have the same content. By this condition the agreements respectively that P, that Q and that <P and Q> are distinct from each other, as they have different contents and may be made at different times. It might be replied that, if the agreements that P and that Q are made at different times, the agreement that <P and Q> is made at the same time as the later of them; but, whether or not that is true, the objection fails because the conditionals are not propositions about identity. It does not follow, from the fact that the three agreements are distinct, that the existence of the first two does not imply that of the third, or the converse.

Two objections might be raised to (134) in particular. Suppose that X and Y, who are planning a party, agree to invite Z. Later, having forgotten that agreement, they agree to invite W. They would never dream of agreeing to invite both Z and W, for they know that Z and W hate each other. Since this case is possible, it is possible that the antecedent of (134) is true and the consequent false, and so (134) is false. The objection is at best inconclusive, for it may be replied that, whatever X and Y may or may not dream of agreeing, they saddle themselves with the third agreement by making the first two.

A stronger objection runs as follows. On Monday X and Y agree that on Tuesday they clean the house; on Thursday they agree that on Friday they do the gardening. Absent special circumstances, the first agreement ends on Tuesday and the second starts on Thursday, and so there is no time at which both agreements exist. In that case it does not follow that they ever have an agreement with this content: on Tuesday they clean the house and on Friday they do the gardening. Since this instance of (134) is false, (134) itself is false. The objection is persuasive, but can be avoided by rewriting (134) so that it applies only to the period, if any, in which both the agreements in its antecedent exist. A corresponding proviso could be added to (135).

An objection that might be made to (135) is based on a simplified version of the principle of obligation in sections 2.3 and 3.3: in this version, each party to an agreement is obligated to perform, but his obligation ceases if the other party fails to perform. Given that the content of an agreement is typically of the conjunctive form (1) (X does Ax and Y does Ay), let P and Q themselves be conjunctions – respectively 'X does Ax1 and

Y does Ay1' and 'X does Ax2 and Y does Ay2'. Suppose that the antecedent of (135) is true: X and Y agree that <<X does Ax1 and Y does Ay1> and <X does Ax2 and Y does Ay2>>. It is debatable how the simplified rule of obligation applies to agreements with complex conjunctive contents of this kind, but it is plausible to read it as here implying that, if X fails to do one or other or both of Ax1 and Ax2, all Y's obligations arising from[22] the agreement cease; such obligations might be <to do Ay1>, <to do Ay2> and/or <to do Ay1 and to do Ay2>. Suppose that X fails to do Ax1. Then, other things equal, Y is not obligated to do Ay2. By (135), X and Y agree that <X does Ax2 and Y does Ay2>. By the simplified principle, Y is obligated to do Ay2. Since the content of this agreement does not refer to Ax1, X's failure to do Ax1 does not cancel this obligation. So Y both is and is not obligated to do Ay2. By reductio ad absurdum, (135) is false.

In reply to this objection it may be said that the simplifed principle of obligation is in relevant respects *too* simple. As indicated by the discussion, in section 1.2314, of the rules in English contract law on rescission for breach, one party's partial failure to perform may not release the other from all his obligations under the agreement. A stronger reply is that no contradiction has been generated. Grant that no obligation on Y arises from the agreement with the complex conjunctive content. In that case, other things equal, Y has no obligation to do Ay2. But, if (135) is true, other things are not equal: X and Y have the other agreement, which imposes[23] such an obligation on Y.

A more fruitful approach to the assessment of the conditionals is to reflect on the factors that determine the content of an agreement. There are various such factors: where the question arises whether X and Y have agreements that P and that Q, an agreement that <P and Q>, or all three, each factor present may weigh in favour of a particular answer, but the answer depends on the factors taken together, as some may outweigh others. (Compare the theses in section 5.1 about reasonable belief.) For example, the parties' words are relevant: if X says to Y 'I propose that <P and Q> and I'm not interested in one without the other', and Y accepts, their actions weigh in favour of their having an agreement that <P and Q>. The same is true if they include P and Q in a single memorandum of agreement. X might instead say 'I propose that P and I propose that Q:

22 As explained in section 1.1 above, talk of an obligation's arising from, or being imposed by, an agreement can be explicated in terms of grounding. On the grounds of obligations to perform agreements, see sections 3.3 ff above.

23 See the previous n.

these are independent offers and you can accept one, the other, or each of them', in which case, if Y accepts each, their actions weigh in favour of their having agreements that P and that Q, but not an agreement that <P and Q>. The same applies if X offers and Y accepts that P, and much later, in a quite different context and without reference to that offer and that acceptance, X offers and Y accepts that Q. (This confirms the point in section 5.2, that elements of the identity condition for simple agreements are interconnected, as it shows that the content of an agreement may depend on the time at which the agreement is made.) The last factor might be outweighed if X and Y previously agree that all agreements between them are to be incorporated in a single agreement and are not to be treated as separate agreements.

There is no reason to suppose that, in all cases, let alone all possible cases, where the relevant factors together determine that there are separate agreements that P and that Q, they also together determine that there is an agreement that <P and Q>, or vice versa. (134) and (135) should therefore be rejected.

5.32 Closure

To say that the property F is closed under the relation *R* is to say that, for any two things A and B, if A both has F and bears *R* to B, then B has F. For example, the property of being a dog is closed under the relation . . . is a sibling of . . . , for anything of which a dog is a sibling is a dog; conversely, the property of being male is not closed under that relation, for some males are siblings of females. A question that arises in law concerns the closure properties of agreement – specifically, where X agrees that P, the closure of the property of being agreed by X[24] under relations borne by P to other propositions. This again is distinct from the question of identity discussed in section 5.2: it does not follow, from the fact that (i) X agrees that P, (ii) P bears a certain relation to Q and (iii) if (i) and (ii) then X agrees that Q, that X's agreement that P and his agreement that Q are the same.

In *Barnard*[25] it was held to be an error to think that a conspiracy to steal is merely a lesser form of a conspiracy to rob. It is not quite clear what that means but, given that a conspiracy is a form of agreement, the

24 A narrow concept of a property might exclude being agreed by X. For the metaphysics of properties, see Loux (2002), 23 f., 42 ff., 96 ff., 187 ff.

25 (1980) 70 Cr. App. R. 28, 33. See also Richardson (2011), paras. 33 ff.

judge may have thought it erroneous to reason thus: if X robs, X steals; so, if X agrees to rob, X agrees to steal.[26] The premiss is true,[27] but the conclusion follows only on the additional premiss that agreement by X is closed under simple conditionality, i.e., that, if both X agrees that P and if P then Q, then X agrees that Q. That this is false, at least for one ordinary sense of 'agree', can be seen by adapting an example from the Introduction: you agree to take the plane that leaves at 9.30; if you take that plane, you will die in an explosion; but you do not agree to die in an explosion.[28] The original example was used to impugn the thesis that 'agrees that . . . ' is referentially transparent: if that thesis is false, so is the premiss of closure, but the converse does not hold.

By contrast it seems that, for sufficiently strong forms of necessity, agreement by X is closed under necessary simple conditionality known by X: if X both agrees that P and knows that necessarily if P then Q, then X agrees that Q. Intuition is not precise enough to rule on various intermediate principles of closure: suppose, for example, that the conditional is, but is not believed by X to be, necessary; or that X believes correctly, but without justification, that the probability of Q given P is 90 per cent. Stipulation is needed to decide such cases and the decision is likely to depend in part on the consequences for the parties. If X would lose much and Y would gain little from a finding that X, by agreeing with Y that P, agrees with Y that Q, there is reason to deny that agreement by X is closed under relations borne by P to Q.

Some guidance is provided by comparing agreement to intention. (On the relations between the two, see sections 5.1–5.17.) In English criminal

26 A similar but different inference was rejected in *Patel* (CACD, 7 Aug. 1991, 14A), where it was stated that 'if you believe you are joining one conspiracy with one objective, that does not make you guilty of a conspiracy which has a different and less serious objective'. For that doctrine, see also *Siracusa* (1990) 90 Cr. App. R. 340; *Hussain* [2002] EWCA Crim. 6, para. 29. In *Barnard* it is clear that the judge was concerned, at least in part, with identity conditions, for he stated that a conspiracy to steal is 'a different agreement' from a conspiracy to rob. 'There has to be another agreement if a conspiracy to steal is to become a conspiracy to rob' (33).

27 Under section 8(1) of the Theft Act 1968, '[a] person is guilty of robbery if he steals, and immediately before or at the time of doing so, and in order to do so, he uses force on any person or puts or seeks to put any person in fear of being then and there subjected to force'. Read literally, this states a sufficient condition of robbery, but part of the intended meaning appears to be that stealing is a necessary condition: see Ormerod (2008), 799.

28 For another implied denial of closure in the context of conspiracy, see G. Williams (1977), 1165: 'he has agreed to a course of conduct, and the course of conduct will amount to an offence, but he has not agreed to the elements of the conduct that amount to the offence, because he did not know of them'.

law the rules on intention are messy, but there is authority for the rule that, if you recognise something to be a virtually certain consequence of your action, you intend that thing, whereas, if you merely foresee it to be a consequence of your action, you do not intend it.[29] Assume that an action is intended by its agent (see further section 6.1). Regimenting and simplifying: if X intends that P and recognises it to be virtually certain that if P then Q, then X intends that Q; but it is false that, if X intends that P and merely foresees that if P then Q, then X intends that Q. An alternative formulation reverses the scopes of 'recognises it to be virtually certain that' and 'foresees that' on the one hand and 'if' on the other, to produce 'if P then X recognises it to be virtually certain / foresees that Q'. This version is perhaps preferable, at least in the case of mere foresight. Suppose that X hits Y and that in consequence Y dies. X, at the time he hits Y, may foresee Y's death, but it is odd to say that X foresees, rather than simply believes, that if he hits Y then Y will die: the intuitive thought – which raises issues that need not be pursued[30] – is that, although the death is later than the hitting, the conditional is already true at the time of the hitting.

On this version, the property of being intended by X is, according to the law, closed under the relation expressed by 'if . . . then X recognises it to be virtually certain that . . . ' but not under that expressed by 'if . . . then X merely foresees that . . . '.[31] By analogy, it may be argued that, at least for some purposes, agreement by X is closed under the former but not the latter relation. (In either version, the principle of the closure of intention disregards the difference between simple conditionality and

29 Virtual certainty sufficient for intention: *Woollin* [1999] AC 82; on the meaning of 'virtually certain', see Simester et al. (2010), 136 f. Mere foresight insufficient: *Hancock and Shankland* [1986] 1 AC 455, 472; *Nedrick* [1986] 1 WLR 1025; *Woollin* (ibid.); *Mathews* [2003] EWCA Crim. 192. For general discussion of intention in English criminal law, see Allen (2009), 55 ff.; Ashworth (2009), 170 ff.; Buzzard (1978); Clarkson et al. (2010), 136 ff.; Duff (1990); Herring (2010), 136 ff.; Horder (1995); Kaveny (2004); Lacey (1993); Lacey (1995); Ormerod (2008), 97 ff.; Simester et al., ibid., 126 ff.; J. Smith (1974); J. Smith (1978a); J. Smith (1978b); G. Williams (1989).

30 On the temporality of truth values, and its implications for the nature of their bearers, see Haack (1978), 79 ff.; Lemmon (1966b).

31 For different concepts of intention, and their implications for closure, see O. Black (1995), 356 f. It is argued there that 'narrow' intention is not closed under conditionality, reasonably believed conditionality, or entailment; that belief is the same as narrow intention in that respect; but that 'imputed' intention is closed under the latter two relations. The article invokes the closure properties of intention and belief in order to illuminate those of acceptance of a restriction under the Restrictive Trade Practices Act 1976 (repealed). On the closure of intention under abstraction, see section 8.11 below.

the relevant, presumably causal, relation of consequence; compare the distinction, in sections 2.63 and 4.11, between the former and the means-end relation. The principle also controversially implies that X's intentions may be directed at things other than his own actions: see further section 8.121.)

5.4 Agreement to agree

The discussion of obligation, in section 2.3 and Chapter 3, illuminates the concept of an agreement to agree.[32] It might be suggested that there is no difference between an agreement to agree to φ and an agreement to φ; or that the former is merely a special case of the latter in which the details of the agreement have not been specified; or that, in any event, if X agrees to agree to φ then X agrees to φ.[33] All those claims are false, unless 'agree to agree' is given a special meaning. Normally, if X agrees to φ then X is obligated to φ, whereas if X agrees to agree to φ then he is obligated to agree to φ; but it is not the case that if X agrees to agree to φ then he is obligated to φ. Hence the existence of an agreement to φ – detailed or not – does not follow from that of an agreement to agree to φ. The same argument leaves room for higher-order agreements, although, as noted in section 4.4, people rarely if ever agree to agree to agree.

5.5 Agreement with oneself

You can agree with nobody, in the sense that you do not agree with anybody; but, if you agree, you must agree with someone. Agreement is thus relational. It is a further question whether the relation is irreflexive in the sense that you cannot agree with yourself.[34] Light is cast on this question by the account, in section 2.4, of the functions of agreement.

Imagine that, when considering whether to go to the cinema, X says to himself 'How about going to the cinema? – All right'. The words have

32 On the treatment of such agreements in English law, see *Walford* v. *Miles* (1992) 2 AC 128; *Petromec* v. *Petrolio Brasiliero* [2005] EWCA Civ 891; *Butters* v. *BBC Worldwide* [2009] EWHC 1954; Peel (2007), paras. 2–104 ff.; S. Smith (2005), 44.

33 Peel (2007), paras. 2–104 ff. suggests that the phrases 'agreement to agree' and 'contract to make a contract' cover an agreement to execute a formal document or to negotiate. Simester et al. (2010), 281 says that, although there is no legal objection to a charge of conspiracy to conspire, it is 'hard to envisage a conspiracy to conspire which is not, more straightforwardly, a conspiracy to commit a substantive offence'.

34 On promises to oneself, see Rosati (2011).

the form of an offer and an acceptance, but it is at best odd to say that he has made an agreement with himself: this looks like a charade. One purported explanation is that an agreement is made by speech acts, which are instances of communication, and you cannot communicate with yourself. But section 1.1 left open the question whether all speech acts are communicative, and the last claim assumes a narrow and disputable view of communication. As noted in that section, a person making a private vow may be said to talk to, and thus to communicate with, himself. It might now be said that talking to oneself is not a conversation; but that is unsatisfactory, for it raises the question why a conversation, rather than a monologue, is necessary for the making of an agreement.

A third purported explanation is that offeror and offeree cannot be the same person; but, for agreements which the offer–acceptance model fits, that begs the question[35] against the possibility of an agreement with oneself. A fourth refers to the functions of an offer to put it in the offeree's power to agree and to impose obligations: the thought is that, if X gives a power to Y, X must have the power; so, if X is Y, Y has the power; so X does not need to, or perhaps cannot, give it to Y. But that trades on a metaphor. In making an offer, X 'gives' those powers to Y only in the sense that the offer results, and normally is intended by X to result, in Y's having the powers. It does not follow that X himself has them.

It is more helpful to invoke the main function of an agreement, to enable rational self-interested parties to benefit from each other's actions. The central idea – amplified by the account, in sections 4.1–4.12, of the instrumental reasoning that leads such parties to make agreements – is that X wants Y to do Ay and makes an agreement with Y as a means of getting Y to do Ay. If X is Y, he can usually just do Ay; there is no need for an agreement. This redundancy explains our reluctance to count the soliloquy about the cinema as an agreement. It might be suggested that the fact mentioned in section 2.4, that sometimes the parties to an ordinary bilateral agreement would have performed the actions in question even if they had not agreed to do so, is a reason to classify the soliloquy as at least a peripheral example of agreement. But the cases can be distinguished on epistemic grounds: even if Y ($\neq$ X) would have done Ay without agreeing with X, the agreement might be justified and/or motivated by the fact that X does not believe this; but X will usually have a good idea of the actions he himself will perform. The difference between the cases is thus, roughly, one between mere redundancy and known redundancy.

35 For a general defence of question-begging, see Shafer-Landau (2009), 192 ff.

In some situations X's desire to do Ax will not issue in his doing it: there are external obstacles, or he has a greater desire to do something else which is incompatible with Ax, or he is weak-willed. (On certain assumptions – in particular, that the concept of doing, like that of action (see the Introduction), covers omissions – the third case is an instance of the second.) It might be suggested that weakness of will provides scope for agreements with oneself. X wants to lose weight, but doubts his resolution, and so he says to himself 'Now then, you go to the gym and I'll buy you a new suit: how about it? – All right'. One reason against classifying this as an agreement is that, as noted in section 1.21, the content of an offer and an acceptance, and thus of an agreement, is typically a conjunctive proposition. 'You go to the gym and I'll buy you a new watch' is conjunctive on its face, but is arguably a colloquial expression of a conditional: if you go to the gym, I shall buy you a new watch. (Compare the similar but less plausible claim, in section 1.22, used to defend conditional versions of the promise model.) A stronger reason is that talk of an agreement is unnecessary in order to explain this case, which is just a matter of X's forming intentions: one, to go to the gym; the other, to buy himself a suit if he goes to the gym. The second intention is formed to protect him from failing to fulfil the first.

Another suggestion is that examples of agreement with oneself can be found in the law of conspiracy. Despite the statement by the US Supreme Court that 'it is impossible in the nature of things for a man to conspire with himself',[36] certain American states, and the American Law

36 *Morrison* v. *California* 291 US 82, 92 (1934). Compare the statement in the Illinois case *People* v. *Ambrose* 28 Ill App 3d 627, 329 NE 2d 11 (1975): 'It would be absurd to claim a conspiracy could be entered into by one individual alone. By the terms of our statute the crime of conspiracy involves an agreement. The definition of agreement implies an intent to agree between a minimum of two people'. The last sentence excludes the possibility, identified in section 5.12 above, of a person's making an agreement without intending to. See also *Rogers* v. *United States* 340 US 367, 375 (1951). It is standardly asserted that a conspiracy must have at least two parties: see Allen (2009), 281; Clarkson et al. (2010), 478; Herring (2010), 804; Hooper and Ormerod (2011), para. A6.38; Marcus (1992), 23; Richardson (2011), para. 33–25; J. Smith (1996b), 387. Section 1(1) of the Criminal Law Act 1977 (as amended) provides that a conspiracy exists where 'a person agrees with any other person or persons' and certain conditions are met. Marcus (1977), 958 says that 'conspiracy requires an agreement between two or more persons; if only one person is found to have actually agreed, there is no agreement and no conspiracy'. Although this statement, which talks of persons rather than parties, makes it clear that there is no conspiracy in the absence of an agreement between at least two persons, it less clearly excludes the possibility of a one-person agreement, for that possibility is arguably contemplated by 'only one person is found to have actually agreed'. The phrase is better

Institute's Model Penal Code, recognise so-called unilateral conspiracy[37] (mentioned in section 5.11). This, as will be argued in section 9.4, is best viewed as an ordinary agreement between two or more persons; the alternative view, which seems to be favoured by some commentators, is that it is a counterexample to the truism that a conspiracy requires an agreement. On neither view is a unilateral conspiracy an agreement with oneself.

In English law, if X and Y are alleged to have conspired with each other, X may be convicted even if Y is acquitted.[38] This principle recognises that the evidence against X may be stronger than that against Y;[39] it does not imply that, where only one of the defendants is convicted, he has an agreement with himself. English law also contains certain exceptions to the liability for criminal conspiracy: see further section 9.4. Statute provides that a person is not liable if the only other person with whom he agrees is his spouse,[40] the historical root of this exception being the fiction that husband and wife are one person.[41] As it is a fiction, it does not yield genuine examples of agreements with oneself. *McDonnell* is authority for the rule that, absent other factors, a director solely responsible for a company's affairs does not conspire with the company if he decides

understood to refer to the situation in which there is only enough evidence to prove that one defendant agreed: see the next paragraph of the main text.

37 See Chap. 9 n. 172 below.

38 Criminal Law Act 1977 (as amended), section 5(6). For the position in the USA, see the Model Penal Code, 5.03, nn. of decisions, 24; Burgman (1979), 82 f.; Marcus (1977), 957 ff.; Marcus (1992), 23 ff.; Rogers (1989).

39 See Ormerod (2008), 435.

40 Criminal Law Act 1977 (as amended), section 2(2)(a).

41 See Ormerod (2008), 432; Simester et al. (2010), 322 f., describing the exception as 'anomalous and anachronistic'; *Chrastny* [1991] 1 WLR 1381, 1383, quoting the judge at first instance: 'it goes back to the very old law when the husband and wife were said to be one, and in those very far-off days, it was said that the husband was that one'. (See further Chap. 9 n. 132 below, and contrast Gilbert (1996b) on the fusion of egos in marriage.) Law Commission (1976), paras. 1.46 ff. supported the exception as safeguarding 'the stability of marriage'; contrast Law Commission (2007), pt. 9. Clarkson et al. (2007), 523 describes it as 'a policy provision aimed at exempting marital confidences from the ambit of the criminal law'; compare Herring (2010), 804 f. Ashworth (2009), 453 notes that in other areas of the criminal law the public interest overrides marital confidence. On criminal conspiracies involving spouses, see *Robinson* (1746) 1 Leach 37; *Whitehouse* (1852) 6 Cox C.C. 38; *Lovick* [1993] Crim. LR 890, CA. Commentary: Allen (2009), 281; Card (1973), 679; Hooper and Ormerod (2011), para. A6.38; Richardson (2011), para. 33–27. On the liability of spouses for tortious conspiracy, see *Midland Bank Trust Co. Ltd.* v. *Green (No. 3)* [1982] Ch 529, [1981] 3 All ER 744 CA; Ormerod (2008), 432 n. 379.

to commit an offence in its name.[42] The judge rejected the charge of conspiracy because:

> where the sole responsible person in the company is the defendant himself, it would not be right to say that there were two persons or two minds. If it were otherwise, I feel that it would offend against the basic concept of a conspiracy, namely, an agreement of two or more to do an unlawful act, and I think it would be artificial to take the view that the company, although it is clearly a separate legal entity, can be regarded here as a separate person or a separate mind, in view of the admitted fact that this defendant acts alone so far as these companies are concerned.[43]

It is not clear whether this means that there is no agreement; or that there is an agreement, but it does not have two or more parties; or that it has two or more parties, but they are not separate persons or minds (the judge did not entertain the possibility of a mindless person or personless mind); or that, even if they are separate persons or minds, the agreement is not a conspiracy. Only the second reading supports the claim that one can have an agreement with oneself; but it supports only an uninterestingly weak version of that claim, as there is a clear respect in which the director and the company are distinct. As the passage says, they are separate legal entities.

The judgment reviewed certain Canadian cases supporting the proposition that a conspiracy may exist where, in addition to these facts, the director agrees with the company in his capacity as a person responsible for the acts of another corporation.[44] Irrespective of the law of conspiracy, an agreement in which one person acts in two capacities is a more

42 *McDonnell* [1966] 1 QB 233. Commentary: Allen (2009), 281; Card (1973), 679; Hooper and Ormerod (2011), para. A6.38; Herring (2010), 805; Richardson (2011), para. 33–31; Simester et al. (2010), 322. The rule is sometimes carelessly stated; for example, Simester et al. write merely that liability will not arise if the only other party to the agreement is a limited company.

43 At 245. Simester et al. (2010), 324 f. argues that the same artificiality would have existed if there had been other parties to the agreement: 'Whenever a company is convicted for conspiracy an artificial duality is involved to the effect that the state of mind of D (a person of requisite seniority) is not merely her own state of mind but, additionally, a state of mind attributable to the company'. But, if one of the parties is not solely responsible for the company's affairs, the objection to the finding of an agreement is removed, even if it is artificial to find that the company and its responsible director are separate parties. The complaint is arguably just an instance of a general objection to the attribution of criminal liability to a corporation on the basis of the mental state of one of its officers. On this 'identification principle', see Ashworth (2009), 149 ff. See further section 6.1 below, which discusses the imputation of actions and reasons to the state on the basis of those of its officials, and sections 7.32 and 7.37 on the mental states of contracting parties.

44 *McDonnell* (n. 42 above), at 245. See Ormerod (2008), 432 n. 378; Richardson (2011), para. 33–31.

interesting candidate for an agreement with oneself: the Secretary of State agrees to pay compensation to a landowner for a compulsory acquisition, and the Secretary of State and the landowner are the same person. There is no harm in calling this an agreement with oneself. It may certainly amount to a contract – but, as explained in sections 7.3–7.38 and 7.64, not all contracts are agreements.

Here is another candidate,[45] which concerns not capacities, in the above sense, but epistemic limitations. X, who is absent-minded, has a property business with a large portfolio of houses. He decides to sell a certain house and so instructs an estate agent to put a For Sale sign outside it. Later, X walks past the house and sees the sign. Forgetting that he is the owner, he phones the agent with an offer. Then he remembers that he owns the house but forgets that he has made the offer. The agent phones him with the news of the offer. X tells him to accept it and thereby makes an agreement with himself.

5.6 Appendix: conditional intention

In section 5.11 I used 'conditional intention' to mean 'internally conditional intention', in accordance with the stipulation in section 1.1; as noted, all intentions are externally conditional. In this appendix the external conditions of internally unconditional intentions will be under discussion, and so it will be convenient to talk explicitly of internally conditional intentions and to use 'externally conditional intention' to signify intentions that are merely externally conditional and thus are internally unconditional.

Internally and externally conditional intentions connect differently to the circumstances, including the other mental states and the actions, of the person intending. Sometimes those differences can be exploited to ascertain, in a case of doubt, whether his intention is internally or externally conditional. Consider the externally and internally conditional intentions represented respectively by:

(136) <X intends to do Ax> if and only if P;
(137) X intends <to do Ax if and only if P>.

If X has only the intention in (136), whether he intends to do Ax depends on whether P. If X has only the intention in (137), then, if X is rational,

45 Proposed by Christopher Hughes in conversation.

whether he intends to do Ax depends on whether he *believes* that P: if X is rational, he obeys requirements of rationality; his intending to do Ax is rationally required by his having the intention in (137) and the belief that P; his not having the intention to do Ax is rationally required by his having the intention in (137) and lacking the belief. These claims rely on an intuitive understanding of rationality and rational requirement[46] and may need qualification, but a rough account is sufficient here. The analysis is the same if P concerns a belief of X, for example if P is 'X believes that Q'. If X has only the intention in (136), his intending to do Ax depends on whether he believes that Q; if he has only the intention in (137) and is rational, it depends on whether he believes that he believes that Q.

Suppose that you want to know whether X has the intention in (136) or the intention in (137) and that X cannot tell you: there is an obstacle to communication or he is himself unsure of the answer. It may be possible to tell which intention he has by contriving a situation in which P is true but X does not believe that P, or one in which P is false but X believes that P. Assume that <X does Ax if and only if X intends to do Ax> and that X is rational. In the first situation, X's doing Ax is consistent with his having the intention in (136) but inconsistent with his having the intention in (137), and so if he does Ax he has either the former intention or neither; whereas his not doing Ax is inconsistent with his having the intention in (136) but consistent with his having the intention in (137), and so if he does not do Ax he has either the latter intention or neither. The reverse is the case in the second situation: X's doing Ax is inconsistent with his having the intention in (136) but consistent with his having the intention in (137); his not doing Ax is consistent with his having the former but inconsistent with his having the latter.

This method is based on connections among (136), (137), P and propositions as to X's intending to do Ax, his doing Ax, his believing that P and his rationality: the truth values of the first two are inferred from those of the remainder. It can be adapted to make inferences in other directions; for example, the truth of 'X believes that P' can be inferred from certain assignments of truth values to other members of the set. The method does not work where the question is whether X has the intention in (137) or the externally conditional intention represented by:

46 Rational requirement is a species of normative requirement, as to which see Chap. 4 n. 5 above. For criticism of the concept of rational requirement, see A. Price (2008).

(138) <X intends to do Ax> if and only if X believes that P,

for on the same assumptions, whichever of these two intentions he has, he does Ax if and only if he believes that P. But it can work in the case mentioned above, where P itself concerns a belief of X.

6

Intervention by the state

6.1 The state and its reasons

What reasons, if any, does the state have to enforce, prohibit or promote certain types of agreement? 'The state' here is a general expression, denoting anything that is a state, and the question is a normative one, concerning reasons for the state to act: it does not concern either the motivation for the state's actions or their explanation.[1] I do not distinguish in meaning between the claim that the state (or anything else) has a reason to φ and the claim that there is a reason for it to φ; in particular, I do not take the former to say that the state believes that it has such a reason.[2] One further preliminary clarification: the question's subject-matter, the state's reasons, differs from that of Chapter 4, the parties' reasoning: not only do most agreements not have the state as a party but, as noted in sections 4.11 and 4.21, correct reasoning is, if Broome is right, a matter not of giving or discovering reasons but of meeting normative requirements.[3]

It might be argued, from the following premisses, that the state has no such reasons. If it has them, it has reasons for action; if a thing has a reason for action, it is capable of action; if it is capable of action, it is capable of intention (see section 5.32);[4] if it is capable of intention, it has a mind; and the state does not have a mind. The core of the answer is the proposition that actions and reasons can correctly be (for short I shall say 'are') imputed to the state on the basis of those of individuals, in particular of officials who represent the state.[5] The relations between the actions and reasons imputed to the state and the actions and reasons of the relevant individuals are complex and varied; an important issue is

1 On the distinctions between normative, motivating and explanatory reasons, see Chap. 1 n. 58 and Chap. 3 n. 48 above.

2 Here I agree with Alvarez (2010), 22 f. See also R. Audi (2001), 119.

3 See Chap. 4 nn. 5 and 27 above.

4 See also Stout (2005), 3; Chap. 3 n. 83 above.

5 Compare Chap. 5 n. 43 above, on the 'identification principle' in criminal law, and the discussion, in sections 7.32 and 7.37 below, of the mental states of contracting parties.

whether, and if so in what sense, the former can be reduced to the latter.[6] Those matters cannot be pursued here. Let it be granted that the state has at least imputed actions and reasons. Provided that our question is understood to cover those, the argument fails.

It matters little which premiss is rejected. It might, for example, be held that the state may be capable of imputed action without being capable of intention, in which case the third premiss is false; or that although it must be capable of imputed intention – and so the third premiss is true if read as covering such intention – it need not have a mind, in which case the fourth is false; or that although it must have an imputed mind – and so the fourth premiss is true if read as covering such minds – the state has an imputed mind, in which case the fifth, so read, is false. On one view, it has an imputed mind if it is appropriate to take the 'intentional stance' towards the state; on a stronger view, if that stance is appropriate then the state has a mind simpliciter,[7] in which case the fifth premiss is false even if read as covering only such minds. The stronger view might be combined with the thesis that there is no difference between a mind simpliciter and an imputed mind.

Although there is broad consensus as to the main features that a political organisation must have in order to be a state in the modern sense[8] – a territory, a self-reproducing and socially interrelated population, a single government,[9] legal and political independence, and recognition by other states – views of the activities proper for the state are contested,[10] value-laden and variable over times and places.[11] Moreover, the phrase 'activity

6 Hollis (1994), 106 ff. is an introduction to the literature on individualism in social science. See also Ryan (1973), esp. chaps. 3, 6 f.; Sheinman (2011a), 371 f. On reduction, see C. Hooker (1981).

7 Dennett (1981), 7 maintains that, if the intentional stance towards a system is appropriate, the question whether the system really has beliefs and desires is misplaced.

8 'State' can be used in a broader sense to mean any independent political organisation: see Nicholson (1998), 120, which also discusses the distinctions between state, government, society and nation. Horton (1992), 15 prefers 'polity' to a broad use of 'state'. On the evolution of the concept of the state, see D. MacCulloch (2010), 12; Schiemann (2007); Skinner (1978), esp. vol. 2, 349 ff.

9 See Nicholson (1998), 120. Nicholson holds that the consensus extends to various features of the government: it is a distinct 'body of rule', supported by a judicial, administrative and military machine; is the ultimate prescriber and enforcer of law for all those within its jurisdiction; claims exclusive control, and has preponderant control, of the use of force within the territory; and claims and receives authority for its existence and actions.

10 On 'essentially contested' concepts, see Gallie (1956). Compare R. Dworkin (1978), 134 ff. and R. Dworkin (1986a), 71 f. on the distinction between concepts and conceptions.

11 See Nicholson (1998), 120 f.

proper for the state' is ambiguous: it may relate, for example, to the state's functions, powers (normative or positive), rights, obligations, duties, or authority, or to the things that the state ought or is required to do, or that it would be right for the state to do, or wrong for it not to do, or to some combination of these.

An anarchist or libertarian might argue that, since it is not an activity proper for the state to enforce, prohibit or promote agreements, the state has no reason to do so.[12] Even if the premiss is true, the conclusion does not follow on any of the readings listed; for example, the state might have a reason to do something that it would be wrong for it to do. It would trivially follow if an activity proper for the state were defined as one that the state has reason to perform, but then the definition would be strained and the premiss implausible. The issue is pursued, as regards a reading of 'proper activity' in terms of functions, in the appendix to the chapter. The question whether the enforcement etc. of agreements is an activity proper for the state is one of several with which our question might, but should not, be confused. Others, in the case of enforcement, are whether agreements need an enforcer; whether enforcement is consistent with the autonomy of the parties; and whether the state is the only capable enforcer.

Another objection at the threshold is that the question is uninteresting because reasons are, and reasons are uninteresting because they are weak: as already conceded, it may be true both that the state has a reason to φ and that φing is not an activity proper for the state in any of the senses listed. Whether something is interesting is at least partly a matter of opinion; judging by the large philosophical literature on reasons, the opinion that reasons are interesting is widely shared. The objector may say that the literature is concerned more with analytical questions than with substantive ones such as ours; but even if that is true – even if, more specifically, the analytical/substantive distinction can be sustained – the former questions would have little interest if the latter had none. He might now retort that, although some substantive questions about reasons may be interesting, this one is not. But there is ample justification for taking an interest in it. In particular – to revert to an earlier charge – it is connected to questions about the state's proper activities in the listed senses. For example, section 3.2 explained that (roughly) ≪X is obligated to φ> if and only if a reason for X to φ is a ground of an obligation on X to φ>;

12 For the varieties of anarchism, see Horton (1992), chap. 5 and Woodcock (1963); of libertarianism, N. Barry (1986).

it follows that if enforcing agreements were not a proper activity of the state, in the sense that the state had no obligation to enforce them, then any reason which the state had to enforce them would not ground such an obligation.

6.2 Reasons for enforcement

The main agreements enforced by the state are contractual. The discussion will be restricted to those, although it can be argued that the state enforces agreements of other kinds, such as certain agreements covered by doctrines of estoppel; conversely it can be argued that some contractual agreements – certain illegal ones, for example – are not enforced by the state. The arguments can be deflected by defining a contractual agreement as one enforced by the state; as noted in section 7.1, there are various ways to define a contract, and the boundaries of contract law are blurred and shifting. I shall talk of contracts, for short, but some contracts are not agreements, just as some agreements are not contracts. Sections 7.2–7.5 and 7.64 discuss the relations between the two.

The question about enforcement is more precisely framed to concern reasons not for enforcement but for providing an apparatus – the courts and other institutions – to which the parties can resort, if they choose, for the enforcement of contracts.[13] In many cases X's awareness that the apparatus exists, and that Y is willing to use it if X breaches his contract with Y, is enough to ensure that X performs. I shall be referring to reasons for providing such an apparatus when, again for short, I talk of reasons for enforcement. The word 'enforcement' should accordingly be read, when the context so requires, as shorthand for 'provision by the state of

13 This distinction is not explicit, but is probably intended, in S. Smith (2005), 3. At 22 f. Smith notes that contracts are often made and performed with little concern for the law of contract, and that, when a contract is broken, parties rarely stand on their legal rights and even more rarely seek or even threaten redress in the courts. Compare Kötz in Chap. 4 n. 28 above. Smith motivates the question about enforcement by referring to two features (or – he is not clear on the point – one feature under two aspects) which, he suggests, impugn the legitimacy of enforcement by the state, namely that contracts are voluntary undertakings (see Chap. 2 n. 52 above and n. 62 below) and are private. Whether the claim that contracts are voluntary and private is true depends on the senses given to those words. For a definition of the voluntary, see Feinberg (Chap. 3 n. 67 above); on contract law as a part of private law, see S. Smith (2005), 1; on voluntary obligations, see section 3.3 above. Chapters 1 and 2 above give reasons to deny that contracts are, or need be made by, undertakings.

an apparatus which the parties to a contractual agreement can use for the enforcement of the agreement'.

6.21 Consequential reasons

Consequential reasons for the state to enforce contracts relate, in the way set out in (139) below, to the achievement of goods or to the avoidance of bads. The goods may result from the performing or the making of contracts, or from neither. They may consist inter alia of benefits enjoyed, expressive acts, or the performing of obligations. Benefits may be enjoyed by the parties to the contract – see the description, in section 2.4, of the main function of agreements – or by others, and they may or may not be intended by one or more parties when the contract is made or performed; a plausible thought is that unintended benefits form an especially good reason for enforcement, as they may not otherwise motivate the parties. This talk of goods and bads, and of their consisting of such-and-such, can be made more precise (in part by using the concept of grounding, described in section 3.2) but it is clear enough. The following points apply to the goods; similar ones apply to the bads.

Benefits may be caused by, or in some other way result causally from, the performing or the making of contracts, whereas expressive acts and the performing of obligations are likely to be results of some other kind, perhaps involving a relation of constitution: compare section 4.11 on the means-end relation. It might be objected that in certain cases the expressive act or the performing of the obligation is not the result of, but is identical to, the performing or the making of the contract: in particular, when a party, in performing the contract, expresses something or performs an obligation, the expression, or the performing of the obligation, is the same action as the performing of the contract. A full response would require an excursion into the philosophy of action, but the objection can be avoided by allowing resultance to include identity as a limiting case. For present purposes there is no need to pursue the analysis of resultance[14] – or of the means-end relation, to which corresponding points apply. (See section 4.3, on an action's being a means to itself, and section 2.1 on the 'in'/'by' distinction.)

14 Dancy appears to use 'resultance' more narrowly, to mean the inverse of grounding: see Chap. 3 n. 33 above.

For each category of good, the argument is the same:

(139) (a) The state's enforcing contracts is a means to G.
(b) G is good.
(c) If (a) and (b), then the state has a reason to enforce contracts.
So:
(d) The state has a reason to enforce contracts.

It can be generalised over agents and actions:

(140) (a) X's φing is a means to G.
(b) G is good.
(c) If (a) and (b), then X has a reason to φ.
So:
(d) X has a reason to φ.

(140)(c), being schematic and hence general, entails:

(141) For any good, any agent, and any action the agent's performance of which is a means to the good, the agent has a reason to perform the action.[15]

(Compare the move from (52) to (53) in section 3.4.) Of the various objections that might be raised to (141), and hence to (140)(c) and (139)(c), I shall consider only one, that (141) generates too many reasons: you have a reason to enforce contracts that do not concern you, as your doing so is a means to the goods described above; the state has a reason to send you a birthday present, as its doing so is a means to your enjoyment of the present. One response is to reject each of the examples, on the basis that the relevant instance of (140)(a) or (140)(b) is false. As to the former example, it might be said that your, rather than the state's, enforcing contracts is not a means to the goods in question; this claim might be reinforced by an analysis of the means-end relation. As to the latter, the claim might be that it is not good for you to enjoy gifts from the state. A second response is that it does not follow, from the proposition that (140)(c) is false and (139)(c) instantiates (140)(c), that (139)(c) is false; this could be supplemented by an explanation of the difference in truth value among the instances of (140)(c).

15 Kagan (1998), 26 states a similar principle. (141) is a form of consequentialism, broadly defined. Scheffler (1988) is an introduction to the large literature on consequentialism.

The best response is that (141) is true. Reasons are weak, as noted in section 6.1, and so the examples are no embarrassment. The state's having a reason to send you a birthday present does not imply that it does not have a stronger reason not to, or that its sending you one is among its proper activities in any of the senses listed in that section. The same applies to the other example. It might now be objected that, if reasons are so weak, they are uninteresting; but that objection has already been answered.

6.211 Goods resulting from performance

Consider the reasons relating to those goods that result from the performing of contracts. A detailed account of the mechanism that makes true the relevant instances of (139)(a) (the state's enforcing contracts is a means to G) would require an analysis of the means-end relation, but an outline can be given without one. Assume that, if enforcement is a means to performance, it is a means to the results of performance. This assumption, which leaves open the possibility that enforcement is a means to the results even if it is not a means to performance, follows from the propositions that the means-end relation is the inverse of resultance and that it is transitive.[16] On one understanding of those relations, the latter proposition is true and the former false: A's being a means to B implies, and B's resulting from A does not, that B can be controlled via A. Whatever the truth values of the propositions, the assumption is plausible, and so the discussion can be directed at the question how enforcement is a means to performance.

Premisses from which the parties may correctly reason to an intention to perform include the premiss that other things are equal: see (72), (94)(b) and (99)(b) (sections 4.21 and 4.22). That is needed, as was explained, to exclude cases of outweighing, for example, – in a simple case of the instrumental reasoning (70)–(105)–(72)–(98) (section 4.22) – where X wants not to perform more than he wants Y to perform. The enforcement of contracts increases the likelihood that other things *are* equal, by reducing the likelihood that an outweighing consideration obtains (see further sections 7.2 and 7.38). Roughly, if X and Y contract with each other, then, if X is to reason correctly from a desire not to perform to an intention not to perform, his desire normally needs to be stronger, given that contracts are enforced, than it would need to be if they were not; for in the normal case he needs to weigh that desire against

16 On inverse relations, see Chap. 3 n. 42 above; on transitivity, n. 34 to that chapter.

not only the desire that Y perform but also the desire to avoid the possible consequences of enforcement. Those consequences may include the remedy of specific performance, in which case X may be compelled to perform anyway.[17] As section 4.11 explained, the point is more accurately stated in terms not of X's desires but of the desires he believes himself to have. As also explained there, his reasoning needs to take into account the probabilities of the various outcomes – in particular, the probabilities that if he breaches the contract then Y will apply to the court for a remedy and that if Y does so then the court will grant one. If X believes either of these to be low enough, the reasoning may conclude in an intention not to perform, even if his desire to avoid the consequences of enforcement is strong.

As noted, this is only an outline; a full explanation would need, among other things, to accommodate the gaps between fact and mental state, between mental state and action, and between probability and instrumentality. As to the first (one instance of which has already been identified), X might be, or believe that Y is, unaware that contracts are enforced. As to the second, it might be that, even though X intends to perform, he fails to do so; this gap could be bridged by an assumption of reliability, as described in section 4.11. As to the third, even if enforcement increases the likelihood that other things are equal, it need not be a means to X's performing. More specifically, even if it increases that likelihood, it need not increase the likelihood that X performs; and, even if it does increase this likelihood, it need not be a means to his performing – just as it does not follow, from the fact that your having fair hair increases the likelihood of your being a member of the Jones family, that having fair hair is a means to becoming one of the Joneses. Conversely, in a case of overdetermination or pre-emption, A can be a means to B without increasing B's likelihood: it might be that, even if it were certain that without enforcement X would perform, enforcement would be a means to his performing. (As noted in section 4.11, such cases could be excluded by a narrow definition of means. Compare the discussion, in that section, of the relation between instrumentality and conditionality.)

In any event, the account describes only the generality of contracts: in a particular instance enforcement may not be a means to performance. A universal apparatus of enforcement may nevertheless be a better means to performance in cases where it is a means than would an apparatus that tried to isolate those cases.

17 On the differences among legal systems as to the availability of specific performance, see Zweigert and Kötz (1998), chap. 35.

6.2111 Benefits to the parties and others As to (139)(b) (G is good), the benefits that result to the parties from performance are highly varied. As noted in section 6.21, they may be unintended – the lucky formation of a friendship, for example. Of course, in some cases one or more parties fail to benefit from performance: if X and Y contract that <X does Ax and Y does Ay>, X may enter into the contract purely for Y's sake, being unwilling to do Ax and not wanting Y to do Ay (on the question whether Y has a performance obligation in such a case, see section 3.3); or the situation may change so that, although at the time of making the contract X wants Y to do Ay, he has ceased to do so when the time comes for Y to perform; or Y's doing Ay may be desired by X, but not be a benefit to him except in the thin sense identified in section 4.11.

An example of a contract the performance of which benefits a third party is one between X and Y providing that Y will look after X's mother: see section 3.52. As noted there, X may also benefit from the arrangement. The benefit to the mother is presumably intended by X and Y when they make the contract, but third parties can benefit in ways unintended by the parties to a contract. Such cases sometimes fall within the economist's definition of positive externalities – roughly, benefits arising from an economic activity that affect someone other than the people engaged in that activity and hence are not fully reflected in prices.[18]

Smith suggests that the performance of contracts benefits both the contracting parties and others. Contract law is justified:

> on the basis that it facilitates mutually beneficial exchanges, and so promotes overall social welfare or social 'wealth' (broadly defined). The underlying idea is that where two parties freely agree on a contract involving, say, a simple exchange of money for goods, the seller does so because he thinks he will be better off with the money than with the goods, and the buyer does so because she prefers the goods to the money. Both parties thus emerge from the exchange 'better off' (in one sense) than they were before, and since society's wealth is made up of the total wealth of its members, even a simple exchange of this kind can improve social wealth. In short, contract law (and the officials needed to enforce the law) is a justified use of the state's resources because it helps everyone to become better off.[19]

18 See Lipsey (1989), 400 f., 424 f. On externalities as contributing to the decline in freedom of contract, see S. Smith (2005), 11.

19 S. Smith (2005), 3. Smith develops this point into the theses that the purpose of contract law is to secure co-operation, particularly in exchange, and that contract law supports the institution of credit (4). On the first thesis, see Chap. 2 n. 30 above; on contract as exchange, see sections 6.213 and 7.1 below. Other works on the economic efficiency of contracts are cited in Chap. 3 n. 79 above.

The qualifiers 'broadly defined' and 'in one sense' are revealing. Smith notes that this argument is associated with economic approaches to law; it can therefore be assumed that 'welfare' and 'better off' have senses used in economics. ('Wealth' appears to be used here as a synonym for 'welfare'.) The difficulty is to understand why it is a benefit to have welfare, or to be better off, in those senses.

On a common view in welfare economics, to say that you are better or worse off, or that there is an increase or decrease in your welfare, is to say that your utility[20] increases or decreases. Utilities are generally understood to be numerical values of a utility function that represents a person's preferences, and his preferences to be revealed in the choices he makes. As to the first half of this thought, it can be proved that if his preferences conform to certain axioms of rationality – in particular, that they are complete and transitive[21] – they can be represented by a utility function in the sense that, for any pair of options, the function assigns a higher utility to the one preferred.[22] As to the second half, talk of revealed preference is entrenched in the literature but is misleading, for the main results of general equilibrium theory can be derived without distinguishing preferences from the acts of choice that 'reveal' them.[23] Thus utility functions can be viewed as directly representing acts of rational choice,[24] and utility as that which is maximised in rational choice. On this view utilities are neither states or qualities of mind nor objects of choice – we

20 On the various meanings of 'utility', see Broome (1991), 1 ff.; Griffin (1986), 7; Hampton (1998), 93 f.; Kahneman and Varey (1993), 127 ff.; Kymlicka (2002), 13 ff.; Leibenstein (1980), 192; Little (1957), 20; Millgram (2000), 114; Roemer (1996), 13; Sen (1981), 199 f.; Sen (1982d), 344; Sen (1985), 187; Sen (2002a), 27.

21 To say that preferences are complete is to say that, for any two bundles of commodities A and B, A is preferred to B, B is preferred to A, or they are ranked equally; to say that they are transitive is to say that if A is preferred to B, and B to C, then A is preferred to C. On transitivity generally, see Chap. 3 n. 34 above. For other axioms, see Boadway and Bruce (1984), 34 ff.

22 Technical accounts are given in Boadway and Bruce (1984), 33 ff.; Frank (2003), 91; Johansson (1991), 147 ff.; Roemer (1996), 15 f. For informal accounts, see Allingham (2002), 22 ff.; Broome (1991), 3; Hampton (1998), 91 ff.; Hargreaves Heap et al. (1992), 4 ff., 265 ff.; Hausman and McPherson (1993), 680; D. Sobel (1994), 787; Weintraub (1998), 308.

23 'Thus, the consumer's market behaviour is explained in terms of preferences, which are in turn defined only by behaviour': Samuelson (1970), 91. By contrast, Sen (1982a), 55 ff. argues that economics cannot dispense with a non-behavioural concept of preference. See also Sen (1982c), 9; Hampton (1998), 91 ff.; Keita (1999), 347; n. 27 below. On the divergence between preference and choice, see O. Black (2005b), 59 f. and references there.

24 See Little (1957), 29. This approach is criticised in Sen (1985), 187 f.

do not choose to increase or maximise our utility[25] – but are numbers associated with choices by utility functions. 'Welfare' and 'better off' thus have senses too thin for it to be clear why they signify a benefit.[26]

The obvious response is to maintain that welfare in the sense at issue is a test or proxy for welfare in the more intuitive sense in which a person's welfare is, roughly, that which makes his life go well for him.[27] This notion has been amplified in various philosophical theories of welfare, which fall on a spectrum from the subjective/positive to the objective/normative:[28] welfare has been conceived as a mental state;[29] as the satisfaction of actual

25 'You do not choose to go riding rather than skiing because it gives you more utility; on the contrary, a greater utility is assigned to riding because you choose it': Allingham (2002), 23 f. See also Hausman (1995), 473 f.; Hausman and McPherson (1993), 680; Little (1957), 29; Sumner (1996), 115 ff.

26 For other objections, see O. Black (2005b), 38 f. Various authors note that the present sense of 'utility' is purged of the notions of pleasure and satisfaction used by earlier theorists (see n. 27 below) to define the term: Hargreaves Heap et al. (1992), 7; Hausman and McPherson (1993), 680; Samuelson (1970), 90 f.; Sumner (1996), 116.

27 In welfare economics the behaviourist approach has an older rival according to which choice behaviour is regarded as evidence of welfare, which in turn is taken to consist of a mental state or of the satisfaction of preferences or desires. This approach, which was taken by Pigou (see Pigou (2002), 10 ff.), is exemplified in two textbooks: Boadway and Bruce (1984), 11, 39, 56 and Johansson (1991), 3 f., 40, 147; see also Sen (1982a). Pigou's theory is analysed in Sumner (1996), 113 ff. On the differences between 'old' and 'new' welfare economics, see Samuelson (1970), 249. Compare Bermúdez (2009), 47 ff. on the distinction between operational and substantive understandings of utility.

Approximate synonyms for 'welfare' in the intuitive sense are 'well-being', 'interest' (but see Raz (1986), 295 ff., which conceives of self-interest as narrower than well-being) and 'flourishing'. 'Your good' is also close to 'your welfare', 'what is good for you' less so: spinach is good for you but is at best a partial cause, not a component, of your welfare. The present sense of 'welfare' should be distinguished from the one at issue in discussions of the welfare state: these concern, roughly, social programmes designed to secure a fair distribution of basic goods and services or to establish a safety net for the disadvantaged: Sumner (1996), vii. A. Moore and Crisp (1996), 599 distinguishes the minimal case, in which a life of well-being is a life worth living, from the case of the fortunate, for whom it is a matter of life's going well. Raz regards well-being as comprising not only that which makes a person's life go well for him but that which makes him a good person: Raz (1994), 36. Parfit (1984), 493 talks of that which makes a person's life go for him as well as possible.

28 For classifications of theories of welfare, see B. Barry (1973), 38 f.; O. Black (2005b), chap. 2; Brock (1993), 96 f.; Buchanan and Brock (1990), 31 ff.; G. Cohen (1993); Elster and Roemer (1993b), 5; A. Goldman (1995), 711; Hausman and McPherson (1998), 206 ff.; Kagan (1998), 29 ff.; Kymlicka (2002), 13 ff.; A. Moore and Crisp (1996), 599 f.; Parfit (1984), 493 ff.; Qizilbash (1997); Scanlon (1993b), 186 ff.; Scoccia (1987), 584; Sen (1982c), 29 f.; Skorupski (2000), 250 f.; Sumner (1996), chaps. 2 ff.; Weale (1998).

29 Such theories are usually hedonistic. They were advanced by the classical utilitarians (see, e.g., Bentham (1948) and, for a review of utilitarian theories, Sumner (1996), 83 ff.) and

choice, preference or desire;[30] as the satisfaction of the choices (etc.) that a subject would make in favourable conditions, or that an idealised subject would make;[31] and as participation in various forms of good.[32] The two questions now are whether 'economic' welfare is indeed a test or proxy for 'philosophical' welfare, presumably in the sense that the former correlates reliably with the latter and perhaps also that it is easier to discern, and whether philosophical welfare is a benefit.

The answers vary depending on the philosophical theory applied, but it seems that no such theory provides a firm basis for the answer yes to both questions. For example, actual-desire theories call into doubt that answer to the second, given the distinction already drawn between desiring something and benefiting from it[33] – a distinction which likewise impugns the adequacy of such theories as accounts of welfare. Likewise, an objection to theories of welfare as participation in forms of good is that they fail to recognise the perspectival character of welfare – the fact that a person's welfare is what makes his life go well *for him*:[34] if benefits are similarly perspectival, these theories also impugn an affirmative answer. (Possible responses are to deny that benefits are perspectival or to propose a perspectival understanding of participation in the forms of good.) The same is true of the first question. Various lists have been given of the relevant forms of good. Griffin suggests: accomplishment; the components of a characteristically human existence (specifically autonomy, minimum material provision and liberty – all of which he claims to be components of agency); understanding, at least of certain basic personal and metaphysical matters; enjoyment; and deep personal relations.[35] It is

still have their defenders, e.g., Bernstein (1998); Kawall (1999); Tännsjö (1996). Epicurean ancestors are found in Diogenes Laertius (1980), bk. 10, para. 34. For objections, see O. Black (2005b), 40 ff. and references there.

30 See the references in the first paragraph of n. 27 above.

31 See Goodin (1989); Griffin (1986), chap. 2; Harsanyi (1982); Kymlicka (2002), 16 ff.; Scoccia (1987); and compare the analysis of 'a man's future good on the whole' in Sidgwick (1907), 111 f. For objections and further references, see O. Black (2005b), 45 f.

32 In some versions the theory is perfectionist, treating the goods as elements of a life that fully realises the distinctive and essential features of human nature. See Griffin (1986), chap. 4; Hurka (1993); Kagan (1998), 40. Hill (2002), 164 ff. describes the transition from objective perfectionist accounts of happiness, in ancient philosophy, to modern subjectivist accounts.

33 For other objections and further discussion, see O. Black (2005b), 42 ff. and references there.

34 See O. Black (2005b), 47 and references there.

35 Griffin (1993), 63, discussed in A. Moore (2000), 75, where a shorter list is proposed, and in Qizilbash (1997), 237 ff. Qizilbash (1998), 63 ff. extends Griffin's list. Different lists

not obvious that economic welfare is a test or proxy for participation in any of these.[36]

6.2112 Expression and obligation The next type of good that results from the performing of contracts consists of expressive acts. To pursue an example from section 4.3: a couple, in performing – or making – a contract to marry, express their commitment to each other.[37] This is often a good, but clearly some expressive acts are bad. Expression by the parties is distinct from expression by the state: the enforcement of contracts is a means for the state to express a positive valuation of contractual performance or of the institution of contract. If such expression is itself good then, by (139), the state has a reason for enforcement:[38] see section 6.213.

It was suggested in section 6.21 that, among the goods that result from the performing of contracts, some consist of the performing of obligations. The main obligations in question are the performance obligations of contractual parties. Section 3.3 maintained – subject to refinements and provisos that can be ignored here – that if X agrees to do Ax then X is obligated to do Ax. As explained there, I use 'performance obligation' to cover indifferently that obligation and (if it is a different one) X's obligation to perform the agreement: 'perform a performance obligation' is thus not a pleonasm. These points apply in particular to contracts. In terms of (139):

(142) (a) The state's enforcing contracts is a means to the parties' performing their performance obligations.
(b) The parties' performing those obligations is good.

are given in Finnis (1980), 85 ff.; Gewirth (1998), 80; Griffin (1986), 64 ff.; Kagan (1998), 39; G. Moore (1959), 188 ff.; Rawls (1972), 69, 92, 440; Rawls (1993), 180 f. (under the heading 'primary goods'); Sumner (1996), 180.

36 Research indicating that economic growth above a certain threshold does little to improve happiness is relevant here: see A. Campbell (1981); Diener (1984); Duncan (1975); Easterlin (1974); Inglehart (1996); Kahneman and Varey (1993), 141; Lane (1994), 229; Scitovsky (1992), chap. 7.

37 On the ends served by marriage contracts, see Aquinas (1894), suppl. q 41, a 1, and the discussion in Gordley (1991), 15 f. On the treatment of marriage in English contract law, see Furmston (2007), 515 ff.; Peel (2007), paras. 11–032 ff.

38 In one of the many meanings of 'liberal', it is characteristic of liberal political views to allow only a narrow scope for the state to favour particular values, e.g., by expressing them. That position is naturally formulated as a limit on the activities proper for the state: see section 6.1 above. On the evaluative element of liberalism, see R. Dworkin (1986b). On the varieties of liberalism, see Fawcett (forthcoming); Kymlicka (1989), chap. 1; Kymlicka (2002), chap. 3; Waldron (1987); Wolff (1996), chap. 4.

(c) If (a) and (b), then the state has a reason to enforce contracts.
So:
(d) The state has a reason to enforce contracts.

There is no confusion here between consequential and deontological reasons for enforcement: deontological reasons apply to the parties in the way summarised above, the consequential one applies to the state, and the latter refers to the former.[39] Nor is it assumed that a party's only motive for performing is the fear of enforcement; there is thus no scope for an objection based on either of the propositions – contentious in any event – that if he acts only from the fear then he does not perform the obligation and that, even if he did perform it in those circumstances, his doing so would not be good.

Premiss (a) follows from the combination of the proposition argued in section 6.211, that enforcement is a means to the performing of contracts, and two assumptions already made, the first that if enforcement is such a means then it is a means to the results of the performing of contracts (see section 6.211), the second that the parties' performing their performance obligations results from their performing the contract (see section 6.21).

39 The distinction is blurred in the discussion in S. Smith (2005), 3 ff. of the justifications for the state's enforcement of contracts. As mentioned in Chap. 2 n. 30 above, Smith distinguishes the 'economic' or 'utilitarian' justification discussed in section 6.2111 above from a 'moral' or 'individualist' one to the effect that enforcement protects duties owed by the contracting parties to each other. In those terms, the reason under discussion, being consequential, comes under the 'utilitarian' heading; but, in so far as it also concerns the parties' mutual moral obligations (see the main text below), it also comes under the 'moral' one. Smith does not consider deontological reasons of the kind discussed in section 6.22 below.

He suggests that the two justifications are in tension as they 'have opposite starting points. The economic view supposes that society's interests take precedence over those of the individual, while the moral view supposes the opposite' (5). That is an artificial problem. Although those suppositions can be built into the justifications, they need not be. Each justification can be read simply as identifying a certain reason for enforcement; it need not be read as claiming that the reason outweighs the one identified by the other.

Zweigert and Kötz (1998), 325 ff. also distinguishes a utilitarian from an individualist justification for enforcement by the state, but expresses the individualist justification in terms not of the parties' duties but of their autonomy. The authors note that the idea of freedom of contract as a manifestation of individual autonomy is connected to the 'will theory' of contract, as to which see sections 6.213 and 7.12 below. See also Kötz (1997), 5, 7 f.; Eisenberg (2001), 223 ff., distinguishing autonomy theories and revealed-preference theories as two types of 'single-value normative theory'. Gordley objects to both utilitarian/economic and 'Kantian' accounts of contract law, as he does to the will theory, on the ground that they seek to 'build contract doctrine around the single idea of choice or commitment': Gordley (1991), 244. On commitment, see Chap. 3 n. 149 above.

As to (b), it is perhaps more accurate to say that the parties' breaching their obligations is bad than that their performing them is good, in which case the argument can be reformulated accordingly. (b) may be supported as follows. It was argued in section 3.6 – subject to refinements which also can be ignored – that, for any agreement, the fact of agreement, FA, is a ground of the parties' performance obligations; that, for some but not all agreements, some other fact grounds a moral performance obligation on a party; hence that, if an obligation grounded only in FA is moral, the parties have moral performance obligations in every case, and, if not, it is only in some cases that a party has such an obligation; and that, whatever the moral status of an obligation grounded only in FA (a question left open), the obligation is important for its bearing on social co-operation. A plausible view is that to perform a moral obligation is good, at least morally and pro tanto.[40] A corresponding point (which may need to be qualified, depending on the explication of 'important') applies to the performing of important obligations, moral or not. The argument can be refined to allow that not every performance obligation is either moral or important: the state's enforcing contracts is a means to the parties' performing their performance obligations in cases where those obligations are moral or important; the parties' performing them in those cases is good; and so on. The remaining cases, if any, are no more problematic than the possibility, contemplated in section 6.211, that in certain cases enforcement is not a means to the performing of a contract.

As regards the moral obligations, a liberal might object that it is not the business of the state to enforce morality. Thus stated, the objection is an extreme one, which excludes much of the criminal law from the state's business; questions of more interest are which aspects of morality it is the business of the state to enforce and what its role in enforcement should be.[41] These need not be pursued, for the objection misses the argument. Talk of the state's business seems to concern the activities proper for the

40 Compare M. Zimmerman (1996), 14 f.: 'to have the *deontic status* of being obligatory, an act's *deontic value* must be greater than that of any other alternative action' (emphasis in original; see further ibid., 21 ff.). Zimmerman here restricts 'deontic' to 'the moral realm'. It is also plausible to view the performance of a moral obligation as involving iterated grounding: in short, the goodness is grounded in compliance with the obligation, and the obligation in FA or some other fact. Compare Dancy on 'resultance trees' (Chap. 3 n. 34 above); n. 50 below.

41 Loci classici are Devlin (1959); Hart (1963); Mill (1910a). For a minimalist conception of the state's business, see Nozick (1974), pt. 1, and compare Hart (1961), 189 ff. on the 'minimum content of natural law'.

state, in one or more of the senses listed in section 6.1. In that case the objector first needs to move from the premiss that the enforcement of morality is not such an activity to the lemma that the enforcement of contracts also is not: that inference might be supported by the further premisses that the state's enforcement of contracts stands in a certain relation to its enforcement of morality and that the property of being an activity proper for the state is closed under that relation. (On closure, see section 5.32. On at least some readings of 'activity proper for the state', the premiss of closure is false for certain obvious candidates for the relation – such as conditionality, contingent or necessary.) As explained in section 6.1, however, even if the enforcement of contracts is not among the state's proper activities, the state may have a reason to enforce contracts. If the objector retorts that it has a stronger reason not to, the answer is that the argument's conclusion is consistent with his claim: see the discussion of (141) in section 6.21.

As noted in that section, it might be argued that the expressive act or the performing of the obligation is identical to the performing of the contract and that, contrary to an assumption in that section, resultance excludes identity. In that case the goods in question are not goods that result from the performing of contracts but fall in the category, discussed in section 6.213, of 'other goods': compare the treatment of autonomy there.

6.212 Goods resulting from formation

Some reasons for enforcement relate to goods that result from the making of contracts; the connection is similar to that between reasons for enforcement and goods that result from the performing of contracts. There is a superficial puzzle here, for enforcement seems to secure performance rather than formation, i.e., the making; but the puzzle is removed by reflecting that, first, goods resulting from performance are indirect results of formation – so that those already considered can be described as such results – and, second, the making of certain contracts is a result of the general enforcement of contracts.

If counterfactual dependence is taken as a proxy for resultance, an intuitive gloss of the second point is to say that in many cases X would not make a contract with Y unless Y was then going to perform it, and Y would not perform it unless contracts were enforced.[42] The point also is supported

42 This ignores the fact that unrestricted transitivity does not hold for counterfactual conditionals: see Chap. 4 n. 19 above.

(I do not set out the argument in detail) by the analysis, in section 4.11, of the reasoning that X may use to reach an intention to make an agreement with Y. The reasoning includes the premiss (84), that Y is reliable. The premiss – which ensures that if X and Y agree then, absent certain contingencies, Y performs – is underpinned, in the sense explained in that section, by Y's reasoning, in one of the ways described in sections 4.2–4.22, from his agreeing to do Ay to his doing Ay. That reasoning includes ceteris paribus clauses, which may be true only because agreements are enforced: compare the remarks in section 6.211 about the mechanism that makes true the relevant instances of (139)(a) (the state's enforcing contracts is a means to G).

Goods that result from the making of contracts, other than goods that result from the performing of them, are miscellaneous, fact-specific, relatively rare and generally minor. A resulting benefit to one party might be that he gains information about the other party's preferences, which might be relevant to possible future contracts between them; a benefit to both parties might be that they form a friendship; a benefit to a third party Z might be that, if X contracts with Y, X stops pestering Z to contract with X; or X's contracting with Y might be good in that X thereby complies with a moral obligation – say, one of friendship – or it constitutes a certain kind of expressive act (see section 6.2112).

Kimel would agree that considerations of friendship are normally unimportant in the context of contract. He holds that although contracts and promises have the same instrumental value, of securing reliance and co-operation, they differ in their intrinsic values: the intrinsic value of promises is grounded in their promoting special relationships, central to which are expressive acts;[43] that of contracts relates to 'personal detachment'. It is unclear in what sense and why Kimel takes these values to be intrinsic ('promote' and, in the passage quoted below, 'provide' suggest instrumentality, and the intrinsic and the instrumental are naturally conceived as mutually exclusive) and whether he thinks that special relationships and detachment are always valuable. It appears to depend on cases: there need be nothing valuable about the special relationship

43 Kimel (2003), 66, 69; compare Stoljar (1988), 204 f.; contrast Markovits (2011); see also Sheinman (2004). On the desirability of special bonds, see Raz (1982). The combination of the view that political obligations are special bonds (as to which, see Gilbert (1996c), 361 ff.; Simmons (1979), 3 f.) and Kimel's view that such bonds are not typical of contracts provides reason to reject an account of political obligation in terms of a social contract.

between a child-molester and his victim. As to detachment, Kimel writes that the intrinsic value of contracts:

> consists in the very framework contracts provide for doing certain things with others not only outside the context of already-existing relationships, but also without a commitment to the future prospect of such relationships, without being required to know much or form opinions about the personal attributes of others, and without having to allow others to know much and form opinions about oneself.[44]

This thesis can be taken as an account of the function of contracts[45] – in which case it supplements my account, in section 2.4, of the function of agreements – but can also be read as describing a good resulting from their formation. Read thus, it does not apply to every case: the parties to a marriage contract, for example, often have an existing relationship and know a fair amount about each other[46] (see further section 6.3). Even where the parties do have the characteristics Kimel describes, the good – if any – normally results from their performing the contract, not just from their making it.

6.213 Other goods

Some writers maintain that contract law protects or promotes autonomy: parties typically exercise autonomy in making contracts and, perhaps to a lesser extent, in performing them. Related concepts, such as those of self-determination, freedom and the voluntary, are sometimes used instead or as well in this context, and the thesis in its different versions has been linked to the 'will theory' of contract and to the doctrine of freedom of contract.[47] For the theory, the doctrine and the relation between them, see section 7.12.

The supposed connection between contract and autonomy can be argued to generate reasons for intervention by the state. Those reasons might be brought within various categories reviewed in this chapter: they might be reasons for enforcing or for promoting contracts; they might be consequential or deontological; if consequential, they might relate to

44 Kimel (2003), 78.

45 Kimel uses 'value' and 'function' interchangeably: Kimel (2003), 65 f., 78.

46 Kimel argues that his thesis accommodates 'relational' contracts: Kimel (2003), 80 ff. On relational contracts generally, see Eisenberg (1995); Goetz and Scott (1981); Kimel (2007); McKendrick (1995); Macneil (1974); Macneil (1981); Schwartz (1992). Kötz (1997), 15 doubts that such contracts require special treatment.

47 See n. 39 above (final paragraph); n. 62 below; Chap. 3 n. 67 above.

goods resulting from the performing or just from the making of contracts, or to goods of some other kind. The easiest argument is in terms of a consequential reason for enforcement. Applying (139):

(143) (a) The state's enforcing contracts is a means to the exercise of autonomy.
(b) The exercise of autonomy is good.
(c) If (a) and (b), then the state has a reason to enforce contracts.
So:
(d) The state has a reason to enforce contracts.

The good mentioned in (b) is not readily classified as resulting from the performing or the making of contracts, for it is plausible to hold that the performing or the making does not merely result in, but is itself, an exercise of autonomy; hence the location of the argument in the present section. However, as noted in section 6.21 in relation to expressive acts and the performing of performance obligations, the objection could be avoided by treating identity as a limiting case of resultance.

Premiss (a) might in turn be derived from:

(144) The state's enforcing contracts is a means to parties' making and performing contracts.
(145) In making and performing contracts, parties exercise autonomy.
(146) If (144) and (145), then the state's enforcing contracts is a means to parties' exercising autonomy.

The two arguments are valid and their premisses have some plausibility; in particular, (144) is supported by the accounts of the way in which enforcement is a means to performance (section 6.211) and of the way in which the making of certain contracts is a result of general enforcement (section 6.212). (143)(b), on the other hand, looks crude; any refinements or qualifications required may entail further changes. The main task in an assessment of the arguments would be to clarify the relevant meaning or meanings of 'autonomy'.[48]

It can be argued that there are other reasons for intervention by the state that fall in the same category: consequential reasons for enforcement that relate to goods that do not result from the performing or from the making of contracts. An example was given in section 6.2112: enforcement is a means for the state to express certain valuations; so, if such expression is good, the state has a reason for enforcement. Here, it seems (but see the

48 See Chap. 3 n. 67 above.

next paragraph), the good results from neither the performing nor the making, but directly from the enforcement. A task which I do not pursue is to identify the sense or senses in which the state or its officials, acting as such, can be truly said to express valuations; for example, it seems that a premier can apologise for, and thus express a negative valuation of, his state's conduct even though he privately does not judge that the state acted wrongly.[49] One approach is to say that he expresses a judgment of the majority of citizens; but that need not be so.

Another possible example is based on the thought that contracts typically, although not always, involve an exchange (see section 7.1), and so enforcement makes available a reliable framework for exchange (RFE). In terms of (139): the state's enforcing contracts is a means to RFE, RFE is good, and so on. It might be suggested that the reason here relates to goods resulting from the performing and/or the making of contracts. As regards performance, the argument is: RFE is good not in itself but as a means to goods (which may in turn be instrumental) that result from exchanges; so RFE is a means to those goods; they include goods that result from the performing of contracts; so RFE is a means to such goods; enforcement is a means to RFE; the means-end relation is transitive (see section 6.211); so enforcement is a means to goods that result from the performing of contracts; so, by (139), the state has a reason to enforce contracts that relates to such goods. Even if the argument is sound, it may be replied that these goods are distinct from the instrumental good of RFE (it is plausible to say that the fact that the results in question are good is, in the terminology of section 3.2, a partial ground of the fact that RFE is good[50]) and that, correspondingly, the reason relating to the former is distinct from the one relating to the latter. To settle the issue, the principles for identifying and individuating goods and reasons would need investigation. A similar argument and reply could be applied to the reason relating to the good of the state's expressing valuations.

6.22 Deontological reasons

As already noted, a rough summary of a thesis from section 3.2 is: <X is obligated to φ> if and only if a reason for X to φ is a ground of

49 On political apologies, see Faraji and Pendharkar (2009); Griswold (2007), chap. 4; Harris et al. (2006); Hook (2008); Radzik (2011); N. Smith (2008).

50 Given that the former fact is grounded, this is another case of iterated grounding: see n. 40 above.

an obligation on X to φ. The thesis can be extended to certain other deontological concepts that were used in section 6.1 to explicate the idea of an activity proper for the state – *duty*, *right* and *ought*, for instance (there is no need here to draw precise boundaries around the category of the deontological (see section 4.21)) – but then needs qualification to forestall such counterexamples as the fact that, although a knife ought to cut, it has no reason to. The obvious way to deal with this case is to limit the thesis to actions: in cutting, a knife does not act. (The grounds are weak here for imputing actions and reasons in the way described in section 6.1. The limitation is implicit in the use of 'φ', which, as explained in the Introduction, is a placeholder for a verb of action.) This highlights a difference between *ought* and *obligation*:[51] the latter typically relates to actions,[52] including mental ones, but the former has a broader extension – or at least 'ought' signifies various concepts which together do so.[53]

The deontological reasons, if any, for the state to act depend on the normative foundations of the state. If you take the state to be a product of, or a party to, some form of social contract, you may find a reason in the ground of an obligation that somehow follows from an obligation to perform that contract; if you take it to be a product or expression of the divine will, you may find a reason in the ground of a duty derived from the duty to obey God; if you take it to be a phase of the unfolding of the Absolute, you may find one in the ground of some demand imposed by that process.

It might be suggested that deontological reasons for the state to enforce contracts can be identified that do not depend on, or at least are fairly insensitive to, particular theories of the state's normative foundations. One thought in this vein invokes the 'ideal utilitarian' view – which might, however, itself be understood as, or as implying, a theory of those foundations – that the, or a, ground of the fact that X ought to φ is the fact that X's φing would result in more good than would result from any other action open to X.[54] From the combination of that view

51 See further Chap. 3 n. 87 above.

52 For the thesis that moral obligation involves a reason that is 'agency-specific', see Pink (Chap. 3 n. 22 above).

53 See Anscombe (1997), 30 on the connection between *ought*, *good* and *bad*.

54 'Ideal utilitarianism' is Ross's label for the theory in G. Moore (1966): see D. Ross (1930), 19. On that theory, *right* is weaker than *ought* in that a ground of its being right for X to φ is the fact that X's φing would not result in less good than would result from any other action open to X: G. Moore (1966), 14 f. D. Ross (1939), 43 draws a similar distinction between *right* and *obligatory*. On the relations between *right*, *ought* and *obligatory*, see

and the thesis that it is best for the state to enforce contracts, it follows (on certain auxiliary assumptions) that there is a deontological reason for the state to do so. This approach assimilates the deontological reason to the consequential reasons discussed above, although here the claim is that the result of enforcement is not merely good but the best.[55]

6.3 Reasons for prohibition or promotion

The two main types of reason – consequential and deontological – for enforcement apply equally to the prohibition and promotion of certain types of agreement; the arguments are similar to those already presented, and so the discussion here can be brief. The state has reason to prohibit criminal conspiracies, for example, in that its doing so prevents or reduces the bad results of performing or just making them; prohibition also arguably has the good result of expressing disapproval, or something stronger; and it can be argued, along the lines just considered, that the state has an obligation or duty, or ought, to prohibit them. The concept of agreement in the law of conspiracy is discussed in Chapter 9.[56]

Not all agreements prohibited by the state are criminal. For example, competition law, the subject of Chapter 8, prohibits cartels, but treats them as criminal only in limited circumstances.[57] The supposed reasons for the prohibition derive mainly from those for economic competition. Again some are consequential – it is said, for example, that competition encourages the survival of the economically fittest – and some are either deontological or, like the one in (142), connected to deontological reasons: competition is sometimes said to embody certain moral rights or political liberties.[58] The claim usually made nowadays by theorists

Chap. 3 nn. 10, 14, 87 and 122 above. Anscombe (1997), 36 ff. rejects ideal utilitarianism, and consequentialist accounts of *right* and *ought* generally, as ethically repugnant.

55 Harman (1977), 85 f. identifies a weaker, 'evaluative', sense of 'ought', in which to say that X ought to φ is to say that the state of affairs in which X φs would be good, but not necessarily the best. See also ibid., chap. 10 and Harman (1978) on the different senses of 'ought'. On the distinction between binding and non-binding senses, see n. 21 to the Introduction above.

56 On the arguments for the recognition of inchoate crimes, and of conspiracy in particular, see n. 4 to that chapter.

57 See nn. 2 and 5 to that chapter.

58 The distinction between consequential and deontological arguments about competition is central to Wolff (2006). For arguments for and against competitive markets, see Buchanan (1985), which provides a survey; Gaus (1998), 29 ff.; Hargreaves Heap et al. (1992), chap. 4; Lipsey (1989), chap. 23; Samuelson (1970), 204 ff.; Whish (2009), 3 ff. Buchanan

and practitioners is a consequential one, that competition maximises welfare;[59] correspondingly, the law is advocated in terms of its effect on welfare.[60] I have argued elsewhere[61] against that orthodoxy. In outline the argument is that 'welfare' has either a meaning in which welfare is good but competition does not maximise it, or one in which competition does maximise welfare but the fact that it does so gives no reason for competition, because welfare in this sense is not worth maximising: compare the discussion, in section 6.2111, of the alleged welfare-based reason for the enforcement of contracts. In that case competition and its law are either ineffective means to a valuable end or effective means to a worthless one.

By the promotion of a type of agreement I primarily mean the promotion of the making of such agreements; promotion of performance has already been largely covered in the discussion of enforcement – although there are other ways of promoting performance, such as propaganda and education. Section 6.212 also discussed a way in which enforcement promotes formation. If the state's acting in a certain way is a means to the making of agreements of a given type, its so acting promotes the making of those agreements. Where acting as a means to something increases that thing's probability (as to which, see section 6.211), the difference between promotion of making and promotion of performing can be represented as one between unconditional and conditional probabilities: the former increases the probability that the agreements are made; the latter, the probability of their being performed if made.

Marriage contracts are a type of agreement which some would argue the state has reasons to promote. Consequential reasons are most likely to be alleged, on the basis, for example, of the thought that, if a couple intend to live together and raise a family, it is good for them to make a

(2 ff.) divides the arguments into those based on efficiency and those based on morality, but acknowledges that the distinction is not sharp. Sen (2002b) proposes a justification of markets on the basis of freedom, contrasting it with welfare-based justifications.

59 US cases: *Reiter* v. *Sonotone Corp.* 442 US 330, 99 S Ct 2326, 60 L Ed 2d 931 (1979); *McGahee* v. *Northern Propane Gas Co.* 858 F. 2d 1487 (11th Cir. 1988); *Atlantic Richfield Co.* v. *USA Petroleum Co.* 495 US 328, 100 S Ct 1884, 109 L Ed 2d 333 (1990). Commentary: S. Bishop and Walker (2002), paras. 2.22 ff.; Bork (1978); Burns (1990), 33 f.; Gellhorn et al. (2004), 47 f.; Kovacic (1990); Whish (2009), 4 ff. There is debate as to whether the welfare in question is consumer welfare or social welfare. Bork, who defines competition in terms of welfare (see Chap. 8 n. 41 below), is concerned with social welfare, but that is obscured by the fact that in his terminology producers are a subclass of consumers.

60 For the various ends that have been pursued in the name of competition, see Chap. 8 n. 41 below.

61 O. Black (2005b), chap. 2.

formal commitment, and that the state's promoting marriage contracts – say, through tax allowances – is a means to that good. The claim about formal commitment is of course debatable and may be developed in various ways, in terms of goods resulting from the performing, or of other goods resulting from the making, of a marriage contract: they might for instance be said to include goods consisting of benefits enjoyed by the couple and their children (emotional security), or by society more broadly (the likelihood of separation and of the consequent burdens on the taxpayer, such as the provision of housing, is reduced), or of the performing of an obligation – possibly a religious one – by the parties, or of the very expression of the commitment. It might also be argued to be good that the state, in promoting marriage contracts, expresses approval of the commitment.

6.4 Appendix: reason and function

In section 6.1 I rejected the argument that, since it is not an activity proper for the state to enforce, prohibit or promote agreements, the state has no reason to do so. The argument may appear to work if expanded in terms of functions:[62]

(147) If the state has a reason to enforce, prohibit or promote agreements, then a function of the state is to do so.[63]
(148) It is not a function of the state to do so.
Therefore:
(149) The state has no reason to do so.

62 On functions, see Chap. 2 n. 29 above. S. Smith (2005), 22 maintains that contracts are of fundamental political importance, as '[t]he idea that economic relations should be governed by voluntary contracts is another way of saying that the market, not the state, should be the primary means of organising economic life. Our ideas about contracts cannot be separated, in other words, from our ideas about the state's role in organising social relations'. (See also n. 13 above.) If a role is the same as a function, Smith seems to say that one of 'our ideas' is that it is a function of the state to enforce contracts but not to be the primary means of organising economic life. For his view of the economic benefits resulting from the performance of contracts, see section 6.2111 above. Compare Kötz (1997), 6; von Mehren (1992), paras. 4, 112, 120.

63 This premiss might be viewed as an instance of an extended form of the 'instrumentalism' attacked in Shafer-Landau (2009): that is the thesis that the only reasons there can be are ancillary to the agent's 'commitments'. For defences of the thesis, see B. Williams (1981); B. Williams (1995).

Where the state has a reason to φ, a proponent of the expanded argument might hold either that the fact that it is a function of the state to φ is part of the reason[64] – more strictly, in accordance with the analysis in section 3.2, that the fact is a part of the reason's factual element – or merely that the absence of the fact would exclude the state's having a reason to φ.[65]

He might support the argument by drawing a comparison with government departments. Suppose that the adoption of some immunisation programme would promote public health. Then, the reasoning goes, the department of health has a reason to adopt the programme, but the ministry of defence does not. The difference is that the department does, but the ministry does not, have the function of promoting public health.

It might be replied that, if in some emergency the department broke down, the ministry could have a reason to step in and adopt the programme even though promoting public health was not one of its functions. It is doubtful that this is the best way to describe such a case. We can imagine that individuals in the ministry start dealing with health and have reasons to do so, but it is not clear that the same is true of the ministry itself: actions and reasons are imputed to government departments, as they are to the state, on the basis of actions and reasons of individuals, and it is unclear that the relations needed to justify the imputation obtain here.

An attempt might be made to strengthen the case for the imputation by redescribing the example. Suppose that the prime minister and the cabinet agree that the ministry will take over responsibility for promoting public health: surely now the ministry itself has reasons to deal with health. Perhaps, but the grounds are equally strong for the view that the promotion of public health has become a function of the ministry, in which case the reasons do not outrun the function. Alternatively it might be said that the ministry has been replaced by a new department, the functions of which include the promotion of public health; whether that is so depends on the criteria for identifying and individuating departments.

Nevertheless the argument, although valid, is unsound: the conclusion follows from the premisses, but at least one of the premisses is false. Since there are agents that have reasons but no functions,[66] it is false that if X has a reason to φ then φing is a function of X. Recognising that this

64 Compare Raz (1990), 22 ff. on 'complete reasons'.

65 An excluding condition is different from an outweighing reason. For this and related distinctions, see Chap. 3 n. 88 above.

66 A neo-Aristotelian such as Gordley might deny this. See Gordley (1991), 245.

principle is false helps one to see that (147), an instance of the principle, is also false (although it could be that the principle was false and (147) true). Granted that (147) is false, the argument fails even if (148) is true.

A possible rejoinder is that, since the state has functions, the relevant principle is more complicated: if X has functions then, if X has a reason to φ, φing is a function of X. The argument can be further expanded so that one of its premisses instantiates that principle:

(150) The state has functions.
(151) If the state has functions, then, if the state has a reason to enforce, prohibit or promote agreements, a function of the state is to do so.
Therefore . . .

and so on as above. The more complicated principle is false: a policeman has a function; if he has an itch, he has a reason to scratch it; but scratching his itch does not fulfil his policing function or any other function he might have. (151), an instance of that principle, is false too. Hence, whether or not (150) is true, the revised argument is unsound.

Another possible rejoinder is that, since the state is unlike a human individual in that it is an abstract object which is nothing over and above its functions, the relevant principle is more complicated still: if X has functions and is nothing over and above its functions, then, if X has a reason to φ, φing is a function of X. The argument can be revised again so that one of its premisses instantiates that principle:

(150) The state has functions.
(152) The state is nothing over and above its functions.
(153) If the state has functions and is nothing over and above its functions, then, if the state has a reason to enforce, prohibit or promote agreements, a function of the state is to do so.
Therefore . . .

As before, the principle at issue and its instance, here (153), might be attacked; but, whether or not (153) is true, the argument is unsound because (152) is false. The notion of something's being nothing over and above its functions is obscure, but on a plausible explication (152) implies the false proposition that the state's only properties are functional. 'The state' is, as noted in section 6.1, a general expression denoting anything that is a state, and any such thing has many non-functional properties.

It might now be proposed that the argument be recast in terms of the reasons which the state has qua state:

(154) If the state qua state has a reason to enforce, prohibit or promote agreements, then a function of the state is to do so.
(148) It is not a function of the state to do so.
Therefore:
(155) The state qua state has no reason to do so.

It might be added that the example of the policeman is irrelevant to this argument because, even if he has a reason to scratch his itch, he does not qua policeman have such a reason.

The notion of the state qua state is little clearer than that of a thing's being nothing over and above its functions, but (154) may plausibly be read as true by definition. In that case, if (148) is true, the argument is sound. But even if (155) is true the state may, albeit not qua state, have reasons to enforce, prohibit or promote certain types of agreement. The argument therefore does not baulk a discussion of those reasons. It might be objected that in that case the concept of the state is superfluous to the discussion, as the question at the start of the chapter has been reduced to one about the reasons that anyone or anything might have. One reply is that certain reasons might be had only by the state even if not qua state. Another is that in modern societies the state is the most, or at least a, prominent enforcer and prohibiter of agreements. (The corresponding claim about promotion is more debatable; for example, the main promoters of sale agreements are arguably potential vendors and purchasers – by advertising, among other things.) It is therefore reasonable to put the question in terms of the state's reasons.

Just as its being a function of the state to enforce, prohibit or promote agreements is not necessary, so it is not sufficient, for the state to have a reason to do so. More generally, the principle is false that if φing is a function of X then X has a reason to φ. The principle misconceives the respective scopes of the conditional and the reason: X has a conditional reason, to see to it that if X's function is to φ then X φs. In Broome's terminology, the function normatively recommends X's φing.[67] It is also arguable – the issue turns on the strength of the concept of a function – that the function normatively *requires* the action, in Broome's sense, i.e., that X ought to see to it that the conditional is true: see section 4.11. For at least one kind of compliance (varieties are discussed in sections 1.22 and

67 Broome (2000), 82 f.

8.122), X can comply with both the recommendation and the requirement either by φing or by not having the function.[68]

It might be replied that there is no confusion of scope in cases where X's φing is good, and hence that the following argument is sound:

(156) If:
  (a) a function of the state is to enforce, prohibit or promote agreements; and
  (b) it is good that the state does so;
  then the state has a reason to do so.
(157) A function of the state is to do so.
(158) It is good that the state enforces, prohibits or promotes agreements.
Therefore:
(159) The state has a reason to do so.

Here the concept of a function is idle, for the argument can be simplified, without loss of plausibility, to:

(158) It is good that the state enforces, prohibits or promotes agreements.
(160) If (158) then the state has a reason to do so.
Therefore:
(159) The state has a reason to do so.

There is thus no interesting argument from the state's functions to its reasons. On certain of the readings of 'activity proper for the state' that were listed in section 6.1, however, its being an activity proper for the state to φ is sufficient for the state to have a reason to φ. In particular, if φing is such an activity in the sense that the state is obligated to φ, then, as explained in section 3.2, X has a reason to φ.

68 Compare Broome on conforming to normative requirements: Chap. 1 n. 44 above.

PART II

Law

7

Contract

7.1 Elements of contract law

There are various ways of defining a contract in English law,[1] but a standard definition is 'an agreement giving rise to obligations which are enforced or recognised by law'.[2] A similar approach is taken in other legal families;[3] for example, Article 1101 of the French Civil Code provides that a contract 'is an agreement by which one or several persons bind themselves [*s'obligent*], to one or several others, to transfer, to do or not to do something'.[4]

An agreement, without more, is not a contract: requirements in English law are that the parties intend to create legal relations, that any relevant formalities are fulfilled and, usually, that consideration is provided.[5] The first two requirements are considered in section 7.21; the third is a peculiarity of common-law systems.[6] Both the definition and the function of

1 Atiyah (1986b), 16 rejects the idea that there is a single model of a contract; see also the strictures in Atiyah (1986j) on the attempt in Fried (1981) to reduce contract to a single principle. For a similar view of contract in Roman law, see Nicholas (1962), 159 ff.; n. 39 below. Atiyah (1986c), 11 f. and Atiyah (1986l), 5 f. present and criticise a 'classical model' of contract. Atiyah (1986i), 63 suggests that in some cases a contract is better characterised as a joint act than as an agreement or an exchange of promises; Atiyah derives that claim from Holmes (2005). See further n. 10 below. On the relation between agreement and joint action, see section 8.5222 below.

2 Peel (2007), para. 1–001.

3 On the concept of a legal family, see Zweigert and Kötz (1998), 63 ff.

4 On the concept of contract as agreement in French law, see Kötz (1997), 3 (citing Pothier's definition, which combines talk of agreement with talk of promises); Nicholas (1992), 61; von Mehren (1992), para. 6. On that concept in German law, see Markesinis et al. (1997), 47; von Mehren (1992), para. 6. On European definitions of contract generally, see Whittaker (2008), para. 1–007.

5 Blackstone (1765–9), vol. ii, 442 defined a contract as 'an agreement upon sufficient consideration to do or not to do a particular thing'. Consideration is not required for a promise in a deed. For the view that such a promise is not a contract, see n. 54 below.

6 See Zweigert and Kötz (1998), 390 ff. On the relation between consideration and French law's concept of *cause*, see Nicholas (1992), 118 ff.

consideration are disputed,[7] but one expression of the central idea is that 'something of value in the eye of the law' must be given for a promise in order to make it contractually enforceable.[8] On that basis it is sometimes said that a contract is an exchange or bargain;[9] but there are objections to this view,[10] for example that a peppercorn consideration represents no real bargain. In any event, an account of consideration in terms of promises causes problems for a definition of a contract as a kind of agreement, if, as argued in Chapters 1 and 2, promises are neither necessary nor sufficient for agreement. (See further section 7.5.)

7.11 Offer and acceptance

Contract law analyses agreement in terms of offer and acceptance. Peel defines an offer as 'an expression of willingness to contract on specified terms, made with the intention that it is to become binding as soon as it is accepted by the person to whom it is addressed'[11] and an acceptance as 'a final and unqualified expression of assent to the terms of an offer'.[12] If 'become binding' means 'impose an obligation', the first definition implies

7 The doctrine of consideration is intricate and doubtfully coherent, and some have argued for its abolition; see, e.g., Fried (1981), chap. 3. Smith writes that 'it is evident that the consideration doctrine serves a number of different roles, that these roles are sometimes in tension . . . and, finally, that the doctrine is not transparent, in the sense that its purpose is not obvious': S. Smith (2005), 109. For surveys of the law on consideration, see ibid., 106 ff.; Beale (2008), chap. 3; Fuller (1941); Furmston (2007), chap. 4; Peel (2007), chap. 3.

8 Peel (2007), para. 3–002. The quoted phrase is from *Thomas* v. *Thomas* (1842) 2 QB 851, 859.

9 See Kötz (1997), 8; von Mehren (1992), para. 7; S. Smith (2005), 28, 35, 57; Whittaker (2008), para. 1–001; compare Eisenberg (1994). On fairness of exchange as a concern of contract law, see Atiyah (1986b). On the principle, expressed in the late Roman doctrine of *laesio enormis*, that legal protection of a contract requires that performance and counterperformance be equivalent, see Gordley (1981); Kötz (1997), 10, 125 ff., which describes the devices used by courts to reconcile substantive fairness with freedom of contract; Nicholas (1962), 175. On the view that consideration is conditional, see section 2.63 above.

10 See Atiyah (1986a), 206 ff.; Atiyah (1986g), 75 f.; Atiyah (1986i), 66 ff.; Fried (1981), chap. 3; S. Smith (2005), 107 f.; Whittaker (2008), para. 1–001 n. 6. For objections to the idea that an agreement, contractual or otherwise, is an exchange of promises, see Gilbert (1996d); Chap. 1 above.

11 Peel (2007), para. 2–002, citing *Storer* v. *Manchester C.C.* [1974], 1 WLR 1403.

12 Peel (2007), para. 2–015. On contractual assent, see Gordley (1991), 135 f., 176; Markesinis et al. (1997), 47; von Mehren (1992), para. 7, citing the 1932 US Restatement of Contracts. See further Chap. 1 n. 3 (mutual assent) and Chap. 2 n. 3 above, and Chap. 8 n. 53 and Chap. 9 n. 36 below.

that an offer can impose an obligation on the offeror to perform; but, as argued in sections 2.62 and 3.6, it is the fact of agreement, rather than of the offer or acceptance, that is a ground of the parties' performance obligations. (Section 1.1 noted that 'impose' can be understood in terms of grounding.)

In Smith's formulation:

> an offer [is] an expression of willingness to undertake an obligation (typically made conditional on the offeree agreeing to do something in return). An acceptance, in turn, is regarded as expressing agreement to the terms of the offer (and thus typically is an agreement to do the requested act in return for the offeror's undertaking).[13]

On one reading, this passage conflicts with the offer–acceptance model in two respects. First, it says that an acceptance expresses or is an agreement, rather than that – as explained in section 2.1 – it is an element of one. Section 2.66 rejected the thought that the concept of acceptance is identical to that of agreement. Second, the passage appears to attribute a conditional content to the offer and the acceptance. (Section 2.63 identified different respects in which agreements are conditional.) The statement that an offer is 'an expression of willingness to undertake an obligation' leaves unclear the relation between the undertaking on the one hand and, on the other, the offer and the agreement. Section 2.62 argued against the view that an offer or an agreement is itself a promise; the argument extends to undertakings, of which – as noted in section 1.1 – promises are one kind.

7.12 Consent and the will

Peel's definition links acceptance to assent, which differs by a shade of meaning from consent: both offer and acceptance are often said to express the parties' consent to the contract's terms.[14] The concept of consent is prominent in the rules about mistake and duress: in *Bell* v. *Lever Bros.* it was said that '[i]f a mistake operates at all, it operates so as to negative or in

13 S. Smith (2004), 168 f.

14 Atiyah (1986l), 5 says that contract law is 'about' co-operative activity, of which consent is a key element. Kötz (1997), 16 says 'At the very outset of their studies students are told that contracts need consent and that consent is always manifested in two declarations, an *offer* by one party matched by an *acceptance* by the other' (emphasis in original). Kötz goes on to argue that, to form a contract, consent can be manifested otherwise than by offer and acceptance. On the place of consent in the history of contract doctrine, see Gordley (1991), 2, 41, 82, 109, 112, 162 f., 201; Nicholas (1962), 175 ff. See further Chap. 1 n. 4 (mutual consent) above, and Chap. 8 n. 54 and Chap. 9 n. 37 below.

some cases to nullify consent'.[15] Mistake is said to 'negative' consent where it puts the parties at cross-purposes so as to prevent them from reaching an agreement, to 'nullify' consent where the parties reach an agreement based on a fundamental mistaken assumption; the legal consequences of negation and nullification are different.[16] Similarly duress has been described as 'a coercion of the will, so as to vitiate consent'.[17] The content and the suitability of the concept of vitiated consent have been debated:[18] on Peel's view, to say that consent is vitiated is to say not that it is negatived but that it has been improperly obtained.

The concept of the will is also central to the related law on undue influence: a transaction can be set aside in equity if, having been procured by undue influence exerted by X over Y, it cannot 'fairly be treated as the expression of [Y]'s free will'.[19] Historically the idea of a contract as an expression of the parties' will has been central to contract doctrine: in some versions of the 'will theory', the supposed fact that the parties willed themselves to be bound by the contract was taken to be the ground of their contractual obligations.[20] That theory reached its zenith in the

15 [1932] AC 161, 217.

16 For the law on mistake, see Peel (2007), chap. 8. On the need for negativing consent to induce the contract and to be operative, see ibid., paras. 8–045 ff. On the theory, which Peel rejects (para. 8–054), that negativing consent is a superfluous category, as the cases can be explained by the rule that offer and acceptance must correspond, see para. 8–054. There are other surveys of the law in Beale (2008), chap. 5; Furmston (2007), chap. 8; S. Smith (2005), 172 ff. On mistake in other jurisdictions, see Zweigert and Kötz (1998), 410 ff.; in Roman law, Nicholas (1962), 176 ff.

17 *Pau On* v. *Lau Yiu Long* [1980] AC 614, 636. See also *The Atlantic Baron* [1979] QB 705; *The Proodos C* [1980] 2 Lloyds Rep 390, 393; *Re T* [1993] Fam 95, 115 f.; Peel (2007), chap. 10.

18 See *Crescendo Management Pty Ltd.* v. *Westpac Banking Corp.* (1989–90) 19 NSWLR 40; *The Evia Luck (No. 2)* [1992] 2 AC 152, 166; *Huyton SA* v. *Peter Cremer GmbH* [1999] 1 Lloyd's Rep 620, 638; Atiyah (1982), 197; Beatson (1991), 113 ff.; Coote (1980), 40; Peel (2007), para. 10–002.

19 *Royal Bank of Scotland* v. *Etridge (No. 2)* [2001] UKHL 44; [2002] 2 AC 733, para. 7.

20 See Atiyah (1979b), 212 f., 407 ff.; Gordley (1991), chap. 7; Kötz (1997), 7 f.; Nicholas (1992), 32 ff.; A. Simpson (1975), 266; A. Simpson (2001), 13; von Mehren (1992), para. 4, n. 7; Chap. 3 nn. 67 and 72 above; also the discussions of assumed, created and attracted obligations, in Chap. 3 n. 91 above, and of agreement as 'concurrence of wills', in section 8.1 below. On the prominence of the will theory in the French law of contract, see Nicholas (1992), 32 ff. (noting at 36 that the requirement that there be an agreement 'has no necessary connection with the theory of the autonomy of the will'). De Moor (1987), 115 holds that the idea of a unity of will is evoked by the statement that two people are in agreement, but not by the statement that there is an agreement between them. On the phrase 'in agreement', see n. 16 to the Introduction above, n. 59 below and the passage from Peel quoted below (and cited in n. 62).

nineteenth century, at about the same time as did the doctrine of freedom of contract, with which it has been associated[21] – although the links are not as clear as some authors assume. Since then, both have been partly supplanted by a more interventionist conception of contract, which allows the courts to find liabilities on the basis, in particular, of benefits or detrimental reliance: such liabilities may diverge from anything the parties may be said to have willed. Atiyah has argued that the decline of freedom of contract since about 1870 reflects – again, the connection is not as clear as he assumes – a broader shift of values: 'the traditional liberal values of free choice' sustain freedom of contract; in imposing benefit-based liability, the law strives for 'a reasonable or just balance in the reciprocity of benefit'; and the values 'involved' in reliance-based liability are 'closely associated with a paternalist social philosophy, and a redistributive economic system'.[22]

The will theory has been widely criticised,[23] and it is implausible, for it seems that a person may make an agreement, contractual or not, against his will and yet without being subject to any such coercion as would exclude his being obligated to perform. (See section 3.3 and compare the example, in section 1.2314, of the pauper's promise to the rich doctor.) An advocate of the theory might try to answer the objection by distinguishing senses of 'will'; one problem with the various claims that have been identified with the will theory is the imprecision and plurality of the senses in play. A narrow sense might be invoked, according to which willing is no more than intending[24] (compare the discussion, in

21 See Whittaker (2008), paras. 1–010 f., 1–019.

22 Atiyah (1979b), 6 f. See also Gordley (1991), 214 ff.; S. Smith (2005), 9 ff. On the resurgence of freedom of contract since about 1980, see Atiyah (1979b), chap. 22; S. Smith (2005), 16 ff. On reliance and benefit as grounds of contractual obligation, see Chap. 3 nn. 59 and 65 above.

23 See Atiyah (1981), 17 ff.; Gordley (1991), 163, 175, 200 ff. (including strictures on the failure of 'objective' theories to answer the criticisms); Hart (1949); Hart (1973); Hume (1978), bk. 3, pt. 3, chap. 5; Melden (1956). De Moor (1990), 640 ff. argues that the will theory poses unnecessary problems for an objective principle of contractual interpretation; but de Moor's own 'intention theory' is similar to the will theory to the extent of holding that it is impossible to undertake an obligation without intending to do so (ibid., 645; see further n. 92 below). On voluntary obligations, see section 3.3 above and n. 88 below.

24 On contractual intention, see Atiyah (1986c), 12; Markesinis et al. (1997), 47; Peel (2007), chap. 4; von Mehren (1992), paras. 129 f. (intention determining the passage from precontractual negotiation to offer and acceptance), 181 (offer and acceptance as declarations of intention); sections 7.1 above and 7.21 below (intention to create legal relations).

section 8.11, of 'concurrence of wills'): the thought is that one cannot make an agreement without intending to. That thought was refuted in section 5.12.

7.13 Rules of offer and acceptance

Contract law has developed – partly through cases, partly through legislation – a number of rules on offer and acceptance. They are fully described in the textbooks,[25] and so I give only an outline. An offer or acceptance need not be in words: in some cases it may be constituted by conduct, or possibly even by silence. 'Constitute', here and in the following chapters, has the meaning identified in section 1.1: to say that X's φing constitutes his χing is to say that <X χs in or by φing>. Thus, to say that an offer is constituted by silence is to say that someone offers in or by being silent. On the 'in'/'by' distinction, see section 2.1, which contemplates a narrower definition of 'constitute' in terms of 'by' rather than 'in'.

An offer is different from an invitation to treat; more generally, offer and acceptance are distinguished from the negotiations that may lead to them. Detailed rules explicating the distinction between offer and invitation to treat apply to auctions, displays of goods for sale, advertisements, timetables, tickets, tenders and sales of shares. There are also rules, discussed later, as to when and where an offer is made or accepted.

Peel's definition of acceptance requires the acceptance (strictly, the expression of assent) to be unqualified, but there may be exceptions to the requirement; an arguable one is the case in which ten widgets are offered and the offeree replies that he will buy twenty[26] (see further below). In general, however, an attempt to vary an offer is not an acceptance but a counter-offer. Usually an acceptance is not effective until communicated to the offeror, but this rule has exceptions relating to agency, the offeror's conduct, the offer's terms and acceptance by post (see section 7.31). It is generally held that acceptance, or alleged acceptance,[27] in ignorance

25 Beale (2008), chap. 2; Furmston (2007), chap. 3; Peel (2007), chap. 2; S. Smith (2005), chap. 3. For other jurisdictions, see Braucher (1965); Kahn (1955); Kötz (1997), chap. 2; Litvinoff (1968); Markesinis et al. (1997), 46 ff.; Nicholas (1992), 61 ff.; von Mehren (1992), paras. 112 ff.; Zweigert and Kötz (1998), 356 ff.

26 Kötz (1997), 31, says that it is a matter of construction whether the offeree is accepting the offer and asking for more or rejecting the offer, the rejection being on the basis that he will take the larger number or none.

27 Peel (2007), para. 2–047, conflates the two.

of an offer cannot create a contract;[28] that has been said[29] to explain the rule that if two people make identical cross-offers, neither knowing of the other's when he makes his own, there is no contract. An act motivated wholly by factors other than the existence of an offer does not constitute an acceptance – a doctrine discussed in section 7.631 in connection with independent promises. There are rules on acceptance in unilateral contracts; the distinction between unilateral and bilateral contracts is explained in section 7.36.

The general rule is that an offer may be withdrawn[30] at any time before acceptance:[31] the usual requirement is that the withdrawal be brought to the mind of the offeree, although it need not be communicated by the offeror. Another way in which an offer may terminate is by rejection, which, to have effect, must be communicated to the offeror. A rejection may be constituted by an attempt to accept an offer on new terms, as in the example of the widgets; an offeree who makes such an attempt cannot later accept the original offer. An offer may terminate through lapse of time or on the occurrence of a certain condition, express or implied. There are rules on the incapacity of a party and conflicting opinions as to whether an offer is terminated by the death of either party (see section 7.32).

The rules on offer and acceptance are not all the rules on contractual agreement – there are rules on vagueness, incompleteness and conditionality – and the rules on agreement are only part of the law of contract: intention, formalities, consideration, mistake, duress, undue influence and agency have already been mentioned; there are also rules on terms, illegality and invalidity, assignment, performance, breach, frustration, remedies and so on. Questions which lead into general legal philosophy, and which I shall not pursue, concern the nature of the rules. Are they constitutive of contract, in the sense described in section 2.2? How are they known? Are they made or discovered? In what ways do they

28 Authority for the contrary view was cited in Chap. 1 n. 65 above; see also n. 68 to that chapter, and section 7.36 and n. 119 below.

29 In Peel (2007), para. 2–048.

30 As mentioned in Chap. 2 n. 54 above, von Mehren (1992), para. 134 distinguishes withdrawal from revocation, the former occurring before, the latter after, the offer has legal effects. Both are forms of termination.

31 For the more restrictive rules in civil systems, see Kessler and Fine (1964); Kötz (1997), 22 ff.; S. Smith (2004), 195 ff.; von Mehren (1992), paras. 135 ff.; R. Zimmerman and Whittaker (2000), 236 ff.; Zweigert and Kötz (1998), 359 ff. On the scope for revocation of an acceptance, see von Mehren (1992), paras. 190 ff.

result from, or are they subject to, interpretation? What are the semantic, moral and political constraints on interpretation?[32] Similar questions arise about those elements of contract law and doctrine that are perhaps better classified as principles than as rules, notably freedom of contract.[33]

7.14 *Varieties of contract*

Contracts are classified in various ways:[34] according to their subject-matter (commercial contracts are distinguished from non-commercial ones, for example, and there are specific statutory regimes for the sale of goods and for consumer credit), their parties (a distinction is drawn between those contracts that involve public bodies and those that do not), their form or means of formation (a contract may be formal or informal, or express or implied, or it may be a distance contract or a relational contract) and their effect. The distinction, already mentioned, between unilateral and bilateral contracts can arguably be classified as one of effect. A more clearly effect-based distinction is between valid, void, voidable and unenforceable contracts. On a strict view, 'void contract' is a contradiction, voidness excluding the existence of a contract; but the term has an established use and a so-called void contract may have legal effects (see section 7.22). A contract is voidable if one or more of its parties have the power, by manifesting an election, to avoid the legal relations created by the contract or, by affirming the contract, to extinguish the power of avoidance; until the right to avoid is exercised, the contract is valid. An unenforceable contract is valid in all respects save that one or more parties cannot be sued on it.

7.15 *Boundaries*

The boundaries of contract law are blurred and shifting; for example, the relations between contract and tort[35] and between contract and trust[36] have been debated, and the law of restitution, which concerns unjust enrichment, is an offshoot of contract law:[37] the same form of action was previously used to remedy breaches of contract and to enforce claims

32 On interpretation, see Chap. 8 nn. 158 ff. below.

33 See Whittaker (2008), para. 1–010. On the distinction between rules and principles, see R. Dworkin (1978), 22 ff. Eisenberg (2001), 241 proposes a 'basic contracts principle': see n. 52 below.

34 See Whittaker (2008), paras. 1–067 ff.

35 Ibid., paras. 1–117 ff.

36 Ibid., paras. 1–188 f.

37 Ibid., para. 1–192. See also S. Smith (2005), 31, 69 f.

that would now be classified as restitutionary, the latter having been held to arise *quasi ex contractu*.[38] The notion that all claims in restitution are quasi-contractual has been abandoned.

The modern English law of contract grew from the action of *assumpsit*, which did not necessarily involve an agreement; an established concept of a contract as an agreement, constituted by offer and acceptance and creating legal rights and obligations, dates only from the end of the eighteenth century.[39] Since my account of agreements borrows from contract law, it might be objected that the account is temporally parochial. A charge of spatial parochialism would be harder to sustain, this concept of contract being standard in Western legal systems;[40] but in any event the temporal objection fails because the fact that agreements, conceived in terms of offer and acceptance, only recently formed the basis of a body of law does not imply that this concept of agreement is equally recent, nor that the parties to agreements, thus conceived, only recently became, or were held to be, subject to non-legal performance obligations. Granted, it would be anachronistic to project on to agreements made long ago all the detailed rules that contract law has generated; for that matter, it is artificial to suppose that all those rules, or non-legal analogues to them, apply to every recent agreement. That concession does not preclude the use of the rules, as proposed in sections 2.1 and 2.3, to develop the offer–acceptance model.

7.2 Agreement not sufficient for contract

The main function of a contract is the same as that of a non-contractual agreement: to enable self-interested parties, if rational, to benefit from

38 On quasi-contract in Roman law, see Nicholas (1962), 159, 227 ff.

39 For the history of English contract law, see Atiyah (1979b); Furmston (2007), chap. 1; Holdsworth (1923), esp. vols. 3 and 8; Ibbetson (1999); Milsom (1981), pt. 3, esp. chap. 12; A. Simpson (2007). Nicholas (1962), 159 ff. notes that in Roman law the idea of a contract as an agreement emerged slowly, probably from an undifferentiated idea of debt, and that Roman law had a list of contracts rather than a single concept of contract. See also Kötz (1997), 16; Nicholas (1992), 40 f. For the view that modern contract law likewise contains no unitary concept of contract, see the works of Atiyah cited in n. 1 above.

Gordley (1991) argues that modern contract doctrine resulted from a synthesis, achieved by the late scholastics, of Roman law and concepts taken from Aristotle and Aquinas, and that, as a result of the decline of Aristotelian philosophy, it lacks adequate theoretical foundations. This is an analogue of the ethical thesis in MacIntyre (1985), although Gordley mentions MacIntyre only in passing (20); see Chap. 3 n. 21 above.

40 See Nicholas (1992), 61; Zweigert and Kötz (1998), 356.

each other's actions (see section 2.4). As with agreements generally, the main mechanism for this is the parties' reasoning – in ways described in Chapter 4 – to the formation and the performance of the contract and their acting on the conclusions of that reasoning. It was explained in sections 4.21 and 4.22 that the premisses from which they may correctly reason to an intention to perform include the premiss that other things are equal, this being needed to exclude cases of outweighing; and, as explained in section 6.211, the enforcement of contracts increases the likelihood that other things *are* equal, by reducing the likelihood that an outweighing consideration obtains (see further section 7.38). Sections 6.21–6.213 reviewed a variety of goods that flow from enforcement; it can be left open whether other functions of contracts can be specified by reference to those. (Compare the discussion, in section 6.212, of Kimel's account of the intrinsic value of contracts.)

Despite the commonality of function, most agreements are not contracts. It follows, given the first assumption in the next sentence, that an agreement is not sufficient for a contract.[41] The assumption is that, if some actual or merely possible agreement is not a contract, the thesis of insufficiency is true; I likewise assume, for the purpose of the next section, that if some contract, actual or merely possible, is not an agreement then an agreement is not necessary for a contract.[42] The indefinite article in 'an agreement' here imports generality: for example, the thesis of insufficiency is that not every agreement is sufficient for a contract. That is consistent with the possibility that some agreements are sufficient. (The point is taken up in section 9.22.) It might be objected that not only are some agreements not contracts, and vice versa, but – as a matter of metaphysics rather than law – no agreement is a contract and no contract an agreement: rather, in certain circumstances, parties' agreeing *constitutes*, or stands in some other relation to, their contracting. If the objection is conceded, talk of an agreement's being a contract, and conversely, may

41 This is distinct from the point that an agreement or contract may give rise to legal rights and obligations that are non-contractual. Examples – some controversial – of agreements creating such rights and obligations are found in company law, trust law, the law of estoppel and the law of collective agreements. Non-contractual obligations in contractual settings may be negative (not to tell falsehoods, not to breach confidence, not to discriminate) or positive (to reverse an unjust enrichment, to act in good faith (but only in limited circumstances – see Whittaker (2008), paras. 1–022 ff.)). See S. Smith (2005), 65 ff., 85 ff. On the distinction between positive and negative obligation, see O. Black (1993); see further Chap. 3 n. 122 above.

42 As explained in n. 4 to the Introduction above, these statements can be expanded into statements about actual or possible facts.

be treated as another convenient abbreviation, covering cases where the relevant relation obtains. The same applies to similar locutions, as in the statement, considered in section 7.33, that simultaneous exchanges may be contracts.

7.21 Agreements that are not contracts

As noted in section 7.1, an agreement is not a contract if the parties do not intend to create legal relations.[43] This condition covers various things: informal social or domestic arrangements;[44] statements not meant seriously, as when a defendant 'affirmed and published that he would give £100 to him that should marry his daughter with his consent';[45] statements inducing a contract that are mere representations rather than terms; highly vague statements; provisions expressly negativing an intention to be legally bound, such as honour clauses or agreements 'subject to contract'; agreements giving wide discretion to one party; letters of intent or comfort; and certain collective agreements on wages and conditions of work. In some cases – for example, those to do with representations or vague statements – there may, depending on the facts, be no agreement, rather than, or as well as, no intention to create legal relations.

The general rule is that a contract can be made informally,[46] but it was also noted in section 7.1 that in some cases an agreement that fails to meet certain formal requirements is not a contract.[47] Those exceptions are now covered by legislation, which provides that some contracts, for example a lease for more than three years, must be made by deed; that some, such as regulated consumer credit agreements, must be made in writing; and that others, for example contracts of marine insurance, must be evidenced in writing.

A third category – likewise noted in section 7.1 – of agreements that are not contracts comprises those not supported by consideration. A more debatable one concerns cases of incapacity, which can arise where one

43 See Beale (2008), paras. 2–158 ff.; Furmston (2007), chap. 5; Peel (2007), chap. 4; S. Smith (2005), 37 ff., suggesting that in some cases of this sort it is better to say that the parties do not intend to create any relations, legal or other.

44 See Litvinoff (1968), 204 f.

45 *Weeks* v. *Tybald* (1605) Noy 11.

46 The English authority is *Beckham* v. *Drake* (1841) 9 M & W 79, 92. On the general principle of informality in modern legal systems, see Zweigert and Kötz (1998), 366; at 377 ff. the authors trace a decline and resurgence of formal requirements.

47 On formalities, see Atiyah (1986f); Beale (2008), chap. 4; Peel (2007), chap. 5; S. Smith (2005), 94 ff. On consideration as form, see Fuller (1941); Holmes (2005), 273.

party is a minor, suffers from a mental disorder, or made the agreement when under the influence of drugs. Incapacity can also affect agreements made by corporations. The legal effects of a party's falling into one of these classes depends on the circumstances;[48] for example, an agreement with a minor may be a valid or a voidable contract, but section 1 of the Infants Relief Act 1874 (repealed) provided that contracts, other than for necessaries, with minors were 'absolutely void'. On the strict view stated in section 7.14, that is a self-contradiction, which can be resolved by interpreting the provision to say that agreements for non-necessaries with minors are not contracts. Such an agreement could nevertheless have legal effects;[49] in particular, the other party could be bound.

Certain illegal agreements are said to be void.[50] Some agreements – such as gaming and wagering agreements, and certain anticompetitive agreements (see Chapter 8), are void by operation of statute.[51] Again, on the strict view, no such agreement is a contract. Other factors – some already mentioned, in sections 7.12 and 7.13 – that can prevent an agreement from being a contract are incompleteness, uncertainty, mistake, misrepresentation, duress and undue influence.

7.22 The divergence explained

It might be suggested that no explanation for this divergence between agreement and contract is required, as the fact that some agreements are contracts gives no reason to expect all to be. A more illuminating response is that contracts are subject to conditions that do not apply to non-contractual agreements; in particular, the making of a contract brings to bear a potentially cumbersome and intrusive apparatus of enforcement which would be undesirable for some agreements. The explanation applies, for example, to certain cases where there is no intention to create legal relations: family life would be grim if every casual agreement between family members were subject to legal sanctions. A supplementary explanation in such cases is that, if the parties not only do not intend,

48 See Beale (2008), pt. 3; Furmston (2007), chap. 13; Peel (2007), chap. 12.

49 *Stocks* v. *Wilson* [1913] 2 KB 235, KBD.

50 On illegal agreements, see Beale (2008), chap. 16; Furmston (2007), chaps. 11 f.; Peel (2007), chap. 11, which at para. 11–108 cites the authorities on voidness; S. Smith (2005), chap. 8. On the requirement in French law for the object of a contract to be licit, see Nicholas (1992), 117.

51 On statutory voidness, see Beale (2008), para. 16–144; Furmston (2007), chap. 10; Peel (2007), chap. 11; S. Smith (2005), chap. 8; Treitel (2003), chap. 12.

but intend not, to create legal relations, the law respects their intention.[52] Some conditions apply only to particular types of contract: in the case of some important contracts it is especially desirable that their terms be certain, that their existence and content be capable of proof, and that the parties enter them cautiously and seriously. Those objects can be achieved by formalities.[53]

7.3 Agreement not necessary for contract

Most but not all contracts are agreements, and so, by the assumption in section 7.2, an agreement is not necessary for a contract. A promise in a deed is a contract but not an agreement.[54] A contract constituted by independent promises is not an agreement: see further section 7.64.

7.31 Posting

A harder case is presented by the law on postal acceptance. Although the general rule is that an acceptance is ineffective until communicated to the offeror (see section 7.13), it is also a rule that a postal acceptance takes effect when the letter is posted.[55] In that situation, if the other necessary

52 Compare the first limb of the 'basic contracts principle' in Eisenberg (2001), 241: 'If but only if appropriate conditions are satisfied, and subject to appropriate constraints, the law should effectuate the objectives of parties to a promissory transaction'.

53 Zweigert and Kötz (1998), 375 notes that a formal requirement can become detached from its original justification. The authors cite para. 766 of the German Civil Code, which provides that an oral promise of guarantee is void even if there is no problem of proof and the guarantor would not have considered the matter more carefully had it been reduced to writing.

54 That is the dominant view: see S. Smith (2005), 58; Whittaker (2008), para. 1–003. Peel (2007), para. 3–164, however, holds that '[t]he binding force of such a promise does not depend on contract at all'. Compare Smith on public announcements of rewards: n. 87 below.

55 *Adams* v. *Lindsell* (1818) 1 B & Ald 681; *Potter & Sanders* (1846) 6 Hare 1; *Harris's Case* (1872) LR 7 Ch App 587; *Henthorn* v. *Fraser* [1892] 2 Ch 27, 33. The same principle applies to telegrams: *Bruner* v. *Moore* [1904] 1 Ch 305. Gordley (1991), 140 argues that the reasoning in *Adams* v. *Lindsell* confuses the question when an acceptance is effective with the question whether a contract can be formed without both parties' knowing that they are bound. On the reasons for the posting rule, see Peel (2007), para. 2–029. For criticism, see Macneil (1964); S. Smith (2004), 189 ff.; Zweigert and Kötz (1998), 359. Different rules on the time of acceptance are used in other jurisdictions: see Kahn (1955), 254 ff. (distinguishing declaration, expedition, reception and information); Kötz (1997), 25 ff.; Litvinoff (1968), 153 ff.; von Mehren (1992), paras. 182 ff. (drawing distinctions similar to Kahn's, but in relation to declarations of intention); Nicholas (1992), 72; S. Smith (2004), 188.

elements of a contract, such as the intention to create legal relations, are present, a contract exists between the time the letter is posted and the time the offeror receives it, even though normally he is unaware of the acceptance until the time of receipt. Thus there can be a contract where the offeror is unaware of the acceptance: call it a 'contract in ignorance'.[56] If he is unaware of the acceptance, it has not been communicated to him – otherwise than in an unnaturally thin sense of 'communicate'[57] – and so the posting rule is an exception to the general rule.

I said that conditions CM and CS of the analysis of agreement in section 2.1 are placeholders for conditions that include ones imposed by informal counterparts of certain rules of contract law, but our ordinary concept of agreement seems not to be fine-grained enough to reflect the posting rule; indeed, intuition is uncertain whether CM and CS cover any condition as to the offeror's awareness of the acceptance. One possibility is to distinguish strong agreements, for which they cover an exceptionless condition that he is thus aware, from weak ones, for which they do not: see the remarks in section 2.1 on a narrow view of agreement. If CM and CS cover that condition, the analysis does not fit a contract in ignorance; but, since the analysis gives only a sufficient, not a necessary, condition of agreement (more strictly, (36) gives a sufficient condition for the making of an agreement, and (37) for the state of agreement), it does not follow that such a contract is not an agreement. That conclusion does follow on the assumption – which, unless justified, begs the question[58] against the view that contracts in ignorance are agreements – that the parties to such a contract meet no other sufficient condition of agreement.[59]

56 On the converse case, of acceptance in ignorance of an offer, see section 7.13 above, section 7.36 and n. 119 below, and Chap. 1 nn. 65 and 68 above.

57 See Chap. 1 n. 13 above; section 8.32 below.

58 See Chap. 5 n. 35 above.

59 Compare S. Smith (2004), 188 f.: 'The postal rule thus appears prima facie inconsistent with the idea of contracts as agreements, since it contemplates an "agreement" being formed prior to one of the parties to it having communicated to the other his willingness to enter the agreement. In such a case, the parties might well be "in agreement" in their minds, that is, each party might at the moment of posting be willing to enter an agreement. But to make an agreement, both parties must communicate their willingness to enter the agreement. If mere agreement "in one's mind" were sufficient, the entirety of an agreement could be constructed in silence'. On the phrase 'in agreement', see n. 16 to the Introduction above, n. 20 above and the comment, in the main text below, on the passage quoted next from Peel. The passage from Smith does not distinguish between the communication and the manifestation of acceptance (the distinction in French doctrine between *information* and *émission*: see Nicholas (1992), 72 and compare Kahn and von Mehren: n. 55 above): the penultimate sentence concerns the former, the final sentence the latter. Normally communication is sufficient for manifestation (as it is for awareness,

The posting rule does not apply to withdrawal of an offer: as noted in section 7.13, the withdrawal must normally be brought to the mind of the offeree.[60] In *Byrne* v. *van Tienhoven*[61] an offer to sell was posted on 1 October and reached the offerees on 11 October; they immediately accepted it by a telegram which they confirmed on 15 October by a letter. On 8 October the offerors had posted a letter withdrawing the offer, but this letter did not reach the offerees until 20 October. The court held that there was a contract, as the withdrawal had not been communicated when the offer was accepted. Peel comments:

> Thus there was a contract in spite of the fact that the parties were demonstrably not in agreement, for when the offerees first knew of the offer, the offerors had already ceased to intend to deal with the offerees. The rule is based on convenience; for no one could rely on a postal offer if it could be withdrawn by a letter already posted but not yet received.[62]

I suggested in the Introduction that the phrase 'in agreement' generally signifies factual rather than active agreement, but Peel appears to have active agreement in mind.[63] The first sentence of the passage is consistent with CM's exclusion of the possibility that the offeror withdraws the offer before the offeree accepts it (see section 2.1): given that exclusion, the analysis does not fit the contract in the present case. As before, the conclusion that the contract was not an agreement follows on the assumption that the parties met no other sufficient condition of agreement than the one given by the analysis.

7.32 Death

Another argument, again based on termination of an offer, concerns the death of a party. One view is that it terminates the offer, as the parties can no longer reach agreement;[64] but Peel, again referring to

by the person to whom communication is made, of the thing communicated – see the main text above), but not vice versa. See further Chap. 8 n. 133 below.

60 For the rules in other jurisdictions, see Kahn (1955), 267 ff.; von Mehren (1992), paras. 149 ff.

61 (1880) 5 CPD 344.

62 Peel (2007), para. 2–058. In the judgment, at 348, convenience and justice are given as reasons for the rule. The judgment is limited to questions about offers and does not state whether the parties had an agreement.

63 See n. 16 to the Introduction above; nn. 20 and 59 above.

64 *Dickinson* v. *Dodds* (1876) 2 Ch D 463, 475.

convenience, submits that the death of either party should terminate the offer only in the case of certain 'personal' contracts, such as contracts of employment.[65] In certain cases, he maintains, there may be a contract without an agreement. The reasoning is not clear: the thought appears to be that these cases include ones in which death does not terminate the offer; but, if the offer subsists, there is pro tanto no reason to deny the existence of an agreement. If X and Y can contract even though one of them is dead, why should death prevent them from agreeing?

Peel might reply that an agreement, unlike a contract, requires that the parties be in certain mental states.[66] The reply would need to be refined to deal with agreements between corporations, states and so on.[67] It is also in tension with contract law's objective test of agreement, which he accepts, but they might be squared on the basis of an interpretationist theory of mental states: see section 7.37. Two objections remain. If the suggested distinction between an agreement and a contract is correct, it is plausible to suppose that an offer is like an agreement: the offeror must be in a certain mental state. In that case, on the assumption that his death ends his mental states, it ends his offer. But Peel allows that an offer may survive the death of the offeror. In any event, the reply, stated thus baldly, begs the question: granted, in paradigm cases of agreement, the parties have certain mental states, but it is presumably common ground that this is not a paradigm case.

7.33 Simultaneous exchange

Section 2.4 noted that simultaneous exchanges need not involve agreement; but it is sometimes held that they may be contracts,[68] in which case, given that the class of such exchanges that are not agreements overlaps the class of them that are contracts, they form another example of contract without agreement. The analysis is debatable: Smith suggests that simultaneous exchanges are not contracts, because the parties neither agree nor promise.[69] On that basis he suggests that many ordinary consumer

65 Peel (2007), paras. 2–067 ff. Kötz (1997), 24 notes that in several legal systems an offer is acceptable despite intervening death or incapacity. On incapacity, see n. 48 above.

66 On the mistaken view that agreement is itself a mental state, see the quotation from Furmston, in section 7.37 below, and Chap. 9 n. 23 below.

67 On the attribution of minds to corporations, see Chap. 5 n. 43 above; on their attribution to states, section 6.1 above.

68 On the need for a contract in certain cases of simultaneous exchange, see Kötz (1997), 7.

69 S. Smith (2005), 70 ff. See also Atiyah (1986g), 75 f.

sales are better described as mere 'conditional transfers. The customer hands over his money on the condition that the shopkeeper hand over the goods (or vice versa)'.[70] It is unclear what that means, but the thought may be that the customer's belief that the shopkeeper is handing over, or about to hand over, the goods is a causally necessary condition of the customer's handing over the money, and conversely. Another reading is that the parties' actions are based on their respective beliefs. On certain analyses of the basing relation – but not the one in terms of causal explanation, proposed in section 1.23 – the latter reading entails the former.

7.34 Imposed contracts

Other debatable instances of contract without agreement are certain cases in which it is said that, contrary to the principle of freedom of contract, the law imposes a contract on the parties. One example is a collateral contract on an implied warranty[71] or on a third party's assurance as to the quality of goods;[72] another arises from the rule that common carriers must accept goods tendered for transport.[73] It is doubtful that these are best classified as contracts; Smith describes both collateral contracts and simultaneous exchanges as 'fictional' contracts and proposes alternative bases for the liabilities arising.[74] It might be suggested that, even if the law does impose a contract in such cases, it likewise imposes an agreement. The parties to the alleged agreement will usually not meet the sufficient condition given by the analysis in section 2.1 – at most there will be a fictional or deemed offer and acceptance (compare the discussion in section 7.37 on the objective view of agreement) – but, as explained in section 7.31, the suggestion may be true if the parties meet some other sufficient condition. In some cases it seems clear that the law imposes a contract and an agreement, at least in the sense that it requires someone to make or accept an offer and that, given certain conditions, the acceptance of the offer is sufficient for both an agreement and a contract. Utilities and firms in a dominant position are sometimes subject to such a requirement.[75]

70 S. Smith (2005), 75. A similar view is proposed in S. Smith (2004), 176 ff. See also Corbin (1952), section 4. Kötz (1997), 16 cites Roman law to argue that face-to-face contracts need not be analysed in terms of offer and acceptance.

71 *Collen* v. *Wright* (1857) 8 E & B 647.

72 *Shanklin Pier Ltd.* v. *Detel Products Ltd.* [1951] 2 KB 854.

73 See S. Smith (2005), 8.

74 Ibid., 70 ff.

75 See Litvinoff (1968), 203 f.; Markesinis et al. (1997), 54.

7.35 *Negotiations*

There is also debate as to whether, and if so when and to what extent, negotiations that on a narrow view are classified as precontractual give rise to a contract.[76] If they can, and given that they need not involve an agreement, then – on an assumption of overlapping classes, corresponding to the assumption made in section 7.33 for simultaneous exchange – they provide another category of contracts that are not agreements. Haupt maintained that obligations arising from such negotiations fall into the class he described as arising from 'social contact': this is one of three subclasses of obligations that he held to arise from the factual context (*faktische Vertragsverhältnisse*), others being obligations due to 'involvement in a common enterprise' or 'commonly understood and accepted practices'.[77] His view was that such obligations are contractual. The doctrine of *culpa in contrahendo* also applies to certain negotiations and is treated in German law as the basis of a contractual claim.[78]

Although the point is controversial, it appears that, as regards the boundary between negotiation and agreement, contract law falls between competition law and the criminal law of conspiracy: it is more likely than the former, and less likely than the latter, to classify a borderline case as mere negotiation. If that is true, an explanation might be given by reference to the purposes of the three bodies of law (the explanation could be cast in terms of a purposive approach to the interpretation of legal expressions – as to which, see section 8.51) and/or to the consequences of a finding of unlawfulness: for example, given the potential severity of the punishment for conspiracy, it may be argued that a narrow view of conspiratorial agreement is appropriate.

7.36 *Unilateral contracts*

Unilateral contracts are sometimes said not to be agreements.[79] The distinction between unilateral and bi- or multilateral contracts has been drawn in various ways. According to Peel:

76 For overviews of the doctrinal discussion and of the relevant law in various jurisdictions, see Kötz (1997), 34 ff.; von Mehren (1992), paras. 112 ff. On the use of umbrella agreements in this context, see Mouzas and Furmston (2008). See further n. 102 below.

77 Haupt (1943), 9. For criticism, see von Mehren (1992), paras. 20 ff.

78 See Jhering (1861). The doctrine is discussed in Kötz (1997), 9 f., 35; von Mehren (1992), paras. 23 ff., 121.

79 See S. Smith (2004), 183 ff.; S. Smith (2005), 56 ff.; Tiersma (1992). The law on unilateral contracts is reviewed in Peel (2007), paras. 2–050 ff., 3–152, 6–036; S. Smith (2005), 53 ff.

> An offer of a unilateral contract is made when one party promises to pay the other a sum of money if the other will do (or forbear from doing) something without making any promise to that effect . . . The contract which arises in these cases is called 'unilateral' because it arises without the offeree's having made any counter-promise to perform the required act or forbearance; it is contrasted with a bilateral contract, in which each party undertakes an obligation and in which acceptance, as a general rule, takes the form of a communication by the offeree of his counter-promise.[80]

In a famous case, X told Y that he would pay Y £100 to walk from London to York;[81] a different type of example concerns the public announcement of a reward, say for the return of lost property.[82] On the orthodox analysis, a unilateral contract is an agreement comprising offer and acceptance:[83] the offer is accepted by fully performing the specified action, there being no need to give advance notice of acceptance. There are conflicting views on the legal position where the offer is withdrawn once the offeree has partly but not wholly performed the specified action; it is also doubtful whether, for a contract to arise, the offeree need be aware of the offer when he performs.

Suppose that X says to Y 'I will pay you £100 if you walk to York' and Y does so. Although X's utterance does not contain the word 'promise',

80 Peel (2007), para. 2–050. In a footnote Peel acknowledges that the promise may be to do some act other than paying money or to forbear from doing something. He also observes that the unilateral/bilateral distinction causes difficulty in some cases, as a contract unilateral in its inception may become bilateral in the course of performance. For other versions of the bilateral/unilateral distinction, see Furmston (2007), 63; S. Smith (n. 79 above); Whittaker (2008), para. 1–079. In the 1981 US Restatement of Contracts, unilateral contracts are termed 'option contracts'. On the distinction in Roman law, see Nicholas (1962), 162 f. On the distinction in French law – and its application respectively to juridical acts, contracts and promises – see Nicholas (1992), 37 ff. On the treatment of unilateral acts in German law, see Markesinis et al. (1997), 649 ff.; von Mehren (1992), para. 14.

81 *Rogers* v. *Snow* (1573) Dalison 94.

82 Such cases are discussed in Kahn (1955), 248 ff.

83 S. Smith (2005), 57, attacking the orthodox analysis of unilateral contracts, says that 'the rules on offer and acceptance are essentially tests for an agreement'. At 59 ff. Smith, citing Raz (1977), identifies three areas in which the analysis creates difficulty: revocation of the offer, communication of acceptance, and acceptance in ignorance of the offer. On the last point, see also Whittaker (2008), para. 1–003 n. 15; section 7.13 above; the main text and n. 119 below. In this context Smith proposes, as a partial explanation for the courts' tendency to interpret contracts as created by offer and acceptance, the fact that the interpretation works well for most commercial contracts: 64 ff.; see also Ibbetson (1999), 221 ff.

in the normal case it is, as Peel indicates, a conditional promise.[84] (On an utterance's being a speech act, see section 1.1.) It is therefore not an offer in the relevant sense, for the reasons given in section 2.62. Similarly, Y's walking to York is not an acceptance in the relevant sense, for, as noted in section 1.1, a promise cannot in that sense be accepted.[85] There is some strain in classifying as a promise the public announcement of a reward[86] – the unintuitive implication is that the public, or every member of it, is a promisee – but it is still an undertaking,[87] to which, as noted in section 7.11, the reasons in section 2.62 apply equally. There is a sense in which the reward is 'offered', but to say that it is offered in that sense is just to say that someone undertakes to provide it. As in the case of promises, other undertakings cannot be accepted in the relevant sense, and so an action performed in order to receive the reward is likewise not in that sense an acceptance.

The conclusion is that unilateral contracts do not comprise an offer and an acceptance and thus do not meet the sufficient condition given by the analysis of agreement in section 2.1. Granted that they meet no other sufficient condition for agreement, such contracts are not agreements.

7.37 Objectivity

English law is said to take an objective view of contract: a party is bound, 'whatever [his] real intention may be', if 'a reasonable man would believe that he was assenting to the terms proposed by the other party and that other party upon that belief enters into a contract with him'.[88] (There are

84 The quoted passage implies that the offer in a unilateral contract is a promise, and that both the offer and the acceptance in a bilateral contract are promises. More strictly, Peel says that, in a bilateral contract, acceptance 'takes the form of a communication' of a promise. Section 2.62 above denies that acceptances are promises.

85 S. Smith (2004), 184 reasons from the impossibility of acceptance, in the case of a unilateral contract, to the absence of an offer.

86 S. Smith (2005), 60 calls it a 'promise to the world'.

87 Ibid., 56 ff. gathers under the heading 'unilateral undertakings' conditional promises, deeds, promises to pay for requested acts, announcements of auctions and calls for tenders. At 60 f. Smith suggests that a 'promise to the world' (see the previous n.) is more similar to a vow or a declaration than to a standard promise. S. Smith (2004), 186 f., maintaining that public announcements of rewards 'do not belong on the map of contract law at all' (compare Peel on deeds – n. 54 above), assimilates them to oaths. On vows and oaths as undertakings, see section 1.1 above. For the view, which Smith seems to accept, that agreements are undertakings, see Chap. 2 n. 52 above.

88 *Smith* v. *Hughes* (1871) LR 6 QB 597, 607. On the characteristics of the reasonable man, see sections 5.1 and 5.13 above. Judge Learned Hand gave a resounding statement of the

exceptions, in particular where the other party actually knows that the hypothesised belief of the reasonable man is mistaken.[89]) Various justifications and explanations are given for the objective principle: obvious points are that it promotes certainty, reliance, fairness and ease of administration and enforcement.[90] A more controversial one is that it reflects the ascendancy of 'collective values' that are the same as or similar to those sometimes invoked, as noted in section 7.12, to explain the decline of freedom of contract.[91] One author grounds a version of the principle in the fact that people sometimes give unconventional meanings to their words.[92]

objective principle: 'A contract has, strictly speaking, nothing to do with the personal, or individual, intent of the parties. A contract is an obligation attached by the mere force of law to certain acts of the parties, usually words, which ordinarily accompany and represent a known intent. If, however, it were proved by twenty bishops that either party, when he used the words, intended something else than the usual meaning which the law imposes upon them, he would still be held, unless there were some mutual mistake, or something else of the sort'. *Hotchkiss* v. *National City Bank of New York* 200 F. 287, 293 (SDNY 1911), aff 201 F. 664 (2 Cir. 1912), aff 231 US 50 (1913). For criticism of the objective approach, see Solan (2007).

For various versions of the objective/subjective distinction in this context, see DiMatteo (1998), esp. chap. 4; Howarth (1984); Spencer (1973); and the works cited in n. 92 below. Atiyah (1986c), 21 notes that the objective principle is hard to reconcile with the view that contractual obligations are assumed voluntarily; compare the quotation from de Moor in n. 92. Von Mehren (1992), 44 holds that the subjective theory is an 'entailment' of the will theory (see section 7.12 above). On voluntary obligations generally, see section 3.3 above.

For the position in other jurisdictions, see Nicholas (1992), 35; von Mehren (1992), paras. 43 ff. (noting, at para. 44, that in some cases the reasonable man is supposed to be a party to the contract and in others to be an observer). Broadly, French law takes a more subjective approach than English law, German law falling in between; in practice, evidential constraints reduce the differences between the approaches. On the subjective approach in Roman law, see Nicholas (1962), 176.

89 See Atiyah (1986h), 364; Peel (2007), para. 1–002. von Mehren (1992), para. 33 notes that neither a subjective nor an objective principle, if rigidly applied, yields satisfactory results, a point implied by Peel.

90 See de Moor (1990), 633; Peel (2007), para. 1–002; von Mehren (1992), paras. 31, 43 ff.

91 See Atiyah (1986c), 25; Atiyah (1986l), 9; de Moor (1990), 633; von Mehren (1992), para. 45.

92 De Moor (1990), 638 ff.; compare S. Smith (2005), 79 and the quotation from Hand in n. 88 above. De Moor distinguishes the parties' 'substantive' intention – what they take the terms of the contract to mean – from their 'formal' intention to enter into a contract at all. (For other taxonomies of intention, see Chap. 5 n. 1 above.) She proposes the objective principle, on the basis explained, only for substantive intention, but argues to a subjective principle for formal intention from the premiss that 'it is not possible to undertake an obligation without intending to do so' (645). The premiss is true by definition, given a sufficiently strong reading of 'undertake'.

If agreements are not also conceived objectively, there may be contracts that are not agreements (or vice versa – and so the objective principle could have been treated in the section on the insufficiency of agreement for contract). Similarly, a wedge could be driven between agreement on the one hand and offer and acceptance on the other, by conceiving agreement objectively and offer and acceptance subjectively, or conversely. (Compare the possibility of mixed readings of the conditionals in the discussion of intention: section 5.1.) For non-legal agreements the position varies according to context: a subjective approach may be taken to an informal and casual agreement between friends; an objective one may be appropriate to an agreement to abide by the rules of a club.

In some circumstances the latter is a contract: compare the discussion of *The Satanita* in section 2.612. The common view, already noted in section 5.1, is that contract law takes an objective view of agreement; for example, Peel writes that contract law is concerned 'with the objective appearance, rather than with the actual fact, of agreement'.[93] These words are unclear, however, for they suggest that a contract may exist even though an agreement only appears to – in which case there can be a contract without an agreement. Furmston likewise may have in mind the appearance rather than the reality of an agreement: the relevant chapter is called not 'Agreement' but 'The Phenomena of Agreement', a title he explains by saying that the chapter is 'concerned not with the presence of an inward and mental assent but with its outward and visible signs'.[94] This too is cloudy, for it may mean either that contract law concerns the appearance of an agreement, whether or not an agreement exists, or that for the purposes of contract law an agreement exists where there is the appearance of assent, whether or not the assent exists. Earlier he writes:

> Agreement . . . is not a mental state but an act, and, as an act, is a matter of inference from conduct. The parties are to be judged not by what is in their minds, but by what they have said or written or done.[95]

De Moor's article is one of several works on the objective principle of contract that were provoked by *The Hannah Blumenthal* ([1981] 3 WLR 823, [1983] 1 AC 854), a case on the questions whether and when a contract can be created by silence (see further Chap. 1 n. 68 above). Others are Atiyah (1986h); Beatson (1986); Vorster (1987). Owsia (1991) is a comparative treatment of silence in English and French contract law.

93 Peel (2007), para. 1–002. See also Beale (2008), para. 2–002.

94 Furmston (2007), 39.

95 Ibid., 38. This formulation is used in Whittaker (2008), para. 1–076, to explain the distinction between express and implied contracts. On agreement as a mental state, see n. 66 above and Chap. 9 n. 23 below.

This fails to clarify the analysis, for it is misleading to separate mental states from acts: on a plausible view, an act typically involves both a mental state and a bodily movement. (Compare the discussion, in section 1.1, of the place of intentions in speech acts. Explication of 'involves' here is a task for the philosophy of action.) Moreover, if 'conduct' is taken to signify acts, and 'a matter of inference' means 'inferred', an act need not be a matter of inference from conduct: rather, conduct *consists* of acts. That seems to be the intended meaning of 'conduct', for Furmston appears to view as conduct 'what they have said or written or done', a phrase which does not comfortably apply to mere bodily movements. If, on the other hand, 'conduct' signifies only bodily movements, an act may be inferred from it; but, as just noted, the inference is to something involving a mental state.[96]

There are various ways of reading the objective principle: it could state a condition of existence, for an actual or for a deemed contract or agreement,[97] or be a principle of evidence. On certain philosophical theories of mind, the distinctions between existence and evidence, and between subjective and objective, are blurred: some philosophers hold that, roughly, the mental states a person has are those that it would be reasonable, given a principle of charity, to interpret him as having.[98] The mental states in question here are those mentioned in Peel's definitions, quoted in section 7.11, of offer and acceptance: willingness, intention and assent. Provided that, as seems to be the case, contract law takes contracts and agreements to be objective in the same sense, the objective principle cannot be used to argue that there may be a contract that is not an agreement, or vice versa.

7.38 The divergence explained

Given that most contracts are agreements, what explains the classification of the exceptions as contracts? One explanation is that the exceptional

96 The same objection arises to Lord Denning's application of the objective principle in *Oscar Chess Ltd.* v. *Williams* [1957] 1 WLR 370, 375: 'The question whether a warranty was intended depends on the conduct of the parties, on their words and behaviour, rather than on their thoughts'. The dichotomy is false, because words and behaviour involve thoughts. Parrots and radios are parasitic cases.

97 Atiyah (1986h), 366 implies that the objective principle relates only to deemed agreements: Atiyah writes of 'a real, genuine agreement, in which both parties did subjectively intend to abandon the arbitration'.

98 Davidson was a prominent advocate of such a theory: see Davidson (1984), chaps. 9 ff.; Evnine (1991), chap. 6; LePore (1986), pt. 4. Compare Dennett on the 'intentional stance': Chap. 6 n. 7 above.

cases are suited to the doctrines and techniques of contract law. Consider deeds: such doctrines and techniques as those relating to mistake, misrepresentation, duress, undue influence, capacity, performance, breach, frustration, remedies, and the construction of content, generally work as well for deeds as they do for contractual agreements. Another explanation is similarity of function. Suppose that an aunt makes a deed, when her nephew is seventeen, in which she promises to pay him £50,000 on his twenty-first birthday. On the strength of that, the nephew borrows money from a bank to pay for his education at university. The aunt is a person of limited and erratic altruism: had she made an informal promise, she might have changed her mind before the nephew reached twenty-one. Because she knows that the nephew can enforce the promise by law, she pays on the due date and the nephew enjoys the benefit of graduating without a large debt. The deed has the function, fulfilled in this example, of enabling a rational self-interested promisee to benefit from the promise of someone self-interested enough to be unreliable in the performing of an informal promise. (Whether the promisor gains any benefit from making or performing the promise – other than the negative 'benefit' of not being sued – will depend on the facts.) This is a variant of the more general function of a contract or a non-contractual agreement: to enable rational self-interested parties to benefit from each other's actions.

As in those cases, the mechanism for fulfilling the function is the parties' practical reasoning – the promisor's to the making and the performance of the promise, the promisee's to action in reliance – and their acting on its conclusions. The forms of reasoning are broadly similar to those discussed in Chapter 4. Where the reasoning uses the premiss that other things are equal, the existence of an apparatus of enforcement increases the likelihood that the premiss is true, in the way described in sections 6.211 and 7.2.

7.4 Contractual agreement without offer and acceptance

The cases so far discussed do not directly threaten the offer–acceptance model of agreement, for they concern the relations that agreement bears to contract, not to offer and acceptance. But contract law also covers situations which appear to involve an agreement but in which the analysis of the agreement in terms of offer and acceptance is difficult or seems artificial.[99] These include cases where one or other party is silent or otherwise inactive;[100] where the time at which an offer can be said to have been made is unclear, a point bearing on the question whether an offer has lapsed;[101] where it is unclear whether the parties have progressed from negotiation to offer and acceptance;[102] where they sign a written agreement;[103] where, on a sale of land, they agree 'subject to contract' but are not bound until formal contracts are exchanged;[104] where the agreement has more than two parties;[105] where reference is made to a third party;[106] and where, in the 'battle of forms', the offeree seeks, or both parties seek, to contract on his/their standard terms.[107]

99 For judicial dicta that an offer–acceptance analysis should be abandoned in such cases, see *Butler Machine Tool Co. Ltd.* v. *Ex-Cell-O Corp. (England) Ltd.* [1979] 1 WLR 401, 404; *Gibson* v. *Manchester C.C.* [1978] 1 WLR 520, 523, reversed [1979] 1 WLR 294. See also *Port Sudan Cotton Co.* v. *Govindaswamy Chettiar & Sons* [1977] 2 Lloyd's Rep 5, 10; *Interfoto Picture Library Ltd.* v. *Stiletto Visual Programmes Ltd.* [1989] Ch 433, 443. Peel (2007), para. 2–076 rejects that approach on the ground that it gives too little guidance to the courts in determining whether agreement has been reached. It is favoured by S. Smith (2005), 64 f.; see also 22, where Smith maintains that it is often artificial to analyse the formation of a contract into discrete moves of offer and acceptance. He gives a more favourable view of the analysis at 36. For the general view that human action is a continuous *durée*, see Giddens (1984), 3.

100 See n. 92 above.

101 See *Adams* v. *Lindsell* (n. 55 above) and the discussion in Peel (2007), para. 2–014.

102 See nn. 76 ff. above. von Mehren (1992), para. 112 notes that the characteristics of negotiation vary from case to case: at one extreme, it reduces to offer and acceptance; at the other, it may be a protracted process. 'Views respecting the arising of "contractual" obligation in the course of negotiation may . . . affect views as to when the offer and acceptance phases begin. E.g. an unwillingness to recognise certain forms of precontractual obligation may cause a legal system to pass more easily and quickly from the negotiation phase to the phases of offer and acceptance.' Kötz (1997), 35 suggests that it makes little difference to the solution of actual cases which juridical basis is adopted; see also Zweigert and Kötz (1998), 356 f.; compare the final paragraph of n. 88 above, on the objective and subjective approaches. At para. 133 von Mehren suggests that use of the concepts of offer and acceptance in this context serves a channelling and cautionary function by imposing a structure on the negotiations. A similar point is made in S. Smith (2005), 36.

103 See Kahn (1955), 247; Pollock (1950), 5.

104 See Peel (2007), paras. 2–079, 2–090 ff.

105 See ibid., para. 2–077.

106 See Kahn (1955), 247; Kötz (1997), 17; Peel (2007), para. 2–078; S. Smith (2005), 36; Zweigert and Kötz (1998), 356.

107 See Beale (2008), paras. 2–034 ff.; Furmston (2007), 209 ff.; Furmston et al. (1997), chap. 4; Peel (2007), paras. 2–019 f.; S. Smith (2005), 53 ff. Contracts on standard terms are known as contracts of adhesion. See Litvinoff (1968), 205 ff.; Rakoff (1994). On adhering, compare Chap. 8 n. 58 and Chap. 9 n. 37 below.

The response is the same as that to the objection in section 2.61. I identified various views, consistent with the model, that may be taken of conduct for which the conditions in (36) and (37) – the propositions at the heart of the model – appear not to hold: (a) the conditions are proposed as sufficient, not necessary, for an agreement, and so their failing to hold does not entail that the conduct is not an agreement; (b) either (i) the parties meet the conditions if minor adjustments to the conditions are made or (ii) the parties stand in a certain relation to a set of normal agreements – the parties to which do meet the conditions (with or without minor adjustments to the conditions) – and in case (i) their meeting the adjusted conditions, and in case (ii) their so standing in that relation, is sufficient for them to agree; (c) the conduct does not amount to an agreement; (d) the conditions hold after all. For example, in some cases where it is unclear whether the parties have moved beyond negotiation, (c) is true; in others, (d) is. As to multipartite agreements, (b)(i) is true of simple agreements with more than one offeree, (b)(ii) of 'wheel' agreements.

7.5 Contract as promise

Whittaker identifies two definitions of a contract in common law: one is Peel's, quoted in section 7.1 – 'an agreement giving rise to obligations which are enforced or recognised by law'; the other, 'a promise or set of promises which the law will enforce'.[108] The difficulties with the definition in terms of an agreement have been discussed in sections 7.2–7.4. In favour of the other definition, Whittaker says that in English doctrine the idea of a contract as an agreement dates only from the nineteenth century (slightly later than the starting point given in section 7.1) and that a justification for the enforcement of contracts is said to lie in the moral obligation to perform a promise. But he notes problems facing the definition in terms of promises: the courts often talk of agreement rather than promise, particularly in the context of offer and acceptance; the doctrine of consideration, related to the definition (see section 7.1), is under attack; and the definition 'does not give full force to the interrelationship of the obligations of the parties which exists in many contracts'.[109] (Compare the Interdependence criterion discussed in section 1.2314.)

Whittaker describes the definitions as 'competing', but they can be squared by holding that promises are necessary and/or sufficient for agreement. That, however, revives the objections in Chapters 1 and 2

108 Whittaker (2008), para. 1–001. 109 Ibid., para. 1–002.

to the promise model. Two solutions, best combined, are to break one or more links in the chain <contract – agreement – offer and acceptance – promise> and to distinguish senses. As to the first, the link between contract and agreement is fairly strong, notwithstanding that an agreement is neither sufficient nor necessary for a contract. Likewise, and despite the difficulties identified in the previous section and in sections 2.6–2.66, the analysis of agreement in terms of offer and acceptance is well entrenched in contract law. But section 2.62 showed that offer and acceptance are not promises.

The fact remains that, in the cases and commentaries, not only offers and acceptances but also agreements and contracts are often described as promises.[110] The description fits some cases: as noted in section 7.3, a promise in a deed is a contract. It almost fits the situation discussed in the next section, that of a contract constituted by independent promises – almost, because it does not follow, from the fact that a contract is so constituted, that it is itself a promise. In other instances the talk of promises can either be dismissed as a confusion or allowed as using a different or at least an extended sense of 'promise'. (The possibility of stretching the sense of 'promise' was considered in section 2.62.) Given the prominence of the locution in the literature, and of contract law in our society,[111] and given the democratic character of linguistic correctness, the latter course is perhaps more comfortable, but it raises the question how that sense is to be defined. It seems to come to no more than 'contract, agreement, offer, acceptance or (in the narrower sense) promise, as the case may be', in which case to describe any of these things as a promise is uninformative.

7.6 Independent promises

In certain circumstances, promises that are independent of each other (I shall call them independent promises, for short) constitute a contract.[112] That is implied by the fact that there is a special rule on the rescission of such contracts: the rule would be pointless if there were no circumstances in which independent promises constituted a contract. The rule is that

110 For the theory of 'contract as promise', see Fried (1981); Sheinman (2004). For the view that agreements are undertakings, even if not promises, see Chap. 2 n. 52 above.

111 Chap. 2 n. 1 above gives citations for the view that the concept of agreement is infused with contract law. For the view that promises contain a contractual element, see Fogelin (1983), 296 f.

112 See McKendrick (2008), paras. 24–035 f.

neither party can rescind[113] the contract for failure by the other party to perform:[114] the defaulting party can still enforce the injured party's promise. Where, on the other hand, the promises depend on each other, rescission is sometimes but not always available, the main determining factor being the seriousness of the failure to perform. A fuller statement of the rules of rescission was given in section 1.2314.

In textbooks of contract law, independent promises are usually discussed in chapters on performance rather than on the nature of agreement, but they provide the basis for two arguments that an agreement is unnecessary for a contract. One of the arguments was briefly stated in section 7.3; both are considered in section 7.64. They presuppose an analysis, presented first, of the distinction between independent and dependent promises. The distinction has been treated unsatisfactorily in the literature, and so the analysis is worth pursuing irrespective of the argument as to necessity.

7.61 Versions of the distinction

Neither the cases nor the textbooks give a clear account of the independent/dependent distinction: in *Stavers* v. *Curling*, for example, it was held to be a matter of the intention of the parties;[115] but that merely raises the question what the content of the relevant intention is. Peel gives some help by contrasting independent promises with conditions precedent and concurrent and by identifying three situations in which it is appropriate to classify promises as independent,[116] but he does not give a general account of the independent/dependent distinction. McKendrick proposes this analysis:

> Promises are said to be independent when the obligation of one party is absolute and not conditional upon the performance by the other of his part of the bargain. They are said to be dependent when the obligation of

113 On the issues raised by the use of 'rescind' in this context, see Chap. 1 n. 89 above.

114 *Fearon* v. *Earl of Aylesford* (1884) 14 QBD 792, 800 (action on a separation deed); *Taylor* v. *Webb* [1937] 2 KB 283 (tenant's covenant to pay rent) (compare *Regis Property Co. Ltd.* v. *Dudley* [1959] AC 370; *Johnstone* v. *Milling* (1886) 16 QBD 460, 468; *Tito* v. *Waddell* (No 2) [1977] Ch 106, 290; *Yorbrook Investments Ltd.* v. *Batten* (1986) P & CR 51); *Winstone* v. *Linn* (1823) 1 B&C 460 (covenants of master and apprentice) (compare *Ellen* v. *Topp* (1851) 6 Exch 424).

115 (1836) 3 Bing NC 355, 368. Other authorities on the distinction are *Pordage* v. *Cole* (1669) 1 Wms Saund 319; *Ritchie* v. *Atkinson* (1808) 10 East 295, 306; *Huntoon Co.* v. *Kolynos* [1930] 1 Ch 528, 558 f.; *Guy-Pell* v. *Foster* [1930] 2 Ch 169.

116 Peel (2007), paras. 17–014 ff.

one party depends upon the performance, or the readiness and willingness to perform, of the other.[117]

This complicates the issue by transferring the relation from the promises to the obligations which, McKendrick must be assuming, they generate; the questions then arise, when and in what sense promises do generate obligations. (See sections 1.1 and 1.2312, and the principles of obligation in sections 7.632 and 7.633. As noted in section 1.1, talk of an obligation's being generated by a promise can be explicated in terms of grounding, a relation discussed in section 3.2. The same point was made in section 7.11 about a promise's 'imposing' an obligation.) The analysis is in any event unsatisfactory because, first, it is unclear what is meant by 'absolute and not conditional' (specifically, whether 'absolute' and 'not conditional' mean the same) and, second, the account of 'dependent' is circular in that it contains 'depends'.[118]

7.611 Dependence

To gain a better understanding of the distinction, it is helpful to start with the notion of dependence. One approach is to analyse it in terms of a reason – that is, a motivating practical reason, as described in section 1.23 – why someone gives a promise. Consider a contract comprising mutual promises Px and Py between, respectively, X and Y. Then:

(161) Px depends on Py if and only if X's reason for giving Px is that Y gives Py.

As in section 1.23, 'X's reason' includes the case where X has more than one reason and the case where Y's giving Py is only part of X's reason.

An alternative approach, closer to McKendrick's, is to analyse dependence in terms of the conditionality of a promise. Let Ax and Ay be the actions that X and Y respectively promise (conditionally or unconditionally) to perform; then dependence may be analysed in terms either of Px's conditionality on Py or of Px's conditionality on Ay. ((161) could be modified to say that Y's doing Ay, rather than Y's giving Py, is X's reason for giving Px; but that would be an implausible analysis.) The former option is closer to the intuitive concept of one promise's depending on another, the latter to judicial dicta. To start with the former, the analysis might be proposed:

117 McKendrick (2008), para. 24–035, cited with approval in *Denmark Productions Ltd.* v. *Boscobel Productions Ltd.* [1969] 1 QB 699, 733.

118 On circularity, see Chap. 2 n. 69 above.

(162) Px depends on Py if and only if:
- (a) X promises to Y that X does Ax if Y promises to X that Y does Ay;
- (b) Y promises to X that Y does Ay;
- (c) Px is X's promise in (a); and
- (d) Py is Y's promise in (b).

(162)(a) is ambiguous: depending on the scope given to 'X promises to Y that' and to 'if', it can be interpreted to describe a promise that is either externally or internally conditional. (For that distinction, see section 1.1.) (162) therefore divides into two analyses:

(163) Px depends on Py if and only if:
- (a) if Y promises to X that Y does Ay, then X promises to Y that X does Ax;
- (b) Y promises to X that Y does Ay;
- (c) Px is X's promise in (a); and
- (d) Py is Y's promise in (b).

(164) Px depends on Py if and only if:
- (a) X promises to Y that, if Y promises to X that Y does Ay, then X does Ax;
- (b)–(d) (as in (163)).

As to (c) in (163): (a) and (b) together entail that X gives the promise in (a). In (164), (c) refers to the revised (a). Variants of these analyses, and of the ones introduced below, would use different conditional relations, but I shall not consider those.

On the second option, which is to analyse dependence in terms of Px's conditionality on Ay, the analyses are:

(165) Px depends on Py if and only if:
- (a) if Y does Ay, then X promises to Y that X does Ax;
- . . .

(166) Px depends on Py if and only if:
- (a) X promises to Y that if Y does Ay then X does Ax.
- . . .

The other clauses again remain the same, with (c) referring to the revised (a).

7.612 Independence

Corresponding to these are analyses of independence. An analysis in terms of reasons can be given by negating the right-hand side of (161), so:

(167) Px is independent of Py if and only if it is not the case that X's reason for giving Px is that Y gives Py.

Analyses corresponding to (163) and (164) cannot be formed by simply negating their right-hand sides. There corresponds to (163):

(168) Px is independent of Py if and only if:
(a) X promises to Y that X does Ax;
(b) Y promises to X that Y does Ay;
(c) Px is X's promise in (a);
(d) Py is Y's promise in (b); and
(e) it is not the case that if (b) then (a).

A first attempt at an analysis corresponding to (164) is to say: Px is independent of Py if and only if, first, it is not the case that the content of Px is, or is equivalent (in a sense that would need clarification) to, 'If Y promises to X that Y does Ay, then X does Ax', second, Y promises to X that Y does Ay, and, third, Py is that promise. But that is unsatisfactory because it does not say what the content of Px *is*. The simplest course is to say that it is 'X does Ax'; that yields a rather narrow analysis of independence, but its narrowness causes no difficulties. So the analysis is:

(169) Px is independent of Py if and only if:
(a)–(d) (as in (168)),

that is, the same as (168) with (e) deleted. By the same reasoning, (169) corresponds to (166). Corresponding to (165) is:

(170) Px is independent of Py if and only if:
(a)–(d) (as in (168));
(e) it is not the case that if Y does Ay then (a).

7.62 Logical properties of dependence and independence

A relation *R* is symmetric if and only if, for any A and B, <A stands in *R* to B if B stands in *R* to A>; asymmetric if and only if <A does not stand in *R* to B if B stands in *R* to A>; and non-symmetric if it is neither symmetric nor asymmetric. Dependence is non-symmetric if analysed by (161), (163) or (165), asymmetric if analysed by (164) or (166); independence is non-symmetric if analysed by (167), (168) or (170), symmetric if analysed by (169). Thus, on (167), (168) or (170), Px may be independent of Py while Py is not independent of Px. The rule of rescission fails to acknowledge this, for it applies only where Px and Py are reciprocally independent. That is an unnecessary restriction, for the rule's justification – discussed in section 7.632 – applies equally to reciprocal independence and to the one-way independence of the injured party's promise of the defaulting party's.

Now consider the questions of exhaustion – whether Px is either dependent on or independent of Py – and mutual exclusivity – whether Px is not both dependent on and independent of Py. McKendrick is unclear on the point, but leaves room for the view that dependence and independence are neither exhaustive nor mutually exclusive, for he uses different phrases to characterise the two relations: the analysis of independence says 'absolute and not conditional' where that of dependence says 'depends', and the former says 'the performance' where the latter says 'the performance, or the readiness and willingness to perform'. The position is this: analysed respectively by (161) and (167), dependence and independence are exhaustive and mutually exclusive; analysed respectively by (163) and (168), by (164) and (169), by (165) and (170), or by (166) and (169), they are mutually exclusive but not exhaustive. There is no need to review other combinations, for example, of (161) and (168).

7.63 The case for internal conditionality

7.631 Against the reason-based analysis

If (167) (Px is independent of Py if and only if it is not the case that X's reason for giving Px is that Y gives Py) were the correct analysis of independence, the stated rule of rescission would conflict both with the rules of offer and acceptance and with the doctrine of consideration. Take offer and acceptance first. The rule of rescission presupposes that the independent promises in question constitute a contract, as explained in section 7.6, and hence that the circumstances required for them to do so obtain. Given that a contract is constituted by an offer and an acceptance, it is reasonable to suppose that one promise, Py, is the offer and the other, Px, the acceptance. Objections to the identification of offer and acceptance with promises were raised in section 2.62, but the point can be conceded arguendo, as the objections apply equally to all the analyses of an independent promise and thus provide no ground for preferring one to another. The relation of independent promises to agreements is discussed in section 7.64.

As noted in section 7.13, one rule of acceptance is that an act motivated wholly by factors other than the existence of an offer does not constitute an acceptance.[119] In (167), as in (161), 'X's reason' signifies a motivating reason. Suppose that by (167) Px is independent of Py. Then the fact that Y gives Py is not a reason motivating X's act of giving Px. (On reasons as facts, see sections 1.23 and 3.2; the arguments here can be reformulated to accommodate the alternative view mentioned in those sections, that reasons are mental states.) Grant that the existence of Py does not motivate that act in any other way. Then, by the rule on motivation, and contrary to the supposition above, Px is not an acceptance. Note that this argument concerns only the acceptance's independence of the offer: it allows that the offer may be independent of the acceptance – a possibility admitted by the non-symmetricality of independence as analysed by (167). That does not reduce the argument's potency against the use of (167) to interpret the rule of rescission; for, as noted in section 7.62, the rule applies only to cases of reciprocal independence.

The conflict with the doctrine of consideration likewise arises from the fact that (167) concerns a motivating reason. Given the doctrine and the assumption, implicit in the rule of rescission, that Px and Py constitute a contract, Py is consideration for Px.[120] Normally the consideration for a promise motivates the promise.[121] So Py motivates Px. Suppose that by (167) Px is independent of Py. Then the fact that Y gives Py is not a reason motivating X's act of giving Px. Grant that Py does not motivate Px in any other way. Again an inconsistency results. This argument, unlike the previous one, applies equally to the supposition that Py, the offer, is independent of Px, the acceptance; for normally, if Px and Py constitute a contract, each is consideration for the other.

119 *Lark* v. *Outhwaite* [1991] 2 Lloyd's Rep 132, 140. This is hard to square with the doubtful rule that a party may accept an offer of which he is ignorant: sections 7.13 and 7.36 above; Chap. 1 nn. 65 and 68 above. The authority is clear – e.g., in the posting rule (section 7.31 above) – for the converse rule that a contract may arise where the offeror is ignorant of the acceptance: see also section 7.13 and Chap. 1 n. 68 above.

120 On the limited legal effects of promises without consideration, see Beale (2008), para. 3–013.

121 *Thomas* v. *Thomas* (1842) 2 QB 851, as interpreted in Beale (2008), para. 3–011. Cases of nominal or invented consideration are exceptions.

7.632 Justification for the rule of rescission

(167) may thus be eliminated as an analysis of independence within the meaning of the rule of rescission, and (161) can correspondingly be excluded from the discussion. That leaves (168), (169) and (170). To repeat:

(168) Px is independent of Py if and only if:
 (a) X promises to Y that X does Ax;
 (b) Y promises to X that Y does Ay;
 (c) Px is X's promise in (a);
 (d) Py is Y's promise in (b); and
 (e) It is not the case that if (b) then (a).
(169) Px is independent of Py if and only if:
 (a)–(d) (as in (168)).
(170) Px is independent of Py if and only if:
 (a)–(d) (as in (168));
 (e) It is not the case that if Y does Ay then (a).

Assume:

(171) If X promises to Y that X does Ax, then:
 (a) X has an obligation, Ox, that X does Ax; and
 (b) X can be released from Ox only with Y's consent.

(171) elaborates principle (12) (section 1.2312) and, like it, is arguably subject to exceptions. ((171)(b) may be true even if, contrary to the view taken in section 1.1, Y cannot release X from Ox.)

The cases and textbooks give little justification for the rule that parties cannot rescind independent promises; Peel for example asserts that it 'follows from the nature of an independent promise',[122] but without explaining how. Given (171) and any of (168), (169) and (170), a justification is forthcoming. Px and Py constitute a contract. Suppose that Y fails to perform Py and that Px is independent of Py. By (168), (169) or (170), Px is X's promise to Y that X does Ax. By (171)(a), X has Ox. Suppose that X rescinds the contract. For him to do so is in part for him to release himself from those of his contractual obligations that have not

122 Peel (2007), para. 17–023, putting the point in terms of termination rather than rescission; contrast the previous edition of the book, Treitel (2003), 765. See Chap. 1 n. 89 above.

accrued at the time of rescission.[123] Assume that Ox is such an obligation. Rescission does not require the consent of the defaulting party, and so X can rescind without Y's consent. In that case X can release himself from Ox without Y's consent. Suppose that he does so. Then he does something precluded by (171)(b). Hence he cannot rescind the contract. The argument assumes only that Px is independent of Py; it applies a fortiori to the narrower situation covered by the rule, where the independence is reciprocal.

7.633 Against externally conditional analyses

The trouble now is that similar arguments appear to show that X cannot rescind where Px *depends* on Py according to any of:

(163) Px depends on Py if and only if:
- (a) If Y promises to X that Y does Ay, then X promises to Y that X does Ax;
- (b) Y promises to X that Y does Ay;
- (c) Px is X's promise in (a); and
- (d) Py is Y's promise in (b).

(164) Px depends on Py if and only if:
- (a) X promises to Y that, if Y promises to X that Y does Ay, then X does Ax;
- (b)–(d) (as in (163)).

(165) Px depends on Py if and only if:
- (a) If Y does Ay, then X promises to Y that X does Ax;
- . . .

If so, the conclusion is that X can rescind only where Px neither is independent of Py nor depends on Py according to those analyses. Since dependence and independence, analysed respectively by (163) and (168), by (164) and (169), or by (165) and (170), are not exhaustive (see section 7.62), such situations may exist; nevertheless the conclusion unduly limits the availability of rescission.

By (163) or (165), the two analyses in terms of external conditionality, Px is X's promise to Y that X does Ax: the argument therefore runs as before. By (164), however, Px is X's promise to Y that, if Y promises to

123 *Heymans* v. *Darwins Ltd.* [1943] AC 356, 399; *Photo Production Ltd.* v. *Securicor Transport Ltd.* [1980] AC 827, 849. See also *Moschi* v. *Lep Air Services Ltd.* [1973] AC 331, 345, 350 f.; *Thompson* v. *Corroon* (1993) 42 WIR 157, 172 f.

X that Y does Ay, then X does Ax. Py is the promise in the antecedent of Px's content. Assume:

(172) If X promises to Y that, if Y promises to X that Y does Ay, then X does Ax, then:
  (a) X has an obligation that, if Y promises to X that Y does Ay, then X does Ax;
  (b) if Y promises to X that Y does Ay, then X has Ox (the obligation that X does Ax); and
  (c) X can be released from those obligations only with Y's consent.

(172), which also is arguably subject to exceptions, specifies and elaborates principle (15) (section 1.2312). By (164)(a) and (172)(a), X has an obligation that, if Y promises to X that Y does Ay, then X does Ax. By (164)(a) and (b) and (172)(b), X has Ox. For each of those obligations the argument runs as before.

Now take the remaining analysis of dependence:

(166) Px depends on Py if and only if:
  (a) X promises to Y that if Y does Ay then X does Ax.
  . . .

Parallel reasoning yields the result that X has the conditional obligation that if Y does Ay then X does Ax, but the conclusion that X has Ox cannot be derived. Here the principle corresponding to (172) is:

(173) If X promises to Y that if Y does Ay then X does Ax, then:
  (a) X has an obligation that if Y does Ay then X does Ax;
  (b) if Y does Ay, then X has Ox; and
  (c) X can be released from those obligations only with Y's consent.

As before, that X has a conditional obligation follows from (166)(a) and (173)(a); but, if (173)(b) is to be used to infer that X has Ox, the premiss is needed that Y does Ay. That premiss is not contained in (166): clause (b) of the analysis says not that Y does, but that Y promises that Y does, Ay. Indeed, in a situation where the question of rescission by X for Y's failure to perform arises, the negation of the required premiss is true. As to the conditional obligation, X's inability to release himself from it is unimportant in such a situation, as the antecedent of the obligation's content is false: compare the discussion of (18) and (19) in section 1.2313.

These arguments favour (166) as the analysis of dependence and, correspondingly, (169) as the analysis of independence; but possible responses to the arguments concerning (163), (164) and (165) deserve consideration. One is to reject (172), which, like its counterpart (15) in section 1.2312, is controversial. Another is to claim that the arguments work only on the assumption that the dependence is not reciprocal, i.e., that Py does not depend on Px. Even if that is true, it admits rescission only where each party's promise depends on the other's, whereas the rule of rescission precludes it only where each party's promise is independent of the other's: the response is thus not as liberal as the rule. That is not very important, for, as noted in section 7.62, there is good reason to extend the rule to certain cases of one-way independence. But in any event the claim is false for (163) and (165) and trivial for (164). Whether or not the dependence is reciprocal, (163) and (165) have it that X promises to Y that X does Ax: the argument therefore works for the case of reciprocity. By (164) that case never arises, for dependence so analysed is asymmetric: see section 7.62.

A more promising response as regards (164) is based on the caducity of promises. (Compare section 1.2314.) In outline it goes as follows. We are concerned with cases where the question of rescission for failure to perform arises; so assume that Y fails to do Ay. If he fails, he ceases to promise – that is, to be in the state of promising – to do Ay. In that case, on the assumption that (164) and (172) concern the state, (172)(b) cannot be used to infer that X has Ox. X is left with the conditional obligation that, if Y promises to X that Y does Ay, then X does Ax; but that obligation is unimportant, for, given that Y ceases so to promise, it does not require X to do anything. Compare the conditional obligation derived from (166)(a) and (173)(a). This response could be elaborated, as in sections 2.3 and 5.11, to refer to the times of the giving of the promises and to the time for Y's doing of Ay: see the next paragraph.

It might be objected that the response proves too much. If Y ceases to promise to do Ay, (164)(b) (Y promises to X that Y does Ay) ceases to be true, and so it ceases to be the case that, by (164), Px depends on Py. Since (b) is common to all the conditional analyses of dependence, the result is the same for (163), (165) and (166): the response identifies a way in which one promise may cease to depend on another, but leaves no room for the possibility, admitted by the law on rescission, that the giver of a dependent promise may rescind if the other party fails to perform. One option is to reject the response, and in particular to deny the premiss that, if Y fails to do Ay, he ceases to be in the state of promising to do Ay. The denial is uncomfortable once times are specified – on Monday Y promises to mow the lawn on Tuesday, on Tuesday he fails to do so, but on Wednesday he is still in the state of promising to mow the lawn on Tuesday – but comfort is increased if the state of promising is identified with the state of having promised. Another option is to develop the response by interpreting the law as implicitly distinguishing the period before from the period after the time for Y to do Ay: before that time, Px depends on Py; after that time, X may rescind although it is no longer the case that Px depends on Py.

The outcome is this. Of the four analyses of dependence in terms of conditionality, the externally conditional ones, (163) and (165), fall to the objection that they unduly limit the availability of rescission. Of the two internally conditional analyses, (166) withstands the objection and, for the reasons discussed in the preceding two paragraphs, (164) may do so. There is no need to reach a firm conclusion on (164), as it matters little which of (164) and (166) is chosen. In the context of the case – resumed in the next section – that an agreement is unnecessary for a contract, the main object is to identify the best analysis of *in*dependence. That is the analysis corresponding to both (164) and (166):

(169) Px is independent of Py if and only if:
- (a) X promises to Y that X does Ax;
- (b) Y promises to X that Y does Ay;
- (c) Px is X's promise in (a);
- (d) Py is Y's promise in (b).

7.64 Independence, dependence and agreement

Section 7.3 argued that, since a contract constituted by independent promises is not an agreement, an agreement is not necessary for a contract. As indicated there, a more explicit statement of the argument is:

(174) A contract constituted by independent promises is not an agreement.

(175) If some contract is not an agreement, then an agreement is not necessary for a contract.

So:

(176) An agreement is not necessary for a contract.

Another argument for the same conclusion uses the premisses:

(177) If X and Y give independent promises to each other, then they contract.

(178) It is not the case that, if X and Y give independent promises to each other, then they agree.

(177) and (178) are shorthand for fuller versions that include a limiting condition: for example, (177) expands to 'If X and Y give independent promises to each other and condition C obtains, then . . . ', this in turn expanding to a version that specifies the content of C. For present purposes the shorthand formulations are accurate enough. Subject to minor refinements, both arguments are sound.

(178) does not follow from the offer–acceptance model: although it is false that if X and Y give independent promises to each other then they meet the condition given by the model, that condition is only sufficient, not necessary, for them to agree. Firmer support for (178) is given by the objections in section 1.21 to analyses of agreement in terms of unconditional promises. In particular, having introduced:

(1) X does Ax and Y does Ay,
and:
(2) X and Y agree that (1),
I rejected:
(3) (2) if:
  (a) X promises to Y that X does Ax; and
  (b) Y promises to X that Y does Ay.

The objections to (3) are not removed by adding to the conjuncts of the antecedent the propositions that Px is X's promise in (a) and that Py is Y's promise in (b). Hence by (169) – the right-hand side of which is the conjunction of (a), (b) and those two propositions – it is false that, if Px is independent of Py, then (2). It is likewise false that, if the parties' promises are independent of each other (a proposition that follows from Px's independence of Py, given the symmetry of independence as analysed by (169) (see section 7.62)), then (2). Trivially, the parties give independent promises to each other if and only if the promises in question are independent of each other. So it is false that, if the parties give independent promises to each other, then (2). Absent any other factors, it is false that if they give such promises then they agree something other than (1). So (178) is true.

What if X's promise *depends* on Y's? For reasons discussed in section 7.633, the strongest analysis of dependence is:

(166) Px depends on Py if and only if:
- (a) X promises to Y that if Y does Ay then X does Ax;
- (b) Y promises to X that Y does Ay;
- (c) Px is X's promise in (a); and
- (d) Py is Y's promise in (b).

(166) recalls the second mixed-promise analysis of agreement in section 1.23:

(10) (2) if:
- (a) X promises to Y that if Y does Ay then X does Ax;
- (b) Y promises to X that Y does Ay;
- (c) Y's reason for giving his promise in (b) is that X gives his promise in (a); and
- (d) X has the justified belief that (b).

(By (10)(c), Y's promise stands to X's in the relation in which, according to (161), X's promise stands to Y's.) The consequent of (10) is the same as the right-hand side of (166), save as regards clauses (c) and (d). The objections raised in section 1.232 against (10) are not removed by replacing its (c) and (d) respectively with the (c) and (d) of (166). Hence by (166) it is false that, if X's promise depends on Y's, then (2). Again, absent any other factors, it is false that if X's promise so depends then the parties agree something other than (1). Therefore, just as it is false that if X's promise is independent of Y's then X and Y agree, so it is false that if X's promise depends on Y's then X and Y agree.

8

Competition

One of the main ways in which competition law ('antitrust law' in American English[1]) protects and promotes economic competition is by prohibiting anticompetitive agreements, such as those that fix prices, rig bids, limit production or supply, or divide markets.[2] An early piece of

1 In British English, 'antitrust' is useful as a noun signifying the body of law and policy designed to protect or promote economic competition: see O. Black (2005b), 1. It is also, in British English, increasingly used more narrowly to signify just the law on cartels and abuse of dominance; in this use it excludes, e.g., the law on merger control, state aid and public procurement.

2 These are the 'hard-core' matters covered by section 188(2) of the Enterprise Act 2002, which turned certain forms of anticompetitive conduct into crimes by introducing the 'cartel offence'. Section 188(1) of the Act provides: 'An individual is guilty of an offence if he dishonestly agrees with one or more other persons to make or implement, or to cause to be made or implemented, arrangements of [the kind in paragraph 2] relating to at least two undertakings'. The leading English case on dishonesty is *R* v. *Ghosh* [1982] 2 All ER 689, 986; for commentary see Elliott (1982); Griew (1985); Ormerod (2008), 782 ff.; G. Williams (1983), 728 f. On the problems of applying *Ghosh* to the cartel offence, see O. Black (2005b), 127 ff.; Dean (2003), 910; Joshua (2003), 626; A. MacCulloch (2003), 622; Peretz and Lewis (2003), 99; S. Taylor and Mansell (2003), 24. On the relation between the cartel offence and conspiracy to defraud, see Chap. 9 n. 3 below.

A question with no clear answer is how agreement and arrangement here relate to each other and to agreement under Article 101 of the Treaty on the Functioning of the European Union and the corresponding provision (section 2) of the Competition Act 1998: see Parr and McKenzie (2008). One suggestion is that 'arrangement' means 'agreement or concerted practice' within the meaning of Article 101; but its meaning appears to be broader: see Ainsworth (2008). Explanations of the cartel offence sometimes omit any mention of an arrangement, thus implying that the concept is superfluous; for example, Richards Butler (2003), 49 says, 'Under section 18[8], the cartel offence is committed where one person (or more than one) . . . dishonestly agrees with another (or more) that two or more businesses will engage in one of the following cartel activities' – and then lists those in section 188(2). 'Arrangement' was used in section 43(1) of the Restricted Trade Practices Act 1976 (repealed) and often assumed by practitioners and commentators to mean much the same as 'concerted practice': see O. Black (1992), 200; Whish (1993), 127 ff. Confusingly, that provision stated that '"agreement" includes any agreement or arrangement'. See further n. 15 below.

competition legislation, the Sherman Antitrust Act, enacted in the USA in 1890,[3] provides in section 1:

> Every contract, combination in the form of trust or otherwise, or conspiracy, in restraint of trade or commerce among the several States, or with foreign nations, is hereby declared to be illegal.

The word 'agreement' is not used,[4] and some have distinguished agreements from contracts, combinations and conspiracies,[5] but the modern consensus is that agreement is the central element of all three.[6] The main

3 For the historical background, see Hazlett (1992); Letwin (1981). Canada introduced competition legislation before the Sherman Act: see Katz et al. (2008).

4 Contrast section 3 of the (US) Clayton Act 1914, which prohibits certain sales and leases made 'on the condition, agreement, or understanding' that the lessee or purchaser shall not use or deal in goods of a competitor of the lessor or seller. Agreement is not needed for a breach of section 5 of the (US) Federal Trade Commission Act 1914, which prohibits 'unfair methods of competition in or affecting commerce'. Section 1 of the Sherman Act also does not use 'compete' or any of its cognates (a point noted by Holmes J. in his dissent in *Northern Securities Co.* v. *United States* 193 US 197 (1904)), although Senator Sherman's Bill was directed against 'all arrangements [etc.] . . . made with a view, or which tend to prevent free and full competition'; see O. Black (2005b), 65 n. 10, 69 n. 18; Joliet (1967), 21.

5 See *Northern Securities* (n. 4 above), 403; J. Baker (1969). For the suggestion that an agreement is unnecessary for a combination, see Gellhorn et al. (2004), 265; Jones (1986), 2000; n. 141 below. Some judgments have been read as holding that an agreement is unnecessary for a conspiracy under section 1 of the Sherman Act: see *Interstate Circuit, Inc.* v. *United States* 306 US 208 (1939), 226 f.; *American Tobacco Co.* v. *United States* 328 US 781 (1946), 809 f.; *United States* v. *Paramount Pictures, Inc.* 334 US 131 (1948), 142. That reading is rejected in Werden (2004), 739 ff., which cites decisions of lower courts. On combination in the law of conspiracy, see Chap. 9 n. 27 below; section 9.4 below discusses the idea of a conspiracy without an agreement.

On the disadvantages of importing the concept of conspiracy into competition law, see Gellhorn et al. (2004), 265 f.; Hammond and Penrose (2001), para. 1.9; Macdonald and Thompson (2003), 99 f.; Chap. 9 n. 3 below. For the advantages, see Joshua and Jordan (2004), 655: these authors maintain that a conspiracy is not identical to, but is constituted by and is the result of, an agreement (653; see Chap. 2 n. 7 above and Chap. 9 n. 22 below); they also note the opprobrium attached to conspiracy. On the change – reflected in the introduction of the cartel offence into UK law (n. 2 above) – in moral attitudes to anticompetitive conduct, see O. Black (2005b), 128; Hammond and Penrose (2001), para. 2.5; Joshua (2003), 625, 640; Peretz and Lewis (2003), 99; Whish (2009), 14. Conspiracy under section 1 of the Sherman Act differs from ordinary criminal conspiracy in that the conduct that is the object of the conspiracy – restraint of trade – is not in itself illegal, a point noted in Joshua and Jordan (2004), 652 and Burns (1990), 3 f.; on criminal conspiracies the object of which is not itself a crime, see Chap. 9 n. 5 below. Burns maintains that vertical arrangements do not fit the 'traditional conspiracy model' as easily as horizontal arrangements do (13 f.); on vertical cases, see section 8.51 below.

6 See Areeda (1986), vol. 6, para. 1403; Burns (1990), 3; Calvani (2006), 1028; Gellhorn et al. (2004), 26; Hay (2006), 879; Joshua and Jordan (2004), 654; Rahl (1950), 744; Turner

topic of this chapter, Article 101 of the Treaty on the Functioning of the European Union, provides in paragraph 1:

> The following shall be prohibited as incompatible with the common market: all agreements between undertakings, decisions by associations of undertakings and concerted practices which may affect trade between Member States and which have as their object or effect the prevention, restriction or distortion of competition within the common market . . . [7]

Similar wording is used in the competition statutes of EU member states and other jurisdictions.

The Treaty does not define 'agreement', and the case law has applied the word broadly.[8] Contracts, including those on standard terms, are normally agreements, but so are 'gentlemen's agreements' or 'protocols' that are not enforceable either legally or in other ways. An agreement may be informal or incomplete and need not be in writing. A party normally cannot avoid Article 101 by claiming that it was forced into an agreement, although the European Commission – the EU institution primarily responsible for enforcement – will consider that claim when deciding how to deal with a breach of the Article. An undertaking may be party to an agreement if it facilitates a cartel without operating in the market to which the cartel relates. The preparation for a full agreement may constitute an agreement, as may 'inchoate understandings and conditional or partial agreement'[9] during a process of negotiation. (See section 7.35 for a comparison, on this point, between competition law, contract law and the criminal law of conspiracy.) The same is true of the consequences of an agreement, even if the agreement has expired. As discussed in section 8.4, the fluid arrangements that make up a complex cartel may constitute an agreement. I shall also discuss cases in which an agreement has been found in seemingly unilateral behaviour, for example a manufacturer's issuing of a notice to its supplier.

(1962), 656; Werden (2004), 734. Kovacic (2006), 820 ff. gives a brief review of the cases on agreement under section 1 of the Sherman Act.

7 'Undertaking' in this context means, broadly, an economic enterprise: see Odudu (2006), chap. 3 and cases cited there. Elsewhere in this book it is used to signify promises and related phenomena: see section 1.1 above.

8 See Whish (2009), 97 f. and the authorities cited there. Other leading textbooks are Faull and Nikpay (2007); Rose and Roth (2008); van Bael and Bellis (2009).

9 *Pre-Insulated Pipes* OJ [1999] L 24/1, [1999] CMLR 402, para. 133, substantially upheld on appeal: cases T-9/99 etc. *HFB Holding* v. *Commission* [2002] ECR II-1487, [2002] 5 CMLR 571.

8.1 Concurrence of wills

Chapter 1 noted various expressions that have been used to try to illuminate the nature of agreement. Most of those listed there can be found in the cases and commentaries on competition law;[10] others

10 'Meeting of minds': EU cases: cases C-89/85 etc. *A. Ahlström Osakeyhtiö* v. *Commission* ('*Wood Pulp II*') [1993] ECR I-1307, AG Opinion para. 166 n. 71; cases C-2/01 P, C-3/01 P, *Bundesverband der Arzneimittel-Importeure eV and Commission* v. *Bayer AG* ('*Bayer* (ECJ)') [2004] ECR I-23, paras. 117, 122. US cases: *American Tobacco* (n. 5 above), 809 f.; *Milgram* v. *Loew's, Inc.* 192 F. 2d 590 f. (3rd Cir. 1951) (Hastie J. dissenting); *Copperweld Corp.* v. *Independence Tube Corp.* 467 US 752, 771 (1984); *Monsanto* v. *Spray-Rite* 465 US 752, 754 n. 9 (1984); *Apex Oil Co.* v. *DiMauro* 822 F. 2d 246, 257 (2d Cir. 1987); *Wallace* v. *Bank of Bartlett* 55 F. 3d 1166, 1168 (6th Cir. 1995); *Systemcare, Inc.* v. *Wang Labs Corp.* 117 F. 3d 1137, 1143 (10th Cir. 1997); *Rossi* v. *Standard Roofing, Inc.* 156 F. Ed 452, 465 (3d Cir. 1998). Commentary: Albors-Llorens (2006), 859; Antunes (1991), 67, 72; O. Black (2005b), 103; Burns (1990), 24; Dashwood et al. (1976), 486; Gellhorn et al. (2004), 273, 319; Guerrin and Kyriazis (1993), 790, 792 ff.; Hay (2006), 892, 899; Henry (2004), 3; Jones (1986), 1992; Kovacic (1993), 23; Lopatka (1996), 851 ff.; Odudu (2006), 72; Posner (1969), 1576 f.; Posner (2001), 60, 94 f., 98; P. Rey and Venit (2004), 154; Sousa Ferro (2007), 207; Turner (1962), 664; Werden (2004), 742, 777. Compare Chap. 1 n. 1 above and Chap. 9 nn. 2 and 26 below.

'Common intention' and variants: EU: case 41–69 *ACF Chemiefarma NV* v. *Commission* [1970] ECR 661, para. 112; cases 209/78 etc. *Heintz van Landewyck SARL and others* v. *Commission* [1980] ECR 3125, [1981] 3 CMLR 134, para. 86; case T-7/89 *SA Hercules Chemicals NV* v. *Commission* [1991] ECR II-1711, para. 256; case T-1/89 *Rhône-Poulenc SA* v. *Commission* [1991] ECR II-867, para. 120; case T-2/89 *Petrofina* v. *Commission* [1991] ECR II 1087, para. 211; case T-347/94 *Mayr-Melnhof Kartongesellschaft mbH* v. *Commission* [1998] ECR II-1751, para. 65; case T-41/96 *Bayer AG* v. *Commission* ('*Bayer* (CFI)') [2000] ECR II-3383, [2001] 4 CMLR 176, para. 67; *Bayer* (ECJ) (above), paras. 97, 118; case T-208/01 *Volkswagen AG* v. *Commission* ('*Volkswagen II* (CFI)') [2003] ECR II-5141, para. 30. UK: cases 2005/1071 etc. *Argos Limited and Littlewoods Limited* v. *Office of Fair Trading, JJB Sports PLC* v. *Office of Fair Trading* ('*Argos/JJB*') [2006] EWCA Civ 1318, para. 23. Commentary: Albors-Llorens (2006), 841, 848 ff., 872; Antunes (1991), 72, 74 ff.; Broberg and Jakobsen (2002), 132; Faull and Nikpay (2007), paras. 3.47, 3.50, 3.67, 3.78; Jephcott (2005), 20; Lidgard (1997), 354, 359; Odudu (2006), 60 ff.; Wessely (2001), 744; Wickihalder (2006), 90 f.; Willis and Hughes (2007), 123. Compare Chap. 1 n. 2 above and Chap. 9 nn. 34 and 126 below.

'Consensus': EU: *Polypropylene* [1986] OJ L230/1, [1988] 4 CMLR 347, para. 81; *British Sugar* [1999] OJ L76, 11. UK: *Argos/JJB* (above), paras. 22, 32, 138. Commentary: Albors-Llorens (2006), 841, 843, 849; Bailey (2006), 237, 240, 243 f., 250; Faull and Nikpay (2007), 3.50; Gellhorn et al. (2004), 266; Goyder (2003), 66; Jephcott (2005), 20; Jones (1986), 1998; Mann (1973), 36; Office of Fair Trading (2004), paras. 2.8 f. Compare Chap. 1 n. 5 and Chap. 3 n. 73 above; Chap. 9 nn. 2 and 23 below.

'Understanding': US: *FTC* v. *Beech-Nut Packing Co.* 257 US 441 S Ct 150, 66 L Ed 307, 373 (1922); *American Tobacco* (n. 5 above), 810. Commentary: Antunes (1991), 67; Burns (1990), 8; Gellhorn et al. (2004), 273, 319, 373 f., 376; Hay (2006), 913; Hovenkamp (2005), 98, 101; Kovacic (1993), 23; Kovacic (2006), 820; Lopatka (1996), 848, 853, 858 (attributing to Turner a distinction between 'actual agreement' and 'prior understanding'

are 'common design',[11] 'common plan',[12] 'common course of action',[13] 'unity of purpose',[14] 'arrangement',[15] 'exchange of assurances',[16] 'collective commitment',[17] 'conscious commitment to a common scheme'[18] and 'concert of action'.[19] In the EU jurisprudence, a phrase that has become canonic is 'concurrence of wills'.[20] In *Bayer*, the facts of

(see further n. 170 below)), 859; Macdonald and Thompson (2003), 99; Posner (1969), 1575 ff.; Turner (1962), 677, 687, 694; Werden (2004), 742; Wessely (2001), 746; Whish (2009), 97. Compare Chap. 1 n. 6 above and Chap. 9 n. 35 below.

11 *American Tobacco* (n. 5 above), 810. Commentary: Antunes (1991), 75 ('joint purpose'; at 60 Antunes writes that a 'common objective' is unnecessary for an agreement); Burns (1990), 24; Gellhorn et al. (2004), 273, 319; Joshua and Jordan (2004), 656 n. 35 ('common purpose'); Kovacic (1993), 23; Kovacic (2006), 820; Lopatka (1996), 853; Werden (2004), 742. Compare Chap. 9 n. 126 below.

12 Burns (1990), 13, 24, 34; Jephcott (2005), 20 ('consensus on a plan'); Kovacic (1993), 8.

13 Kovacic (1993), 7; Turner (1962), 683.

14 *American Tobacco* (n. 5 above), 810; Burns (1990), 8, 14, 24, 34; Gellhorn et al. (2004), 273, 319; Kovacic (1993), 23; Kovacic (2006), 820; Lopatka (1996), 853; Werden (2004), 742. Compare Chap. 9 n. 126 below for 'unity of design and purpose'.

15 *American Tobacco* (n. 5 above), 810; *Paramount Pictures* (n. 5 above), 142. Commentary: Kovacic (1993), 23; Kovacic (2006), 820 f. See also n. 2 above.

16 Gellhorn et al. (2004), 266 ff., 314, 318; Kovacic (1993), 7, 13, 18 f., 23, 25; Kovacic (2006), 818, 821.

17 Kovacic (2006), 819.

18 The phrase used in *Monsanto* (n. 10 above) 764, 768, quoting *Edward J. Sweeney & Sons, Inc.* v. *Texaco, Inc.* 637 F. 2d 105, 111 (3d Cir. 1980). Werden (2004), 777 states that this appears to be the formulation most often used recently in relation to section 1 of the Sherman Act; that article cites other cases at 777 n. 270. See also Burns (1990), 24; Gellhorn et al. (2004), 269, 277, 375; Hawk (1988); Jones (1986), 1992; Kovacic (1993), 16, 24, 27; Kovacic (2006), 821; Lopatka (1996), 853. In EU competition jurisprudence, 'commitment to a common scheme' was used by the Commission in *British Sugar* (n. 10 above), para. 22. Compare Chap. 9 n. 30 below for 'deliberate and preconcerted scheme'.

19 Or 'concerted action' or 'concerted behaviour': *Paramount Pictures* (n. 5 above), 142; Gellhorn et al. (2004), 269 ff., 319; Kovacic (1993), 23; Kovacic (2006), 821; E. Levi (1947), 177 f.; Werden (2004), 741. On one reading, an agreement is not necessary for a concert of action: for discussion, see Handler (1953), 42 ff.; E. Levi (1947), 177 f.; Werden (2004), 739 ff. On the distinction in EU law between agreements and concerted practices, see sections 8.2, 8.3 and 8.5222 below. Compare Chap. 9 nn. 32, 44, 59 and 61 below on 'concerted activity' and 'acting in concert'.

20 EU: *Volkswagen II* (CFI) (n. 10 above), para. 56. UK: *Unipart Group Ltd.* v. *O2 (UK) Ltd.* [2004] EWCA Civ 1034, paras. 35, 41, 44, 49, 51 f., 55, 61, 79, 90 f., 96, 103; *Argos/JJB* (n. 10 above), paras. 21, 23. Albors-Llorens (2006), 840 calls this the 'standard' definition (see 848, 850, on 'common will'). See also Bailey (2006), 243, 245; O. Black (2005b), 103; O. Black (2008); Faull and Nikpay (2007), paras. 3.47, 3.50, 3.67; Henry (2004), 3; Odudu (2006), 60; Ratliff (2005), 59; P. Rey and Venit (2004), 155, 157 (n. 20 speaks of 'concordance of the wills'); Schulz (2004), 19; Sousa Ferro (2007), 205 (calling this the 'common sense notion of agreement'), 207 f.; Whish (2009), 110; Wickihalder (2006), 88, 90 f., 96, 103, 106, 108, 110, 116 f.; Willis and Hughes (2007), 123, 128. For uses of

which are set out in section 8.51, the Court of First Instance[21] (CFI) stated:

> [I]n order for there to be an agreement within the meaning of Article [101](1) of the Treaty it is sufficient that the undertakings in question should have expressed their joint intention to conduct themselves on the market in a specific way . . .
>
> It follows that the concept of an agreement within the meaning of Article [101](1) of the Treaty, as interpreted by the case-law, centres around the existence of a concurrence of wills between at least two parties, the form in which it is manifested being unimportant so long as it constitutes the faithful expression of the parties' intention.[22]

This is Delphic. It is obscure, for example, both how the statement about concurrence of wills is supposed to 'follow' from the one about expression of a joint intention[23] and what is meant by 'centres around':[24] in particular, what is it for a concept to centre around the existence of something? Various readings are available, some of which entail and/or stand in explanatory relations to others. The passage might be drawing a connection, perhaps of identity or containment, between the meanings of 'agreement' and 'concurrence of wills'. This reading, like those that follow, divides into others, respectively concerning the making of, the performance of, and compliance with, an agreement; in the present context, the agreement's content is presumably not in question and it can be assumed that the state of agreement raises no separate issues. (For these distinctions, and other meanings of 'agreement', see the Introduction.)

the phrase in other contexts, see de Moor (1986); de Moor (1987), 115 ff.; Owsia (1991), 805. On 'concurrence' as an ingredient of criminal conspiracy, see Chap. 9 n. 38 below.

21 Renamed, by the Lisbon Treaty, the General Court.

22 *Bayer* (CFI) (n. 10 above), paras. 67, 69; see also paras. 173 f., 176. The judgment was upheld by the European Court of Justice (ECJ) (renamed, by the Lisbon Treaty, the Court of Justice) in *Bayer* (ECJ) (n. 10 above); see para. 97 (which repeats the CFI's formulation) and para. 102, which says: 'For an agreement within the meaning of Article [101](1) of the Treaty to be capable of being regarded as having been concluded by tacit acceptance, it is necessary that the manifestation of the wish of one of the contracting parties to achieve an anti-competitive goal constitute an invitation to the other party, whether express or implied, to fulfil that goal jointly . . . '. The words 'fulfil that goal jointly' come close to the CFI's 'joint intention', save that here the jointness is predicated of the fulfilment rather than the goal or intention; in this respect the ECJ's wording seems closer to 'common course of action' (n. 13 above).

23 Albors-Llorens (2006), 840 f. seems to say that joint intention is an 'example' of concurrence of wills.

24 Wickihalder (2006), 91 also uses 'it follows that' but substitutes 'is characterised by' for 'centres around'. The substitution is unhelpful, as the two phrases are equally obscure.

On another reading the connection is between the concepts of agreement and concurrence of wills; if meanings are concepts, these readings may coincide. That the Court had in mind a conceptual identity is suggested by a statement later in the judgment, that a concurrence of wills is 'the subjective element that characterises the very concept of an agreement'.[25]

The idea might be rather that, although there is no significant connection of meanings or concepts, there is one of conditionality: the condition might be sufficient or necessary for agreement, or might be something more complex – say a minimal sufficient condition (see section 3.2). Here, as in sections 2.66 and 5.1, I assume for convenience a strict-implication analysis of the conditional: <if P then Q> if and only if it is not possible that both P and not Q. (As noted in sections 1.22 and 5.1, the analysis can be reformulated in terms of truth values or in mixed terms; for example, 'If P then Q' is true if and only if it is not possible that both P is true and Q is false.) Since the quoted passage says that expression of the relevant joint intention is sufficient for there to be an agreement, a possible reading is that the existence of a concurrence of wills, or of an expressed or manifested concurrence of wills (it is unclear whether 'expressed' and 'manifested' are intended as synonyms), is likewise a sufficient condition.

It might be objected, on the following grounds, that the reading is uncharitable. The passage forms part of an argument that, where there was no agreement, the Commission held there to be one; it is therefore natural to understand the judgment as saying that a condition which the Commission thought to be sufficient for agreement is not sufficient. The claim that A is sufficient for B is not refuted by the claim that C is, for both claims may be true; a way to refute the first claim is to show that D, which is not necessary for A, is necessary for B. So the Court may have had in mind a necessary condition for agreement. An answer is that the Court's reasoning may have included the claim of sufficiency, roughly as follows: every agreement is such that a concurrence of wills is sufficient for it; a concurrence of wills is not sufficient for the conduct in question; so that conduct is not an agreement. The Court's reasoning is discussed further in section 8.51.

On another reading of the passage, there is no conditionality, but merely a contingent correlation between agreement and concurrence of wills: the claim might be that there is no agreement in the absence of a concurrence of wills. (A different reading of 'correlation' is given in section 8.5222.) 'In the absence of' would need to be made more precise – for example, to avoid

25 *Bayer* (CFI) (n. 10 above), para. 173. See further n. 33 below.

the claim's being made true simply by the existence of any concurrence of wills; 'no agreement' might be weakened to 'rarely an agreement'; and various standards could be imposed for the application of 'rarely', or whichever other adverb is chosen. The converse claim of correlation, that there is no concurrence of wills in the absence of an agreement, would not be a sympathetic reading of *Bayer*, for it is consistent with the proposition that most agreements occur in the absence of a concurrence of wills: that is hard to square with the Court's assertion that the concept of an agreement centres around the existence of a concurrence of wills. Similar objections apply to weaker formulations.

The claim that there is no concurrence of wills in the absence of an agreement does, however, support a sympathetic reading, that a concurrence of wills is useful evidence of an agreement.[26] Variants would employ the (or a) concept of a test, or sign, or criterion,[27] and the specified epistemic relation might be more or less strong: the evidence could be conclusive or only defeasible, or the relation formulated by reference to any of a number of mental states with various strengths – belief, justified belief or knowledge, say.

The objection in Chapter 1, to the use of certain phrases for the purpose of illuminating the nature of agreement, might be raised in respect of 'concurrence of wills': the phrase's meaning is unclear.[28] A fiercer variant

26 'Imply' and 'indicate', in Turner (1962), 660 appear to signify evidence rather than conditions for existence. The distinction is unclear in Albors-Llorens (2006), 848 ff. Albors-Llorens starts by writing that 'for an agreement to exist, there must be an *expression* of the joint intention of the undertakings concerned' (emphasis in original). This echoes the words quoted in the main text above from *Bayer* (CFI) and is a point about existence rather than evidence. A page later she writes 'By contrast, in a concerted practice, and [*sic*] while the undertakings must have communicated, the joint intention of the undertakings involved would not have been formally expressed in any way and would have had to be wholly inferred from other parameters, such as direct or indirect contacts between them or market behaviour'. The mention of inference suggests that evidence, rather than existence, is now in question. This reading is supported by the sentence that follows: 'Once we accept this basic distinction between the two categories encompassed in Article [101](1)... it becomes clear that the main question is not *which* form of cooperation we apply to a particular set of facts but *how to prove* the existence of collusion' (emphasis in original). Compare Calvani (2006), 1029; Joshua and Jordan (2004), 660, which suggests that the Commission has sometimes mistaken for a concerted practice an agreement proved entirely by circumstantial evidence (as to which, see section 8.521 below). Compare O. Black (2005b), 162 on the importance of distinguishing evidential and constitutive questions about concerted practices.

27 See Chap. 5 n. 17 above.

28 For similar complaints about the words of section 1 of the Sherman Act, and the phrases used to explicate them, see Burns (1990), 5; Kovacic (1993), 24 f.; Lopatka (1996), 853 f.

of the objection is that 'concurrence of wills' is no more than a label which an authority may apply ex post to conduct that it has already decided amounts to an agreement; on this view, it means 'whatever an authority takes to be an agreement' and the statement that the concept of an agreement centres around the existence of a concurrence of wills is vacuous. But the objection even in its milder form is unconvincing because, as I shall maintain, a fairly clear meaning, which concerns the parties' intentions, can be found for the phrase.

A more forceful objection is that, on any of the readings of the passage that were set out above, the judgment's claim of a relation between agreement and concurrence of wills is either false or uninteresting. Given that concurrence of wills is a matter of intention, this objection supports the thesis, stated in the Introduction and section 5.1, that bad law results from the drawing of too tight a connection between agreement and intention. Further support is given by the discussion, in section 8.2, of 'common intention' (and, in section 9.4, of 'unilateral conspiracy'). I shall argue the objection for simple conditional readings only, and the argument will be illustrative, not exhaustive.

8.11 *Intention and concurrence of wills*

To say that there is a concurrence of wills between X and Y is perhaps to say that X and Y both will the same thing: on the assumption that willing is a propositional attitude (see the Introduction), there is a proposition P such that X and Y both will that P. Alternatively it might be to say that they will things that are compatible: there are propositions P and Q such that X wills that P, Y wills that Q, and it is possible that both P and Q. Another reading, which captures in one way an idea prominent in *Bayer*, that the parties to an agreement need to co-operate,[29] is: there are P and Q such that X wills that P, Y wills that Q, and P only if Q.

In any of these formulations, 'will' is naturally understood in terms of intention or desire; so, for example, the first reading might be expanded to say that X and Y both intend that P, or desire that P, or that X intends and Y desires that P. Given that the quoted passage talks of intention but not desire, a reading purely in terms of intention is better. The passage

See also nn. 5 f. above. The problem is sometimes said to be the lack of an operational definition: Kovacic (2006), 822 ('operational means'); Werden (2004), 777 f.

29 *Bayer* (CFI) (n. 10 above), para. 71; *Bayer* (ECJ) (n. 10 above), para. 101. See also Bailey (2006), 243; Faull and Nikpay (2007), para. 3.77; Sousa Ferro (2007), 207; Wickihalder (2006), 107 f.

suggests a stronger reading, on which the parties express or manifest their intentions or desires; indeed it is reasonable to suppose that the Court had in mind not merely expression or manifestation but communication.[30] The judgment leaves it unclear whether communication is part of or additional to a concurrence of wills,[31] and it matters little which reading is taken. On the former, the simplest analysis of concurrence of wills that both embodies an intuitive understanding and is sympathetic to the Court's words is:

(179) X and Y have a concurrence of wills if and only if, for some P:
- (a) X intends that P;
- (b) Y intends that P;
- (c) X communicates his intention that P to Y; and
- (d) Y communicates his intention that P to X.

It might be objected that (a) and (b) are trivial because, at a high enough level of abstraction, any two people with intentions can be represented as having the same one. X turns a key, intending to unlock a door; Y dusts a shelf, intending to clean it: both have the same intention – to alter the state of some physical object. The objection assumes that intention is closed under abstraction, i.e., that if <X intends that P> and <Q abstracts from P> then X intends that Q. A broad sense of 'intend' can be stipulated that makes this principle true by definition, but I shall assume an ordinary and narrower sense in which it is false.[32]

Consider an agreement between competitors X and Y that:

(180) X sells only in France and Y sells only in Germany,

(180) having a sense entailing that X and Y respectively sell in France and in Germany. Assume that the agreement is made through an exchange of the sort captured by the offer–acceptance model: X: 'How about this – I sell only in France and you sell only in Germany?' Y: 'Fine.' A concurrence of wills might relate to the making or the performance of, or to compliance with, the agreement. Although, as explained in the Introduction, performance and compliance are distinct, the former can be ignored here, as the argument concerning compliance can be extended to

30 See Chap. 7 n. 59 above; n. 133 below.

31 Faull and Nikpay (2007), para. 3.50 juxtaposes the phrases 'expression of a joint intention' and 'concurrence of wills'; this suggests that communication, or at least expression, is built into the concept of a concurrence of wills.

32 On other closure properties of intention, see Chap. 5 n. 31 above.

performance. If (179) is applied to the making of the agreement, candidates for the content of the intentions are (180) and:

(181) X and Y agree that (180),

where 'agree' signifies the making of the agreement. If (179) is applied to compliance, candidates for the intentions' content are (180) and:

(182) X and Y comply with their agreement that (180).

Substituting:

(183) (a) X intends that (180);
(b) Y intends that (180);
(c) X communicates his intention that (180) to Y; and
(d) Y communicates his intention that (180) to X.

(184) and (185) respectively substitute (181) and (182) for (180) in (183).

8.12 Conditionality

I now argue that the existence of a concurrence of wills is neither necessary nor interestingly sufficient either for the making of or for compliance with an agreement. That conclusion is reached by generalising from the lemma that, of the following conditionals, the even-numbered ones are false and the odd-numbered ones either false or uninterestingly true:

(186) If (181) then (183).
(187) If (183) then (181).
(188) If (181) then (184).
(189) If (184) then (181).
(190) If (182) then (183).
(191) If (183) then (182).
(192) If (182) then (185).
(193) If (185) then (182).

The lemma is true, whether the conditionals use subjective or objective concepts of agreement and intention,[33] whether they are about prior

33 It is debatable whether the concept of agreement for the purposes of Article 101 is objective and, if so, in what sense. The statement quoted, in section 1.1 above, from *Bayer* (CFI), that a concurrence of wills is 'the subjective element that characterises the very concept of an agreement', can be read as implying that the concept of agreement is itself subjective, in which case it is plausible, when interpreting the conditionals, to apply a correspondingly subjective concept of intention. On the other hand, a more recent judgment of the ECJ

intentions or intentions in action, and whichever kind of compliance they concern. The refutations of the false conditionals overlap the arguments applied in sections 5.11–5.16 to propositions (116)–(121) and to their elaborations. As in the discussion there, which explained the distinctions between subjective and objective and between kinds of intention, I shall only give examples – in this case, one concerning the making of the agreement and one concerning compliance.

8.121 First case: (186) – subjective concepts, prior intention

The argument in section 5.11 against (122) can be adapted to refute (186) where (186) is read subjectively and in terms of prior intention. Assume that the agreement is made at time Ta and provides that in period Ts, starting after Ta, X sells only in France and Y sells only in Germany. A natural reading of (186) is:

(194) If at Ta X and Y agree that <in Ts, X sells only in France and Y sells only in Germany>, then:
- (a) at Ta X intends that <in Ts, X sells only in France and Y sells only in Germany>;
- (b) at Ta Y intends that <in Ts, X sells only in France and Y sells only in Germany>;
- (c) X communicates his intention in (a) to Y; and
- (d) Y communicates his intention in (b) to X.

It is possible that, although at Ta X and Y make the agreement, at Ta X does not intend that in Ts he sells only in France. He may intend to breach the agreement. Even if he does not, his intentions, if any, as to the selling are likely to be conditional, as explained in the discussion, in section 5.11, of sincere agreement. If at Ta X does not intend that in Ts he sells only in France, then at Ta he does not intend that <in Ts, he sells only in France and Y sells only in Germany>: this conditional might be deduced by contraposing the principle – attractive but perhaps needing qualification – that intentions distribute over conjunction.[34] (See further the discussion, in section 5.31, of the distributivity of propositional attitudes over conjunction.) In that case (a) is false. If (a) is false, so is (c). The

appears to say that the parties' subjective intentions do not determine the object of an agreement: case C-209/07 *Competition Authority* v. *Beef Industry Development Society Ltd, Barry Brothers (Carrigmore) Meats Ltd.* [2008] ECR I-8637, para. 21. See further the discussion in O. Black (2005b), 116 ff. of Odudu (2001), 70.

34 For discussion of similar principles, see Bratman (1987), 146 ff.; Bratman (1990), 25 ff.; Chisholm (1976), 74 f.

possibility follows that the antecedent of (194) is true but the consequent false. Therefore (194) is false. Although (c) is false if (a) is, (c) may be false even if (a) is true: another refutation of (194) invokes the possibility that, although both the antecedent and (a) are true, (c) is false because X keeps his intention to himself. Parallel arguments apply to Y, (b) and (d).

Where X intends that P, and P entails that X performs some action, say that X's intention is 'directed at' an action of X; similarly, if P entails that Y performs some action, X's intention is directed at an action of Y. A third refutation of (194) invokes the possibility that (i) the antecedent of (194) is true, (ii) at Ta X intends that in Ts he sells only in France, but (iii) each of X's intentions at Ta is directed only at an action of X. If (i)–(iii) are true, (a) and (c) are still false, as (a) concerns an intention of X directed at an action of Y. Again it follows that (194) is false and again a parallel argument applies to Y, (b) and (d).

A possible reply is that X's intention in (a) is directed at a single joint action of geographically partitioned selling, performed by both X and Y, and hence that X's intention is directed at an action of his own, even though it is also an action of Y's. If, to forestall this reply, (iii) is reworded to provide that X's intentions at Ta are directed at actions that are X's alone, it might be claimed that X and Y form a 'plural subject' which both has the intention and would alone perform the action (see section 2.62). Three objections to this claim are that it is obscure;[35] that it fails to support (194), the consequent of which describes intentions held severally by X and Y; and that, since X is distinct from the plural subject, an action performed only by the latter is not one performed only by the former. To the second and third objections it might be replied that in (194) 'X' and 'Y' co-refer to the plural subject; but then (c) and (d) have the plural subject communicating with itself. Even if, as section 1.1 allowed, talking to oneself may be considered a limiting case of communication, it is possible that, although the antecedent of (194) is true, (c) and (d) on this reading are false. So again (194) is false.

A variant of the refutation from the compossibility of (i)–(iii) uses the controversial premiss that necessarily a person's intentions are directed only at actions of his own.[36] (This might in turn be derived from the

35 See Chap. 2 n. 55 above.

36 For similar principles, see O. Black (2005b), 124; Bratman (1999b); Ormerod (2008), 407; Simester et al. (2010), 319; Tuomela (1995), chap. 2. Evnine (2008), 131 appears to contemplate intentions directed at the actions of others, but Evnine writes that 'where our plans require the actions of others, we must always, to a greater or lesser extent, take

thesis that necessarily the content of an intention has the form 'I φ'.) The argument runs thus: the consequent of (194) purports to concern intentions each of which is directed at actions of X and Y; by the premiss, the consequent is false; on the assumption that (181) is true, so is (194)'s antecedent; a conditional with a true antecedent and a false consequent is false; so (194) is false.

The controversial premiss can also be used to show that each of the odd-numbered conditionals, read in terms of subjective intention, is true. Each of (180)–(182) concerns actions of X and Y; correspondingly, each of (183)–(185) purports to concern intentions each of which is directed at actions of X and Y; by the premiss, (183)–(185) not only are false but cannot be true; so each of the odd-numbered conditionals, read in the way specified, has an impossible antecedent; by the strict-implication analysis, 'If P then Q' is true if and only if it is not possible that both P and not Q; and this condition is met if P is impossible. The result – an instance of one of the paradoxes of strict implication[37] – is uninteresting, as it follows from the modal status of the antecedent alone, irrespective of any relation between its subject matter and that of the consequent. In any event, it does not hold where the conditionals are read in terms of objective intention, for then the antecedents have the form 'the reasonable man [RM] believes that R': see section 5.13. Even if R cannot be true, RM may believe it; this strengthens the claim, included in section 5.1's description of RM, that he may believe a false proposition. It follows that the antecedents, on the objective reading, are possibly true.

A more general point is that, if the controversial premiss is true, a concurrence of wills as analysed by (179) cannot exist, save in the limiting case of one between a person and himself. (Compare the remark above on talking to oneself.) According to (179), if X and Y have a concurrence of wills, then, for some P, both X intends that P and Y intends that P. From the premiss it follows that necessarily: if P entails that X performs some action, then Y does not intend that P; if P entails that Y performs some action, then X does not intend that P; and, if P does not entail either, then neither X nor Y intends that P. But necessarily, for any P, at least one of these three conditionals has a true antecedent. This result is hard to

measures to ensure fulfilment of our intentions'. Distinguish: (a) X's intention is directed at Y's action; (b) each of X and Y has an intention directed at Y's action; (c) X and Y share a single intention directed at Y's action; (d) X and Y, in intending, form a 'plural intender'; (e) X and Y, in acting, form a 'plural agent'.

37 See Chap. 1 n. 42 above.

reconcile with the statement in *Bayer* that the concept of an agreement centres around the *existence* of a concurrence of wills between at least two parties. It also narrows the range of readings that can charitably be given to the judgment: if, for example, the judgment is interpreted to say that the existence of a concurrence of wills is necessary for the making of an agreement, then, given the premiss and (179), it entails, absurdly, that an agreement cannot exist.

8.122 Second case: (191) – subjective concepts, prior intention

As section 1.22 noted, various kinds of compliance are distinguishable. I shall consider one which involves certain intentions in action and for which this biconditional is true:

(195) (182) if and only if:
- (a) (181);
- (b) X sells only in France;
- (c) Y sells only in Germany;
- (d) X, in selling only in France, intends to sell only in France; and
- (e) Y, in selling only in Germany, intends to sell only in Germany,

(181) being the proposition that X and Y agree that (180) X sells only in France and Y sells only in Germany, and (182) the proposition that X and Y comply with their agreement that (180). Let (191) be read subjectively and, so far as the concurrence of wills is concerned, in terms of prior intention, the relevant prior intentions being those in (194); the intentions in the compliance are, as just noted, intentions in action. Then, given (195), (191) is true if and only if:

(196) If:
- (a) at Ta X intends that <in Ts, X sells only in France and Y sells only in Germany>;
- (b) at Ta Y intends that <in Ts, X sells only in France and Y sells only in Germany>;
- (c) X communicates his intention in (a) to Y; and
- (d) Y communicates his intention in (b) to X;

then:
- (e) at Ta X and Y agree that <in Ts, X sells only in France and Y sells only in Germany>;
- (f) in Ts X sells only in France;
- (g) in Ts Y sells only in Germany;

(h) X, in selling only in France, intends to sell only in France; and
(i) Y, in selling only in Germany, intends to sell only in Germany.

(196), and hence (191), is false for three reasons. It is possible that, although the antecedent is true, (e) is false because X and Y do not agree anything:[38] they may tell each other that, in having and communicating their intentions in (a)–(d), they are not agreeing and, in particular, are neither accepting nor imposing any such obligations as would arise from an agreement. That is consistent with the offer–acceptance model, for a mere declaration of intention is neither an offer nor an acceptance. It is also possible that (a)–(e) are true but that X breaches the agreement and hence that (f) and (h) are false. As shown by the following example, it is possible that (a)–(f) are true but that (h) is false: in Ts, X sends goods to addresses that he thinks are in Germany but in fact are in France, his intention being to sell in Germany and thus to breach the agreement. Corresponding arguments apply to Y, (g) and (i).

8.13 Defences and further objections

One defence against these objections is to look for other substitutions in (179) – the proposed analysis of concurrence of wills – for which conditionals replacing (186)–(193) are interestingly true. There are no candidates. A second defence is to analyse concurrence of wills otherwise than by (179). One version of this defence removes the clauses about communication; another recasts (179) in terms of desire rather than intention. The latter is unappealing both because, as noted in section 8.11, *Bayer* talks of intention, not desire, and because in any event the objections can be adapted to apply to the revised analysis. The former is consistent with the wording of the judgment and excludes certain counterexamples, but the excluded cases are not needed in order to refute the conditionals.

A third version runs as follows. The offer–acceptance model gives only a sufficient condition of agreement; if a sufficient condition is good enough for an analysis of agreement, it is good enough to analyse a concurrence of wills; so (179) can be weakened to:

38 Compare *Mulcahy* (1868) LR 3 HL 306, para. 11, a case on criminal conspiracy: 'A conspiracy consists not merely in the intention of two or more, but in the agreement of two or more to do an unlawful act, or to do a lawful act by unlawful means. So long as such a design rests in intention only, it is not indictable'. See also *Quinn* v. *Leathem* [1901] AC 495, 529. Both cases are discussed further in Chap. 9 below.

(197) X and Y have a concurrence of wills if, for some P:
 (a) X intends that P;
 (b) Y intends that P;
 (c) X communicates his intention that P to Y; and
 (d) Y communicates his intention that P to X.

The objections concern only 'normal' concurrences of wills – those the parties to which meet (a)–(d) of (197). As (197) gives only a sufficient condition, it allows that there may be abnormal concurrences of wills. Hence the objections fail.

In this version the defence works only if the judgment in *Bayer* is understood to concern abnormal cases. (197) says nothing about such cases, and so the price of the defence is to deprive the judgment of any support from an analysis of the relevant kind of concurrence of wills. It might be replied that, because, as admitted in section 8.11, we have an intuitive understanding of 'concurrence of wills', no such support is needed. The objection now is that our intuitive understanding is represented either by clauses (a)–(d), which do not apply to abnormal cases, or by the revisions which were contemplated in the first two versions of the defence and to which similar objections apply. If there is any residual intuitive understanding, not represented thus, it is too thin to establish the judgment's claim of a relation between agreement and concurrence of wills, on any of the proposed readings of that claim.

A third defence is to maintain that the objections based on the specimen agreement about sales in France and Germany miss their mark because, whereas they concern an agreement in the ordinary sense, 'agreement' in Article 101 is a term of art. The objection to this is that the absence of a definition in the Treaty makes it clear that the word has its ordinary meaning (or meanings): if it were a term of art, a definition would be needed and supplied, for otherwise those using it would have no guidance as to its meaning.[39] The following reply might now be given. The reason for omitting a definition was to allow the meaning of 'agreement' to develop through interpretation in the case law; such flexibility, which would be impaired by an explicit definition that every decision or judgment had

39 Compare Burns (1990), 32 f., which rejects the proposal to give 'agreement' a special meaning for the purposes of the Sherman Act. The objection might be developed by reference to paradigm-related reasons for legal interpretations (see section 8.51 below); but a possible reply, in those terms, would be that the paradigms for the application of 'agreement', within the meaning of Article 101, differ from those for the word's application in its ordinary sense.

to fit,[40] helps authorities to bring anticompetitive conduct within Article 101, thereby advancing the provision's purposes.[41] Although the process

40 Gellhorn et al. (2004), 39 says that in the USA '[t]he open texture of the foundational statutes gives the antitrust system an inherent flexibility and evolutionary quality that a fully-specified statutory statement of standards and an elaborate definition of terms would lack'. See further n. 158 below.

41 Burns (1990), 2 f. maintains that the US Supreme Court has failed to recognise that, as regards vertical arrangements, 'the definition of "agreement" is intricately related to antitrust policies'. (Vertical arrangements are discussed in section 8.51 below.) Burns identifies 'two obvious, but easily overlooked, propositions. First, how one defines "agreement" may affect what will be an offence under section 1 of the Sherman Act. Second, the definition of "agreement" will, itself, be coloured by one's view of the goal or goals of the antitrust laws'. See further Gellhorn et al. (2004), 43 ff.; Wickihalder (2006), 92; nn. 144 f. below. Gellhorn et al. note also, at 39, the relevance of the purpose and effect of specific business practices. The point could be developed by reference to purpose-related reasons for legal interpretations: see section 8.51 and compare n. 123 below.

On the various and conflicting purposes that have been proposed or assumed for competition law, see O. Black (1997), 246 ff.; O. Black (2005b), 6 f., 33, 65 f., 68 f.; Bork (1978), 58 ff. Bork writes 'Antitrust policy cannot be made rational until we are able to give a firm answer to one question: What is the point of the law – what are its goals? Everything else follows from the answer we give. Is the antitrust judge to be guided by one value or by several? If by several, how is he to decide cases where a conflict in values arises? Only when the issue of goals has been settled is it possible to frame a coherent body of substantive rules'. Bork (1978), 50. See also Gavil (1991); Posner (1975), 297. Bork and his opponents have been criticised for tendentiously selecting from the historical record to support their favoured answers: see Ernst (1990), 885; Gellhorn et al. (2004), 44. Gellhorn et al., at 45, argue against settling the purpose of competition law by reference to the legislators' intention; contrast Bork (1978), chap. 2. For general arguments against legislative intention as a guide to legal interpretation, see R. Dworkin (1986a), chap. 1; on legal interpretation, see nn. 158 ff. below.

Examples of the purposes, other than the protection or promotion of competition, that have been proposed or assumed are: fairness; diversity of choice; protection of consumers and small firms; dispersal of power; access to markets; redistribution of wealth; promotion of various industrial and social policies concerning employment, working hours and so forth; dissemination of information on market conditions; reduction of risk; technological innovation; the allocation of commercial decisions between firms on the one hand and competition authorities on the other; and, in the case of EU competition law, the integration of the internal market. Article 101 itself includes desiderata additional to competition, paragraph 3 providing that the prohibition in paragraph 1 may, subject to certain conditions, be declared inapplicable to an agreement (etc.) 'which contributes to improving the production or distribution of goods or to promoting technical or economic progress, while allowing consumers a fair share of the resulting benefits'.

EU cases mentioning purposes other than competition are case 26/76 *Metro SB-Grossmärkte GmBH & Co. KG* v. *Commission* [1977] ECR 1875, paras. 21, 43; *Synthetic Fibres* [1984] OJ L207/17, para. 37; case 42/84 *Remia BV* v. *Commission* [1985] ECR 2545, para. 42; case 75/84 *Metro SB-Grossmärkte GmbH & Co. KG* v. *Commission* [1986] ECR 3021, para. 65; *Ford/Volkswagen* [1993] OJ L20/14, paras. 23, 36; cases T-528/1993 etc. *Metropole Télévision SA* v. *Commission* ('*Eurovision*') [1996] ECR II-649, para. 112;

of interpretation started from the ordinary meaning of 'agreement', the result is that the word has become a term of art. A fuller statement of the reply would explain how meaning can be changed by interpretation.

Whatever the explanation, an objection is that it is at best doubtful whether the case law for Article 101 has changed the meaning of 'agreement', and that, even if it has, the result has been an expansion of the ordinary meaning to cover more kinds of conduct (see the list at the start of the chapter), not to exclude ordinary agreements such as the specimen. The respondent might concede this but hold that *Bayer* expands the

Albany International BV v. *Stichting Bedrijfspensioenfonds Textielindustrie* [1999] ECR I-5751, AG opinion, paras. 126, 193; *CECED* [2000] OJ L187, 47, paras. 8, 24; case C-309/99 *Wouters* v. *Algemene Raad van de Nederlandse Orde van Advocaten* [2002] ECR I-1577, AG opinion, para. 113. Commentary: Banks (1997); Bengoetxea et al. (2001), 67 ff.; B. Bishop (2000), 43; B. Bishop and S. Bishop (1996), 208; Boni and Manzini (2001), 244; Bouterse (1994), 22, 41 ff.; Calvani (2006), 1032; J. Cooke (2000), 61 ff.; Cosma and Whish (2003), 41 f.; de Gaay Fortman (1966), 151 ff.; Ehlermann (1995), 479 ff.; Ehlermann (2000), 549; Ellis (1963), 263 ff., 271 ff.; European Commission (1997), para. 191; Fels and Edwards (1998), 54, 63 f.; Gerber (1994), 131 f.; Gerber (2001), 417 ff.; Gyselen (2002), 185 f.; Hawk (1988), 56; Hawk (1995), 987 f.; Hildebrand (1998), 12 ff.; Hornsby (1987); House of Lords Select Committee (2000), paras. 54, 58, 130 ff., 149; Ichino (2001), 187; Joliet (1967), 24, 60, 71 ff., 113 f.; Korah (1986), 85; McNutt (2000), 50, 56 ff.; Marsden (1997), 237; Monti (2002), 1069 ff.; Odudu (2006), chap. 7; Prosser (2005), 24 ff.; Scherer and Ross (1990), 328 ff.; Schmid (2000), 167 ff.; Siragusa (1998), 665 f.; Siragusa (2000), 1101; Snyder (1990), 94 f.; van den Bergh and Camesasca (2001), 159 ff.; Wesseling (1999), 423 ff.; Wesseling (2000), 18, 33, 61, 33 ff., 62 ff., 83 ff., 94 ff., 103 ff.; Whish (2009), 19 ff.; Whish and Sufrin (2000), 147 ff.

US cases mentioning such purposes are *Northern Securities* (n. 4 above); *Board of Trade of the City of Chicago* v. *United States* 246 US 231, 238 (1918); *Appalachian Coals Inc.* v. *United States* 288 US 344, 359 f. (1933); *United States* v. *Associated Press* 52 F. Supp 362 (1943); *United States* v. *Aluminium Company of America* 148 F. 2d 416, 427 (2d Cir. 1945); *Paramount Pictures* (n. 5 above); *Standard Oil Co.* v. *United States* 337 US 293, 318 f. (1949) (Douglas J. dissenting); *Times-Picayune Publishing Co.* v. *United States* 345 US 594, 614 ff. (1953); *Brown Shoe Co.* v. *United States* 370 US 294, 344 (1962); *United States* v. *Penn-Olin Chemical Co.* 378 US 158, 176 f. (1964); *United States* v. *Topco Associates Inc.* 405 US 596, 610 (1972). Commentary: O. Black (1997), 148; O. Black (2005b), 68; DiLorenzo (1985); E. Fox (1981); Gellhorn et al. (2004), 23 ff., 43 ff.; Hazlett (1992); Lande (1982); J. May (1989), 391 ff.; Millon (1988); Peeters (1989), 521 ff.

Even as regards competition, the jurisprudence is inconsistent because there is debate as to the meaning of 'competition': see O. Black (1997), 146; O. Black (2005b), chap. 1, and texts cited there. Bork (1978), 58 ff. identifies five definitions: the process of rivalry; the absence of restraint over one firm's economic activities by another firm; the state of the market in which the individual buyer or seller does not influence the price by his purchases or sales; the existence of fragmented industries and markets; and – Bork's preferred definition – a state of affairs in which consumer welfare cannot be increased by moving to an alternative state of affairs through judicial decree: see Chap. 6 n. 59 above. Competition is understood as rivalry in Bork (1966), 377 n. 5.

meaning far enough to make interestingly true the judgment's claim of a relation between agreement and concurrence of wills: in particular, given the expanded meaning, a concurrence of wills is interestingly sufficient for the making of or for compliance with an agreement. In that case the argument from the specimen to the uninteresting truth, or the falsity, of the claim fails for illegitimate generalisation.

The objection now is that, if the meaning is stretched that far, it is incoherently disjunctive: 'agreement' in Article 101 applies to a congeries of situations that have little significant in common.[42] In that case the judgment in *Bayer* has the very fault of which it accuses the Commission's decision – that it pushes the boundaries of the category of agreement too far: see section 8.51. A disjunctive meaning could be avoided by positing a disjunction of meanings, i.e., an ambiguity, but that would merely change the form of incoherence: Article 101 would be like a provision on banks that applied equally to financial institutions and the sides of rivers.

The discussion has already hinted that the competition authorities would do better to talk of offer and acceptance. The cases and commentaries occasionally mention offer and acceptance[43] but, when they do, sometimes seem to use those words with meanings different from the ones they bear in contract law: the next section gives an example. In any event, the words are often used to describe conduct distant from that at the centre of contract law's doctrines of offer and acceptance:[44]

42 An application of the objection in O. Black (2005b), 94. For a similar complaint about section 1 of the Sherman Act, see *Holiday Wholesale Grocery Co.* v. *Philip Morris, Inc.* 231 F. Supp 2d 1253, 1270 (ND Ga 2002), affd sub nom *Williamson Oil Co.* v. *Philip Morris USA* 346 F. 3d 1287 (11th Cir. 2003).

43 EU: case 107/82 *AEG-Telefunken* v. *Commission* [1983] ECR 2151, [1984] CMLR 325, para. 38; cases 25 and 26/84 *Ford-Werke AG and Ford of Europe Inc.* v. *Commission* [1985] ECR 2725, [1985] 3 CMLR 528, para. 21; *Konica* [1988] OJ L78/34, para. 36; *Eco System/Peugeot* [1992] OJ L66/1, para. 23; case T-43/92 *Dunlop Slazenger International Ltd.* v. *Commission* [1994] ECR II-441, para. 60; case C-338/00P *Volkwagen AG* v. *Commission* ('*Volkswagen I* (ECJ)') [2003] ECR I-9189, para. 65; *Volkswagen II* (CFI) (n. 10 above), para. 52; *Bayer* (ECJ) (nn. 10 above and 163 below). US: *In re High Fructose Corn Syrup Antitrust Litigation* 216 F. 3d 621 (7th Cir. 2002) (dictum). Commentaries: Bailey (2006), 246 n. 76 (see further n. 162 below); Broberg and Jakobsen (2002), 134; Gellhorn et al. (2004), 271, 322; Jones (1986), 1992; Posner (1969), 1576; Posner (2001), 94; Schulz (2004), 19; Wickihalder (2006), 97.

44 In *Konica* (n. 43 above), para. 36 the Commission spoke of an 'offer of an agreement'; i.e., the agreement is the object of the offer, rather than, or as well as, the offer's being an element of the agreement (compare Chap. 2 n. 51 above, and see further nn. 45 and 164 below). Broberg and Jakobsen (2002), 134 says that in a vertical agreement it may be that '[t]he manufacturer "offers" distributors the option of sanctions not being imposed in return for the distributors refraining from engaging in parallel trade in the product in

specifically, it may be an instruction or non-linguistic conduct that is said to be accepted[45] – the talk in this context often being, instead, of 'acquiescence'[46] (see section 8.51), which arguably connotes a greater degree of passivity and/or reluctance than does 'acceptance'.[47] A number of other phrases are also used which are akin to 'offer' and 'accept': examples are 'instruct',[48] 'require',[49] 'exhort',[50] 'request'[51] and 'invite';[52]

question'. On vertical agreements, see section 8.51 below. See also Odudu (2006), chap. 4, discussed in section 8.2 below; Wickihalder (2006), 97.

45 Posner (1969), 1576; Posner (2001), 94 says that in oligopolies (discussed in sections 8.52–8.5222 below) it may be that a seller 'communicates his "offer" by restricting output, and the offer is "accepted" by the actions of his rivals in restricting their outputs as well'. Posner as judge made a similar statement in *High Fructose* (n. 43 above), although there he talked of an offer of a contract; compare the Commission in *Konica* (nn. 43 f. above); see also *Volkswagen I* (ECJ) (n. 43 above), paras. 64 f. on acceptance of a contract. Contrast Werden (2004), 776 f., describing co-ordination of prices in an oligopoly: '[t]he bargain was struck without an explicit offer or acceptance. None was required'. These statements can be reconciled by taking Posner to be talking about offer and acceptance that are not explicit; on tacit agreements, see section 8.521 below. Alternatively, his inverted commas may signify that the parties' actions do not amount to genuine offer and acceptance; see section 8.521 on 'tacit' as an alienans predicate. For further discussion of Posner's view, see Gellhorn et al. (2004), 322.

46 EU cases: *Adalat* [1996] OJ L201/1 ('*Bayer* (Commission)'), paras. 172, 176; *Volkswagen II* (CFI) (n. 10 above), paras. 35 f.; *Bayer* (CFI) (n. 10 above), paras. 71 f., 169, 173; *Bayer* (ECJ) (n. 10 above), paras. 125 ('de facto'), 130 ('tacit'). UK: *Argos/JJB* (n. 10 above). Commentary: Albors-Llorens (2006), 842 n. 10; Broberg and Jakobsen (2002), 132; Burns (1990), 24; Faull and Nikpay (2007), paras. 3.67 ff.; Henry (2004), 3; Jones (1986), 1992; Lidgard (1997), 359; Ratliff (2005), 59; P. Rey and Venit (2004), 155 f.; Schulz (2004), 20; Sousa Ferro (2007), 205; Turner (1962), 684, 689, 692, 694, 705 f.; Wickihalder (2006), 96 ff. Compare *Prior* [2004] EWCA Crim. 1147, an English case on criminal conspiracy: 'an acceptance of, or acquiescence in, an offer' (para. 16). In *State* v. *King* 104 Iowa 724, 74 NW 691 (1898), a US criminal conspiracy case, there was found to be acquiscence but no conspiratorial agreement: see Burgman (1979), 90.

47 Wickihalder (2006) appears to use them interchangeably.

48 Albors-Llorens (2006), 849 n. 38.

49 *Bayer* (ECJ) (n. 10 above), para. 90, AG opinion, para. 60; Wickihalder (2006), 103.

50 *Volkswagen* [2001] OJ L262/14, para. 62; Ratliff (2005), 59.

51 *Volkswagen II* (CFI) (n. 10 above), para. 52; Schulz (2004), 19; Wickihalder (2006), 103, 106, 108.

52 EU: *Bayer* (ECJ) (n. 10 above), para. 102. UK: *Argos/JJB* (n. 10 above), para. 25. US: *Interstate Circuit* (n. 5 above); *United States* v. *Masonite Corp.* 316 US 265, 275 (1942). Commentary: Albors-Llorens (2006), 849, 872; Bailey (2006), 244; Faull and Nikpay (2007), para. 3.76; Gellhorn et al. (2004), 272; Hay (2006), 891 f.; Henry (2004), 3; Hovenkamp (2005), 98, 101; Kovacic (1993), 22; Kovacic (2006), 820; Sousa Ferro (2007), 207; Turner (1962), 683, 689, 696; Werden (2004), 740; Wickihalder (2006), 108 ff., 117; Willis and Hughes (2007), 124. On the relation between inviting and inducing, see section 3.51 above; on the distinction in contract law between an offer and an invitation to treat, see section 7.13 above.

and 'assent',[53] 'consent',[54] 'endorse',[55] 'subscribe',[56] 'abide',[57] 'adhere',[58] 'conform',[59] 'comply',[60] 'co-operate'[61] and 'participate'.[62]

8.2 Common intention

Odudu appears to hold that, although offer and acceptance are evidence for an agreement under Article 101, 'common intention is central to the meaning of agreement in both Article [101] and contract'.[63] It is unclear whether he takes his view to be the same as that of the CFI in *Bayer*. 'Common intention' and 'is central to' are close to the Court's 'joint intention' and 'centres around', but distinctions can be drawn. It is perhaps pedantic in this context to distinguish 'common' and 'joint', although they are not always interchangeable: two people may have an illness in common or a common illness, without having a joint illness. More substantial differences are that, whereas the Court says that the

53 Turner (1962), 683. See further Chap. 1 n. 3 (mutual assent), Chap. 2 n. 3 above and Chap. 9 n. 36 below.

54 *Eco System* (n. 43 above), para. 23; *Volkswagen I* (ECJ) (n. 43 above), para. 65; *Bayer* (ECJ) (n. 10 above), para. 132; Antunes (1991), 75; Broberg and Jakobsen (2002), 135, 139; Lidgard (1997), 354; Wickihalder (2006), 98, 101. See further Chap. 1 n. 4 (mutual consent) above, Chap. 7 n. 14 above and Chap. 9 n. 37 below.

55 Albors-Llorens (2006), 849 n. 38.

56 Cases C-204/00 etc. *Aalborg Portland et al.* v. *Commission* [2004] ECR I-123.

57 Albors-Llorens (2006), 849 n. 38.

58 EU: *AEG* (n. 43 above), 38. US: *Interstate Circuit* (n. 5 above), 226; *FTC* v. *Cement Institute* 333 US 683, 716 n. 17 (1948). Commentary: Gellhorn et al. (2004), 272; Kovacic (1993), 7, 22; Kovacic (2006), 820; Turner (1962), 696; Werden (2004), 741. See also Chap. 7 n. 107 above and Chap. 9 n. 37 below.

59 *Paramount Pictures* (n. 5 above); Gellhorn et al. (2004), 273 n. 4.

60 Jones (1986), 1992.

61 Cases 48/60 etc. *ICI* v. *Commission* ('*Dyestuffs*') [1972] ECR 619, [1972] CMLR 557, para. 64; Albors-Llorens (2006), 872.

62 *Bayer* (CFI) (n. 10 above), para. 71.

63 Odudu (2006), 61. Contrast Willis and Hughes (2007), 126, which states that '"agreement" has an autonomous meaning under Article [101] and catches arrangements that do not constitute agreements for the purposes of contract law'. If this means that an agreement within Article 101 need not be a contract, it is true; but it is doubtful that 'agreement' means different things in competition law and contract law. (Chapter 7 above shows that an agreement is neither necessary nor sufficient for a contract.) The doubtful thesis is not supported by the citation the authors give – *Chemiefarma* (n. 10 above), paras. 107, 110 ff. – which relates to a gentlemen's agreement. In any event, criteria of synonymy are not sharp: see Haack (1978), 76 f.; Quine (1961). In the context of the law of conspiracy, Farrell (1992), 23 distinguishes 'common object' from 'object in common': see Chap. 9 n. 126 below.

intention is expressed, Odudu is unclear on the point,[64] and that for Odudu it is a common intention, but for the Court a concurrence of wills, that is the 'centre' of agreement; as noted in section 8.1, the relation between joint intention and concurrence of wills is obscure.

Odudu's account raises various concerns. 'Is central to' is no clearer than 'centres around' – Odudu seems to intend it to connote a necessary and sufficient condition[65] – and 'common intention' is little clearer than 'concurrence of wills'. In particular, he gives no reason for his assertion that '[c]ommon intention is not a continuum concept; either there is a concurrence of wills, or there is not'[66] – a remark implying that common intention and concurrence of wills are the same. As to the connection with contract, he quotes Beatson's assertion that contract 'involves . . . an outward expression of common intention';[67] but that assertion not only is clearly untrue of at least some contracts that are not agreements (see sections 7.3–7.38) but is exposed to variants of the objections in sections 8.1–8.13 to *Bayer*. Moreover, the meanings Odudu gives to 'offer' and 'acceptance' appear different from those that they have in contract law – an instance of the phenomenon mentioned in the previous section. He glosses 'offer' as 'communication', and 'acceptance' as 'commitment'.[68] The making of an offer is a speech act (see section 2.1); there is a natural sense of 'communication' in which speech acts are, typically at least, forms of communication (see section 1.1); and an acceptance may, in normal cases, naturally be said to involve a commitment.[69] But offer and communication are not identical, and nor are acceptance and commitment, for a person can communicate without offering and commit himself without accepting. In any case, even if a contractual agreement is constituted, it is not always evidenced, by an offer and an acceptance.[70]

Odudu's statements about evidence are puzzling. He writes that common intention is evidenced *by* offer and acceptance, but moves on to discuss evidence *for* offer and acceptance.[71] The shift might perhaps be

64 He quotes (ibid., 60) both the passage from *Bayer* (CFI) (n. 10 above), para. 67, which says that the intention is expressed, and the statement in Beatson (2002), 27, that contract involves 'an outward expression of common intention' (see the main text below); but he then writes that common intention, not expressed common intention, is necessary and sufficient for agreement.

65 See the previous n. 66 Ibid., 83. Compare Chap. 9 n. 35 below.

67 See n. 64 above. 68 Odudu (2006), 61.

69 On commitment, see Chap. 3 n. 149 above.

70 An agreement is sometimes referred to as the object of an offer or acceptance: see n. 44 above. On constitution, see sections 1.1 and 7.13 above.

71 Odudu (2006), 61.

defended on the basis that there can be chains of evidence, so that A is evidence for B, which is evidence for C; but his claims about the evidence needed to prove an agreement are hard to reconcile. Later, when rejecting the theory that a concerted practice is likewise a matter of common intention, he writes:

> it seems strange for the . . . Treaty to provide a means of establishing common intention [constituting a concerted practice] with evidence that is too weak to establish common intention as agreement.[72]

The weak evidence seems to be non-verbal conduct, for he writes that, on the common-intention theory of concerted practice:

> Written and parol evidence of common intention establishes agreement; evidence of common intention inferred from conduct establishes concerted practice.[73]

But he also writes that, although the existence of an offer and an acceptance may be established by written or parol evidence, it 'may also be inferred from other forms of conduct'.[74] So he appears to be saying that non-verbal conduct establishes offer and acceptance, that offer and acceptance establish agreement, but that non-verbal conduct does not establish agreement. He might try to defend this triad by distinguishing types of non-verbal conduct, or by arguing that the various phrases he uses – 'established by', 'inferred from', 'evidenced by' – signify different evidential relations,[75] or that the relevant relation is non-transitive.[76] But his position is an uncomfortable one.

8.3 Concerted practices

Like 'agreement', 'concerted practice' is undefined in the Treaty. The courts also tend to shun definitions, preferring to draw pragmatically on such dicta from previous cases as help with the matter in hand.[77] The judgment in *Dyestuffs*, however, contains a statement commonly treated as the standard definition:

72 Ibid., 81. 73 Ibid., 76. 74 Ibid., 61 f. 75 Compare Chap. 9 n. 59 below.

76 On transitivity, see Chap. 3 n. 34 above. On the non-transitivity of reasons and confirmation, see O. Black (1987), chap. 7; O. Black (1988), 430 ff.; Klein (1976), 806 f.; Lehrer (1970), 122; Post (1980), 39.

77 See, e.g., *Argos/JJB* (n. 10 above), para. 21; case 1032/1/1/04 *Apex Asphalt and Paving Co. Limited* v. *Office of Fair Trading* [2005] CAT 4, para. 206. In the latter case my account of concerted practices as instances of joint action (see section 8.31 below) was cited (at paras. 134, 139 and 155), but the Tribunal declined to engage with it.

> a form of coordination between undertakings which, without having reached the stage where an agreement properly so-called has been concluded, knowingly substitutes practical cooperation between them for the risks of competition.[78]

This is unhelpful, for the relevant meanings of 'co-ordination' and 'co-operation' are unclear. The same is true of a cluster of words beginning with 'co' – co-ordinate, co-operate, concord, correlate, collude, conspire, consensus – which are often used in competition law, in economics and in game theory, but without any clear indication of their meanings and relations to each other.[79] The objection corresponds to the one raised in Chapter 1 against the use of certain expressions for the purpose of illuminating the nature of agreement.

The commentaries shed little light. Faull and Nikpay write:

> First, some form of contact between undertakings is necessary... Secondly, there must [be] some meeting of minds or consensus between the parties to cooperate rather than compete.[80]

'Meeting of minds' is a hallowed but cloudy phrase, and the gloss 'consensus' is unilluminating; nor is the difficulty removed by truistically saying, as Whish does, that the consensus is 'mental'.[81] Phlips writes that a concerted practice exists where:

> a concordance of wills leads to collusive outcomes without there being any explicit cooperation between the colluders.[82]

'Concordance of wills' is just as bad, and Phlips compounds the problem by failing to explain the relations between concordance, collusion and co-operation.

A proposal for avoiding the problem of defining 'concerted practice' is to abandon the phrase and to bring all the relevant forms of conduct under the heading 'agreement'.[83] The distinction is not drawn in section 1 of the Sherman Act:[84] even if the meanings of the words 'contract', 'combination'

78 *Dyestuffs* (n. 61 above), para. 64.

79 For observations on the terminological anarchy, see O. Black (1996a); O. Black (2005b), 141 f., 185; Whish (2009), 544, 547 f.

80 Faull and Nikpay (2007), paras. 3.108 f.

81 Whish (2009), 105. 82 Phlips (1995), 2.

83 See Antunes (1991); O. Black (2005b), 163. As mentioned in n. 26 above, Joshua and Jordan (2004), 600 criticises the confusion between an agreement proved by circumstantial evidence and a concerted practice.

84 Calvani (2006), 1028 contrasts the Sherman Act's broad definition of agreement with the 'legalistic' definition used in EU law. See also Calvani and Davies (2006), 688.

and 'conspiracy' in that provision are different from each other, the lines between them appear not to correspond to that between an agreement and a concerted practice. Other points in favour of the proposal are that, as noted above, 'agreement' already has a broad application in the cases on Article 101;[85] that it is established case law that the Commission may prove a breach of the Article by proving the existence of an agreement 'and/or' a concerted practice, without specifying which (see section 8.4); that there is authority for the principle – the meaning and scope of which is debatable – that a concerted practice, like an agreement, need not be put into effect;[86] and that it is sometimes said that the concepts of agreement and concerted practice are fluid and may overlap,[87] or even – a claim which is implied by the passage from *Dyestuffs* and which I shall question in section 8.5222 – that a concerted practice is a pale or diluted form of agreement.[88]

8.31 The joint action model

A reason for rejecting that proposal is that, if the account I gave in an earlier book is correct, a concerted practice is quite different from an agreement. I there considered two analyses[89] of a concerted practice: one an analogue of Grice's analysis of speaker meaning,[90] the other – which I

85 Albors-Llorens (2006), 843 says that the broad definition of 'agreement' under Article 101 blurs the boundary between agreements and concerted practices.

86 Leading cases on the principle are cases 40/73 etc. *Suiker Unie* v. *Commission* [1975] ECR 1663, 1942, [1976] 1 CMLR 295, 425; case C-49/92 P, *Commission* v. *Anic Partecipazioni SpA* [1999] ECR I-4125, paras. 118 f.; cases C-199/92 P etc. *Hüls AG* v. *Commission* [1999] ECR I-4287, [1999] 5 CMLR 1016; *HFB Holding* (n. 9 above), para. 213; *British Sugar* (n. 10 above), paras. 95 ff. For discussion, see Albors-Llorens (2006), 846 ff.; Antunes (1991), 64 ff.; O. Black (2005b), 159 f.; Wessely (2001), 743 ff.; Whish (2009), 106 f.

87 See O. Black (2005b), 166; Faull and Nikpay (2007), para. 3.120; Joshua and Jordan (2004), 675. Antunes (1991), 76 f. maintains that the distinction between agreements and concerted practices is, although conceptually fundamental, usually unimportant in practice.

88 See also *Suiker Unie* (n. 86 above), para. 26; *van Landewyck* (n. 10 above), AG opinion [1980] ECR 3310, [1981] 3 CMLR 185; *Polypropylene* (n. 10 above), 1; *Ahlström* (n. 10 above), para. 63; *Anic* (n. 86 above), para. 131; *Hüls* (n. 86 above), 158; Albors-Llorens (2006), 840 n. 6; Antunes (1991), 60, 72, 75; Kerse (1988), 7; Wessely (2001), 748 f.; Whish (2009), 104 ff.

89 The approach was in terms of a 'model', in the sense indicated there, rather than of necessary or sufficient conditions: O. Black (2005b), 4, 142 f. This book uses 'model' in a different sense.

90 Ibid., 144 ff.

preferred – representing concerted practices as instances of joint action.[91] If concerted practices are instances of joint action, then:

(198) If X and Y engage in a concerted practice, then X and Y act jointly.

Another sufficient condition for joint action is given by:

(199) X and Y act jointly if:
(a) X, in doing Ax, relies on Y to do Ay;
(b) Y, in doing Ay, relies on X to do Ax;
(c) X, in relying on Y to do Ay, has the goal Gx;
(d) Y, in relying on X to do Ax, has Gy;
(e) Gx = Gy;
(f) X knows (a)–(e);
(g) Y knows (a)–(e);
(h) (f) partly because Y communicates (b) and (d) to X; and
(i) (g) partly because X communicates (a) and (c) to Y.[92]

(a) and (b) can be expanded in accordance with (25), the analysis of reliance in section 1.5; assume that Gx and Gy, mentioned in (199)(c)–(e), are the same as the goal mentioned in clauses (b) and (c) of (25). Although it does not follow, from (198) and (199), either that clauses (a)–(i) of (199) severally state necessary conditions or that they jointly state a sufficient condition for X and Y to engage in a concerted practice, the following are plausible:

(200) X and Y engage in a concerted practice if (199)(a)–(i) are true.
(201) In most or at least many cases where X and Y engage in a concerted practice, (199)(a)–(i) are true.

If (198) and (200), then (199). (200) and (201) together – the joint action model of concerted practice – are an account of concerted practices that corresponds to the offer–acceptance model of agreement: section 2.1 maintained that (36) and (37) give sufficient conditions for agreement and that the parties to most or at least many agreements meet those conditions. If it is objected that the antecedent of (200) is too weak, because 'concerted practice' in this context applies only to conduct of concern to competition law[93] (roughly, conduct by commercial entities

91 Ibid., 150 ff.
92 For other accounts of joint action, see Gilbert (1989); Gilbert (1996e); Gilbert (2000b); Gilbert (2006); S. Miller (1992); S. Miller (2001); Tuomela (1984); Tuomela (1995).
93 Compare O. Black (2005b), 157 f.

that damages economic competition), the answer is that the limitation is secured by other words in Article 101, which talks of undertakings and of the prevention, restriction or distortion of competition.

8.32 Communication

As to (199)(h) and (i), I commented in the earlier book that communication[94] comes in various forms and degrees, covering a spectrum from full-blown linguistic communication down to (as I put it) somewhere short of the case where one person simply causes another to believe something.[95] The comment was too sketchy, for it is often important, in determining whether a concerted practice exists, to identify the kind of communication, if any, between the parties. On that basis the objection in section 8.3 might be applied to the analysis: it uses a 'co' word – 'communicates' – with an unclear meaning. It can be replied that a word with a clear meaning ('triangle', say) may signify something that has different kinds (equilateral and right-angled triangles); but the need to specify the relevant kinds of communication remains.

In response I shall present a Gricean analysis of degrees of communication. This has the pleasing feature that it brings together the two approaches: the Gricean one is no longer an alternative to, but a component of, the one in terms of joint action. Even if the analysis of a concerted practice in terms of joint action is rejected,[96] the analysis of degrees of communication should be of interest, given the high plausibility of the view that concerted practices involve communication.[97]

Consider the proposition, entailed by (199)(i), that X communicates (a) (X, in doing Ax, relies on Y to do Ay) to Y. X does so in performing some action Ax* which may or may not be identical to Ax:

(202) X, in doing Ax*, communicates (a) to Y.

On a very weak concept of communication, (202) is equivalent to:

(203) X, in doing Ax*, intends to cause Y to believe (a).

94 The looser term 'contact' is often used: see, e.g., *Suiker Unie* (n. 86 above), para. 174; Albors-Llorens (2006), 846, 852, 876 (n. 26 above). Antunes (1991), 77 talks of 'contact or communication', leaving it unclear whether Antunes views these as the same. See further Chap. 9 n. 53 below.

95 O. Black (2005b), 154.

96 It is defended against objections, ibid., 158 ff.

97 *Suiker Unie* (n. 86 above) is authority for that view.

'Cause', here and below, stands for the relevant causal relation, which need not be specified precisely but may be more complex than simple causing – appropriate, indirect and/or partial causing, for example. (On appropriate causal chains, see section 1.23.) (203) leaves it open whether X causes Y to believe (a). It might be said that if X does not there is communication, but of an unsuccessful kind; but it is more natural to say that only if X causes Y to believe (a) does X communicate (a) to Y. In that usage, the truth of (203) is not sufficient, even if it is necessary, for that of (202). This motivates the conjoining of (203) and:

(204) X, in doing Ax*, causes Y to believe (a).[98]

The core of Grice's analysis of speaker meaning is the idea that the speaker intends his utterance to produce an effect in the hearer by means of the hearer's recognition of that intention.[99] One element of the analysis is the proposition that the speaker intends the hearer to recognise the speaker's intention. An analogue, which may be conjoined with (203) and (204), is:

(205) X, in doing Ax*, intends to cause Y to recognise X's intention in (203).

'X intends to cause Y to recognise' makes it clear – as 'X intends Y to recognise' would not – that the object of X's intention is an action by X: this avoids the controversy, mentioned in section 8.121, as to whether one person's intention can be directed at another's action. Standing to (205) as (204) does to (203) is:

(206) X, in doing Ax*, causes Y to recognise X's intention in (203),

which may be conjoined with (203)–(205). Another element of Grice's analysis is the proposition that the speaker intends the hearer's recognition of the speaker's intention to be a means to the production of the effect in the hearer. An analogue, which may be conjoined with (203)–(206), is:

(207) X, in doing Ax*, intends that Y's recognition in (206) cause Y to believe (a),

for Grice's analysis is best read as concerning causal rather than constitutive means (see section 4.11). (207), unlike (205), does not imply that the

98 (204) by itself represents the concept of communication identified in J. Bennett (1976), 127 f.

99 See Chap. 1 n. 22 above.

object of X's intention is an action by X; but that consequence could be avoided by replacing (205) and (207) with the proposition – stronger than their conjunction – that X in doing Ax* intends to cause a recognition by Y, of X's intention in (203), that causes Y to believe (a). Standing to (207) as (206) does to (205) is:

(208) Y's recognition in (206) causes Y to believe (a),

which may be conjoined with (203)–(207). The conjunction of (203), (205) and (207) is an analogue of Grice's analysis of speaker meaning. (204), (206) and (208) say that the intentions in question are fulfilled: that is one difference between meaning and communicating. I shall call communication represented by the conjunction of (203)–(208) Gricean communication, or communication in the Gricean sense.

An objection to that conjunction as an analysis of communication[100] is that (203)–(208) leave open the possibility of X's contriving that Y fails to recognise X's intention in (205): if that possibility is realised, the objection goes, the parties are at cross-purposes in a way that is inconsistent with communication. One response is to add to the conjunction:

(209) X, in doing Ax*, intends to cause Y to recognise X's intention in (205).

Standing to (209) as (206)–(208) do to (205) are:

(210) X, in doing Ax*, causes Y to recognise X's intention in (205).
(211) X, in doing Ax*, intends that Y's recognition in (210) cause Y to believe (a).
(212) Y's recognition in (210) causes Y to believe (a).

These may be added too. But X may now contrive that Y fails to recognise X's intention in (209), in which case it may be said that the parties are still at cross-purposes in a way inconsistent with communication. This objection can in turn be blocked by adding a further clause, that X in doing Ax* intends to cause Y to recognise X's intention in (209), and perhaps also clauses corresponding to (210)–(212); but that is to start down a regress. In the earlier book I considered ways of dealing with this sort of problem.[101]

100 The objection is analogous to one raised in Strawson (1971a), 28 f., to Grice's analysis.
101 O. Black (2005b), 148 f. See also J. Bennett (1976), 126 f.; D. Lewis (1969), 52 ff.; Schiffer (1972), 30 ff., criticised in Harman (1974), 224 ff.

(203)–(208), and whatever further clauses are needed to deal with the problem of cross-purposes, represent increasing degrees of communication from X to Y: (203) represents the lowest; the conjunction of (203) and (204) represents a higher one; the conjunction of (203)–(205) represents one higher still; and so on. Our intuitive concept of communication is not sharp enough to be identified with just one degree – arguably it embraces them all – but it seems that we often implicitly or explicitly think of communication as represented by the conjunction of (203)–(208), i.e., as Gricean. The step from meaning to communication is small,[102] and so the considerations that favour Grice's analysis of meaning apply, with adjustments, to that conjunction as an analysis of communication. Grice and others refined his analysis to answer various objections,[103] including the one just considered, and it may be that the analysis of degrees of communication likewise needs refinement; but the basic approach seems sound. The claim is not that this analysis covers every case of communication: most obviously, it does not as it stands deal fully with the case in which X simply *says* to Y 'In doing Ax, I am relying on you to do Ay'.[104] It does however illuminate cases of communication where neither party says or writes anything but one draws inferences from the other's conduct. Such inferences are typical of cases that give rise to the 'oligopoly problem': the analysis will be applied to these in sections 8.5221 and 8.5222.

It needs to be refined to account for the fact that a concerted practice can arise by communication through one or more intermediaries. That situation would already be covered if communication, analysed in these terms, were transitive, but it is not transitive. The solution is to analyse the degrees of communication in terms of the proper ancestrals of the relations represented by the conjunctions in the existing analysis. (For proper ancestrals, see section 1.23; for transitivity, section 3.2.) Communication through intermediaries was central to the *Argos* and *JJB* cases decided jointly by the Court of Appeal.[105] In *JJB* the Competition Appeal Tribunal (CAT) had proposed the following as a sufficient condition for a concerted practice:

102 Lycan (2000), 102 f. and Strawson (1971a), 28 talk of communication when discussing Grice's theory.

103 See Schiffer (1987), chap. 9; Lycan (2000), chap. 7.

104 Grice had a further theory as to how the meaning of linguistic expressions derives from speaker meaning: Grice (1989g).

105 Bailey (2006) gives a summary and commentary.

> if one retailer X privately discloses to a supplier Y its future pricing intentions in circumstances where it is reasonably foreseeable that Y might make use of that information to influence market conditions, and Y then passes that pricing information on to a competing retailer Z, then in our view X, Y and Z are all to be regarded on those facts as parties to a concerted practice having as its object or effect the prevention, restriction or distortion of competition. The prohibition on direct *or indirect* contact between competitors on prices has been infringed.[106]

If this is communication between the parties, it falls well short of Gricean communication: all that seems to be involved in X's disclosing its future pricing intentions to Y is X's intending to cause, and causing, Y to believe that X has those intentions.[107] That corresponds only to (203) and (204). On appeal, the Court of Appeal proposed a stronger condition:

> if (i) retailer X discloses to supplier Y its future pricing intentions in circumstances where X may be taken to intend that Y will make use of that information to influence market conditions by passing that information to other retailers (of whom Z is or may be one), (ii) Y does, in fact, pass that information to Z in circumstances where Z may be taken to know the circumstances in which the information was disclosed by X to Y and (iii) Z does, in fact, use the information in determining its own future pricing intentions, then X, Y and Z are all to be regarded as parties to a concerted practice having as its object the restriction or distortion of competition.[108]

This comes closer, but still does not amount, to Gricean communication. X discloses its future pricing intentions to Y; as before, that corresponds to (203) and (204). X also 'may be taken' to intend that Y will make use of that information, and so presumably Y recognises that intention. It can also be supposed that X intends to cause, and causes, Y's recognition. Here, then, are analogues to (205) and (206), save that the intention that

106 *JJB and Allsports* v. *OFT* [2004] CAT 17, para. 659 (emphasis in original; for uniformity I have changed the schematic names here and in the following quotation from the Court of Appeal's judgment). Earlier EU cases on such 'triangular' concerted practices are *Suiker Unie* (n. 86 above) paras. 282 f.; *Musique Diffusion Française* v. *Commission* [1983] ECR 1825, [1983] CMLR 221; case 86/92 *Hasselblad* v. *Commission* [1984] ECR 883, paras. 24 ff.

107 Albors-Llorens (2006), 869 criticises the CAT's test for using 'a far-reaching construction of the notion of reciprocal communication'. Even if these conditions amount to communication, it is surely not reciprocal. See further nn. 108, 113 and 120 below.

108 *Argos/JJB* (n. 10 above), para. 141. The passage continues: 'The case is all the stronger where there is reciprocity: in the sense that Z disclosed to supplier Y its future pricing intentions in circumstances where Z may be taken to intend that Y will make use of that information to influence market conditions by passing the information to (amongst others) X, and Y does so'. See further nn. 107 above and 113 and 120 below.

is the object of Y's recognition does not correspond to the intention in the analogue of (203). It is pleasing to view the judgment as groping towards the concept of Gricean communication and to speculate that, if the concept had been put before the Court, the Court would have adopted it.[109]

An example, not involving intermediaries, shows how the concept could be applied. X and Y are duopolists and usually a price rise by X is quickly followed by one on Y's part. To decide whether X and Y are parties to a concerted practice, an authority may apply the relevant instances of (199)(a)–(i) (which give a sufficient condition of joint action). In applying the instance of (i), it considers whether X communicates the instance of (a) to Y in the Gricean sense. Let that instance be:

(213) X, in raising prices by 5 per cent, relies on Y to raise prices by 5 per cent.

The authority must identify X's action of communication Ax*. Suppose that Ax* is Ax, i.e., X's action of raising prices by 5 per cent. The relevant instance of (203) is:

(214) X, in raising prices by 5 per cent, intends to cause Y to believe that X, in raising prices by 5 per cent, relies on Y to raise prices by 5 per cent.

The authority must determine whether (214) is true, and likewise for the relevant instances of (204)–(208). The evidence it needs to review concerns X's actions, X's intentions in action, the effects of X's actions, Y's beliefs and Y's recognitions (recognition presumably entails belief). Questions of evidence as to action, intention, causation, belief and recognition are commonplace in the law, but, given the complexity of some of the relevant propositions, establishing Gricean communication is a challenge for an authority.[110] It is unlikely to be easy, for example, to establish the instance of (207):

(215) X, in raising prices by 5 per cent, intends that Y's recognition that X, in raising prices by 5 per cent, intends to cause Y to believe that X, in raising prices by 5 per cent, relies on Y to raise prices

109 O. Black (2005a), 345 proposes an analysis of concerted practices in terms of Gricean communication.

110 On the evidential difficulties of using the concept of a concerted practice to deal with the oligopoly problem, see Whish (2009), 552 ff. The oligopoly problem is discussed in sections 8.52–8.5222 below.

by 5 per cent cause Y to believe that X, in raising prices by 5 per cent, relies on Y to raise prices by 5 per cent.

This supports the charge that the concept of a concerted practice, analysed according to the joint action model, is too complex to serve as a tool of antitrust.[111] One reply is that the model does not offer necessary conditions of a concerted practice: X and Y may engage in a concerted practice without the relevant instances of all of (199)(a)–(i) being true. Another is that, even if they are true, application of the instances of (h) and (i) does not in every case require application of those of (203)–(208). In particular, the instances of (203)–(208) need not be applied in cases of straightforward linguistic communication: if X says to Y 'In raising prices by 5 per cent I am relying on you to raise prices by 5 per cent', it can be defeasibly presumed that he communicates that to Y. A third reply is that, even if it is appropriate to apply the instances of some of (203)–(208), it may not be necessary to apply those of all of them: as already noted, the CAT and the Court of Appeal found a concerted practice in the absence of Gricean communication. This point is developed in section 8.5222. Finally, it may be replied that the position is little or no worse here than in some other areas of law: for example, in criminal law[112] – where the standard of proof is higher – certain types of mens rea have complex analyses. Conspiracy, discussed in the next chapter, is a case in point.

8.33 Reduction of uncertainty

Odudu and I agree that concerted practices differ from agreements, but our views of the former diverge more widely than our views of the latter, which are aligned to the extent of giving prominence to offer and acceptance. Odudu proposes a much thinner account of concerted practices. He rejects the thought that common intention, which he invokes to illuminate agreement, is involved in a concerted practice; rather, he holds that agreements and concerted practices have in common the reason for which people engage in them – to reduce uncertainty about the future.[113]

111 The charge is answered in O. Black (2005b), 162 f.

112 On the overlap of competition law and criminal law, see nn. 2 and 5 above; Posner (2001), 53 ff.

113 On reduction of uncertainty as the aim of parties to a concerted practice, see also Antunes (1991), 68. Albors-Llorens (2006), 846 cites *Dyestuffs* (n. 61 above) and *Suiker Unie* (n. 86 above) in support of the proposition that 'direct or indirect reciprocal contacts between undertakings aimed at knowingly removing uncertainty as to future market behaviour' is necessary for a concerted practice. 'Knowingly' imports a stronger

As to proof, he writes that '[c]ommunication reduces uncertainty and evidence of communication seems sufficient to establish a concerted practice'.[114] 'Seems' here appears to be a hesitant variant of 'is', rather than to imply that evidence of communication is in fact insufficient to establish a concerted practice. As in the case of agreement, he perhaps has in mind a chain of evidence – evidence of communication, which in turn is evidence of a concerted practice; otherwise the passage suggests, implausibly, that a concerted practice and communication are the same thing, a reading made even harder by his earlier use of 'communication' as a gloss for 'offer'. (He might reply that the suggestion does not amount to an entailment, as a single piece of evidence may suffice to establish the existence of two things.) The mention of communication – not analysed by Odudu – does not bridge the gap between our views: in particular, the joint action model ((200) and (201)) gives no reason to think that evidence of communication is sufficient to establish a concerted practice.

His remarks about uncertainty are unclear. 'Risk,' he writes, 'and uncertainty go together'[115] – a statement that can be read loosely enough to ensure its truth (but, if it is read so loosely that 'risk' and 'uncertainty' are taken as synonyms, it is at best misleading: compare 'Vixens and female foxes go together'). There is, however, a clear sense in which it is false: you may be uncertain whether 12 times 23 equals 276, but there is no risk that the sum is wrong. The distinction between risk and uncertainty is a commonplace of decision theory. Odudu continues:

> Competition requires uncertainty; the risks of competition are that an undertaking does not know how competitors, trading partners, and customers will act in the future; it is this uncertain environment that provides the impetus to engage in the competitive struggle. In *Suiker Unie*, the need for uncertainty and the competitive risk that this entails are recognised . . . [116]

Later he writes that 'it is uncertainty as to the future that forces undertakings to engage in a competitive struggle'.[117] These passages combine

condition than Odudu's, although in practice there is little between them, for it would be odd for parties to aim at an unknowing reduction of uncertainty. (On reciprocity, see nn. 107 f. above and 120 below.) Bailey (2006), 246 says that any behaviour reducing or removing uncertainty as to the risks of competition falls within the mischief of section 2 of the Competition Act 1998, a provision that corresponds to Article 101 (see n. 2 above). Bailey does not distinguish concerted practices from agreements in that respect; also his words appear to concern the actual reduction or removal of such uncertainty, rather than the aim of reducing or removing it.

114 Odudu (2006), 84. 115 Ibid., 82. 116 Ibid., 83. 117 Ibid., 96.

various claims about the relation between uncertainty and competition: that uncertainty is a necessary condition of competition; that it is a causal antecedent ('provides the impetus', 'forces') of competition; and – more obscure – that it entails competitive risk. It is not obvious whether he intends to assert all of them and what he takes the relations between them to be.

An objection to Odudu's account is that, although he talks of reasons and evidence, he does not say what a concerted practice *is*; indeed, the question seems not to interest him.[118] One of his grounds for rejecting an analysis in terms of common intention is that common intention is unnecessary for a concerted practice; but it is unclear whether or how this claim is supported by the points he cites in favour of it: that in *Suiker Unie* the court found that concerted practices 'in no way require the working out of an actual plan'; that commentators held this to establish that a meeting of minds is unnecessary for a concerted practice; and that in *Dyestuffs* the court said that a concerted practice does not have all the elements of a contract.[119] The obscurity of the inference results in part from that, noted in sections 8.2 and 8.3, of the crucial phrases 'common intention' and 'meeting of minds'.

Unless the communication that Odudu has in mind is reciprocal[120] – which seems not to be the case – his evidential thesis is implausibly lax even if 'evidence of communication' is charitably interpreted to mean 'conclusive evidence of communication from one party to another about the first party's future behaviour in a market in which both compete'; for the thesis still entails that, if the evidence is merely that X has received an unsolicited and unwanted email message of this nature from his competitor Y, who was previously unknown to X, there is enough to establish that X is party to a concerted practice with Y.[121] A gerrymandered interpretation of 'concerted practice' might support this result, but that would

118 'Rather than ask what agreements and concerted practices are, we should consider why undertakings enter into agreements or engage in concerted practices': ibid., 82. But both questions are important and an answer to the former illuminates the latter.

119 Ibid., 80.

120 On reciprocal communication in concerted practices, see nn. 107 f. and 113 above. On one-way communication, see O. Black (2005b), 161.

121 Compare the case imagined in Albors-Llorens (2006), 865: 'an undertaking receives an unsolicited telex, e-mail or fax from a competitor disclosing, for example, pricing intentions and suggesting collusion'. This also grounds a persuasive objection to Odudu's thesis, albeit a weaker one, as this example includes the suggestion of collusion. Albors-Llorens writes that 'the only safe course of action for the undertaking would be to disassociate itself from the information or to inform the competition authorities'

break the link with the (rather hazy) ordinary meaning (or meanings) which, as is implied by the absence of a definition in Article 101, the phrase must be taken to have: the position is the same as for 'agreement'. Since I conceded in section 8.13 that the case law for Article 101 may have expanded the ordinary meaning of 'agreement', Odudu might reply that the corresponding concession should be made for 'concerted practice'; but, even if that is right, the meaning of 'concerted practice' has not expanded to the point of accommodating his evidential thesis.

Odudu is not worried by the objection that his account makes Article 101 too broad:

> the conception can be defended if the collusive terms enumerated in Article [101] are jurisdictional, serving merely to capture conduct capable of causing the substantive harm the provision seeks to guard against.... Whether there is collusion and whether collusion has or will cause [*sic*] a restriction of competition in particular circumstances are separate questions, though sometimes evidence of collusion overlaps with evidence that competition is restricted.[122]

The objection and the reply here are similar respectively to the objection that the antecedent of (200) is too weak, because 'concerted practice' applies only to conduct of concern to competition law, and the reply that the limitation is secured by other words in Article 101; but Odudu's reply faces difficulties that mine avoids. As the caveat at the end of the passage perhaps acknowledges, the line between the jurisdictional and the substantive can be unclear.[123] Even if it is clear in this instance,[124] there might be strong evidence that the imagined case had an anticompetitive effect. Suppose the evidence to establish this: the information gained by X from Y's message influences X's behaviour on the market in an anticompetitive way despite the facts that X intends not to let it do so, that he has sent a reply of repudiation to Y and that he has even informed the competition authorities. Given Odudu's view that there is also enough evidence to establish that X is party to a concerted practice (and on the

(see further n. 132 below). But that, on Odudu's view, would not save it from being party to a concerted practice. See also Willis and Hughes (2007), 128.

122 Odudu (2006), 86 f.

123 Another point that could be developed by reference to purpose-related reasons for legal interpretations: see n. 41 above.

124 A claim impugned in Broberg and Jakobsen (2002), 137: 'the Commission has an eye to the grossness of the "infringement" when it assesses whether a given action or conduct [*sic*] falls within the scope of Article [101](1)'. Compare Goebel (1987), 622; Thompson (1990), 599.

assumption that there is enough evidence to establish that the other conditions of Article 101 are satisfied), Odudu is forced to the perverse conclusion that X is in breach of Article 101, in which case X may have to pay a fine and damages: see section 8.4. In theory Odudu could avoid the conclusion by denying that 'There is enough evidence to establish that <P and Q>' follows from 'There is enough evidence to establish that P' and 'There is enough evidence to establish that Q' (the relevant P and Q being the propositions respectively that X has received the message from Y and that the information in the message influences X's behaviour anticompetitively); but, even if the denial is correct, it provides only a desperate solution. The conclusion is compatible with justice only if, and arguably not even if, the competition authorities decline to impose a remedy against X – a procedural palliative for a jurisdictional disease.[125]

Odudu might retort that, if his account of concerted practices is too weak, mine is too strong; for example, the sufficient condition stated by the Court of Appeal in *Argos / JJB* does not include actions in mutual reliance. A short reply is that, as noted in section 8.32, the joint action model does not offer necessary conditions of a concerted practice: (201) allows that (199)(a)–(i) are not true of the parties to some concerted practices. Material for a longer reply is supplied by my earlier book.[126]

8.4 Complex cartels

Article 101 would be feeble if it could not be used against complex cartels; but these pose a problem, well expressed by Whish:

> Many cartels are complex and of long duration. Over a period of time some firms may be more active than others in the running of a cartel; some may 'drop out' for a while but subsequently re-enter; others may attend meetings or communicate in other ways in order to be kept informed, without necessarily intending to fall in line with the agreed plan; there may be few occasions on which all the members of a cartel actually meet or behave precisely in concert with one another. This presents a problem for a competition authority: where the shape and active membership of a cartel changes over a period of time, must the authority prove a series of discrete agreements or concerted practices, and identify each of the parties to each of those agreements and concerted practices? This would require a considerable amount of evidence and impose a very high burden

125 Calvani (2006), 1028 ff. states other objections to Odudu's account of concerted practices.

126 O. Black (2005b), 159 ff.

> on the competition authority. It might also mean that it would not be possible to impose fines in relation to 'old' agreements and concerted practices, in relation to which infringement proceedings had become time-barred . . . [127]

A similar problem, discussed in section 9.27, arises for conspiracy. The Commission, upheld by the courts, has responded in two ways, the first being to develop the doctrine noted in section 8.3, that a breach of Article 101 can be established without either proving the existence of an agreement or proving the existence of a concerted practice, provided that it is proved that one or the other exists.[128] This evidential doctrine does not entail the claim, also mentioned in that section, that the concepts of agreement and concerted practice are fluid and may overlap, or its stronger version, that a concerted practice is a pale or diluted form of agreement: you might prove that a box contains chalk or cheese, without proving which.

The second response is to use a concept of a 'single overall agreement' for which all members of the cartel are responsible, whatever their involvement from day to day.[129] (On the implications for the identity conditions for agreements, see section 5.2.) The precise scope of the concept is hard to discern, but it is clear that the mere existence of various agreements between a number of undertakings is not enough to establish a single overall agreement.[130] One way of reconciling this response with the offer–acceptance model would be to maintain that 'single overall' is an alienans

127 Whish (2009), 99. See also Vesterdorf AG in *Rhône Poulenc* (n. 10 above), section I.A.1.

128 Cases T-305/94 etc. *NV Limburgse Vinyl Maatschappij* v. *Commission* [1999] ECR II-931, [1999] 5 CMLR 303, paras. 692 ff. See also Antunes (1991), 71 ff.; Faull and Nikpay (2007), paras. 3.121 ff.; Joshua and Jordan (2004), 676; Wessely (2001), 764 f. (citing *Anic* (n. 86 above), *Hüls* (n. 86 above) and case C-235/92 P *Montecatini* v. *Commission* [1999] ECR I-4539); Whish (2009), 99 f.

129 Commission decisions: *Polypropylene* (n. 10 above); *PVC* OJ [1986] L 74/1, [1990] 4 CMLR 345; *LdPE* OJ [1989] L74/21, [1990] 4 CMLR 382, paras. 49 ff.; *PVC* OJ [1994] L 239/14, paras. 30 f.; *Pre-Insulated Pipes* (n. 9 above); *Amino Acids* OJ [2001] L142/24, [2001] 5 CMLR 322, paras. 221, 237 f. CFI judgments: *Rhône Poulenc* (n. 10 above), para. 126; cases T-10/92 etc. *Cimenteries CBR SA* v. *Commission* [1992] ECR II-2667, paras. 1353, 1389, 3199; case T-141/89 *Tréfileurope* v. *Commission* [1995] ECR II-791, para. 85; case T-311/94 *BPB de Eendracht NV* v. *Commission* [1998] ECR II-1129, para. 203; *Limburgse Vinyl* (n. 128 above), para. 773; cases T-141/94 etc. *Thyssen Stahl* v. *Commission* [1999] ECR II-347, [1999] 4 CMLR 810. Commentary: Faull and Nikpay (2007), paras. 3.57 ff.; Joshua and Jordan (2004), 670 ff. (maintaining that this amounts to an importation of the concept of conspiracy into EU competition law (see n. 5 above, and section 9.27 below on complex conspiracies)); Whish (2009), 100 ff.

130 *Cimenteries* (n. 129 above), paras. 4027, 4060, 4109, 4112; Faull and Nikpay (2007), paras. 3.61 f.; Whish (2009), 101.

predicate,[131] so that a single overall agreement is not an agreement; but that would be unhelpful because Article 101 concerns agreements. It is better to follow again the approach set out in sections 2.61 and 7.4. I identified various views, consistent with the model, that may be taken of conduct for which the conditions in (36) and (37) – the propositions at the heart of the model – appear not to hold: (a) the conditions are proposed as sufficient, not necessary, for an agreement, and so their failing to hold does not entail that the conduct is not an agreement; (b) either (i) the parties meet the conditions if minor adjustments to the conditions are made or (ii) the parties stand in a certain relation to a set of normal agreements – the parties to which do meet the conditions (with or without minor adjustments to the conditions) – and in case (i) their meeting the adjusted conditions, and in case (ii) their so standing in that relation, is sufficient for them to agree; (c) the conduct does not amount to an agreement; (d) the conditions hold after all.

Suppose that W, X, Y and Z are all producers of widgets. W proposes to X that they fix a price of £1 per widget and that they persuade Y to join them. X says OK. Here there is an offer by W, an acceptance by X and hence (on the assumption – made, where relevant, throughout this discussion – that CM and CS in (36) and (37) are met) a normal agreement between W and X. Later W tells Y of his conversation with X and makes the price-fixing proposal to Y, who also says OK. Here there is likewise a normal agreement between W and Y: only a minor adjustment is needed ((b)(i) above) to accommodate the fact that the content of the agreement partly concerns an action of someone – X – who is not a party. An authority applying Article 101 is likely also to find a trilateral agreement between W, X and Y, the basis of the finding being that the three parties stand in a certain relation to the two normal agreements and that their doing so is sufficient for the trilateral one: (b)(ii). The nature of the relation is unclear from the jurisprudence: that is the main reason why the scope of the concept of a single overall agreement is unclear. One proposal for specifying the relation is to import concepts used in criminal law to characterise complex conspiracies: see section 9.27.

There is now a meeting between W, X, Y and Z, at which the first three discuss their price-fixing plan. Z does not say that he will join them – indeed, he expresses reservations – but he does not repudiate the plan or complain to the authorities. Case law indicates that this is

131 See Chap. 5 n. 10 above.

enough for Z to be in breach of Article 101.[132] If the breach is due to his engaging in a concerted practice, there is no conflict with the model; but, even if he is party to an agreement with W, X and Y, the parties to that agreement meet the conditions in (36) and (37) provided, first, that minor adjustments to the conditions are made – (b)(i) again – to cover the fact that the agreement is multipartite and, second, that 'accept' is understood broadly. Z's statements at the meeting appear to amount not to an acceptance but to a rejection of the plan; but an acceptance may be found in his failure to repudiate or to complain and/or in the fact – if it obtains – that, despite his reservations, he goes on to align his price with that of the other parties. How broad an understanding of 'offer' is needed depends on the facts. If one or more of W, X and Y explicitly ask Z to join them, there is an offer; but an offer might also be constituted by their talking in a way which indicates that they want Z to do so. At the limit, such an indication might be seen in the mere fact that they discuss the plan in Z's presence. Section 2.1 has already granted broad understandings of 'offer' and 'accept', and the present case resembles the cases of fluidity and voting described in section 2.613.

After the cartel has been operating for some time, Y fails for a period to keep his price to £1. A finding that he continues to be party to an agreement during that period is consistent with the model, for it is one thing to be party and another to perform: Y is a party by virtue of his entering into the agreement, and, as already shown, that fits the model. Suppose now that, for the period in question, Y not only fails to perform but repudiates the agreement and that later, through a new process of offer and acceptance, he rejoins. Absent special facts, an authority is unlikely to find that he is party to an agreement during the period of repudiation ((c) above), although it might do so if doubtful that Y's acts or omissions – perhaps a failure to attend meetings with or to respond to messages from the others – amount to repudiation in a strong enough sense: as explained in section 5.31, for repudiation to exclude Y's being a party, it must amount to more than a mere denial by Y that he is. In any event, the model can accommodate, under (b)(ii), a finding that Y is a party during that period: the basis of the finding would be that the preceding

132 *Anic* (n. 86 above), para. 96; *Thyssen* (n. 129 above), para. 177; case T-202/98 *Tate & Lyle* v. *Commission* [2001] ECR II-2035, para. 54; *Aalborg Portland* (n. 56 above), paras. 81 ff.; case T-99/04 *AC-Treuhand AG* v. *Commission* [2008] ECR II-1501, paras. 130 ff.; case C-510/06P *Archer Daniels Midland* v. *Commission*, judgment of 19 Mar. 2009, paras. 119 f.; Albors-Llorens (2006), 864 f. (n. 121 above); Bailey (2008); Faull and Nikpay (2007), para. 3.51; section 8.33 above.

and subsequent agreements between W, X, Y and Z are normal, that in the intervening period the parties stand in the relevant relation to those agreements, and that their doing so is sufficient for them to agree in that period. Similarly, a single overall agreement may be found to cover all the phases just described, its parties standing in the relation to the normal agreements identified.

8.5 Unilateral action

In my earlier book, in an attempt to introduce order among the 'co' words listed in section 8.3 above, I defined 'X and Y collude' to mean that X and Y either agree or engage in a concerted practice. On that definition, communication is characteristic of collusion.[133] The communicative aspect of concerted practices was examined in section 8.32, and section 2.1 analysed agreement in terms of offer and acceptance: the acts of offering and accepting are speech acts, which are typically if not always communicative[134] (see sections 1.1 and 8.2). The definition entails that

133 Compare O. Black (2005a), 344; O. Black (2005b), 190 for a distinction, in terms of communication, between collusive and non-collusive co-ordination; see further the degrees of correlation discussed in section 8.5222 below. On communication among oligopolists (discussed in that section and in section 8.521 below), see Kaysen (1951), 268 f.; Kovacic (2006), 827 f.; Lopatka (1996), 852; Turner (1962), 664 f.; Wang (2008); Werden (2004), 780. Albors-Llorens (2006), 848 f. infers that agreements and concerted practices involve communication from the proposition that they are forms of 'co-operation'. Albors-Llorens distinguishes them by writing that for an agreement, but not for a concerted practice, to exist there must be 'an *expression* of the joint intention of the undertakings involved'. She also writes that, in *AEG* and *Ford*, both of which concerned agreements (see section 8.51 below), 'at least one party had *manifested* formally the intention to pursue an anticompetitive goal'. (Emphases in original.) This is hard to understand because, as implied in section 8.11 above, it is plausible to hold that expression and manifestation are necessary for communication (compare Chap. 7 n. 59 above) and hence – if Albors-Llorens is right – also for a concerted practice, in which case her distinction between concerted practices and agreements breaks down. No doubt senses of 'express', 'manifest' and 'communicate' can be contrived for which this necessary condition does not obtain, or it may be that she has in mind a distinction between formal and informal expression/manifestation. (Compare the definition of tacit collusion in Hovenkamp (2005), 405 as collusion that exists among competitors even though they have not 'explicitly or formally' created a cartel; on tacit collusion, see nn. 171, 186 and 188 below.) But this distinction either uses an artificially weak sense of 'formal' – which arguably fits certain concerted practices – or is irrelevant, for, as noted at the start of the chapter, an agreement under Article 101 can be informal.

134 Contrast Habermas's view that agreement is the goal of communicative action: Habermas (1981), vol. 1; Habermas (1998), chap. 7.

the distinction between agreements and concerted practices is one within the category of collusion.[135] The category itself contrasts with that of unilateral action,[136] which is most simply defined as collusion's complement within the category of action, so that action is unilateral if and only if it is not collusive. The simple definition may be too crude for some purposes, but is good enough here.

If decisions by associations of undertakings are left out of account (they will be from now on), collusion is necessary for Article 101 to apply. The Treaty's main provision against anticompetitive but unilateral action is Article 102, which prohibits abuse of a dominant position. There is thus a jurisdictional gap between Articles 101 and 102: they do not catch anticompetitive unilateral action by a non-dominant undertaking.[137] Such action may, however, be controlled, prevented or stopped under other provisions – for example, under Part 4 of the Enterprise Act, which provides for market investigations, or, where there is a concentration, under legislation on merger control. The same division exists in other jurisdictions: section 1 of the Sherman Act deals with collusion, whereas section 2 covers unilateral action amounting to monopolisation or an attempt to monopolise. (Section 2 also applies to combinations and conspiracies to monopolise; given that these involve agreement (see above), they are collusive. Article 102 has been interpreted to cover abuses of 'collective' dominance, and it is debatable whether such cases need involve collusion.[138])

A difficulty for the distinction between collusion and unilateral action is posed by the possibility, discussed in section 5.5 above, of an agreement with oneself: if it is an agreement, it is collusive; if it is with oneself, it looks unilateral. In the jurisprudence on Article 101 a candidate for that description is an agreement between two firms that constitute a single

135 A view supported by *Polypropylene* (n. 10 above); Albors-Llorens (2006), 843; Antunes (1991), 72; Odudu (2006), 57; Wessely (2001), 748; Wickihalder (2006), 87 n. 1.

136 Calvani (2006), 1026 talks of 'duality' in connection with Article 101.

137 *Bayer* (CFI) (n. 10 above), paras. 174, 176. See also Henry (2004), 2; Lidgard (1997), 359.

138 Leading decisions and cases on collective dominance are *Italian Flat Glass* OJ [1989] L33/44, 4 CMLR 535; cases T-68/89 etc. *Società Italiano Vetro SpA* v. *Commission* [1992] ECR II-1403, [1992] 5 CMLR 302, para. 358; case C-393/92 *Almelo* v. *NV Energiebedrijf Ijsselmij* [1994] ECR I-1477, paras. 42 f.; case C-396/96 P *Compagnie Maritime Belge Transports* v. *Commission* [2000] ECR I-1365, [2000] 4 CMLR 1076. Commentary: O. Black (1996a); O. Black (2005b), 188 ff.; Soames (1996); Stroux (2000); Whish (2009), 556 ff., and works cited there.

undertaking,[139] for example a parent and a subsidiary which 'although having separate legal personality, enjoys no economic independence'.[140] Such agreements are not caught by Article 101: they are normally viewed merely as internal allocations of functions.[141] If the agreement is between separate legal persons, there is also a clear sense in which it is not an agreement with oneself. In any event, the distinction between collusion and unilateral action can be reconciled with the arguable cases of an agreement with oneself, by drawing the distinction, and if necessary sharpening it, in such a way that they fall clearly into one category or the other.

Two other problems relating to the distinction are posed by certain vertical relationships and by oligopolies.[142] The rest of the chapter shows how the distinction can accommodate these phenomena.

8.51 Vertical relationships

A vertical relationship in this context is one between firms at different levels of the supply chain, for example between a producer and a wholesaler, or between a wholesaler and a retailer; a horizontal one is between firms at the same level. Vertical arrangements are generally less harmful to competition than are horizontal ones and are therefore treated more leniently by competition law.[143] A charge sometimes made is that the law wrongly transfers to vertical cases definitions and principles suited

139 Faull and Nikpay (2007), para. 3.48 is unclear on the point: the paragraph's heading reads 'Requires At Least Two *Undertakings*', but the first sentence of the paragraph is 'In order for an agreement to exist the concurrence of wills must, as common sense dictates, be between at least two *parties*' (emphasis added). On the concept of an undertaking in this context, see n. 7 above.

140 Case 22/71 *Beguelin Import* v. *GL Import Export* [1971] ECR 949, [1972] CMLR 81, para. 8.

141 That they fall outside Article 101 does not follow from the use of the plural 'undertakings' in Article 101(1), for the relevant phrase also uses 'agreements'. On the rule that for an agreement to fall within Article 101 it must be between at least two undertakings, see Faull and Nikpay (2007), paras. 3.87 ff.; Schaeffer and Kon (1997), 130 f.; Whish (2009), 91 ff. That section 1 of the Sherman Act does not apply to unilateral action is established in *Copperweld Corp.* v. *Independence Tube Corp.* 467 US 752 (1984), 767 f.; see also *Gall* v. *Home Box Office, Inc.* 1992–2 Trade Cas (CCH) 69,949; Gellhorn et al. (2004), 25 f., 263 ff. (suggesting that 'combination' appears flexible enough to include unilateral action (see n. 5 above)); Kovacic (1993), 14 f.

142 These are the central issues in Turner (1962): see 656. On the problem posed by the 'unilateral approach' in the law of conspiracy, see Marcus (1977) and section 9.4 below.

143 On the treatment of vertical arrangements in EU law, see Whish (2009), chap. 16. For US law, see Gellhorn et al. (2004), chap. 8; Hovenkamp (2005), chaps. 4 ff.; Lidgard (1997), 358 f.; Posner (2001), 171 ff.

only to horizontal ones.[144] Some commentators have tried to introduce clarity by proposing, or claiming to discern already in the cases, distinct types of agreement for the two categories.[145] That is either truistic or both extravagant and clumsy: truistic if the suggestion is merely that vertical agreements and horizontal agreements can be called two types of agreement; extravagant if it means that, apart from the vertical/horizontal distinction, there is some difference between the agreements which is so great that it requires them to be analysed in different ways; and clumsy in replacing unity with duality. Notwithstanding the point, noted in section 8.33, that the line between the jurisdictional and the substantive can be unclear, the questions whether certain conduct amounts to an agreement and what its effects are on competition are distinct. Competition law should be able adequately to separate vertical and horizontal issues in terms of the second question, without distinguishing analyses of agreement.

144 See Hawk (1988), 75 f.; Burns (1990), 2 f., 16, 38. Burns maintains that, whereas 'the horizontal arrangement . . . easily fits the various proffered goals of the antitrust laws', 'the vertical arrangement forces courts to choose between the competing goals . . . ' (11 f.; see also 32). This seems to mean that, if the finding that a horizontal arrangement is an agreement furthers one goal of the laws, it furthers all of them, but that this conditional is not true of vertical arrangements. On the purposes of competition law, see n. 41 above.

145 Burns (1990) is unclear. On the one hand Burns writes that 'there has been a pervasive (but erroneous) assumption that the agreement element for a Sherman Act section one *vertical* violation will basically be the same as the agreement element in a *horizontal* offense' (2; emphasis in original). She suggests that the difference, or an important one, is that '[i]n the vertical area, unlike the horizontal area, the anticompetitive nature of the arrangement is not linked to a finding of a common plan or unity of purpose between the firms. On the contrary . . . an anticompetitive vertical arrangement is likely to involve some coercion between the two levels of distribution' (31; see also 34). She also writes that 'the word "agreement" is not a Platonic ideal with fixed metes and bounds. On the contrary, in the vertical context the concept of an agreement is thoroughly intertwined with the antitrust policies to be advanced . . . ' (39; see also n. 41 above). This suggests not merely that vertical and horizontal agreements are agreements of different types, but that different *concepts* of agreement are at issue in the two cases. (It is obscure how a word could be a Platonic ideal.) On the other hand, Burns may intend the distinction between common plan and coercion to relate not to the existence, but only to the anticompetitive nature, of an agreement. She also proposes that 'agreement', for the purposes of section 1 of the Sherman Act, has its 'ordinary, everyday use' (32 f.); as her choice of the singular suggests, it is at least doubtful that everyday use separates vertical from horizontal agreements, otherwise than in the truistic way described in the main text below.

Gellhorn et al. (2004), 377 f. suggests that in the Sherman Act jurisprudence, as a result partly of historical accident and partly of the courts' increased grasp of economics, the tests for a horizontal agreement and for a vertical agreement are different. That is a point about types of evidence, not – other than truistically – about types of agreement.

The distinction at issue now, however, is not between vertical and horizontal agreements but between vertical agreements and unilateral action. In a line of decisions, the Commission argued with increasing audacity that certain seemingly unilateral actions constituted agreements between entities at different levels of the supply chain; this approach was endorsed by the courts until, in the *Bayer* case cited in section 8.1, the CFI found that the Commission had pushed the boundaries of the category of agreement too far.[146]

AEG concerned AEG's refusal to supply retail outlets that were suitable to handle its goods but were not willing to adhere to its policy of maintaining high prices and excluding modern channels of distribution. The European Court of Justice[147] (ECJ) upheld the Commission's conclusion that the refusal amounted in the circumstances to an agreement. The Court said:

> Such an attitude on the part of the manufacturer does not constitute, on the part of the undertaking, unilateral conduct which, as AEG claims, would be exempt from the prohibition contained in Article [101](1) of the Treaty. On the contrary, it forms part of the contractual relations between the undertaking and resellers. Indeed, in the case of the admission of a distributor, approval is based on the acceptance, tacit or express, by the contracting parties of the policy pursued by AEG which requires inter alia the exclusion from the network of all distributors who are qualified for admission but are not prepared to adhere to that policy.[148]

Ford[149] concerned the refusal by Ford's German subsidiary to supply cars with right-hand drive to German distributors. The purpose of the refusal was to prevent parallel imports: because prices were higher in the UK, British customers were ordering from the German distributors, to the detriment of both Ford and its British distributors. The Court agreed with the Commission that the refusal was not a unilateral action but was attributable to the contractual relationship between Ford AG and

146 *Bayer* (CFI) (n. 10 above). For the development of the case law leading to *Bayer*, see Broberg and Jakobsen (2002); Sousa Ferro (2007); Whish (2009), 107 ff.; Wickihalder (2006) (which, at 115 ff., also cites cases referring to *Bayer*). The CFI reached a similar result in *Volkswagen II* (CFI) (n. 10 above); the judgment was largely upheld by the ECJ: case C-74/04 P *Commission* v. *Volkswagen AG* [2006] ECR I-6585 ('*Volkswagen II* (ECJ)'). There is commentary on *Volkswagen II* in Faull and Nikpay (2007), paras. 3.70 ff.; Ratliff (2005), 58 f.; Sousa Ferro (2007) (emphasising the differences between the conclusions of the CFI and the ECJ); Wickihalder (2006), 94.

147 Since renamed: see n. 22 above.

148 *AEG* (n. 43 above), para. 38.

149 *Ford-Werke AG and Ford of Europe Inc.* v. *Commission* [1985] ECR 2725, [1985] 3 CMLR 528.

the German distributors. This extended the line of thought in *AEG*, for, whereas in that case the distributors that were held to be party to the agreement were those that benefited – by being protected against cut-price outlets – from the refusal to supply, in *Ford* it was the German distributors that were held to be parties but the British distributors that benefited.

In *Sandoz* there was no written contract between producer and distributors, but the producer sought to prevent parallel imports by sending to the distributors invoices bearing the words 'export prohibited'. The Commission, upheld by the Court, stated:

> Although no written general contract exists between Sandoz PF and its customers, it must be considered that the type of agreement referred to in Article [101] is represented by the continuous commercial relationship set up and concretised by the whole of the above-described commercial procedures normally provided for by Sandoz PF in its relations with its customers and at least implicitly accepted by them. . . . Consequently, the invoice cannot be seen as the expression of a merely unilateral act but forms part of such an agreement of which it constitutes the documentary evidence. The fact that the invoices have been constantly and systematically used leads to the conclusion that Sandoz PF's clients implicitly agreed with it and accepted it. . . . Hence the words 'export prohibited', which appear on the invoices used by Sandoz PF, represent, with regard to Article [101], a contractual clause forming an integral part of the agreement on which Sandoz PF and its customers base their transactions.[150]

As these cases indicate, an important ground for the finding of an agreement is the fact that the prima facie unilateral action is an element of a continuing commercial relationship between the parties.[151]

Bayer was another case about parallel imports:[152] Bayer sought to stop its French and Spanish distributors from supplying the drug Adalat to the UK, where prices were higher, and thereby undercutting the British

150 *Sandoz* [1987] OJ L222/28, paras. 25 ff.

151 P. Rey and Venit (2004), 156 n. 15 maintains that in *Bayer* the disagreement between the Commission and the CFI 'crystallises around the issue of whether, as the Commission argued, the mere continuation of commercial relations is sufficient to establish the existence of an agreement'. See also Faull and Nikpay (2007), para. 3.68; Schaeffer and Kon (1997), 130; Sousa Ferro (2007), 205; Wickihalder (2006), 93 ff.

152 For commentary on the various phases of *Bayer*, see Broberg and Jakobsen (2002), 131 ff.; Eilmansberger (2004); Faull and Nikpay (2007), paras. 3.75 ff.; Henry (2004); Lidgard (1997); P. Rey and Venit (2004) (discussing the case's implications for parallel trading in medicines); Schaeffer and Kon (1997), 128 ff.; Souto Soubrier (2007), 83 f., 91 f.; Schulz (2004); Whish (2009), 110 f.; Wickihalder (2006), 104 ff.

distributors. Bayer's method was to impose quotas on the French and Spanish distributors: the quantities it delivered to them were intended to be just enough to satisfy domestic demand, but no prohibition on export was imposed. The distributors objected and tried in various ways to obtain additional quantities for sale into the UK; nevertheless the Commission found that they had, albeit reluctantly, concluded an unwritten agreement not to export, the agreement forming part of their continuing relationship with Bayer.[153]

The CFI, distinguishing earlier cases, rejected that interpretation. It acknowledged that apparently unilateral action by a producer may give rise to an agreement with its distributors, in particular where the distributors tacitly or impliedly acquiesce in the action;[154] here, however, there was active resistance rather than acquiescence.[155] The ECJ, upholding the judgment, talked in terms of tacit acceptance[156] – as it had in the passage from *AEG* quoted above – but the idea seems much the same. A related point is that Bayer could achieve its aim without the distributors' participation or assistance.[157] Further case law is needed to clarify the concept or concepts of tacit/implicit acquiescence/acceptance (the notion of a tacit *agreement* is considered in section 8.521) and to identify the minimum level of assistance needed, in such circumstances, for an agreement.

Section 8.1 discussed the statement, in the CFI's judgment, that 'the concept of an agreement within the meaning of Article [101] . . . centres

153 *Bayer* (Commission) (n. 46 above), paras. 156 ff.

154 *Bayer* (CFI) (n. 10 above), paras. 71 f. The English version of the judgment uses 'tacit' and 'implied', seemingly as synonyms; the French version uses only 'tacite'. Turner (1962), 695 adopts a stronger position: 'any substantive legal distinction between vertical agreement and acquiescence resulting from refusals to deal should be wiped out'. This is a reaction to the elusive distinction in *US* v. *Colgate & Co.* 250 US 300, 39 S Ct 465 (1919), which grounds an exception to the per se rule in the USA against minimum retail price maintenance. The rule was established in *Dr Miles Medical Co.* v. *John D Park & Sons Co.* 220 US 373, 31 S Ct 376, 55 L Ed 502 (1911). *Colgate* provided that, if a producer merely announces that it will not deal with distributors that charge less than the specified price, and then later refuses to deal with such a distributor, there is no violation of section 1 of the Sherman Act, because there is no agreement between the parties. For discussion of the *Colgate* doctrine – described in Gellhorn et al. (2004), 372 as 'both necessary and illogical' – and its modifications in subsequent cases, see Areeda (1986), vol. 7, 54 ff., 79 ff., 107 ff.; Burns (1990), 16 ff.; Hawk (1988), 76 f.; Hovenkamp (2005), 225 f.; Jones (1986), 1991 ff.; Posner (2001), 178 ff. On the distinction between per se rules and rules of reason, see O. Black (1997); O. Black (2005b), chap. 3.

155 See *Bayer* (CFI) (n. 10 above), para. 129.

156 See n. 22 above.

157 *Bayer* (CFI) (n. 10 above), para. 71; *Bayer* (ECJ) (n. 10 above), para. 101. See also Bailey (2006), 243; Faull and Nikpay (2007), para. 3.77; Sousa Ferro (2007), 207; Wickihalder (2006), 107 f. The point was taken up by the Court of Appeal in *Argos/JJB* (n. 10 above).

around the existence of a concurrence of wills'. In these terms, the Court's reasoning can be represented schematically thus: every agreement has a certain property F that involves concurrence of wills; the conduct in issue does not have F; so the conduct is not an agreement. F might be specified in accordance with any of the readings of the statement that were set out in section 8.1: for example (and roughly), as the property of falling under a concept that contains that of a concurrence of wills; the property of being sufficient, or the property of being necessary, for a concurrence of wills; or the property of belonging to a class no member of which exists in the absence of a concurrence of wills. The judgment does not distinguish the readings, and the Court may have intentionally chosen the vague phrase 'centres around' to leave room for further interpretation of 'agreement' in later cases.

The concept of interpretation[158] can be used to develop the Court's reasoning, again in a way that goes beyond the wording of the judgment. Reasons for an interpretation of a legal expression may relate to paradigms for the expression's application[159] or to purposes of the body of law in question.[160] Suppose that X, in applying a body of law B, is considering whether to interpret expression E as applying to case C. Roughly, if C is unlike paradigms for the application of E, then that fact is a reason

158 On interpretation in law, see Marmor (1992); Marmor (1995); on statutory interpretation, J. Bell and Engle (1987); on law itself as an interpretive concept, R. Dworkin (1986a). Dworkin distinguishes (at 50) four kinds of interpretation: conversational, scientific, artistic and interpretation of a social practice. He is primarily interested in the fourth, which he classifies with the third as a form of 'creative' interpretation. The interpretation involved in applying 'agreement' in competition law does not perfectly fit any of Dworkin's categories: conversational interpretation seems the closest. For an overview of Dworkin's theory, see Guest (1992), esp. chap. 2; for criticism, Fish (1989), chap. 4. On interpretation more generally, see A. Barnes (1988); C. Taylor (1985a), chaps. 1 f.; C. Taylor (1985b), chap. 1.

The proposition that a given word, meaning, concept etc. is interpretive is sometimes confused with other propositions – that it is vague (see Williamson (1994)) or has open texture (see Chap. 3 n. 94 above), that it is contested (see Chap. 6 n. 10 above), or that its application is uncertain or involves discretion (on the meanings of 'discretion', see O. Black (1997), 160 f.; O. Black (2005b), 91 ff.; R. Dworkin (1978), 32 ff., 68 ff.; Hawkins (1992)). Gellhorn et al. (2004), 39 f. appears to merge interpretation, open texture and discretion: n. 40 above.

159 On the function of paradigms in interpretation, and the scope for discarding them, see R. Dworkin (1986a), 72 f.

160 On the purposive approach to statutory interpretation, see J. Bell and Engle (1987), 17 ff., 55 ff., 92 ff. On the use of this approach in EU law, see Albors-Llorens (1999), 381 ff.; Arnull et al. (2000), 539 ff.; L. Brown and Kennedy (2000), 334 ff., 339 ff.; P. Craig and de Búrca (2003), 98; Koopmans (1986), 928 f.; Odudu (2006), 160.

for X to interpret E as not applying to C; but, if X's interpreting E as applying to C would advance B's purposes, then that fact is a reason for X to interpret E as applying to C. The reasons are normative practical reasons (as in sections 3.2 and 6.1) and either might outweigh the other.

These principles need refinement, but the refinements need not detain us. The Court's reasoning can now be developed, in outline, as follows. Paradigms for the application of 'agreement' have the property F. The conduct in issue does not have F. So the conduct is unlike the paradigms. So, by the relevant principle, there is a reason for the Commission to interpret 'agreement' as not applying to the conduct. The Commission's interpreting 'agreement' as applying to the conduct would bring certain anticompetitive behaviour within Article 101. If it would, then it would advance the purposes of competition law.[161] So the Commission's thus interpreting 'agreement' would advance those purposes. So, by the relevant principle, there is a reason for the Commission to interpret 'agreement' as applying to the conduct. The first reason outweighs the second. (This claim might in turn be derived from further premisses – for example, that the conduct is highly unlike the paradigms and that the Commission's interpreting 'agreement' as applying to it would advance the purposes to only a small degree.) So, absent other reasons, the Commission is wrong to interpret 'agreement' as applying to the conduct.

It was implied in section 8.13 that the CFI's judgment would have been better cast in terms of offer and acceptance than of concurrence of wills. On the assumption that these cases were rightly decided, a plausible thought is that *Bayer* did not, but the earlier cases did, comprise an offer and an acceptance.[162] The thought is consistent with, although not entailed by, the offer–acceptance model and fits both the ECJ's mention of acceptance, in *Bayer* and in the passage quoted from *AEG*, and the statement by the Advocate General in *Bayer* that, for an agreement to be

161 For those purposes, see n. 41 above.

162 Bailey (2006), 246 appears to assimilate offer and acceptance to concurrence of wills, at least in vertical cases, but does not make clear the relation between them. Bailey writes that 'in a vertical case, such as *Bayer*, the Community courts have normally insisted on proof of reciprocity or acquiescence on the part of the recipient', adding in a footnote: 'The actual proof of offer and acceptance – as opposed to invoking evidential presumptions – means that the vertical cases more closely resemble the concurrence of wills paradigm'. Note that it is just as hard to fit *Bayer* into a promise-based model of agreement: specifically, the conduct of the distributors cannot plausibly be viewed as amounting to a promise not to export.

made by tacit acceptance, there must be an 'offer or requirement'.[163] Likewise in *Sandoz* the Commission mentioned acceptance (see the quotation above) and, on appeal, the ECJ spoke of 'the consent of the supplier to the establishment of business relations with each customer prior to any delivery and the tacit acceptance by the customers of the conduct adopted by the supplier in their regard'.[164]

It is debatable, however, whether *AEG* and *Ford*, and similar cases where an agreement was found, all involved offer and acceptance. It might be suggested that the verbal exchanges that took place between AEG and its distributors were respectively offers and acceptances along the lines of 'AEG will supply the goods and the distributor will maintain prices etc.', but an objection is that, in the Commission's decision and the Court's judgment, many of the responses by the distributors are described as undertakings: section 1.1 noted that promises are undertakings, and the arguments in section 2.62, that offers and acceptances are not promises, can be extended to show that they are not undertakings (see sections 7.11 and 7.36). *Ford* looks still more difficult. The judgment indicates that Ford AG announced to the distributors that it would no longer accept their orders for right-hand-drive cars. Whether or not the announcement was an offer, it is hard to find any conduct by the distributors that constituted acceptance even in the attenuated form that amounts to mere acquiescence (see above): they merely ceased exporting to the UK because they had no cars to export. The case is like *Bayer* in that the distributors' assistance was unnecessary for the producer to achieve its aim. To that extent there is reason for the cases to have been decided in the same way.[165]

In the search for offer and acceptance among these facts, a better approach is to recall that the parties were found to be acting in the context of a broader commercial relationship. Offer and acceptance might therefore be found – the judgments do not give enough information to tell – in the earlier formation of the relationship, and specifically of any contract that gave rise to it.

163 *Bayer* (ECJ) (n. 10 above), AG opinion, paras. 60 f., 94.

164 Case C-277/87 *Sandoz prodotti farmaceutici SpA* v. *Commission* [1990] ECR I-45, para. 1. See also *Konica* (nn. 43 f. above), another case involving apparently unilateral action: the Commission found that Konica's behaviour was an offer of an agreement which was accepted by dealers.

165 For criticism of the judgment in *Ford*, see Broberg and Jakobsen (2002), 130; C. Brown (2004), 388; Eilmansberger (2004), 299 ff.; Wickihalder (2006), 94, 110. Hawk (1988), 77 suggests that a US court would not have found an agreement on the facts of this case.

8.52 Oligopolies

An oligopoly is a market in which there are few sellers. According to the theory of oligopolistic interdependence,[166] sellers in such a market may engage in anticompetitive conduct that is parallel but unilateral. The notion of unilateral parallelism is only superficially paradoxical. The definition of parallelism can be left open, as the idea is reasonably clear from examples: one is the case in which, when one firm cuts its price, the others follow in order to avoid losing customers and profits. The 'oligopoly problem' is how, if at all, competition law should deal with such cases.[167] In particular they risk falling into the gap between Articles 101 and 102: Article 101 does not apply if the conduct is unilateral, Article 102 does not apply if the firms are not dominant.[168]

There are three questions here: whether the theory of interdependence is true, how common the problematic cases are, and the oligopoly problem itself. As to the first, the theory has drawn various objections,[169] for example that it overstates the degree of interdependence, that it presupposes a simplistic picture of market structures, that it is inconsistent with the existence of vigorous competition in some oligopolies and – the fundamental objection – that it does not explain how parallelism occurs without collusion.

166 Lopatka (1996), 861 ff. and Werden (2004), 722 ff. describe the theory's historical development. Turner (1962), 658 appears to define interdependent decisions as ones that are 'consistent with the self-interest of those concerned only if they are all decided in the same way' (658). On self-interest in this context, see n. 182 below. For the use of 'interdependence' in relation to oligopolies, see also Kovacic (2006), 824 ff.; Posner (2001), 55 ff.; Werden (2004), 779. See further nn. 170 and 175 below.

167 The terms of modern discussion of the problem were set in Turner (1962) and Posner (1969); Lopatka (1996), 908 maintains that the positions of Turner and Posner 'are probably more similar than dissimilar'. Gateways to the large literature are J. Baker (1993); S. Bishop and Walker (2002), paras. 2.28 ff., 7.28 ff.; O. Black (2005a); O. Black (2005b), chap. 6; Bork (1978), chap. 8; Carlton and Perloff (2000), chaps. 4 ff.; Gellhorn et al. (2004), 270, chap. 7; Hovenkamp (2005), 98 ff.; Joshua and Jordan (2004), 661; Lipsey (1989), chap. 14; National Economic Research Associates (1999); Scherer and Ross (1990), chaps. 6 ff.; Whish (2009), chap. 14. On the problem's intractability and the consequent persistence of debate, see Gellhorn et al. (2004), 319; Lopatka (1996), 846, 893 (questioning the contribution of game theory), 903. For game-theoretic approaches, see Franzosi (1988); Phlips (1995); Scherer and Ross (1990), 208 ff.; Tirole (1988), 205 ff.; Yao and DeSanti (1993); Werden (2004).

168 Hovenkamp (2005), 99 shows how they similarly fall between sections 1 and 2 of the Sherman Act.

169 See Bork (1978), chap. 8; Posner (1969); Posner (2001), chap. 3; Werden (2004), 780; Whish (2009), 548 ff.

8.521 Tacit agreement

If the second question is taken to concern only actual cases, it is empirical; but it may also be read as concerning merely possible cases. The following discussion covers both readings. One answer, for which the argument runs as follows, is that the problematic cases are less common than at first appears. Anticompetitive unilateral parallelism among oligopolists (AUPO) is a kind of unilateral action. As explained in section 8.5, unilateral action is collusion's complement within the category of action. By the definition in that section, collusion includes agreement. An agreement may be explicit or tacit.[170] Because the category of agreement includes tacit agreements, it is larger – and hence the category of collusion is

170 '[T]here may be no agreement in the traditional sense. But since each seller is fully aware of the interdependence and the consequences of his taking advantage of it, it is not at all preposterous, to say the least, to classify what transpires as a "tacit agreement"': Turner (1962), 663; see also 689, 692, n. 188 below. At 687 Turner writes of 'tacit or implied agreements' but leaves unclear the relation between 'tacit' and 'implied'; he may regard them as synonyms. (Compare the objection in n. 171 below to Posner's 'overt or detectable'.) He does not explain what an 'agreement in the traditional sense' is. He also writes – no more clearly – of 'actual' and 'overt' agreement (660 ff.) and of agreement 'of the usual sort' (668); see further n. 10 above and n. 190 below. Compare the US conspiracy cases *Castro* v. *Superior Court* 9 Cal App 3d 675, 686, 88 Cal Rptr 500, 508 (1970) ('not necessary to show that the parties met and actually agreed'); *State* v. *St Christopher* 232 N W 2d 798 (Minn 1975) ('true agreement'); and see Marcus (1977), 950 n. 89, 958 f., 965; Marcus (1992), 18, 21; Robbins (1989), 80.

In *High Fructose Corn Syrup* (n. 43 above), Judge Posner said that the language of section 1 of the Sherman Act is broad enough 'to encompass a purely tacit agreement to fix prices, that is, an agreement made without any actual communication among the parties to the agreement'; but he acknowledged the prevailing judicial view of section 1 to be that 'an express, manifested agreement, and thus an agreement involving actual, verbalised communication, must be proved in order for a price-fixing conspiracy to be actionable under the Sherman Act' (654); see also Posner (2001), 93. For discussion, see Hovenkamp (2003), 922 f.; Werden (2004), 775 ff. It is unclear whether 'actual' here is merely an intensifier or Posner thinks that there is such a thing as non-actual communication. Compare Turner on 'actual' agreement; Turner also writes of 'overt communication' (ibid., 661).

For other US cases indicating that a tacit agreement may violate competition law, see *United States* v. *United States Gypsum Co.* 438 US 422, 457 (1978); *Apex Oil Co.* v. *DiMauro* 822 F. 2d 246, 253 (2d Cir. 1987); *Rosefelde* v. *Falcon Jet Corp.* 701 F. Supp 1053, 1064 (DNJ 1988); *In re Co-ordinated Pretrial Proceedings in Petroleum Products Antitrust Litigation* 906 F. 2d 432, 446 ff. (9th Cir. 1990), cert. denied, 500 US 959 (1991); *Alvord-Polk, Inc.* v. *F. Schumacher & Co.* 37 F. 3d 996, 1013 (3d Cir. 1994). An example from EU jurisprudence is *Bayo-n-ox* [1990] OJ L21/71. Commentary: Chamberlin (1929), 65; Fellner (1949), 15 f., 229 ('quasi-agreement'); Gellhorn et al. (2004), 281 n. 8 (citing Posner in *High Fructose*); Lopatka (1996), 848 f., 899 f.

larger and that of unilateral action correspondingly smaller – than at first appears.

The argument is incomplete: even if the category of unilateral action is smaller, it does not follow that the category of AUPO is also smaller. The argument can be elaborated to avoid that objection. A deeper objection is that, if the question is read naturally, as concerning the category's current boundaries (a different and more forced reading is considered in section 8.522), a reply in terms of tacit agreement is unhelpful.[171]

On one account a tacit agreement is a non-verbal agreement.[172] For present purposes the limits of the verbal need not be drawn precisely:

171 Various meanings, often unclear, are given to 'tacit agreement' in the cases and commentaries; for a complaint on that score, see Werden (2004), 735 f. O. Black (2005b), 154, 189 f. rejects talk of tacit communication and tacit co-ordination. The phrase 'tacit collusion' is also used in this context: see, e.g., Albors-Llorens (2006), 851; Cooper (1986); Gellhorn et al. (2004), 269 f. (seemingly identifying tacit agreement and tacit collusion); Hay (2006), 891 n. 38; Hovenkamp (2005), 100, 404; Joshua and Jordan (2004), 662 n. 55; Kovacic (1993), 14 ff., 59 ff.; Kovacic (2006), 819; Tirole (1988), chap. 6; Yao and DeSanti (1993); nn. 133 above and 186 and 188 below. On the misleading connotation of 'tacit collusion', see Whish (2009), 547 f.; on the broader terminological confusion, see Kovacic (1993), 19 f., 35, and n. 79 above. Posner (2001), 52 f. identifies as tacit collusion the situation in which 'competing sellers might be able to co-ordinate their pricing without conspiring in the usual sense of the term – that is, without any overt or detectable acts of communication'. (Compare Turner on the 'traditional sense' of 'agreement': n. 170 above.) This too is unsatisfactory because, first, 'co-ordinate' is no clearer than 'collude' (see section 8.3 above), second, it does not explain what amounts to communication and, third, 'overt or detectable' is unclear. (Compare the objection in n. 170 above to Turner's 'tacit or implied'.) Does 'overt' mean the same as 'detectable'? If not, are they coextensive? What is the threshold for the application of these predicates? It is correspondingly unclear what the fourteen types of evidence, which Posner identifies at 79 ff., are evidence *of*: see further n. 179 below. 'Tacit collusion' is often used to signify the absence of an agreement: see *Brooke Group Ltd.* v. *Brown & Williamson Tobacco Corp.* 509 US 209, 227 (1993); J. Baker (1993), 145; Clark (1983); Werden (2004), 736. In that case a tacit agreement amounts to tacit collusion only if the first 'tacit' is alienans: see the main text below. Contrast Kovacic (1993), 20, which notes the use of 'tacit collusion' to signify an agreement established by circumstantial evidence (again see the main text below). Compare Horton (1992), 29 f., 82 on tacit consent.

172 Werden (2004), 735 f. prefers to distinguish between 'co-ordination', 'spoken agreement' and 'unspoken agreement': 'Without prejudging the existence of an agreement, oligopoly pricing near monopoly levels is said to be "co-ordinated".... A "spoken agreement" results from communications using anything akin to language... Because winks, nods, and the like communicate much as words do, and because the law does not require the exchange of explicit mutual assurances, there are no legally important distinctions among essentially linguistic means of communication. An "unspoken" agreement results from communications purely in the form of marketplace actions. It does not stretch the meaning of the term to say that communication occurs when rivals observe each other's marketplace actions, e.g., which customers each seller supplies and at what prices'. This is unsatisfactory because, first, Werden does not explain what it is for communication to

we need not decide whether an agreement made in Morse code is verbal. Suppose that X says to Y 'If I raise my price by £10, you are to take that as an offer that we both raise our prices by £10 and that for six months we hold them at the new level'. Y replies 'If I then raise my price by £10, you are to take that as an acceptance of your offer'. They then raise their prices in the manner described. Given certain conditions – notably that at the relevant times they actually or constructively remember their exchange – it is plausible to say that X's raising his price constitutes such an offer and that Y's raising his price constitutes an acceptance of the offer. Assume that the relevant instances of CM and CS in (36) and (37) (section 2.1) obtain. Then, by the offer–acceptance model, X and Y agree that they both raise their prices (etc.). It is also plausible to say that, since the offer and the acceptance are non-verbal, the agreement is too.

The point is debatable: an objection is that, if the verbal exchange had not occurred, the raising of the prices would not constitute an offer and an acceptance. A reply is that nevertheless the offer and the acceptance themselves are non-verbal; but the objection might be strengthened, the claim now being that the acts of offering and accepting are partly constituted by the verbal exchange. The debate need not be pursued, for a cleaner example of a non-verbal agreement can be given. X performs a non-verbal action Ax* and the relevant instances of (203)–(208) are true, so that X in doing Ax* communicates, in the Gricean sense, to Y that <X offers to Y that <X does Ax and Y does Ay≫ (see section 8.32); Ax and Ay might be the parties' raising and holding of prices, as in the previous example. Y performs a non-verbal action Ay* and in so doing communicates, in the Gricean sense, to X that Y accepts X's offer. It is plausible to say, on these facts, that X makes and Y accepts the offer. Assume again that the relevant instances of CM and CS obtain. Then, by the offer–acceptance model, X and Y agree that <X does Ax and Y does Ay>. Since the offer and the acceptance are non-verbal, so is the agreement.

The argument that AUPO is less common than at first appears turns on the point that, since the category of agreement includes tacit agreements,

be 'akin to language' (at 765 ff. he merely gives two examples from case law) and, second, it does stretch the meaning of 'communicate' to apply it to unspoken agreements in his sense; in particular, mere mutual observation in the marketplace does not constitute any of the degrees of communication identified in section 8.32 above. Werden's remarks on unspoken agreements echo the statement in Turner (1962), 665: 'Considered purely as a problem in linguistic definition, there is no reason to exclude oligopolistic behaviour from the scope of the term agreement simply because the circumstances make it possible to communicate without speech'. See further nn. 188 f. below.

that category is larger than at first appears. But on the present account of tacit agreements the argument fails, for it is obvious at first sight that the category includes non-verbal agreements. On another account a tacit agreement is an agreement the existence of which can be proved but only by circumstantial evidence.[173] There is no sharp line between circumstantial and direct evidence: it is perhaps better to conceive of a spectrum of evidence shading away from the most direct forms, such as spoken testimony by a party.[174] The case law in both the European Union and the USA is clear that parallelism by itself is not enough for the finding of an agreement[175] – after all, prices move in parallel in a

173 See Gellhorn et al. (2004), 269; Hay (2006), 891 n. 38; Joshua and Jordan (2004), 660, 662 n. 55 (see further n. 186 below); Kovacic (1993), 19 f.; Kovacic (2006), 819. Hovencamp writes of 'circumstantial evidence of express collusion' (Hovencamp (2005), 8 f., 100 ff.); this is compatible with the view that tacit agreement, thus defined, and express collusion are mutually exclusive. On the distinction between circumstantial and direct evidence, see the following note.

174 Compare Gellhorn et al. (2004), 266 ff. applying the distinction to section 1 of the Sherman Act: 'Documents and testimony typically stand atop the hierarchy of proof because they tend to give the court greater confidence that the defendants acted jointly'. This is expressed as a positive claim but may be intended as a normative one, about the degree of confidence that a court ought to have. See also Hay (2006), 878 ('hard' evidence), 883; Kovacic (2006), 819. Hawk (1988), 77 complains about the lack of evidential rules in EU competition law.

175 Leading EU cases, which deal with concerted practices but can be extended to apply to agreements, are *Dyestuffs* (n. 61 above); case 172/80 *Züchner* v. *Bayerische Vereinsbank AG* [1981] ECR 2021, [1982] 1 CMLR 313, para. 14; *Wood Pulp* OJ [1985] L85/1, [1985] 3 CMLR 474. Commentary: Faull and Nikpay (2007), para. 3.113; Joshua and Jordan (2004), 663 ff.; Whish (2009), 552 ff. In the Sherman Act jurisprudence, the observation from *Theatre Enterprises, Inc.* v. *Paramount Film Distribution Corp.* 346 US 537, 541 (1954) is often cited: 'Circumstantial evidence of consciously parallel behaviour may have made heavy inroads into the traditional judicial attitude toward conspiracy; but "conscious parallelism" has not read conspiracy out of the Sherman Act entirely'. It has been argued, however, that these words are less restrictive than they appear: see, e.g., Posner (2001), 95 f.; Turner (1962), 658. Other significant US cases are *United States* v. *International Harvester Co.* 274 US 693, 708 f. (1927); *Interstate Circuit* (n. 5 above); *American Tobacco* (n. 5 above); *Matsushita Electric Industrial Co.* v. *Zenith Radio Corp.* 475 US 574, 106 S Ct 1348 (1986); *Williamson Oil* (n. 42 above). Commentary: Broder and Alexander (2006); Broder and Alexander (2007); Gellhorn et al. (2004), 273 ff., 318 ff.; Hay (2006), 884; Hovenkamp (2005), 100 ff.; Kovacic (2006), 821; Werden (2004). Marcus (1977), 952 states a similar principle for agreement in the offence of conspiracy.

The phrase 'conscious parallelism' is often used in this context. 'Conscious' can be interpreted more or less strongly, it often being unclear which degree of strength is intended. On a weak reading, it means that each party is aware that other parties are acting in parallel; on a strong one, that the parallelism is common knowledge among the parties. (On common knowledge, see Chap. 1 n. 67 above.) Turner (1962), 671 appears to hold that parallel price-setting is conscious where the parties 'take into account the

perfectly competitive market[176] – but there is debate as to what 'plus factors' are required,[177] whether in an oligopoly or elsewhere. In outline, further circumstantial evidence may relate to the market generally[178] – showing that it conduces to the making or the performance of agreements – or to the specific agreement alleged.[179] Where, for example, it is claimed that sellers have a price-fixing agreement, evidence of the former kind might be the fact that the market is highly concentrated on the sellers' side; that barriers to entry, and economies of scale in particular, are large; that buyers are many, small and poorly informed; or that the product is homogeneous. Evidence of the latter kind might consist of very stable market shares; a rigid price structure; or the widespread use of facilitating practices[180] such as (i) standardisation of products or terms, (ii) the use of delivered or base-point pricing, or (iii) straightforward exchanges of information.[181] A court is likely to find good evidence of agreement in

probable reactions of competitors'. Just as parallelism and conscious parallelism are often not clearly distinguished, so Turner slides between talk of interdependence and of conscious or recognised interdependence: ibid., 672, 676, 681. On the definition of interdependence, and on other obscurities of Turner's terminology, see nn. 166 and 170 above.

176 As noted in Hay (2006), 884 and Turner (1962), 659.

177 On plus factors, see Gellhorn et al. (2004), 274 ff.; Hay (2006), 884 ff.; Hovencamp (2005), 9 f., 102 ff.; Joshua and Jordan (2004), 666; Kovacic (2006), 824 ff.; Werden (2004), 745 ff. The phrase is from US case law (reviewed in Gellhorn et al. and Werden), but the concept is also used in other jurisdictions.

178 Joshua and Jordan (2004), 663 argues that such evidence poses a dilemma which impugns the finding of an agreement: 'Where economic analysis of a market suggests that the economic environment is not conducive to co-ordination, it will be irrational for the firms to reach an agreement not to compete. If co-ordination is implausible, circumstantial evidence is unlikely to demonstrate an agreement for the court. However, where the industry is shown to be conducive to co-ordination, an agreement may be unnecessary for the industry to reach the co-ordinated outcome. The court could conclude that absent any direct evidence it will not infer the existence of an agreement'. On the general difficulty of using economic evidence to establish an agreement, see Posner (2001), 98 f. On the use of expert economic testimony for that purpose, see Werden (2004), 780 ff.

179 Posner (2001), 69 ff. lists seventeen kinds of evidence of the former kind and fourteen of the latter: see n. 171 above.

180 See *United States* v. *Container Corp. of America* 393 US 333, 334 f. (1969); *US Gypsum* (n. 170 above), 457 ff.; *Ethyl Corp.* 101 FTC 425 (1983), reversed *EI du Pont de Nemours & Co.* v. *FTC* 729 F. 2d 128 (2d Cir. 1984); *Todd* v. *Exxon Corp.* 275 F. 3d 191, 198 (2d Cir. 2001); Blechman (1979); Carstensen (1983); Clark (1983); Cooper (1986); Gellhorn et al. (2004), 275; Hay (1982); Hay (2000); Holt and Scheffman (1987); Hovencamp (2005), 103 f.; Joshua and Jordan (2004), 675; Neilson and Winter (1993); Vita (2000); Werden (2004), 751; Whish (2009), 554 f.; Yao and DeSanti (1993), 121.

181 On information exchange, see M. Bennett and Collins (2010).

the fact, if present, that the conduct of the sellers would not be in their self-interest unless each had reason to believe that the others would act in the same way.[182] There is some authority for the strong abductive principle that, for parallel conduct to be caught by the part of Article 101 that concerns agreements, the existence of an agreement must be not only the best but the only explanation for the presence of the relevant plus factors of the latter kind.[183] A fuller statement of the principle might use, and explain, the concept of an *available* explanation.[184] (Compare the concept of an available means: section 4.11.)

This account makes the existence of a tacit agreement a relative matter. First, it depends on the standard of proof: in particular, tacit agreements are likely to be rarer in the criminal than in the civil context[185] – the standard of proof, as regards both circumstantial and direct evidence, being higher in the former than in the latter (see section 8.32). Second, one person (a complainant, perhaps) may have only circumstantial evidence when another (one of the parties) has direct evidence; likewise an explanation may be available to one person but not to another. More objectionable is the fact that the account conflates a thesis about a condition for the existence of a type of agreement with one about a type of

182 Compare Turner's definition of interdependence: n. 166 above. This test is sometimes labelled 'action contrary to self-interest'; as noted by Werden (2004), 748 f. (citing cases), the label is inaccurate because no actor who is rational by classical standards of economics does anything contrary to self-interest. There is nevertheless authority for the proposition that an agreement within Article 101 can be found where the conduct in question is not in the interest of all the parties: see case 30/78 *Distillers Company Limited* v. *Commission* [1980] ECR 2229; *Johnson & Johnson* [1980] OJ L377/16, para. 28; *Fisher-Price/Quaker Oats Ltd.-Toyco* [1988] OJ L49/19, para. 19; *Gosme/Martell-DMP* [1991] OJ L185/23, para. 33; *Bayer* (CFI) (n. 10 above), para. 129; *Bayer* (ECJ) (n. 10 above), para. 121 ('genuine wishes'); Lidgard (1997), 356; Wickihalder (2006), 92.

183 See *Ahlström* (n. 10 above), para. 71; cases 29 and 30/83 *CRAM & Rheinzink* v. *Commission* 1984 ECR 1679, 1702; Albors-Llorens (2006), 857; Antunes (1991), 77; Whish (2009), 554; Willis and Hughes (2007), 129. The test extracted by Gellhorn et al. (2004), 274 from the US cases is that the parallelism 'more likely than not was the result of a jointly determined course of action'; see also Kovacic (2006), 821. Stronger tests in the US jurisprudence are stated in Hay (2006), 883 ('no plausible explanation for the conduct other than some kind of agreement'); Kovacic (1993), 42 ('cannot be explained rationally except as the product of concerted action'). Compare the test, stated in J. Smith (1996b), 386, for conspiracy in English law: the parties' acts and declarations 'are not reasonably explicable except on the basis that they had made the agreement alleged'. On abductive inference, see Boyd (1991); N. Cartwright (1983), chap. 4; Ennis (1968); Harman (1965); Harman (1968); Lipton (1991); Peirce (1931–58), vol. 5; Railton (1989).

184 Ruben (1993) is an introduction to the philosophy of explanation.

185 On the overlap of competition law and criminal law, see nn. 2, 5 and 112 above.

evidence for an agreement's existence.[186] The latter thesis is partly dubious, in that there is no firm theoretical basis for the identification of plus factors:[187] why these and not others, and how do these prove the existence of an agreement? It is also partly trite, for it is obvious at first sight that the category of agreement includes some instances the existence of which can be proved but only by circumstantial evidence. On this account, therefore, the argument as to the extent of AUPO fails, for the reason that it failed on the account of tacit agreement as non-verbal agreement.

A bolder claim is that the combination of parallelism and plus factors is not (or not merely) evidence, but is a sufficient condition, for tacit agreement.[188] Apart from facing the objection about the theoretical basis of the plus factors, the claim distorts the ordinary meaning of 'agreement' – possibly by breaking the link, argued in Chapter 3, between agreement and obligation (whether it breaks the link is disputable) and in any event by blurring the distinction between making and performing an agreement.[189]

186 Joshua and Jordan (2004), 662 n. 55 maintains that, under the influence of the Chicago School, courts have often used 'tacit collusion' to denote an agreement proved by circumstantial evidence. (On tacit collusion, see nn. 133 and 171 above and 188 below.) See also ibid., 660 on the confusion between such an agreement and a concerted practice (n. 26 above) and compare J. Baker (1993), 144 f. On inferring a concerted practice from circumstantial evidence, see Faull and Nikpay (2007), para. 3.11.

187 Compare Gellhorn et al. (2004), 276: 'Variation in judicial analyses of plus factors suggests that decisions often depend on the court's unarticulated intuition about the likely cause of observed parallel behaviour'. See also Kovacic (2006), 825.

188 Versions of this approach are advocated in Hay (2006), 891 n. 38, proposing 'a substantive, not merely evidentiary, basis for the concept of tacit collusion', and Jones (1986), 1990 f. Compare the definition of 'concerted practice' in Joshua and Jordan (2004), 666: 'the concerted adoption of a facilitating practice in circumstances where there is no obvious agreement' (clearly flawed, as 'concerted' occurs in the definiens). Hay contrasts tacit agreements with 'formal' and 'explicit' agreements (877, 881), but leaves unclear the relation – possibly identity – between the latter pair. (Compare the distinction, in n. 133 above, between formal and informal expression or manifestation.)

As mentioned in n. 170 above, Turner proposes an account of tacit agreements in terms of interdependence: 'I . . . find considerable appeal, as a general matter, in defining "agreement" for purposes of Sherman Act law in terms of interdependence of decisions, if for no other reason than that it seems to me to be a clearer and more workable standard than any other standard, of acceptable scope, which requires something more. Once one goes beyond the boundaries of explicit, verbally communicated assent to a common course of action – a step long since taken and from which it would not seem reasonable to retreat – it is extraordinarily difficult if not impossible to define clearly a plausible limit short of interdependence' (683). For the definition of interdependence, see n. 166 above; on the confusion between interdependence and recognised interdependence, n. 175 above.

189 Turner is impatient of a purely 'semantic' approach to the definition of 'agreement' for the purposes of section 1 of the Sherman Act (Turner (1962), 671 f., 676) and says that

With some strain the distinction can be sustained in certain cases: for example, where there is parallel pricing, the raising of prices could be viewed as the making of an agreement to hold them at the new level, and the subsequent holding them at that level as the performance of the agreement.

The reply that 'agreement' in Article 101 is a term of art faces difficulties discussed in section 8.13; but the claim might be defended as consistent with the ordinary meaning of 'agreement', on the basis that 'tacit' here is alienans[190] (compare the corresponding reading, rejected in section 8.4, of 'single overall'), X and Y tacitly agreeing only if they do not agree. This necessary condition might be strengthened: they do not agree, but they act as if they did. In that case, by the claim under discussion, parallelism and plus factors are together sufficient for parties to act as if they agreed. In either form, the condition undermines the argument as to the extent of AUPO, for the argument uses the premiss that the category of agreement includes tacit agreements. If parties' not agreeing is necessary for them tacitly to agree, the premiss is false.

8.522 Reducing the problem

A plausible view is that, however large the category of AUPO now is, it can be shrunk: the proposal is to shrink it by narrowing the boundaries of the category of unilateral action. The proposal faces, and can be elaborated to avoid, an objection in section 8.521: even if the category of unilateral action is smaller, that of AUPO may not be. Since the boundaries of the former are not sharp, it may be hard to distinguish in substance a proposal to redraw them from a description of their current position; the difficulty is not removed by the definitions of unilateral action as the complement of collusion, and of collusion as agreement or concerted practice, for the boundaries of the categories of agreement and concerted practice are themselves not sharp.

the reasons for his own account 'are derived from the context of the Sherman Act itself. I believe these results would improve the prospects of putting future Sherman Act law on more solid foundations' (ibid., 706; see also Lopatka (1996), 853 f.).

190 Turner's use of 'actual agreement' (n. 170 above) might be construed as excluding a tacit agreement in this sense. Kovacic (1993), 20 notes that in a minority of cases courts seem to use 'express' and 'tacit' as synonyms respectively for 'collective' and 'unilateral'. On the assumptions that no conduct is both unilateral and collusive and that agreements are a form of collusion (see section 8.5 above), either 'tacit' on this reading is alienans or 'tacit agreement' is a contradiction.

The proposal is naturally understood as answering the third question, how competition law should deal with AUPO; but it could be understood as answering the second, as to the extent of AUPO, if that question were (rather artificially) interpreted to concern not the current situation but the situation after the shrinking. The proposal is taxonomic rather than substantive: it is not directly a proposal to change or eliminate any conduct falling within the current category of unilateral action; rather, it is to recategorise certain cases of such conduct. It does not follow that the proposal is either trivial or delusive, for a change in categorisation may entail a change in jurisdiction, which in turn may extend the range of available remedies:[191] if the boundaries of the category of unilateral action are redrawn to bring certain conduct, currently categorised as AUPO, within the category of collusion, the conduct may thereby fall within Article 101 and hence be subject to the remedies for breach of it.

Unless all cases of AUPO are recategorised, a full answer to the oligopoly problem will say how the residual ones should be treated. A conservative approach, on which I shall not try to improve, is to use provisions mentioned in section 8.5, so far as they apply – on market investigations, mergers and abuse of dominance (including collective dominance). Remedies under those provisions are broadly of three kinds: structural, behavioural and regulatory.[192] Examples are, respectively, the break-up of large firms; the prohibition of parallel pricing[193] or, more realistically, of certain facilitating practices; and the imposition of prices by, or their notification to, a government agency.[194]

The proposal has two versions: shrink the category of unilateral action but leave the category of collusion unchanged; or expand the latter and in consequence shrink the former. The first version is unhelpful, as it does not make the recategorised cases any more tractable; in particular, they are not brought within Article 101, for that applies only to collusion. A similar objection applies to one variant of the second version: that variant is the proposal to add to the category of collusion a subcategory comprising

191 Compare the passage from Burns in n. 41 above, and also the 'characterisation problem' of determining whether conduct falls into a category to which a per se prohibition applies or into one that is subject to a rule of reason: see O. Black (1997), 154; O. Black (2005b), 80; and texts cited there.

192 See Gellhorn et al. (2004), 318 ff.; Hovenkamp (2005), 99 ff.; Whish (2009), 550 ff.

193 Whish (2009), 551 asserts the common view that this would be 'quite inappropriate: it would be absurd to forbid firms from behaving in a parallel manner if this is an inevitable consequence of the structure of the market'.

194 On the role of such agencies in elaborating policy, see Gellhorn et al. (2004), 41 f.

neither agreements nor concerted practices. A more promising variant is the proposal to expand the category of agreement and/or that of concerted practice.

8.5221 Agreements As to agreement, this proposal might be developed by taking ideas from the discussion of tacitness. The claim that parallelism and plus-factors are together sufficient for a tacit agreement is more persuasive as a recommendation for expanding the category of agreement than as a description of its present extent; but, even if the claim is taken as a recommendation, it requires the meaning of 'agreement' to be stretched to the point of incoherence. This is the counterpart of an objection raised in section 8.13 in relation to concurrence of wills.

Here is a more promising idea. I suggested that, if X and Y perform certain acts of Gricean communication, they non-verbally agree. If a person communicates in the Gricean sense, he communicates at each lower degree in the spectrum described in section 8.32: that follows from the facts that each degree is represented by a conjunction (the lowest is the limiting case represented by (203) alone) and that, for any two degrees, all the conjuncts of the conjunction representing the higher are conjuncts of the one representing the lower. For example, Gricean communication is represented by the conjunction of (203)–(208), and one of the lower degrees by that of (203)–(206): if the former conjunction is true, so is the latter. If, however, he communicates in the Gricean sense, he does not communicate at *only* a lower degree: if the conjunction of (203)–(208) is true, that of (203)–(206), <not (207)> and <not (208)> is false. It might accordingly be argued that, if the category of agreement does not now include cases of communication at only lower degrees, it can be expanded to do so; a corresponding argument could be made in respect of communication at any higher degrees. The objection of semantic incoherence has less force here, as the various degrees are obviously connected.

8.5222 Concerted practices A similar approach might be taken to the category of concerted practice. Recall:

(199) X and Y act jointly if:
- (a) X, in doing Ax, relies on Y to do Ay;
- (b) Y, in doing Ay, relies on X to do Ax;
- (c) X, in relying on Y to do Ay, has the goal Gx;
- (d) Y, in relying on X to do Ax, has Gy;
- (e) Gx = Gy;

(f) X knows (a)–(e);
(g) Y knows (a)–(e);
(h) (f) partly because Y communicates (b) and (d) to X; and
(i) (g) partly because X communicates (a) and (c) to Y.

(200) X and Y engage in a concerted practice if (199)(a)–(i) are true.
(201) In most or at least many cases where X and Y engage in a concerted practice, (199)(a)–(i) are true,

(200) and (201) together being the joint action model of concerted practice. A way of potentially expanding the category of concerted practice is to replace (200) and (201) with two weaker propositions that respectively differ from them only in this respect: where (200) and (201) refer to (199)(a)–(i), the substituted propositions both refer to the members of the same proper subclass of {(199)(a)–(i)}. The expansion is potential, because it results from the replacement only if, given the present boundaries of the category, at least one of the substituted propositions is false. Their falsity does not follow from (200) and (201): the truth of (200) does not determine the truth value either of (200)'s replacement or of (201)'s; the truth of (201) entails the truth of its replacement but does not determine the truth value of (200)'s. One refinement substitutes propositions referring to the members of a disjunction of proper subclasses: for example, either {(a)–(f), (h)} or {(a)–(e), (g), (i)}. Another amends certain clauses of (199) to reflect the exclusion of others from the relevant subclass: for example, if (e) is excluded, (f) is amended to say that X knows (a)–(d) rather than (a)–(e).

A version of this proposal refers to a spectrum of (as I shall label them) degrees of correlation;[195] this last is one of the troublesome 'co' words discussed in section 8.3, but the specification of the spectrum clarifies its relevant meaning. The first degree – call it *independent action* – is the limiting case where there is no correlation:

(216) X does Ax;
(57) Y does Ay;
(217) Ax and Ay are independent of each other.

Independence can be left undefined;[196] (217) entails, for example, that X neither expects Y to do Ay nor relies on him to do so. The conjunction

195 O. Black (2005b), chap. 6 contains a cruder version. For different spectra, see Hay (2006), 894, 901; Kovacic (2006), 817 f.; Willis and Hughes (2007), 125 ff.
196 Mintoff (2004), 46 distinguishes independent action from individual action.

of (216), (57) and (217) states a necessary and sufficient condition for independent action, just as the conjunctions specified below state such conditions for their respective degrees of correlation.

The next degree is *mutual belief*, for which the conjuncts of the relevant conjunction are (216), (57) and the propositions:

(218) X believes that Y does Ay;
(67) Y believes that X does Ax.

Belief here includes expectation. The reference to mutual belief can be strengthened, so that belief is replaced by justified belief, or by knowledge, or by iterations of these – for example, X believes that Y believes – or by common versions of them, for example common knowledge. Alternatively it can be weakened so that, for example, X and Y merely hope rather than believe. (In either case, this degree would need to be renamed.) Section 1.23 explained the notion of a common propositional attitude; section 1.5 considered a similar weakening of clause (e) of the analysis of reliance (25) proposed there.

The next degree is *mutual reliance*, for which the conjuncts are:

(219) X, in doing Ax, relies on Y to do Ay;
(58) Y, in doing Ay, relies on X to do Ax.

(219) and (58) replace (216) and (57), rather than being conjoined with them as (218) and (67) were, because (219) entails (216) and (58) entails (57). If each party meets the condition specified in (25) as sufficient for reliance, they are together in a state stronger than mutual belief (but not stronger than all variants of the latter) in that clauses (a)–(f) of (25) together entail (218) – which is identical to (25)(e) – but not vice versa. The analysis of reliance, and hence of mutual reliance, can itself be strengthened or weakened in various ways (one of them just noted) within the vague limits imposed by our intuitive concept: see section 1.5.

For *mutual reliance with a common goal* the conjuncts are (219), (58) and:

(220) X, in relying on Y to do Ay, has the goal Gx;
(221) Y, in relying on X to do Ax, has Gy;
(222) Gx = Gy.

For *mutual reliance with a common goal and with knowledge* another two conjuncts are added:

(223) X knows (219), (58) and (220)–(222);
(224) Y knows (219), (58) and (220)–(222).

As before, these can be strengthened or weakened, by substituting for knowledge the other states already considered.

The next degree adds:

(225) (223) partly because Y communicates (58) and (221) to X;
(226) (224) partly because X communicates (219) and (220) to Y.

Since (219), (58) and (220)–(226) are identical to (199)(a)–(i), this degree might be called *narrow joint action* – 'narrow' to reflect the fact that, although, by (199), the conjunction of (219), (58) and (220)–(226) states only a sufficient condition for joint action, it states a condition both necessary and sufficient for this degree of correlation. By the joint action model, if X and Y meet the condition, they engage in a concerted practice; and, in most or at least many cases where they engage in a concerted practice, they meet the condition.

It is tempting to think that a necessary and sufficient condition for agreement is given by adding further conjuncts, but the temptation should be resisted, because (219), (58) and (220)–(226) do not state necessary or sufficient conditions for agreement (other than, possibly, for a peripheral case of agreement): as noted in section 8.31, on the joint action model a concerted practice is quite different from an agreement. Section 1.5 gave reason to think that the parties to some agreements do not rely on each other, in which case (219) and (58) do not state necessary conditions. Moreover, if (219), (58) and (220)–(226) stated such conditions, then, by the offer–acceptance model, their truth would be necessary for that of clauses (a)–(c) of (36) or (37) (section 2.1); but it is not. It is therefore misleading to view agreement as the highest degree of correlation,[197] forming one end of a spectrum of which the other is independent action: agreement is better described as falling outside the spectrum. That impugns the claim that a concerted practice is a pale or diluted form of agreement; indeed, it might be argued that an agreement is a pale or diluted concerted practice, people only making agreements when they do not have enough in common to act jointly.[198]

197 Contrast Antunes (1991), which says, at 72, that the concepts of agreement and concerted practice 'reflect different degrees of co-ordination' and, at 75, that an agreement amounts to 'a higher degree of collusion' than does a concerted practice.

198 O. Black (2005b), 166 argues thus. Sheinman (2011a) argues that the making, but not the performance, of an agreement is a joint action, but not as characterised by (199).

If independent action is set aside, the degrees of correlation are similar to those of communication in that, if the parties instantiate one degree, they instantiate the lower ones. AUPO may fall at any point on the spectrum, short of narrow joint action; for example, firms that move their prices in parallel may, in so doing, exhibit mutual reliance with a common goal, but fail to reach the next degree as they fall short of knowledge – oligopolists often having to rely on fragile inferences about each other's behaviour. If (200) and (201) are replaced with weaker propositions that respectively differ from them only in the respect that, where (200) and (201) refer to (199)(a)–(i), the substituted propositions refer to (199)(a)–(e) (= (219), (58), (220)–(222)), the category of concerted practice catches such cases and thus potentially expands. Different replacements yield corresponding results for different degrees of correlation. (If (200) and (201) were replaced – implausibly, in the case of (200) – with propositions that concerned only mutual belief, the substituted propositions would not refer to members of a subclass of {(199)(a)–(i)}, for (216), (57), (218) and (67) are not among (199)(a)–(i). Nevertheless, if (a) and (b) are true, so are (216) and (57); and, at least in the normal case, if (f) and (g) are true, so are (218) and (67). Moreover, as already noted, (218) is true if X meets the condition in (25) for the truth of (a).)

A different approach is to expand the category of concerted practice by leaving (200) and (201) as they are but expanding the category of communication at issue in (199)(h) and (i). The proposal, which corresponds to the one about communication in non-verbal agreements, is unclear because the cases – such as *Argos/JJB*, discussed in section 8.32 – leave it open how broad the latter category now is: the point is similar to one made in section 8.522 about unilateral action. Given that there are degrees of communication, there is potentially a spectrum (degrees of communication) within a spectrum (degrees of correlation). If (199)(h) and (i) are currently interpreted as concerning only communication at a given degree – say, Gricean communication – and are reinterpreted as also concerning communication at only lower degrees or at higher degrees, the reinterpretation expands the category.

9

Conspiracy

9.1 Statutory conspiracy

English law recognises both a crime and a tort of conspiracy.[1] This chapter is concerned with the former,[2] one of the inchoate crimes: others are attempt and the crimes of encouraging and assisting.[3] There are various

1 On the relation between the two, see Sayre (1922), 424 f. On tortious conspiracy, see *Kuwait Oil Tanker Company SAK and anr* v. *Al Bader and others* [2000] EWCA Civ 160, esp. paras. 106 ff.; n. 61 below.

2 For the English criminal law of conspiracy, see Allen (2009), 280 ff.; Ashworth (2009), 453 ff.; Clarkson et al. (2010), 469 ff.; Herring (2010), 802 ff.; Hooper and Ormerod (2011), paras. A6.33 ff.; Ormerod (2008), 399 ff.; Richardson (2011), paras. 33–1 ff.; Simester et al. (2010), 300 ff. For the history and the political aspects of this area of criminal law – in particular, its use against trade unions and Irish nationalists – see *Knuller* (1972) 56 Cr. App. R. 633, 669 ff.; Ashworth (2009), 448 ff.; Farrell (1992), 22; Goldstein (1959), 415 ff.; Hazell (1974), 13 ff.; Holdsworth (1923), vol. 3, 400 ff.; Richardson (2011), para. 33–1; Robertson (1974); Sayre (1922), 394 ff.; Simester et al. (2010), 316; Spicer (1981); R. Wright (1873).

Conspiracy is the crime in which agreement is most prominent: see Macdonald and Thompson (2003), 98. The law of accessories might also be said to involve agreement, if a meeting of minds or a consensus amounts to an agreement (as to which see Chap. 1 nn. 1 and 5, Chap. 3 n. 73 and Chap. 8 n. 10 above, and nn. 23 and 26 below): of aiding, abetting, counselling and procuring, Allen (2009), 225 says 'What seems to be necessary is some meeting of minds or consensus, namely that the offence committed is the one encouraged and the principal is aware of that encouragement even if he would have committed it without encouragement'. For a contrary view, see Ormerod (2008), 186. See further nn. 12 and 78 below.

3 On inchoate crimes generally, see Allen (2009), chap. 8; Ashworth (2009), chap. 11; Clarkson et al. (2010), chap. 5; Herring (2010), chap. 14; Law Commission (2007), para. 1.3; Ormerod (2008), chap. 13; Richardson (2011), chap. 33; Simester et al. (2010), chap. 9. Ashworth maintains that certain substantive crimes, notably those that need not cause harm, are 'defined in an inchoate mode' (ibid., 437). Burgman (1979), 84 maintains that conspiracy has an inchoate and a substantive dimension.

Macdonald and Thompson (2003), 99 f. suggests that the inchoateness of conspiracy was a reason why 'agree' was preferred to 'conspire' in the formulation of the cartel offence in section 188 of the Enterprise Act 2002. A related reason which the authors also propose is that it is bad practice to bring a charge of conspiracy when the facts disclose the commission of a substantive crime the indicting of which adequately reflects the degree of criminality:

arguments for and against the recognition of inchoate crimes, and of conspiracy in particular – for example, on the one hand, that it allows intervention at an early stage to prevent harm, and that an agreement to commit a crime makes it more likely that the crime will be committed; on the other, that people do not deserve punishment for merely making an agreement which they never implement and from which they quickly withdraw, and that adequate protection against the danger posed by conspiracy is provided by other parts of the criminal law.[4]

Criminal conspiracy is now mainly covered by statute, which deals with conspiracies to commit crimes, but there is a residual category of common law conspiracy – traditionally defined as an 'agreement of two or more to do an unlawful act, or to do a lawful act by unlawful means'[5] – which includes conspiracies to defraud and agreements to engage in conduct

see further n. 56 below; Hammond and Penrose (2001), para. 1.9. For the definition of the cartel offence, and the concept of dishonesty it uses, see Chap. 8 n. 2 above. *Norris* v. *United States of America* [2008] UKHL 16 raises the question of the relation between the cartel offence and conspiracy to defraud: in that case, which concerns facts antedating the cartel offence, the House of Lords found that a price-fixing agreement by itself – without aggravating elements such as misrepresentation, intimidation or inducement of breach of contract – did not amount to a conspiracy to defraud. See Bellamy (2008); Pullen and Vernon (2005), 40. For other aspects of the relation between conspiracy and agreement for the purposes of competition law, see Chap. 8 n. 5 above; on the relation between complex conspiracies and complex cartels, section 9.27 below.

4 For these and other arguments, and proposals for reform, see *Boulton* (1871) 12 Cox C.C. 87; *Bhagwan* (1970) 54 Cr. App. R. 460, 472; *Knuller* (n. 2 above), 671 f. (see further nn. 24, 44 and 61 below); *Doot* [1973] AC 807, 817 f.; the US cases *Rabinowich* 238 US 78, 88 (1915), *Pinkerton* 328 US 640, 644 (1946); Abbate (1992), 56 ff.; Alexander and Kessler (1997); Anon. (1948) and cases and commentaries cited there; Ashworth (2009), 448 ff.; Broderick (1985), 896; Card (1973), 674 ff.; Clarkson et al. (2010), 470 ff.; Darrow (1932), 64; Dennis (1977); Farrell (1992), 22; Fitzpatrick (1993), 3; Goldstein (1959); Herring (2010), 778, 818 ff., 836 ff.; Hodgson (1978); Holdsworth (1921), 467; Husak (1995), 170 ff.; P. Johnson (1973), 1157 f.; Law Commission (2007), pt. 2; M. Levi and Smith (2002), 16; Katyal (2003), 1316 ff.; Marcus (1977); Marcus (1992); Orchard (1974), esp. 343 f.; Ormerod (2006), 227 ff.; Ormerod (2008), 380, 436 f.; Sayre (1922); Simester et al. (2010), 285 f., 326 ff.; J. Smith (1994). Hand J., referring to the prejudice to defendants, called conspiracy the 'darling of the modern prosecutor's nursery' (*Harrison* 7 F. 2d 259, 263 (2d Cir. 1925)); compare Grant (2006); Marcus (1977), 946 ff.; Ormerod (2006), 186. The arguments are sensitive to conceptions of the purposes of the criminal law, as to which see n. 111 below.

5 *Mulcahy* (1868) LR 3 HL 317; see further section 9.22 below. This is sometimes known as 'Lord Denman's Antithesis'. Joshua and Jordan (2004), 652 n. 21 states that Lord Denman 'did not invent it; when he said it, he did not intend it as a definition, and when it was quoted back to him he said it was incorrect'. On criminal conspiracies the object of which is not itself a crime, see Anon. (1948), 283 n. 48; Goldstein (1959), 413 f., 416 f.; D. Harrison (1924), 146 f.; Marcus (1977), 963; Sayre (1922); Chap. 8 n. 5 above.

that (i) tends to corrupt public morals or outrages public decency but (ii) would not be criminal if carried out by a single person otherwise than in pursuance of an agreement.[6] The range of conduct that meets both (i) and (ii) is debatable.[7] This chapter primarily discusses statutory conspiracy, although the same concept of agreement is central to both forms of criminal conspiracy.[8] I shall use 'conspiratorial agreement' to mean an agreement that falls within section 1(1) of the Criminal Law Act 1977 (as amended) ('CLA'),[9] which provides:

> Subject to the following provisions of this Part of this Act, if a person agrees with any other person or persons that a course of conduct shall be pursued which, if the agreement is carried out in accordance with their intentions, either –
>
> (a) will necessarily amount to or involve the commission of any offence or offences by one or more parties to the agreement, or
>
> (b) would do so but for the existence of facts which render the commission of the offence or any offences impossible,
>
> he is guilty of conspiracy to commit the offence or offences in question.[10]

6 Section 5 of the Criminal Law Act 1977 (as amended).

7 See Allen (2009), 297 ff.; Clarkson et al. (2010), 477; Herring (2010), 813, 817; Hooper and Ormerod (2011), para. A6.33; Ormerod (2008), 429 ff.; Richardson (2011), para. 33–41.

8 Allen (2009), 280 makes the seemingly weaker statement that agreement is an element common to statutory and common law conspiracies. Hooper and Ormerod (2011), para. A6.50 states that in conspiracy to defraud '[t]he agreement may . . . be wider in certain respects than that required in respect of the statutory offence'; this, however, is a point not about the concept of agreement but, as the paragraph goes on to make clear, about the questions whether the agreement in issue, if carried out, would necessarily involve the commission of a substantive offence and whether it must be envisaged that the fraud will be carried out by the conspirators themselves. For present purposes, there is no need for precise identity conditions for concepts of agreement. (On identity conditions for agreements themselves, see section 5.2 above.)

9 This reading has the mildly paradoxical consequence that, where section 1(2) CLA – discussed in section 9.3 below – applies to a conspiratorial agreement, its parties are not (without more) guilty of a conspiracy.

10 Section 1 CLA has been much criticised. G. Williams (1977), 1190 states a common view: 'A combination of inferior draftsmanship, inept amendments in the House of Lords (not resisted by the Government), stubborn[n]ess on the part of the Government in not eliminating defects when they were pointed out, and lack of interest in the whole matter by MPs with legal knowledge, has, unhappily, produced a measure that creates more doubts than it resolves'. See also Elliott (1978), 202; J. Smith (1977), 652; Spicer (1981), 137. On the difficulty of defining conspiracy, see Harno (1941), 624; Sayre (1922), 393. Marcus (1977), 928, citing *Pinkerton* (n. 4 above), 647, maintains that it is easy: 'Criminal conspiracy is an agreement between two or more persons formed for the purpose of committing a crime. The basic definition is straightforward enough. Legitimate protest

This can be read in various ways. For example, 'the commission of any offence or offences by one or more parties' contemplates a situation in which two parties, X and Y, commit an offence: this could mean (i) that, for each of X and Y, there is an offence such that he commits it, or (ii) that there is an offence such that X and Y commit it (this is the distinction, explained in section 9.27, between AE and EA propositions); (ii) could refer to several or joint commission of the offence; and 'offence' could signify a type of offence (murder, say) or a token of that type (a particular murder) (compare section 9.25).[11] The phrase should probably be read as covering all those possibilities.

Then there are ambiguities of scope. To simplify, the headpiece and paragraph (a) of section 1(1) CLA might together be read as having any of these forms:

(227) (a) X and Y agree that P.
(b) Necessarily if P then Q.
(228) (a) X and Y agree that P.
(b) If P then necessarily Q.
(229) X and Y agree that:
(a) P;
(b) necessarily if P then Q.
(230) X and Y agree that:
(a) P;
(b) if P then necessarily Q.

For example, if read in accordance with (227), the words mean that (a) persons agree that a course of conduct shall be pursued and (b) necessarily if that course of conduct is pursued then an offence is committed; read in accordance with (230), they mean that persons agree that (a) a course of conduct shall be pursued and (b) if that course of conduct is pursued then necessarily an offence is committed. These readings do not

goes not to the definition of the crime, but . . . to its application and to the evidence necessary to prove the existence of the agreement'. On the distinction between evidence and conditions for existence, see section 9.2 below.

As to paragraph (b), the rules on impossibility differ between statutory and common law conspiracy: see *Nock* [1978] AC 979; Allen (2009), 292, 299; Clarkson et al. (2010), 487; Herring (2010), 813, 817 f.; Hooper and Ormerod (2011), paras. A6.5, A6.45; Richardson (2011), para. 33–12. On agreements to do the impossible, see Chap. 3 n. 83 above. Compare Chap. 1 n. 28 above on promises to do the impossible. On the doctrine of unilateral conspiracy as a limit to the defence of impossibility, see n. 172 below.

11 On the type/token distinction, see Chap. 5 n. 18 above and n. 133 below.

purport to capture every element of the statutory provision – in particular, they reduce 'amount to or involve'[12] to simple conditionality and do not mention the agreement's being carried out in accordance with the parties' intentions – but the simplification does not distort the discussion.

The use of 'which' – a word that, narrowly construed, introduces a non-defining relative clause – in the headpiece of section 1(1) CLA suggests that the connection between the course of conduct and the commission of an offence is not part of the agreement's content; in that case readings (227) and (228) are to be preferred to (229) and (230). This view is reinforced by J. Smith's comment ((1977), 601) that '[t]he "agreement" referred to in section 1(1) is clearly the agreement that "a course of conduct shall be pursued"' and by section 12(1) of the Criminal Justice Act 1987 – concerning conspiracy to defraud at common law – which begins:

> (1) If –
> (a) a person agrees with any other person or persons that a course of conduct shall be pursued; and
> (b) that course of conduct will necessarily amount to or involve the commission of any offence . . .

It appears that only paragraph (a) of this provision relates to the content of the agreement, and hence that the connection, stated in (b), between the course of conduct and the commission of an offence is not part of the content.[13] Of course, few if any agreements have the content 'a course of conduct shall be pursued': those words normally refer to, rather than state, the content, which might for example be 'We'll poison Eric'.[14]

Given the reduction of 'amount to or involve' to simple conditionality, the words 'will necessarily amount to or involve' seem to indicate that the

12 On the meaning of 'amount to or involve the commission of any offence', and specifically its implied exclusion of participation as an accessory, see *Hollinshead* [1985] 1 All ER 850, 858 (Court of Appeal), [1985] AC 975 (House of Lords); Clarkson et al. (2010), 486 f.; Herring (2010), 805 f.; Ormerod (2008), 408 f. On participation as an accessory, see nn. 2 above and 78 f. below.

13 The same inference can be drawn from the manner in which the elements of section 1(1) CLA were divided in *Anderson* [1986] AC 27, 37: 'it is perhaps convenient to isolate the three clauses each of which must be taken as indicating an essential ingredient of the offence as follows: (1) "if a person agrees with any other person or persons that a course of conduct shall be pursued" (2) "which will necessarily amount to or involve the commission of any offence or offences by one or more parties to the agreement" (3) "if the agreement is carried out in accordance with their intentions"'. *Anderson* is discussed in section 9.3 below.

14 On the notion of content, see n. 15 to the Introduction above. See further n. 166 below.

scope of 'necessarily' includes the relevant conditional: necessarily if the course of conduct is pursued then an offence is committed. The contrary construal, which puts the necessity within the scope of the conditional, is however possible, for 'necessarily' comes after 'will', which forms a compound with 'amount to or involve'. On the former construal, (227) and (229) are better than (228) and (230). Given that (227) is better than (229), the favoured reading is (227). But Clarkson et al. give this analysis:

> There must be an agreement that:
> (a) a course of conduct be pursued
> (b) which if carried out in accordance with their intentions, and [*sic*]
> (c) will necessarily amount to (or involve) a crime.[15]

Although this supports the first interpretation of the scope of 'necessarily', it indicates that the conditional is part of the agreement's content, in which case (229) is the best.

Section 1(1) CLA is best read in accordance with (227), which avoids objections to the other readings. (230) faces objections that are the same as or similar to ones to (228) and (229). (228) is unacceptable because it allows detachment of a false proposition of necessity. Suppose that X and Y agree to murder Z. By (228)(b), if they murder Z then necessarily they commit an offence. Now suppose that they carry out the agreement. Then necessarily they commit an offence. But that conclusion is false; even if they commit an offence, they might not have done (certain forms of determinism aside), and so it is not necessary that they do. If there is a necessary truth here, it is only the conditional 'If they murder Z then they commit an offence', which does not license the detachment. (Compare the discussion of conditional and unconditional obligation, in sections 1.2312 and 3.3.)

There are three objections to (229), the first being that it creates an awkward hybrid of an active agreement and a factual agreement: for example, X and Y actively agree that they will murder Z; they factually agree that necessarily if they do so then they commit an offence. (On the active/factual distinction, see the Introduction.) One response is to represent the agreement as purely active, thus: X and Y agree to perform respectively actions Ax and Ay such that, first, Ax and Ay are murderings, or jointly are a murdering, of Z and, second, necessarily if X and Y perform them then they commit an offence. The next objection is that (229)

15 Clarkson et al. (2010), 478.

is logically problematic by virtue of including a modal operator ('necessarily') within the scope of an attitude-word ('agree');[16] the problem is more acute if 'agrees that . . . ' is not referentially transparent – as to which, see the Introduction. Even if that objection too can be answered, there remains the third and simplest objection, that a conspiratorial agreement need not, and rarely if ever will, have a conditional content of either kind described. If X and Y agree to murder Z, and certain further conditions are met, X and Y are guilty of conspiracy whether or not they agree that necessarily if they murder Z then they commit an offence, or that they will perform actions such that necessarily if they perform them then they commit an offence.[17] A corresponding objection applies to (230)(b).

9.2 Actus reus: the agreement

Criminal law traditionally distinguishes a crime's external elements, the actus reus, from its mental elements, the mens rea.[18] The actus reus usually is or includes an action by the defendant.[19] The distinction is serviceable but problematic,[20] for action itself normally has a mental aspect; in particular, paradigmatic actions are intentional.[21] The point is obvious in the case of conspiracy, the actus reus of which is said to be the agreement,[22] for agreements are typically made by speech acts – if

16 For introductions to the literature, see Gallois (1998); Linsky (1971); K. Taylor (1998).

17 This is distinct from the point, also true, that they are guilty of conspiracy even if they do not know that the thing they agree to do constitutes an offence. On that point, see *Clayton* (1943) 33 Cr. App. R. 113; *Jacobs* [1944] KB 417; *Churchill* v. *Walton* [1967] 2 AC 224, 236 f. (HL); Ashworth (2009), 454; Herring (2010), 805; Orchard (1974), 335 f. (noting the exception where commission of the substantive offence agreed upon is defined to require knowledge of the law); Richardson (2011), para. 33–16. See also the American Law Institute's Model Penal Code, section 5.03, explanatory note.

18 See Allen (2009), 17 ff.; Clarkson et al. (2010), 69 ff.; Herring (2010), 72 ff.; Ormerod (2008), 42 ff.; Simester et al. (2010), 67 f.

19 Arguable counterexamples are being 'found drunk on any highway or other public place' (Licensing Act 1872, section 12) and being 'in possession' of a controlled drug (Misuse of Drugs Act 1971, section 5(2)). See Law Commission (2007), para. 4.8; Ormerod (2008), 58 ff.

20 Allen (2009), 17 goes so far as to say that 'the terms *actus reus* and *mens rea*, are simply useful labels to be attributed to the constituent parts of any crime being analysed; they do not have any meaning in themselves. They have no greater meaning than, for example, the terms "obverse" and "reverse" used when describing coins'.

21 See Chap. 3 n. 83 above.

22 See Anon. (1948), 278; Marcus (1977), 950; Orchard (1974), 298. Herring (2010), 804 says that an agreement is 'the key element' of the actus reus, the other elements apparently being the relevant circumstances (see 803); see further n. 24 below. In *Nock* (n. 10 above),

the parties to the agreement meet the conditions of the offer–acceptance model, the speech acts are the acts of offering and accepting – and these are typically intentional:[23] see sections 1.1 and 2.1. Sections 5.11 and 5.12 argued that nevertheless a person who agrees to φ may neither intend to φ nor even intend to agree to φ – a point taken up in sections 9.21, 9.23, 9.27, 9.3 and 9.4. (To be more accurate: the argument was against propositions (116) and (117) (section 5.1), but this shorthand formulation is trivially derivable. Section 5.32 briefly discussed the rules on intention in English criminal law.)

Agreement is often called the essence of conspiracy,[24] although in this area of law, as in others, different phrases are sometimes used

994, the actus reus was said to be 'the fact of agreement' – 'the fact of' probably being verbiage; the same phrase is used in Simester et al. (2010), 316 (see further n. 23 below and n. 4 to the Introduction above). Joshua and Jordan (2004), 653 says that a conspiracy is not identical to, but is constituted by and is the result of, an agreement (see Chap. 2 n. 7 and Chap. 8 n. 5 above, and n. 29 below).

23 The problem of separating actus reus from mens rea in conspiracy is noted in Allen (2009), 283 f.; Anon. (1948), 278, 280; Grammel (2001), 16 ('The agreement is also part of the mens rea'); Harno (1941), 635; Simester et al. (2010), 312, which goes on to say that 'the presence of a consensus does not exhaust what is required by way of a mental element for this offence. Agreements operate on the surface of things and the fact of agreement may coexist with secret reservations or betrayals that one or more of the parties may have in mind'. The authors suggest that such reservations or betrayals exclude liability for conspiracy by excluding the necessary mens rea; contrast Alexander and Kessler (1997), 1179, quoted in n. 63 below. The metaphor of operating on the surface needs careful construal to ensure consistency with the principle, discussed in section 9.22 below, that the criminal law of conspiracy uses a subjective concept of agreement; see further nn. 62 f. and 179 below. Some authors err in the other direction, maintaining that agreement is 'in itself a state of mind' (Farrell (1992), 22), a 'purely mental state' (Orchard (1974), 302) or 'essentially a mental operation' (Ormerod (2008), 413). There is a distinction between the making of an agreement and the resultant state of agreement, but it is only in a loose sense that the latter is a state of mind: the agreement may subsist even if the parties are not thinking, and even if they have forgotten, about it. See further n. 18 to the Introduction and Chap. 7 n. 66 above.

24 See *Doot* (n. 4 above), 821; *O'Brien* (1974) 59 Cr. App. R. 222; *Kuwait Oil Tanker* (n. 1 above), para. 110; *Hussain* [2002] EWCA Crim. 6, para. 25; *Saik* [2007] 1 AC 18, para. 75; Allen (2009), 280; Ashworth (2009), 448, 453 ('basic element'), 461; Burgman (1979), 79, 84, 90 (citing US cases for 'gist of the offence' and 'gravamen'), 90 ('gravamen'); Grammel (2001), 15 (citing US cases for 'gravamen'); Herring (2010), 804 ('key element' (see n. 22 above)); Hooper and Ormerod (2011), para. A6.37; Richardson (2011), para. 33–5; J. Smith (2002), 407. Fisher (2006), 3 says 'The essence of the offence is the agreement. Therefore the agreement must have been expressed verbally, in writing, or by the actions of the parties involved'. The 'therefore' is baffling. On the need for an overt act and for communication, see section 9.21 below. For the view that the emphasis on agreement is misguided, see *Bhagwan* and *Knuller* (cited respectively in nn. 4 and 2 above and both discussed in n. 44 below); Farrell (1992), 22; P. Johnson (1973), 1142 n. 17 (criticised in Marcus (1977), 956). For different views of the essence of conspiracy, see the Australian case *Coffey* [1971] 1 NSWLR 434, 445 ('participation in a design'); Burgman (1979), 87

instead of 'agreement': it is not always clear whether a phrase is being used to explicate, or to add to, the requirement that there be an agreement. Examples[25] – some familiar from earlier chapters – are 'meeting of minds',[26] 'combination',[27] 'confederacy',[28] 'partnership',[29] 'deliberate

('a uniting with another who also intends to carry out the plan'); Ormerod (2003), 413 ('the intent to cause the forbidden result').

Some legislation uses concepts that are akin to that of conspiracy but cover arrangements looser than agreement: examples are 'arrangement' within the meaning of section 328 of the Proceeds of Crime Act 2002 – 'arguably a conspiracy in all but name' (McCluskey (2006), 2 (see also Law Society (2005), paras. 3.1 ff.)) – and 'enterprise' within the meaning of the Racketeer Influenced and Corrupt Organisations ('RICO') provisions of the US Organized Crime Control Act 1970, a concept that includes 'any group of individuals associated in fact although not a legal entity': see M. Levi and Smith (2002), which also contains examples from legislation on organised crime in other jurisdictions; Tarlow (1980); nn. 117 and 126 below. Marcus (1992), 15 notes that 'RICO, combined with conspiracy, has always had the potential to cause serious definition and application problems, especially with large multi-defendant prosecutions. After all, it is hard to imagine two terms more difficult to confine in such cases than "enterprise" and "agreement"'. On 'arrangements' in section 188 of the Enterprise Act 2002, see Chap. 8 n. 2 above.

25 See further nn. 126 and 131 below on phrases used to distinguish a single complex conspiracy from a plurality of conspiracies.

26 Allen (2009), 225, 283; Ashworth (2009), 453 (contrasting 'physical meeting of the persons' (on conspiracy without meeting, see *Murphy* (1837) 8 C. & P. 297, 311; *Parnell* (1881) 14 Cox 508, 515; *Meyrick* (1929) 21 Cr. App. R. 94, 99, 101; *Hammersley* (1958) 42 Cr. App. R. 207, 217; *Doot* (n. 4 above), 823; Grammel (2001), 16; Hooper and Ormerod (2011), para. A6.38; Macdonald and Thompson (2003), 99; Marcus (1977), 950; Richardson (2011), para. 33–25; and the discussion, in section 9.27 below, of complex conspiracies)); Barnard (2005), 2; Burgman (1979), 90 f., 93; Card (1973), 678; Clarkson et al. (2010), 478; Fitzpatrick (1993), 1180; Law Commission (2007), para. 1.47; M. Levi and Smith (2002), iv, 16; Macdonald and Thompson (2003), 99; Marcus (1977), 959; Simester et al. (2010), 312. For the variant 'union of two or more minds', see *Odneal* 117 Tex. Crim. 97, 101, 34 S.W. 2d 595, 597 (1931); Burgman (1979), 90. Compare Chap. 1 n. 1 and Chap. 8 n. 10 above.

27 *Quinn* v. *Leathem* [1901] AC 495, 507, citing *Allen* v. *Flood* [1898] AC 1 ('there was no case of conspiracy or even combination', implying that combination is weaker than conspiracy, but not that it is weaker than agreement); *Tibbits* [1902] 1 KB 77, 90; Anon. (1948), 277, citing US cases; Anon. (2005), 2; Orchard (1974), 301; Rogers (1989), 549 n. 1, citing *Black's Law Dictionary*. In *Kuwait Oil Tanker* (n. 1 above), para. 111, it was said to be sufficient, both for criminal and for tortious conspiracy, that 'two or more persons combine with a common intention, or, in other words, that they deliberately combine, albeit tacitly, to achieve a common end': a liberal reading is needed for the second half of this statement to amount to the first half 'in other words'. This wording was followed in *Tower Hamlets* v. *Chavda et al.* [2005] EWHC 2183 (QB), para. 18. See further n. 61 below. On combinations in competition law, see Chap. 8 n. 5 above.

28 *Simmonds* (1967) 51 Cr. App. R. 316, 332; Rogers (1989) (n. 27 above).

29 *Kessel* 218 US 601, 608 (1910); *Socony-Vacuum Oil Co.* 310 US 150, 253 (1940); *Ong Way Jong* 245 F. 2d 392, 394 n. 2 (9th Cir. 1957); Burgman (1979), 91. Compare Joshua and Jordan (2004), 653; n. 22 above.

and preconcerted scheme',[30] 'concerted purpose',[31] 'concerted activity',[32] 'joint project',[33] 'common purpose',[34] 'understanding',[35] 'assent',[36] 'consent'[37] and 'concurrence'.[38] The cases and commentaries say fairly little about the concept of agreement in this context,[39] beyond noting that it is flexible.[40] One object of the chapter is to show the importance, in the law of conspiracy, of respecting the distinctions drawn earlier in the book between agreement and intention (see sections 5.1–5.17) and

30 *Gregory* v. *Duke of Brunswick* [1843] 1 Car & K 25, 698, citing *Leigh* (1775) 1 Car & K 28n and *Clifford* v. *Brandon*. Compare the citations in Chap. 8 n. 18 above for 'conscious commitment to a common scheme'. On the notion of a scheme in complex conspiracies, see section 9.27 below.

31 *Peoni* 100 F. 2d 401, 402 (2d Cir. 1938); Burgman (1979), 90.

32 *Hanley* 92 Misc 2d 465, 468, 400 NYS 2d 319, 321 (1977); Burgman (1979), 95; Herring (2010), 804 ('acting in concert'); see further nn. 44, 59 and 61 below. Compare Chap. 8 n. 19 above on 'concert of action'; on concerted practices in EU competition law, see sections 8.3–8.33 above.

33 Herring (2010), 804. Compare Simester et al. (2010), 303, quoted in section 9.28 below.

34 See n. 126 below. Compare Chap. 1 n. 2 and Chap. 8 n. 10 above, on 'common intention'; Chap. 8 nn. 11 and 14 give references respectively for 'common design' and 'unity of purpose'.

35 *Direct Sales Co.* 319 US 703, 714 (1943); *Lauria* 251 Cal. App. 2d 471, 475, 59 Cal. Rptr. 628 630 (1967); Abbate (1992), 56; Herring (2010), 837; Marcus (1977), 950 f.; Model Penal Code, section 5.03, nn. of decisions, pt. 2. Compare Chap. 1 n. 6 and Chap. 8 n. 10 above.

According to Macdonald and Thompson (2003), 99, 'whether a mere understanding amounts to an agreement is a question of degree'. (A similar point, expressed more tentatively ('may be a matter of degree'), is made in Ashworth (2009), 453, which links it to the distinction between agreement and negotiation: see n. 67 below.) The statement is unclear, but can be squared with the view that the existence of an agreement is a binary matter, i.e., all or nothing (as to which, see P. Johnson (1973), 1157, citing the Model Penal Code, and compare Odudu (2006), 83, quoted in section 8.2 above); for the statement can be read as meaning that understanding must reach a certain degree in order to amount to an agreement. (Compare the discussion of grasp and dependence of concepts, in section 2.66 above.)

36 *Thomson* (1966) 50 Cr. App. R. 1, 3 f.; *Anderson* (n. 13 above), 37; Clarkson et al. (2010), 484; Herring (2010), 809; Orchard (1974), 301; Ormerod (2008), 413 ('assent or agreement'). See further Chap. 1 n. 3 (mutual assent), Chap. 2 n. 3 and Chap. 8 n. 53 above.

37 'Consent, that is the agreement or adherence to the agreement': *Siracusa* (1990) 90 Cr. App. R. 340, 349; Allen (2009), 290; Herring (2010), 812. Compare Chap. 1 n. 4 (mutual consent), Chap. 7 n. 14 and Chap. 8 n. 54 above. On adhering, see further Chap. 7 n. 107 and Chap. 8 n. 58 above.

38 *Tibbits* (n. 27 above), 90; Orchard (1974), 301. Compare 'concurrence of wills' in competition law: Chap. 8 nn. 20 and 22 above.

39 For observations on the absence of a definition of agreement, see Burgman (1979), 78 n. 14, 108 f.; Ormerod (2008), 402.

40 See Orchard (1974), 297 f.

between evidence, and conditions for the existence, of an agreement (see sections 8.1, 8.2 and 8.521). Another is to show that conspiratorial agreements are accommodated by the offer–acceptance model.

9.21 Agreement and action

Once a conspiratorial agreement has been made, the actus reus is complete: nothing need be done to carry out the agreement – failure and lack of opportunity are immaterial – and withdrawal, termination and repentance (concepts that are not always clearly distinguished from each other or from mere failure to carry out the agreement[41]) go to mitigation only.[42] In the USA, federal law and the law of certain states requires that, for a conspiracy to occur, an overt act be done in pursuance of the agreement,[43] but this requirement, which obscures the distinction between conspiracy and attempt, is not part of English law.[44]

41 See, e.g., *Walker* (1962) Crim LR 459 ('abandoning' an agreement); Fisher (2006), 3 ('reneging'). Hooper and Ormerod (2008), para. A6.17, distinguishes abandonment of an agreement from failure to carry it out; the corresponding sentence in Hooper and Ormerod (2011), para. A6.40, does not mention failure to carry out. Clarkson et al. (2010), 487 says 'repents and withdraws'.

42 *O'Connell* (1843) 5 St Tr (NS) 593; *Mulcahy* (n. 5 above), 317; *Warburton* (1870) LR 1 CCR 274; *Aspinall* (1876) 2 QBD 48, 58; *Quinn* v. *Leathem* (n. 27 above), 530; *Tibbits* (n. 27 above), 89; *Meyrick* (n. 26 above), 99; *Thomson* (n. 36 above), 2; *Simmonds* (n. 28 above), 332; *Doot* (n. 4 above), 821 ff., 825, 827; *Gortat* [1973] Crim LR 648; *Nock* (n. 10 above), 991, 994; *Bolton* [1992] 94 Cr. App. R. 74, 80; *Kuwait Oil Tanker* (n. 1 above), para. 110; *Hussain* (n. 24 above), para. 25; *Saik* (n. 24 above), paras. 3, 75, 93; Allen (2009), 281, 285; Ashworth (2009), 453; Clarkson et al. (2010), 487; Grant (2006), 1120; Herring (2010), 804; Hooper and Ormerod (2011), para. A6.40; Macdonald and Thompson (2003), 100; Marcus (1977), 965; Richardson (2011), para. 33–5; J. Smith (2002), 407; compare Katz et al. (2008), 2. On arguments for and against a defence of withdrawal, see Card (1973), 688 f. Ormerod (2008), 415 argues that a more limited defence based on an intention to frustrate the object of the conspiracy may exist in English law; compare Hooper and Ormerod (2011), para. A6.43 ('frustrate or sabotage'), and see further n. 180 below. On 'abandonment' as a defence under the Model Penal Code, see its section 5.03(7). For a similar defence in competition law, see Chap. 8 n. 132 above. Section 2.62 above distinguishes withdrawing from an agreement and withdrawing an agreement, and discusses withdrawal of offers and acceptances; section 1.1 discusses withdrawal of promises. On withdrawal of an 'offer to supply' a controlled drug, see *Prior* [2004] EWCA Crim. 1147, paras. 7, 16, 28, 30 (discussed in Chap. 2 n. 4 above).

43 See Burgman (1979), 101; Perkins and Boyle (1982), 685 ff.; Simester et al. (2010), 286, 308. The requirement is included in the Model Penal Code, section 5.03(5).

44 Australian law follows English in this respect: *Coffey* (n. 24 above), 445. For the view that the definition of criminal conspiracy is misconceived in turning on the agreement rather than on actions done pursuant to it, see the statements by Lord Diplock in *Bhagwan*, 472, and *Knuller*, 671 f. (nn. 4 and 2 above): 'The least systematic, the most irrational branch

There is some English authority for the principle that the agreement need not be made before actions are taken to carry it out:[45] it appears that X and Y conspire if X is taking steps towards the commission of a crime, Y comes to his aid and they then act in concert. (On the relation between agreement and joint action, see section 8.5222 and the discussion below of proof of conspiratorial agreement.) It might be objected that this is not an instance of the principle at issue; rather, Y's coming to X's aid constitutes the making of an agreement the content of which concerns only actions to be performed thereafter. To hold otherwise, the objection runs, is to confuse the making with the carrying out of an agreement. Whether or not the principle is part of English law, it appears that the law does not include the following stronger principle: there may be a conspiracy even if the agreement is not made until all the actions specified in its content have been performed and thus until (in the normal case) the crime in question has been committed. Even if persons can conspire to φ while they are already φing, they cannot when they have already

of English penal law, it still rests upon the legal fiction that the offence lies not in the overt acts themselves which are injurious to the common weal but in an inferred anterior agreement to commit them'. '[I]t may be rational to hold that there are some kinds of acts which, if done by a number of people acting in concert, have consequences sufficiently harmful to call for punishment by the State, but which, if done by one person acting on his own, have consequences that are not grave enough to demand penal sanctions. But it is the height of sophistry to say that the doing of the acts in concert which alone can have harmful consequences is not what the law regards as meriting punishment, but that the prior agreement to do them is. This is to turn the common law doctrine of "overt act", which was the origin of the crime of conspiracy, upon its head. In most cases of conspiracy the prior agreement is itself only inferred from the acts which have been done in pursuance of it. They are a consequence of the conspiracy, not a step taken towards it; whereas a conspiracy, like an attempt, became a crime because it was a step taken towards the commission of a crime.' These passages do not deny that in the situations in question there is an agreement (although, in the first passage, the indefinite article in 'an inferred anterior agreement' could be taken to cast doubt as to whether an agreement exists): the alleged legal fiction is not that an agreement exists but that 'the offence lies' in the agreement. Similarly, 'the height of sophistry' is not the inference to the agreement but the claim that the agreement rather than the doing of the acts merits punishment. Contrast Fitzpatrick (1993), 3 on 'the philosophical tortuousness that accompanies proof of an agreement'; Goldstein (1959), 410 on conspiratorial agreement as a 'theoretical construct' (nn. 48 and 60 below). See further Farrell (1992), 22; Marcus (1992), 45; Ormerod (2008), 404 n. 173. Note 61 below quotes Lord Diplock on the tort of conspiracy.

45 See *Leigh* (n. 30 above); *Tibbits* (n. 27 above); Orchard (1974), 299 f.; Ormerod (2008), 403.

φd.[46] If they could, conspiracy would not be an exclusively inchoate crime.[47]

Conspiracy's inchoateness and the doctrine that an inchoate crime is committed only when 'the accused has moved from mere mental planning to the stage of performing overt acts which manifest his intention'[48] are together consistent with the principle that for a conspiracy to occur no overt act need be done in pursuance of the agreement, for the overt acts in a conspiracy may be done in making rather than pursuing the agreement.[49] On a natural understanding of 'overt',[50] the making of an agreement is, at least in the normal case, overt – a thesis supported by the propositions that an agreement is typically made by speech acts and that these are overt; the latter proposition is in turn supported by the propositions that speech acts are typically communicative (see sections 1.1, 8.2 and 8.5) and that communication is by its nature overt.[51] Given the point already recalled from sections 5.11 and 5.12, however, the acts by which a party makes an agreement to φ need not 'manifest his intention' to φ or his intention to agree to φ – unless 'manifest' is given an artificially weak sense in which something non-existent may be manifested. They may of course manifest some other intention – for example, and at the minimum, to utter certain sounds (see section 1.1).[52]

46 On the problem this can cause in prosecuting latecomers to a complex conspiracy, see Richardson (2011), para. 33–10. See also *Murphy* (n. 26 above), 311; *Doot* (n. 4 above), 823; *Zezev* [2002] Crim. LR 648 (CA); Orchard (1974) 342 f.; Herring (2010), 804 n. 59; nn. 117 f. below.

47 Compare Orchard (1974), 301. It is not clear whether Orchard is concerned with the stronger or the weaker principle, or both: in one sentence he writes of a continuing offence's having been 'initiated'; in the next, of a substantive offence's having been 'actually committed': 343 f.

48 Allen (2009), 272. Compare Goldstein (1959), 405 f. on the 'act requirement', according to which mere intention is insufficient for a crime. Goldstein maintains that '[m]ore than any other important crime, conspiracy impinges on the act requirement', as the alleged agreement 'is almost as much a theoretical construct as the "intent" it is supposed to carry over the threshold from fancy to fact' (410). Later on the same page he writes that the agreement has an 'illusory quality'. See further nn. 44 above and 60 below.

49 Ferguson (1986a), 225 says that '[t]he "overt act" which completes the crime of conspiracy . . . is the agreement which must therefore be unqualified'. The inference marked by the 'therefore' is obscure. Compare Goldstein (1959), 409.

50 On the meaning of 'overt', see Chap. 8 nn. 170 f. above.

51 On communication, see Chap. 1 n. 13 above; section 8.32 above.

52 Compare the passage quoted from Ormerod (2008) in n. 157 below.

The previous paragraph connected overtness and communication, and there is some authority for the principle that the latter is necessary for a conspiracy.[53] This principle is in turn consistent with its being in the nature of conspiracies that the agreements in question are usually hard to detect by anyone other than the conspirators.[54] Often the only evidence will be circumstantial – in particular the actions, if any, that the conspirators perform in pursuance of their agreement.[55] In some cases those actions will constitute the substantive crime that is the object of the conspiracy, but it is normally bad practice to charge conspiracy as

53 Orchard (1974), 298, 302 speaks of 'physical communication': it is unclear what, other than telepathy, is ruled out by 'physical'. (Compare Macdonald and Thompson (2003), 99 on 'physical contact'.) Marcus (1977), 950 says that a conspiratorial agreement 'need not be a formal transaction involving meetings and communications' (see also n. 61 below), but this can be read as consistent with the requirement of some communication. *Scott* (1979) 68 Cr. App. R. 164, 166 f. is authority for the principle that '[a]n intention to enter into an agreement must, to become effective as an agreement, be communicated to the other party by some means or other' (see also Richardson (2011), para. 33–8) – an example of the blurring of the distinction between agreement and intention. There is a similar blurring of the distinction between agreement and decision in Clarkson et al. (2010), 478 ('decisions must have been communicated between the parties' (see further n. 68 below)) and Herring (2010), 804. On the relations between conspiracy, agreement, intention and decision, see n. 68 below. On communication or 'contact', or the alleged lack of it, between parties to complex conspiracies, see *Meyrick* (n. 26 above), 101 ff.; *Varelli* 407 F. 2d 735 (7th Cir. 1969), paras. 1 f.; *Saik* (n. 24 above), para. 113; Allen (2009), 281; Card (1973), 678; Herring (2010), 804; Marcus (1977), 950; Orchard (1974), 336; n. 26 above (on conspiring without meeting). Complex conspiracies are discussed in section 9.27 below. For the use of the word 'contact' in the context of Article 101 TFEU, see Chap. 8 n. 94 above.

54 See *Varelli* (n. 53 above), para. 1 ('the mark of a successful conspiracy is secrecy'); Spicer (1981), 120. Contrast Orchard (1974), 299, which cites *O'Connell* (n. 42 above), 593 ff., *Parnell* (n. 26 above), 516, and *Clayton* (n. 17 above), 119, for the propositions that secrecy is not an essential element and that 'there need not be anything particularly sinister about the object'. A secret agreement is different from an implied agreement, unless the meanings of 'secret' and/or 'implied' are gerrymandered. On implied agreements, see *Kuwait Oil Tanker* (n. 1 above), para. 111; Allen (2009), 280; Anon. (2005), 2; Joshua and Jordan (2004), 655. Compare sections 7.14 and 8.521 above, respectively on implied contracts and the various ways in which an agreement may be tacit. On tacit agreements in the context of conspiracy, see the Model Penal Code, section 5.03, notes of decisions, pt. 3: 'tacit agreement may be inferred from circumstances'. That follows from one of the accounts of tacitness proposed in section 8.521. See further the following note.

55 See *Cooper* [1947] 2 All ER 701; *Hammersley* (n. 26 above), 213; *Varelli* (n. 53 above), paras. 1 f.; *Coffey* (n. 24 above), 445 f.; *Doot* (n. 4 above), 821; *Siracusa* (n. 37 above), 349; Orchard (1974), 298; Ormerod (2008), 404; J. Smith (1996b), 386. On the more general use of circumstantial evidence in this context, see Spicer (1981), 120, 128 f.; Model Penal Code, section 5.03, notes of decisions, pt. 48. For complaints about inferences of conspiracy from such evidence, see Ferguson (1986a), 224; Goldstein (1959), 411, citing US cases; Marcus (1977), 951 ff., also citing US cases.

well as charging the substantive crime.[56] The actions may exhibit one of the degrees of correlation described in section 8.5222, and specifically may constitute narrow joint action as specified by propositions (219), (58) and (220)–(226);[57] the fact, noted in that section, that narrow joint action is neither necessary nor sufficient for agreement does not prevent the former from being evidence of the latter or – as may sometimes happen – the latter from evidencing the former.[58] In either case there is likely to be an evidential chain, as described in sections 8.2 and 8.33: where, for example, narrow joint action is adduced in proof of an agreement, further evidence may be needed to prove that the conditions for narrow joint action are met.[59] As Chapter 8 showed, questions of evidence and of conditions for existence are not always clearly separated: that is true of the law of conspiracy,[60] it being sometimes suggested that joint action of

56 See *Boulton* (n. 4 above), 93; *Jones* (1974) 59 Cr. App. R. 120; Practice Direction [1977] 2 All ER 540; Ashworth (2009), 451; Ormerod (2008), 431 f.; n. 3 above. For cases where the practice is justified, see Law Commission (2007), para. 1.18 n. 15.

57 Joshua and Jordan (2004), 655, citing *American Tobacco Co.* v. *United States* 328 US 781, 810 (1946), a US competition case, states that conspiracy for the purposes of the Sherman Act 'may be demonstrated by concert of action between the participants all working together for a common purpose'. See also Ashworth (2009), 454: 'the typical process is to infer a prior agreement from behaviour which appears to be concerted'. Orchard (1974), 298 f. says 'the fact that different persons have pursued the same unlawful end is only of evidential importance and it is certainly true that "the mere fact that two persons independently pursue the same end" does not render them conspirators'. The phrase quoted by Orchard is from G. Williams (1961), 667. Pursuit, and a fortiori independent pursuit, of the same end is not by itself one of the specified degrees of correlation: rather, the conditions for a common goal ((220)–(222) in section 8.5222 above) are conjoined with further conditions ((219) and (58) in the same section) which themselves are necessary and sufficient for mutual reliance. See also *Kuwait Oil Tanker* (n. 1 above), paras. 111 f.; Simester et al. (2010), 327, quoted in n. 59 below.

58 Compare Simester et al. (2010), 303: a conspiratorial agreement 'must be indicative of a collaboration'. A longer passage from which these words are taken is quoted in section 9.28 below.

59 See *Doot* (n. 4 above), 822: 'A conspiracy is usually proved by proving acts on the part of the accused which lead to the inference that they were acting in concert in pursuance of an agreement to do an unlawful act'. This seems to say that the acts are evidence not, or not only, of the agreement but of the concertation. Compare Simester et al. (2010), 327: 'Typically, evidence for a conspiracy is inferred from concerted criminal activity'. Not the conspiracy, but the evidence for it, is inferred from the concerted activity; so it seems that the activity is evidence for evidence. These readings might be resisted by distinguishing 'is evidence for' from either or both of 'leads to the inference that' and the inverse of 'is inferred from'; compare the distinctions proposed on Odudu's behalf in section 8.2 above.

60 Examples: (a) It is unclear whether Goldstein's criticism of conspiracy for impinging on the 'act requirement' is a point about evidence, existence or both. The statement,

some kind is a condition for the existence of a conspiratorial agreement.[61] Some of the expressions cited in section 9.2 – 'joint project' and 'common

quoted in n. 48 above, that the conspiratorial agreement 'is almost as much a theoretical construct as the "intent" it is supposed to carry over the threshold from fancy to fact' seems to concern existence, but is immediately followed by a statement about evidence: 'Indeed, in most cases, it is proved by the very same evidence from which intent will be inferred'. Goldstein might reply that the first statement is also evidential, since a theoretical construct is merely an entity inferred from evidence on the basis of a theory. The counter-reply is that 'construct' appears to say something about the nature of the thing in question, not just about the evidence for it. The same applies to Goldstein's subsequent statement that the agreement has 'an illusory quality'. (b) In Marcus (1977), 951 f. an alleged condition 'sufficient to sustain the existence' of an agreement is described in a discussion of evidence. For warnings against such confusion, see Allen (2009), 290; Orchard (1974), 298 f., quoted in n. 57 above; Ormerod (2008), 404.

61 Examples: (a) Herring (2010), 804: 'In some cases it can be difficult to decide whether many people happen to be pursuing the same crime independently . . . or whether they are acting in concert'. In context – a section on the nature of conspiratorial agreements – this could be read as implying that action in concert is a condition for the existence of such an agreement. (On the problem of deciding whether crimes are 'the same', see n. 133 below.) (b) Marcus (1977), 950 f.: 'The agreement . . . need not be a formal transaction involving meetings and communications. The prosecution need only show concert of action . . . '. The word 'show' suggests that the point concerns evidence; but, as the second sentence appears to amplify the first, which appears to concern existence conditions, the second might be read as meaning that concert of action is such a condition. (c) There is similar ambiguity in *Varelli* (n. 53 above), para. 1: 'The agreement may be shown . . . if there be concert of action . . . '. (d) The passage from Simester et al. (2010), quoted in n. 59 above, may be intended to concern existence conditions; see further section 9.28 below.

The agreement may be to act jointly, and, as noted in Ashworth (2009), 454, 'if the charge is conspiracy, it is the conduct agreed upon and not the conduct actually carried out that is the basis of the offence'; compare the quotation from *Bolton* in n. 70 below. Ashworth criticises *El-Kurd* [2001] Crim. LR 234 for failing to recognise that distinction. The position is different in tort: it appears that action taken pursuant to an agreement is necessary but not sufficient for tortious conspiracy. 'Regarded as a civil tort . . . conspiracy is a highly anomalous cause of action. The gist of the cause of action is damage to the plaintiff; so long as it remains unexecuted the agreement, which alone constitutes the crime of conspiracy, causes no damage; it is only acts done in execution of the agreement that are capable of doing that. So the tort, unlike the crime, consists not of agreement but of concerted action taken pursuant to agreement'. Lord Diplock in *Lonrho Ltd.* v. *Shell Petroleum Co. Ltd.* [1982] AC 173, 188; see also *Kuwait Oil Tanker* (n. 1 above), paras. 109 ff., and compare Lord Diplock's animadversions on criminal conspiracy in *Bhagwan* and *Knuller*, quoted in n. 44 above. The present passage is consistent with the propositions that concerted action is neither necessary nor sufficient for agreement and that agreement is necessary for tortious conspiracy; indeed, it entails the latter.

Kuwait Oil Tanker arguably leaves room for tortious conspiracy without agreement. The relevant words are 'A conspiracy . . . is actionable where the claimant proves that he has suffered loss or damage as a result of action taken pursuant to a combination or agreement . . . ' (para. 108). First, the word 'where' may be read as signifying only a sufficient condition. Second, even if 'where' means 'if and only if', 'combination or purpose', for example – apply at least as happily to joint action as to agreement.

9.22 *Conspiracy and contract*

The requirement of communication is also consistent with the principle that the concept of agreement used in the criminal law of conspiracy is subjective – roughly, that it has regard to the content of the parties' minds[62] – and thus differs from the objective concept, used in contract law, according to which (again roughly) the existence and/or the content of an alleged agreement depends on the view that a reasonable man would take of the situation (see sections 5.1 and 7.37):

> When a man makes an agreement, he assents with his mind to the offer of the other party and communicates his assent to the other party by words or conduct. For the purposes of the law of contract, the words or conduct by which a man manifests his assent are binding on him and the law does not allow him to say that his mind did not go with his conduct. The criminal law, however, is concerned with punishing wrongdoing; the essential element in any crime, other than in the limited class of absolute offences, is a guilty mind. Evidence that the accused person acted and spoke as if he was making and had made an agreement may provide cogent evidence of a guilty mind; but it is only evidence and can be rebutted by other evidence.

agreement' may be read as meaning not 'combination or, in other words, agreement' but 'combination or, instead or as well, agreement'. On the latter reading, there can be an agreementless conspiracy, provided that an agreement is not necessary for a combination; if it were necessary, a combination could exist only as well as, not instead of, an agreement. For the suggestion, in the context of competition law, that an agreement is unnecessary for a combination, see Chap. 8 n. 5 above; compare n. 27 above. Third, 'prove' may be given a non-factive reading, so that the claimant can prove something that is not the case; in tort the standard of proof is the balance of probabilities, and there are some false propositions that are more likely than not to be true. The words from para. 108 of *Kuwait Oil Tanker* are like the passages from the criminal law, quoted earlier in this note, in blurring the evidence/existence distinction. The same is true of para. 111 (already quoted in part in n. 27 above), which can also be read as saying that agreement is unnecessary: 'it is not necessary to show that there is anything in the nature of an express agreement, whether formal or informal. It is sufficient if two or more persons combine with a common intention . . . '. An alternative reading is that an agreement is necessary, but need not be express. On implied conspiratorial agreements, see n. 54 above.

62 See Orchard (1974), 298. Anon. (1948), 280 conflates this principle with a requirement of conspiracy's mens rea, discussed in section 9.3 below, that there be an intention to agree: 'the criminal "act" is an agreement, which is itself subjective and involves as an essential element an intent to agree'. As noted in section 5.12 above, a person can agree without intending to; and, as explained in section 5.1 above, there are subjective and objective concepts of intention.

These words from *Thomson*[63] reinforce the point that in conspiracy the boundary between actus reus and mens rea is blurred. They also, in the mention of an offer, support the view that the offer–acceptance model fits conspiratorial agreements; if such an agreement is subjective and is made by an offer and an acceptance, the offer and acceptance are subjective too. The passage speaks of assent rather than acceptance, but, as noted in section 2.1, 'accept' for the purposes of the model has a broad sense similar to the sense of 'assent'. Read literally, the passage says only that an agreement is made by one who assents to, not by one who makes, an offer: the wording may be loose, or the idea may be that it is not until the assent has been given that the agreement comes into existence.

Orchard invokes the difference between conspiracies and contracts when rejecting an analysis of conspiratorial agreements in terms of offer and acceptance:

> it seems clear that in the context of conspiracy the courts have not analysed the concept of agreement in terms of offer and acceptance, and furthermore the Court for Crown Cases Reserved rejected the need for any such "contractual" agreement in *Tibbits*.[64]

The first claim is hard to square with the mention in *Thomson* of an offer. The second seems to refer to the passage from *Tibbits* in which the judge cited Willes J. in *Mulcahy*:

> Willes J . . . never said that when the unlawful purpose has been carried out no indictment for conspiracy can be maintained unless the concerted action has been preceded by such a contract between the conspirators as, if the purpose had been lawful, would have given ground for a lawsuit.[65]

63 *Thomson* (n. 36 above), 3; see further n. 152 below. Conspiracy is distinguished from contract in *Walker* (n. 41 above), 459; *Doot* (n. 4 above), 827; *Anderson* (n. 13 above), 37; *Prior* (n. 42 above), para. 28; Burgman (1979), 93 (maintaining that the Model Penal Code abandons a subjective concept of agreement in order to account for so-called unilateral conspiracies (as to which, see section 9.4 below)); Joshua and Jordan (2004), 653 (see further Chap. 2 n. 7 above); Ormerod (2008), 402, 434; Richardson (2011), paras. 33–5. Contrast Alexander and Kessler (1997), 1179, which, after noting that a person may agree without intending to carry out the agreement, says 'Mental reservations do not relieve the defendant of or negate his commitment if they are unexpressed. Conscious awareness that one is objectively "agreeing" suffices as the requisite mental state for declaring one morally and legally bound'. The authors here cite a textbook of contract law. Their formulation is partly subjective ('conscious awareness') and partly objective ('objectively "agreeing"'). Compare n. 23 above.

64 Orchard (1974), 300 f.

65 *Tibbits* (n. 27 above), 89. The relevant passage from *Mulcahy* was quoted in section 9.1 above.

There is no route from these words to the conclusion that the offer–acceptance model does not fit conspiratorial agreements. (For replies to objections that the model does not fit certain other agreements, see sections 2.61–2.613.) Ignore, for simplicity, any distinction between 'no indictment for conspiracy can be maintained' and 'there is no conspiracy'. The first objection is that *Tibbits* does not say that *Mulcahy* denies, at most it says that *Mulcahy* does not assert:

(231) If there is a conspiracy, then there is a contract.

The negation of a legal proposition does not follow from the fact that the proposition is not asserted in a judgment, let alone from the fact that one judgment asserts that another does not assert it; indeed, it would be a caricature of the doctrine of precedent to say that a legal proposition follows from the fact that a judgment asserts it. So the silence of *Mulcahy* is compatible with (231).

Grant arguendo that <not (231)>. Suppose, again for simplicity, the statement that the model fits conspiratorial agreements to mean this:

(232) X and Y conspiratorially agree if and only if X makes to Y an offer which Y accepts.

(232) is inaccurate in that it does not distinguish the making of an agreement from the state of agreement (see section 9.23) and does not mention various elements in section 1(1) CLA, but those points do not affect the discussion. Also, given that the model provides a sufficient condition, not a necessary one, for agreement, and that the condition includes elements beyond offer and acceptance, (232) is too strong; but, since Orchard presumably denies the claim of fit, to read it as (232) is charitable to him, for <not (232)> is correspondingly weak and so should be easy to prove. <Not (232)> might be derived from the combination of <not (231)> and:

(233) If there is a conspiracy, then there is a conspiratorial agreement;
(234) If there is a contractual agreement, then there is a contract;
(235) If X makes to Y an offer which Y accepts, then there is a contractual agreement.

But the argument would fail for equivocation, both because offer and acceptance should be understood subjectively in (232) but objectively in (235) (see the quotation from *Thomson*) and because 'contractual agreement' has two meanings, one of which falsifies (235), the other of which falsifies (234). Sections 7.2–7.22 showed that an agreement is not sufficient for a contract. As explained in section 7.2, the indefinite article in 'an agreement' imports generality: the thesis is that not every agreement is sufficient for a contract. Certain agreements are sufficient: these have properties identified in section 7.1 – the property of having parties who intend to create legal relations, the property of being supported by consideration, and so on. If 'contractual agreement' signifies such an agreement, (235) is false, because X's making to Y an offer which Y accepts is not sufficient for their agreement to have the relevant properties. If the phrase signifies an agreement which would, if it had those properties, be sufficient for a contract, (234) is false, because the phrase is true of agreements that lack the properties. This horn of the dilemma assumes that the indefinite article in 'a contractual agreement' again imports generality – (234) meaning that every contractual agreement is sufficient for a contract. With some strain, (234) might be read as concerning a particular agreement: if that agreement is contractual not only in the second but also in the first sense, (234) is true. But then, to avoid another equivocation, (235) must be read as concerning the same agreement. On that reading, given that (235)'s schematic antecedent imports generality, (235) is true if and only if:

(236) For any two parties, if one makes to the other an offer which the other accepts, then the particular contractual agreement in question exists.

(Compare the move from (52) to (53) in section 3.4.) (236) is false. Hence (235), on that reading, is false.

9.23 Duration

A conspiratorial agreement is often informal,[66] but it exists only if the parties have passed beyond the stage of mere discussion or negotiation.[67]

66 See *Coffey* (n. 24 above), 446; *Varelli* (n. 53 above), para. 1; Joshua and Jordan (2004), 655; Marcus (1977), 950; Orchard (1974), 299; Model Penal Code, section 5.03. The same is true of tortious conspiracy: *Kuwait Oil Tanker* (n. 1 above), para. 111; *Tower Hamlets* v. *Chavda* (n. 27 above), para. 18; Anon. (2005), 2.

67 *Walker* (n. 41 above) is often cited as authority for this principle, but the report is unclear. First the question is said to be whether 'what had occurred so far as the appellant was concerned had passed from the sphere of negotiation or intention and had become a matter of agreement'; then whether 'at the time when he pulled out the negotiations had passed from a matter of intention and had become a matter of agreement' (458 f.).

Section 7.35 compared conspiracy law with contract law and competition law as regards their approaches to the distinction between negotiation and agreement: as in these two areas of law, the distinction can be hard to draw in practice. The practical problem is sometimes compounded by a failure to separate this distinction clearly from those between agreement in principle and agreement in detail, between conditional and unconditional agreement (see section 9.26) and between agreement and intention or decision.[68]

The criminal law of conspiracy is concerned not only with the making of an agreement but also with the resultant state of agreement:

> When there is agreement between two or more to commit an unlawful act all the ingredients of the offence are there and in that sense the crime is complete. But a conspiracy does not end with the making of the agreement. It will continue so long as there are two or more parties to it intending to carry out the design.[69]

The first passage implies that agreement is distinct from, the second that it is a phase of, negotiation. The relation between negotiation and intention is also left obscure: in 'negotiation or intention', does 'or' mean 'or in other words' or 'or instead or as well'? The latter reading is allowed by the phrase 'the negotiations had passed from a matter of intention', which suggests that intention is not necessary for negotiation; compare the discussion of 'combination or agreement' in n. 61 above. See also *Chrastny* [1991] 1 WLR 1381, 1383 ('actually concluded the agreement', 'positive agreement' (see further n. 132 below)); *O'Brien* (n. 24 above), 225 f.; Ashworth (2009), 453 (explicating the claim that '[w]hether the understanding amounts to an agreement may be a matter of degree' (see n. 36 above)); Ferguson (1986a), 225; Herring (2010), 804 ('clear' agreement); Hooper and Ormerod (2008), para. A6.14 ('firm' (omitted from Hooper and Ormerod (2011), para. A6.37)); Law Commission (1976), para. 1.22 ('full'); Orchard (1974), 339 ('true' (see further n. 127 below)), 343 ('serious' and 'concluded'); Simester et al. (2010), 307 ('final').

68 For example, as to agreement in principle and in detail, see Simester et al. (2010), 307. As to conditional and unconditional agreement: *Mills* (1963) 47 Cr. App. R. 49, 53 ff.; *O'Brien* (n. 24 above), 225 f.; Ferguson (1986a), 225 (see n. 49 above); Richardson (2011), para. 33–6; see further n. 99 below. Agreement and intention: *Mills* 53 ff. Agreement and decision: *Walker* (n. 41 above), 459; Herring (2010), 804 (see also n. 53 above); Ormerod (2008), 402; G. Williams (1961), 212. For the idea that conspiracy involves a decision, see also Clarkson et al. (2010), 478 (quoted in n. 53 above). If the thought is that a decision to φ, or to agree to φ, is necessary for an agreement to φ, it faces variants of the arguments in sections 5.11 and 5.12 above against the corresponding thought about intention. On the difference between intention and decision, see Bratman (1999c), 32 f.; on joint decisions, Gilbert (1996a), 292 ff.

69 *Doot* (n. 4 above), 822; there are similar statements at 825 and 827. See also *Simmonds* (n. 28 above), 332; *Prior* (n. 42 above), paras. 28, 30; Allen (2009), 280 f.; Farrell (1992), 22; Marcus (1977), 951, 965; Model Penal Code, section 5.03(7); Orchard (1974), 302; Richardson (2011), para. 33–9.

If X and Y agree to rob the bank, their 'intending to carry out the design' is presumably their intending to rob the bank. (In this chapter there is no need to distinguish that intention from others with coextensive contents, such as an intention to perform the agreement, or – on the assumption, made here, that carrying out is the same as performance (see further section 9.26) – to carry out the agreement: compare the points on performance, in the Introduction, and on performance obligations, in section 3.3. Likewise the fact – important in section 8.121 – that the parties are likely to have distinct intentions relating to their respective parts of the agreement can be ignored.) In that case the passage seems to imply that a conspiracy between X and Y to rob the bank exists for just as long as it is the case both that X and Y agree to rob the bank and that they intend to rob it. From this it follows that the conspiracy ends if either (i) X and Y terminate the agreement but continue to have the intention or (ii) they cease to have the intention but leave the agreement in place;[70] that each of (i) and (ii) is possible was admitted in Chapter 5. The claim that the conspiracy ends if (ii) is the case goes beyond the wording of section 1(1) CLA, for although that provision mentions the parties' intentions ('if the agreement is carried out in accordance with their intentions') it does not say that the intentions in question are to carry out the agreement, let alone that the parties' intending to carry out the agreement is necessary for a conspiracy to exist. This point recurs in section 9.3.

9.24 Course of conduct

The phrase 'course of conduct' causes difficulty.[71] One set of questions concerns its breadth:[72] Does it include just the actions to which the agreement relates, or also the consequences that the parties intend or foresee those actions to have?[73] Does it include the circumstances that the

70 *Bolton* (n. 42 above), 79 f. appears not to recognise that the agreement may come apart from the intention: a paragraph discussing the distinction between the way in which conspirators intend to achieve their objective and the way in which they actually achieve it concludes that 'it is what is agreed to be done and not what was in fact done which is all important'. Compare the quotation from Ashworth in n. 61 above.

71 On the varieties of courses of conduct, see *Anderson* (n. 13 above), 37; Herring (2010), 808 f.

72 See Allen (2009), 284 ff.; Ashworth (2009), 454; Herring (2010), 805 f.; Ormerod (2008), 405 ff.; Simester et al. (2010), 309 ff.

73 'The phrase "course of conduct" here does not refer purely to physical actions, but must be taken to include intended consequences – in short, the plan': Clarkson et al. (2010), 479; see also 486. On plans in conspiracy, see also Herring (2010), 811; nn. 24 above

parties believe will exist when the actions are performed? How, in any case, are the boundaries to be drawn between action on the one hand and consequences and circumstances on the other?[74] Further questions concern the identity of courses of conduct: if X and Y agree to burgle and, if they are disturbed, to kill the intruder, how many courses of conduct does the agreement cover and what do they comprise?[75]

The passive construction – persons agree 'that a course of conduct shall be pursued' – seems to admit the possibility of the agreement's providing that persons other than its parties are to pursue the course of conduct.[76] It might be suggested that the possibility is excluded by the fact that, first, section 1(1) CLA requires the agreement to be carried out in accordance with the parties' intentions and, second, a person's intentions are directed only at his own actions.[77] Even if this last thesis – which follows from a stronger one considered in section 8.121 – is true, the possibility remains, for the actions intended by the parties might be distinct from the pursuit of the course of conduct. Another suggestion for excluding the possibility is that, under paragraph (a), pursuit of the course of conduct necessarily amounts to or involves the commission of an offence by one or more

and 95, 126, 136, 144 and 179 below. On the relation between intentions and plans, see Bratman (1987); Bratman (1990).

74 See Law Commission (2007), paras. 4.6 ff. On the austere view, in Davidson (1980b), 59 'our primitive actions, the ones we do not do by doing something else, mere movements of the body – these are all the actions there are. We never do more than move our bodies: the rest is up to nature'. This thesis is more palatable when it is recognised that an action may be described by reference to other things, its consequences in particular: the assassin's moving of his finger may be described as the killing of the archduke. See further Chap. 3 n. 83 above. For discussion of Davidson's theory and its place in the philosophy of action, see Evnine (1991), chap. 3. Compare Simester et al. (2010), 309 (citing Feinberg (1965), 146, on the 'accordion effect'): 'In ordinary English speech, it is perfectly permissible to describe the same incident in a manner whereby X's conduct includes consequential results (as in "X killed Y by shooting him") or in a manner which separates X's conduct from its consequence (as in "X fired a gun at Y causing Y to die")' (schematic names changed). It is not clear what 'consequential' adds to 'results'. See also Anscombe (1963), 37 ff.

75 See Simester et al. (2010), 311 f. Compare the proposal, discussed in sections 5.31 above and 9.26 below, for analysing an internally conditional agreement into two agreements, one of which is not internally conditional.

76 Compare *Harmer* [2005] EWCA Crim. 1, para. 13: 'The offence of conspiracy . . . is not simply an agreement with another to commit a crime, but an agreement that a crime be committed'. Passive constructions are also used in clause 48 of the Draft Criminal Code Bill (Law Commission (1989)); see Clarkson et al. (2007), 532 f.

77 In *Saik* (n. 24 above), para. 4, it was held that the mens rea of conspiracy included 'the intention to pursue a course of conduct', not the intention that a course of conduct be pursued; see Clarkson et al. (2010), 480. On mens rea, see section 9.3 below.

parties to the agreement, and that this is so only if such a party carries out the course of conduct. But X and Y might agree to procure the commission of an offence by Z: in that case, it might be objected, Z carries out the course of conduct, but X and Y commit an offence as accessories.[78] In *Hollinshead*, however, the Court of Appeal rejected a finding of conspiracy on such facts.[79]

The law appears to be that, despite the passive construction, the course of conduct agreed upon must, in order for there to be a conspiracy, be one that is to be pursued by one or more parties to the agreement.[80]

9.25 Material object

In *Harmer*, a case about money-laundering, the judge said:

> Although the offence of conspiracy comprises an agreement to commit an offence (not the subsequent committing of the agreed offence), the agreement has to have a material object. In the present case, the appellant was not alleged to have been party to an abstract agreement to convert or transfer theoretical property which might turn out opportunistically to be the proceeds of crime. The alleged agreement concerned the particular money to which the Crown's evidence related . . . [81]

Although the point is debatable, the first sentence appears to apply to conspiratorial agreements generally – not just to the particular agreement alleged, or even just to agreements to commit the substantive offence in question. If so, the principle appears to be that, although an agreement

78 On the law of accessories – which covers aiding, abetting, counselling and procuring – see Allen (2009), 221 ff.; Ashworth (2009), chap. 10; Clarkson et al. (2010), chap. 6; Herring (2010), chap. 15; Ormerod (2008), 183 ff.; Simester et al. (2010), chap. 7. See further nn. 2 and 12 above.

79 *Hollinshead* (n. 12 above). See also *Kenning* [2009] QB 221; Hooper and Ormerod (2011), para. A6.39.

80 According to Herring (2010), 'a conspiracy is an agreement . . . to engage in a course of conduct . . . '; similarly, the agreement must be 'to pursue a course of conduct . . . ' (802 f.; Herring uses 'engage in' and 'pursue' interchangeably). This implies that the parties to the agreement are to pursue the course of conduct. See also Hooper and Ormerod (2011), para. A6.39: 'To be the subject of a conspiracy, the course of conduct proposed must be something that will be done by one or more of the parties to the agreement'. It might be argued that this conflicts with the passage from *Anderson* discussed in section 9.3 below; but *Anderson* primarily concerned the parties' intentions, not their agreement. In any event, as noted in that section, *Anderson* is widely regarded as bad law. Ormerod (2008), 416 says that 'notwithstanding *Anderson*, the parties must intend that at least one of them will pursue the course of conduct agreed upon'.

81 *Harmer* (n. 76 above), para. 24.

may lack a material object, a conspiratorial agreement must have one. This claim is obscure and, when clarified, at best doubtful.

'Material' is not happily translated as 'physical' in this context, for although money can take the form of cash, in the sense of notes or coins, it is not in any ordinary sense a physical object. (The facts of the case included cash payments and non-cash transfers between bank accounts.) A more promising suggestion is that the statement that an agreement has a material object may mean either (i) that the agreement refers or (ii) that it makes an identifying reference.[82] Consider three agreements: to murder the Prime Minister, to murder some vivisectors, to murder the Man in the Moon. The first has a material object in both senses, as it refers to a person in a way that identifies him; the second has one in sense (i) but not sense (ii), as it refers to vivisectors but does not identify any one; and the third has a material object in neither sense, as there is no Man in the Moon to which the agreement can refer.[83] The phrase 'the particular money' supports a reading of the quoted passage in terms of (ii).

This needs refinement, given that the content of an agreement between X and Y is typically a proposition of the form 'X does Ax and Y does Ay' (see section 1.21). If an expression that makes an identifying reference (a name or pronoun, say) is substituted for 'X' or 'Y', the agreement in question makes an identifying reference: if you and I agree that you and I will murder the Man in the Moon, our agreement makes such references to you and me. (By contrast, 'Ax' and 'Ay' are usually not proxies for expressions that identify token actions;[84] in the example just given, the agreement does not identify a particular murdering. Compare section 9.1.) It is therefore necessary to specify the class in respect of which reference succeeds or fails: an agreement has a material object if and only if it refers, or makes an identifying reference, to one or more things in that class.

One idea is that the class contains only the victim or victims of the relevant substantive crime. That is unsatisfactory for various reasons. First, some crimes – money-laundering is an example – have no victims in any clear sense, and so for these the class is empty. It follows that an agreement to commit such a crime has no material object and hence, according to

82 On an alternative definition it means that the agreement is de re rather than de dicto; but this terminology covers several distinctions and it appears that, whichever one is applied, the principle in *Harmer* faces objections similar to those raised in the main text below. For introductions to the de dicto / de re distinctions and to the theory of reference, see respectively Gallois (1998) and Devitt (1998).

83 *Pace* Meinong: see Chap. 3 n. 40 above.

84 See Chap. 5 n. 18 above and n. 133 below.

Harmer, is not conspiratorial. That conflicts with the proposition, clearly implied in the quoted passage, that the agreement in *Harmer* had a material object. Second, even if there is an agreement to murder, there is no victim if the agreement is not carried out. It follows, absurdly, that an agreement, not carried out, to murder an identified person has no material object and hence again, according to *Harmer*, is not conspiratorial. It will not do to reply that there is still an *intended* victim: as already noted, the parties to the agreement may not intend to perform the murder. Third, the definition of the class in terms of victims, actual or intended, does not fit the view, likewise clearly implied in the passage, that the material object of the agreement in *Harmer* was money, for the money was not a victim.

A simpler idea is that the class contains everything but the parties to the agreement; this implies that an agreement to murder the Man in the Moon by hitting him with the Koh-i-Noor diamond has a material object, since the agreement makes identifying reference to the diamond, which falls in the class. Whatever the best definition of the class, it is clear that in English law an identifying reference to a member of the class is not needed in order for an agreement to be conspiratorial; for example, an agreement to plant bombs may be conspiratorial whether or not the parties make further agreements to plant particular bombs at particular places and times.[85] It is also at best doubtful whether non-identifying reference is necessary: if X and Y agree to kill anyone who comes round the corner, but no one does, it is arguable that they conspire to murder.

9.26 Conditionality

The agreement just mentioned is implicitly conditional: the parties agree that if anyone comes round the corner they will kill him. The application of section 1(1) CLA to conditional agreements causes problems,[86] in

85 See *Greenfield* (1973) 57 Cr. App. R. 849; *Coughlan* (1976) 63 Cr. App. R. 33; M. Levi and Smith (2002), 16; Ormerod (2008), 403, 405; Simester et al. (2010), 308. Compare *Prior* (n. 42 above), para. 34.

86 See Alexander and Kessler (1997); Allen (2009), 287 f.; Ashworth (2009), 454 f.; Broderick (1985); Clarkson et al. (2010), 482 ff.; Herring (2010), 806 f.; Hooper and Ormerod (2011), para. A6.40; Law Commission (2007), pt. 5; Ormerod (2008), 409 ff.; Richardson (2011), paras. 33–6 f.; Simester et al. (2010), 307 f.; J. Smith (1977), 606 ff.; J. Smith (1985), 442 f.; G. Williams (1983), 356; Yaffe (2004), 276 f. Some of these works concern conditional intention or purpose (a matter of mens rea), rather than agreement; the distinction is blurred in much of the literature on conditionality in conspiracies. On the difficulty of distinguishing mens rea from actus reus, see section 9.2 above.

part because of the word 'necessarily' in paragraph (a). It might be said that the carrying out of the present agreement in accordance with the intentions of X and Y does not necessarily involve the commission of an offence, because if no one comes round the corner the parties carry out the agreement without killing anyone. A possible response is to deny that 'necessarily' means 'inevitably',[87] but that seems to be a distinction with no significant difference. A better response is to deny that in those circumstances the agreement is carried out. This response is reinforced by identifying carrying out with performance, in the sense given in the Introduction, and by distinguishing performance from those kinds of compliance – one was considered in section 1.22 – for which it is true that, in the circumstances described, the parties comply.

Some commentators maintain that problems of this nature are rife, as every conspiratorial agreement is explicitly or implicitly conditional:[88] an agreement to rob the bank is implicitly conditional on its not being the case that the police are there.[89] Two distinctions need to be made, between internal and external conditionality[90] of the agreement and between conditionality of the agreement and conditionality of performance.[91] (For the internal/external distinction, see section 1.1; on respects in which

87 See *Jackson* [1985] Crim. LR 442; Herring (2010), 807.

88 See J. Smith (1985), 443. Some argue from the premiss that an intention or purpose is directed towards the future to the conclusion that it is conditional: Alexander and Kessler (1997), 1172 f., 1181; Broderick (1985), 899. The idea presumably is that the intention might cease to exist before the time for the performance of the action intended. That is a point about external conditionality of the intention and the action, not internal conditionality of the intention. See the main text below for corresponding distinctions about the conditionality of agreement.

89 A frequently used example: see *Mills* (n. 68 above), 54; *Saik* (n. 24 above), para. 5; Clarkson et al. (2010), 482; Herring (2010), 807; Macdonald and Thompson (2003), 99; Richardson (2011), para. 33–6.

90 Alexander and Kessler (1997), 1139 f. gives a version of the distinction in the case of purposes. The formulation is unclear but appears to confuse the questions whether the condition is part of the purpose's content and whether it is contemplated by the subject. Normally, if the answer to the former is yes, then – on a liberal enough reading of 'contemplated' – so is the answer to the latter, but the converse is untrue; for example, X may have the internally unconditional purpose of robbing a bank but reflect that if certain conditions obtained – such as his not wanting any money – then he would not have that purpose.

91 Ashworth (2009), 454 f. fails to draw the latter distinction: 'this unduly concrete term ["necessarily"] seems to run counter to the proposition that all agreements are conditional in some way or another, and thus to ignore the possibility of an unexpected failure (the bomb which fails to detonate, the shot which misses, etc.)'. The next sentence talks of 'fallible' agreements. Unexpected failure or fallibility bears on conditionality of performance, not of the agreement. Ashworth might reply that 'in some way or another'

agreements are conditional, section 2.63.) Suppose that X says to Y 'Let's rob the bank' and Y replies 'Yes, let's do it'. They may mean no more than they say, in which case the content of the agreement is not a conditional proposition and so the agreement is not internally conditional. It is externally conditional, as all agreements are, in the sense that there are certain conditions on which it exists; for example, as noted in section 2.63, it would not exist if X and Y did not exist, and it ceases to exist when the conditions for its termination are met. Assume that if, on arriving at the bank, X and Y find the police there they do not carry out the robbery: then performance is conditional on the police's absence.

The question is how to separate those internal conditions that do from those that do not prevent an agreement from falling within section 1(1) CLA.[92] It might be suggested that some internally conditional agreements are easily dealt with as they are logically equivalent to unconditional agreements. Suppose that X and Y agree that even if Z is unarmed they will kill him. 'P even if Q' is equivalent to 'P whether or not Q', which is equivalent to 'P if Q, and P if not Q', which is equivalent to P.[93] Hence, the argument runs, X and Y agree to kill Z tout court, in which case – given other conditions – the agreement falls within section 1(1).[94] This inference makes the debatable assumption that agreement is closed under logical equivalence; the assumption is the less plausible, the weaker the concept of equivalence used. (On closure properties of agreement, see section 5.32.)

The application of section 1(1) CLA to some internally conditional agreements is uncontroversial – it seems clear, absent unusual circumstances, that the provision covers an agreement <to rob the bank provided that the police are not there> but not one <to rob the bank provided that each of the parties wins the National Lottery jackpot>[95] – but a general

an agreement is conditional if performance of it is. There is the same confusion in J. Smith (1985), 443.

92 For various kinds of internal condition (mainly of intention rather than agreement), see *Saik* (n. 24 above), paras. 97, 121; Broderick (1985), 899; K. Campbell (1982), 84 f.; Ormerod (2006), 221 ff.

93 This is implicitly recognised in *Saik* (n. 24 above), paras. 98 f.; K. Campbell (1982), 84 f.; Ormerod (2006), 224.

94 Law Commission (2007), paras. 5.3, 5.23 ff. proposes that such cases be treated as ones of recklessness rather than of conditionality. See further n. 112 below.

95 For other fanciful conditions, see *Saik* (n. 24 above), para. 5; Broderick (1985), 899, 903. In *Saik* it was stated that 'the condition could be so far-fetched that it would cast doubt on the genuineness of a conspirator's expressed intention to do an unlawful act'. Whether or not that is true, the same does not apply to the genuineness of the agreement. As to

principle of distinction is elusive. At one extreme it has been asserted that any internal conditionality,[96] at the other extreme that none,[97] puts an agreement outside section 1(1). Other proposals are that whether an agreement falls within the provision depends on (dependence here can be explicated in various ways) the probability, or the parties' estimate of it, that the condition will be met;[98] the condition's not being substantial;[99] the project's being intrinsically criminal;[100] the agreement's not being part of a wider agreement;[101] its having an unconditional component or being analysable into two agreements, one of which is not internally

intention, suppose that X says that provided that P he will φ. Its being highly unlikely that P is neither necessary nor sufficient to raise a doubt that X intends to φ: it is unnecessary, as there may be other reasons for doubt; it is insufficient, as it may be clear that X wrongly believes it to be highly likely that P. Even if X's believing (rightly or wrongly) that P is highly unlikely is enough to cast doubt on his intention to φ, it is a further question whether his having that belief casts doubt on his conditional intention, to φ provided that P. One argument that it does might use the debatable premisses that intentions are, or are similar to, plans (see n. 73 above) and that plans concern only outcomes which the planner believes to be reasonably likely. For the bearing on a person's intentions of his recognition of the virtual certainty of a consequence, rather than a condition, of his action, see Chap. 5 n. 29 above.

96 'Nor . . . is it conspiracy to agree to commit the crime if certain conditions are met, because then the agreement is not complete but dependent on the perfection of a future condition': Ferguson (1986a), 225. Depending on the meaning of 'complete', that is either false or empty. If X offers to Y, and Y accepts, that if P then they will φ, then – on the other conditions in the offer–acceptance model – nothing further is needed for them to agree, and so in that natural sense their agreement is complete. If 'complete' means 'not internally conditional', Ferguson's claim is a tautology. If 'complete' means 'not externally conditional', no agreement is complete, for, as shown in the main text above, all agreements have external conditions. Where an external necessary condition is not met, the agreement is not merely incomplete: it does not exist. The view proposed by Ferguson was rejected in *Mills* (n. 68 above), 54.

97 See Simester et al. (2010), 312.

98 See Broderick (1985). For objections, see Alexander and Kessler (1997), 1143 ff. Compare n. 95 above.

99 Richardson (2011), para. 33–6, following *Mills* (n. 68 above), 54 f., maintains that where there is a substantial reservation 'the arrangement may amount only to negotiation falling short of conspiracy'. On the confusion between the question whether there has been a transition from negotiation to agreement and the question whether the agreement is conditional or unconditional, see n. 68 above.

100 See Simester et al. (2010), 307.

101 J. Smith (1985), 443 finds this principle in the 'driving to Edinburgh' example in *Reed* [1982] Crim LR 819, 820 – an example that can be interpreted in various ways: see Allen (2009), 287; Ashworth (2009), 455; Hooper and Ormerod (2011), para. A6.40; Ormerod (2005), 371 f.; Richardson (2011), paras. 33–6 f.; Simester et al. (2010), 307 f., 311; n. 107 below.

conditional[102] (this raises questions about the identity and logical properties of agreements, as to which see sections 5.2–5.31); the main object of the agreement;[103] the condition's not casting doubt on the genuineness of a party's intention to do an unlawful act;[104] the necessity of committing a crime in order to attain the parties' goal[105] or to pursue the course of conduct to a successful conclusion;[106] the intrinsic rather than contingent nature of that necessity;[107] the parties' not hoping that the condition is not met, or their not regretting that it is met;[108] or their being dangerous or culpable.[109]

Each of these proposals faces objections,[110] and I can offer no better solution. Part of the trouble is the wording of section 1 CLA, but there is a more general problem of policy – the problem of identifying the category of agreements fit for criminalisation as conspiracies. A despairing conclusion would be that there is no principled way of specifying a subclass of internal conditions that exclude conspiracy, in which case it might be maintained, as above, that no internally conditional agreement is conspiratorial. That is a slippery slope, for it might then be argued further that, since for the purposes of the criminal law[111] there is no relevant difference between unconditional agreements and some internally conditional ones, conspiracy should be removed from the list of crimes. That argument could be reinforced by other arguments against the recognition of inchoate offences[112] (see section 9.1).

102 See Allen (2009), 287 f.; Simester et al. (2010), 311. Compare the question in section 9.24 above on the identity of courses of conduct. See also the discussion, in section 5.31 above, of conjunctive agreements.

103 See Allen (2009), 287. Compare 'the true object of the agreement' in *Attorney-General's Reference (No. 1 of 1982)* [1983] QB 751, a case on conspiracy to defraud.

104 *Saik*, para. 5, quoted in n. 95 above.

105 See Simester et al. (2010), 311.

106 See Clarkson et al. (2010), 486; Lynch (1978), 205; J. Smith (1977), 606 f.; J. Smith (1978b).

107 Simester et al. (2010), 311 finds this distinction in the 'driving to Edinburgh' example; see n. 101 above.

108 Rejected in Alexander and Kessler (1997), 1146 f.

109 Rejected ibid., 1147 ff.

110 Alexander and Kessler (1997) raises objections to several of the proposals.

111 For those purposes, see Broderick (1985), 896; Feinberg (1984); Feinberg (1985); Feinberg (1986); Feinberg (1990); Husak (1995), 155 ff.; Law Commission (2007), 1.5; Marcus (1977), 929 ff., 950: Sayre (1922), 412 ff.

112 Alexander and Kessler (1997) argues from the problems of conditionality – of purposes rather than agreements – to the conclusion that inchoate crimes generally should be eliminated and their domain covered, so far as appropriate, by liability for recklessness. (Compare the more limited proposal by the Law Commission in n. 94 above.) According to these authors, the source of the problem is 'the idea that acting with a purpose or forming a purpose to commit a future crime is itself a culpable act' (1182).

9.27 Complex conspiracies

The law on complex conspiracies is similar to the law on complex cartels, described in section 8.4.[113] A conspiracy may be complex as regards its content or its membership. As to content, it may (as the phrase 'offence or offences' in section 1(1) CLA implies) be a conspiracy to commit more than one crime,[114] or crimes in the alternative,[115] or the content may be in general terms that cover a number of crimes or provide for later specification of the actions to be done.[116] Complexity as to membership may be diachronic or synchronic. Parties may join or leave over the course of the conspiracy:[117] this is sometimes said to follow from the fact noted in section 9.23, that conspiracy is a continuing offence comprising the state of agreement;[118] but the continuing nature of the offence is at most

113 On the place of conspiracy in competition law, see Chap. 8 n. 5; n. 3 above.

114 On multiple-object conspiracies and the problems they cause, see *Siracusa* (n. 37 above); *Roberts* [1998] 1 Cr. App. R. 441; *Suchedina* [2004] EWCA Crim. 1944, paras. 14 f.; Orchard (1974), 341 ff.; Richardson (2011), para. 33–10.

115 See *El-Kurd* (n. 61 above); *Hussain* (n. 24 above), para. 27; *Suchedina* (n. 114 above), para. 14; Richardson (2011), para. 33–11 (confusingly calling an agreement to commit crimes in the alternative 'permissible'); J. Smith (2002), 407. Contrast the point in sections 8.3 and 8.4 above, that a breach of Article 101 TFEU can be proved by establishing the existence of an agreement and/or a concerted practice. In that case the probandum is (inclusively) disjunctive: that there is an agreement or a concerted practice. In the present case it is non-disjunctive – that there is an agreement – but the agreement has a disjunctive content.

116 See *Hammersley* (n. 26 above); *Coughlan* (n. 85 above), 35; M. Levi and Smith (2002), 16; Ormerod (2008), 403, 405; Richardson (2011), para. 33–57.

117 See *Hunt* (1820) 1 St Tr (NS) 172; *Murphy* (n. 26 above), 311; *Sweetland* (1957) 42 Cr. App. R. 62, 67; *Hammersley* (n. 26 above), 438; *Griffiths* (1965) 49 Cr. App. R. 279, 290 (see the passage quoted in the main text below); *Simmonds* (n. 28 above), 332; *Scott* (n. 53 above), 165; *Siracusa* (n. 37 above), 111; *Kuwait Oil Tanker* (n. 1 above), para. 111; *Saik* (n. 24 above), para. 113; Card (1973), 678; Orchard (1974), 341 f.; Spicer (1981), 120; Model Penal Code, section 5.03, nn. of decisions, pt. 15. See *Varelli* (n. 53 above), paras. 1 ff., on the possibility of there being 'a small group of core conspirators'. A similar principle applies to membership of an 'enterprise' within the meaning of the RICO legislation: see nn. 24 above and 126 below.

118 Macdonald and Thompson (2003), 100 appears to say not merely that one point follows from the other but that they amount to the same thing: 'it is settled law that a criminal conspiracy is a continuing offence. *That is to say* individuals may join and depart over time and they need not all be parties to the agreement during the same period' (emphasis added). Orchard (1974), 302 says that it is a 'result' of the continuing nature of the offence that people may join the same conspiracy at different times. Allen (2009), 281 uses 'As conspiracy is a continuing offence . . . '. J. Smith and Tausz (2002), 650 merely conjoins the points: '[c]onspiracy is a continuing offence and a person who is not a party to a conspiracy at the moment of its formation may become one by subsequently joining

necessary, not sufficient, for the possibility of a changing membership. At a given time a conspiracy may have the form of a wheel,[119] a fork, a chain, a net, or something more exotic.[120] It may include sub-conspiracies,[121] which in turn may include further conspiracies, there being no limit to the possible number of levels in such a hierarchy.

It can be important to ascertain whether there is a single complex conspiracy or only a plurality of simpler ones:[122] the answer may determine whether the charge is bad for duplicity,[123] how serious it is[124] and how wide a range of evidence is admissible.[125] In cases of complex membership the courts have used various phrases to try to identify the property or properties that create a single conspiracy from simpler arrangements. 'Common purpose' is often used,[126] but is unsatisfactory because

in it or aiding and abetting it'; there is a similar conjunctive formulation in *Doot* (n. 4 above), 821 (see also 823, 825).

119 Contrary to the headnote to *Griffiths* (n. 117 above), 280. See *Ardalan* [1972] 1 WLR 463, 470; Richardson (2011), para. 33–55.

120 For general statements as to the various forms a conspiracy may take, see *Anderson* (n. 13 above), 37; *Siracusa* (n. 37 above), 349 ('Participation in a conspiracy is infinitely variable'); Allen (2009), 290; Herring (2010), 809. On wheels and chains, see *Coffey* (n. 24 above), 446; *Saik* (n. 24 above), para. 113; Card (1973), 678 n. 30; Hooper and Ormerod (2011), para. A6.37; Law Commission (1976), para. 1.22; Richardson (2011), paras. 33–53, 33–55. On forks, see the Model Penal Code, section 5.03, nn. of decisions, pt. 13.

121 See the references in n. 117 above; also *Varelli* (n. 53 above), paras. 8 f. Compare the concept of a 'single overall agreement' used in EU competition law to deal with certain complex cartels. As noted in section 8.4 above, the scope of that concept is unclear; but it appears to cover similar structures.

122 On the difficulty of doing so, see Hooper and Ormerod (2011), para. A6.37; Orchard (1974), 341. For the proposition that the importance increases, the longer the conspiracy is alleged to have lasted, see *Greenfield* (n. 85 above), 857. See also Richardson (2011), para. 33–55, on the factual nature of the question; *Varelli* (n. 53 above), paras. 3 f.

123 In outline, the rule against duplicity is that no more than one offence should be charged in a single count; the detail is in rule 14.2 of the Criminal Procedure Rules 2010. For application of the rule to conspiracy, see *Hammersley* (n. 26 above), 210; *Griffiths* (n. 117 above); *Ardalan* (n. 119 above), 469 f.; *Greenfield* (n. 85 above), 857; Hooper and Ormerod (2011), para. A6.37; Richardson (2011), para. 33–52. Grant (2006), 1121 proposes a relaxation of the rule in this context. The rule concerns not the charge of a complex conspiracy, but that of multiple conspiracies, simple or complex.

124 See Orchard (1974), 341.

125 On the admissibility of evidence in this context, see Joshua and Jordan (2004), 655 f.; Macdonald and Thompson (2003), 100; Marcus (1992), 25 ff.; Orchard (1974), 341.

126 See *Marino* 91 F. 2d 691, 694 (9th Cir. 1937); *Varelli* (n. 53 above), para. 5, citing other US cases; *Coffey* (n. 24 above), 445; *Ardalan* (n. 119 above), 469; *Blodgett* 310 A 2d 629 (Del 1973); *Greenfield* (n. 85 above), 856; *Coates* (1989), 15 May, 3471/B1/88; *Siracusa* (n. 37 above), 349; *Saik* (n. 24 above), 113; Allen (2009), 281; Burgman (1979), 91; Card (1973), 678; Farrell (1992), 23; Marcus (1977), 951; Richardson (2011), paras. 33–53,

purpose is close to intention: the arguments in sections 5.11 and 5.12, that a person who agrees to φ may neither intend to φ nor intend to agree to φ, can be extended to show that parties may agree without having either the purpose of carrying out the agreement or the purpose of agreeing. (By contrast, the condition which proposition (199) (section 8.31) gives as sufficient for joint action, and which (219), (58) and (220)–(226) (section 8.5222) give as necessary and sufficient for narrow joint action, mentions goals, which in this context need not be distinguished from purposes. See the discussion, in section 9.21, of proof of conspiratorial agreement.)

One possible reply is that common purpose relates not to agreements generally but only to certain complex ones; but that does not work, because the arguments apply equally to complex agreements. Another is

33–68. On the insufficiency, for conspiracy, of common purpose without agreement, see Card (1973), 678; Law Commission (1976), para. 1.22. On common purpose in cases covered by the RICO legislation, see M. Levi and Smith (2002), para. 3.2; see further nn. 24 and 117 above.

Variants are 'common object/design/goal/intention/end/enterprise' (compare the concept of an enterprise in the RICO legislation (nn. 24 and 117 above)), 'unity of design and purpose', 'single, over-all, comprehensive plan', 'single design', 'same objective' and the pleonastic 'same common object' and 'share the same object': see *Parnell* (n. 26 above), 515; *Meyrick* (n. 26 above), 99 ff.; *Kotteakos* 328 US 750 (1946); *Griffiths* (n. 117 above), 290; *Simmonds* (n. 28 above), 332; *Varelli*, paras. 1 ff.; *Coffey*, 445 f., 450; *Ardalan*, 469; *Bastone* 526 F. 2d 971, 980 (7th Cir. 1975); *Kuwait Oil Tanker* (n. 1 above), para. 111; Abbate (1992), 56; Burgman (1979), 91; Herring (2010), 837; Orchard (1974), 339, 341; Ormerod (2008), 404; Richardson (2011), paras. 33–65, 33–70; Spicer (1981), 120; n. 34 above. Hooper and Ormerod (2011), para. A6.37 says that 'the alleged conspirators must each be shown to be party to a common design, and they must be aware that there is a larger scheme to which they are attaching themselves', leaving unclear the relations between (a) being party to a common design, (b) attaching oneself to a larger scheme and (c) being aware that one is so attaching oneself. See further n. 137 below.

Farrell (1992), 23 distinguishes a common object from an object in common and maintains that, where only the latter is present, conspiracy should not be charged. Farrell gives the example of 'a crowd arriving by train on the south side of the Thames and together crossing London Bridge all to go to work in the city. All have an object in common, which is to cross the bridge and to go to work, but no common object, because they have not agreed to go across together'. The implied definition of 'common object' is 'agreed object', in which case it is a term of art, for there is an ordinary sense in which it can be said that the commuters have the common object of crossing the bridge and going to work (even if they also have different objects – X to go to X's work, Y to go to Y's). The sense given to 'common object' by Farrell differs from that given to 'common purpose' by Card and the Law Commission: as indicated above, they held that common purpose is not enough for agreement. Farrell's sense is of little practical use in ascertaining whether a complex conspiracy exists, for usually the question is precisely whether the alleged parties all have an agreement; but Farrell might reply that he is not trying to identify evidence.

that it relates to the mens rea but not to the agreement: the common purpose binds separate agreements into a single conspiracy. That reply fails to fit the cases:[127] it is hard to square with the statements in *Ardalan*, that for there to be a conspiracy the parties must have 'entered into an agreement . . . to effect a common purpose',[128] and in *Coates*, that in a conspiracy 'the purpose of the agreement must be common to all who are said to be party to it',[129] and it implies that X may conspire with Y even if they do not agree with each other. The implication contradicts the assertion in *Griffiths* that 'in law all must join in the one agreement, each with the others, in order to constitute one conspiracy'.[130] The judge continued:

> They may join in at various times, each attaching himself to that agreement; any one of them may not know all the other parties, but only that there are other parties; any one of them may not know the full extent of the scheme to which he attaches himself; but what each must know is that there is coming into existence, or is in existence, a scheme which goes beyond the illegal act which he agrees to do.[131]

This condition is partly epistemic: the party *knows* that there is a scheme with other parties.[132] It seems that his knowledge of the others need

127 It also conflicts with the statement in Orchard (1974), 339 that 'common purpose' has 'merely been used to emphasise the need for true agreement'.

128 *Ardalan* (n. 119 above), 469, quoting with approval the judgment at first instance.

129 *Coates* (n. 126 above); see also Farrell (1992), 23.

130 *Griffiths* (n. 117 above), 290. See also *Saik* (n. 24 above), para. 113; *Varelli* (n. 53 above), para. 5; Law Commission (1976), para. 1.22; Richardson (2011), para. 33–53.

131 See also *Coffey* (n. 24 above), 451; *Barratt* (1996) Crim. LR 495; *Kuwait Oil Tanker* (n. 1 above), para. 111. US cases: *Falcone* 311 US 205 (1940); *Kotteakos* (n. 126 above); *Varelli* (n. 53 above), para. 5 ('one overall general scheme'). Commentaries: Farrell (1992), 23; Orchard (1974), 337, 341; Spicer (1981), 120 ('general scheme').

132 The epistemic aspect is emphasised in *Chrastny* (n. 67 above), 1383 ff. The question in that case was clumsily phrased: '[w]hether a defendant can be convicted of conspiracy when, though knowing that there are other parties to the conspiracy, the only other person with whom he or she agrees is his or her spouse' (1385). The dangling of the participle apart, the answer is too easy: if the defendant agrees only with her husband, she does not agree with the other parties to the conspiracy and therefore does not conspire with them; her agreement with her husband falls within the exception in section 2(2)(a) CLA (see section 9.4 below and Chap. 5 nn. 40 f. above); so she cannot be convicted of conspiracy. This reading is not excluded – rather the question is made murkier – by the use of the phrases 'positive agreement' (1383) and (in the headnote) 'actually concluded the agreement' (see n. 67 above). The real issue is whether, by agreeing with her husband, she agrees with the others. The judge recognised this in stating that 'if . . . a wife, knowing that her husband is involved with others in a particular conspiracy, agrees with her husband that she will join the conspiracy and play her part, she is thereby

only be existential, not identificatory: he must know that there are other parties, but need not know who they are.[133] Identification, rather than personal acquaintance, appears to be in question, although the words 'know all the other parties' could be read as concerning the latter.[134] By contrast, a requirement of common purpose need not be conceived epistemically: if X and Y have the same purpose but do not know this, there is an ordinary sense in which they have a common purpose.[135]

agreeing with all those whom she knows are the other parties to the conspiracy' (1384). See further the following note.

133 Counsel for the Crown, quoted in the judgment at 291, likewise used an existential locution. Compare *Saik* (n. 24 above), para. 113; Abbate (1992), 56; Card (1973), 678; Herring (2010), 837; Orchard (1974), 336; Richardson (2011), para. 33–53; Spicer (1981), 39 f. In the passage from *Chrastny* quoted in the previous note, the phrase 'those whom she knows are the other parties' is unhappy, for it suggests that the woman has identificatory rather than merely existential knowledge of those parties. By contrast, 'knowing that her husband is involved with others' is implicitly existential, and (on the same page) 'knows that there are others' and 'know that there are any parties' are explicitly so. See also *Varelli* (n. 53 above), paras. 1 f., 6 f. On identificatory knowledge generally, see Boër and Lycan (1986).

The Model Penal Code provides, at section 5.03(2): 'If a person guilty of conspiracy . . . knows that a person with whom he conspires to commit a crime has conspired with another person or persons to commit the same crime, he is guilty of conspiring with such other person or persons, whether or not he knows their identity, to commit such crime'. In some cases it is unclear whether crimes are 'the same' (compare n. 61 above): it is not the case (without more) that, if V and W conspire to murder X, Y knows this, and Y conspires with W to murder Z, then Y conspires with V – even though there is a respect, murder, in which the substantive crimes are the same; but, if V and W conspire to plant bombs in one part of town, Y knows this, and Y conspires with W to plant bombs in another part of town, do Y and V conspire to commit the same crime? The phrase 'the specific crime', in the explanatory n. to the provision (compare *Saik* (n. 24 above), para. 113, Law Commission (1976), para. 1.22), does not provide an answer. Nor is it helpful to distinguish types of crime from tokens of a type (see sections 9.1 and 9.25 and Chap. 5 n. 18 above). In the first place, when the conspiracy is formed, the crime has not yet been committed (see section 9.21 above), and so there is no relevant token. Even if that difficulty can be avoided by talking of a token or tokens that would exist if the conspiracy were carried out, the question can be rephrased in terms of tokens: would the planting of bombs by V and W and the planting of bombs by Y and W be elements of the same token? One way of dealing with hard cases is to apply the conditions that determine whether there is one conspiracy or more: on that approach, the identity conditions for conspiracies and for the crimes that are their objects partly coincide.

134 The same is true of 'knew each other' in *Meyrick* (n. 26 above), 101; see also the Model Penal Code, section 5.03, nn. of decisions, pt. 2. Both identifying knowledge and personal acquaintance are distinct from knowledge of someone's name, as to which see *Parnell* (n. 26 above), 515; *Meyrick*, 99; *Coffey* (n. 24 above), 445.

135 That the same applies to common design is suggested by 'conscious understanding of a common design', in *Coffey* (n. 24 above), 446. The phrase implies that parties may have a common design without consciously understanding that they do; it might similarly

Stronger senses of 'common purpose' can be specified that do import an epistemic condition: on a very strong one, to say that X and Y have a common purpose is to say that it is common knowledge between them that they have the same purpose. (On common knowledge, see section 1.23.)

The quoted passage is not clear[136] – 'scheme' in particular needs to be amplified and, in order to avoid the objection above, distinguished from purpose[137] – but, together with the actual and hypothetical cases discussed in the judgment,[138] it gives some guidance. It can usefully be supplemented by the list of factors which, in order to distinguish a single conspiracy from multiple conspiracies, the American Law Institute's Model Penal Code extracts from US case law. These include:

> the number of overt acts in common; the overlap of personnel; the time period during which the alleged acts took place; the similarity in methods of operation; the locations in which the alleged acts took place; the extent to which the purported conspiracies share a common objective; and the degree to which interdependence is needed for the overall operation to succeed.[139]

The list is better read as adding to than as merely explicating the conditions in *Griffiths*, although there may be some overlap in substance. As the passage is preceded by the words 'In determining whether evidence presented has established a single or multiple conspiracies, several factors

be held that they may have one without knowing that they do – although there are senses of 'consciously understand' and 'know' in which something may be consciously understood by someone without his knowing it, and vice versa.

136 Orchard (1974), 344 says that '[t]he idea that the existence of a "scheme" or a "plan" can provide a sufficient unifying element is objectionable as being too vague'.

137 It is doubtful that the judge would have recognised that distinction; at 292 the judgment cites with approval a textbook referring to 'a criminal purpose held in common between' the conspirators – the phrase used in *Meyrick* (n. 26 above), 102. The passage quoted from Hooper and Ormerod (2011) in n. 126 above leaves room for a distinction between a 'common design' and a 'larger scheme'.

138 See the examples of the accountant and the Post Office clerk, at 291 f.

139 Model Penal Code 5.03, nn. of decisions, pt. 13, describing this as a 'multifactor totality of the circumstances analysis' and citing case law. Law Commission (2007), para. 6.9, discussing the application of the rule against duplicity (n. 123 above) to conspiracies, identifies other relevant factors. See also J. Smith (1996a), 497 on the relevance of the character of the actions in question: 'The idea that parties agreed in 1992 to commit a series of burglaries over the coming years seems utterly far-fetched . . . It may be different where the allegation is that the defendants were carrying on an unlawful business like brothel keeping or drug dealing for such an activity may well be the product of a single agreement'.

can be considered', the listed items are arguably intended as categories of evidence, rather than of conditions for the existence, of a single conspiracy. They can, however, be taken as classifying existence conditions which form a cluster in the sense that, although not all of them are (and possibly none of them is) necessary, the members of certain subclasses are jointly sufficient, for a single conspiracy to exist;[140] as indicated in section 5.2, referring to such a cluster is a way of expanding the simple identity condition for agreements, presented there, into a condition that covers complex cases. By itself, an abstract list of this sort does not draw a clear line between a single conspiracy and multiple conspiracies.

Complex conspiracies are accommodated by the offer–acceptance model in the same ways as complex cartels are: see section 8.4. In particular, the parties to a complex conspiracy often stand in a certain relation to a set of normal agreements – the parties to which meet the conditions specified by propositions (36) and (37) (section 2.1) as sufficient for an agreement (or they meet them if minor adjustments to the conditions are made) – and their standing in that relation to those agreements is sufficient for them to agree. In one kind of chain conspiracy, for example, X makes an offer to Y which Y accepts and Y makes an offer to Z which Z accepts. It excessively stretches the meanings of 'offer' and 'accept' to say that the relation expressed by '. . . makes an offer to__which__accepts' includes its own proper ancestral and hence that, because X and Z are linked by such a chain, X makes an offer to Z which Z accepts. (Compare the similar objection in the case of the wheel agreement: section 2.612. On proper ancestrals, see section 1.23.) But, given that conditions CM and CS in (36) and (37) obtain as regards the offers by X and Y and their acceptance by Y and Z, X and Z have an agreement with each other by virtue of standing in a certain relation to normal agreements between X and Y and between X and Z: the relation could be specified by reference to the factors described in *Griffiths* and/or the Code.

The same approach works for a fork conspiracy in which X makes offers to Y and Z which they accept. The difference between chains and forks can be expressed in terms of the logical distinction, mentioned in section 9.1, between AE and EA propositions, that is, between propositions of the forms 'For every *x*, there is a *y* such that . . . ' and 'There is a *y* such that, for

140 For cluster theories in other domains, see Searle (1958); Searle (1969), 162 ff.; Searle (1979), chap. 3 (proper names); Davies (2006); Gaut (2000) (definition of art).

every *x*, . . . ':[141] for every member of the chain, there is a member such that one makes an offer to the other which the other accepts, whereas there is a member of the fork who makes an offer to every other member which the other member accepts. The usual concept of a wheel conspiracy makes a wheel the same as a fork[142] (similarly, the wheel agreement in section 2.612 could just as well have been described as a fork), but on a stronger concept – plausible in the abstract, but seldom if ever instantiated – a wheel amounts to a fork plus a looping chain: W makes offers to X, Y and Z which they accept; X makes an offer to Y which Y accepts; Y makes an offer to Z which Z accepts; Z makes an offer to X which X accepts. To continue the mixing of metaphors, the fork's prongs are the spokes, and the chain the rim, of the wheel;[143] an agreement of this sort could also be described as a net. Such conspiracies can be reconciled with the model in the same way. At the limit – where there are only two parties – chain, fork, wheel and net reduce to a normal agreement.

9.28 Collaboration

According to Simester et al.:

> It is not enough that X and Y agree a course of conduct which necessarily involves the commission of an offence. The commission of that offence must constitute a project that they have in common; their agreement must be indicative of a collaboration to achieve that end.[144]

This seems not to be intended as a condition distinguishing a single complex conspiracy from a plurality of simpler ones; rather, the authors appear to maintain that the requirement must be met in all cases of conspiracy, even those comprising a simple bilateral agreement. They give an example in which X and Y arrange a rendezvous at which X can

141 The distinction, which was introduced in section 3.4 above, is illustrated by the ambiguity of 'Every boy loves a certain girl' – an example attributed in Lemmon (1971), 100 to Peter Geach.

142 See, e.g., the definition in Card (1973), 678 n. 30.

143 For warnings about such metaphors, see *Ardalan* (n. 119 above) 469; Orchard (1974), 336 n. 56; Richardson (2011), para. 33–55; Model Penal Code, section 5.03, nn. of decisions, pt. 13.

144 Simester et al. (2010), 303 (see n. 33 above; schematic names changed). Compare Burgman (1979): 'there must be a uniting with another who also intends to carry out the plan' (87); '"agreement" has to be an agreement to work together toward one goal' (90). See also *Mills* (n. 68 above), 53 f.: 'there was an agreement in the sense that what both parties intended became an agreement with a common design'. It is hard to see how the words following 'in the sense that' give the sense of 'there was an agreement'.

hand over drugs for cash to Y: X's selling of drugs constitutes the crime of drug-trafficking, but there is no conspiracy between X and Y to commit that crime, as the project of selling drugs is X's alone.

There are several reasons to reject this thesis. It is no clearer than the talk of a 'common purpose' or 'scheme' considered in section 9.27; in particular, the authors leave doubt whether collaboration on a project is an element of, or something separate from, the agreement. The former is suggested by the words that precede the passage just quoted:

> Agreement is the essence of conspiracy . . . Yet the term must be regarded with some caution, particularly by lawyers familiar with the concept of agreement as used in other areas of law such as contract.

The latter is suggested by their writing that the agreement is 'indicative of' the collaboration: this implies that the collaboration is not an element of, but is evidenced by, the agreement. Here is another instance of the failure to distinguish clearly between evidence and conditions for existence,[145] in this case the issue being whether an agreement is evidence of something, not whether something is evidence of an agreement.

More important, it is not clear what the requirement adds to the truism that an agreement is necessary for a conspiracy. In the example, the parties can without strain be described as collaborating to achieve their common project of X's selling drugs to Y. It will not do to reply that 'project' signifies a purpose ulterior to the subject matter of the agreement,[146] for then the requirement excludes undoubted conspiracies, such as an agreement to murder someone without any further end in view. Reference to purposes also faces the objection discussed in section 9.27.

Even if the crucial phrases can be defined to capture the undoubted cases but to exclude the example, the requirement appears to be at best an unwarranted generalisation from the special case of complex conspiracies. The authority for its application to simple cases is weak. There is nothing on the point in section 1(1) CLA. There is contrary authority in *Drew*, where it was stated that Y could lawfully be charged with conspiring with X to commit the crime consisting of X's supply of heroin to Y.[147] The words from *Ardalan* that the authors purport to quote in support[148] do not occur either in the All England report of the case, which they cite, or in

145 See nn. 60 f. above.
146 Compare Chap. 5 n. 1 above, on ulterior intentions.
147 *Drew* [2000] 1 Cr. App. R. 91, 96. See also Ormerod (2008), 416, noting that under section 1(1) CLA a conspiracy may exist where only one party would carry out the substantive crime.
148 Simester et al. (2010), 303.

the Weekly report. *Sokoloski*,[149] from which they take their example, was before the Supreme Court of Canada and hence is not binding in English law; the majority judgment was that a conspiracy existed; the judgment of the minority did not state the requirement; even if the requirement was implicit in the minority judgment, it was arguably limited to the facts; and the minority acknowledged conflicting decisions in US law.[150] Other cases cited by the authors concerned complex conspiracies.[151]

9.3 Mens rea

Granted first that, subject to reservations noted in section 9.2, actus reus and mens rea are distinct and second that the agreement is conspiracy's actus reus, there is no need here to discuss at length the problems concerning its mens rea, for this is a book about agreements. A few points should be mentioned. Commentators differ as to the definition of the mens rea: Ormerod writes that it comprises an intention to agree, an intention to carry out the agreement, and intention or knowledge as to any circumstances forming part of the substantive offence.[152] Simester et al. give a list that is longer[153] but does not include all the items on Ormerod's: in particular, they do not state that the defendant must intend to agree. They may think that the requirement of such an intention is too obvious to be worth mentioning, as the intention follows from the agreement;[154] if so, they are wrong, for the reason given in section 5.12.[155] It is debatable whether, and if so in how strong a sense, the parties must *share* their intentions.[156]

149 [1977] 2 SCR 523. 150 At para. 10. 151 Simester et al. (2010), 282 f.

152 Ormerod (2008), 413 ff.; see also Ormerod (2006), 188. *Thomson* (n. 36 above) does not clearly distinguish between the first two intentions.

153 Simester et al. (2010), 312 ff. For other statements of the mens rea, see *Nock* (n. 10 above), 994; *Saik* (n. 24 above), para. 4; Allen (2009), 288 ff.; Ashworth (2009), 455 ff.; Clarkson et al. (2010), 479 f.; Herring (2010), 805 f. (expressed partly as an answer to the question 'what exactly must the conspirators know if they are to be said to have agreed to commit a crime?' and thus showing the difficulty, identified in section 9.2 above, of distinguishing mens rea from actus reus for this crime); Orchard (1974), 335; Richardson (2011), paras. 33–15 ff.

154 Compare Law Commission (2007), para. 1.39: 'an agreement to commit an offence implies an intention that it should be committed . . . .'

155 For examples, in the context of conspiracy, of agreement without intention to agree, see Ormerod (2008), 413, discussed in n. 157 below.

156 Conflicting answers are given in the citations in the Model Penal Code, section 5.03, nn. of decisions, pts. 2, 4. On shared intention generally, see Bratman (1999e); Gilbert (1996g); Gilbert (2000d); Searle (1990); Tuomela and Miller (1988); Velleman (2000b).

The first two elements mentioned by Ormerod go beyond section 1(1) CLA, which is silent as to an intention to agree.[157] Nor, as noted in section 9.23, does it say that the parties to the agreement intend to carry out the agreement;[158] rather, it provides for certain situations that arise 'if the agreement is carried out in accordance with their intentions'. On its face this admits the possibilities, first, that persons other than the parties carry out the agreement (compare the discussion, in section 9.24, of 'a course of conduct shall be pursued') and second that, although the parties have some intentions – for 'their intentions' appears to have existential import – and although 'in accordance with' implies that those intentions bear in some way on the carrying out of the agreement, the content of the intentions concerns something other than the carrying out of the agreement.[159] The second possibility appears to have been contemplated in *Anderson*,[160] where it was held that:

157 'Clearly, if X is unaware that his conduct is being construed by Y as an assent or agreement to a criminal proposal he will have no liability for conspiracy since he will not be intending to form the necessary agreement. It might be argued that there are two elements to this part of the *mens rea*. First, it must be shown that X intended to perform the acts / speak the words that were capable of constituting an offer or acceptance of the agreement. This provides a very limited scope for denial of *mens rea*, but this might succeed where X is so intoxicated that he uses language or actions without being aware of their likely interpretation. Secondly, the requirement of *actus reus* that there is an agreement suggests a corresponding *mens rea* requirement that X intentionally used conduct that he was aware might be understood to constitute an offer/acceptance in the non-contractual sense.' Ormerod (2008), 413 (schematic names (inconsistent in the original) are changed). This is partly false and partly obscure. As to the first sentence, it might be that, although X is unaware that his words are being construed by Y as an assent, X intends in uttering those words to make an agreement with Y; for example, X has no means of detecting Y's reaction but hopes that Y is taking his words in the intended way. As to the two 'elements', suppose that X utters sounds that in normal circumstances would be understood as the words 'Let's murder Z'. It is unclear which of the two elements includes which of the following intentions (or which others) on X's part: (a) to utter sounds; (b) to utter those sounds; (c) to utter words; (d) to utter those words; (e) to utter those words with their normal meaning and force; (f) to cause Y to understand that X is agreeing to murder Z. In a personal communication, Ormerod agreed with the suggestion that (a)–(d) are covered by the first element, (e) and (f) by the second.

158 For other statements that the mens rea includes an intention to carry out the agreement, see *Yip* [1995] 1 AC 111, 118; *Saik* (n. 24 above), paras. 3 f.; Clarkson et al. (2010), 486; Grant (2006), 1120; Herring (2010), 804; Hooper and Ormerod (2011), para. A6.43; Simester et al. (2010), 312 f.

159 In the definition of conspiracy in clause 48 of the Draft Criminal Code Bill 1989 (Law Commission (1989)), the parties' intention is 'that the offence or offences shall be committed'.

160 And, earlier, in Orchard (1974), 338.

> the necessary mens rea of the crime is . . . established if, and only if, it is shown that the accused, when he entered into the agreement, intended to play some part in the agreed course of conduct in furtherance of the criminal purpose which the agreed course of conduct was intended to achieve.[161]

Anderson is now widely regarded as bad law,[162] although one of the main objections raised – that it implies the supposed absurdity of a conspiracy that no one intends to carry out – appears to be based on the false assumption that if a person agrees to do something then he intends to do it (see section 5.11).[163] The objection can be recast to avoid the assumption, the principle then being that, even if no party to an agreement need intend to carry it out, if X and Y agree that <X does Ax and Y does Ay> then, if their agreement is conspiratorial, either X intends to do Ax or Y intends to do Ay.[164] The principle might be justified on grounds of policy: the thought is that the law has little or no reason to concern itself with agreements that are inert.[165] (Compare the objection, mentioned in section 9.1, to the recognition of conspiracy as a crime.) But it threatens to narrow the offence unduly, by excluding cases where such an intention is absent. The intention is naturally taken to be a prior intention existing at the time the agreement is made; but, as section 5.11 argued, such an intention may be absent even if the parties are sincere in making the agreement. The principle would be better revised to provide that the intention is appropriately conditional: for example, it might be one

161 *Anderson* (n. 13 above), 39.

162 The case is discussed in *Yip* (n. 158 above), 117 f.; Allen (2009), 288 ff.; Ashworth (2009), 456 f., proposing a reconsideration of the distinctions between conspiracy and complicity; Clarkson et al. (2010), 483 ff.; Ferguson (1986b); Fitzpatrick (1993), 1180; Herring (2010), 808 ff.; Law Commission (2007), paras. 1.52 ff., 4.23 ff.; Ormerod (2008), 414 ff.; Reed (2005), 3, urging clarification by the House of Lords; Richardson (2011), para. 33–15; Simester et al. (2010), 313 ff.

163 The assumption appears to underlie the versions of the objection in Allen (2009), 288 f. and Ormerod (2008), 414 f., but reasons might be given for rejecting this reading. Ormerod identifies as 'an absurdity, if not an impossibility' a conspiracy, not an agreement, that no one intends to carry out; compare Law Commission (2007), para. 1.39, and see further n. 179 below. Allen does not here write of intention-to but uses the passive constructions 'intention that the course of conduct be pursued' and 'intended the substantive offence to be committed'; compare the discussion, in section 9.24 above, of courses of conduct. (Ormerod uses both the passive form and 'intends to'.)

164 Compare Hooper and Ormerod (2011), para. A6.41.

165 O. Black (2003a), 224, O. Black (2003c), 74 f., and O. Black (2005b), 160 make a similar point about concerted practices in the context of Article 101 TFEU. On concerted practices, see sections 8.3–8.33 above.

of the conditional intentions proposed in that section as sufficient for sincere agreement.

The third element in Ormerod's description of the mens rea is intended to reflect section 1(2) CLA, which provides that:

> Where liability for any offence may be incurred without knowledge on the part of the person committing it of any particular fact or circumstance necessary for the commission of the offence, a person shall nevertheless not be guilty of conspiracy to commit that offence by virtue of subsection (1) above unless he and at least one other party to the agreement intend or know that the fact or circumstance shall or will exist at the time when the conduct constituting the offence is to take place.

The purpose of this provision is to ensure that, even if strict liability or recklessness is sufficient mens rea for the substantive offence, it is not enough for conspiracy;[166] the underlying principle seems to be that, since the commission of an inchoate crime does not inflict harm, a higher degree of fault is necessary to justify criminalisation.[167] Section 1(2) achieves its purpose clumsily; for example, it can be read as imposing a heavier mens rea for conspiracy to commit a crime of strict liability than to commit a crime for which knowledge or intention as to circumstances is required.[168]

166 See *Saik* (n. 24 above), paras. 6 ff., discussed in Grant (2006). Macdonald and Thompson (2003), 99 inaccurately describes this element of the mens rea as an intention that the substantive offence be committed. Barnard (2005), 1 says that section 1(2) CLA 'does no more than ensure that conspiracies can exist only when unlawfulness is *an ingredient of the agreement* rather than an *unknown and unforeseen consequence of it*' (emphasis in original). That formulation is problematic in two respects. First, it appears to confuse agreeing that P with intending or knowing that P. Second, 'ingredient' is unclear. The word seems to mean something that need not be part of the agreement's content: if, for example, X and Y agree to murder Z, the content of their agreement may just be 'We'll murder Z', which makes no mention of unlawfulness. If Barnard insists that an ingredient is part of the content, he could distinguish between referring to content and stating it – a distinction drawn in section 9.1 above – or between different concepts of content: see n. 15 to the Introduction above.

167 See *Saik* (n. 24 above), para. 95; Ashworth (2009), 456 f.; Ormerod (2006), 187.

168 See Elliott (1978), 205, stating that the apparently lax condition for mens rea in the latter case creates a 'scandalously paradoxical position'. As to the phrase 'intend or know', Allen (2009), 285 objects that '[i]t is not strictly accurate to state that X intends a fact or circumstance to exist if he has no control over whether or not it exists' (schematic name changed); this is similar to but distinct from the proposition, entertained in section 8.121 above, that necessarily a person's intentions are directed only at actions of his own (see also sections 5.32 and 9.24 above). For discussion of the problems arising from section 1(2) CLA, and for possible solutions, see Law Commission (2007), paras. 4.44 ff.; Ormerod (2006). For strictures on section 1 CLA generally, see n. 10 above.

9.4 Parties

There are various exceptions to the liability for statutory conspiracy. Section 2(1) CLA provides that an intended victim is not liable; section 2(2) that a person is not liable if the only other person with whom he agrees is his spouse[169] or civil partner, a person under the age of criminal responsibility, or an intended victim; and there is authority in case law for the rule that, absent other factors, a director solely responsible for a company's affairs does not conspire with the company if he decides to commit an offence in its name.[170] It is wrong to describe any of these as an exception to the requirement in section 1(1) CLA that a person agree 'with any other person or persons',[171] for in these cases one person does or may agree with another; as section 5.5 argued for two of the cases, they are not examples of an agreement with oneself.

Another rejected candidate for an agreement with oneself was so-called unilateral conspiracy, which is recognised in some states of the USA and in the Model Penal Code.[172] The concept is unclear,[173] but a rough definition is this: X does something with the intention of, and believing that he is, making an agreement with Y to commit a crime,[174] but in fact there is no agreement. A paradigm often mentioned is the case where Y is an undercover police officer who, in order to prevent the crime, pretends to agree with X.[175] Of the various objections that have

169 See n. 132 above; Chap. 5 nn. 40 f. above. 170 See Chap. 5 n. 42 above.

171 Ormerod (2008), 432 describes the cases in section 2(2) CLA as an exception to the requirement of two or more parties; Ormerod does not there distinguish parties from persons.

172 See Burgman (1979); Emanuel (2007), 186 f.; Grammel (2001); LaFave (2003), 500 ff.; Marcus (1977), 957 ff.; Marcus (1992), 21 f.; Robbins (1989), 27 f., 81 (explaining how the doctrine of unilateral conspiracy limits the defence of impossibility); Singer and La Fond (2007), 346 ff. These works cite penal codes and case law and give the arguments for and against the doctrine.

173 For example, Burgman (1979), 76 says that 'the unilateral approach assesses the subjective, individual behaviour of a defendant', leaving obscure the sense in which behaviour can be subjective.

174 'Guilt as a conspirator is measured by the situation as the actor views it; he must . . . agree (or believe that he is agreeing) with another . . . ': Model Penal Code, section 5.03, explanatory note. This suggests that belief without intention may be sufficient: compare Grammel (2001) and Singer and La Fond (2007), 348, which likewise talk only of belief. Marcus (1992), 21 talks of a 'culpable state of mind'. See also Burgman (1979), 93; Emanuel (2007), 187; Robbins (1989), 27.

175 For variations on this theme, see *DiDominick* 94 Misc 2d 392, 393 f., 406 NYS 2d 420, 421 (NY Sup Ct 1978); Burgman (1979), 77, 89; Grammel (2001) and cases cited there; Marcus (1992), 21; Robbins (1989), 80; Singer and La Fond (2007), 348; Model Penal

been raised to this idea, an obvious one is that the notion of a conspiracy without an agreement is self-contradictory: to be more precise, 'X and Y conspire' and 'X and Y do not agree' are contraries, i.e., cannot both be true.

One suggestion is that the example is best viewed not as a conspiracy but as an attempt by X to agree: the attempt fails because Y only pretends to agree.[176] In *Harmer*, the English case discussed in section 9.25, the court 'found the concept of attempting to make an agreement an odd one',[177] but it is not very odd: I attempt and fail to make an agreement with you if I press you to accept my offer and you refuse to do so; or we might both attempt and fail if we try to make an agreement over a bad phone line that prevents us from hearing each other. Nevertheless, if the example is to be caught by English law, the suggestion does not work, as English law does not include a crime of attempting to conspire.[178] A distinction might be drawn between attempting to conspire and attempting to agree: the parties only attempt to agree, but they do conspire. But that again leaves a conspiracy without an agreement.

There is no need to countenance the notion of an agreementless conspiracy in order to deal with the cases that it is meant to cover. Suppose that drug dealer X says to undercover officer Y 'How about this? I supply you with heroin and you sell it on the street' and Y says 'Done'. Since Y's purpose is to prevent the sale of the heroin, he does not intend to sell it, but – a familiar point by now – a person can agree to perform an

Code, section 5.03, nn. of decisions, pt. 41. In the context of English law, compare *O'Brien* (1974) 59 Cr. App. R. 222, 227; *Yip* (n. 158 above, discussed in n. 186 below); Law Commission (1973), para. 45; Law Commission (1989), vol. 2, para. 13.48; Law Commission (2007), paras. 1.51 ff., 7.38 ff.; G. Williams (1977), 1189.

176 Robbins (1989), 90, 111 reverses the point, stating it to be an advantage of the doctrine of unilateral conspiracy that it eliminates much of the need for charges of attempt to conspire; on the distinction between attempting to conspire and attempting to agree, see the main text below. Burgman (1979), 94 maintains that the availability of the charge of attempt – to commit the substantive crime rather than to conspire to commit it – removes the need for certain applications of the doctrine. In the English context, compare Ormerod (2008), 434.

177 *Harmer* (n. 76 above), para. 27.

178 Section 1(4) of the Criminal Attempts Act 1981. See Allen (2009), 300; Law Commission (1973), para. 45; Law Commission (1989), vol. 2, para. 13.48; Law Commission (2007), paras. 1.93 ff., 7.36 ff.; Ormerod (2008), 396, 434. The converse crime exists, of conspiring to attempt to commit a crime: Herring (2010), 805. For the position in the USA, see Grammel (2001); Robbins (1989), 54 ff. (which discusses double inchoate crimes generally).

action that he does not intend to perform;[179] he may likewise agree to perform it if he not only does not intend but intends not to perform it or even intends to frustrate or sabotage its performance.[180] Absent special circumstances,[181] the exchange between X and Y is an offer and acceptance

179 'There may be many situations in which perfectly respectable citizens, more particularly those concerned with law enforcement, may enter into agreements that a course of conduct shall be pursued which involve commission of a crime without the least intention of playing any part in furtherance of the ostensibly agreed criminal objective, but rather with the purpose of exposing and frustrating the criminal purpose of the other parties to the agreement. . . . The mens rea implicit in the offence of statutory conspiracy must clearly be such as to recognise the innocence of such a person, notwithstanding that he will, in literal terms, be obliged to agree that a course of conduct be pursued involving the commission of an offence': *Anderson* (n. 13 above), 38 f. The phrases 'enter into agreements' and 'he will, in literal terms, be obliged to agree' appear to acknowledge that a person can agree to do something that he does not intend to do, but the point is blurred by 'ostensibly agreed'.

Although Ormerod distinguishes the agreement, as actus reus, from the intention to carry it out, as part of the mens rea, he loses sight of the distinction at this point. He imagines a case in which 'Y purports to conspire with X but has no intention of going through with the plan' – for the present purpose there is no need to distinguish an intention of going through with the plan from an intention to carry out the agreement (compare the corresponding point in section 9.23 above, about an intention to carry out the design) – and rejects the suggestion that the application of an objective, contractual concept of agreement would allow the case to be categorised as a conspiracy; the rejection is based on the proposition, discussed in section 9.22 above, that the criminal law of conspiracy uses a subjective concept of agreement. Ormerod concludes, despite the difficulties he elsewhere identifies in *Anderson* (see n. 163 above), that '[i]f *Anderson* is followed and Y is held to be guilty of conspiracy notwithstanding his lack of intention, the problem disappears' (Ormerod (2008), 434, schematic names changed). There is no need to invoke objective agreement or *Anderson* in order to classify the imagined case as a criminal conspiracy, for Y's lack of intention does not exclude his subjectively agreeing.

Orchard (1974), 338 (quoting from *Thomson* (n. 36 above)) likewise fails to recognise this point; Orchard writes of 'a person who merely pretended to agree – a person who merely led the others to believe that he agreed to carry out the unlawful object, which [*sic*] he really "had no intention of doing anything of the kind"' (see also 343). For other examples of such failure, see Burgman (1979), 89; Marcus (1992), 21 (quoting the phrase 'secret intention' from a draft of the Model Penal Code); Robbins (1989), 80. Burgman maintains, still less plausibly, that for the existence of the agreement requisite for conspiracy it is necessary not merely that the parties intend to make it and to carry it out but that they have the specific intent required for the substantive crime (90).

180 Even if Ormerod is right that in English law there is a defence of intention to frustrate the object of the conspiracy (Ormerod (2008), 415 (n. 42 above)), it need not deny that the defendant was party to the conspiratorial agreement.

181 Notably the lack of certain 'input' or 'output' conditions of the kind described by Searle: Chap. 5 n. 10 above.

and hence, on the other conditions given in the offer–acceptance model, an agreement; the same would be true if the roles of X and Y were reversed. In certain respects the circumstances *are* special – in particular, Y is likely to be insincere; but, as noted in section 5.11, an insincere agreement is an agreement none the less. There is nothing in the example to imply that Y's utterance is not an acceptance but merely a pretence:[182] he is not joking,[183] say, or acting in a play. Situations can be imagined in which a person is only pretending to offer, accept, or agree: a document needs to be signed, he waves his pen near the page, but he makes sure that it leaves no mark. Likewise Y might make his utterance without pretending, but also without intending, to accept X's offer; in that case, if a person accepts only if he intends to do so (a possibility left open in Chapter 5), there is no acceptance and hence no agreement. But Y need not contrive such a situation in order to achieve his purpose.

It might be suggested that Y will want to pretend because he does not want to breach an obligation, that if he makes an agreement he will incur an obligation to perform it, and that he is not going to perform. (On performance obligations, see Chapter 3.) One reply is that, whether Y agrees or only pretends to, he breaks the related obligation not to deceive X, for implicit in the example is the fact that Y deceives X into believing that Y will, on certain conditions, sell the drug. Possible counter-replies are that it is worse to breach two obligations than to breach one and that in any event there is no simple obligation not to deceive.[184] There is no need to pursue the dialectic, for the initial suggestion is unrealistic: in these circumstances, Y is unlikely to worry about such an obligation to X.

182 Talk of pretending, feigning, purporting, supposing, fiction and so forth, and the use of inverted commas, is common in this context: see Burgman (1979), 77, 87, 93, 95, 97, 103, 106, 111, 113; Emanuel (2007), 186 f.; Grammel (2001) and cases cited there; LaFave (2003), 502; Marcus (1977), 959; Marcus (1992), 21 f., n. 119; Robbins (1989), 56, 92; Singer and La Fond (2007), 348. For similar remarks in relation to English law, see Hooper and Ormerod (2011), para. A6.43; Law Commission (2007), para. 8.15; G. Williams (1977), 1189; and the quotations in nn. 179 above and 186 below. One of the earliest conspiracy cases, the *Poulterer's Case* (1611) 9 Co. Rep. 55b, 77 ER 813, spoke of 'fake conspiracy'; see Spicer (1981), 25. On fiction in conspiracy, see the statement by Lord Diplock in *Bhagwan* (n. 44 above). On the concept of pretending, see Austin (1970c); Walton (1990).

183 See Chap. 5 n. 10 above.

184 On deception, see Chap. 1 n. 32; on the ethics of veracity, Chap. 3 n. 69 above.

Another thought is that Y needs to pretend so as to ensure that he is not himself guilty of conspiracy. The answer is that, on the account, in section 9.3, of the mens rea in English law, his lacking an intention to to sell the heroin – and hence, on assumptions made in section 9.23, his lacking an intention to carry out the agreement – entails that he lacks the mens rea and hence is not guilty; a similar answer is available if such an intention is conceived, as suggested in section 9.3, in conditional terms. The English cases contain authority for the principle that, if either party to an agreement is to be guilty of conspiracy, both must intend to carry it out,[185] and so an exception must be read into the principle if X is to be liable; but that modification of the law, if it is one, concerns only the mens rea and does not touch the truism that a conspiracy requires an agreement. An appeal to mens rea does not cover a variant of the example, in which Y does intend – conditionally or not – to carry out the agreement, his purpose being rather to prevent or limit the resulting harm or to forestall the commission of other crimes.[186] One way of dealing with such cases is to introduce a defence, possibly to the effect (suitably specified) that the defendant was acting reasonably.[187]

185 See *Doot* (n. 4 above), 822; *Yip* (n. 158 above), 118; Herring (2010), 805; Hooper and Ormerod (2011), para. A6.43; Law Commission (2007), para. 7.50; Ormerod (2008), 418; Richardson (2011), para. 33–15.

186 In *Yip* (n. 158 above), the Privy Council appeared to find that an undercover agent had conspired because, inter alia, he had intended to commit the substantive crime. The facts were distinguished from those hypothesised in *Anderson* (see the quotation in n. 179 above): 'There may be many cases in which undercover police officers or other law enforcement agents pretend to join a conspiracy in order to gain information about the plans of the criminals, with no intention of taking any part in the planned crime but rather with the intention of providing information that will frustrate it . . . The facts of the present case are quite different' (117 f.). It is unclear why the words 'pretend to' are included. They may evince the mistaken thought that if the agents do not intend to take part they do not agree to do so. Alternatively the idea may be that the pretence relates not to the agreement but to the conspiracy, the reasoning being that if (a) the mens rea of conspiracy includes an intention to carry out the agreement, (b) the agents lack that intention, but (c) they meet all the other conditions for conspiracy, then (d) they are pretending to conspire. But (d) does not follow from (a)–(c). For commentary on *Yip*, see Allen (2009), 71, 251, 290 f.; Ashworth (2009), 457; Clarkson et al. (2010), 367, 485 f.; S. Gardner (1995), 179; Herring (2010), 136, 676 f., 811; Hooper and Ormerod (2011), para. A6.43; Law Commission (2007), paras. 1.53 f., 8.3, 8.11 ff. (citing other cases that take a similar approach); Ormerod (2008), 96, 413 n. 239; Simester et al. (2010), 315 f. See also *Testouri* [2003] EWCA Crim. 3735, (2004) 2 Cr. App. R. 4.

187 For a proposal on these lines, see Law Commission (2007), pt. 8, which requires both action and belief to be reasonable, imposes a burden of proof on the defendant and argues that the defence should not be restricted to agents of the state. Law Commission (2006), paras. 6.1 ff., proposes a more limited defence. Section 50 of the Serious Crime

The conclusion is that unilateral conspiracy is either a monster or a commonplace – the former if it is a conspiracy without an agreement, the latter if it is an agreement which a party does not intend to carry out.

Act 2007 provides a defence of acting reasonably for the crimes of encouraging and assisting.

REFERENCES

Abbate, F. 1992. 'The Conspiracy Doctrine: A Critique'. In M. Gorr and S. Harwood (eds.), *Controversies in Criminal Law*. Boulder, CO: Westview.

Adams, E. 1975. *The Logic of Conditionals*. Dordrecht: Reidel.

Adams, R. 1987. 'A Modified Divine Command Theory of Ethical Wrongness'. In R. Adams, *The Virtue of Faith and Other Essays in Philosophical Theology*. New York: Oxford University Press.

1999. *Finite and Infinite Goods: A Framework for Ethics*. Oxford University Press.

Adler, J. 2002. *Belief's Own Ethics*. Cambridge, MA: MIT Press.

Ainsworth, L. 2008. 'Competition Regime: Chapter I Prohibition'. *PLC Competition Regime*. www.practicallaw.com.

Albors-Llorens, A. 1999. 'The European Court of Justice, More Than a Teleological Court'. *Cambridge Yearbook of European Legal Studies* 2.

2006. 'Horizontal Agreements and Concerted Practices in EC Competition Law: Unlawful and Legitimate Contacts between Competitors'. *Antitrust Bulletin* 51.

Albritton, R. 1968. 'On Wittgenstein's Use of the Term "Criterion"'. In Pitcher (1968).

Alexander, L., and K. Kessler. 1997. 'Mens Rea and Inchoate Crimes'. *Journal of Criminal Law and Criminology* 87.

Allen, M. 2009. *Textbook on Criminal Law*. 10th edn. Oxford University Press.

Allingham, M. 2002. *Choice Theory: A Very Short Introduction*. Oxford University Press.

Altham, J. 1985. 'Wicked Promises'. In I. Hacking (ed.), *Exercises in Analysis*. Cambridge University Press.

Alvarez, M. 2010. *Kinds of Reasons*. Oxford University Press.

Anon. 1948. 'The Conspiracy Dilemma: Prosecution of Group Crime or Protection of Individual Defendants'. *Harvard Law Review* 62.

Anon. 2005. 'Accommodating Asylum Seekers, Fraud and Conspiracy'. *Housing Law Monitor* 12.

Anscombe, G. 1963. *Intention*. 2nd edn. Oxford: Blackwell.

1974. 'Comment on Chisholm's "Practical Reason and the Logic of Requirement"'. In S. Körner (ed.), *Practical Reason*. Oxford: Blackwell.

1981. 'Rules, Rights and Promises'. In G. Anscombe, *Ethics, Religion and Politics*. Minneapolis: University of Minnesota Press.

1997. 'Modern Moral Philosophy'. In R. Crisp and M. Slote (eds.), *Virtue Ethics*. Oxford University Press.

Antunes, L. 1991. 'Agreements and Concerted Practices under EEC Competition Law: Is the Distinction Relevant?'. *Yearbook of European Law* 11.

Aquinas, T. 1894. *Summa Theologiae*. Rome: Vatican Polyglot Press.

Åqvist, L. 1967. 'Good Samaritans, Contrary-to-Duty Imperatives, and Epistemic Obligation'. *Noûs* 1.

Ardal, P. 1976. 'Promises and Reliance'. *Dialogue* 15.

Areeda, P. 1986. *An Analysis of Antitrust Principles and their Application*. Boston, MA: Little, Brown.

Aristotle. 1962. *Nicomachean Ethics*. Indianapolis, IN: Bobbs-Merrill Educational Publishing.

1983. *Physics*. Oxford University Press.

1912. *De Motu*. Oxford: Clarendon Press.

Armstrong, D. 1974. *Belief, Truth and Knowledge*. Cambridge University Press.

2004. *Truth and Truthmakers*. Cambridge University Press.

Arnull, A., et al. 2000. *Wyatt & Dashwood's European Union Law*. 4th edn. London: Sweet & Maxwell.

Ashworth, A. 2009. *Principles of Criminal Law*. 6th edn. Oxford University Press.

Atiyah, P. 1979a. 'Promises and the Law of Contract'. *Mind* 88.

1979b. *The Rise and Fall of Freedom of Contract*. Oxford: Clarendon Press.

1981. *Promises, Morals, and Law*. Oxford: Clarendon Press.

1982. 'Economic Duress and the Overborne Will'. *Law Quarterly Review* 98.

1986a. 'Consideration: A Restatement'. In Atiyah (1986d).

1986b. 'Contract and Fair Exchange'. In Atiyah (1986d).

1986c. 'Contracts, Promises and the Law of Obligations'. In Atiyah (1986d).

1986d. *Essays on Contract*. Oxford: Clarendon Press.

1986e. 'Executory Contracts, Expectation Damages, and the Economic Analysis of Contract'. In Atiyah (1986d).

1986f. 'Form and Substance in Contract Law'. In Atiyah (1986d).

1986g. 'Fuller and the Theory of Contract'. In Atiyah (1986d).

1986h. 'The Hannah Blumenthal and Classical Contract Law'. *Law Quarterly Review* 102.

1986i. 'Holmes and the Theory of Contract'. In Atiyah (1986d).

1986j. 'The Liberal Theory of Contract'. In Atiyah (1986d).

1986k. 'Misrepresentation, Warranty, and Estoppel'. In Atiyah (1986d).

1986l. 'The Modern Role of Contract Law'. In Atiyah (1986d).

Atwell, J. 1978. 'Ross and Prima Facie Duties'. *Ethics* 88.

Audi, P. unpub. 'A Clarification and Defense of the Notion of Grounding'.

Audi, R. 1989. *Practical Reasoning*. London: Routledge.

Audi, R. 2001. *The Architecture of Reason*. Oxford University Press.

1996. 'Intuitionism, Pluralism, and the Foundations of Ethics'. In W. Sinnott-Armstrong and M. Timmons (eds.), *Moral Knowledge?: New Readings in Moral Epistemology*. Oxford University Press.

Aumann, R. 1976. 'Agreeing to Disagree'. *Annals of Statistics* 4.

Austin, J. 1962. *How to Do Things with Words*. Oxford: Clarendon Press.

1970a. 'Performative Utterances'. In Austin (1970b).

1970b. *Philosophical Papers*. 2nd edn. Oxford University Press.

1970c. 'Pretending'. In Austin (1970b).

Axelrod, R. 1984. *The Evolution of Cooperation*. N.p.: Basic Books.

1997. *The Complexity of Cooperation*. Princeton, NJ: Princeton University Press.

Ayer, A. 1947. *Language, Truth and Logic*. 2nd edn. London: Victor Gollancz.

1956. *The Problem of Knowledge*. London: Macmillan.

Bach, K. 1987. *Thought and Reference*. Oxford University Press.

1995. 'Terms of Agreement'. *Ethics* 105.

1998. 'Speech Acts'. In Craig (1998), vol. 9.

Bach, K., and R. Harnish. 1979. *Linguistic Communication and Speech Acts*. Cambridge, MA: MIT Press.

Baier, A. 1985. *Postures of the Mind*. Minneapolis: Minnesota University Press.

1986. 'Trust and Antitrust'. *Ethics* 96.

1997. *The Commons of the Mind*. Chicago, IL: Open Court.

Bailey, D. 2006. 'Contours of Collusion: Football Shirts and Toys and Games'. *Competition Law Journal* 5.

2008. '"Publicly Distancing" Oneself from a Cartel'. *World Competition Law and Economics Review* 31.

Baker, G., and P. Hacker. 1984. *Scepticism, Rules and Language*. Oxford: Blackwell.

Baker, J. 1969. 'Combinations and Conspiracies – Is There a Difference?'. *Antitrust Bulletin* 14.

1993. 'Two Sherman Act Section 1 Dilemmas: Parallel Pricing, the Oligopoly Problem, and Contemporary Economic Theory'. *Antitrust Bulletin* 38.

Bambrough, R. 1968. 'Universals and Family Resemblances'. In Pitcher (1968).

Banks, D. 1997. 'Non-Competition Factors and their Future Relevance under European Merger Law'. *European Competition Law Review* 18.

Barnard, J. 2005. 'A Stupid Agreement: Conspiracy, Money Laundering and Objective Recklessness'. *Archbold News* 5.

Barnes, A. 1988. *On Interpretation*. Oxford: Blackwell.

1990. 'When Do We Deceive Others?'. *Analysis* 50.

1992. 'On Deceiving Others'. *American Philosophical Quarterly* 29.

2007. *Seeing Through Self-Deception*. Cambridge University Press.

Barnes, J. 1969. 'The Law of Contradiction'. *Philosophical Quarterly* 19.

Barnett, R. 1986. 'A Consent Theory of Contract'. *Columbia Law Review* 86.

Barry, B. 1973. *Political Argument*. London: Routledge and Kegan Paul.

Barry, N. 1986. *On Classical Liberalism and Libertarianism*. London: Macmillan.

Bayles, M. 1992. *Hart's Legal Philosophy: An Examination*. Dordrecht: Kluwer.

Beale, H. (ed.). 2008. *Chitty on Contracts*. 30th edn. London: Sweet & Maxwell.

Bealer, G. 1998. 'Analyticity'. In Craig (1998), vol. 1.

Beatson, J. 1986. 'Abandoning the Contract of Abandonment'. *Law Quarterly Review* 102.

1991. *The Use and Abuse of Unjust Enrichment*. Oxford: Clarendon Press.

2002. *Anson's Law of Contract*. 28th edn. Oxford University Press.

Beatson, J., and D. Friedmann (eds.). 1995. *Good Faith and Fault in Contract Law*. Oxford University Press.

Bell, J., and G. Engle. 1987. *Cross: Statutory Interpretation*. 2nd edn. London: Butterworths.

Bellamy, C. 2008. *Norris – The Case and its Implications*. London: Linklaters.

Belzer, M. 1998. 'Deontic Logic'. In Craig (1998), vol. 2.

Bengoetxea, J., et al. 2001. 'The European Court of Justice'. In G. de Búrca and J. Weiler (eds.), *Integration and Integrity in the Legal Reasoning of the European Court of Justice*. Oxford University Press.

Benn, S. 1971. 'Freedom, Autonomy, and the Concept of a Person'. *Proceedings of the Aristotelian Society* 12.

Bennett, J. 1954. 'Meaning and Implication'. *Mind* 63.

1965. Review of A. R. Anderson and N. D. Belnap. 'The Pure Calculus of Entailment'. *Journal of Symbolic Logic* 27 (1962), 19 ff. and Smiley, *Journal of Symbolic Logic* 30 (1959).

1976. *Linguistic Behaviour*. Cambridge University Press.

Bennett, M., and P. Collins. 2010. 'The Law and Economics of Information Sharing: The Good, the Bad and the Ugly'. *European Competition Journal* 6.

Benson, P. 2001a. 'Introduction'. In Benson (2001b).

2001b. *The Theory of Contract Law*. Cambridge University Press.

2001c. 'The Unity of Contract Law'. In Benson (2001b).

Bentham, J. 1948. *An Introduction to the Principles of Morals and Legislation*. Oxford: Blackwell.

Ben-Yami, H. 1997. 'Against Characterizing Mental States as Propositional Attitudes'. *Philosophical Quarterly* 47.

Bergström, K. 2010. 'The Implicit Rules of Board Games: On the Particulars of the Lusory Agreement'. *Proceedings of the 14th International Academic MindTrek Conference: Envisioning Future Media Environments*. New York: ACM.

Bermúdez, J. 2009. *Decision Theory and Rationality*. Oxford University Press.

Bernstein, M. 1998. 'Well-Being'. *American Philosophical Quarterly* 35.

Bigelow, J., and R. Pargetter. 1987. 'Functions'. *Journal of Philosophy* 84.

Binmore, K. 1994. *Playing Fair*. Cambridge, MA: MIT Press.

1998. *Just Playing*. Cambridge, MA: MIT Press.

Binmore, K., and A. Brandenburger. 1990. 'Common Knowledge and Game Theory'. In K. Binmore (ed.), *Essays on the Foundations of Game Theory*. Oxford: Blackwell.

Bishop, B. 2000. 'The Anti-Trust Epidemic – Causes and Prospects'. In Rivas and Horspool (2000).

Bishop, B., and S. Bishop. 1996. 'Reforming Competition Policy: Bundeskartellamt – Model or Muddle?'. *European Competition Law Review* 17.

Bishop, S., and M. Walker. 2002. *The Economics of EC Competition Law: Concepts, Application and Measurement*. London: Sweet & Maxwell.

Bittner, R. 2001. *Doing Things for Reasons*. Oxford University Press.

Bix, B. 1993. *Law, Language, and Legal Determinacy*. Oxford: Clarendon Press.

Black, M. (ed.). 1950. *Philosophical Analysis*. Ithaca, NY: Cornell University Press.

(ed.). 1965. *Philosophy in America*. London: George Allen & Unwin.

1983. 'Reasonableness'. In M. Black, *The Prevalence of Humbug and Other Essays*. Ithaca, NY and London: Cornell University Press.

Black, O. 1987. 'The Infinite Regress of Justification'. Ph.D. thesis, University of London.

1988. 'Infinite Regresses of Justification'. *International Philosophical Quarterly* 28.

1992. 'Communication and Obligation in Arrangements and Concerted Practices'. *European Competition Law Review* 13.

1993. 'Competition and Negative Obligation'. *European Competition Law Review* 14.

1994. 'Ends, Desires and Rationality'. *International Philosophical Quarterly* 34.

1995. 'Accepting a Relevant Restriction by Accepting Something Else'. *European Competition Law Review* 16.

1996a. 'Concertation and Co-ordination: A Distinction Without a Difference?'. *European Competition Law Review* 17.

1996b. 'Infinite Regress Arguments and Infinite Regresses'. *Acta Analytica* 16.

1996c. 'Legal Validity and the Infinite Regress'. *Law and Philosophy* 15.

1997. 'Per Se Rules and Rules of Reason: What are They?'. *European Competition Law Review* 18.

1998. 'The Relation between Reliance and Obligation'. In P. Kampits et al. (eds.), *Applied Ethics*. Kirchberg am Wechsel: Austrian Ludwig Wittgenstein Society.

2002. 'What Makes Me the Person I Am'. *Dialegesthai*, Nov. 2002.

2003a. 'Concerted Practices, Joint Action and Reliance'. *European Competition Law Review* 24.

2003b. 'Infinite Regresses, Infinite Beliefs'. In W. Löffler and P. Weingartner (eds.), *Knowledge and Belief*. Kirchberg am Wechsel: Austrian Ludwig Wittgenstein Society.

2003c. 'Joint Action, Reliance and the Law.' *King's College Law Journal* 14.
2003d. 'What is an Agreement?'. *European Competition Law Review* 24.
2004a. 'Agreements, Undertakings and Practical Reason'. *Legal Theory* 10.
2004b. 'Reliance and Obligation'. *Ratio Juris* 17.
2005a. 'Communication, Concerted Practices and the Oligopoly Problem'. *European Competition Journal* 1.
2005b. *Conceptual Foundations of Antitrust.* Cambridge University Press.
2006. 'Creating Identities, Creating Values?'. *Ratio* 19.
2007. 'Two Theories of Agreement'. *Legal Theory* 13.
2008. 'Agreement: Concurrence of Wills, or Offer and Acceptance?'. *European Competition Journal* 4.

Blackburn, S. 1984. *Spreading the Word.* Oxford: Clarendon Press.
1993a. *Essays in Quasi-Realism.* New York: Oxford University Press.
1993b. 'Moral Realism'. In Blackburn (1993a).
1993c. 'Supervenience Revisited'. In Blackburn (1993a).
1998a. *Ruling Passions.* Oxford: Clarendon Press.
1998b. 'Supervenience'. In Craig (1998), vol. 9.

Blackstone, W. 1765–9. *Commentaries on the Laws of England.* Oxford: Clarendon Press.

Blechman, M. 1979. 'Conscious Parallelism, Signalling and Facilitating Devices: The Problem of Tacit Collusion under the Antitrust Laws'. *New York Law School Law Review* 24.

Blustein, J. 1991. *Care and Commitment.* New York: Oxford University Press.

Boadway, R., and N. Bruce. 1984. *Welfare Economics.* Oxford: Blackwell.

Boër, S., and W. Lycan. 1986. *Knowing Who.* Cambridge, MA: MIT Press.

Bok, S. 1989. *Lying.* New York: Vintage Books.

Boni, S., and P. Manzini. 2001. 'National Social Legislation and EC Antitrust Law'. *World Competition* 24.

Bork, R. 1966. 'The Rule of Reason and the Per Se Concept: Price Fixing and Market Division'. Part 2. *Yale Law Journal* 75.
1978. *The Antitrust Paradox.* New York: The Free Press.

Bouterse, R. 1994. *Competition and Integration: What Goals Count?* Deventer: Kluwer Law and Taxation.

Boyd, R. 1991. 'Observations, Explanatory Power, and Simplicity: Toward a Non-Humean Account'. In R. Boyd et al. (eds.), *The Philosophy of Science.* Cambridge, MA: MIT Press.

Bradley, F. 1927. *Ethical Studies.* 2nd edn. Oxford: Clarendon Press.

Brandt, R. 1958. 'Blameworthiness and Obligation'. In Melden (1958).
1964. 'The Concepts of Obligation and Duty'. *Mind* 73.

Bratman, M. 1987. *Intention, Plans, and Practical Reason.* Cambridge, MA: Harvard University Press.

1990. 'What is Intention?'. In P. Cohen et al. (eds.), *Intentions in Communication.* Cambridge, MA: MIT Press.

1999a. *Faces of Intention.* Cambridge University Press.

1999b. 'I Intend That We J'. In Bratman (1999a).

1999c. 'Practical Reasoning and Acceptance in a Context'. In Bratman (1999a).

1999d. 'Shared Cooperative Activity'. In Bratman (1999a).

1999e. 'Shared Intention'. In Bratman (1999a).

Braucher, R. 1965. 'Offer and Acceptance in the Second Restatement'. *Yale Law Journal* 74.

Brecher, B. 2002. 'Our Obligation to the Dead'. *Journal of Applied Philosophy* 19.

Brewer, T. 2006. 'Three Dogmas of Desire'. In T. Chappell (ed.), *Values and Virtues: Aristotelianism in Contemporary Ethics.* Oxford: Clarendon Press.

Broad, C. 1946. 'Some of the Main Problems in Ethics'. *Philosophy* 21.

1985. *Ethics.* Dordrecht: Martinus Nijhoff.

Broberg, M., and P. Jakobsen. 2002. 'The Concept of Agreement in Article 81 EC: On the Manufacturers' Right to Prevent Parallel Trade within the European Community'. *European Competition Law Review* 23.

Brock, D. 1993. 'Quality of Life Measures in Health Care and Medical Ethics'. In Nussbaum and Sen (1993).

Broder, D., and S. Alexander. 2006. 'US: Procedure – US Supreme Court Appeals – Amicus Curiae Briefs'. *European Competition Law Review* 27.

2007. 'United States: Anti-competitive Agreements – Parallel Conduct'. *European Competition Law Review* 28.

Broderick, P. 1985. 'Conditional Objectives of Conspiracies'. *Yale Law Journal* 94.

Brogaard, B. 2009. 'Perceptual Content and Monadic Truth: On Cappelen and Hawthorne's *Relativism and Monadic Truth*'. *Philosophical Books* 50.

Bromberger, S. 1992. 'Types and Tokens in Linguistics'. In S. Bromberger, *On What We Know We Don't Know.* University of Chicago Press.

Broome, J. 1978. 'Choice and Value in Economics'. *Oxford Economic Papers* 30.

1990a. *Ethics Out of Economics.* Cambridge University Press.

1990b. 'Incommensurable Values'. In Broome (1990a).

1990c. 'Is Incommensurability Vagueness?'. In Broome (1990a).

1991. 'Utility'. *Economics and Philosophy* 7.

2000. 'Normative Requirements'. In J. Dancy (ed.), *Normativity.* Oxford: Blackwell.

2001a. 'Are Intentions Reasons? And How Should We Cope with Incommensurable Values?'. In C. Morris and A. Ripstein (eds.), *Practical Rationality and Preference: Essays for David Gauthier.* Cambridge University Press.

2001b. 'Normative Practical Reasoning'. *Proceedings of the Aristotelian Society.* suppl. vol. 75.

2002. 'Practical Reasoning'. In J. Bermúdez and A. Millar (eds.), *Reason and Nature*. Oxford University Press.

2004. 'Reasons'. In Wallace et al. (2004).

unpub. 'Ought'.

Brown, C. 2004. '*Bayer* v. *Commission*: The ECJ Agrees'. *European Competition Law Review* 25.

Brown, L., and T. Kennedy. 2000. *The Court of Justice of the European Communities*. 5th edn. London: Sweet & Maxwell.

Brown, P. 1966. 'Infinite Causal Regression'. *Philosophical Review* 1966.

Buchanan, A. 1985. *Ethics, Efficiency, and the Market*. Totowa, NJ: Rowman & Allanheld.

Buchanan, A., and D. Brock. 1990. *Deciding for Others*. Cambridge University Press.

Buckley, F. (ed.). 1999. *The Fall and Rise of Freedom of Contract*. London: Duke University Press.

Burge, T. 1977. 'Belief *de re*'. *Journal of Philosophy* 74.

Burgman, D. 1979. 'Unilateral Conspiracy: Three Critical Perspectives'. *DePaul Law Review* 29.

Burns, J. 1990. 'Rethinking the "Agreement" Element in Vertical Antitrust Restraints'. *Ohio State Law Journal* (1990).

Buzzard, J. 1978. 'Intent'. *Criminal Law Review*.

Byron, M. 1998. 'Satisficing and Optimality'. *Ethics* 109.

(ed.). 2004. *Satisficing and Maximizing*. Cambridge University Press.

Calvani, T. 2006. Review of Odudu 2006. *Antitrust Bulletin* 51.

Calvani, T., and J. Davies. 2006. 'Guest Editors' Note'. *Antitrust Bulletin* 51.

Cameron, J. 1972. 'The Nature of Institutional Obligation'. *Philosophical Quarterly* 22.

Cameron, P. 2008. 'Turtles All the Way Down: Regress, Priority and Fundamentality in Metaphysics'. *Philosophical Quarterly* 58.

Campbell, A. 1981. *The Sense of Well-Being in America*. New York: McGraw-Hill.

Campbell, A. H. 1954. *The Structure of Stair's Institutions*. Glasgow: Jackson.

Campbell, J. 1994. *Past, Space, and Self*. Cambridge, MA: MIT Press.

Campbell, K. 1982. 'Conditional Intention'. *Legal Studies* 2.

Cappelen, H., and J. Hawthorne. 2009. *Relativism and Monadic Truth*. Oxford University Press.

Card, R. 1973. 'The Working Paper on Inchoate Offences: (2) Reform of the Law of Conspiracy'. *Criminal Law Review*.

Carey, S. 2009. *The Origin of Concepts*. Oxford University Press.

Carlton, D., and J. Perloff. 2000. *Modern Industrial Organization*. 3rd edn. Reading, MA: Addison-Wesley.

Carroll, L. 1895. 'What the Tortoise Said to Achilles'. *Mind* 4.

Cartwright, J. 1984. 'An Evidentiary Theory of Promises'. *Mind* 93.

Cartwright, N. 1983. *How the Laws of Physics Lie*. Oxford University Press.
Carstensen, P. 1983. 'Commentary: Reflections on Hay, Clark, and the Relationship of Economic Analysis and Policy to Rules of Antitrust Law'. *Wisconsin Law Review* 953.
Cassam, Q. (ed.). 1994. *Self-Knowledge*. Oxford University Press.
Castañeda, H. 1977. 'Ought, Time, and Deontic Paradoxes'. *Journal of Philosophy* 74.
1999. *The Phenomeno-Logic of the I*. Bloomington: Indiana University Press.
Cavell, S. 1979. *The Claim of Reason*. New York: Oxford University Press.
Chamberlin, E. 1929. 'Duopoly: Value Where Sellers are Few'. *Quarterly Journal of Economics* 44.
Chang, R. (ed.). 1997. *Incommensurability, Incomparability, and Practical Reason*. Cambridge, MA: Harvard University Press.
2004. 'Can Desires Provide Reasons for Action?'. In Wallace et al. (2004).
Charles, D. 1984. *Aristotle's Philosophy of Action*. London: Duckworth.
Chellas, B. 1980. *Modal Logic: An Introduction*. Cambridge University Press.
Chisholm, R. 1957. *Perceiving: A Philosophical Study*. Ithaca, NY: Cornell University Press.
1964. 'The Ethics of Requirement'. *American Philosophical Quarterly* 1.
1974. 'Practical Reason and the Logic of Requirement'. In S. Körner (ed.), *Practical Reason*. New Haven, CT: Yale University Press.
1976. *Person and Object*. Chicago: Open Court.
Christiano, T., and S. Sciaraffa. 2003. 'Legal Positivism and the Nature of Legal Obligation'. *Law and Philosophy* 22.
Christman, J. (ed.). 1989. *The Inner Citadel*. New York: Oxford University Press.
Chwang, E. 2011. 'On Coerced Promises'. In Sheinman (2011c).
Clark, D. 1983. 'Price-Fixing without Collusion: An Antitrust Analysis of Facilitating Practices after *Ethyl Corp*'. *Wisconsin Law Review* 887.
Clarke, M. 1972. 'Obligations'. *Proceedings of the Aristotelian Society* 53.
Clarkson, C., et al. 2007. *Clarkson and Keating Criminal Law*. 6th edn. London: Sweet & Maxwell.
2010. *Clarkson and Keating Criminal Law*. 7th edn. London: Sweet & Maxwell.
Cohen, G. 1993. 'Equality of What? On Welfare, Goods, and Capabilities'. In Nussbaum and Sen (1993).
Cohen, L. 1964. 'Do Illocutionary Forces Exist?'. *Philosophical Quarterly* 14.
Cohen, M. (ed.). 1984. *Ronald Dworkin and Contemporary Jurisprudence*. London: Duckworth.
Colburn, B. 2010. *Autonomy and Liberalism*. New York: Routledge.
Cole, P., and J. Morgan (eds.). 1975. *Syntax and Semantics*. New York: Academic Press.
Coleman, J. 2001. *The Practice of Principle*. Oxford University Press.

Coleman, J., and S. Shapiro (eds.). 2002. *The Oxford Handbook of Jurisprudence and Philosophy of Law.* Oxford University Press.

Cooke, J. 2000. 'Changing Responsibilities and Relationships for Community and National Courts: The Implications of the White Paper'. In Centre for European Legal Studies Occasional Paper 4, *The Modernisation of European Competition Law: The Next Ten Years.* Faculty of Law, University of Cambridge.

Cooke, P., and D. Oughton. 1993. *The Common Law of Obligations.* London: Butterworths.

Cooper, T. 1986. 'Most-Favored-Customer Pricing and Tacit Collusion'. *Rand Journal of Economics* 377.

Coote, B. 1980. 'Duress by Threatened Breach of Contract'. *Cambridge Law Journal* 39.

Corbin, A. 1952. *Corbin on Contracts.* St Paul, MN: West Publishing.

Cosma, H., and R. Whish. 2003. 'Soft Law in the Field of EU Competition Policy'. *European Business Law Review* 14.

Craig, E. 1990. *Knowledge and the State of Nature.* Oxford: Clarendon Press.

(ed.). 1998. *Routledge Encyclopedia of Philosophy.* London: Routledge.

Craig, P., and G. de Búrca. 2003. *EU Law: Text, Cases, and Materials.* 3rd edn. Oxford University Press.

Craswell, R., and A. Schwartz. 1994. *Foundations of Contract Law.* New York: Oxford University Press.

Creswell, M. 1973. *Logics and Languages.* London: Methuen.

Crisp, R., and B. Hooker (eds.). 2000. *Well-Being and Morality: Essays in Honour of James Griffin.* Oxford: Clarendon Press.

Cummins, R. 1975. 'Functional Analysis'. *Journal of Philosophy* 72.

Dagger, R. 1982. 'Harm, Utility and the Obligation to Obey the Law'. *Archiv für Rechts- und Sozialphilosophie* 68.

Dancy, J. 1993. *Moral Reasons.* Oxford: Blackwell.

2000. *Practical Reality.* Oxford University Press.

Daniels, N. 1979. 'Wide Reflective Equilibrium and Theory Acceptance in Ethics'. *Journal of Philosophy* 76.

Darrow, C. 1932. *The Story of My Life.* New York: Charles Scribner's Sons.

Darwall, S (ed.). 2003. *Contractarianism/Contractualism.* Malden, MA: Blackwell.

2006. *The Second-Person Standpoint.* Cambridge, MA: Harvard University Press.

2010. 'Moral Obligation: Form and Substance'. *Proceedings of the Aristotelian Society* 110.

2011. 'Demystifying Promises'. In Sheinman (2011c).

Dashwood, A., et al. 1976. 'The Sugar Industry Marathon'. *European Law Review* 23.

Davidson, D. 1980a. 'Actions, Reasons, and Causes'. In Davidson (1980d).

1980b. 'Agency'. In Davidson (1980d).

1980c. 'Causal Relations'. In Davidson (1980d).

1980d. *Essays on Actions and Events.* Oxford: Clarendon Press.

1980e. 'Mental Events'. In Davidson (1980d).

1984. *Inquiries into Truth and Interpretation.* Oxford: Clarendon Press.

Davies, S. 2006. *The Philosophy of Art.* Malden, MA: Blackwell.

Dean, N. 2003. 'Creating a Stir'. *New Law Journal* 153.

de Chiara-Quenzer, D. 1994. 'To Lie or Not to Lie: Plato's *Republic*'. *Polis* 13.

de Gaay Fortman, B. 1966. *Theory of Competition Policy.* Amsterdam: North-Holland.

DeMarco, J., and R. Fox. 1992. 'Putting Pressure on Promises'. *Southern Journal of Philosophy* 30.

de Moor, A. 1986. 'Contract and Agreement in English and French Law'. *Oxford Journal of Legal Studies* 6.

1987. 'Are Contracts Promises?'. In J. Eekelaar and J. Bell (eds.), *Oxford Essays in Jurisprudence.* Oxford University Press.

1990. 'Intention in the Law of Contract: Elusive or Illusory?'. *Law Quarterly Review* 106.

Dennett, D. 1981. 'Intentional Systems'. In D. Dennett, *Brainstorms.* Brighton: Harvester Press.

Dennis, I. 1977. 'The Rationale of Criminal Conspiracy'. *Law Quarterly Review* 93.

DePaul, M. 1987. 'Supervenience and Moral Dependence'. *Philosophical Studies* 51.

Devitt, M. 1998. 'Reference'. In E. Craig (1998), vol. 8.

Devlin, P. 1959. *The Enforcement of Morals.* Oxford University Press.

Diener, E. 1984. 'Subjective Well-Being'. *Psychological Bulletin* 95.

DiLorenzo, T. 1985. 'The Origins of Antitrust: An Interest Group Perspective'. *International Review of Law and Economics* 5.

DiMatteo, L. 1998. *Contract Theory.* East Lansing: Michigan State University Press.

Diogenes Laertius. 1980. *Lives of Eminent Philosophers.* Cambridge, MA: Harvard University Press.

Dixit, A., and S. Skeath. 1999. *Games of Strategy.* New York: Norton.

Dodd, J. 2007. *Works of Music.* Oxford University Press.

Domat, J. 1713. *Les Loix civiles.* Paris: Pierre Debats.

Donagan, A. 1977. *The Theory of Morality.* University of Chicago Press.

Donnellan, K. 1967. 'Paradigm-Case Arguments'. In P. Edwards (ed.), *The Encyclopedia of Philosophy.* New York: Macmillan: vol. 6.

Downie, R. 1985. 'Three Accounts of Promising'. *Philosophical Quarterly* 35.

Downie, R., and E. Telfer. 1971. 'Autonomy'. *Philosophy* 15.

Dreier, J. 1992. 'The Supervenience Argument against Moral Realism'. *Southern Journal of Philosophy* 30.

Driver, J. 1983. 'Promises, Obligations, and Abilities'. *Philosophical Studies* 44.

2011. 'Promising Too Much'. In Sheinman (2011c).
Duff, R. 1990. *Intention, Agency and Criminal Liability*. Oxford: Blackwell.
Dummett, M. 1973. *Frege: Philosophy of Language*. London: Duckworth.
Duncan, O. 1975. 'Does Money Buy Satisfaction?'. *Social Indicators Research* 2.
Duncan-Jones, A. 1935. 'Is Strict Implication the Same as Entailment?'. *Analysis* 2.
Dworkin, G. 1988. *The Theory and Practice of Autonomy*. Cambridge University Press.
Dworkin, R. 1978. *Taking Rights Seriously*. London: Duckworth.
1986a. *Law's Empire*. London: Fontana.
1986b. 'Liberalism'. In R. Dworkin, *A Matter of Principle*. Oxford: Clarendon Press. 1986.
Earlenbaugh, J., and B. Molyneux. 2009. 'Intuitions are Inclinations to Believe'. *Philosophical Studies* 145.
Easterlin, R. 1974. 'Does Economic Growth Improve the Human Lot? Some Empirical Evidence'. In P. David and M. Reder (eds.), *Nations and Households in Economic Growth*. New York: Academic Press.
Edgington, D. 1991. 'Do Conditionals Have Truth-Conditions?'. In Jackson (1991).
Ehlermann, C. 1995. 'Reflections on a European Cartel Office'. *Common Market Law Review* 32.
2000. 'The Modernisation of EC Antitrust Policy: A Legal and Cultural Revolution'. *Common Market Law Review* 37.
Eilmansberger, T. 2004. 'Die Adalat-Entscheidung des EuGH'. *Zeitschrift für Wettbewerbsrecht*.
Eisenberg, M. 1994. 'The Principles of Consideration'. In Craswell and Schwartz (1994).
1995. 'Relational Contracts'. In Beatson and Friedmann (1995).
2001. 'The Theory of Contracts'. In Benson (2001b).
Elliott, D. 1978. 'Mens Rea in Statutory Conspiracy'. *Criminal Law Review*.
1982. 'Dishonesty in Theft: A Dispensable Concept'. *Criminal Law Review*.
Ellis, J. 1963. 'Source Material for Article 85(1) EEC'. *Fordham Law Review* 247.
Elster, J., and J. Roemer (eds.). 1993a. *Interpersonal Comparisons of Well-Being*. Cambridge University Press.
1993b. 'Introduction'. In Elster and Romer (1993a).
Emanuel, S. 2007. *Criminal Law*. Austin, TX: Wolters Kluwer.
Ennis, R. 1968. 'Enumerative Induction and Best Explanation'. *Journal of Philosophy* 65.
Ernst, D. 1990. 'The New Antitrust History'. *New York Law School Law Review* 35.
European Commission. 1997. *Green Paper on Vertical Restraints in EC Competition Policy*. *Common Market Law Review* 519.
Evans, G. 1982. *The Varieties of Reference*. Oxford University Press.
Evnine, S. 1991. *Donald Davidson*. Cambridge: Polity Press.

2008. *Epistemic Dimensions of Personhood.* Oxford University Press.

Faraji, F., and J. Pendharkar. 2009. 'Art of the Political Apology'. *Berkeley Political Review.* 23 Apr. 2009.

Farrell, S. 1992. 'Criminal Conspiracy'. *Legal Action.*

Faull, J., and A. Nikpay (eds.). 2007. *The EC Law of Competition.* 2nd edn. Oxford University Press.

Fawcett, E. forthcoming. *Liberalism: A Biography.*

Feinberg, J. 1965. 'Action and Responsibility'. In M. Black (1965).

1973. *Social Philosophy.* Upper Saddle River, NJ: Prentice Hall.

1984. *Harm to Others.* New York: Oxford University Press.

1985. *Offense to Others.* New York: Oxford University Press.

1986. *Harm to Self.* New York: Oxford University Press.

1990. *Harmless Wrongdoing.* New York: Oxford University Press.

Feldman, F. 1986. *Doing the Best We Can.* Dordrecht: Reidel.

Fellner, W. 1949. *Competition among the Few.* New York: Knopf.

Fels, A., and G. Edwards. 1998. 'Competition Policy Objectives'. In C. Ehlermann and L. Laudati (eds.), *European Competition Law Annual 1997: The Objectives of Competition Policy.* Oxford: Hart.

Ferguson, P. 1986a. 'The Agreement in Criminal Conspiracy'. *Juridical Review* 2.

1986b. 'Intention, Agreement and Statutory Conspiracy'. *Law Quarterly Review* 26.

Finnis, J. 1980. *Natural Law and Natural Rights.* Oxford: Clarendon Press.

Fish, S. 1989. *Doing What Comes Naturally.* Oxford: Clarendon Press.

Fisher, J. 2006. 'Criminal Law'. *Tax Journal* 821.

Fitzpatrick, D. 1993. 'Variations on Conspiracy'. *New Law Journal* 143.

Flathman, R. 1972. *Political Obligation.* New York: Atheneum.

Flume, W. 1975. *Das Rechtsgeschäft.* 2nd edn. Berlin: Springer.

Fodor, J. 1975. *The Language of Thought.* New York: Crowell.

1998. *Concepts.* Oxford: Clarendon Press.

2008. *LOT 2: The Language of Thought Revisited.* Oxford University Press.

Fogelin, R. 1983. 'Richard Price on Promising: A Limited Defence'. *Journal of the History of Philosophy* 21.

Føllesdal, D., and R. Hilpinen. 1970. 'Deontic Logic: An Introduction'. In R. Hilpinen (ed.), *Deontic Logic: Introductory and Systematic Readings.* Dordrecht: Reidel.

Foot, P. (ed.). 1967. *Theories of Ethics.* Oxford University Press.

1978. 'Morality as a System of Hypothetical Imperatives'. In P. Foot, *Virtues and Vices and Other Essays in Moral Philosophy.* Oxford: Blackwell.

Forbes, G. 1989. 'Cognitive Architecture and the Semantics of Belief'. In P. French et al. (eds.), *Midwest Studies in Philosophy*, vol. 14. Minneapolis: University of Minnesota Press.

Foster, M. 1957. '"We" in Modern Philosophy'. In B. Mitchell (ed.), *Faith and Logic*. London: George Allen & Unwin.
Fox, E. 1981. 'The Modernization of Antitrust: A New Equilibrium'. *Cornell Law Review* 66.
Fox, J. 1987. 'Truthmaker'. *Australasian Journal of Philosophy* 65.
Fox, R., and J. DeMarco. 1993. 'The Immorality of Promising'. *Journal of Value Inquiry* 27.
Frank, R. 2003. *Microeconomics and Behavior*. 5th edn. New York: McGraw-Hill Irwin.
Frankena, W. 1950. 'Obligation and Ability'. In M. Black (1950).
Frankfurt, H. 1999. 'Autonomy, Necessity, and Love'. In H. Frankfurt, *Necessity, Volition, and Love*. Cambridge University Press.
Franzosi, M. 1988. 'Oligopoly and the Prisoner's Dilemma: Concerted Practices and "As If" Behaviour'. *European Competition Law Review* 9.
Frazier, R. 1998. 'Intuitionism in Ethics'. In E. Craig (1998), vol. 4.
Fried, C. 1981. *Contract as Promise*. Cambridge, MA: Harvard University Press.
Friedrich, D., and N. Southwood. 2011. 'Promises and Trust'. In Sheinman (2011c).
Fuller, L. 1941. 'Consideration and Form'. *Columbia Law Review* 41.
Fuller, L., and W. Perdue. 1936. 'The Reliance Interest in Contract Damages'. *Yale Law Journal* 46.
Furmston, M. 2007. *Cheshire, Fifoot and Furmston's Law of Contract*. 15th edn. Oxford University Press.
Furmston, M., et al. 1997. *Contract Formation and Letters of Intent*. Chichester: Wiley.
Gallie, B. 1956. 'Essentially Contested Concepts'. *Proceedings of the Aristotelian Society* 56.
Gallois, A. 1998. 'De Re / De Dicto'. In E. Craig (1998), vol. 2.
Gardner, J., and H. Jung. 1991. 'Making Sense of Mens Rea: Antony Duff's Account'. *Oxford Journal of Legal Studies* 11.
Gardner, J., and T. Macklem. 2002. 'Reasons'. In Coleman and Shapiro (2002).
Gardner, S. 1995. 'Criminal Defences by Judicial Discretion'. *Law Quarterly Review* 177.
Gaus, G. 1998. 'Why All Welfare States (Including Laissez-Faire Ones) are Unreasonable'. *Social Philosophy and Policy* 15.
Gaut, B. 2000. '"Art" as a Cluster Concept'. In N. Carroll, *Theories of Art Today*. Madison: University of Wisconsin Press.
Gavil, A. 1991. 'Antitrust Casebooks: Ideology or Pedagogy?'. *New York University Law Review* 66.
Gazdar, G. 1979. *Pragmatics: Implicature, Presupposition, and Logical Form*. New York: Academic Press.
Geach, P. 1958. 'Entailment'. *Proceedings of the Aristotelian Society*. suppl. vol. 32.
1967. 'Good and Evil'. In Foot (1967).

Geanakoplos, J. 1992. 'Common Knowledge'. *Journal of Economic Perspectives* 6.
Gellhorn, E., et al. 2004. *Antitrust Law and Economics in a Nutshell*. 5th edn. St Paul, MN: West Publishing.
Gerber, D. 1994. 'The Transformation of European Community Competition Law?'. *Harvard International Law Journal* 35.
2001. *Law and Competition in Twentieth-Century Europe: Protecting Prometheus*. Oxford University Press.
Gettier, E. 1967. 'Is Justified True Belief Knowledge?'. In A. Phillips Griffiths (ed.), *Knowledge and Belief*. Oxford University Press.
Gewirth, A. 1998. *Self-Fulfillment*. Princeton, NJ: Princeton University Press.
Gibbard, A. 1990. *Wise Choices, Apt Feelings*. Oxford: Clarendon Press.
Giddens, A. 1984. *The Constitution of Society*. Cambridge: Polity Press.
Gilbert, M. 1989. *On Social Facts*. Princeton, NJ: Princeton University Press.
1996a. 'Agreements, Coercion, and Obligation'. In Gilbert (1996e).
1996b. 'Fusion: Sketch of a "Contractual" Model'. In Gilbert (1996e).
1996c. 'Group Membership and Political Obligation'. In Gilbert (1996e).
1996d. 'Is an Agreement an Exchange of Promises?'. In Gilbert (1996e).
1996e. *Living Together*. Lanham, MD: Rowman & Littlefield.
1996f. 'Notes on the Concept of a Social Convention'. In Gilbert (1996e).
1996g. 'On Feeling Guilt for What One's Group Has Done'. In Gilbert (1996e).
1996h. 'On Language and Convention'. In Gilbert (1996e).
1996i. 'Walking Together: A Paradigmatic Social Phenomenon'. In Gilbert (1996e).
2000a. 'Obligation and Joint Commitment'. In Gilbert (2000b).
2000b. *Sociality and Responsibility*. Lanham, MD: Rowman & Littlefield.
2000c. 'Social Rules: Some Problems with Hart's Account, and an Alternative Proposal. In Gilbert (2000b).
2000d. 'What is it for *Us* to Intend?'. In Gilbert (2000b).
2004. 'Scanlon on Promissory Obligation: The Problem of Promisees' Rights'. *Journal of Philosophy* 101.
2006. *A Theory of Political Obligation*. Oxford: Clarendon Press.
Gilmore, G. 1995. *The Death of Contract*. Columbus: Ohio State University Press.
Ginet, C. 1979. 'Performativity'. *Linguistics and Philosophy* 3.
Goble, L. 1993. 'The Logic of Obligation, "Better" and "Worse"'. *Philosophical Studies* 70.
Godfrey-Smith, P. 1993. 'Functions: Consensus Without Unity'. *Pacific Philosophical Quarterly* 74.
1994. 'A Modern History Theory of Functions'. *Noûs* 28.
Goebel, R. 1987. '*Metro II*'s Confirmation of the Selective Distribution Rules: Is This the End of the Road?'. *Common Market Law Review* 24.
Goetz, C., and R. Scott. 1981. 'Principles of Relational Contracts'. *Virginia Law Review* 67.

Goldman, A. 1995. 'Simulation and Interpersonal Utility'. *Ethics* 105.

2007. 'Philosophical Intuitions: Their Target, their Source, and their Epistemic Status'. *Grazer Philosophische Studien* 74.

Goldman, H. 1976. 'Dated Rightness and Moral Imperfection'. *Philosophical Review* 85.

Goldstein, A. 1959. 'Conspiracy to Defraud the United States'. *Yale Law Journal* 68.

Goodin, R. 1989. 'Laundering Preferences'. In J. Elster and A. Hylland, *Foundations of Social Choice Theory*. Cambridge University Press.

Goodman, N. 1973. *Fact, Fiction, and Forecast*. 3rd edn. Indianapolis: Bobbs-Merrill.

Goodman, N., and W. Quine. 1947. 'Steps toward a Constructive Nominalism'. *Journal of Symbolic Logic* 12.

Gordley, J. 1981. 'Equality in Exchange'. *California Law Review* 69.

1991. *The Philosophical Origins of Modern Contract Doctrine*. Oxford: Clarendon Press.

Goyder, D. 2003. *EC Competition Law*. 4th edn. Oxford University Press.

Grammel, T. 2001. 'Justice and Discipline: Recent Developments in Substantive Criminal Law'. *Army Lawyer*. Apr. 2001.

Grant, G. 2006. 'The End of the Affair?'. *New Law Journal* 156.

Green, G. 1989. *Pragmatics and Natural Language Understanding*. Hillsdale, NJ: Lawrence Erlbaum.

Green, L. 1988. *The Authority of the State*. Oxford: Clarendon Press.

1989. 'Associative Obligations and the State'. In A. Hutchinson and L. Green (eds.), *Law and the Community: The End of Individualism?* Toronto: Carswell.

2002. 'Law and Obligations'. In Coleman and Shapiro (2002).

Greenspan, P. 1975. 'Conditional Oughts and Hypothetical Imperatives'. *Journal of Philosophy* 72.

Grice, P. 1989a. 'Further Notes on Logic and Conversation'. In Grice (1989f).

1989b. 'Indicative Conditionals'. In Grice (1989f).

1989c. 'Logic and Conversation'. In Grice (1989f).

1989d. 'Meaning'. In Grice (1989f).

1989e. 'Meaning Revisited'. In Grice (1989f).

1989f. *Studies in the Way of Words*. Cambridge, MA: Harvard University Press.

1989g. 'Utterer's Meaning, Sentence-Meaning, and Word-Meaning'. In Grice (1989f).

1991. *The Conception of Value*. Oxford: Clarendon Press.

Grice, P., and P. Strawson. 1991. 'In Defense of a Dogma'. In Grice (1989f).

Griew, E. 1985. 'Dishonesty: The Objections to Feely and Ghosh'. *Criminal Law Review*.

Griffin, J. 1986. *Well-Being*. Oxford: Clarendon Press.

1993. 'Against the Taste Model'. In Elster and Roemer (1993a).

Griffiths, P. 1993. 'Functional Analysis and Proper Functions'. *British Journal of Philosophy of Science* 44.

Griswold, C. 2007. *Forgiveness: A Philosophical Exploration*. Cambridge University Press.

Grotius, H. 1925. *The Law of War and Peace*. New York: Carnegie Endowment for International Peace.

Guerrin. M., and G. Kyriazis. 1993. 'Cartels: Proof and Procedural Issues'. In B. Hawk (ed.), *International Antitrust Law and Policy 1992*. New York: Transnational Juris.

Guest, S. 1992. *Ronald Dworkin*. Edinburgh University Press.

Gyselen, L. 2002. 'The Substantive Legality Test under Article 81(3) EC Treaty – Revisited in Light of the Commission's Modernization Initiative'. In A. Bogdany et al. (eds.), *European Integration and International Co-ordination*. The Hague: Kluwer Law International.

Haack, S. 1974. *Deviant Logic*. Cambridge University Press.

1978. *Philosophy of Logics*. Cambridge University Press.

Habermas, J. 1981. *Theorie des Kommunikativen Handelns*. Frankfurt: Suhrkamp.

1998. *On the Pragmatics of Communication*. Cambridge, MA: MIT Press.

Hammond, A., and R. Penrose. 2001. *Proposed Criminalisation of Cartels in the UK*. London: Office of Fair Trading.

Hampton, J. 1998. 'Rationality, Practical'. In E. Craig (1998), vol. 8.

Handler, M. 1953. 'Contract, Combination or Conspiracy'. *ABA Antitrust Section Report* 3.

Hanfling, O. 1975. 'Promises, Games and Institutions'. *Proceedings of the Aristotelian Society* 13.

Hanna, R. 1998. 'Conceptual Analysis'. In E. Craig (1998), vol. 2.

Hare, R. 1952. *The Language of Morals*. Oxford University Press.

1963. *Freedom and Reason*. Oxford University Press.

1967. 'The Promising Game'. In Foot (1967).

1981. *Moral Thinking*. Oxford: Clarendon Press.

Hargreaves Heap, S., et al. 1992. *The Theory of Choice*. Oxford: Blackwell.

Harman, G. 1965. 'The Inference to the Best Explanation'. *Philosophical Review* 74.

1968. 'Enumerative Induction as Inference to the Best Explanation'. *Journal of Philosophy* 65.

1974. Review of S. Schiffer, *Meaning*. Oxford University Press. 1972. *Journal of Philosophy* 71.

1977. *The Nature of Morality*. New York: Oxford University Press.

1978. 'Reasons'. In Raz (1978).

Harno, A. 1941. 'Intent in Criminal Conspiracy'. *University of Pennsylvania Law Review* 89.

Harrington, B. (ed.). 2009. *Deception*. Palo Alto, CA: Stanford University Press.

Harris, S., et al. 2006. 'The Pragmatics of Political Apologies'. *Discourse and Society* 17.

Harrison, B. 1979. *An Introduction to the Philosophy of Language*. London: Macmillan.

Harrison, D. 1924. *Conspiracy as a Crime and as a Tort in English Law*. London: Sweet & Maxwell.

Harsanyi, J. 1982. 'Morality and the Theory of Rational Behaviour'. In Sen and Williams (1982).

Hart, H. 1949. 'The Ascription of Responsibility and Rights'. *Proceedings of the Aristotelian Society*. suppl. vol. 49.

1958. 'Legal and Moral Obligation'. In Melden (1958).

1961. *The Concept of Law*. Oxford: Clarendon Press.

1963. *Law, Liberty and Morality*. Oxford University Press.

1967. 'Are There Any Natural Rights?'. In A. Quinton (ed.), *Political Philosophy*. Oxford University Press.

1973. 'Acts of Will and Responsibility'. In H. Hart, *Punishment and Responsibility*. Oxford: Clarendon Press.

1982. 'Commands and Authoritative Reasons'. In H. Hart, *Essays on Bentham*. Oxford: Clarendon Press.

Haupt, G. 1943. 'Über Faktische Vertragsverhältnisse'. *Leipziger Rechtswissenschaftliche Studien* 124.

Hausman, D. 1995. 'The Impossibility of Interpersonal Utility Comparisons'. *Mind* 104.

Hausman, D., and M. McPherson. 1993. 'Taking Ethics Seriously: Economics and Contemporary Moral Philosophy'. *Journal of Economic Literature* 31.

1998. 'Economics and Ethics'. In E. Craig (1998), vol. 3.

Hawk, B. 1988. 'The American (Anti-Trust) Revolution: Lessons for the EEC'. *European Competition Law Review* 9.

1995. 'System Failure: Vertical Restraints and EC Competition Law'. *Common Market Law Review* 32.

Hawkins, K. (ed.). 1992. *The Uses of Discretion*. Oxford: Clarendon Press.

Hay, G. 1982. 'Oligopoly, Shared Monopoly, and Antitrust Law'. *Cornell Law Review* 67.

2000. 'The Meaning of "Agreement" under the Sherman Act: Thoughts from the "Facilitating Practices" Experience'. *Review of Industrial Organization* 16.

2006. 'Horizontal Agreements: Concept and Proof'. *Antitrust Bulletin* 51.

Hazell, R. 1974. *Conspiracy and Civil Liberties*. London: Bell & Hyman.

Hazlett, T. 1992. 'The Legislative History of the Sherman Act Re-examined'. *Economic Inquiry* 30.

Heal, J. 1978. 'Common Knowledge'. *Philosophical Quarterly* 28.

Hegel, G. 1952. *Philosophy of Right*. Oxford University Press.

Hellman, G., and F. Thompson. 1975. 'Physicalism: Ontology, Determination, and Reduction'. *Journal of Philosophy* 72.

Hempel, C. 1965. 'The Logic of Functional Analysis'. In C. Hempel, *Aspects of Scientific Explanation*. New York: Free Press.

Henderson, G. 1966. '"Ought" Implies "Can"'. *Philosophy* 41.

Henry, D. 2004. 'The Bayer Judgment: To Agree or Not to Agree'. *EU Focus* 140.

Herring, J. 2010. *Criminal Law*. 4th edn. Oxford University Press.

Hertzberg, L. 1988. 'On the Attitude of Trust'. *Inquiry* 31.

Hick, J. 1971. *Arguments for the Existence of God*. London: Macmillan.

Hildebrand, D. 1998. *The Role of Economic Analysis in the EC Competition Rules*. The Hague: Kluwer Law International.

Hill, T. 1991. *Autonomy and Self-Respect*. Cambridge University Press.

2002. 'Happiness and Human Flourishing'. In T. Hill, *Human Welfare and Moral Worth: Kantian Perspectives*. Oxford: Clarendon Press.

Hilpinen, R. 1970. *Deontic Logic: Introductory and Systematic Readings*. Dordrecht: Reidel.

1981. *New Studies in Deontic Logic*. Dordrecht: Reidel.

Hindricks, F. 2004. 'A Modest Solution to the Problem of Rule-Following'. *Philosophical Studies* 121.

Hintikka, J. 1970. 'Some Main Problems in Deontic Logic'. In Hilpinen (1970).

Hobbes, T. 1968. *Leviathan*. Harmondsworth: Penguin Books.

1983. *De Cive: The Latin Version*. Oxford: Clarendon Press.

Hodgson, D. 1978. 'Law Com. No. 76 – A Case Study in Criminal Law Reform'. In P. Glazebrook (ed.), *Reshaping Criminal Law: Essays in Honour of Glanville Williams*. London: Stevens.

Hofweber, T. 2009. 'Ambitious, Yet Modest, Metaphysics'. In D. Chalmers et al., *Metametaphysics: New Essays on the Foundations of Ontology*. Oxford University Press.

Hohfeld, W. 1985. 'Fundamental Conceptions as Applied in Judicial Reasoning'. In D. Lloyd and M. Freeman (eds.), *Lloyd's Introduction to Jurisprudence*. London: Stevens.

Holdcroft, D. 1978. *Words and Deeds*. Oxford University Press.

Holdsworth, W. 1921. 'Conspiracy and Abuse of Legal Process'. *Law Quarterly Review* 37.

1923. *History of English Law*. London: Methuen.

Hollis, M. 1994. *The Philosophy of Social Science*. Cambridge University Press.

Holmes, O. 2005. *The Common Law*. Clark, NJ: The Lawbook Exchange.

Holt, C., and D. Scheffman. 1987. 'Facilitating Practices: The Effects of Advance Notice and Best-Price Policies'. *Rand Journal of Economics* 18.

Holton, R. 1994. 'Deciding to Trust, Coming to Believe'. *Australasian Journal of Philosophy* 72.

Holtzman, S., and C. Leich. 1981. *Wittgenstein: To Follow a Rule.* London: Routledge and Kegan Paul.

Hook, G. 2008. 'The Road to Reconciliation Begins with an Apology'. *MAI Review* 2.

Hooker, B. 1990. 'Rule Consequentialism'. *Mind* 91.

2011. 'Promises and Rule-Consequentialism'. In Sheinman (2011c).

Hooker, B., and M. Little. 2000. *Moral Particularism.* Oxford: Clarendon Press.

Hooker, C. 1981. 'Toward a General Theory of Reduction'. *Dialogue* 20.

Hooper, A., and D. Ormerod (eds.). 2008. *Blackstone's Criminal Practice.* Oxford University Press.

2011. *Blackstone's Criminal Practice.* Oxford University Press.

Horder, J. 1995. 'Intention in the Criminal Law – A Rejoinder'. *Modern Law Review* 678.

Hornsby, S. 1987. 'Competition Policy in the 80s: More Policy Less Competition'. *European Law Review* 12.

Horton, J. 1992. *Political Obligation.* Basingstoke: Macmillan.

Horty, J. 2001. *Agency and Deontic Logic.* Oxford University Press.

House of Lords Select Committee. 2000. *Fourth Report: Reforming EC Competition Procedures.* London: House of Lords.

Hovenkamp, H. 2003. 'The Rationalization of Antitrust'. *Harvard Law Review* 116.

2005. *Antitrust.* 4th edn. St Paul, MN: West Publishing.

Howarth, W. 1984. 'The Meaning of Objectivity in Contract'. *Law Quarterly Review* 100.

Hudson, W. 1969. *The Is-Ought Question.* London: Macmillan.

Hughes, G., and M. Cresswell. 1968. *An Introduction to Modal Logic.* London: Methuen.

1984. *A Companion to Modal Logic.* London: Methuen.

Hume, D. 1963. 'Of the Original Contract'. In D. Hume, *Essays Moral, Political and Literary.* Oxford University Press.

1978. *A Treatise of Human Nature.* Oxford: Clarendon Press.

Hurka, T. 1993. *Perfectionism.* New York: Oxford University Press.

Hurley, S. 1989. *Natural Reasons.* New York: Oxford University Press.

Husak, D. 1995. 'The Nature and Justifiability of Nonconsummate Offenses'. *Arizona Law Review* 37.

Husi, S. 2011. 'Is Promising a Practice and Nothing More?'. In Sheinman (2011c).

Hutcheson, F. 1969. *Inquiry Concerning the Original of our Ideas of Beauty and Virtue.* In D. Raphael (ed.), *British Moralists 1650–1800.* Oxford: Clarendon Press. vol. 1.

Hutton, C. 1990. *Abstraction and Instance: The Type-Token Relation in Linguistic Theory.* Oxford: Pergamon.

Hyman, J. 2006. *The Objective Eye.* University of Chicago Press.

Ibbetson, D. 1999. *A Historical Introduction to the Law of Obligations*. Oxford University Press.

Ichino, P. 2001. 'Collective Bargaining and Antitrust Laws: An Open Issue'. *International Journal of Comparative Labour Law and Industrial Relations* 17.

Inglehart, R. 1996. 'The Diminishing Utility of Economic Growth: From Maximizing Security Toward Maximizing Subjective Well-Being'. *Critical Review* 10.

Irwin, T. 2007–9. *The Development of Ethics*. Oxford University Press.

Isenberg, A. 1964. 'Deontology and the Ethics of Lying'. *Philosophy and Phenomenological Research* 24.

Jackson, F. 1985. 'On the Semantics and Logic of Obligation'. *Mind* 94.

(ed.). 1991. *Conditionals*. Oxford University Press.

1998a. *From Metaphysics to Ethics: A Defence of Conceptual Analysis*. Oxford: Clarendon Press.

1998b. 'Indicative Conditionals'. In E. Craig (1998), vol. 4.

Jackson, F., and R. Pargetter. 1987. 'Two Puzzles about Conditional Obligation'. *Philosophical Papers* 16.

Jephcott, M. 2005. *Horizontal Agreements and EU Competition Law*. London: Richmond Law and Tax Ltd.

Jhering, R. 1861. 'Culpa in Contrahendo oder Schadenersatz bei nichtigen oder nicht zur Perfektion gelangten Verträgen'. *Jahrbücher für die Dogmatik des Heutigen: Römischen und Deutschen Privatrechts* 1.

Johansson, P. 1991. *An Introduction to Modern Welfare Economics*. Cambridge University Press.

Johnson, C. 1975. 'Moral and Legal Obligation'. *Journal of Philosophy* 72.

Johnson, P. 1973. 'The Unnecessary Crime of Conspiracy'. *California Law Review* 61.

Joliet, R. 1967. *The Rule of Reason in Antitrust Law*. The Hague: Nijhoff.

Jones, W. 1986. Review of P. Areeda, *Antitrust Law*, vols. 6 and 7. *Harvard Law Review* 99.

Joshua, J. 2003. 'The UK's New Cartel Offence and its Implications for EC Competition Law: A Tangled Web'. *European Law Review* 28.

Joshua, J., and S. Jordan. 2004. 'Combinations, Concerted Practices and Cartels: Adopting the Concept of Conspiracy in European Community Competition Law'. *Northwestern Journal of International Law and Business* 24.

Kagan, S. 1989. *The Limits of Morality*. Oxford: Clarendon Press.

1998. *Normative Ethics*. Boulder, CO: Westview Press.

Kahn, E. 1955. 'Some Mysteries of Offer and Acceptance'. *South African Law Journal* 72.

Kahneman, D., and C. Varey. 1993. 'Notes on the Psychology of Utility'. In Elster and Roemer (1993a).

Kant, I. 1929. *Critique of Pure Reason*. London: Macmillan.

1969. *Fundamental Principles of the Metaphysic of Ethics.* London: Longmans, Green.

Katkov, G. 1937. *Untersuchungen zur Werttheorie und Theodizee.* Brunn: Rohrer.

Katyal, N. 2003. 'Conspiracy Theory'. *Yale Law Journal* 112.

Katz, M., et al. 2008. 'Cartel Enforcement in Canada: What Asian Companies Should Know'. *Asia-Pacific Antitrust Review* 2008.

Kaveny, M. 2004. 'Inferring Intention from Foresight'. *Law Quarterly Review* 120.

Kawall, J. 1999. 'The Experience Machine and Mental-State Theories of Well-Being'. *Journal of Value Inquiry* 33.

Kaysen, C. 1951. 'Collusion under the Sherman Act'. *Quarterly Journal of Economics* 65.

Keefe, R. 2002. 'When Does Circularity Matter?'. *Proceedings of the Aristotelian Society* 102.

Keita, L. 1999. 'Welfare Economics and Positive Neoclassical Economics'. *Journal of Value Inquiry* 33.

Kemmerling, A. 1986. 'Utterer's Meaning Revisited'. In R. Grandy and R. Warner (eds.), *Philosophical Grounds of Rationality.* Oxford University Press.

Kenny, A. 1963. *Action, Emotion and Will.* London: Routledge and Kegan Paul.

1969. *The Five Ways.* London: Routledge and Kegan Paul.

Kerse, C. 1988. *EEC Antitrust Procedure.* London: European Law Centre.

Kessler, F., and E. Fine. 1964. '*Culpa in Contrahendo,* Bargaining in Good Faith, and Freedom of Contract: A Comparative Study'. *Harvard Law Review* 401.

Kim, J. 1971. 'Causes and Events: Mackie on Causation'. *Journal of Philosophy* 68.

1993a. 'Concepts of Supervenience'. In Kim (1993d).

1993b. 'Postscripts on Supervenience'. In Kim (1993d).

1993c. '"Strong" and "Global" Supervenience Revisited'. In Kim (1993d).

1993d. *Supervenience and Mind.* Cambridge University Press.

1993e. 'Supervenience as a Philosophical Concept'. In Kim (1993d).

Kimel, D. 2003. *From Promise to Contract.* Oxford: Hart.

2007. 'The Choice of Paradigm for a Theory of Contract: Reflections on the Relational Model'. *Oxford Journal of Legal Studies* 27.

King, J. 2008. *The Nature and Structure of Content.* Oxford University Press.

Kitcher, P. 1988. 'Function and Design'. In P. French et al. (eds.), *Midwest Studies in Philosophy* 18. Notre Dame: Indiana University Press.

Klagge, J. 1984. 'An Alleged Difficulty Concerning Moral Properties'. *Mind* 93.

1988. 'Supervenience: Ontological and Ascriptive'. *Australasian Journal of Philosophy* 66.

Klein, P. 1976. 'Knowledge, Causality, and Defeasibility'. *Journal of Philosophy* 73.

Knapp, C. 1984. 'The Promise of the Future – and Vice Versa: Some Reflections on the Metamorphosis of Contract Law'. *Michigan Law Review* 82.

Knobe, J., and S. Nichols (eds.). 2008. *Experimental Philosophy*. New York: Oxford University Press.

Kohn, M. 2008. *Trust*. Oxford University Press.

Koopmans, T. 1986. 'The Role of Law in the Next Stage of European Integration'. *International and Comparative Law Quarterly* 35.

Korah, V. 1986. 'EEC Competition Policy – Legal Form or Economic Efficiency'. *Current Legal Problems* 39.

Korsgaard, C. 1996a. *The Sources of Normativity*. Cambridge University Press.

1996b. 'Kant's Analysis of Obligation: The Argument of *Groundwork I*'. In C. Korsgaard, *Creating the Kingdom of Ends*. Cambridge University Press.

unpub. 'Natural Motives and the Motive of Duty: Hume and Kant on our Duties to Others'.

Kötz, H. 1997. *Formation, Validity, and Content of Contracts: Contract and Third Parties*. Vol. 1 of H. Kötz and A. Flessner, *European Contract Law*. Oxford: Clarendon Press.

Kovacic, W. 1990. 'The Antitrust Paradox Revisited: Robert Bork and the Transformation of Modern Antitrust Policy'. *Wayne Law Review* 36.

1993. 'The Identification and Proof of Horizontal Agreements Under the Antitrust Laws'. *Antitrust Bulletin*. Spring 1993.

2006. 'An Integrated Competition Policy to Deter and Defeat Cartels'. *Antitrust Bulletin* 51.

Kripke, S. 1982. *Wittgenstein on Rules and Private Language*. Cambridge, MA: Harvard University Press.

Kronman, A., and R. Posner (eds.). 1979. *The Economics of Contract Law*. Boston, MA: Little, Brown.

Kuhn, S. 1998. 'Modal Logic'. In E. Craig (1998), vol. 6.

Kupfer, J. 1982. 'The Moral Presumption against Lying'. *Review of Metaphysics* 36.

Kymlicka, W. 1989. *Liberalism, Community, and Culture*. Oxford: Clarendon Press.

2002. *Contemporary Political Philosophy*. 2nd edn. Oxford University Press.

Lacey, N. 1993. 'A Clear Concept of Intention: Elusive or Illusory?'. *Modern Law Review* 56.

1995. 'In(de)terminable Intentions'. *Modern Law Review* 58.

LaFave, W. 2003. *Principles of Criminal Law*. St Paul, MN: West Publishing.

Lagenspetz, O. 1992. 'Legitimacy and Trust'. *Philosophical Investigations* 15.

Lande, R. 1982. 'Wealth Transfers as the Original and Primary Concern of Antitrust: The Efficiency Interpretation Challenged'. *Hastings Law Journal* 34.

Lane, R. 1994. 'Quality of Life and Quality of Persons: A New Role for Government?'. *Political Theory* 22.

Langford, C. 1952. 'Moore's Notion of Analysis'. In P. Schilpp (ed.), *The Philosophy of G. E. Moore*. 2nd edn. New York: Tudor.

Law Commission. 1973. *Inchoate Offences: Conspiracy, Attempt and Incitement*. Working Paper No. 50. London: The Law Commission.

1976. *Report on Conspiracy and Criminal Law Reform.* London: Her Majesty's Stationery Office.

1989. *Draft Criminal Code Bill (Law Com. No. 177).* London: The Law Commission.

2006. *Inchoate Liability for Assisting and Encouraging Crime (Law Com. No. 300).* London: The Law Commission.

2007. *Conspiracy and Attempts: A Consultation Paper (Law Com. No. 183).* London: The Law Commission.

Law Society. 2005. *Guidance on* Bowman *v.* Fels. London: The Law Society.

LeBuffe, M. 2003. 'Hobbes on the Origin of Obligation'. *British Journal for the History of Philosophy* 11.

Lehrer, K. 1970. 'Justification, Explanation, and Induction'. In M. Swain (ed.), *Induction, Acceptance and Rational Belief.* Dordrecht: Reidel.

Leibenstein, H. 1980. *Beyond Economic Man.* Cambridge, MA: Harvard University Press.

Leibniz, G. 1934a. *The Monadology.* In Leibniz (1934c).

1934b. *On the Ultimate Origination of Things.* In Leibniz (1934c).

1934c. *Philosophical Writings.* London: Dent.

Lemmon, E. 1965. 'Deontic Logic and the Logic of Imperatives'. *Logique et Analyse* 6.

1966a. *An Introduction to Modal Logic.* Oxford: Blackwell.

1966b. 'Sentences, Statements and Propositions'. In B. Williams and A. Montefiore (eds.), *British Analytical Philosophy.* London: Routledge and Kegan Paul.

1971. *Beginning Logic.* London: Nelson.

Lemos, R. 1980. 'Duty and Ignorance'. *Southern Journal of Philosophy* 18.

LePore, E. (ed.). 1986. *Truth and Interpretation: Perspectives on the Philosophy of Donald Davidson.* Oxford: Blackwell.

Letwin, W. 1981. *Law and Economic Policy in America: The Evolution of the Sherman Antitrust Act.* University of Chicago Press.

Levi, E. 1947. 'The Antitrust Laws and Monopoly'. *University of Chicago Law Review* 14.

Levi, M., and A. Smith. 2002. *A Comparative Analysis of Organised Crime Conspiracy Legislation and Practice and their Relevance to England and Wales.* London: Home Office.

Levinson, S. 1983. *Pragmatics.* Cambridge University Press.

Lewis, C., and C. Langford. 1959. *Symbolic Logic.* New York: Dover.

Lewis, D. 1969. *Convention.* Cambridge, MA: Harvard University Press.

1973. *Counterfactuals.* Oxford: Blackwell.

1986. 'Causation'. In D. Lewis, *Philosophical Papers.* New York: Oxford University Press. vol. 2.

Lewis, H. (ed.). 1963. *Clarity is Not Enough.* London: George Allen & Unwin.

Lewy, C. 1950. 'Entailment and Necessary Propositions'. In M. Black (1950).

1958. 'Entailment'. *Proceedings of the Aristotelian Society*. suppl. vol. 32.

Lidgard, H. 1997. 'Unilateral Refusal to Supply: An Agreement in Disguise?'. *European Competition Law Review* 18.

Liebermann, M. 1998. *Commitment, Value, and Moral Realism*. Cambridge University Press.

Linsky, L. (ed.). 1971. *Reference and Modality*. Oxford University Press.

Lipsey, D. 1989. *An Introduction to Positive Economics*. 7th edn. London: Weidenfeld and Nicolson.

Lipton, P. 1991. *Inference to the Best Explanation*. London: Routledge.

List, C., and P. Pettit. 2011. *Group Agency*. Oxford University Press.

Little, D. 1957. *A Critique of Welfare Economics*. 2nd edn. Oxford University Press.

Litvinoff, S. 1968. 'Offer and Acceptance in Louisiana Law: A Comparative Analysis'. *Louisiana Law Review* 28.

Loar, B. 1981. *Mind and Meaning*. Cambridge University Press.

Locke, D. 1972. 'The Object of Morality, and the Obligation to Keep a Promise'. *Canadian Journal of Philosophy* 2.

Locke, J. 1965. *An Essay Concerning Human Understanding*. London: Dent.

Loewer, B., and M. Belzer. 1991. 'Prima Facie Obligation: Its Deconstruction and Reconstruction'. In E. Lepore and R. van Gulick (eds.), *John Searle and his Critics*. Cambridge, MA: Blackwell.

Lopatka, J. 1996. 'Solving the Oligopoly Problem: Turner's Try'. *Antitrust Bulletin* 41.

Loux, M. 2002. *Metaphysics: A Contemporary Introduction*. 2nd edn. London: Routledge.

Luce, R., and H. Raiffa. 1989. *Games and Decisions*. New York: Dover.

Lycan, W. 1984. *Logical Form in Natural Language*. Cambridge, MA: MIT Press.

2000. *Philosophy of Language: A Contemporary Introduction*. London: Routledge.

Lynch, A. 1978. 'A Further Comment'. *Criminal Law Review*.

Lyons, D. 1965. *Forms and Limits of Utilitarianism*. Oxford: Clarendon Press.

McCloskey, H. 1963. 'Ross and the Concept of Prima Facie Duty'. *Australasian Journal of Philosophy* 41.

1973. 'Utilitarianism: Two Difficulties'. *Philosophical Studies* 24.

McCluskey, D. 2006. 'The Proceeds of Crime Act: A Review'. *Tolley's Insolvency Law and Practice* 22.

McConnell, T. 1989. '"Ought" Implies "Can" and the Scope of Moral Requirements'. *Philosophia* 19.

MacCormick, N. 1972. 'Voluntary Obligations and Normative Powers (I)'. *Proceedings of the Aristotelian Society*. suppl. vol. 46.

1978. *Legal Reasoning and Legal Theory*. Oxford: Clarendon Press.

1981. *H. L. A. Hart*. Palo Alto, CA: Stanford University Press.

1982. 'Voluntary Obligations'. In N. MacCormick, *Legal Right and Social Democracy*. Oxford: Clarendon Press.

1983. 'What is Wrong with Deceit?'. *Sydney Law Review* 10.

MacCulloch, A. 2003. 'The Cartel Offence and the Criminalisation of United Kingdom Competition Law'. *Journal of Business Law*. Nov. 2003.

MacCulloch, D. 2010. Review of D. Womersley, *Divinity and State. Times Literary Supplement*. 10 Sept. 2010.

Macdonald, K., and R. Thompson. 2003. 'Dishonest Agreements'. *Competition Law Review* 4.

McDowell, J. 1979. 'Virtue and Reason'. *Monist* 62.

1982. 'Reasons and Actions'. *Philosophical Investigations* 5.

McGinn, C. 1984. *Wittgenstein on Meaning*. Oxford: Blackwell.

MacIntyre, A. 1985. *After Virtue*. London: Duckworth.

McKeever, S., and M. Ridge. 2006. *Principled Ethics*. Oxford: Clarendon Press.

McKendrick, E. 1995. 'The Regulation of Long-Term Contracts in English Law'. In Beatson and Friedmann (1995).

2008. 'Discharge by Breach'. In Beale (2008), vol. 1.

Mackie, J. 1974. *The Cement of the Universe*. Oxford University Press.

1977. *Ethics: Inventing Right and Wrong*. Harmondsworth: Penguin Books.

1993. 'Causes and Conditions'. In E. Sosa and M. Tooley (eds.), *Causation*. Oxford University Press.

MacKinnon, J. 2000. 'Scruton, Sibley, and Supervenience'. *Journal of Aesthetics and Art Criticism* 58.

2001. 'Aesthetic Supervenience: For and Against'. *British Journal of Aesthetics* 41.

McMahon, C. 1989. 'Promising and Co-ordination'. *American Philosophical Quarterly* 26.

Macneil, I. 1964. 'Time of Acceptance: Too Many Problems for a Single Rule'. *University of Pennsylvania Law Review* 112.

1974. 'The Many Futures of Contract'. *Southern California Law Review* 47.

1981. 'Economic Analysis of Contractual Relations'. *Northwestern University Law Review* 75.

McNeilly, F. 1971. 'Promises De-Moralized'. *Philosophical Review* 81.

McNutt, P. 2000. 'The Appraisal of Vertical Agreements: Competitiveness, Efficiency, Competitive Harm and Dynamic Conduct'. In Rivas and Horspool (2000).

McPherson, T. 1967. *Political Obligation*. London: Routlege and Kegan Paul.

2009. 'Unnatural Normativity?'. *Philosophical Books* 50.

Mann, F. 1973. 'The Dyestuffs Case in the Court of Justice of the European Communities'. *International and Comparative Law Quarterly* 22.

Mannison, D. 1969. 'Lying and Lies'. *Australasian Journal of Philosophy* 47.

Marcus, P. 1977. 'Conspiracy: The Criminal Agreement in Theory and in Practice'. *Georgetown Law Journal* 65.

1992. 'Criminal Conspiracy Law: Time to Turn Back from an Ever Expanding, Ever More Troubling Area'. *William and Mary Bill of Rights Journal* 1.
Marc-Wogau, K. 1962. 'On Historical Explanation'. *Theoria* 28.
Margalit, A. 1981. *Meaning and Use*. Amsterdam: Reidel.
Markesinis, B., et al. 1997. *The Law of Contracts and Restitution: A Comparative Introduction*. Vol. 1 of B. Markesinis, et al., *The German Law of Obligations*. Oxford: Clarendon Press.
Markovits, D. 2011. 'Promise as an Arm's-Length Relation'. In Sheinman (2011c).
Marmor, A. 1992. *Interpretation and Legal Theory*. Oxford: Clarendon Press.
(ed.). 1995. *Law and Interpretation*. Oxford: Clarendon Press.
Marsden, P. 1997. 'Inducing Member State Enforcement of European Competition Law: A Competition Policy Approach to Antitrust Federalism'. *European Competition Law Review* 18.
Martin, C. (ed.). 2009. *The Philosophy of Deception*. Oxford University Press.
Martinich, A. 1985. 'A Solution to a Paradox of Promising'. *Philosophia* 15.
1987. 'Obligation, Ability and Prima Facie Promising'. *Philosophia* 17.
1998. 'Ordinary Language Philosophy'. In E. Craig (1998), vol. 7.
May, J. 1989. 'Antitrust in the Formative Era: Political and Economic Theory in Constitutional and Antitrust Analysis, 1880–1919'. *Ohio State Law Journal* 50.
Meinong, A. 1915. *Über Möglichkeit und Wahrscheinlichkeit*. Leipzig: Barth.
1972. *On Emotional Presentation*. Evanston, IL: Northwestern University Press.
Melden, A. 1956. 'On Promising'. *Mind* 65.
(ed.). 1958. *Essays in Moral Philosophy*. Seattle: University of Washington Press.
Mele, A. 2003. *Motivation and Agency*. Oxford University Press.
Mellor, D. 2000. 'The Semantics and Ontology of Dispositions'. *Mind* 109.
Mendola, J. 1987. 'The Indeterminacy of Options'. *American Philosophical Quarterly* 26.
Menzies, P. 2008. 'Counterfactual Theories of Causation'. *Stanford Encyclopedia of Philosophy*. http://plato.stanford.edu/.
Merricks, T. 2007. *Truth and Ontology*. Oxford: Clarendon Press.
2009a. 'Propositional Attitudes? *Proceedings of the Aristotelian Society* 109.
2009b. 'Truth and Freedom'. *Philosophical Review* 118.
Milgrom, P. 1981. 'An Axiomatic Characterization of Common Knowledge'. *Econometrica* 49.
Mill, J. 1910a. *On Liberty*. London: Dent.
1910b. *Utilitarianism*. London: Dent.
Miller, A. 1998. *Philosophy of Language*. London: Routledge.
2003. *An Introduction to Contemporary Metaethics*. Cambridge: Polity Press.
Miller, J. 2011. *Examined Lives*. New York: Farrar, Straus and Giroux.
Miller, S. 1992. 'Joint Action'. *Philosophical Papers* 21.
2001. *Social Action*. Cambridge University Press.

Millgram, E. 2000. 'What's the Use of Utility?'. *Philosophy and Public Affairs* 29.
(ed.). 2001. *Varieties of Practical Reasoning*. Cambridge, MA: MIT Press.
Millikan, R. 1984. *Language, Thought, and Other Biological Categories*. Cambridge, MA: MIT Press.
1993. *White Queen Psychology and Other Essays for Alice*. Cambridge, MA: MIT Press.
Millon, D. 1988. 'The Sherman Act and the Balance of Power'. *Southern California Law Review* 61.
Milsom, S. 1981. *Historical Foundations of the Common Law*. Oxford University Press.
Mintoff, J. 2004. 'Is an Agreement an Exchange of Intentions?'. *Pacific Philosophical Quarterly* 85.
Mints, G. 1992. *A Short Introduction to Modal Logic*. Palo Alto, CA: Center for the Study of Language and Information, Stanford University.
Misztal, B. 1996. *Trust in Modern Societies*. Cambridge: Polity Press.
Montague, M. 2007. 'Against Propositionalism'. *Noûs* 41.
Montefiore, A. 1958. '"Ought" and "Can"'. *Philosophical Quarterly* 8.
Monti, G. 2002. 'Article 81 EC and Public Policy'. *Common Market Law Review* 39.
Moore, A. 1990. *The Infinite*. London: Routledge.
2000. 'Objective Human Goods'. In Crisp and Hooker (2000).
Moore, A., and R. Crisp. 1996. 'Welfarism in Moral Theory'. *Australasian Journal of Philosophy* 74.
Moore, G. 1959. *Principia Ethica*. Cambridge University Press.
1966. *Ethics*. Oxford University Press.
Morris, C. 1991. 'Some Notes on "Reliance"'. *Minnesota Law Review* 75.
Mouzas, S., and M. Furmston. 2008. 'From Contract to Umbrella Agreement'. *Cambridge Law Journal* 67.
Mulligan, K., et al. 1984. 'Truth-Makers'. *Philosophy and Phenomenological Research* 44.
Nagel, E. 1961. *The Structure of Science*. London: Routledge and Kegan Paul.
Nagel, T. 1970. *The Possibility of Altruism*. Princeton, NJ: Princeton University Press.
Narveson, J. 1967. *Morality and Utility*. Baltimore, MD: Johns Hopkins University Press.
Nash, J. 1950. 'The Bargaining Problem'. *Econometrica* 18.
National Economic Research Associates. 1999. *Merger Appraisal in Oligopolistic Markets*. OFT Research Paper 19. London: Office of Fair Trading.
Neilson, W., and H. Winter. 1993. 'Bilateral Most-Favored-Customer Pricing and Collusion'. *Rand Journal of Economics* 24.
Nelson, E. 1930. 'Intensional Relations'. *Mind* 39.
Nicholas, B. 1962. *An Introduction to Roman Law*. Oxford: Clarendon Press.
1992. *The French Law of Contract*. Oxford: Clarendon Press.
Nicholson, P. 1998. 'State, the'. In E. Craig (1998), vol. 9.

Nielsen, L. 1984. 'Common Knowledge, Communication, and Convergence of Beliefs'. *Mathematical Social Sciences* 8.

Nietzsche, F. 1966. *Zur Genealogie der Moral.* In F. Nietzsche, *Werke.* Munich: Hanser. vol. 2.

Noordhof, P. 2001. 'Believe What You Want'. *Proceedings of the Aristotelian Society* 101.

Norcross, A. 2011. 'Act-Utilitarianism and Promissory Obligation'. In Sheinman (2011c).

Nozick, R. 1974. *Anarchy, State, and Utopia.* Oxford: Blackwell.

1981. *Philosophical Explanations.* Oxford: Clarendon Press.

Nussbaum, A. 1936. 'Comparative Aspects of the Anglo-American Offer-and-Acceptance Doctrine'. *Columbia Law Review* 36.

Nussbaum, M., and A. Sen (eds.). 1993. *The Quality of Life.* Oxford: Clarendon Press.

Odudu, O. 2001. 'Interpreting Article 81(1): Object as Subjective Intention'. *European Law Review* 26.

2006. *The Boundaries of EC Competition Law.* Oxford University Press.

Office of Fair Trading. 2004. *Article 81 and the Chapter I Prohibition.* London: Office of Fair Trading.

Olafson, F. 1967. *Principles and Persons: An Ethical Interpretation of Existentialism.* Baltimore, MD: Johns Hopkins Press.

Oliver, A. 1996. 'The Metaphysics of Properties'. *Mind* 105.

Orchard, G. 1974. '"Agreement" in Criminal Conspiracy'. *Criminal Law Review.*

Ormerod, D. 2005. *Smith & Hogan: Criminal Law.* 11th edn. Oxford University Press.

2006. 'Making Sense of *Mens Rea* in Statutory Conspiracies'. *Current Legal Problems* 59.

2008. *Smith & Hogan: Criminal Law.* 12th edn. Oxford University Press.

Owens, D. 2011. 'The Problem with Promising'. In Sheinman (2011c).

Owsia, P. 1991. 'Silence: Efficacy in Contract Formation. A Comparative Review of French and English Law'. *International and Comparative Law Quarterly* 40.

Page, C. 1991. 'The Truth about Lies in Plato's *Republic*'. *Ancient Philosophy* 11.

Papineau, D. 2009. 'The Poverty of Analysis'. *Proceedings of the Aristotelian Society,* suppl. vol. 83.

Pappas, G. 1979. 'Basing Relations'. In G. Pappas (ed.), *Justification and Knowledge.* Dordrecht: Reidel.

Parfit, D. 1984. *Reasons and Persons.* Oxford: Clarendon Press.

Parikh, R., and P. Krasucki. 1990. 'Communication, Consensus and Knowledge'. *Journal of Economic Theory* 52.

Parr, N., and R. McKenzie. 2008. 'Competition Regime: The Enterprise Act 2002 Cartel Offence'. *PLC Competition Law.* www.practicallaw.com.

Parsons, G., and A. Carlson. 2008. *Functional Beauty.* Oxford: Clarendon Press.

Paseau, A. 2010. 'Defining Ultimate Ontological Basis and the Fundamental Layer'. *Philosophical Quarterly* 60.

Pateman, C. 1985. *The Problem of Political Obligation: A Critique of Liberal Theory.* 2nd edn. Oxford: Polity Press.

Patterson, D. 1992. 'The Value of a Promise'. *Law and Philosophy* 11.

Peacocke, C. 1979. *Holistic Explanation.* Oxford: Clarendon Press.

1986. *Thoughts: An Essay on Content.* London: Blackwell.

1992. *A Study of Concepts.* Cambridge, MA: MIT Press.

Peel, E. 2007. *Treitel: The Law of Contract.* 12th edn. London: Sweet & Maxwell.

Peeters, J. 1989. 'The Rule of Reason Revisited: Prohibition on Restraints of Competition in the Sherman Act and the EEC Treaty'. *American Journal of Comparative Law* 37.

Peirce, C. 1931–58. *Collected Papers of Charles Sanders Peirce.* Cambridge, MA: Harvard University Press.

Peretz, G., and J. Lewis. 2003. 'Go Directly to Jail: Losing Badly in "Monopoly"'. *New Law Journal* 153.

Perkins, R., and R. Boyle. 1982. *Criminal Law.* 3rd edn. Mineola, NY: Foundation Press.

Perry, J. 1993. *The Problem of the Essential Indexical and Other Essays.* Oxford University Press.

Peter, F., and H. Schmid (eds.). 2007. *Rationality and Commitment.* Oxford University Press.

Peters, R. 1958. *The Concept of Motivation.* London: Routledge and Kegan Paul.

Pettit, P. 2002. *Rules, Reasons, and Norms.* Oxford: Clarendon Press.

Phillips, J. 1976. 'Contracts between Users of a Service Supplied by a Third Party'. *Law Quarterly Review* 92.

Phlips, L. 1995. *Competition Policy: A Game-Theoretic Perspective.* Cambridge University Press.

Pickard-Cambridge, W. 1932. 'Two Problems about Duty'. *Mind* 41.

Pietroski, P. 1993. 'Prima Facie Obligations, Ceteris Paribus Laws in Moral Theory'. *Ethics* 103.

Pigou, A. 2002. *The Economics of Welfare.* New Brunswick, NJ: Transaction Publishers.

Pink, T. 2004. 'Moral Obligation'. In A. O'Hear (ed.), *Modern Moral Philosophy.* Cambridge University Press.

2007. 'Normativity and Reason'. *Journal of Moral Philosophy* 4.

2009. 'Promising and Obligation'. *Philosophical Perspectives* 23.

Pitcher, G. (ed.). 1968. *Wittgenstein: The Philosophical Investigations.* London: Macmillan.

Plowden, E. 1792. *The Commentaries or Reports of Edmund Plowden.* Dublin: Watts.

Pollock, F. 1885. *Principles of Contract.* 4th edn. London: Stevens.

1950. *Principles of Contract.* 13th edn. London: Stevens.

Pollock, J. 1966. 'The Paradoxes of Strict Implication'. *Logique et Analyse* 34.

Posner, R. 1969. 'Oligopoly and the Antitrust Laws: A Suggested Approach'. *Stanford Law Review* 21.

1975. 'Antitrust Policy and the Supreme Court: An Analysis of the Restricted Distribution, Horizontal Merger and Potential Competition Decisions'. *Columbia Law Review* (1975).

1986. *Economic Analysis of Law*. 3rd edn. Boston: Little, Brown.

2001. *Antitrust Law*. 2nd edn. University of Chicago Press.

Post, J. 1980. 'Infinite Regresses of Justification and of Explanation'. *Philosophical Studies* 38.

Postow, B. 1980. 'A Possible Ground of Political Obligation'. *Southern Journal of Philosophy* 18.

Pothier, R. 1802. *A Treatise on Obligations Considered in a Moral or Legal View*. Newburn, NC: Martin and Ogden.

Powers, L. 1967. 'Some Deontic Logicians'. *Noûs* 1.

Preston, B. 1998. 'Why is a Wing Like a Spoon? A Pluralist Theory of Functions'. *Journal of Philosophy* 115.

Price, A. 2008. 'Against Requirements of Rationality'. *Proceedings of the Aristotelian Society* 108.

Price, R. 1948. *Review of the Principal Questions in Morals*. Oxford: Clarendon Press.

Prichard, H. 2002a. 'Does Moral Philosophy Rest on a Mistake?'. In Prichard (2002e).

2002b. 'Duty and Ignorance of Fact'. In Prichard (2002e).

2002c. 'Exchanging'. In Prichard (2002e).

2002d. 'Moral Obligation'. In Prichard (2002e).

2002e. *Moral Writings*. Oxford: Clarendon Press.

2002f. 'The Obligation to Keep a Promise'. In Prichard (2002e).

2002g. 'The Time of an Obligation'. In Prichard (2002e).

Priest, G. 2005. *Towards Non-Being: The Logic and Metaphysics of Intentionality*. New York: Oxford University Press.

Prior, A. 1957. *Time and Modality*. Oxford: Clarendon Press.

Prosser, T. 2005. *The Limits of Competition Law*. Oxford University Press.

Pufendorf, S. 1934. *On the Law of Nature and Nations*. Oxford: Clarendon Press.

Pullen, M., and K. Vernon. 2005. 'Corporate Compliance and Regulatory Enforcement'. *In-House Lawyer*. Sept. 2005.

Putnam, H. 1975. 'The Meaning of "Meaning"'. In H. Putnam, *Mind, Language and Reality*. Cambridge University Press.

Qizilbash, M. 1997. 'Well-Being and Despair: Dante's Ugolino'. *Utilitas* 9.

1998. 'The Concept of Well-Being'. *Economics and Philosophy* 14.

Quine, W. 1961. 'Two Dogmas of Empiricism'. In W. Quine, *From a Logical Point of View*. 2nd edn. Cambridge, MA: Harvard University Press.

1979. *Mathematical Logic*. rev. edn. Cambridge, MA: Harvard University Press.

1987. *Quiddities: An Intermittently Philosophical Dictionary.* Cambridge, MA: Harvard University Press.
Quinn, P. 2002. 'Obligation, Divine Commands and Abraham's Dilemma'. *Philosophy and Phenomenological Research* 64.
Radford, C. 1984. 'I Will, If You Will'. *Mind* 93.
Radzik, L. 2011. *Making Amends.* Oxford University Press.
Rahl, J. 1950. 'Conspiracy and the Antitrust Laws'. *Illinois Law Review* 44.
Railton, P. 1989. 'Explanation and Metaphysical Controversy'. In P. Kitcher and W. Salmon (eds.), *Scientific Explanation.* Minneapolis: University of Minnesota Press.
Rakoff, T. 1994. 'Contracts of Adhesion: An Essay in Reconstruction'. In Craswell and Schwartz (1994).
Ratliff, J. 2005. 'Major Events and Policy Issues in EC Competition Law, 2003–2004: Part 1'. *International Company and Commercial Law Review* 16.
Rawls, J. 1964. 'Legal Obligation and the Duty of Fair Play'. In S. Hook (ed.), *Law and Philosophy.* New York University Press.
1967. 'Two Concepts of Rules'. In Foot (1967).
1972. *A Theory of Justice.* Oxford University Press.
1993. *Political Liberalism.* New York: Columbia University Press.
Raz, J. 1972. 'Voluntary Obligations and Normative Powers (II)'. *Proceedings of the Aristotelian Society.* suppl. vol. 46.
1977. 'Promises and Obligations'. In P. Hacker and J. Raz (eds.), *Law, Morality, and Society.* Oxford University Press.
(ed.). 1978. *Practical Reasoning.* Oxford University Press.
1982. 'Promises in Morality and Law'. *Harvard Law Review* 916.
1984. 'On the Nature of Rights'. *Mind* 93.
1986. *The Morality of Freedom.* Oxford: Clarendon Press.
1990. *Practical Reason and Norms.* Princeton, NJ: Princeton University Press.
1994. 'Liberating Duties'. In J. Raz, *Ethics in the Public Domain.* Oxford: Clarendon Press.
1999. 'When We are Ourselves: The Active and the Passive'. In J. Raz, *Engaging Reason.* Oxford University Press.
Reath, A. 1998. 'Autonomy, Ethical'. In E. Craig (1998), vol. 1.
Recanati, F. 1993. *Direct Reference: From Language to Thought.* Oxford: Blackwell.
Reed, A. 2005. 'Court of Appeal: Conspiracy: Mens Rea'. *Journal of Criminal Law* 69.
Regan, D. 1985. 'On Preferences and Promises: A Response to Harsanyi'. *Ethics* 96.
Restall, G. 1996. 'Truthmakers, Entailment and Necessity'. *Australasian Journal of Philosophy* 74.
Rey, G. 1998. 'Concepts'. In E. Craig (1998), vol. 2.
Rey, P., and J. Venit. 2004. 'Parallel Trade and Pharmaceuticals: A Policy in Search of Itself'. *European Law Review* 29.

Richards Butler. 2003. *The Enterprise Act 2002: The Competition Provisions.* London: Richards Butler.

Richardson, P. (ed.). 2011. *Archbold: Criminal Pleading, Evidence and Practice.* London: Sweet & Maxwell.

Richman, R. 1983. *God, Free Will, and Morality.* Dordrecht: Reidel.

Rivas, J., and M. Horspool (eds.). 2000. *Modernisation and Decentralisation of EC Competition Law.* The Hague: Kluwer Law International.

Robbins, I. 1989. 'Double Inchoate Crimes'. *Harvard Journal on Legislation* 26.

Robertson, G. 1974. *Whose Conspiracy?* London: National Council for Civil Liberties.

Robins, M. 1976. 'The Primacy of Promising'. *Mind* 85.

1984. *Promising, Intending, and Moral Autonomy.* Cambridge University Press.

Robinson, R. 1971. 'Ought and Ought Not'. *Philosophy* 46.

Roemer, J. 1996. *Theories of Distributive Justice.* Cambridge, MA: Harvard University Press.

Rogers, J. 1989. '*United States* v. *Andrews*: Conspirators May Go it Alone These Days'. *American Journal of Trial Advocacy* 12.

Rosati, C. 2011. 'The Importance of Self-Promises'. In Sheinman (2011c).

Rose, V., and P. Roth (eds.). 2008. *Bellamy & Child: European Community Law of Competition.* 6th edn. London: Sweet & Maxwell.

Ross, A. 1941. 'Imperatives and Logic'. *Theoria* 7.

Ross, D. 1930. *The Right and the Good.* Oxford: Clarendon Press.

1939. *Foundations of Ethics.* Oxford: Clarendon Press.

Rotenstreich, N. 1972. 'On Confidence'. *Philosophy* 47.

Routley, R., and V. Routley. 1975. 'The Role of Inconsistent and Incomplete Theories in the Logic of Belief'. *Communication and Cognition* 8.

Ruben, D. (ed.). 1993. *Explanation.* Oxford University Press.

Russell, B. 1956. 'On Denoting'. In B. Russell, *Logic and Knowledge.* London: George Allen & Unwin.

1970. 'The Elements of Ethics'. In W. Sellars and J. Hospers (eds.), *Readings in Ethical Theory.* 2nd edn. Englewood Cliffs, NJ: Prentice-Hall.

1979. *The Principles of Mathematics.* London: George Allen & Unwin.

Ryan, A. (ed.). 1973. *The Philosophy of Social Explanation.* Oxford University Press.

Salmon, N., and S. Soames (eds.). 1988. *Propositions and Attitudes.* Oxford University Press.

Samuelson, P. 1970. *Foundations of Economic Analysis.* New York: Atheneum.

Sartor, G. 2000. 'Legal Validity as Doxastic Obligation: From Definition to Normativity'. *Law and Philosophy* 19.

Sartorius, R. 1987. 'Positivism and the Foundations of Legal Authority'. In R. Gavison (ed.), *Issues in Contemporary Legal Philosophy: The Influence of H. L. A. Hart.* Oxford: Clarendon Press.

Sayre, F. 1922. 'Criminal Conspiracy'. *Harvard Law Review* 35.
Sayre-McCord, G. 1986. 'Deontic Logic and the Priority of Moral Theory'. *Noûs* 20.
Scanlon, T. 1982. 'Contractualism and Utilitarianism'. In Sen and Williams (1982).
1990. 'Promises and Practices'. *Philosophy and Public Affairs* 19.
1993a. 'The Moral Basis of Interpersonal Comparisons'. In Elster and Roemer (1993a).
1993b. 'Value, Desire, and Quality of Life'. In Nussbaum and Sen (1993).
1998. *What We Owe to Each Other*. Cambridge, MA: Harvard University Press.
2001. 'Promises and Contracts'. In Benson (2001b).
Schaeffer, F., and S. Kon. 1997. 'Parallel Imports of Pharmaceutical Products: A New Realism or Back to Basics?'. *European Law Review* 22.
Schauer, F. 1991. *Playing by the Rules*. Oxford: Clarendon Press.
Scheffler, S. (ed.). 1988. *Consequentialism and its Critics*. Oxford University Press.
Schelling, T. 1980. *The Strategy of Conflict*. Cambridge, MA: Harvard University Press.
Scherer, F., and D. Ross. 1990. *Industrial Market Structure and Economic Performance*. 3rd edn. Boston: Houghton Mifflin.
Schiemann, K. 2007. 'Europe and the Loss of Sovereignty'. *International and Comparative Law Quarterly* 56.
Schiffer, S. 1972. *Meaning*. Oxford University Press.
1987. *Remnants of Meaning*. Cambridge, MA: MIT Press.
Schmid, C. 2000. 'Diagonal Competence Conflicts between European Competition Law and National Regulation – A Conflict of Laws Reconstruction of the Dispute on Book Price Fixing'. *European Review of Private Law* 8.
Schneewind, J. 1986. 'The Use of Autonomy in Ethical Theory'. In T. Heller et al. (eds.), *Reconstructing Individualism*. Palo Alto, CA: Stanford University Press.
1998. *The Invention of Autonomy*. Cambridge University Press.
Schueler, G. 1995. *Desire*. Cambridge, MA: MIT Press.
2003. *Reasons and Purposes*. Oxford University Press.
Schulz, A. 2004. 'Bayer/Adalat – A Unilateral Decision?'. *European Law Reporter* 1.
Schwartz, A. 1992. 'Relational Contracts in the Courts: An Analysis of Incomplete Agreements and Judicial Strategies'. *Journal of Legal Studies* 21.
Scitovsky, T. 1992. *The Joyless Economy*. New York: Oxford University Press.
Scoccia, D. 1987. 'Autonomy, Want Satisfaction, and the Justification of Liberal Freedoms'. *Canadian Journal of Philosophy* 17.
Scruton, R. 1974. *Art and Imagination*. London: Methuen.
Seabright, P. 2010. *The Company of Strangers*. 2nd edn. Princeton, NJ: Princeton University Press.

Searle, J. 1958. 'Proper Names'. *Mind* 67.

1965. 'What is a Speech Act?'. In M. Black (1965).

1967. 'How to Derive "Ought" from "Is"'. In Foot (1967).

1969. *Speech Acts: An Essay in the Philosophy of Language*. Cambridge University Press.

1978. '*Prima Facie* Obligations'. In Raz (1978).

1979. *Expression and Meaning*. Cambridge University Press.

1984. *Minds, Brains and Science*. Cambridge, MA: Harvard University Press.

1990. 'Collective Intentions and Actions'. In P. Cohen et al. (eds.), *Intentions in Communication*. Cambridge, MA: MIT Press.

Sen, A. 1981. 'Plural Utility'. *Proceedings of the Aristotelian Society* 81.

1982a. 'Behaviour and the Concept of Preference'. In Sen (1982b).

1982b. *Choice, Welfare and Measurement*. Cambridge, MA: Harvard University Press.

1982c. 'Introduction'. In Sen (1982b).

1982d. 'Personal Utilities and Public Judgments: Or What's Wrong with Welfare Economics?'. In Sen (1982b).

1985. 'Well-Being, Agency and Freedom: The Dewey Lectures 1984'. *Journal of Philosophy* 82.

2002a. 'Introduction: Rationality and Freedom'. In Sen (2002c).

2002b. 'Markets and Freedoms'. In Sen (2002c).

2002c. *Rationality and Freedom*. Cambridge, MA: Belknap Press.

Sen, A., and B. Williams (eds.). 1982. *Utilitarianism and Beyond*. Cambridge University Press.

Seung, T., and D. Bonevac. 1992. 'Plural Values and Indeterminate Rankings'. *Ethics* 102.

Shafer-Landau, R. 2009. 'A Defence of Categorical Reasons'. *Proceedings of the Aristotelian Society* 109.

Shaw, P. 1965. '"Ought" and "Can"'. *Analysis* 23.

Sheinman, H. 2004. 'Are Normal Contracts Normal Promises?'. *Oxford Journal of Legal Studies* 24.

2011a. 'Agreement as Joint Promise'. In Sheinman (2011c).

2011b. 'Introduction: Promises and Agreements'. In Sheinman (2011c).

(ed.). 2011c. *Promises and Agreements*. Oxford University Press.

Shoemaker, S. 1963. *Self-Knowledge and Self-Identity*. Ithaca, NY: Cornell University Press.

1984. 'Self-Reference and Self-Awareness'. In S. Shoemaker, *Identity, Cause, and Mind*. Cambridge University Press.

1996. *The First-Person Perspective and Other Essays*. Cambridge University Press.

Shute, S., and J. Horder. 1993. 'Thieving and Deceiving: What is the Difference?'. *Modern Law Review* 56.

Sidgwick, H. 1907. *The Methods of Ethics.* 7th edn. London: Macmillan and Co.

Simester, A., et al. 2010. *Simester and Sullivan's Criminal Law.* 4th edn. Oxford and Portland, OR: Hart.

Simmonds, N. 1986. *Central Issues in Jurisprudence.* London: Sweet & Maxwell.

Simmons, A. 1979. *Moral Principles and Political Obligation.* Princeton, NJ: Princeton University Press.

1981. 'Reasonable Expectations and Obligations: A Reply to Postow'. *Southern Journal of Philosophy* 19.

1984. 'Consent, Free Choice, and Democratic Government'. *Georgia Law Review* 18.

Simon, H. 1957. *Models of Man.* New York: Wiley.

1978. 'Rationality as a Process and Product of Thought'. *American Economic Review* 68.

1983. *Reason in Human Affairs.* Palo Alto, CA: Stanford University Press.

Simpson, A. 1975. 'Innovation in Nineteenth Century Contract Law'. *Law Quarterly Review* 91.

2007. 'Historical Introduction'. In Furmston (2007).

Simpson, D. 1992. 'Lying, Liars and Language'. *Philosophy and Phenomenological Research* 52.

Singer, R., and J. La Fond. 2007. *Criminal Law.* 4th edn. Austin, TX: Wolters Kluwer.

Sinnott-Armstrong, W. 1985. '"Ought to Have" and "Could Have"'. *Analysis* 45.

1987. 'A Resolution of a Paradox of Promising'. *Philosophia* 17.

1988a. *Moral Dilemmas.* Oxford: Blackwell.

1988b. 'Promises which Cannot be Kept'. *Philosophia* 18.

Siragusa, M. 1998. 'The Millennium Approaches: Rethinking Article 85 Competition Rules'. *Fordham International Law Journal* 21.

2000. 'A Critical Review of the White Paper on the Reform of the EC Competition Law Enforcement Rules'. *Fordham International Law Journal* 23.

Skinner, Q. 1978. *The Foundations of Modern Political Thought.* Cambridge University Press.

1996. *Reason and Rhetoric in the Philosophy of Hobbes.* Cambridge University Press.

Skorupski, J. 2000. 'Quality of Well-Being: Quality of Being'. In Crisp and Hooker 2000.

Skyrms, B. 1996. *Evolution of the Social Contract.* Cambridge University Press.

Slote, M. 1990. 'Rational Dilemmas and Rational Supererogation'. In P. Moser (ed.), *Rationality in Action.* Cambridge University Press.

Smart, A. 1999. 'Expressions of Interest: Friendship and *Guanxi* in Chinese Societies'. In S. Bell and S. Coleman (eds.), *The Anthropology of Friendship.* Oxford: Berg.

Smiley, T. 1959. 'Entailment and Deducibility'. *Proceedings of the Aristotelian Society* 59.

Smith, A. 1976. *The Theory of Moral Sentiments*. Oxford: Clarendon Press.

1978. *Lectures on Jurisprudence*. Oxford University Press.

Smith, B. 1999. 'Truthmaker Realism'. *Australasian Journal of Philosophy* 77.

Smith, J. 1974. 'Intention in Criminal Law'. *Current Legal Problems* 27.

1977. 'Conspiracy under the Criminal Law Act 1977'. *Criminal Law Review*.

1978a. 'A Reply'. *Criminal Law Review*.

1978b. 'Some Answers'. *Criminal Law Review*.

1985. Comment on *R.* v. *Jackson, Golding and Jackson*. *Criminal Law Review*.

1994. 'Secondary Participation in Crime – Can We Do Without It?'. *New Law Journal* 144.

1996a. Commentary on *R.* v. *Barratt and Sheehan*. *Criminal Law Review*.

1996b. 'Proving Conspiracy'. *Criminal Law Review*.

2002. 'Indictment: Count Charging Conspiracy to Launder Proceeds either of Drug Trafficking or of Other Crime'. *Criminal Law Review*.

Smith, J., and D. Tausz. 2002. 'Computer Misuse: Whether Sending an E-mail which Did Not Come from the Purported Source Affected the Reliability of Data'. *Criminal Law Review*.

Smith, M. 1994. *The Moral Problem*. Oxford: Blackwell.

Smith, N. (ed.). 1982. *Mutual Knowledge*. London: Academic Press.

2008. *I was Wrong*. Cambridge University Press.

Smith, S. 2004. *Contract Theory*. Oxford University Press.

2005. *Atiyah's Introduction to the Law of Contract*. 6th edn. Oxford: Clarendon Press.

Snare, F. 1974. 'The Definition of Prima Facie Duties'. *Philosophical Quarterly* 24.

Snyder, F. 1990. *New Directions in European Community Law*. London: Weidenfeld and Nicolson.

Soames, T. 1996. 'An Analysis of the Principles of Concerted Practice and Collective Dominance: A Distinction without a Difference?'. *European Competition Law Review* 17.

Sobel, D. 1994. 'Full Information Accounts of Well-Being'. *Ethics* 104.

Sobel, J. 1968. 'Rule-Utilitarianism'. *Australasian Journal of Philosophy* 46.

Sober, E. 1993. *Philosophy of Biology*. Oxford University Press.

Solan, L. 2007. 'Contract as Agreement'. *Notre Dame Law Review* 83.

Sosa, E., and M. Tooley (eds.). 1993. *Causation*. Oxford University Press.

Sousa Ferro, M. 2007. 'Reassessing Borders between Agreements and Unilateral Practices after Case 74/04 *Volkswagen II*'. *European Competition Law Review* 28.

Souto Soubrier, L. 2007. 'The Concept of an Agreement and Beyond: How to Block Parallel Imports of Pharmaceuticals to Protect the Heart of Competition'.

In G. Amato and C. Ehlermann (eds.), *EC Competition Law: A Critical Assessment*. Oxford and Portland, OR: Hart.

Spencer, J. 1973. 'Signature, Consent, and the Rule in *L'Estrange* v. *Graucob*'. *Cambridge Law Journal* 32.

Spicer, R. 1981. *Conspiracy: Law, Class and Society*. London: Lawrence and Wishart.

Stalnaker, R. 1991. 'A Theory of Conditionals'. In Jackson (1991).

Stevenson, C. 1944. *Ethics and Language*. New Haven, CT: Yale University Press.

1959. 'The Emotive Meaning of Ethical Terms'. In A. Ayer (ed.), *Logical Positivism*. Glencoe, IL: Free Press.

Stocker, M. 1970. 'Moral Duties, Institutions, and Natural Facts'. *Monist* 54.

1971. '"Ought" and "Can"'. *Australasian Journal of Philosophy* 49.

1990. *Plural and Conflicting Values*. Oxford: Clarendon Press.

Stoljar, S. 1988. 'Promise, Expectation and Agreement'. *Cambridge Law Journal* 47.

Stout, R. 1996. *Things That Happen Because They Should*. Oxford University Press.

2005. *Action*. Montreal: McGill-Queen's University Press.

Stoutland, F. 1998. 'Intentionalists and Davidson on Rational Explanation'. In G. Meggle (ed.), *Actions, Norms, Values: Discussions with Georg Henrik von Wright*. Berlin and New York: de Gruyter.

Strasser, M. 1985. 'Dependence, Reliance and Abortion'. *Philosophical Quarterly* 35.

Strawson, P. 1948. 'Necessary Propositions and Entailment-Statements'. *Mind* 57.

1963. *Introduction to Logical Theory*. London: Methuen.

1971a. 'Intention and Convention in Speech Acts'. In J. Searle (ed.), *The Philosophy of Language*. Oxford University Press.

1971b. 'On Referring'. In P. Strawson, *Logico-Linguistic Papers*. London: Methuen.

Stroux, S. 2000. Case Note on *Compagnie Maritime Belge and Others* v. *Commission*. *Common Market Law Review* 37.

Suárez, F. 1944. 'A Treatise on Laws and God the Lawgiver'. In *Selections from Three Works of Francisco Suárez, SJ*. Oxford: Clarendon Press, vol. 1.

Sumner, L. 1996. *Welfare, Happiness, and Ethics*. Oxford: Clarendon Press.

Takahiro, I. 1999. 'What Can We Learn from Lewis Carroll's Paradox?'. *Memoirs of the Faculty of Education, Miyazaki University: Humanities* 86.

Tännsjö, T. 1996. 'Classical Hedonistic Utilitarianism'. *Philosophical Studies* 81.

Tarlow, B. 1980. 'RICO: The Darling of the Prosecutor's Nursery'. *Fordham Law Review* 49.

Taylor, C. 1985a. *Human Agency and Language*. Cambridge University Press.

1985b. *Philosophy and the Human Sciences*. Cambridge University Press.

Taylor, K. 1998. 'Propositional Attitude Statements'. In E. Craig (1998), vol. 7.

Taylor, M. 1987. *The Possibility of Cooperation*. Cambridge University Press.

Taylor, S., and J. Mansell. 2003. 'White-Collar Crime – Caught in the Act'. *Legal Week* 5.

Textor, M. 2010a. 'Frege on Conceptual and Propositional Analysis'. *Grazer Philosophische Studien* 81.

2010b. 'Proper Names and Practices: On Reference without Referents'. *Philosophy and Phenomenological Research* 81.

Thomason, R. 1981. 'Deontic Logic as Founded on Tense Logic'. In R. Hilpinen (ed.), *New Studies in Deontic Logic*. Dordrecht: Reidel.

Thompson, J. 1990. Case Note on *Sandoz P.F.* v. *Commission* and *Tipp-Ex* v. *Commission*. *Common Market Law Review* 27.

Thomson, J. 1986. *Rights, Restitution, and Risk*. Cambridge, MA: Harvard University Press.

Tiersma, P. 1992. 'Reassessing Unilateral Contracts: The Role of Offer, Acceptance and Promise'. *University of California at Davis Law Review* 26.

1994. 'The Language of Offer and Acceptance'. In Craswell and Schwartz (1994).

Tirole, J. 1988. *The Theory of Industrial Organization*. Cambridge, MA: MIT Press.

Travis, C. 1975. *Saying and Understanding*. New York University Press.

Trebilcock, M. 1993. *The Limits of Freedom of Contract*. Cambridge, MA: Harvard University Press.

Treitel, G. 2003. *The Law of Contract*. 11th edn. London: Sweet & Maxwell.

Trilling, L. 1972. *Sincerity and Authenticity*. Cambridge, MA: Harvard University Press.

Trollope, A. 1982. *The Way We Live Now*. Oxford University Press.

2004. *He Knew He Was Right*. London: Penguin Books.

Tsohatzidis, S. (ed.). 1994. *Foundations of Speech Act Theory*. London: Routledge.

Tunick, M. 2002. 'The Moral Obligation to Obey Law'. *Journal of Social Philosophy* 33.

Tuomela, R. 1984. *A Theory of Social Action*. Dordrecht: Reidel.

1995. *The Importance of Us*. Palo Alto, CA: Stanford University Press.

Tuomela, R., and S. Miller. 1988. 'We-Intentions'. *Philosophical Studies* 53.

Turner, D. 1962. 'The Definition of Agreement under the Sherman Act: Conscious Parallelism and Refusals to Deal'. *Harvard Law Review* 75.

Twining, W., and D. Miers. 1991. *How to Do Things with Rules*. 3rd edn. London: Weidenfeld and Nicolson.

Ullmann-Margalit, E. 1977. *The Emergence of Norms*. Oxford: Clarendon Press.

Utz, S. 2004. 'Associative Obligation and Law's Authority'. *Ratio Juris* 17.

van Bael, I., and J. Bellis. 2009. *Competition Law of the European Community*. 5th edn. The Hague: Kluwer Law International.

van den Bergh, R., and P. Camesasca. 2001. *European Competition Law and Economics: A Comparative Perspective*. Antwerp: Intersentia.

van Eck, J. 1982. 'A System of Temporally Relative Modal and Deontic Predicate Logic and its Philosophical Applications'. *Logique et Analyse* 25.

van Fraassen, B. 1993. 'The Pragmatics of Explanation'. In Ruben (1993).
Velleman, D. 2000a. 'Deciding How to Decide'. In Velleman (2000c).
2000b. 'How to Share an Intention'. In Velleman (2000c).
2000c. *The Possibility of Practical Reason*. Oxford: Clarendon Press.
Vita, M. 2000. 'Fifteen Years after *Ethyl*: The Past and Future of Facilitating Practices'. *Antitrust Law Journal* 68.
Vitek, W. 1986. 'The Humean Promise: Whence Comes its Obligation?'. *Hume Studies* 12.
von Mehren, A. 1992. 'The Formation of Contracts'. In R. David et al. (eds.), *International Encyclopedia of Comparative Law*. Tübingen: Mohr (Siebeck), vol. 7.
von Wright, G. 1957. 'The Concept of Entailment'. In G. von Wright, *Logical Studies*. London: Routledge and Kegan Paul.
1963. *Norm and Action*. London: Routledge and Kegan Paul.
1968. 'An Essay in Deontic Logic and the General Theory of Action'. *Acta Philosophica Fennica* 21.
1978. 'On So-called Practical Inference'. In Raz (1978).
Vorobej, M. 1986. 'Conditional Obligation and Detachment'. *Canadian Journal of Philosophy* 16.
Vorster, J. 1987. 'A Comment on the Meaning of Objectivity in Contract'. *Law Quarterly Review* 104.
Waismann, F. 1965. *The Principles of Linguistic Philosophy*. London: Macmillan.
1968. 'Verifiability'. In A. Flew (ed.), *Logic and Language*. 1st ser. Oxford: Blackwell.
Waldron, J. 1987. 'Theoretical Foundations of Liberalism'. *Philosophical Quarterly* 37.
Wallace, R., et al. (eds.). 2004. *Reason and Value: Themes from the Moral Philosophy of Joseph Raz*. Oxford University Press.
Walton, K. 1990. *Mimesis as Make-Believe*. Cambridge, MA: Harvard University Press.
Walzer, M. 1970. *Obligations: Essays on Disobedience, War and Citizenship*. Cambridge, MA: Harvard University Press.
Wang, Z. 2008. 'Collusive Communication and Pricing Co-ordination in a Retail Gasoline Market'. *Review of Industrial Organization* 32.
Warnock, G. 1971. *The Object of Morality*. London: Methuen.
Warrender, H. 1957. *The Political Philosophy of Hobbes*. Oxford: Clarendon Press.
Weale, A. 1998. 'Welfare'. In E. Craig (1998), vol. 9.
Wedgwood, R. 2007. *The Nature of Normativity*. Oxford: Clarendon Press.
Weintraub, R. 1998. 'Do Utility Comparisons Pose a Problem?'. *Philosophical Studies* 92.
Weir, T. 1992. 'Contracts in Rome and England'. *Tulane Law Review* 1992.

Wellman, C. 2004. 'Political Obligation and the Particularity Requirement'. *Legal Theory* 10.

Werden, G. 2004. 'Economic Evidence on the Existence of Collusion: Reconciling Antitrust Law with Oligopoly Theory'. *Antitrust Law Journal* 71.

Wesseling, R. 1999. 'The Commission White Paper on Modernisation of EC Antitrust Law: Unspoken Consequences and Incomplete Treatment of Alternative Options'. *European Competition Law Review* 20.

2000. *The Modernisation of EC Antitrust Law*. Oxford: Hart.

Wessely, T. 2001. Case Note on the *Polypropylene* Cases. *Common Market Law Review* 38.

Wetzel, L. 1993. 'What are Occurrences of Expressions?'. *Journal of Philosophical Logic* 22.

1998. 'Type/Token Distinction'. In E. Craig (1998), vol. 9.

Whish, R. 1993. *Competition Law*. 3rd edn. London: Butterworths.

2009. *Competition Law*. 6th edn. Oxford University Press.

Whish, R., and B. Sufrin. 2000. 'Community Competition Law: Notification and Individual Exemption – Goodbye to All That'. In D. Hayton (ed.), *Law's Future(s): British Legal Developments in the 21st Century*. Oxford: Hart.

White, A. (ed.). 1968. *The Philosophy of Action*. Oxford University Press.

1975. *Modal Thinking*. Oxford: Blackwell.

White, M. 1950. 'The Analytic and the Synthetic: An Untenable Dualism'. In S. Hook (ed.), *John Dewey: Philosopher of Science and Freedom*. New York: Dial Press.

Whiteley, C. 1952. 'On Duties'. *Proceedings of the Aristotelian Society* 53.

1960. 'On Defining "Moral"'. *Analysis* 20.

Whittaker, S. 2008. 'Introductory'. In Beale (2008), vol. 1.

Wickihalder, U. 2006. 'The Distinction between an "Agreement" within the Meaning of Article 81(1) of the EC Treaty and Unilateral Conduct'. *European Competition Journal* 2.

Widerker, D. 1991. 'Frankfurt on "Ought Implies Can" and Alternative Possibilities'. *Analysis* 51.

Wiggins, D. 1998. 'A Sensible Subjectivism?'. In D. Wiggins, *Needs, Values, Truth*. Oxford: Clarendon Press.

Williams, B. 1973. 'Deciding to Believe'. In B. Williams, *Problems of the Self*. Cambridge University Press.

1981. 'Internal and External Reasons'. In B. Williams, *Moral Luck*. Cambridge University Press.

1993. *Ethics and the Limits of Philosophy*. London: Fontana.

1995. 'Internal Reasons and the Obscurity of Blame'. In B. Williams, *Making Sense of Humanity*. Cambridge University Press.

2002. *Truth and Truthfulness.* Princeton, NJ: Princeton University Press.
Williams, G. 1961. *Criminal Law: The General Part.* 2nd edn. London: Stevens.
1977. 'The New Statutory Offence of Conspiracy'. *New Law Journal* 127.
1983. *Textbook of Criminal Law.* 2nd edn. London: Stevens.
1989. 'The Mens Rea for Murder – Leave it Alone'. *Law Quarterly Review* 105.
Williamson, T. 1994. *Vagueness.* London: Routledge.
1996. 'Knowing and Asserting'. *Philosophical Review* 105.
2000. *Knowledge and its Limits.* Oxford University Press.
2007. *The Philosophy of Philosophy.* Malden, MA: Blackwell.
Willis, P., and P. Hughes. 2007. 'What is an Agreement?'. *Competition Law Journal* 6.
Winch, P. 1958. *The Idea of a Social Science.* London: Routledge.
1972. 'Nature and Convention'. In P. Winch, *Ethics and Action.* London: Routledge and Kegan Paul.
Wittgenstein, L. 1958. *Philosophical Investigations.* Oxford: Blackwell.
1972. *The Blue and Brown Books.* Oxford: Blackwell.
1974. *Philosophical Grammar.* Oxford: Blackwell.
Wolff, J. 1996. *An Introduction to Political Philosophy.* Oxford University Press.
2002. 'Economic Competition: Should We Care about the Losers?'. In H. La Follette (ed.), *Ethics in Practice.* 2nd edn. Oxford: Blackwell.
2006. 'Liberty, Utility and Economic Competition'. *Virginia Law Review* 92.
Wollheim, R. 1980. *Art and its Objects.* 2nd edn. Cambridge University Press.
Wolterstorff, N. 1975. 'Toward an Ontology of Art Works'. *Noûs* 9.
Woodcock, G. 1963. *Anarchism.* Harmondsworth: Penguin Books.
Woodfield, A. 1975. *Teleology.* Cambridge University Press.
Woozley, A. 1981. 'Promises, Promises'. *Mind* 90.
Wright, C. 1992. *Truth and Objectivity.* Cambridge, MA: Harvard University Press.
Wright, L. 1973. 'Functions'. *Philosophical Review* 82.
1976. *Teleological Explanation.* Berkeley: University of California Press.
Wright, R. 1873. *The Law of Criminal Conspiracies and Agreements.* London: Butterworths.
Yaffe, G. 2004. 'Conditional Intent and Mens Rea'. *Legal Theory* 10.
Yalden-Thomson, D. 1964. 'Remarks about Philosophical Refutations'. *Monist* 48.
Yao, D., and S. DeSanti. 1993. 'Game Theory and the Legal Analysis of Tacit Collusion'. *Antitrust Bulletin* 38.
Young, R. 1980. 'Autonomy and the Inner Self'. *American Philosophical Quarterly* 17.
Zagzebski, L. 2002. 'Obligation, Good Motives, and the Good'. *Philosophy and Phenomenological Research* 64.
Zimmerman, M. 1992. 'Cooperation and Doing the Best One Can'. *Philosophical Studies* 65.

1995. 'Prima Facie Obligation and Doing the Best One Can'. *Philosophical Studies* 78.
1996. *The Concept of Moral Obligation*. Cambridge University Press.
Zimmerman, R., and S. Whittaker. 2000. *Good Faith in European Contract Law*. Cambridge University Press.
Zweigert, K., and H. Kötz. 1998. *Introduction to Comparative Law*. 3rd edn. Oxford: Clarendon Press.

List of numbered propositions

This is a list of all the numbered propositions in the book. They are grouped under the chapters in which they first occur. In some cases, for ease of understanding, the formulation here differs trivially from the original.

Chapter 1

(1) X does Ax and Y does Ay.

(2) X and Y agree that (1).

(3) (2) if:
  (a) X promises to Y that X does Ax; and
  (b) Y promises to X that Y does Ay.

(4) (2) if:
  (a) X promises to Y that if Y does Ay then X does Ax; and
  (b) Y promises to X that if X does Ax then Y does Ay.

(5) X complies with the agreement only if he does Ax.

(6) X complies with his promise if Y does not do Ay.

(7) It is not the case that if Y does not do Ay then X does Ax.

(8) If (4) then, if X complies with his promise, X complies with the agreement.

(9) (2) if:
  (a) X promises to Y that, if Y promises to X that Y does Ay, then X does Ax (call this promise Px);
  (b) Y promises to X that Y does Ay (call this promise Py);
  (c) Y's reason for giving Py is that X gives Px; and
  (d) X has the justified belief that (b).

(10) (2) if:
  (a) X promises to Y that (Px) if Y does Ay then X does Ax;
  (b) Y promises to X that (Py) Y does Ay;
  (c) Y's reason for giving Py is that X gives Px; and
  (d) X has the justified belief that (b).

(11) If someone promises that P, then he is obligated that P.

(12) If someone promises that he φs, then he is obligated that he φs.

(13) If someone promises that if P then he φs, then he is obligated that if P then he φs.

(14) Whether or not someone promises that P, he is obligated that if he promises that P then P.

(15) If someone promises that if P then he φs, then:
(a) he is obligated that if P then he φs; and
(b) if P then he is obligated that he φs.

(16) If at T1 someone promises that he φs, then at T1 he gets an obligation that he φs.

(17) If at T2 someone promises that if at T3 event E occurs then he φs, then at T2 he gets an obligation that if at T3 E occurs then he φs.

(18) If at T2 someone promises that if at T3 E occurs then he φs, then:
(a) at T2 he gets an obligation that if at T3 E occurs then he φs; and
(b) if at T3 E occurs, then at T3 he gets an obligation that he φs.

(19) <At T1 X and Y agree that (1)> if:
(a) at T2 X promises to Y that (Px) if at T1 Y promises to X that Y does Ay, then X does Ax;
(b) at T1 Y promises to X that (Py) Y does Ay;
(c) Y's reason for giving Py is that X gives Px; and
(d) X has the justified belief that (b).

(20) (2) if:
(a) X promises to Y that, if Y gives to X the promise in (b), then X does Ax; and
(b) Y promises to X that if X does Ax then Y does Ay.

(21) (2) if:
(a) X promises to Y that (Px):
(i) subject to (ii), if Y gives to X the promise in (b) then X does Ax;
(ii) if Y does not do Ay, then X does not do Ax;
(b) Y promises to X that (Py):
(i) subject to (ii), Y does Ay;
(ii) if X does not do Ax, then Y does not do Ay;
(c) Y's reason for giving Py is that X gives Px; and
(d) X has the justified belief that (b).

(22) (2) if:
(a) X promises to Y that (Px):
(i) subject to (ii), if Y does Ay then X does Ax;
(ii) if Y does not do Ay, then X does not do Ax;

(b) Y promises to X that (Py):
  (i) subject to (ii), Y does Ay;
  (ii) if X does not do Ax, then Y does not do Ay;
(c) Y's reason for giving Py is that X gives Px; and
(d) X has the justified belief that (b).

(23) If Y does not ask X to stop and X does not stop, then X complies with his obligation.

(24) If:
(a) Y gives Py; and
(b) X relies on Y to do Ay,
then Y is obligated to do Ay.

(25) <X, in doing Ax, relies on Y to do Ay> if:
(a) X does Ax;
(b) X has the goal Gx;
(c) If X does Ax, then Gx is achieved if and only if Y does Ay;
(d) X believes (c);
(e) X believes that Y does Ay; and
(f) (a) because <(b), (d) and (e)>.

(26) (a) Subject to (b), if Y gives Py then Y is obligated that he does Ay.
(b) If clauses (a), (c) and (d) of (9) are met, then Y's obligation ceases if X does not do Ax.

(27) (a) Subject to (b), if X gives Px then:
  (i) X is obligated that if Y gives Py then X does Ax; and
  (ii) if Y gives Py then X is obligated that X does Ax.
(b) If (b)–(d) of (9) are met, then X's obligation ceases if Y does not do Ay.

(28) (2) if:
(a) X promises to Y that, only if Y does Ay, X does Ax; and
(b) Y promises to X that, only if X does Ax, Y does Ay.

(29) (2) if:
(a) X promises to Y that, if Y promises to X that Y does Ay, then X does Ax; and
(b) Y promises to X that, if X promises to Y that X does Ax, then Y does Ay.

(30) (2) if:
(a) X promises to Y that, only if Y promises to X that Y does Ay, X does Ax; and
(b) Y promises to X that, only if X promises to Y that X does Ax, Y does Ay.

(31) (2) if:
(a) if Y does Ay, then X promises to Y that X does Ax; and
(b) if X does Ax, then Y promises to X that Y does Ay.

(32) (2) if:
  (a) if X promises to Y that X does Ax, then Y does Ay; and
  (b) if Y promises to X that Y does Ay, then X does Ax.

(33) (2) if:
  (a) if Y promises to X that Y does Ay, then X promises to Y that X does Ax; and
  (b) if X promises to Y that X does Ax, then Y promises to X that Y does Ay.

(34) (2) if:
  (a) if X promises to Y that X does Ax, then Y promises to X that Y does Ay; and
  (b) if Y promises to X that Y does Ay, then X promises to Y that X does Ax.

(35) (2) if:
  (a) X promises to Y that, if X does not have good reason to believe that Y does not do Ay, then X does Ax; and
  (b) Y promises to X that, if Y does not have good reason to believe that X does not do Ax, then Y does Ay.

Chapter 2

(36) <X and Y make an agreement that (1)> if:
  (a) X makes to Y an offer that (1);
  (b) Y accepts X's offer; and
  (c) condition CM obtains.

(37) <X and Y have an agreement that (1)> if:
  (a) X makes to Y an offer that (1);
  (b) Y accepts X's offer; and
  (c) condition CS obtains.

(38) X's making to Y an offer that (1), Y's accepting X's offer and CM's obtaining together count as X's and Y's making an agreement that (1).

(39) Concept C1 depends on concept C2 if <if X grasps C1, then X grasps C2>.

(40) C1 depends on C2 if <if X grasps C1 to degree N1, then X grasps C2 to degree N2>.

(41) If X fully grasps the concepts of offer and acceptance, then X has some grasp of the concept of agreement.

(42) It is not the case that, if X has a fair grasp of the concepts of offer and acceptance, then X has some grasp of the concept of agreement.

(43) In an analysis, the concepts in the analysans do not depend on those in the analysandum.

(44) In the offer–acceptance model, the concepts in the supposed analysans depend on those in the analysandum.

Chapter 3

(45) If (2) then X is obligated that X does Ax.

(46) X is obligated that if (2) then X does Ax.

(47) X and Y agree that Everest is the highest mountain.

(48) If (47) then X is obligated that Everest is the highest mountain.

(49) X is obligated that if (47) then Everest is the highest mountain.

(50) X's obligation in (45) is a moral performance obligation.

(51) Every obligation has a ground.

(52) If (2) then there exists a ground of a moral performance obligation on X.

(53) In every relevant case, there exists a ground of a moral performance obligation on a party.

(54) In some relevant cases, there exists no ground of a moral performance obligation on a party.

(55) X's obligation in (46) is a moral obligation.

(56) If (2) then FA grounds an obligation on X to do Ax.

(57) Y does Ay.

(58) Y, in doing Ay, relies on X to do Ax.

(59) A failure by X to do Ax would cause significant harm to Y.

(60) X induces Y to do Ay.

(61) It would be reasonable for X to believe (57)–(60).

(62) If (57) and (58) and (59) and (60) and (61), then X is obligated to do Ax.

(63) If (57) and (58) and (60) and (61), then X is obligated to do Ax.

(64) Y has the goal Gy.

(65) If Y does Ay, then Gy is achieved if and only if X does Ax.

(66) Y believes (65).

(67) Y believes that X does Ax.

(68) (57) because <(64), (66) and (67)>.

Chapter 4

(69) (a) I want that P.
(b) The best means to its being the case that P is for me to φ.

(c) Other things are equal.
So:
(d) I will φ.

(70) I want that Y does Ay.

(71) The best means to Y's doing Ay is for me to offer to Y that <I do Ax and he does Ay>.

(72) Other things are equal.

(73) I will offer to Y that <I do Ax and he does Ay>.

(74) I do Ax and he does Ay.

(75) I want that X does Ax.

(76) The best means to X's doing Ax is for me to accept X's offer.

(77) I will accept X's offer.

(78) If:
(a) I offer to Y that (74); and
(b) condition C1 obtains;
then Y accepts my offer.

(79) C1 obtains.

(80) If:
(a) I offer to Y that (74);
(b) Y accepts my offer; and
(c) C2 obtains;
then I and Y agree that (74).

(81) C2 obtains.

(82) If:
(a) I and Y agree that (74);
(b) C3 obtains; and
(c) Y is reliable;
then Y does Ay.

(83) C3 obtains.

(84) Y is reliable.

(85) If I offer to Y that (74), then Y does Ay.

(86) A means to Y's doing Ay is for me offer to Y that (74).

(87) No other means to Y's doing Ay is at least as good as my offering to Y that (74).

(88) I want that <I do Ax and Y does Ay>.

(89) If I do Ax and Y does Ay, then Y does Ay.

(90) (a) I want that P.
(b) If P then Q.
So:
(c) I want that Q.

(91) (a) I want that <P and Q>.
So:
(b) I want that Q.

(92) The best means to its being the case that <I do Ax and Y does Ay> is for me to offer to Y that (74).

(93) I will offer to Y that (74).

(94) (a) I am obligated to φ.
(b) Other things are equal.
So:
(c) I will φ.

(95) I and Y agree that (74).

(96) If (95) then I am obligated to do Ax.

(97) I am obligated to do Ax.

(98) I will do Ax.

(99) (a) There is a reason for me to φ.
(b) Other things are equal.
So:
(c) I will φ.

(100) If I am obligated to do Ax, then there is a ground of that obligation.

(101) If there is a ground of my obligation to do Ax, then there is a reason for me to do Ax.

(102) There is a reason for me to do Ax.

(103) If (95) then the fact that (95) is a reason for me to do Ax.

(104) The fact that (95) is a reason for me to do Ax.

(105) The best means to Y's doing Ay is for me to do Ax.

(106) If I do Ax, then Y has an obligation to do Ay.

(107) If Y has an obligation to do Ay, then Y does Ay.

(108) If I do Ax, then Y does Ay.

(109) The best means to its being the case that I do Ax and Y does Ay is for me to do Ax.

(110) I want to avoid a rebuke.

(111) The best means to my avoiding a rebuke is for me to do Ax.

(112) I want to make agreements in future.

(113) The best means to my making future agreements is for me to do Ax.

(114) I will do Ax if and only if I know that Y does Ay.

(115) I know that Y does Ay.

Chapter 5

(116) If X agrees with Y that (1), then X intends to do Ax.

(117) If X agrees with Y that (1), then X intends to agree with Y that (1).

(118) If X offers to Y that (1), then X intends to do Ax.

(119) If X offers to Y that (1), then X intends to offer to Y that (1).

(120) If Y accepts X's offer that (1), then Y intends to do Ay.

(121) If Y accepts X's offer that (1), then Y intends to accept X's offer that (1).

(122) If at Ta X agrees with Y that <at Tx X does Ax and at Ty Y does Ay>, then at Ta X intends to do Ax at Tx.

(123) If X agrees with Y that (1), the agreement being made by X's making to Y an offer which Y accepts, then X in making the offer intends to agree with Y that (1).

(124) If the reasonable man (RM) believes that X agrees with Y that (1), then RM believes that X intends to agree with Y that (1).

(125) It is possible that RM believes that <P and if P then <Q and not R≫.

(126) If RM believes that <P and if P then <Q and not R≫, then RM believes that <Q and not R>.

(127) If RM believes that <Q and not R>, then <RM believes that Q> and <RM believes that not R>.

(128) If RM believes that not R, then RM does not believe that R.

(129) It is possible that RM believes that <X and Y instantiate the Bluff and if X and Y instantiate the Bluff then ≪X agrees with Y that (1)> and <X does not intend to agree with Y that (1)⋙.

(130) If X offers to Y that (1), then X in making the offer intends to do Ax.

(131) If X offers to Y that (1), then X in making the offer intends to offer to Y that (1).

(132) If RM believes that X offers to Y that (1), then RM believes that X in making the offer intends to offer to Y that (1).

(133) It is possible that RM believes that <X and Y instantiate the Auction and if X and Y instantiate the Auction then ≪X offers to Y that (1)> and <X in making the offer does not intend to offer to Y that (1)≫>.

(134) If <X and Y agree that P> and <X and Y agree that Q>, then X and Y agree that <P and Q>.

(135) If X and Y agree that <P and Q>, then <X and Y agree that P> and <X and Y agree that Q>.

(136) <X intends to do Ax> if and only if P.

(137) X intends <to do Ax if and only if P>.

(138) <X intends to do Ax> if and only if X believes that P.

Chapter 6

(139) (a) The state's enforcing contracts is a means to G.
(b) G is good.
(c) If (a) and (b), then the state has a reason to enforce contracts.
So:
(d) The state has a reason to enforce contracts.

(140) (a) X's φing is a means to G.
(b) G is good.
(c) If (a) and (b), then X has a reason to φ.
So:
(d) X has a reason to φ.

(141) For any good, any agent, and any action the agent's performance of which is a means to the good, the agent has a reason to perform the action.

(142) (a) The state's enforcing contracts is a means to the parties' performing their performance obligations.
(b) The parties' performing those obligations is good.
(c) If (a) and (b), then the state has a reason to enforce contracts.
So:
(d) The state has a reason to enforce contracts.

(143) (a) The state's enforcing contracts is a means to the exercise of autonomy.
(b) The exercise of autonomy is good.
(c) If (a) and (b), then the state has a reason to enforce contracts.
So:
(d) The state has a reason to enforce contracts.

(144) The state's enforcing contracts is a means to parties' making and performing contracts.

(145) In making and performing contracts, parties exercise autonomy.

(146) If (144) and (145), then the state's enforcing contracts is a means to parties' exercising autonomy.

(147) If the state has a reason to enforce, prohibit or promote agreements, then a function of the state is to do so.

(148) It is not a function of the state to enforce, prohibit or promote agreements.

(149) The state has no reason to enforce, prohibit or promote agreements.

(150) The state has functions.

(151) If the state has functions, then, if the state has a reason to enforce, prohibit or promote agreements, a function of the state is to do so.

(152) The state is nothing over and above its functions.

(153) If the state has functions and is nothing over and above its functions, then, if the state has a reason to enforce, prohibit or promote agreements, a function of the state is to do so.

(154) If the state qua state has a reason to enforce, prohibit or promote agreements, then a function of the state is to do so.

(155) The state qua state has no reason to enforce, prohibit or promote agreements.

(156) If:
(a) a function of the state is to enforce, prohibit or promote agreements; and
(b) it is good that the state does so;
then the state has a reason to do so.

(157) A function of the state is to enforce, prohibit or promote agreements.

(158) It is good that the state enforces, prohibits or promotes agreements.

(159) The state has a reason to enforce, prohibit or promote agreements.

(160) If (158) then the state has a reason to enforce, prohibit or promote agreements.

Chapter 7

(161) Px depends on Py if and only if X's reason for giving Px is that Y gives Py.

(162) Px depends on Py if and only if:
(a) X promises to Y that X does Ax if Y promises to X that Y does Ay;
(b) Y promises to X that Y does Ay;
(c) Px is X's promise in (a); and
(d) Py is Y's promise in (b).

(163) Px depends on Py if and only if:
- (a) if Y promises to X that Y does Ay, then X promises to Y that X does Ax;
- (b) Y promises to X that Y does Ay;
- (c) Px is X's promise in (a); and
- (d) Py is Y's promise in (b).

(164) Px depends on Py if and only if:
- (a) X promises to Y that, if Y promises to X that Y does Ay, then X does Ax;
- (b) Y promises to X that Y does Ay;
- (c) Px is X's promise in (a); and
- (d) Py is Y's promise in (b).

(165) Px depends on Py if and only if:
- (a) if Y does Ay, then X promises to Y that X does Ax;
- (b) Y promises to X that Y does Ay;
- (c) Px is X's promise in (a); and
- (d) Py is Y's promise in (b).

(166) Px depends on Py if and only if:
- (a) X promises to Y that if Y does Ay then X does Ax.
- (b) Y promises to X that Y does Ay;
- (c) Px is X's promise in (a); and
- (d) Py is Y's promise in (b).

(167) Px is independent of Py if and only if it is not the case that X's reason for giving Px is that Y gives Py.

(168) Px is independent of Py if and only if:
- (a) X promises to Y that X does Ax;
- (b) Y promises to X that Y does Ay;
- (c) Px is X's promise in (a);
- (d) Py is Y's promise in (b); and
- (e) it is not the case that if (b) then (a).

(169) Px is independent of Py if and only if:
- (a) X promises to Y that X does Ax;
- (b) Y promises to X that Y does Ay;
- (c) Px is X's promise in (a);
- (d) Py is Y's promise in (b).

(170) Px is independent of Py if and only if:
- (a) X promises to Y that X does Ax;
- (b) Y promises to X that Y does Ay;
- (c) Px is X's promise in (a);
- (d) Py is Y's promise in (b); and
- (e) it is not the case that if Y does Ay then (a).

(171) If X promises to Y that X does Ax, then:
(a) X has an obligation, Ox, that X does Ax; and
(b) X can be released from Ox only with Y's consent.

(172) If X promises to Y that, if Y promises to X that Y does Ay, then X does Ax, then:
(a) X has an obligation that, if Y promises to X that Y does Ay, then X does Ax;
(b) if Y promises to X that Y does Ay, then X has Ox (the obligation that X does Ax); and
(c) X can be released from those obligations only with Y's consent.

(173) If X promises to Y that if Y does Ay then X does Ax, then:
(a) X has an obligation that if Y does Ay then X does Ax;
(b) if Y does Ay, then X has Ox (the obligation that X does Ax); and
(c) X can be released from those obligations only with Y's consent.

(174) A contract constituted by independent promises is not an agreement.

(175) If some contract is not an agreement, then an agreement is not necessary for a contract.

(176) An agreement is not necessary for a contract.

(177) If X and Y give independent promises to each other, then they contract.

(178) It is not the case that, if X and Y give independent promises to each other, then they agree.

Chapter 8

(179) X and Y have a concurrence of wills if and only if, for some P:
(a) X intends that P;
(b) Y intends that P;
(c) X communicates his intention that P to Y; and
(d) Y communicates his intention that P to X.

(180) X sells only in France and Y sells only in Germany.

(181) X and Y agree that (180).

(182) X and Y comply with their agreement that (180).

(183) (a) X intends that (180);
(b) Y intends that (180);
(c) X communicates his intention that (180) to Y; and
(d) Y communicates his intention that (180) to X.

(184) (a) X intends that (181);
(b) Y intends that (181);

(c) X communicates his intention that (181) to Y; and
(d) Y communicates his intention that (181) to X.

(185) (a) X intends that (182);
(b) Y intends that (182);
(c) X communicates his intention that (182) to Y; and
(d) Y communicates his intention that (182) to X.

(186) If (181) then (183).

(187) If (183) then (181).

(188) If (181) then (184).

(189) If (184) then (181).

(190) If (182) then (183).

(191) If (183) then (182).

(192) If (182) then (185).

(193) If (185) then (182).

(194) If at Ta X and Y agree that <in Ts, X sells only in France and Y sells only in Germany>, then:
(a) at Ta X intends that <in Ts, X sells only in France and Y sells only in Germany>;
(b) at Ta Y intends that <in Ts, X sells only in France and Y sells only in Germany>;
(c) X communicates his intention in (a) to Y; and
(d) Y communicates his intention in (b) to X.

(195) (182) if and only if:
(a) (181);
(b) X sells only in France;
(c) Y sells only in Germany;
(d) X, in selling only in France, intends to sell only in France; and
(e) Y, in selling only in Germany, intends to sell only in Germany.

(196) If:
(a) at Ta X intends that <in Ts, X sells only in France and Y sells only in Germany>;
(b) at Ta Y intends that <in Ts, X sells only in France and Y sells only in Germany>;
(c) X communicates his intention in (a) to Y; and
(d) Y communicates his intention in (b) to X;
then:
(e) at Ta X and Y agree that <in Ts, X sells only in France and Y sells only in Germany>;

(f) in Ts X sells only in France;
(g) in Ts Y sells only in Germany;
(h) X, in selling only in France, intends to sell only in France; and
(i) Y, in selling only in Germany, intends to sell only in Germany.

(197) X and Y have a concurrence of wills if, for some P:
(a) X intends that P;
(b) Y intends that P;
(c) X communicates his intention that P to Y; and
(d) Y communicates his intention that P to X.

(198) If X and Y engage in a concerted practice, then X and Y act jointly.

(199) X and Y act jointly if:
(a) X, in doing Ax, relies on Y to do Ay;
(b) Y, in doing Ay, relies on X to do Ax;
(c) X, in relying on Y to do Ay, has the goal Gx;
(d) Y, in relying on X to do Ax, has Gy;
(e) Gx = Gy;
(f) X knows (a)–(e);
(g) Y knows (a)–(e);
(h) (f) partly because Y communicates (b) and (d) to X; and
(i) (g) partly because X communicates (a) and (c) to Y.

(200) X and Y engage in a concerted practice if (199)(a)–(i) are true.

(201) In most or at least many cases where X and Y engage in a concerted practice, (199)(a)–(i) are true.

(202) X, in doing Ax*, communicates (199)(a) to Y.

(203) X, in doing Ax*, intends to cause Y to believe (199)(a).

(204) X, in doing Ax*, causes Y to believe (199)(a).

(205) X, in doing Ax*, intends to cause Y to recognise X's intention in (203).

(206) X, in doing Ax*, causes Y to recognise X's intention in (203).

(207) X, in doing Ax*, intends that Y's recognition in (206) cause Y to believe (199)(a).

(208) Y's recognition in (206) causes Y to believe (199)(a).

(209) X, in doing Ax*, intends to cause Y to recognise X's intention in (205).

(210) X, in doing Ax*, causes Y to recognise X's intention in (205).

(211) X, in doing Ax*, intends that Y's recognition in (210) cause Y to believe (199)(a).

(212) Y's recognition in (210) causes Y to believe (199)(a).

(213) X, in raising prices by 5 per cent, relies on Y to raise prices by 5 per cent.

(214) X, in raising prices by 5 per cent, intends to cause Y to believe that X, in raising prices by 5 per cent, relies on Y to raise prices by 5 per cent.

(215) X, in raising prices by 5 per cent, intends that Y's recognition that X, in raising prices by 5 per cent, intends to cause Y to believe that X, in raising prices by 5 per cent, relies on Y to raise prices by 5 per cent cause Y to believe that X, in raising prices by 5 per cent, relies on Y to raise prices by 5 per cent.

(216) X does Ax.

(217) Ax and Ay are independent of each other.

(218) X believes that Y does Ay.

(219) X, in doing Ax, relies on Y to do Ay.

(220) X, in relying on Y to do Ay, has the goal Gx.

(221) Y, in relying on X to do Ax, has Gy.

(222) Gx = Gy.

(223) X knows (219), (58) and (220)–(222).

(224) Y knows (219), (58) and (220)–(222).

(225) (223) partly because Y communicates (58) and (221) to X.

(226) (224) partly because X communicates (219) and (220) to Y.

Chapter 9

(227) (a) X and Y agree that P.
(b) Necessarily if P then Q.

(228) (a) X and Y agree that P;
(b) If P then necessarily Q.

(229) X and Y agree that:
(a) P;
(b) necessarily if P then Q.

(230) X and Y agree that:
(a) P;
(b) if P then necessarily Q.

(231) If there is a conspiracy, then there is a contract.

(232) X and Y conspiratorially agree if and only if X makes to Y an offer which Y accepts.

(233) If there is a conspiracy, then there is a conspiratorial agreement.

(234) If there is a contractual agreement, then there is a contract.

(235) If X makes to Y an offer which Y accepts, then there is a contractual agreement.

(236) For any two parties, if one makes to the other an offer which the other accepts, then the particular contractual agreement in question exists.

INDEX